check out:

French marigolds 19

GROW
COOK
NOURISH

DARINA ALLEN

Darina Allen is Ireland's best-known food ambassador. She has run the world-renowned Ballymaloe Cookery School in Shanagarry, Co. Cork, situated in the middle of a 100-acre organic farm, since 1983.

She is the bestselling author of fifteen books, including *30 Years at Ballymaloe, Forgotten Skills of Cooking*, which won the André Simon award in 2009, *Irish Traditional Cooking, Ballymaloe Cooking School Cookbook,* and *Healthy Gluten-free Eating* (with Rosemary Kearney). Darina has hosted nine series of her cooking programme, *Simply Delicious*, on television around the world and has written a weekly food column for the *Irish Examiner* since 1998.

Darina is a tireless campaigner for local produce. She founded the first farmers' markets in Ireland, is on the board of The Soil Association, and is one of the leaders of the Slow Food movement in Ireland. She is a natural teacher, whose enthusiasm and energy for good things is quite contagious, and has won many awards, including the Guild of Food Writers' Lifetime Achievement award in 2013 "for her incalculable contribution to culinary education", and two IACP awards.

pickled red onions 36
potato tart 36
salad dressing 182
heirloom tomato salad 188
peach salad 360
soda bread 458
skewers 498
ravioli w/ sage butter 524
panzanella J563

GROW
COOK
NOURISH

A KITCHEN
GARDEN
COMPANION
IN 500 RECIPES

DARINA ALLEN

PHOTOGRAPHY BY CLARE WINFIELD

KYLE BOOKS

Published in 2017 by Kyle Books
www.kylebooks.com

Distributed by National Book Network
4501 Forbes Blvd, Suite 200,
Lanham, MD 20706
Phone: (800) 462-6420
Fax: (800) 338-4550
customercare@nbnbooks.com

First published in Great Britain in 2017
by Kyle Books an imprint of Kyle Cathie Limited

10 9 8 7 6 5 4 3 2 1

ISBN: 978 1 909487 74 1

Editor: Vicky Orchard
Editorial assistants: Isabel Gonzalez-Prendergast
Nutritional analysis: Alina Tierney
Editorial adaptation for American edition: Christy Lusiak,
Ivy McFadden, Warren Schultz, Christopher Steighner,
Angela Taormina, Claire Rogers
Design: Miranda Harvey
Photography: Clare Winfield
Food styling: Sunil Vijayakar and Rosie Reynolds
Props styling: Hannah Wilkinson
and Polly Webb-Wilson
Production: Nic Jones and Gemma John

Library of Congress Control Number: 2017945590

Color reproduction by ALTA London
Printed and bound in China by C&C Offset Printing Co., Ltd.

*For Tim and his team on the farm and gardens
who have created an organic Garden of Eden
for our nourishment and enjoyment.*

Contents

INTRODUCTION

This is my sixteenth book and may just be the most important one I ever write. In the words of Lady Eve Balfour, founder of The Soil Association: "The health of soil, plant, animal, and man is one and indivisible."

The working title—*For God's sake grow some of your own food and cook it*—sounded convincing when I said it with very deep passion as I always do, but on paper it looked preachy. And so *Grow, Cook, Nourish* came about. This encapsulates the entire process of sowing plants and seeds, nurturing them, harvesting, cooking, and nourishing yourself and others.

When I was a child, people shopped every day. Some say the real turning point when our food became less nourishing was in 1979 when the first premade was sold in the supermarket and so began the start of the rise in allergies, food intolerances, obesity, type 2 diabetes... I doubt that it is that simple but whatever the accumulated causes, there is no doubting that things have gone horribly wrong. We have gone from being a society who shopped for our fresh food and provisions on a daily basis, to one that has handed the power over our food choices to five or six multinational companies that can scarcely be expected to have our best interests, either our health or enjoyment of food, at their heart. Their main responsibility is to their shareholders.

For most people with busy lives a one-stop "shop" at a supermarket once a week is the only choice, but not every society has chosen this option. France, Spain, Italy, and many more European countries still shop daily at markets for their fresh produce far more than we do in the UK.

Since the 1950s, food producers have been encouraged to produce the maximum yield at the minimum cost. These days they are being forced by the cheap food policy in the retail trade and by the public's unrealistic assumption that inexpensive food is our right, to produce food below an economic level. It is quite simply impossible to produce wholesome food for the prices that farmers are now being paid. The result is an unmitigated disaster in health and socioeconomic terms.

As a child in the 1950s and 60s we ate simple, nourishing food from our garden and the local area—there were just three shops in our village and only a handful of processed foods. I can't quite remember when I first learned how to grow or even sow seeds. We always had a vegetable garden with apple trees, gooseberry and currant bushes, a few raspberry canes, and a little row of strawberries that never seemed to produce very many berries. I never knew either of my grandmothers, as they died when I was very young, but both my grandfathers loved their vegetable gardens and orchards. Grandad, my paternal grandfather, designed quite elaborate formal gardens with long paths and many "summer houses" connecting the business and our house in the little village of Cullohill in Co. Laois, Ireland. There were lots of perennials, both fruit and vegetables, nothing particularly exotic because we didn't have a greenhouse but certainly enough to keep us plentifully supplied pretty much year round.

My maternal grandfather, whom we called Granpoppy, was a virtually self-sufficient farmer who also loved his garden. I don't remember the vegetable garden much but I do remember him being inordinately proud of his crop of Golden Wonder potatoes. There were pears and apples and plum trees in the orchard behind the house, and plums and sloes in bushes around the farm. My mother also encouraged us to grow and allocated us little plots behind our house to grow both vegetables and flowers.

Later when I got married, despite the fact than we had a horticultural enterprise with acres of commercial greenhouses, a mushroom farm, and extensive orchards, I was longing for my own little vegetable patch so we cultivated a tiny plot close to the kitchen door and had the best fun planting it. After a few years, we designed a formal kitchen garden. I was inspired by many potagers as well as the gardens at Villandry in the Loire Valley and by those of Robert Carrier at Hintlesham Hall in Suffolk, England.

Anyone can grow, anywhere, in any space. Even if you live in a skyscraper or a high-rise flat with a balcony, you can grow some of your own food. To grow, all you need is a seed, some soil or compost, light, and water. You don't need green fingers, you don't even need a garden. You can grow on a windowsill, a balcony, in a few pots, buckets, baskets, in fact any kind of well-draining container. Obviously, the more space you have the more variety you can grow, but there can be an advantage in limited space because you are forced to be ingenious. I've seen old drawers, rusty wheelbarrows, old chests, and baths bursting with produce.

Gardening and growing is a lifetime of learning curves, every year a new adventure building on the previous year's experience. There's nothing like nature to keep us humble: one never knows it all. Every year there will be new challenges and a few successes, occasionally even a spectacular success or breakthrough that will have you bursting with pride. But from each disappointment and mistake we learn and then there's the thrill of growing something entirely new and exotic or an heirloom variety or a crop from the seeds we've saved ourselves.

A COOK'S GARDEN

I'm often asked if I came to gardening from being a cook, or vice-versa, but actually I realize that it's neither. When I arrived at Ballymaloe House I discovered many exotic perennial vegetables such as seakale, globe and Jerusalem artichokes, and cardoons, that are now my norm and I hope will also become yours.

I've always grown principally for flavor rather than for maximum yield. There are few things more disappointing for a gardener than discovering that, after all the time and effort to grow produce, the end result has little flavor. For this reason the variety is also crucially important so be super fussy when you order seeds and plants, shrubs and trees. There can be the world of difference in flavor between one tomato or bean variety and another.

From the cook's perspective it's all about the freshness of ingredients. Not only do freshly harvested vegetables, fruit, and herbs taste remarkably different, but they cook faster, saving energy, and in some cases the texture is also very different. The skin of some fruit and vegetables toughens as they get older and that is hugely noticeable in vegetables such as eggplant and cucumbers. For cooks and chefs, the secret of the wow factor is freshness and, of course, intensity of flavor.

The other bonus for the gardening cook is having access to different and unusual varieties, in comparison to what's normally available in the grocery store. Many chefs and keen cooks find that unless they grow their own, they simply can't access the unusual and heirloom varieties that are intriguing to cook with and add interest and panache to a menu.

Hence a growing number of chefs are starting to cultivate gardens in the most unlikely spaces, both indoors and outside. René Redzepi at Noma in Copenhagen is growing herbs and salad leaves under LED lights in a large indoor bed on legs beside the kitchen. Research indicates that growing under LED lights can enhance both flavor and yield, since the wavelengths can be controlled and varied for different crops. The chef can literally snip a pea shoot or a nasturtium leaf and pop it straight onto the guest's plate. Others, like Robin Gill at The Dairy overlooking Clapham Common in London, has quite an extensive plastic crate garden on the roof, as has Tom Colicchio at River Park in New York, although the gardener Zach Pickens admits that it's been a learning curve. April Bloomfield of The Spotted Pig, John Dory, and the Breslin, also has all manner of plants growing outside her restaurants, while she actively hunts for a farm in upstate New York. Eric Skokan grows a wide range of fruit, vegetables, and herbs on his 130-acre Black Cat Farm in Colorado, as well as foraging locally for produce to supply his Black Cat Bistro and Bramble and Hare farmhouse kitchen and pub. The bounty from the farm carries them through the winter months. Rick Bayless of Frontera Grill and Topolobampo in Chicago has been growing for his restaurants for 22 years and Brett Graham of the Ledbury in London, Bruno Loubet of the Grain Store and Unleashed, Thomasina Miers, and Wai Tin Ching, all grow their own. Terence Conran grows food at his home in Hampshire for the Albion and Ruth Rogers grows many good things on her terrace at the River Café in London, and has done so since the beginning, as has Ballymaloe House, whose menu for over half a century has been based on the produce of the walled garden and greenhouses, as well as produce from the local area.

Of course, it's difficult to be self-sufficient, but even a little produce adds extra interest to your menu. Chefs who have created their own growing space find that many of their team have found a whole new understanding of how their fresh ingredients are produced. This brings an intangible excitement to the kitchen and a real pride in their achievement, plus a whole new interest in using every scrap and preserving gluts.

If I had my way, no chef or cook would be considered qualified to cook in a restaurant kitchen unless they had spent a year on a farm. That would give them a deep understanding and respect for their artisan and specialty producers, and an insight into why good produce must cost more. My wish would also be that every chef school or hotel would have a garden and see it as a vital part of the chefs' training. I would love to see an edible garden beside every school, from kindergarten upward, and practical cooking embedded in the national curriculum. Imagine how that could change the eating habits and health of the nation.

THE FIRST DAY AT BALLYMALOE COOKERY SCHOOL

On their first day, we introduce the 12-week Certificate students to our gardeners, Eileen, Haulie, and Susan, who will produce much of what they will cook during their stay. I show them a barrow full of rich soil and run my hands through it, instructing them to "Remember, this is where it all starts, in the good earth, and if you don't have clean, fertile soil you won't have good food or pure water." Some of them look askance at this eccentric gray-haired hippy woman with a mission, as I tell them about the millions of organisms and bacteria all working away underground to enrich the soil; denatured soil doesn't have the essential minerals and trace elements we need in our food and our guts.

We walk through the gardens, past the herbs, vegetables, and fruits, down to the compost heap, close to the hen house. Here they get their first recipe—how to make compost. I want them to see it all as part of a cycle starting in the good

earth. Susan Turner, our consultant head gardener who trained at the Henry Doubleday Research Association's organic center, talks them through the theory of making compost. Later they go gathering with the gardeners—a valuable way of learning how and when to harvest food. Trimmings and scraps from their cooking go into the stockpot, to the hens, or into the composting bin. The scraps for the hens come back as eggs a few days later, what goes into the compost bin is returned to enrich the soil, and the stockpot creates the basis for many wonderful soups, stews, and sauces. We teach the students to respect and value the work of the gardeners

and to appreciate how long it takes to grow our food—students won't dare to boil the hell out of a carrot when they realize it's taken three months to grow! They begin to see everything is interconnected and part of a holistic cycle, and to think about how things can be recycled beneficially. After we've had our composting lesson, we come to the greenhouses, where Susan and Eileen show them how to sow seeds. For me this is a very important initiation to the course—I know of no better way to give people a respect for food than for them to plant a seed and to watch it grow. Each and every student gets a broccoli or lettuce plant that they label and sow in the greenhouse, and during the next few weeks they watch it grow.

REASONS TO GROW YOUR OWN

My passion for encouraging virtually everyone I meet to grow some of their own food may seem baffling. Why bother? There's never been a time in history when such a wide variety of foods is available. Every grocery store and supermarket in the country is stacked to the ceiling with tantalizing products, enticingly labeled with a delicious promise of flavor and health benefits—a seemingly endless supply of super processed foods to make our lives easier. But, we now know that this kind of food is, quite simply, killing us. This may sound like a rather extreme reaction but a growing body of research leads us to the undeniable conclusion that a diet high in processed foods is, at the very least, detrimental to our health in a variety of ways. This type of food is being linked to many autoimmune diseases, type-2 diabetes, diverticulitis, cancer, heart disease, and obesity.

But what to do? For many people, it's simply not possible, in the midst of

Cardoons in full flourish in the gardens.

our busy daily lives to find the sort of wholesome nourishing food we would like to feed ourselves and our families.

HEALTH BENEFITS

We know that plants are the most important food group. Vegetables should form the biggest part of your food intake. Vegetable nutrients provide us with a strong gastrointestinal and immune system, a healthy heart, improved eyesight and brain function, help weight management, and seemingly contribute to a far lower risk of almost every known disease. The dietary fiber in vegetables and fruit comes from the indigestible part of the plants that passes relatively unchanged through the intestines. It plays a vital role in maintaining a healthy digestive system, reducing the risk of heart disease by lowering cholesterol, regulating blood sugar, and helping to prevent constipation.

Fresh vegetables, fruit, and herbs are undeniably higher in nutrients than those that have traveled long distances over several days. Think of a green bean—people today expect these to be available all year round—yet their season is 2 to 3 months long. They are flown in from Peru or Kenya and about 10 days old by the time they are on the supermarket shelf. So by growing your own you will reap the benefits of eating fresh produce grown in rich, fertile soil. This includes the beneficial bacteria and enzymes of your local area. Much research is being done into the importance of a healthy gut microbiome and it is becoming increasingly apparent that this is a fundamental to our physical and mental well-being.

Freshness is also vitally important. When vegetables wilt, they lose much of their nutritional value. Research has shown that organic vegetables contain little or no pesticide residues—another convincing reason to grow your own and try to source organic versions of what you can't grow locally. Many, though sadly not all, farmers' markets are excellent for local, seasonal produce.

Much of the fruit, vegetables, and herbs available in our supermarkets is grown hydroponically or aquaponically. Yet the label doesn't reveal this information, so it's difficult for the consumer to differentiate between produce that's grown in rich, fertile soil and similar looking fruit and vegetables that are grown in water with the added chemicals needed to form them into a lettuce or strawberry. Food grown in water is unlikely to be as delicious or as nutritionally complex as food grown in healthy, fertile soil.

If you go to the trouble of growing your own produce then you are more likely to increase your consumption of fruit and vegetables. This should in turn save money on medical bills; doctors I've spoken to estimate that between 60 to 70 percent of the cases they see are caused directly by the food people are eating and can be significantly improved by a change in diet. The new advice of eating 10 portions of fruit and vegetables a day

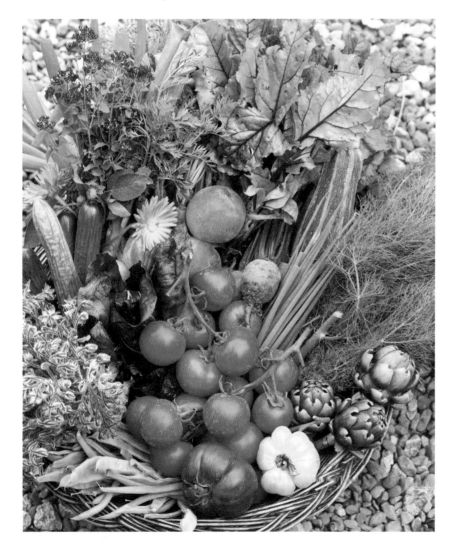

A basket of fresh produce from the farm and gardens in midsummer.

is simply not going to be a reality for most people. Increasing consumption of fruits and veggies and its health benefits is one thing pretty much all health practitioners seem to agree on, but this may also be connected to the alarming decrease in nutrients in those fruits and vegetables we do eat.

Since the 1940s and 50s, the levels of iron, magnesium, and other essential minerals have declined in fruit and vegetables by between a quarter and three-quarters. A study done in 2004 by David Thompson, Professor of Nutrition in King's College, London, showed some vegetables had lost almost half of their calcium and sodium content, a quarter of their iron, and 76 percent of their copper content, due to intensive production. Similarly with fruits, the nutrient levels have declined significantly with iron, copper, and zinc all falling by up to 27 percent. Anne-Marie Mayer of Cornell University's research project measured 20 fruits and 20 vegetables grown in Britain between the late 1930s and the 1990s found similar changes. She too identified significant reductions in levels of calcium, copper, magnesium, and sodium in vegetables and decreased levels of manganese, copper, and potassium in fruits. The most dramatic decrease was in copper levels in vegetables, to less than a fifth of previous levels. To satisfy modern palates, the level of sugar has more than doubled in many fruits—apples, pears, oranges—over the same period.

The rise in sweetness in fruit is partly due to new varieties and is in part due to improved picking and storage techniques, but the new reality has prompted some dentists to reverse their health advice that eating an apple a day is almost as good as brushing teeth. Research has found that fruit acids soften tooth enamel and the sugar encourages the growth of bacteria.

Both Thompson and Mayer link the decline in nutrients to intensive farming practices and suggest that agricultural chemicals and techniques are responsible for stripping plants of minerals. Another study concluded that you need to eat on average 8 oranges a day to get the same amount of vitamin A that our parents would have derived from one.

Nonetheless, vegetables and fruit are still rich in phytonutrients and phytochemicals and one of our best sources of many nutrients.

Michael Pollan, author, journalist, and activist has a much-repeated quote: "Eat food, not too much, mostly plants," which just about sums up all the nutritional advice we need. In these days of widespread nutritional confusion it's comforting to know that the answer to our dilemma is fundamentally very simple. Just seven words of plain English—you don't need a degree in science or biochemistry. We just need to go back to basics.

It's good to remember when we are obsessing about individual nutrients or "superfoods" that nutritional science is young, and the food scientists themselves would tell you that they certainly don't know all the answers. I am not anti-science, but as Pollan says in *An Eater's Manual,* "Foods are more than the sum of their nutrient parts and those nutrients work together in ways that are still only dimly understood."

I can't say it surprised me but I was intrigued to discover that traditional Chinese and Ayurvedic medicine both believe that the type of food you eats can affect your energy levels—food that is mass-produced in a conventional large agri-business has a different energy than food that is locally grown and harvested on a small family farm. So it appears that health and energy can be affected—positively or negatively—by the energy of the plants we consume.

VEGETARIAN AND VEGAN
The number of people becoming vegetarian and flexitarian continues to grow exponentially as awareness increases of the reality of intensive poultry and pig production in particular. There is mounting concern about the use of probiotics and antibiotics in animal feed. As consumers become ever more savvy, these concerns are no longer limited to a small group of animal welfare and environmental activists; they are becoming much more mainstream.

This is evidenced by the increase in those turning to a vegetarian or vegan lifestyle. A recent study showed that 7.3 million US adults follow a vegetarian-based diet, 1 million of whom are vegan. The perceived health benefits of a plant-based vegan diet appear to be driving the trend. It particularly appeals to health-conscious young people. About half the vegans are aged between 15 and 34, compared with 17 percent of over-65s.

Advocates of a plant-based diet claim that vegans typically have lower levels of blood pressure and cholesterol and a reduced risk of cancer and heart disease plus a lower body mass index. Convincing arguments, but the reality is that one needs to be deeply knowledgeable about nutrition and what constitutes a healthy diet, plus have access to wholesome sources of vitamins, such as B12, iron, zinc, and calcium, to maintain optimum health. For many people, this can be quite a challenge. Another incentive to grow even a little of your own organic food in rich, fertile soil so you have the maximum nutrients.

ECONOMIC BENEFITS
Growing some of your own produce reduces the cost of providing your family with a supply of fresh organic produce. A packet of seeds typically costs less than one item of fruit or vegetables.

Composting your garden and food

waste saves on waste charges—there's no need to pay the town to dispose of your garden and food waste. The resulting humus will help to enrich the soil to produce more healthy vegetables and fruit—creating a virtuous triangle.

When you grow and harvest your own, many vegetables have multiple uses, such as beets—root, stalks, and leaves; radishes—bulb and fresh leaves; spinach—stalk and leaves; zucchini—vegetable, flowers, tender leaves, and tendrils; beans—pods, shell beans, dried seeds—eat at many stages; peas—pods, shoots, tendrils; sprouts—sprout tops, peeled stalks. Much more food for your money and effort.

ENVIRONMENTAL BENEFITS
Growing your own food sustainably helps to reduce fossil fuels and the pollution that results from transporting fresh produce by airplane and truck from all over the world to our supermarkets. You are also far less likely to waste food when you have nurtured it from a seed into a plant.

Gardening also connects you to the impact of weather, pests, and the reality of nature—it heightens awareness of the seasons and looking forward to seasonal treats like the first rhubarb or asparagus.

It may sound esoteric to some, but loss of biodiversity should concern all of us deeply. The reality is our lives are inextricably linked with the biodiversity of the planet. Ultimately, its protection is essential for our very survival.

According to the Food and Agriculture Organization of the United Nations, an estimated 75 percent of all agricultural crops have disappeared and 75 percent of the world's food comes from just twelve plant and five animal species. At present, just thirty crops provide 95 percent of the world's nutritional needs; of these wheat, rice, and corn provide more than 60 percent of the calories consumed.

Once again we can each make a difference by growing as wide a variety of plants as possible, and help in the important work of saving seeds and preserving heirloom varieties. Together with the heroic seed saving organizations around the world, home gardeners can grow many more species and have helped save many heirloom varieties from extinction and saved them for posterity. In the 1930s, there were 338 varieties of rock melon (now there are 27), and 164 varieties of celery—there are now just three. In New Zealand in 1950, over 100 varieties of tomatoes were grown, now about five are grown commercially. Many of the lesser known varieties are far more flavorful but often less uniform in appearance, which is what prompts supermarkets from stocking them.

CONTROL/CHOICE
For me the security of knowing exactly how my food is produced and where it comes from—ultimate traceability—is enough reason to grow my own. One needs to worry less about food safety, food adulteration, and food scandals. You will have a supply of fresh organic food ready to harvest at a moment's notice, and there is nothing more *local* than food that comes from your balcony or garden.

FEEL-GOOD FACTOR
There is lots of evidence to show that gardening is good for one's physical and mental health. Gardening is a powerful way to relax, destress and enjoy fresh air and sunshine. Many find it therapeutic and it is increasingly being used as part of treatment for those with mental health conditions and for prisoners and troubled young people. Every gardening activity provides exercise—digging, planting, watering, weeding...you can burn off as many calories in 45 minutes of gardening as in 30 minutes of aerobics.

Growing your own food produces a wonderful feel-good factor and sense of pride and satisfaction at each new achievement. It may also spark new interests in nutrition, botany, landscaping, or photography. Growing even a little of your own food gives you a deeper understanding and appreciation of the time and effort that goes into producing wholesome, nourishing food—you will be less likely to complain about the price of food again!

PASS ON OUR SKILLS
Educate children, grandchildren, nieces, nephews, and neighbors on how to grow and where food comes from and an understanding of how dependent we are on the top 5 to 6 inches of soil around the world. When children are involved in sowing seeds and planting, they eat everything they have helped to grow. Meals will be more personal—we regularly sit down to meals where something or almost everything comes from the farm and gardens.

ORGANIC GROWING
Organic or non-organic? For me there's no choice. Organic means working with nature, not against it. It means higher levels of animal welfare, lower levels of pesticides, no manufactured herbicides or artificial fertilizers, and more environmentally sustainable management of the land and natural environment—this means more wildlife!

We can no longer say we don't know the damage that pesticides and herbicides are doing to our health and to the environment. The emerging body of research, from Professor Carlo Liefert at University of Newcastle among others, is

Left to right: Zaiah checking her carrot crop; Dancing with Smurfs heirloom tomatoes; a lush crop of redcurrants; Amelia with her pockets full of fresh peas.

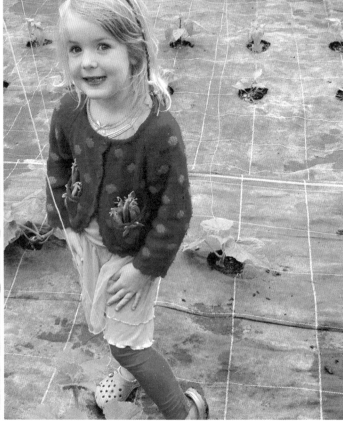

increasingly worrying, so why would you go to the trouble of growing food for your family and friends and then spray it with known poisons.

Farmers too are becoming increasingly concerned about the diminishing fertility of soils that have been intensively farmed since the 1950s and the ever escalating level of resistance to pesticides and herbicides.

This fear has been highlighted by several research projects, such as those of Professor Keith Goulding, past-president of the British Society of Soil Science, who estimated that the world, due to erosion and bad land management in commercial farming, "will run out of soil within 60 years," particularly in the US, UK, and parts of Europe.

There are many large organic farms but the majority are small, family-run operations that use techniques and lighter machinery that limit agricultural impact on the soil, on river and ground water, birds and wildlife, and human health. However, the reality is that organic food production is more labor-intensive and often less profitable. Many crops take longer to grow because no hormones or chemicals are used to speed up the process.

The IAASTD (International Assessment of Agricultural Knowledge, Science and Technology for Development) report published in 2008, entitled "Agriculture at a Crossroads," was the result of research by 400 scientists over a three-year period, whose brief was to look at food production and growing methods that would benefit human health. The press release entitled "Business as Usual is not an Option" was adopted by 58 governments; it spelled out that a thorough and radical overhaul of national and international agriculture policies is necessary to meet the enormous challenges of the twenty-first century. The report recommended an

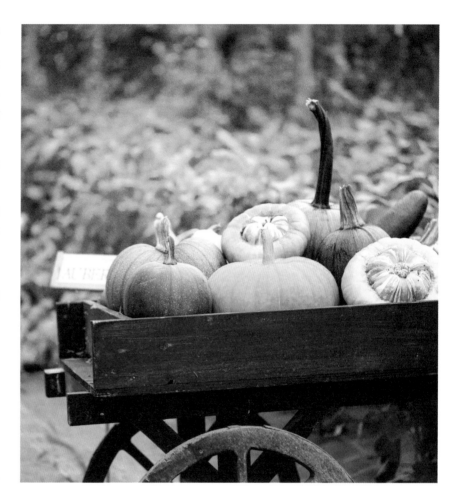

agro-ecological approach or what most of us call organic farming.

Organic guidelines indicate that certified organic fruit and vegetables may not contain growth hormones, antibiotics, preservatives, dyes, or chemical coatings. They cannot be irradiated or genetically engineered. A growing body of research, including the work of Professor Carlo Liefert at University of Newcastle, now indicates that organic food is more nutritious in many instances—including iron, vitamin C, magnesium, and phosphorus.

Consequently, organic food provides better nourishment and protection against disease. Organic foods also retain essential nutrients such as iron and salicylic acid which can be lost in

A cart full of a variety of pumpkins.

conventional food processing.

Organic farmers are obsessed with nourishing and enhancing the fertility of the soil; we take regular soil samples to measure the fertility of the soil and identify deficiencies, such as lime or salt, which we then spread on the land in the correct proportion.

The more we grow and garden the more we realize the value of working closely with nature, rather than against it. If in our arrogance or merely for convenience we decide to spray our crops with pesticides and herbicides, we discover to our dismay that instead of going away, the strain or pest or bacteria gradually gets stronger and stronger, necessitating increased applications or a stronger even more powerful pesticide, to the detriment of the soil, our health, and the environment.

There is no question in my mind that organic produce tastes better, however, it's important to stress the importance of freshness. The flavor also depends on the type and fertility of the soil and the variety of the plant you are growing.

We use organic seed where possible, and find overall that they are hardier and more resilient than F1 hybrids

HOW TO GET STARTED

You'll most likely be brimming with enthusiasm and want to get going right away. Slow down, it's worth investing a little time and thought to check a few fundamental details. Remember that it's all about the soil

Identify your particular type of soil: is it acid, wet, marshy? The plants and weeds that grow naturally will give you a clue as to the nature of the soil but, if you want to be 100 percent accurate, take a sample and send it to your nearest soil testing laboratory. This will also help you to identify any deficiencies. There's simply no point in trying to grow an acid-loving plant in a limey area. Most experienced gardening neighbors will be able to give you a rough guide.

OUTDOORS

It's vital to clear your plot of weeds, particularly perennial weeds, before you start to sow seeds and plant. Learn to recognize a few of the main offenders such as crabgrass, plantain, bindweed, docks, and poison ivy.

If you're starting to grow from scratch, the easy solution is to spray with a weed killer, however, this damages the soil in a variety of ways and residues can remain in the plants and in the soil. If you decide to grow organically then you'll need to employ various methods

to keep on top of the weeds and it is unquestionably more labor-intensive. The options are:

• Spray the entire area with glyphosate to kill the pernicious weeds like crabgrass, docks, bindweed, thistles—this is the fastest method of eradicating perennial weeds.

• Cover with black plastic sheeting for 6 months. It's important to fold it back 2 to 3 times during that time to allow the worms to survive. Seek out the perennial weeds and dig them out.

• Cover the ground with cardboard for at least a year. The advantage of cardboard is that it keeps the weeds down, is biodegradable, and can also be composted.

• Double dig and pick out every scrap of root—this may be practical in a very small area, but virtually impossible in a large garden, even a tiny piece of a perennial root or stem will resprout.

• Harrow the ground regularly during the dry season; the roots will come to the surface and wilt in the dry weather. The longer you spend clearing the ground the better—6 months to a year would be good but is not always practical.

• In a small garden, it is best to pick off and dispose of the roots as they come to the surface.

This can be a frustrating wait, but if you skip this stage it will be virtually impossible to keep on top of the weeds or grow successfully.

INDOORS

We are in the happy position of owning a block of greenhouses—divided up into 20 "bays," each one approx. 20 x 100-feet, the size of several domestic greenhouses or tunnels. Before we plant, we remove the remainder of the last crop and feed the green matter to the pigs. The remainder of the crop plus stalks goes onto the compost heap and eventually will return to the soil as humus to keep feeding it.

We dig, plow, or rotavate the patch of

ground then rake the soil to a fine tilth. When the first flush of weeds emerge—1 to 3 weeks later, depending on time of year—we hoe with a swivel hoe or burn off the weeds with a gas torch at the two-leaf stage. This is a very effective method of weed control that we use both indoors in the greenhouse outdoors in the garden and field.

For some crops, we completely cover the ground a black woven weed control fabric as a barrier. It suppresses the growth of weeds by blocking light, but still allows water and nutrients to filter through to the soil to the plants. We also use this fabric on a limited scale outdoors. At appropriate spacing, make holes in the fabric, either with a blowtorch or by cutting a cross with a sharp Stanley knife, and plant directly through the Mypex. Cover the space between rows with cardboard to suppress weeds.

When the crop is finished, we lift the fabric and give it a thorough brushing, hosing it down if necessary, and then roll it up and store outdoors until we need it to plant the same crop at a later stage. We have our own steam cleaner that we use to clean it as well as the greenhouse walls, glass, and entire structure in the winter. Winter glasshouse hygiene is immensely important and all parts of the greenhouse should be scrubbed down.

If we are sowing directly into the soil, we hoe between the rows of plants with a swivel hoe and hand weed between the plants themselves. This is usually a communal exercise with 3 to 4 people working together and enjoying the experience. We hoe 2 to 3 times a week. I love a bit of gentle weeding and find it immensely therapeutic, but it has to be said that the state of the vegetable garden and greenhouses does not depend on me alone! We rake up the weeds and they too get added to the compost bin, which is added to the compost heap at the end of every week.

Insects are essential for pollination and it is particularly important to open the door to greenhouses and polytunnels to let them in—plant flowers that attract them and encourage bumble bees.

COMPOST AND HUMUS

So how do you increase the fertility of your soil? By adding compost, seaweed, and organic matter. Start a compost heap. Compost can be homemade or acquired from garden centers—try to use organic if you can. Well-rotted compost and humus is like black gold; it's nourishment for the soil. If using mushroom compost, check that it is organic.

Soil pH is a measure of the acidity or alkalinity of the soil and it's essential to know before you start; while some plants are not fussy, others will not thrive if there is an excess of one or other element in the soil. If it's necessary to increase the pH of the soil, add lime in the fall before planting the new season's plantings such as brassicas. On the other hand keep lime away from potatoes, where it could encourage scab.

After reading *The Living Soil* by Lady Balfour, I became interested in the nourishing and healing qualities of feeding the soil with humus. Humus is the stage after the compost has cooled and broken down. It resembles soil and

A handful of humus—so important to help nourish the soil.

offers the perfect medium for the basics of life to inhabit: worms, fungi, and insects. This living medium, when added to soil, helps to lock in moisture and encourages the biodiversity of the soil to produce healthy plants, which in turn then have better resistance to pests and diseases. These health benefits are then passed onto animal and humans.

The composting system we use is simply a series of silos, and we turn the composting material from one silo to the next on a regular basis, so we always need to have at least one or two empty silos. We have builders' bins placed in strategic places, to collect waste material around the farm and garden. Whenever we have a full bin or any organic waste, we dump it into the silo where a new compost pile is being established. This heats up. Compost heat is produced as a byproduct of the microbial breakdown of organic material. The heat production depends on the size of the pile, its moisture content, and aeration. Turning it every 5 to 7 days or so helps aeration. It takes us about 3 months to fill a silo, then another 3 months, turning roughly once a week, until it eventually cools down, then only turn it occasionally.

The longer we leave it the better it is, at least another 6 to 9 months. It is constantly breaking down and, on close inspection, we begin to see tiny worms, fungi spores, flies, and grubs and no seed germination. We are not very scientific about our mixture, I don't ever know what the proportions are, so everything that we need to dispose of goes in, including vegetable waste from the kitchen, garden, or farm.

We have a small herd of cattle that go indoors for 4 to 5 months in winter. When we clean out the cattle sheds in early spring we add the farmyard manure

that comes from their winter bedding to the compost heap. The hen houses are cleaned out about twice a month, so this straw is also added, plus shredded garden prunings, which are added as they become available. We have been adding this humus to the soil for about 10 years and now we all agree that we have fewer problems with pests and diseases and much healthier plants.

SEAWEED

We live close to the long sandy beach at Ballinamona in Ireland and like many generations of coastal dwellers hugely value seaweed as a fertilizer, mulch, and flavor-enhancer.

If you live close to the coast, where the water is unpolluted, think about collecting seaweed, but first check out the regulations that protect the coastline. There shouldn't be a difficulty with collecting a few bags of seaweed after a storm, but if you intend to collect it on a larger scale, you may need to apply for a permit. You need to be vigilant because the tide washes it back to sea if it's not collected within a day or two. The seaweed can be spread directly onto the soil (there's no need to wash unless you have a high sodium content in your soil.) The essential minerals and other chemicals will benefit the plants. It will smell strong, particularly indoors, for a couple of days as it decomposes. We also add it to the compost heap to help activate the compost and speed up the process. Make a seaweed tea to use as a liquid fertilizer. Dry or crisp seaweed can be crumbled and spread on the soil later. Use as a mulch on no-dig beds. Seaweed contains many valuable nutrients, including nitrogen, potassium, phosphate, and trace elements. From the environmental point of view, seaweed is a sustainable, renewable resource.

LEAF MOLD

Pile the autumn leaves under trees in a well-shaded piece of woodland. Alternatively pile the leaves up in a wooden box or chicken wire cage, or better still mix it through the compost. It has little or no nourishment but makes a useful mulch to suppress weeds.

Leaf mold takes 2 to 3 years to break down. Be careful if raking out early, because one can accidentally disturb or even kill a hibernating creature.

COVER CROPS

Cover crops, or "green manure," is an herbaceous plant or crop that is grown primarily for the benefit of the soil, rather than for food or appearance. They are plowed or dug in to enrich the soil. Alternatively in a no-dig system (see page 22), the plants are simply cut down and treated as a mulch as they decompose. The foliage can also be added to the compost heap.

Planting green manures is a great way to add organic matter to the soil and provides nutrients and organic material for succeeding crops. It creates living space for predators and bees as well as attracting beneficial insects. It covers bare soil, which otherwise loses fertility and structure as well as reducing erosion and protecting against leaching. It also helps to break up compacted soil and improve soil structure and can suppress weeds and rest the soil.

Large quantities of nitrates can be lost from bare soil over the winter and the green manures help to stop this leaching.

SUMMER COVER CROPS

These can be legumes (for a quick boost of nitrogen in mid-rotation), red, white, or crimson clover, or summer vetch. Buckwheat, phacelia, mustard, and sunflower also provide seeds for the birds. In the vegetable garden, Eileen O'Donovan cuts the seedheads after the

One of our fancy hens—an essential part of our composting system at the school.

flowers have died and hangs them upside down for the birds.

WINTER COVER CROPS

When sown in the fall, these are a good way of building up the fertility over winter. Try Rye Landsberger mix, Rye with vetch, Phacelia with vetch, or Rye with Phacelia.

HENS

You might ask, what have hens got to do with a growing your own food and cooking your own produce? Well, they are a vital and integral part of our composting and waste disposal system.

The vegetable scraps and peelings from the morning's cooking go into the hens' bucket in each kitchen. These are emptied into the compost bins in the hen run. The hens gobble up whatever tasty morsels they like. Each evening we scatter a layer of straw and perhaps some leaf mold on top. By the end of the week the full bin is added to the compost heap and so on...

WHY KEEP BEES?

It can't have escaped your notice that bees are dying in alarming numbers around the globe. They are being attacked by virulent viruses against which they have no protection. The exact cause is not yet fully understood but there is a growing body of scientific research linking the harmful neonicotinoid pesticide group and other pollutants with the decline in honey bee colonies from colony collapse disorder and the varroa mite. The EU brought in a temporary ban on their use in 2012 but there is strong lobbying from farmers' groups across Europe to lift the ban. Already hundreds of bee species have become extinct, bringing to mind Albert Einstein's warning, "If the bee disappeared off the surface of the globe, then man would only have four years of life left. No more bees, no more pollination, no more plants, no more animals, no more man."

Organic farms and gardens provide important havens for bees and wildlife. Several research projects indicate that organic farms support in excess of 50 percent more wildlife, birds, bees, insects, and butterflies than conventional farms. Think about including bee-friendly flowers in your garden, on your balcony, or windowsill. Bees need to be able to collect pollen and nectar, as they pollinate the plants. Every little action will help in the process, but don't use pesticides.

You can even become a beekeeper! Contact your local beekeeper's association that regularly offers courses for novices and more experienced beekeepers.

Your food scraps will be appreciated by the hens who will reward you with eggs a few days later. Plus you don't have to pay your local council to dispose of the "waste." The byproduct will be chicken manure which is great for activating compost because of its high nitrogen content.

Hens, however can do damage in the vegetable garden, particularly in summer, but are a big bonus for winter maintenance. We open the kitchen garden gate and let them scratch and forage on the beds to clear the area of the occasional slug and beetle.

WHAT TO GROW

Before you decide which plants to grow, it's worth knowing what growing zone you are in and your soil type, so you can determine whether your chosen plant is suited to the temperature fluctuations and extremes in your area. Plant hardiness zones are geographically defined around the globe. Here in Ireland we are in Zone 9, but in the US, zones range all the way from 1 in Alaska to 11 in Hawaii. Go online to discover your zone:planthardiness.ars.usda.gov or in Canada, www.planthardiness.gc.ca. In this book, if a plant is limited to particular zones, then they are listed at the beginning of the entry.

What you decide to grow will also be dictated by your situation. If you have lots of space, the world's your oyster, but even with little or no space, if you are determined to grow some of your own food, it's amazing what you can produce in window boxes, pots, and growbags.

What each person decides to grow will be deeply personal. Grow what you like to eat. Take a pen and paper and make a list. Ask yourself, what do you like to eat and use most? What is expensive and/or difficult to source in good condition and what you would love to be able to dash outside to just snip? Fresh herbs are the

gateway to gardening for many people. Also think about whether you can create a little "veggie co-op" with friends and each agree to grow certain things.

In spring, wait until the soil temperature is right and any danger of frost has past before sowing seed; otherwise they will rot in the ground. The soil should be about 45°F. One could buy a soil thermometer but I just lay my hand on the soil—it shouldn't feel uncomfortably cold.

CROP ROTATION

Crop rotation is vital. If annual vegetable crops are grown in the same place year after year, there is a tendency for soil-borne pests and diseases to become a problem and for plant health to decline. The alternative is to move crops around. This is an ancient practice, known as rotation, which continues to be used to benefit both soil and plants. Plants that belong to the same family are prone to the same soil-loving pests and diseases. Moving crops around helps to prevent the build-up of problems in the soil. Plants require nutrients in varying amounts and take them from different levels within the soil depending on species and root depth. Varying the plants grown in a specific area helps to make best use of the soil.

Group together crops that require the same soil to provide them with the best growing conditions. It also means that the whole growing area will receive the same treatments over the course of the rotation.

Some plants have dense foliage and are good at suppressing weeds. Others, such as carrots or onions, are not. Alternating plants with different growth habits helps to keep weeds under control.

COMPANION PLANTING

Companion planting is nature's little helper. The term refers to the practice

of planting different crops in close proximity to help with pest control, pollination, and to provide habitat for beneficial insects. Certain plants like a type of soil and some maximize space or support each other. Organic gardeners are well aware that a biodiverse environment makes for healthier, stronger, and more beautiful plants. It's well worth experimenting and there are many guides to help. Share experience with gardeners in your area.

Tall plants can provide shade and shelter where needed and attract beneficial insects to help with pollination. They can provide a support for climbing plants to clamber up—as in the famous three sisters example of squash, corn, and beans. By allowing upright plants to grow tall you can maximize the use of limited space.

Ground cover plants repel weeds. Decoy plants can attract insects away from another plant, such as nasturtiums, which attract aphids and other destructive insects. French marigolds exude an odor that deters slugs and we've had success when they are inter-planted with cabbage, cauliflowers, Brussels sprouts, broccoli, cucumbers, radishes, and zucchini.

Basil both repels insects and attracts bees. We like to plant it near tomatoes, apricots, parsley, and asparagus. Summer savory and fava beans is another successful combination and we continue to experiment every season.

Plants with deep roots can grow happily alongside shallow rooted plants without competing. Some plants enhance the fertility and condition of the soil—members of the legume family, such as beans, have the ability to draw nitrogen from the air and release it into the soil through nodules in the roots.

Here are a few suggestions:
Garlic—Grow close to carrots to deter carrot fly. It also repels aphids and

thrips, and helps to fight mildew. It's a natural fungicide and pesticide and both wild and cultivated varieties can be used. Planted under an apple tree, as it discourages scab and under a peach it protects against leaf curl.

Garlic chives—Plant under peaches to prevent leaf curl.

Alliums—The onion scent of chives, scallions, and alliums deters aphids from tomatoes, garlic, and sunflowers.

Roses—Plant feverfew and pennyroyal close to roses to repel aphids.

Thyme—Deters aphids on many plants such as broccoli and strawberries.

Mint—Deters aphids and ants.

French and African Marigolds—Discourage plant parasitic nematodes. We pop them in near potatoes, tomatoes, beans, and lettuces.

Basil—Plant beside tomatoes to repel aphids.

Poached egg plant—Attracts hover flies, which feed on aphids.

Chives—Helps to prevent carrot fly and scab on apples.

Calendula—Plant near tomatoes to ward off white fly and exude a substance that is off-putting to slugs and snails.

Nasturtiums—Entices aphids away from vulnerable crops.

Dill, fennel, angelica, calendula, cosmos, and yarrow—Attract ladybugs, which eat greenfly.

Lemon balm—Credited with improving the flavor of fruit.

Geraniums—Deter Japanese beetles, aphids, and rose beetles.

Yarrow—Attracts beneficial insects into the garden, particularly predatory wasps or ladybugs and hover flies.

Lavender—Repels moths, flies, mosquitos, and fleas.

Sage—Attractive to bees and repels flying insects like mosquitoes, cabbage moths, carrot fly, and ants.

Tansy—Discourages ants.

Hyssop, savory, and dill—Lure insects away if planted close to cabbage, carrots, beans, and grapes.

Chervil—Helps to keep aphids off lettuce and salad crops.

French marigolds, a good companion plant to potatoes, beans, and lettuces.

WATERING

Watering may seem very straightforward, but it is a very definite skill. Successful watering takes real attention to detail and concentration. Different types of plants have different needs—cactus and orchids for example need very little water to survive whereas vegetables, particularly those grown indoors, need regular watering, so one needs to pay attention to the needs of each plant.

Over-watering is more serious than under-watering. The former can kill a plant but you can often revive a distressed plant when it has become a little dry. In the greenhouses, we have a combination of irrigation and hand watering, particularly in the nursery where we sow seeds in trays before they are transplanted into the ground. The irrigation system is on a timer and is carefully regulated, but you may not have this at home in a small garden.

How do you know when a plant needs to be watered? It may seem like a silly question but I'm constantly amazed at the number of people who don't notice when potted plants are in need of water. Drooping leaves are an obvious sign that the plant is dry, but do the "finger test" to feel the soil around the plant—it should feel vaguely moist, unless it is a dry plant. If the soil is totally dry, the plant needs to be watered judiciously, preferably with a hose with an adjustable spray nozzle on top.

Here in Ireland in our damp and unpredictable climate, it's rare to need an irrigation system outdoors. So when we plant in the garden or vegetable field, we choose conditions carefully and the method of planting and watering depends on the specific crop. For brassicas, we water in the plants—one watering is usually enough unless we get a particularly dry spell.

When sowing seeds directly into the ground either in the greenhouse or outdoors, we cover the seeds with a layer of soil, then water them in and continue to water as needed.

FERTILIZING

As organic farmers and gardeners, we are passionate about feeding the soil to maintain and increase the fertility. We do this primarily by adding humus and well-rotted compost and seaweed, and find that we need add less and less inputs. However, some crops get an extra feed of organic fertilizer. For example, with potatoes, we scatter organic pellets of NPK fertilizer into the ground before we plant (see the label for proportions). For brassicas, we put a fistful of NPK around each plant when planting.

When planting tomatoes, cucumbers, bell peppers, and pumpkins in the greenhouse, we make the holes for the plants and add a fistful of organic NPK into each one. This provides adequate nitrogen, potassium, calcium, chlorine, iron, zinc, manganese, phosphorus, sulfur, magnesium, iodine, copper, molybdenum, and boron.

We use seaweed extract to feed many plants, such as eggplant, tomatoes, zucchini, cucumbers, bell peppers, and pumpkins. This is an excellent all-purpose feed containing nitrogen,

potassium, calcium, chlorine, iron, zinc, manganese, phosphorus, sulfur, magnesium, iodine, copper, and boron. Dilute per the instructions into water and spray onto the leaves as a foliar feed as and when needed.

GROWING IN CONTAINERS

Containers enable us to grow food in a tiny space. Many herbs, vegetables, and fruits can be successfully grown in a variety of pots. However, growing in small containers is definitely more challenging and you need to understand a few fundamentals.

1. A source of rich, fertile soil is essential.
2. The container needs to be large and deep enough to allow plenty of room for the roots of the chosen plant or plants to spread. It must have drainage holes so the plant doesn't get water-logged.
3. The greater the soil depth the more choice one has—6 inches is quite enough for salads but at least 12 inches will be needed for carrots, for example.
4. You may need to feed the plants occasionally.
5. There is more danger of the plants drying out on a sunny day.

All manner of boxes, crates, old drawers, baths, zinc buckets or tanks, clean oil drums, old or not so old log baskets, hanging baskets, tin cans, or chipped bowls can be used as containers. A variety of shapes and sizes add interest but standard terracotta pots are also fine and practical. Hanging baskets can also be slung over the railings of a balcony to increase growing space but make sure they don't drip down on neighbors!

It's important that the container is large enough to hold enough soil or compost to provide the plant with nourishment and moisture and allow ample space for roots to spread. Grow bags are convenient for both tomatoes and cucumbers.

Grow what you really like to eat when

space is very limited. Some containers can hold several plants; nasturtiums, marigolds, and borage grow easily, add color, attract beneficial insects, and can be used to embellish your dishes.

GROWING VERTICALLY

You'll be amazed how much you can produce in a small area but it's all about space management. Your choice of plants and using your vertical space is an important part of the equation.

Hang planters on the railings of a balcony garden. This allows you to make best use, from both the inside and outside of the railings. Wooden wine boxes and pallets can be used to grow lots of small plants, such as lettuces, arugula, or a variety of salad leaves, radishes, salad onions, and fresh herbs. Aluminum or PVC gutters or pipes may also be used to grow small plants with shallow roots. They can be mounted on a wall or on balcony railings.

Pots can be hung one above another from a strong chain. Regular watering is crucially important and you'll need to pay attention to leakage. Provide a receptacle to catch the drips and don't forget to consider weight. Plant walls or plant pockets also optimize the space on your balcony or terrace.

Beans, peas, tomatoes, and cucumbers romp happily up trellis or wigwams. A sunflower can also be used as a support for beans. Planters can be also hung from wooden or metal trellises on the wall. Shelves attached to the wall or freestanding can accommodate lots of pots and containers. Hanging baskets can be hung from brackets on a wall or the balcony itself. They are especially good for trailing plants like strawberries, nasturtiums, and cherry tomatoes.

There are a few considerations to bear in mind when planning your vertical garden. Large terracotta pots and soil can be surprisingly heavy so check the strength and weight bearing capacity of your balcony. It shouldn't be an issue but if you have several large containers it is worth checking to ensure you are complying with any weight restrictions. Half barrels of soil can weigh hundreds of pounds when watered.

Plants need lots of light for growth and flavor. Arrange containers carefully to ensure maximum light and minimum shade. In north-facing situations or if you are surrounded by tall buildings, some shade will be inevitable, so choose leafy vegetables like lettuce, cabbage, or greens that can tolerate less light.

Needless to say you will want your balcony to look as beautiful as possible, so tuck some flowers in here and there—pretty little violas and cheery nasturtiums work really well, they are both decorative and edible, plus there are several climbing varieties.

A water tap and hose on the balcony or the terrace makes watering so much easier. In urban areas wind tunnels can cause a problem, so you may need to create a windbreak; acrylic can provide this.

A SQUARE FOOT GARDEN

The square foot garden was devised by Mel Bartholomew in Utah and is a real gem of a little garden. Once you have some planks, nails, bamboo rods, a few bags of potting compost or topsoil, some seedlings and seeds, and a place to assemble them, you have a small, easy-to-care-for garden in an hour or two.

My sister-in-law Natasha Harty frequently demonstrates how to make a square foot garden. This is perfect for those with little space or little confidence or both, and has become a catalyst for many to start to grow their own vegetables and herbs.

HOW TO MAKE A 3 X 4-FOOT GARDEN

Square foot gardens should be at most 4-feet wide so access is available from both sides). Three feet has been found to work better if children are gardening as their arms are shorter.

• Find a sunny, fairly level site. It can be on a hard surface, like gravel or concrete, or on lawn. It must be big enough that you have space to walk all around it, or to push a lawn mower around if on lawn.

• Find some planks approx. 7 inches wide. For a 3 x 4-foot garden either the sides or the ends will need to be longer by twice the thickness of the timber. For example, for 1-inch thick wood, add 2 inches to either the 4-foot or the 3-foot lengths, so that your bed will be an even 1 x 4-foot rectangle.

• Nail your wood together to make a 1 x 4-foot frame.

• On a hard surface place the frame in position, and skip the lawn instructions.

• On a lawn, place the frame where you want the garden to be. With a spade, cut

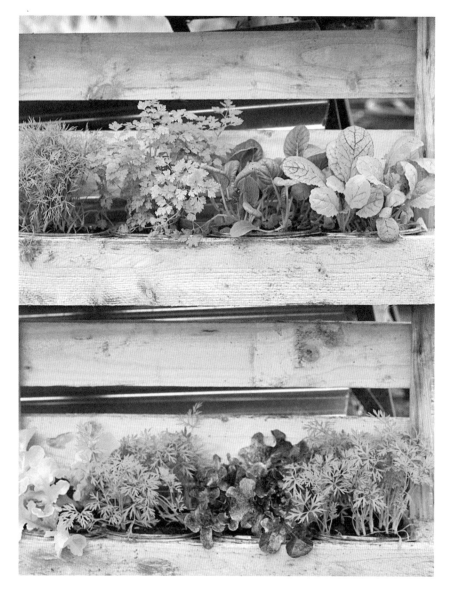

A vegetable garden in a timber pallet.

all along the outside edge of the frame. Lift off the frame and skim off the top sod. This is easier if you cut it into squares with the spade first. Place the frame back into the skimmed off area, making sure it sits down all around, and fill the sods back inside the frame.

• Sprinkle with the optional extras, like a bucket of sand, worm or garden compost, horse manure, etc. Add in the potting compost or topsoil, or a mixture of both, and rake the surface flat. For some extra fertility, sprinkle a layer of organic compost on the top.

• Cut bamboo rods to size, for a 1 x 4-foot bed you need 2 x 4-foot and 3 x 3-foot bamboo rods. These can be laid in place 12 inches apart and tied together securely where they cross. If you have a drill they can be left a little longer, and slipped into holes in the wood 1 foot apart and a little above the soil level.

• Plant the seedlings. Four lettuce plants in one square, 9 onion sets in another, 1 parsley plant in a third, and a pinch of arugula seed, radishes, thyme, and chives.

• Most of the time your garden will grow. Just make sure it has enough water in dry weather.

NO-DIG GARDENS

I first came across Charles Dowding at a Soil Association Conference in 2002 and then visited his smallholding on a fifth of an acre in Somerset, England. It was deep in winter yet there was an impressive selection of vegetables in his "No Dig" garden. I was hugely impressed not only by the variety but also the health of the plants and the fertility of the soil.

The origin of the "No Dig" method is unclear but it seems to date back to pre-industrial or nineteenth-century farming techniques. Masanobu Fukuoka started his pioneering research work in 1938, and published his Fukuokan philosophy of "Do Nothing Farming" in the 1970s. This is now acknowledged by many to be the beginning of the Permaculture movement. Later in 1946 F. C. King, Head Gardener at Levens Hall, in the UK's Lake District, wrote *Is Digging Necessary?* and in 1948 A. Guest published the book *Gardening Without Digging*. No-dig gardening was also promoted by Australian gardener and grower, Esther Deans in the 1970s, and American gardener Ruth Stout advocated a "permanent" mulching

technique in *Gardening Without Work*.

So what are the advantages and how do you start? No digging is the obvious one but proponents find it enhances the fertility of the soil and consistently produces higher yields of healthier crops—this is certainly our experience. However, for No Dig to be successful you need to use lots of mulch material, compost, well-rotted manure, seaweed, leaf mold, and straw.

Start by marking out a bed, ours are about 3-feet wide and whatever length suits the space you have available. Lay a layer of wet sodden cardboard or newspaper directly on the ground. This helps to smother perennial weeds. Then put at least 2 inches and up to 6 inches of compost on top. We have also used a layer of seaweed and some straw. It is important to keep it moist. We plant directly into the ground and have had tremendous success with leeks, onions, and lettuces in particular. In one bed the sets were pushed directly into the compost, in the other we covered the seed with straw, which produced even better results. Our beds don't have edges but one can edge the plots with wood boards, bales of straw, or galvanized iron. Scalloped willow edges also look great, as do stones, bricks, or roof tiles. You will need to replenish the mulch of organic materials every year.

SEED-SAVING

Seed-saving can be intimidating for a novice gardener but once you've harvested your first few crops you might think about saving some seeds from your favorite variety.

If you follow a few basic principles, getting started is not rocket science. This basic skill becomes even more crucial as both vegetable and flower varieties disappear at an alarming rate.

A crop of onions swelling nicely in a no-dig bed.

Borlotti beans drying in a pod.

As a general rule, the larger the seed the easier it is to save, so beginners may like to begin with peas and beans. Ensure the plant is healthy. Allow the seed pods to dry naturally for as long as possible on the plant. The pod will look papery and slightly wizened. When they are bone-dry, shell them; we rub them between our fingers in a large bowl. This will release most of the peas and beans, and we shell the remainder by hand.

Spread them out and let dry in a warm, airy place. In direct sunlight, on a windowsill, or in greenhouse is fine. When they are completely dry, store them in a mason jar, a tin box, or any airtight container.

Tomato seeds are also easy to save, as are potatoes, but it's crucial to choose seeds from plants that are totally disease-free. Leave tomatoes on the vine until fully ripe. Pick, cut, and scoop out the seeds with the tomato juice into a cup. Add a little water if required to keep the seeds from drying out. Mold will develop around the seeds. After 4 to 5 days put the moldy mixture into a strainer and wash clean under the tap. Place the clean seeds on a saucer to dry out for a week or two. Store in a paper envelope—seeds last well if kept in a cool, dry place. If you are saving seeds from different varieties, dry and store them separately in marked envelopes. Apparently allowing mold to develop in the seed-saving process will protect the future tomato plants against diseases when growing.

For potatoes, save a few of the smaller tubers, about the size of an egg. Store them in a cool, dark, frost-free shed out of reach of rodents. They will gradually begin to sprout (chit) and be ready to plant in spring, depending on the variety. One can even halve the potatoes, ensuring there is a sprout on each piece that you plant in the ground.

HARVESTING AND STORING ROOT VEGETABLES

In mild areas, root vegetables such as carrots, parsnips, beets, celeriac, salsify and scorzonera, rutabaga, turnips, and winter radish can usually over-winter in well-drained soil, to be dug as needed. Whereas a light frost will convert the starches into sugar, a hard frost can damage the roots, so you may want to cover the ground with a protective layer of straw or bracken about 6 inches deep. If in doubt you may want to lift the roots. Lift carefully so as not to damage them and use up any that are not in perfect condition. Do not wash the roots. Shake off any loose soil and trim off the foliage.

Beets can be left in the ground but they just become woodier so it's best to harvest them at optimum size. Be careful not to damage the root and trim the leaves about 2 inches from the top (they can be added to the compost heap). Store the beets in layers in damp sand either in boxes or in a heap against an inside wall in a frost-free shed.

Carrots and parsnips can be left in the ground but if you want to store them at their best, trim off leaves and store as above. Carrots can also be stored in an outside pit in a fairly sheltered spot in the garden. Build them up into a mound with the stalk end pointing outward. Cover with a layer of soil at least 2 inches thick. Pat it down well with the spade so it doesn't wash off in the rain. Recover the remaining roots carefully each time you take some carrots out.

Sandboxes are suitable for small quantities of root vegetables. Choose wood or plastic boxes. Store the roots (not touching) in layers of sand. Store in a dark, frost-free garage, shed, or cellar. Keep covered as you extract a few for use.

Root stores in Scandinavia are often dug into the ground to maintain a cool, even temperature. When we visited Fäviken in Sweden, chef Magnus Nilsson showed us his root store. They have double doors, to ensure that not even a crack of light filters into the inner sanctum. Even a split second of light can initiate sprouting and shorten the storage time.

EAT WHAT YOU SOW

The aim of this book is to instil in the reader the vast difference between the many ways of growing food, in whatever space you may have. I hope that the 400 or so recipes for the produce will inspire you to make seasonal and deliciously nourishing dishes and then convince you to find ways of growing more of your own food. Even if it's only a little of your own produce, it will have contributed to helping the planet just that little bit.

VEGETABLES

OKRA *Abelmoschus esculentous (syn. Hibiscus esculentus). Malvaceae* ANNUAL

Okra brings to mind gumbo, the classic American stew from Louisiana. Songs and poems have been written about this beloved stew, which originated in the eighteenth century.

The finger-like green seed pods of okra are unlikely to be on your vegetable A-list, but they are beautiful and really fun to grow. Remember, this is a warm-season crop, so they must be transplanted as starts into the garden in cooler climates. My publisher was baffled that I would want to include them in this book—she is a savvy gardener but her efforts to grow these only resulted in one okra on each plant. We've been growing them in the greenhouse for some years now, though, with considerable success—our plants have yielded about five or six each in a season.

VARIETIES

Red Burgundy—49 inches tall plants with 6 to 8 inch maroon pods—their color even extends into the plant's leaves and stems.

Beautiful Red Burgundy okra.

Clemson Spineless—this is the classic Southern variety. Open-pollinated, so seeds can be saved, it is a prolific producer of light green pods. Matures in 60 days on four-foot tall plants.
Red Velvet—beautiful red-stemmed pants grow four-to-five feet tall. Pick the tender, ribbed pods when they reach three-to-six inches.

HOW TO GROW

Okra enjoys the same growing conditions as cucumbers and melons: rich, fertile, well-drained soil. Sow the seeds in a greenhouse or under lights in early spring, 1 inch deep in trays or peat pots. The temperature needs to be at least 68°F for germination. It speeds up germination if you soak the seeds overnight in tepid water. Transplant before they get pot-bound, which can happen quickly. In southern gardens, you can sow okra directly in the garden in late spring, or after the soil temperature reaches 60 degrees.

CONTAINER GROWING

Okra grows beautifully in pots, in a greenhouse or on a sheltered sunny balcony or roof terrace. Feed and water plants in pots regularly.

HARVESTING

The pods will be ready in mid-summer to mid-autumn. Snip off the pods with a knife or shears while they are still quite small, 2 to 4 inches long.

PESTS AND DISEASES

Red spider mite—leaves turn pale and mottled and tiny red spiders will be clearly visible. Red spider thrives in hot, dry weather, so mist regularly and use insecticidal soap or horticultural oils. Try biological control—the predatory mite *Phytoseiulus persimilis* (see page 627).

Whitefly and aphids—both suck sap and excrete a sticky honeydew, which encourages the growth of a black, sooty mould over the leaves and soft tips. For whitefly, we have had success with sticky traps. Insecticial soap and horticultural oils are also effective. Try biological control—*Encarsia formosa*, order early.

To combat aphids, squash colonies with your finger and thumb or once again spray with plant or fish oils. Try biological control—*Aphidius* or *Aphidoletes* (see page 627).

GOOD FOR YOU...

Okra is naturally low in saturated fat, cholesterol and sodium, and helps stabilize blood sugar.

It's also a good source of protein, niacin, iron, phosphorus, zinc, copper and is rich in fibre. It contains vitamins A, C and K1. Also a source of thiamine, riboflavin, folate, calcium, magnesium, potassium and manganese.

WHAT TO DO WITH A GLUT

Give the seed pods to your friends to try out. They freeze well and can be used directly from frozen.

IN THE KITCHEN

Depending on how they are cooked, okra can be slimy. Smaller pods produce less slime. Frying or roasting them is best—either pan-fry or deep-fry them in hot oil in slices until slightly browned. Drain and toss on paper towels, season, and serve immediately.

Holly & Vinita Waddell's Louisiana Chicken Gumbo

Gumbo is a stew from Louisiana that is made from a well-flavored stock with the addition of meat or shellfish, a thickener, and what Louisianans call "the holy trinity of vegetables"—celery, peppers, and onions. It is characterized by the type of thickener used. This is an authentic Chicken Gumbo from Melville, Louisiana, written in Holly's own words—Holly was a student on our three-month Certificate Course in 2015.

SERVES 6

2 Andouille sausages, sliced into ¼-inch pieces

1 (4½-pound) free-range chicken

1 to 2 tablespoons extra virgin olive oil

1 large onion, chopped (14 ounces)

9 ounces celery, chopped into ⅓-inch dice

3 green bell peppers, seeded and chopped into ⅓-inch dice

3 quarts chicken stock

3 bay leaves

2¼ cups basmati rice

1 to 2 teaspoons cayenne pepper

9 ounces okra, sliced

sea salt and freshly ground black pepper

filé (sassafras) powder, for sprinkling over the top

FOR THE ROUX

1 cup plus 6 tablespoons all-purpose flour

¾ cup vegetable oil

First make the roux. Mix the flour and oil in a big pot (the pot needs to be big enough to add your stock). Stir constantly over medium heat until the mixture is a rich reddish-brown color. Do NOT let it burn.

Lightly brown the Andouille sausage and set aside.

Joint the chicken and brown each piece in oil from the Andouille sausage.

Heat a separate skillet, add the olive oil, and cook the onion, celery, and bell peppers for 10–15 minutes until tender.

Whisk the stock into the piping-hot roux. Season to taste with salt and freshly ground black pepper. Add the bay leaves and browned chicken pieces, bring to a boil, and simmer over medium heat for 30 to 45 minutes until the chicken is cooked and falling off the bone.

When the chicken is cooked, remove the chicken and debone. Remove the skin if you like—I prefer to remove it, it just adds a nice flavor to the stock. Set the chicken aside. Strain the broth and add the vegetables, Andouille sausage, okra, and cayenne pepper. Simmer for 15 minutes or until the okra is cooked to your liking. Add the chicken and season to taste.

In a separate pot, bring 1⅔ cups water to a boil. Add the rice and simmer for 10 to 12 minutes or until it is just cooked.

The gumbo is served over the hot rice (not mixed in) and should be like a thick soup with a serving of rice in the middle. The gumbo filé is served at the table for people to add to their gumbo to taste.

Traditionally gumbo is served with sweetened iced tea, sliced cucumbers from the garden (on the side) and freshly baked, warm cornbread.

DID YOU KNOW?
Okra is a member of the *Mallow Malva* family and has pretty flowers similar to hibiscus, which is in the same family. It originated in North Africa where it still grows wild and was probably brought to America in the 1600s with the slave trade.

Okra Masala

This is a really flavorsome okra dish with none of the slime that is often associated with okra. We love it with chicken or alone with a naan or flaky paratha. Okra is widely used in Indian cooking; this recipe comes from Madra, Uttar Pradesh.

SERVES 6 TO 8

3 green chiles
3 tablespoons vegetable oil
1 teaspoon black mustard seeds
6 ounces red onions, chopped
1 teaspoon toasted ground cumin
1 teaspoon toasted ground coriander
2 teaspoons garam masala
1 teaspoon ground turmeric
3 garlic cloves, minced
½ cup fresh tomato paste (2 large ripe
   tomatoes whizzed together)
pinch of chile flakes or ½ teaspoon mild
   Kashmiri chile powder
1 pound okra, trimmed and cut into
   ¾-inch pieces
sea salt
fresh cilantro, to serve

Split the chiles in half lengthwise and remove and discard the seeds.

Heat the oil in a wok or karahi, add the mustard seeds and onions, and cook until the onions are golden and the mustard seeds pop, then add the cumin, coriander, garam masala, and turmeric and continue to cook over medium heat for 1 minute.

Add the garlic, tomato purée, and chile flakes or chile powder and stir. Add the okra and green chiles to the wok. Fry for 5 to 7 minutes, stirring occasionally, then add ½ cup water or stock a little at a time and stir to make a sauce. Season with salt and simmer for 15 minutes, until the okra is cooked through and the sauce is thick and dry.

Serve with lots of cilantro scattered over the top.

Okra in Batter

These crisp little okra pakoras are pretty irresistible, and when you cook okra like this, there's none of the gloopiness that is sometimes associated with okra stews.

SERVES 4

½ pound okra
scant 1 cup all-purpose flour
1½ tablespoons rice flour
1 tablespoon mild Kashmiri chile powder
½ teaspoon ground cumin
½ teaspoon ground turmeric
1 teaspoon salt
1 teaspoon fresh thyme leaves
olive oil, for frying
lemon wedges, to serve

Slice the tops off the okra and discard. Cut the okra into ⅓-inch-thick rounds. Sift the flour, rice flour, chile powder, cumin, turmeric, and salt into a bowl. Add the thyme leaves and mix well. Make a well in the center and add about 6 tablespoons water, whisking it in a little at a time, to make a light batter about the consistency of heavy cream.

Heat the oil in a deep skillet over a medium-low heat. Fold the slices of okra gently into the batter, then drop tablespoons of the mixture gently into the oil. Fry, turning now and then, until the fritters are crisp and golden. This will take 6 to 7 minutes. Remove with a spider or slotted spoon and drain on paper towels.

Serve immediately with a wedge of lemon.

ONIONS
Allium cepa Allium fistulosum ANNUAL

Onions swelling nicely in our no-dig bed.

You may well wonder, why would one bother to grow onions when they are so widely available and seem to look just fine. Well, that's exactly how I felt I until we started to grow our own again, a few years ago, but now I know how much more delicious home-grown onions are. They are much sweeter and more meltingly tender when cooked, plus when you grow your own you can be sure they are not sprayed with a nasty anti-sprouting chemical or powder.

Scallions or spring onions are also easy to grow and tremendously versatile—they can be grown virtually year round in deep seed trays or planters. There seems to be considerable confusion between spring onions and scallions: spring onions are wispy little onions about the thickness of a child's paint brush while the wide end of scallions are as large as a thick pencil or my little finger.

VARIETIES

Welsh onions, potato onions, and tree or Egyptian oniosn are fun varieties that you may also enjoy growing. Welsh onions are brilliant for a perennial vegetable bed, as these hardy onions are wonderfully versatile with a mild sweet flavor. We've had them in the kitchen garden for over twenty years; they are planted around the base of a bay tree in our formal herb garden and re-emerge every spring. They multiply in perennial clumps and don't form bulbs but have large, decorative, white "pompom" flower heads, so they can also be grown in a flower bed or herbaceous border. As they are evergreen, the leaves can be used as a substitute for scallions or chives.

BULB OR COMMON ONIONS
Growing from sets
Forum—One of the earliest bulbing onions. Plant in Spring for green onion by early July, or bulbs a month later.
Stuttgarter—flattened, globe-shaped yellow onion with a mild flavor, maturing in August or September. Open-pollinated.
Egyptian Walking Onion—These true topsetting onons produce small red topsets above delicious greens, which can be harvested twice a year.

Growing onions from plants
Walla Walla—Big, round, sweet, and mild. Stores up to three months.
Superstar—This hybrid variety can be grown anywhere in North America. It matures much earlier than is typical of white, sweet onions. The bulbs have a mild, sweet flavor and they store well.
Copra—this is the ultimate storage onion, it will keep well for up to 12 months; mildly pungent, 3 to 4 inch bulbs.

Growing bulb onions from seed
Red Baron—Very popular red onion, strong flavor, and stores well.
Ailsa Craig—Old large variety dating from 1899, renowned for its flavor, is hard to beat.
Candy—as its name suggests, this is a sweet onion. A good alternative to Walla Walla for southern gardens.
Purplette—Small bulbs are good for pickling; mildly sweet flavor.
Cortland—large, round, pungent onions, their thick brown skin allows them to store well.
Granex Hybrid—this Vidalia type is suited for southern gardening. The plants produce colossul sweet bulbs.
Red Weathersfiled—sometimes classified as a Spanish onion, the flesh is mildly pungent. The plants are hardy and the bulbs store well.

SPRING ONIONS AND SCALLIONS
Allium fistulosum Guardsman—Also known as the Welsh onion or Japanese onion, this is a cross between a bunching onion and a bulb onion with small greenish flowers in early summer.
Red Welsh Bunching Onion—thick, green stems and hollow, flavorful leaves; does not form a bulb, but side shoots may be replanted.
White Lisbon—Traditional variety, very quick-growing spring onion, plant in succession from early spring to late summer.
Parade—Spring onion with lovely green upright foliage, does not form a bulb, good flavor and fast growing.
Crimson Forest—New red variety bred in the UK, adds color to salads. Hardy enough for autumn sowing.

HOW TO GROW

Both onions and shallots can be grown from plants, sets (mini onions) or seed, which is, of course, much cheaper than buying plants or sets. Seeds require more work but often yield better-quality onions; gardeners entering show competitions will grow their produce from seed.

Onions like well-drained fertile soil, with an ideal pH of 6.5 to 7, and a sunny location. They work well in raised beds. Plant sets in early to mid-spring. In the South, you can buy some varieties that can be planted in mid-autumn for an early summer crop. Autumn-planted onions will be ready to harvest about a month before the spring-sown crop.

TO PLANT SETS

Push each set gently into the well-prepared soil, with the growing point upwards, so the tips are just above the ground. We have had good results from spacing them 4 inches apart with 10 inches between rows. Birds love to pull them out of the ground, so you may want to cover them with row covers held up by pea sticks or try one of the various bird scarers available on the market.

Managing weeds is the biggest challenge, because the shallow roots of the onions grow close to the surface and can easily be damaged by careless hoeing. Some gardeners even plant onions through plastic or weed-control fabric to control weeds, which also helps to keep the soil warm. We have had success mulching with seaweed or straw, too, both of which will naturally break down in the soil.

SETS From planting to harvesting take 3 to 4 months.

SEED We have grown onions from seed very successfully by planting in early spring in trays indoors, sowing three seeds to a cell. Plant out in late spring as soon as the weather gets mild.

We don't separate the seedlings in the cell, just plant them as a group, so there is minimum root disturbance and they get off to a good start.

Bolting can be a problem, particularly with red onions, if the weather is erratic—e.g. a particularly cold spring followed by a hot summer. Smaller sets seem to be less susceptible to bolting than larger ones. Plant in a well-prepared weed-free soil. Also, in our experience, where we have added plenty of humus (see page 16) to the soil, we suffer less from bolting. Don't use farmyard manure as onions don't need high levels of nitrogen.

Spring onions or scallions may be grown either indoors or outdoors. We grow them all year round in the greenhouse. Sow in early spring; buy a deep seed tray, fill with potting compost, then sow the seeds in groups of six (multi-sowing). You can also grow them in cells, putting a pinch of six seeds in each section. This way they grow and can be harvested in bunches of six.

Plant outdoors 3 to 4 weeks before the last frost. They like well-drained soil and they love full sun. We overwinter them in the greenhouse. Outdoors, sow in succession up until late summer to pick up until early spring. Direct sow in drills as thinly as possible because they will fill out. Leave 10 inches between rows for ease of hoeing. If you want to have a very early crop, it's possible to multi-sow them in cell trays indoors in early spring, then plant them out in little clumps 9 inches apart, just don't let them get pot bound.

CONTAINER GROWING

Onions can be grown in a container, but the yield will be smaller. Welsh onions will also grow successfully in a large pot

Bunches of onions curing in an optimum environment in the greenhouse.

or trough. Bunching onions or scallions work brilliantly in all kinds of pots and troughs and can also be scattered through a flower border.

HARVESTING AND STORING

We begin harvesting in midsummer and use both the bulb and the greens.

Spring-planted onions are ready for storing in late summer/early autumn, when the onion stalks turn yellow and fall over.

In a good summer the onions could remain in the ground for a couple of weeks longer, but if the weather is inclement, we pull the onions on a sunny day, tie them in bunches of 8 to 10, bring them into the greenhouse and hang them on wires and allow them to dry until we need them. They are usually gone by early winter.

Good air ventilation is essential while onions are drying. Keep a vigilant eye on them and use any soft ones as soon as possible. Don't cut or trim off the stalks, otherwise the onions won't cure properly. During the drying process the sugars in the stalks go down into the bulb and preserve it. When the onions are properly dry they can be tied into bunches or plaited and hung in a dry frost-free shed or a pantry. In optimum conditions they can last until mid-spring. In our experience, red onion varieties don't tend to store as well as white onions.

Spring onions will be ready to harvest about 70 days from planting. Pull as you need and use every scrap.

PESTS

Crop rotation, always an important factor in vegetable growing, is vital here, so no member of the onion family should be grown on the same piece of ground for four years or more.

Several pests can attack onions—including onion fly and onion eelworm—but the diseases we encounter most often are downy mildew, white rot and neck rot. Keeping them weed-free helps and many gardeners tell me that a row of parsley planted close to onions will keep onion flies away.

Plants whose roots get damaged by careless hoeing are more susceptible to disease, particularly downy mildew. Space plants well apart to reduce risk of damage and to encourage good air circulation.

Spring onions are highly resistant to pests and are almost disease proof.

GOOD FOR YOU...

Spring onions and scallions are a good source of vitamins A, C, K, folate, calcium, iron, potassium, magnesium, phosphorus, manganesae, copper and thiamin.

WHAT TO DO WITH A GLUT

Onions remain in the ground for months on end so use them as you need.

IN THE KITCHEN

Onions can be eaten at the scallion stage, which is a bit of a waste, but still one can sneak off a few green leaves to add to omelets, frittatas, or a potato salad. They are also delicious eaten at new-season spring onion stage when both the bulbs and leaves can be eaten.

Onions roasted in their skins are one of our favorite standby recipes. What could be easier than throwing them into the oven in their skins, where they roast to melting tenderness? Just cook them until they are soft and squishy and will pop out of the charred skin when the root is removed. However, **Roast Onion Halves** have even more flavor. Cut the unpeeled onions in half from top to bottom, then brush the cut side with extra virgin olive oil and season with salt and freshly ground pepper. Arrange, cut-side down, on a baking sheet in a single layer. Roast in a preheated oven at 450°F for 20 to 40 minutes, depending on size, until the cut side is caramelized and the onion is meltingly tender. We use these onions in myriad ways—as an accompanying vegetable, as a starter with goat cheese or curds, and in warm salads.

Welsh onion leaves can be snipped like scallions or spring onions into salad, soups, omelets or deviled eggs.

Every scrap of a spring onion is edible—the green leaves, white bulbs, and even the roots. As with spring onions, you can eat scallions from when they are small and wispy to quite large. The flavor is quite delicate when young and gets progressively stronger as they mature, and the white part has a stronger flavor than the green leaves. They can be eaten raw or cooked; the bottom can be eaten raw but is often sautéed a little first as a base or to add to dishes. Scallions are important in Chinese cooking and are also often sliced and scattered over dishes just before serving.

For **Chargrilled Red Onions with Thyme Leaves** (serves 6), peel 3 large red onions, then halve them through the root and cut into generous half-

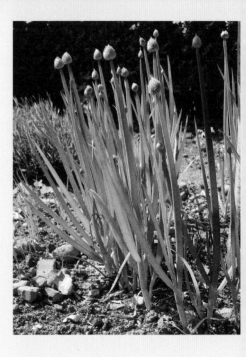

Welsh onions—a perennial worth growing as every part, including the seeds, is edible.

moons. Thread the onion slices onto flat metal skewers, brush both sides with 4 tablespoons extra virgin olive oil and 1 tablespoon balsamic vinegar and sprinkle with 2 teaspoons fresh thyme leaves. Marinate for 15 to 20 minutes. Grill over medium heat on an outdoor grill or on the stovetop in a grill pan. Cook until browned and softish in the center.

For **Melted Scallions with Thyme Leaves** to serve 6 to 8, peel and trim 2 pounds young scallions, leaving the root intact. Slice the white and green parts of the scallions into rounds. Heat 3 to 4 tablespoons extra virgin olive oil in a heavy saucepan and toss the scallions in. Add 2 teaspoons thyme leaves and season with salt and freshly ground pepper. Cook over low heat for about 15 minutes until soft. Season to taste and serve in a hot vegetable dish. They are particularly good with a well-hung sirloin or lamb steak or a duck breast.

Confiture d'Oignons

This superb recipe has become a new basic in recent years and I always have a few jars made up. It is also good served warm, particularly with pan-grilled monkfish or even a lamb chop.

. . . .

MAKES 2 CUPS

⅓ cup butter
1½ pounds white or red onions, peeled
  and thinly sliced
⅔ cup superfine sugar
1 teaspoon salt
½ teaspoon freshly ground black pepper
¼ cup plus 3 tablespoons sherry vinegar
1 cup full-bodied red wine
2 tablespoons Crème de Cassis (page 382)

Melt the butter in the saucepan and hold your nerve until it becomes a deep nut-brown color—this will give the onions a delicious rich flavor—but be careful not to let it burn. Toss in the onions and sugar, add the salt and freshly ground pepper, and stir well. Cover the saucepan and cook for 30 minutes over low heat, keeping an eye on the onions and stirring from time to time.

Add the sherry vinegar, red wine, and cassis. Cook for an additional 30 minutes, uncovered, stirring regularly. This onion jam must cook very gently. When it is cold, skim off and discard any butter that rises to the top and use to sauté and onion and potato soup base, perhaps.

Confiture d'oignons will keep for months in sterilized glass jars and is especially delicious with pâtés and terrines of meat, game, and poultry.

Chicken Tagine with Caramelized Onions & Raisins

This was one of the most delicious tagines I tasted in Marrakesh. It seems like a lot of onions but they reduce during cooking and the sweetness of the caramelized onion combined with the honey and spices is rich and irresistible.

. . . .

SERVES 6 TO 8

4½ ounces raisins
3 to 4 tablespoons extra virgin olive oil
2 pounds 14 ounces sliced onions
2¼ pounds chicken thighs or 4 thighs and
  4 drumsticks
1 teaspoon ground cinnamon
2 teaspoons grated fresh ginger
good pinch of saffron, soaked in 1
  tablespoon water
1¾ cups chicken stock or water
1 good tablespoon honey
sea salt and freshly ground black pepper
fresh flat-leaf parsley, coarsely chopped

Put the raisins into a little bowl and cover with boiling water to plump up.

Heat the olive oil in a tagine or casserole, add the onions, and cook, stirring occasionally, for 10 to 15 minutes until they are soft and slightly colored. Add the chicken pieces, cinnamon, ginger, saffron, salt, and freshly ground pepper. Cook for 8 to 10 minutes until the chicken begins to brown, then add the chicken stock or water to come halfway up, cover, and continue to cook for 40 to 45 minutes, depending on the size of the chicken pieces.

Finally, add the honey and raisins and continue to cook, uncovered, until the sauce reduces and the onions are richly caramelized. Season to taste.

Serve scattered with lots of fresh parsley.

Swansey's Penang Laksa

Many of you will be familiar with the delicious laksa recipe but this is another version given to me by Lay Choo Lim from Penang, who did the Certificate Course here at the school in 2007. The recipe was given to her by her late mother, Swansey. Lay Choo uses local fresh white rice noodles in Malaysia, but over here she uses fine udon noodles, which she cooks like spaghetti until slightly al dente. Penangites like their laksa hot—so use fewer chiles according to your preference; perhaps use 4 chiles and a red bell pepper instead of the fifth.

SERVES 6 TO 8

3 tablespoons sunflower oil

1 pound fish fillet, such as monkfish, cut into ¾-inch dice

9 ounces raw shrimp, peeled and cut into ⅓-inch dice

salt

1⅔ cups coconut milk

¾ cup plus 1 tablespoon tamarind juice (½ cup hot water and 2 ounces dry tamarind squeezed and strained)

2½ cups fish stock (optional)

1 tablespoon palm sugar or soft brown sugar

5¼ ounces round rice noodles or spaghetti

FOR THE CHILE PASTE

8 fresh Thai chiles, seeded

3 stalks lemongrass (white parts only)

1 level tablespoon ground turmeric

10 shallots (approx. 200g)

1 (1¾-ounce) block (2 × 1 × ¼ inch) belachan (shrimp paste)

1 inch galangal (approx. 1 ounce)

TO SERVE

1 cucumber, seeded, cut in very fine strips

½ fresh pineapple, cut in very fine strips (canned pineapple works but the liquid must be fully drained)

½ small head lettuce, cut into very fine strips

1 large red onion, very thinly sliced

3 large (or 6 small) gherkins, cut into thin strips

fresh mint leaves

lime wedges, to serve

Roughly chop all the ingredients for the chile paste. Transfer to a food processor and pulse until a fine paste is formed.

Heat a clay pot (a saucepan works as an alternative) over medium heat and add the oil. When the oil is hot, add the chile paste. Continue to stir, otherwise the chile paste will burn. Cook for 4 to 5 minutes until the aroma is fully released, then add the fish and the shrimp. Stir to coat thoroughly with the cooked chile paste and add salt to taste. After a minute, add the coconut milk and tamarind juice. Depending on how thick you like the laksa sauce, the mixture can be thinned down by adding either fish stock or more tamarind juice, if you want it to be more sour. When the fish and prawns are almost cooked, add the sugar. Taste and, if necessary, add more salt. Simmer for a few minutes after the fish and prawns are cooked until the chile oil comes to the surface. Remove from the heat.

Boil a big pot of water, add the rice noodles or spaghetti, and cook according to the package instructions. Drain once the cooked. Divide the noodles into the serving bowls. Add all the vegetables and fruit, including a few mint leaves on top of the noodles.

Heat the laksa sauce until it is simmering again and ladle into the bowls to cover the noodles, vegetables, and fruit. Make sure there are enough fish and shrimp in the bowl and not just the liquid. A traditional way of warming the noodles and vegetables is to pour the laksa sauce (but not the noodles or the vegetables) back into the pot. Once the sauce comes back to a boil, ladle it out again. Garnish with a few more mint leaves and lime wedges and serve.

DID YOU KNOW?
Welsh onions didn't originate in Wales as one might think, but owe their name to the pre-German word *walhaz*.

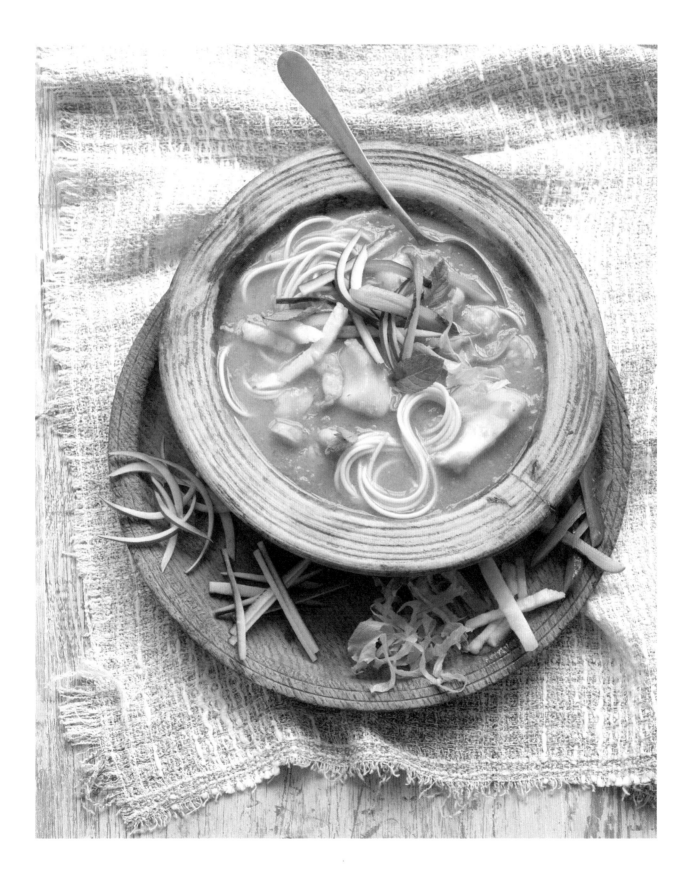

Goat Cheese, Scallion & Potato Tart

The scallions add a delicious sweetness to this tart. A little diced chorizo sausage would also be delicious in this recipe, not more than 1¾ ounces, though, otherwise the flavor will predominate.

SERVES 6

FOR THE SHORTCRUST PASTRY

1¼ cups all-purpose flour, plus extra
   for dusting

5 tablespoons butter

1 organic egg

FOR THE FILLING

1 tablesoon butter

1 tablespoon olive oil

¼ pound scallions, thinly sliced

1¾ ounces chorizo, diced (optional)

4 to 6 small new potatoes, cooked

3 organic eggs

3 tablespoons thyme leaves, plus flowers
   to garnish

¾ cup cream

4 ounces goat cheese

sea salt and freshly ground black pepper

green salad, to serve

First make the shortcrust pastry. Sift the flour into a bowl and rub in the butter until the mixture resembles coarse bread crumbs. Mix 2 tablespoons of water with the egg and add just enough to bind the pastry. Wrap in parchment paper and chill for at least 15 minutes.

Preheat the oven to 350°F. Remove the pastry from the fridge, then roll out on a well-floured worktop until large enough to line an 9-inch tart pan or flan ring to a thickness of about ⅛ inch. Line with waxed paper or parchment paper and fill to the top with dried beans. Rest for 15 minutes, then bake for 20 minutes. Remove the beans and paper, brush the bottom with the remaining egg wash, and return to the oven for 1 to 2 minutes. This seals the pastry and helps to avoid a "soggy bottom."

Now make the filling. Melt the butter in a skillet over medium heat, add the olive oil and onions, and sweat with a good pinch of salt for 4 to 5 minutes until soft but not colored. Add the chorizo, if using.

Cut the cooked potatoes into thick slices or chunks. Whisk the eggs and most of the thyme leaves in a bowl, add the cream, onions, and potatoes. Season well with salt and freshly ground pepper. Pour into the pastry shell.

Drop a few blobs of goat cheese into the tart at regular intervals. Bake for 40 to 45 minutes or until just set in the center. Sprinkle the remaining thyme leaves and flowers (if available), over the top. Serve with a good green salad.

Pickled Red Onions

Dip into the jar of pickled onions to add to a sandwich, salad, or as an accompaniment to beef or fish burgers.

MAKES TWO ½-PINT JARS

1 cup white wine vinegar

½ cup granulated sugar

pinch of salt

3 whole cloves

1 cinnamon stick, broken

1 dried red chile

1 pound red onions, peeled and thinly
   sliced on a mandoline

Put the vinegar, sugar, salt, and spices in a heavy-bottomed pan and bring to a boil. Put in one-third of the sliced onions and simmer for 2 to 3 minutes or until they turn pink and wilt. Lift out the cooked onions with a slotted spoon and transfer them to a sterilized jam jar with a nonreactive lid. Repeat with the remaining onions, cooking them in two batches.

Fill the jars with the hot vinegar, put on the lids, and set aside to cool overnight. Once cold, store in the fridge for up to a week or two.

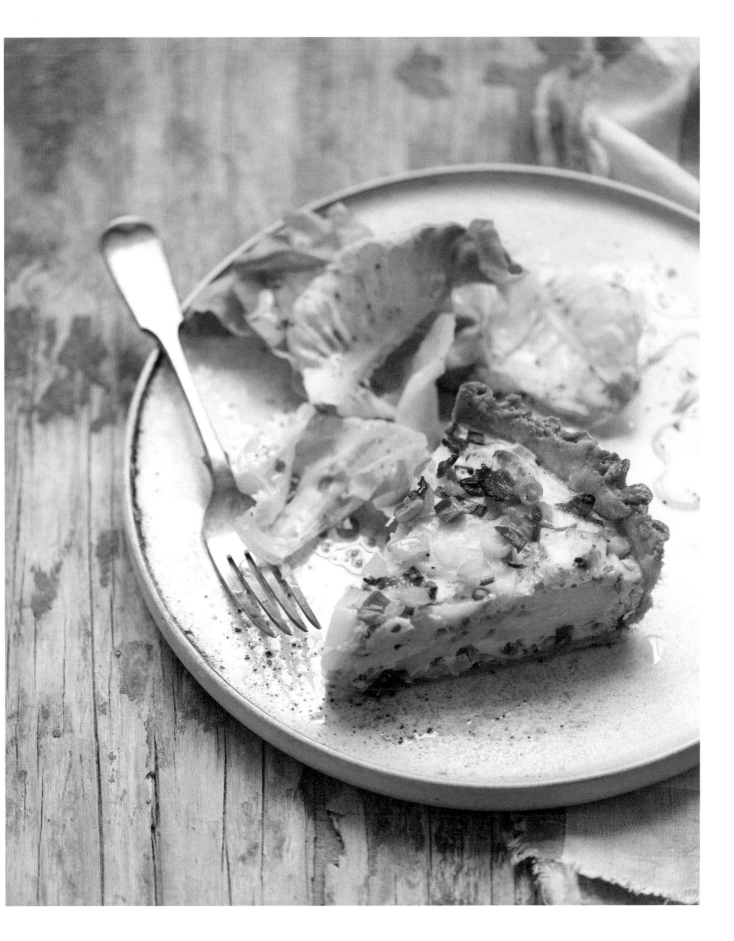

SHALLOTS *Allium cepa* ANNUAL

Chefs love shallots as they give depth of flavor without being overpowering. They deserve to be better appreciated by the rest of us. The flavor is more delicate and the texture more melting than onions. They can also be used fresh like a large spring onion. They are easy to grow and, everywhere you plant one bulb it multiplies to form a cluster of 5 to 8 bulbs.

VARIETIES

Seek out virus-free bulbs, they will be higher yielding and more vigorous.
Conservor—produces long bulbs with coppery red skin and cream-colored flesh. The bulbs peel easily.
Camelot—teardrop-shaped bulbs have red skin and creamy white flesh. Bulbs will store well through winter.
French Red—prolific, 1-2 inch long red skinned bulbs with a sweet, mild flavor.

HOW TO GROW

Sow all the members of the allium family in one area and rotate. Like onions, shallots are easiest to grow from "sets." We plant in mid-spring in well-drained soil, 10 inches apart with 12 inches between the rows. (In warmer climates, shallots can be fall-planted for an early summer crop.) This allows enough room to hoe the weeds between the rows. As with onions, keep shallots weed-free and be careful not to damage the shallow roots if hoeing. Hand weeding is best.

DID YOU KNOW?

The great culinary center of shallots was Bordeaux, hence the inspired culinary partnership of rich red wine and shallots and the classic Sauce Bordelaise.

Red Sun shallots almost ready to harvest.

A plot 2 yards square will yield around 184 shallots if they are planted 10 inches apart with 3 rows in a bed. Enough to last you from late summer to mid-spring.

Bolting can occur some years more than others depending on weather conditions, so do seek out the best-quality sets you can get.

CONTAINER GROWING

Shallots can be grown in containers, ideally in a sunny place. They need well-drained compost and drainage. Keep well watered during dry periods.

HARVESTING

Shallots will be ready to harvest when the leaves start to die back. If the weather is sunny they can be left on the soil surface to dry off for about a week.

Dig and store on chicken wire frames in a single layer so the air can circulate. When dried, tie in bunches some leaf is left, otherwise store in a basket or hang in net onion bags in a well-ventilated, bright shed; check regularly and discard any that are deteriorating—you may have them up to mid-spring.

PESTS AND DISEASES

Shallots can suffer from the same diseases as onions (see page 31).

GOOD FOR YOU...

Shallots contain more antioxidants, minerals and vitamins, weight for weight, than onions. They are a rich source of vitamin A which is a powerful antioxidant. They also contain vitamin B6, folate, thiamine, and vitamin C.

WHAT TO DO WITH A GLUT

Drye as described above. You can also pickle them like onions (see page 36).

IN THE KITCHEN

Shallots can be eaten raw or cooked. Minced and use for béarnaise sauce or beurre blanc and classic French red wine sauces. Snipped fresh leaves can be used in potato salad or whole in soup or stock.

Steak with Béarnaise Sauce & Pommes Frites

Steak, béarnaise, and pommes frites are an unbeatable combination—life doesn't get much better. Shallots are essential to the flavor of a good béarnaise and have always been an integral part of the ingredients for this classic sauce. The consistency of béarnaise sauce should be considerably thicker than that of hollandaise or beurre blanc, both of which ought to be a light coating consistency. If you do not have tarragon vinegar to hand, use a wine vinegar and add some extra chopped tarragon.

SERVES 6

1 garlic clove
6 (6-ounce) sirloin or fillet steaks
a little olive oil
salt and freshly ground black pepper
watercress, to serve

FOR THE POMMES ALLUMETTES
1 pound floury potatoes, such as russets
olive oil, for deep-frying
salt

FOR THE BÉARNAISE SAUCE
¼ cup tarragon vinegar
¼ cup dry white wine
2 teaspoons minced shallots
pinch of freshly ground black pepper
2 organic egg yolks
4 to 6 ounces salted or unsalted butter,
 depending on what it is being served
 with
1 tablespoon chopped fresh French
 tarragon leaves

Prepare the steaks about 1 hour before cooking. Cut a garlic clove in half, rub both sides of each steak with the cut clove, grind some black pepper over the steaks, and sprinkle on a few drops of olive oil. Turn the steaks in the oil and set aside. If using sirloin steaks, score the fat at 1-inch intervals.

Wash and peel the potatoes. Cut them into tiny, even matchsticks and soak in cold water for 15 minutes. Dry them thoroughly with a dishtowel.

To make the béarnaise sauce, boil the first four ingredients together in a low, heavy-bottomed stainless-steel saucepan until completely reduced and the pan is almost dry but the sauce is not browned. Add 1 tablespoon of cold water immediately. Remove the pan from the heat and let cool for 1 to 2 minutes.

Whisk in the egg yolks and add the butter bit by bit over very low heat, whisking all the time. As soon as one piece melts, add the next piece; it will gradually thicken. If it shows signs of becoming too thick or slightly "scrambling," remove from the heat immediately and add a little cold water. Finally, add the French tarragon and season to taste.

If the sauce is slow to thicken it may be because you are excessively cautious and the heat is too low. Increase the heat slightly and continue to whisk until all the butter is added and the sauce is a thick coating consistency. Keep the sauce warm in a heatproof bowl over hot but not simmering water or in an insulated container until you want to serve it.

Heat a grill pan. Season the steaks well with salt and cook to your taste—rare, medium rare, medium—in the hot pan. If using sirloin steaks, then turn them over onto the fat and cook for 3 to 4 minutes or until the fat becomes dry. Put the steaks onto a plate and let them rest for a few minutes in a warm place while you cook the pommes allumettes.

Heat the oil to 375°F. Fry the potatoes until they are golden brown and very crisp. Drain on paper towels. Sprinkle with salt. (If the pommes allumettes are very crisp they will keep in the oven for 10 minutes or even longer.)

Put the steaks onto hot plates. Serve the béarnaise sauce over one end of the steak or in a little bowl on the side of the plate and the pommes allumettes and fresh watercress alongside.

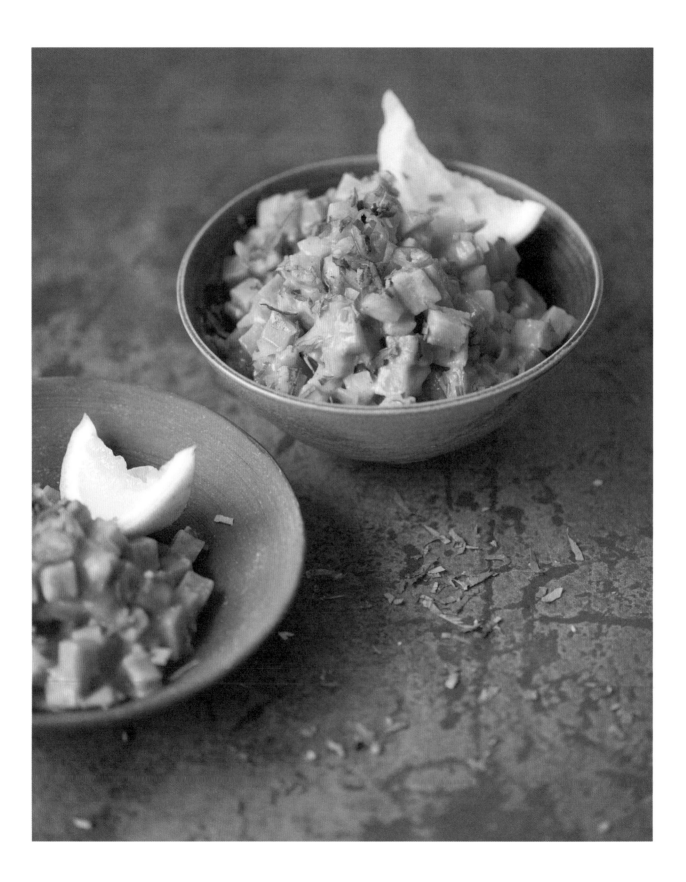

Sri Lankan Carrots with Shallots & Green Chile

Shallots add extra sweetness to this simple spiced carrot dish, which can be fully prepared ahead and gently heated later.

. . . .

SERVES 4

2 tablespoons sunflower or olive oil
2 ounces shallots, chopped
½ green chile, seeded and chopped
1 pound carrots, cut into ¾-inch dice
1 teaspoon freshly ground cumin seeds
1 teaspoon freshly ground coriander seeds
½ teaspoon freshly ground fennel seeds
pinch of cayenne pepper
⅛ teaspoon ground turmeric
½ teaspoon salt
freshly ground black pepper (a few grinds)
¾ cup coconut milk
roughly chopped fresh cilantro, to garnish
lemon wedges, to serve

Put the oil into a heavy, low-sided pan and set over medium heat. When the oil is hot, add the shallots and green chile. Stir-fry for about 2 minutes or until the shallots have softened a bit. Add the carrots, cumin, coriander, fennel, cayenne pepper, turmeric, salt, and pepper and continue to fry, stirring at the same time, over medium heat for 2 to 3 minutes.

Whisk the coconut milk to mix the thick and thin liquid evenly. Add to the base and bring to a simmer. Cover, reduce the heat to low, and simmer very gently for 15 to 20 minutes. Season to taste, scatter some roughly chopped cilantro on top, and serve with lemon wedges.

Italian Beef Stew with Shallots

The shallots add sweetness and a roll of pork fat adds a delicious unctuousness to this gutsy stew.

. . . .

SERVES 6–8

3 pounds well-aged stewing beef or lean
    flank
1 tablespoon extra virgin olive oil
1 pound shallots, peeled
2 large carrots, cut into ½-inch slices
1 heaped tablespoon plain flour
a roll of pork fat tied with cotton string
    (optional)
⅔ cup red wine
⅔ cup beef stock
1 cup homemade tomato paste
5 ounces flat mushrooms, sliced
1 tablespoon chopped flat-leaf parsley,
    plus extra sprigs to garnish
sea salt and freshly ground black pepper
Gremolata (page 513—optional), to garnish
polenta, mashed potatoes or noodles and a
    green salad, to serve

Preheat the oven to 320°F.

Trim the meat of any excess fat and cut into 1½-inch cubes. Heat the olive oil in a Dutch oven and sweat the shallots and carrots over a gentle heat, with a lid on, for 10 minutes.

Heat a little more olive oil in a frying pan until almost smoking. Sear the pieces of meat on all sides, reduce the heat, stir in the flour, cook for a minute, then add the roll of pork fat, if using. Mix the wine, stock, and tomato paste together and add gradually to the Dutch oven. Season with salt and freshly ground pepper. Cover and transfer to the oven for 2½ to 3 hours.

Meanwhile, sauté the mushrooms and add to the Dutch oven, about 30 minutes before the end of cooking. Add lots of chopped parsley and garnish with Gremolata or sprigs of parsley. Serve with polenta, mashed potatoes, or noodles, and a good green salad.

LEEKS *Allium porrum* BIENNIAL BUT WE GROW AS AN ANNUAL

Leeks are part of the extensive allium family so are related to onions, garlic, chives, and scallions. They are easy to grow and immensely versatile—a brilliant standby winter vegetable. Every scrap is edible, including the roots, which can be sauteed or deep-fried.

We grow a fine plot of leeks every year, both outdoors and in the greenhouse—where they didn't work so well. We eat them from the time they are pencil thin until they are the size of a brush handle. If you are short of space, their glaucous spiky leaves work wonderfully in a flower border and will withstand even the harshest winter weather.

The perennial variety, Allium ampeloprasum var. babingtonii, is well worth seeking out. It is frequently mentioned in old Irish manuscripts and

is thought to have been one of the main ingredients, along with potatoes, in an ancient Irish leek and oatmeal soup called Brotchán Roy, meaning "A broth fit for a king"

This perennial leek grows wild on the West and Northwest coast of Ireland, but we have been growing it in our kitchen garden for over two decades, where it re-emerges every year. More recently, we transplanted some into the little wood, where it has started to romp away, providing brilliant ground cover as well as lots of leeks for the stockpot in the spring when our other crop has finished. These wild leeks are tougher in texture, but the flavor is delicious.

VARIETIES

There are many different varieties available, some of which mature in late autumn, some in winter/spring. The winter/spring varieties are invaluable at a time when there isn't much else in the garden and provide a great opportunity to extend the season.

King Richard—Matures early to a large, tender leek. Very attractive plants.
Tadorna—Open-pollinated so seed can be saved from year to year. Grows fast and produces a very reliable crop.
Dawn Giant—Grows up to 15 inches long and 2 inches across. An early variety that can be sown directly in the garden. Matures in about 100 days.
Bandit—Winter/spring. Resistant to bolting, is hardy, tolerating cold conditions, and keeps until mid-spring.
Pandora—Popular late summer/autumn variety, which can be harvested from early autumn to early in the new year, or

Young Musselburgh F1 leeks with a few rosettes of wintercress growing underneath.

longer in milder areas.

HOW TO GROW

For an autumn crop, sow the seeds in modular trays, 1/3 inch deep, in a greenhouse or under lights indoors in early spring. They will take about 6 to 8 weeks to grow to transplanting size, but it's very important not to let them get pot-bound before transplanting, or they will bolt. Alternatively, you can purchase leek starts in garden centers or through seed catalogues

Leeks are tolerant of a variety of soils but do best transplanted into a rich, fertile, alkaline soil with a pH of 6 to 7.5, perhaps after a potato crop, so the soil is loose and crumbly. They are heavy feeders so the soil needs to be enriched with lots of manure or compost in the autumn before planting.

The leeks are ready to transplant when they are about 8 inches high and pencil-thick. Using a dibber, make holes in the soil where you want them to grow, 6 to 8 inches deep and the same distance apart, with 10 to 12 inches between rows. Drop the young leeks down into the hole; if some of the roots stick out of the hole, trim them. We also trim the leaves to about 6 inches above the hole. Fill the hole around the leek with water but not soil—this sounds odd but believe me it works. Keep the bed weed free.

For a supply of leeks from autumn to late winter, make three sowings, starting in early spring with an early variety, followed by a maincrop and then a late variety. We generally just sow one maincrop.

Seeds can also be sown directly into the soil in late spring, but the soil temperature does need to be about 50°F.

Earth up several times so you have

the maximum pale elongated leek—this simply means drawing up the soil around the bottom of the leek, which prevents light getting to the bottom part so that it stays white rather than turning dark green. The spiky green leaves are stronger in flavor than the white stems but can also be used in stock or soup, or if you have a surplus, add them to the compost heap.

Leeks are biennial, they will form edible leaves in the first year and will naturally bolt in the second year. In the first year they can bolt if left in the growing cell too long, or in some years the weather can be difficult and they will bolt.

Some gardeners treat leeks as perennials; they let them bolt and go to flower so that they seed into the ground around them and come back every year. Interestingly, if you dig up a leek that has flowered you may find little cloves underneath, quite late in their second summer, a bit like elephant garlic, *Allium ampeloprasum*.

CONTAINER GROWING

Leeks can be grown in a container filled at least 12 to 14 inches deep with rich soil—the more depth, the better quality the leeks. Make sure the leeks don't dry out.

HARVESTING

Leeks are at their most tender and delicious when young. Baby leeks can be harvested from about ¾ inch in diameter or even smaller. They seem to survive both frost and even a little snow, however the flavor and texture deteriorate as they grow larger, so there's no need to strive for prize-winning giant leeks!

Leeks are all the more valuable because they can stay in the ground and be harvested as needed throughout the winter where the ground doesn't freeze

solid. It's best to dig up leeks, rather than try to pull them, otherwise they'll most likely break. If you need to clear the ground they are growing in, dig up the last of the crop, "heel them in" (temporarily plant them into another bed) in a shady spot and use as soon as you can.

If the leeks bolt and run to seed, don't despair, the pretty allium flowers are edible and if snapped off the leek may produce small white bulbs at the base, which are delicious as baby onions or shallots.

PESTS AND DISEASES

Though we haven't had it, leek rust affects all the allium family and can be an issue. It's an airborne fungus that particularly affects garlic but even though it looks unsightly, with strange orange powdery spots on the leaves, it doesn't affect the taste. The variety *Crusader F1* is resistant to rust.

We have also had occasional problems with white rot, which affects all members of the onion family. As with all vegetables, for maximum success you should be meticulous about rotation and make sure there is a gap of three or preferably four years before leeks or any members of the allium family are grown again in the same ground.

Leek moth has become a problem in the U.S.. Leek moth traps are being used as a method of dealing with this pest, or some people simply cover the leeks with a fine insect-proof net, similar to that used for carrots, to keep the moth out. Similar controls can be used to control the onion fly, the larva of which burrow into the plant tissue.

GOOD FOR YOU...

Leeks are one of the world's healthiest foods. They are rich in vitamins A, C, B6, E and K, and are a good source of manganese, copper, iron folate,

We use both the white and green parts of the leeks and the roots in our kitchen.

potassium and calcium. They are known to reduce blood pressure and block platelet clot formation in the blood vessels, thus decreasing the overall risk of stroke and coronary heart disease.

WHAT TO DO WITH A GLUT

Slice and sweat down then freeze as a soup base, or add cream, grated cheese, and sautéed mushrooms to cooked leeks. We use the tops in our stockpot.

IN THE KITCHEN

Leeks are a reliable standby during the winter—with potatoes and leeks in the kitchen, you will never be short of the basis for a warming soup.

Leeks are milder in flavor than onions or garlic and are super delicious sautéed in melted butter or cooked into soups, stews, gratins, frittatas, sauces, and pasta. More recently I've been charring them, and I love the sweet, smoky flavor that this technique produces.

Leek Flamiche

Similar leek tarts and pies are made in Belgium, France, and many parts of the United Kingdom, including Wales and Cornwall. There are many variations on this theme—some have no cheese, others no bacon. You can use the filling to make a gorgeous pie with pastry underneath and on top, or just on top—either way it is delicious. There's no need to re-cook the ham if it is already cooked.

. . . .

SERVES 6 TO 8

4 tablespoons (½ stick) butter
1 pound white part of leeks, sliced in
⅓-inch rings
extra virgin olive oil, for frying
3½ ounces bacon or raw ham, cut into
¼-inch lardons
2 organic eggs, or 1 large organic egg and
1 egg yolk
1¼ cups heavy cream
2¾ ounces Gruyère cheese, grated
sea salt and freshly ground black pepper

FOR THE PASTRY

1 prebaked 9-inch tart shell made with
1½ cups of plain flour, 6 tablespoons of
butter and 1 organic egg yolk mixed with
a little water (page 36)

Preheat the oven to 350°F.

Melt the butter in a heavy saucepan over low heat. When it foams, add the sliced leeks. Season with salt and pepper, toss, cover, and cook gently for 4 to 6 minutes until soft and almost tender but not colored. Drain and let cool.

Heat a little olive oil in a skillet over medium heat, add the bacon or ham, and cook for 5 to 6 minutes or until slightly golden and cooked through.

Meanwhile, whisk the eggs and cream together, then stir in the cooled leeks and bacon and most of the cheese. Season with salt and pepper.

Spoon into the tart shell, sprinkle the remainder of the cheese over the top, and bake for 35 to 40 minutes or until just set in the center and golden on top.

Serve warm.

Melted Leeks

This my favorite basic way to cook leeks. For maximum flavor choose young leeks rather than monster specimens.

. . . .

SERVES 6 TO 8

8 medium leeks (about 2 pounds)
4 tablespoons (½ stick) butter or extra
virgin olive oil
sea salt and freshly ground black pepper
marjoram, tarragon, parsley, or chervil,
to garnish

Trim the roots and cut off the dark green leaves from the top of the leeks (add to the stockpot). Slit the leeks lengthwise about halfway through and wash well under cold running water. Slice into ¼-inch rounds.

Melt the butter in a heavy casserole and when it foams, add the sliced leeks and toss gently to coat with butter. Season with salt and pepper. Cover with a layer of parchment paper and a close-fitting lid, then reduce the heat and cook very gently for 8 to 10 minutes or until the leeks are semi-soft and moist. We sometimes turn off the heat when the leeks are almost cooked and leave them to finish cooking in the covered saucepan or casserole. Check and stir every now and then. Serve on a warm dish sprinkled with chopped marjoram, tarragon, parsley, or chervil. Extra virgin olive oil can, of course, be substituted for butter.

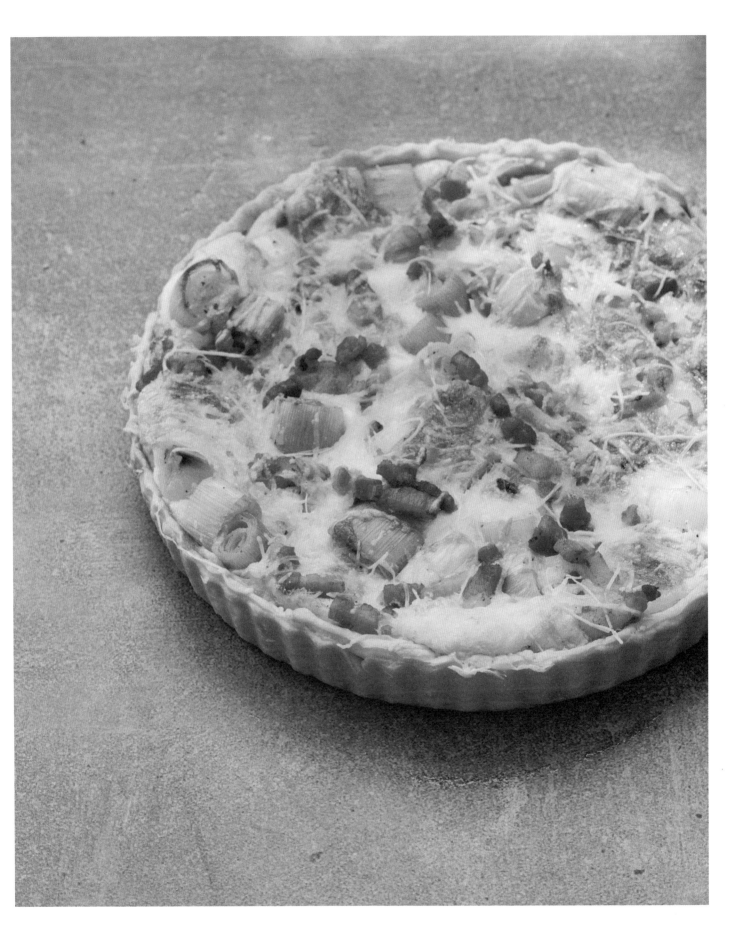

GARLIC *Allium sativum* ANNUAL

We have had tremendous success with garlic in our no-dig beds.

Where would we cooks be without garlic? It is one of the hardiest members of the onion family and is a pretty trouble-free crop to grow. Native to Central Asia, it's been grown for over 5,000 years, which makes it one of the oldest cultivated plants in the world. The Egyptians, Greeks and Romans prized it for its endurance-enhancing effect; soldiers ate it before battle and athletes consumed it before sporting events.

VARIETIES

There are over a hundred varieties of garlic, some white, others in shades of pink and purple. Some cloves are tiny, others huge—hence the food writer's dilemma.

There are two main types, though: hardneck, which produces scapes (flower stems), and autumn-planting softneck, which does not produce flowers and stores longer.

HARDNECK

Hardneck varieties originate from climates with colder winters; they have larger cloves but only store until mid-winter.

Chesnok Red—Crops well in early summer, deep purple veining on the skin and cloves. Good, strong flavor.
Red Sicilian—Well-flavored, early summer variety, good for roasting.
Music—large, pungent cloves; this popular variety stores well.
Spanish Roja—this rocambole type is easy to peel, and produces plenty of cloves on each plant.

SOFTNECK

Purple Moldovan—A heritage variety with large purple cloves, late maturing. New Yorker: a good all purpose garlic; flavor is mild and cloves store very well.
Chinese Pink—this early, attractive garlic matures very early and produces a plethora of bulbs.
Chet's Italian Red—a very pungent and spicy variety that survives cold winters in the garden
Allium ampeloprasum (Elephant perennial garlic)—Huge, plump, mild cloves. Not a true garlic but a variant of the garden leek. Cloves with papery skin, perfect for roasting and baking, can be planted both in spring and autumn and if some is left in the ground it will happily grow as a perennial.

HOW TO GROW

Plant the garlic cloves directly into the ground.

Garlic does not take up much space in the garden. One can grow a 4-yard row from 6 ounces of garlic. In 100 feet one can easily grow enough garlic to provide a bulb a week—on average 10 cloves (could be up to 20). It doesn't sound a lot, but believe me that should be enough to supply the needs of the average household.

Choose a sunny spot with well-prepared, rich, fertile, free-draining light soil. Choose appropriate disease-free bulbs from a reputable source, rather than a random bulb from the supermarket, which may have been grown in southern Europe, won't be hardy and may not suit your soil conditions.

Garlic does not thrive in acid soils (pH below 6.5), so you may need to add lime to the soil in autumn or winter.

Just before planting separate the cloves but don't peel them, plant root downwards, pointy end up. Plant in Fall, late September to early October, depending on your climate, sinking the cloves about two inches deep, 6 to 8 inches apart in the row. After it sprouts and before frost, cover with loose straw.

Autumn planting works best for us, there is still warmth in the soil and it avoids the very heavy wet conditions that might delay spring planting. Practice a four-year rotation otherwise you may suffer from white rot or rust.

CONTAINER GROWING

Garlic can be grown in a container 10 inches in diameter in a sunny spot—an old bath or trough is best.

PESTS AND DISEASES

Birds can pull garlic from the ground so you may need to provide some protective netting until it gets established. Planting deeply will also help. Bugs don't seem to attack garlic but rust and white rot can be a problem. Rotation is vital to help prevent this (see page 18).

HARVESTING

Autumn-sown garlic will be ready to harvest in midsummer. Some of the fresh young leaves can be snipped into salads, omelets and soups, but the bulbs are ready to harvest when the first six leaves turn yellowy/brown, otherwise it can be left too late. Don't wait for the leaves to fall over, dig the bulbs out carefully. Shake off the excess soil from the roots but don't cut the foliage. We leave it to dry in the greenhouse for a couple of weeks, then tie or braid it into bundles and hang in a dry, airy place. We hang garlic and onions from wires in the conservatory beside the Garden Café at the school, which is drier than the greenhouse, with excellent results. The temperature needs to be about 60 to 70°F but they will tolerate cooler conditions once they are in the light.

They should store for 3 months or more in a cool, dry place. You could save the best and healthiest bulbs to plant for next year.

GOOD FOR YOU...

Garlic is an excellent source of calcium, phosphorus and selenium, and also contains significant amounts of vitamins C, B6 and manganese. It's naturally low in sodium, fat, and cholesterol. Peer-reviewed research has shown that garlic lowers blood pressure, is beneficial for the cardio-vascular system and has anti-inflammatory properties. It's antibacterial and antiviral.

Raw garlic is rich in compounds known as allicins, the garlic plant's defence mechanism. Crushing, chopping or bruising garlic activates it, but once it's cooked the healing properties reduce very quickly.

WHAT TO DO WITH A GLUT

Dry the garlic as already mentioned and give braids to your friends. There are also several recipes that use an abundance of garlic, such as **Roast Guinea Fowl with 40 Cloves of Garlic** (page 51) or garlic confit.

IN THE KITCHEN

If you don't have your own garlic, always buy fresh bulbs rather than garlic flakes, powder, or pastes. Cooks should also avoid ready-peeled garlic. Garlic has many flavors depending on how and when it is used—whole, slivered, crushed, chopped, raw, cooked...

When I was an au pair in Besançon in France in the 1960s, Maman rubbed a cut clove of garlic around the base and sides of the salad bowl to perfume the salad. Americans have discovered young green garlic, sometimes called spring garlic, which is a highlight of early spring farmers' markets. Use it anywhere you use garlic—it's delicious in frittatas, stir-fries, pasta, salads, dressings, and quiches.

Garlic Butter is a kitchen basic, made in minutes and so useful for slathering over garlic bread. Keep a roll in the fridge for melting over steaks or chops, or freshly cooked vegetables. To make 4 ounces garlic butter, cream 4 ounces butter, add 2 or 3 crushed garlic cloves, stir in 4 teaspoons minced fresh curly or flat-leaf parsley, and a few drops of lemon juice at a time. Pack into a bowl. Roll into butter pats or form into a roll and wrap in parchment paper or foil, twisting each end so that it looks like a Christmas cracker. Refrigerate to harden. Alternatively, melt the butter over medium heat, add the crushed garlic, and stir for 30 seconds. Add the parsley and a few drops of freshly squeezed lemon juice, if you like.

We dry the garlic bulbs in the greenhouse, warm and well ventilated.

To make **Crispy Garlic** for nibbling and scattering over dishes, choose large garlic cloves. Peel and shave into paper-thin slices, then spread on paper towels and let dry. Heat 1 inch of oil in a pan or use a deep-fryer heated to 300°F or a wok. Cook a little at a time until golden and crisp. Dry on paper towels. Store in a screw-top jar and use within 5 or 6 days, and scatter over Asian-inspired salads.

Garlic scapes can be eaten raw or cooked, whole or chopped—we use them like scallions with green vegetables or in frittatas, omelets, scrambled eggs, salads, or risotto. Use in soup, or add to sauces and dressings. They make delicious pizza toppings and are also great just grilled.

Cian's Garlic Pizza

A pizza for all you garlic addicts out there. Cian worked at the school in summer 2000 and developed this great pizza topping. The beauty of this recipe is that it is so quick and easy, and using this fast-acting yeast does away with the first rising. There's another simple variation on this recipe that I'm very partial to—add 1 tablespoon of chopped red onion and lots of coarsely chopped cilantro to the garlic butter and cook as below.

MAKES 1

FOR THE PIZZA DOUGH
(MAKES EIGHT 10-INCH PIZZAS)

5 cups bread flour or 4½ cups bread
    flour and 1 cup rye flour, plus extra for
    dusting
2 level teaspoons salt
1 tablespoon granulated sugar
4 tablespoons (½ stick) butter
1 (¼-ounce) packet instant yeast
2 to 4 tablespoons olive oil, plus extra
    for brushing
1¾ to 2 cups lukewarm water, plus more
    if necessary

FOR THE PIZZA

semolina (if using a pizza peel)
1 to 2 tablespoons garlic butter
    (see page 47)
wild garlic flowers and leaves, when
    in season
freshly snipped fresh curly or flat-leaf
    parsley

To make the dough, sift the flour into a large wide bowl and add the salt and sugar. Rub in the butter and yeast and mix all the ingredients together thoroughly. Make a well in the center of the dry ingredients and add the oil and most of the lukewarm water. Mix to form a loose dough. You can add more water or flour if needed.

Turn the dough onto a lightly floured worktop, cover, and let relax for about 5 minutes.

Knead the dough for 8 to 9 minutes or until smooth and springy (if kneading in a stand mixer with the dough hook, 5 minutes is usually long enough). Leave the dough to relax again for about 10 minutes, then shape and measure into 8 equal balls of dough, each weighing about 5¼ ounces. Lightly brush the balls of dough with olive oil.

If you have time, put the oiled balls of dough into a plastic bag and chill. The dough will be easier to handle when cold but it can be used immediately.

Preheat the oven to 465°F.

On a well-floured work surface, roll out a ball of pizza dough to a 10-inch disc. Sprinkle a little semolina all over the surface of the pizza peel, if you have one, and put the dough round on top. Spread the garlic butter over the surface of the dough, keeping it about ¾ inch from the edge. Bake for 10 to 12 minutes or until the base is crisp and the top is bubbly and golden. Sprinkle the garlic flowers and leaves and the snipped parsley on top and serve immediately. Repeat with the remaining dough or make a variety of pizzas with different toppings.

> **DID YOU KNOW?**
> In Central European folklore garlic was believed to keep the evil eye at bay, bring good luck, and ward off evil spirits and vampires. It could be worn on the person, or hung from a window or a door. In Greece, midwives hung garlic cloves in birthing rooms to keep the evil spirits away and this practice became common across Europe..

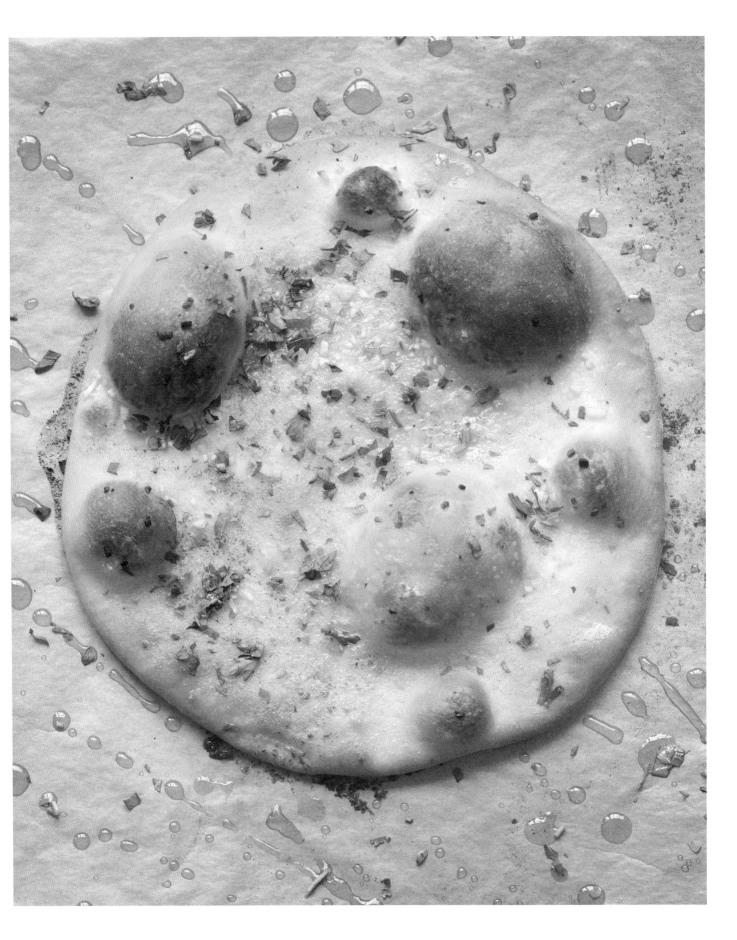

Black Garlic

You can quite easily make black garlic at home. We've been experimenting in a dehydrator and in a rice cooker, and we've had the best results from the latter.

. . . .

Wrap the heads of garlic in plastic wrap and then in foil to trap in the moisture. Pop into a dehydrator at 130°F until the heads are soft and the cloves turn black. This can take a couple of weeks, but keep checking, as the length of time will depend on the size of the garlic cloves. We've also had good results in the rice cooker, set at the lowest setting. Check after 4 or 5 days, but it can take 10 to 12 days depending on size.

Store in an airtight container in the fridge, where it will keep for 2 to 3 months but gradually become drier, or peel and store in glass jars covered with olive oil, in which case it will keep for 2 months or more.

Jared's Black Garlic Chicken

Black garlic is one of the hot "new" culinary ingredients, but in fact it was developed in Korea over 4,000 years ago as a method to preserve garlic. The result is a soft, black garlic with a sweet yet savory flavor once it has been dried slowly at a low temperature of 130°F for three weeks. It is not fermented, as is often claimed, but is the result of long, slow caramelization of the natural sugar in the garlic. This recipe was developed by a past student who has a cult following—Jared Baston, from Nomad in Chicago, and his friends—for a pop-up dinner at the cooking school.

. . . .

SERVES 6

1 organic or free-range chicken, weighing
    4 to 5 pounds, cut into 12 serving pieces
sea salt and freshly ground black pepper
1 tablespoon sunflower oil
3 garlic cloves, mashed
3 black garlic cloves, chopped
2 tablespoons light soy sauce
2 tablespoons oyster sauce
1 tablespoon sesame oil
1 tablespoon honey
1 tablespoon hoisin sauce
½ teaspoon Aleppo pepper (pul biber)
3 or 4 scallions or spring onions—green
    and white parts, cut at an angle, to
    garnish
steamed rice, to serve

Preheat the oven to 350°F.

Season the chicken pieces generously with salt and black pepper, toss to evenly coat, and transfer to a large casserole.

Whisk the sunflower oil, both garlics, the soy sauce, oyster sauce, sesame oil, honey, hoisin sauce, and Aleppo pepper together, drizzle over the chicken, and toss well to coat.

Bake for 20 minutes, then increase the temperature to 450°F and cook for an additional 10 minutes. Baste with some of the pan juices, turn over, and continue to cook for 10 minutes more. Reduce the temperature to 350°F and cook until the chicken is cooked through, about 20 minutes more, basting at least once more.

Remove the chicken pieces to a warm serving dish. Deglaze the pan juices and reduce until syrupy. Season to taste, adding more salt, sauces, or honey as needed. Pour over the chicken. Garnish with the scallions or spring onions. Serve immediately with steamed rice.

Gambas al Ajillo—Garlic Shrimp

Serve lots of crusty bread to mop up the last of the delicious olive oil in the earthenware *casuelas*. We make this simple tapas with the little pink shrimp (*Palaemon serratus*) that the fishermen collect from their pots in Ballycotton. They are much smaller than the Asian shrimp but deliciously sweet, and sustainable. Slice the garlic thinly and be careful not to let it burn.

SERVES 4

4 garlic cloves, thinly sliced
2 dried red chile peppers, broken into
  3 pieces (discard the seeds)
5 tablespoons Spanish extra virgin olive oil
1 bay leaf, cut into 4 pieces
10½ ounces shrimp, peeled and deveined
flaky sea salt
crusty bread, to serve

Divide the sliced garlic and chile peppers more or less evenly among 4 individual fireproof casuelas, ovenproof dishes, or cast-iron pans, or cook in one large pan. Divide the olive oil among them and add one-quarter of the bay leaf to each.

Heat over medium heat until the oil begins to sizzle. Just as the garlic turns pale gold, add the shrimp and cook for 2 to 4 minutes, stirring gently, until just done. Sprinkle with a little sea salt and serve immediately from the cooking pot or pots, with lots of crusty bread to mop up the delicious oil and juices.

Roast Guinea Fowl with 40 Cloves of Garlic

Garlic has many different flavors depending on how you use it. Here we go to one extreme and seemingly throw caution to the wind, roasting our guinea fowl with lots and lots of plump garlic cloves. In France they would usually use chicken. The garlic cooks long and slowly and the flavor is transformed to a mellow sweetness which is quite addictive.

SERVES 4 TO 6

1 × 3⅓ to 5-pound free-range guinea fowl
1 sprig of thyme
2 ounces plump garlic cloves, peeled
1 tablespoon butter, softened
good drizzle of olive oil
1 pound plump garlic cloves, unpeeled
a little homemade chicken stock (optional)
sea salt and freshly ground black pepper
gravy, to serve

Preheat the oven to 355°F. Season the cavity of the guinea fowl with salt and freshly ground black pepper, then put in a sprig of fresh thyme and the peeled garlic cloves. Smear the breast and legs with some soft butter and season with salt and freshly ground pepper. Truss lightly with cotton string. Put the guinea fowl breast-side down into a roasting tin and drizzle with a little olive oil. Roast for 30 minutes, then turn breast-side up and continue to roast. After about 15 minutes add the unpeeled garlic. Continue to roast for 45 minutes to 1 hour until the guinea fowl is golden and fully cooked.

Remove the guinea fowl to a serving dish, surround with the unpeeled garlic, spoon out all the garlic from the cavity and test to make sure the cloves are cooked. I often find that they need a little longer, so I put them in a saucepan with a little stock and continue to cook for a further 5 to 10 minutes or until they are soft, then add them to the carving dish.

Serve the guinea fowl the whole garlic cloves and some gravy.

AMARANTH

A. gangeticus, A. hypochondriacus, A. cruentus, A. caudatus

Though I disapprove of the term "superfood" in general, amaranth comes close to qualifying as one—it's actually more nutritious than kale. It is a multi-use plant, easy to grow and highly nutritious, gorgeous to look at and provides year-round sustenance.

VARIETIES

There at least 60 species of amaranth—some red, some green, and some multi-colored, also ornamental varieties with long red tassels known as "Love-lies-bleeding." In the Caribbean a short variety called callaloo is valued for cooking. You may even have this already, not realizing what a treasure you are growing.
Burgundy—Tall, elegant variety with intense red leaves, which add color to salads as well as being nutritious. Striking rich burgundy flower plumes, and it produces plentiful white seeds.

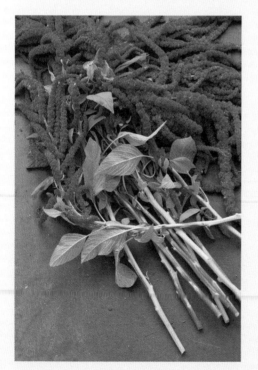

Golden Amaranth—Golden yellow stalks and leaves and bronze-gold seed heads. It is a high-quality Aztec grain amaranth. The young leaves may be used in salads. In a reasonably good summer it will ripen outdoors and can grow to 70 inches tall.

HOW TO GROW

Amaranth likes full sun. It will thrive in virtually any type of soil, but ideally it likes soil high in nitrogen and phosphorus. It requires little water.

Sow the seed under glass in mid-spring, ideally in cells of compost—barely cover the seeds with compost and they will germinate in 3 or 4 days if the temperature is about 68°F. Because the seeds are tiny, it is be difficult to sow singly, so you will need to thin them out as the shoots appear. Plants from cells can be transplanted outdoors after the last frost and planting under a cloche will give them added protection, especially if you are aiming to grow large plants.

Amaranth can be grown outdoors, too, directly into the soil, in rows 20 inches apart, once the danger of the last frost has past. Once the seedlings are large enough to handle, thin them out. Spacing depends on the variety, how large you would like them to grow and how much space can be allocated to the plants. If you would like larger plants, allow up to 39 inches between them, but if you don't have that, 20 inches will be fine.

CONTAINER GROWING

Amaranth has a shallow root system so it can be grown in quite a shallow container. Choose the variety carefully, though, as some can grow up to 14 feet tall. We grow Burgundy in pots and it looks very attractive. It's also an excellent community garden plant as it self-seeds.

Amaranth can also be grown as micro-greens, and red amaranth is especially lovely as a garnish. Put some potting soil on the bottom of a seed tray or container with a few drainage holes in the base. Flatten the soil gently with your hand, then sprinkle on a thin layer of seeds and press down gently.

Cover the seeds with a light layer of compost, water lightly with a plant mister, then cover with a plastic sheet and a newspaper. Mist a couple of times a day until the seedlings appear about a week later, then uncover and allow to sprout. Snip, wash, drain in a colander, then dry gently with paper towels and enjoy in salads or as a garnish.

PESTS AND DISEASES

We haven't had any problems; rabbits don't seem to be tempted by amaranth.

HARVESTING

Amaranth gives double value as both the leaves and the seeds are harvested. The plant will grow and flower and add color to your garden or border and then produce several grams of nutritious and delicious amaranth seeds. When the plant flowers you can collect and dry the seeds.

> **DID YOU KNOW?**
> Amaranth means "everlasting" in Greek. It was a staple and revered food of the Aztecs and is closely related to quinoa.

Amaranth (left) and lemon basil growing in pots around the cookery school.

GOOD FOR YOU...

The leaves are high in vitamins A and C, protein, beta-carotene, iron, fibre and calcium—having three times as much calcium as spinach. The seeds are also protein-rich (16 per cent as opposed to 10 per cent in most whole grains) and high in omega 3. A cup of uncooked amaranth seed contains about six times as much fibre as a similar amount of long grain white rice. Amaranth is rich in amino acids including lysine, and offers 5 per cent of the body's daily requirement of vitamin B6, and 3 per cent of the potassium (per 100 g of cooked amaranth), which helps to lower blood pressure. It is also high in magnesium and manganese and amaranth leaves contain a high level of vitamin K, which contributes to a healthy heart. Another great plus is that amaranth is naturally gluten free so it can be used in cooking for those with gluten intolerance to raise the protein content.

WHAT TO DO WITH A GLUT

Use as much as you can in salads, cook like spinach and freeze to use as a vegetable or in a soup.

IN THE KITCHEN

Young leaves can be eaten in salads, sautéed, steamed, or used in soups or stews. Try chopping them into a pancake batter. Particularly tasty in light Chinese soups or a cannelloni filling. Add a couple tablespoons of seeds to soda or yeast bread, with fantastic results.

Amaranth Shortbread

This simple amaranth shortbread is so good; the seeds create a crunchy sensation that becomes addictive.

MAKES TWENTY-SIX 2-INCH BISCUITS

1¼ cups all-purpose flour
2 tablespoons amaranth seeds
scant ¼ cup superfine sugar
½ cup (1 stick) butter
⅓ cup sesame seeds (optional)

Preheat the oven to 350°F.

Put the flour, amaranth seeds, and sugar into a bowl and rub in the butter as for shortcrust pastry. Gather the mixture together and knead lightly. Roll out to ¼ inch thick and cut into rounds with a 2-inch cutter. Sprinkle with sesame seeds, if using. Transfer to a baking sheet. Bake for 8 to 15 minutes, depending on the thickness of the biscuits, until pale brown. Watch these biscuits really carefully in the oven; because of the relatively high sugar content they burn easily. They should be a pale golden—darker and they will be more bitter. However, if they are too pale they will be undercooked and doughy.

Remove and cool on a wire rack. Best enjoyed fresh but they'll keep pretty well for a couple of days in an airtight container.

Amaranth, Potato & Tomato Stew

Another delicious way to enjoy amaranth leaves—a dish to eat alone or as an accompaniment to either meat or fish. I came across this recipe on a vacation in Goa where they love amaranth and what is also called red spinach.

. . . .

SERVES 4

4 tablespoons extra virgin olive oil
¾ pound potatoes, cut into ¾-inch dice
5½ ounces onions, chopped
½ to 1 red or green chile, seeded and chopped
1 teaspoon grated fresh ginger
2 garlic cloves, crushed to a paste
1 pound ripe tomatoes, peeled and chopped
pinch of brown sugar
¾ to 1½ cups amaranth leaves, chopped
lots of coarsely chopped fresh cilantro
salt and freshly ground black pepper
juice of ½ lemon or to taste

Heat the oil in a wok or sauté pan, add the diced potato, season with salt, and toss continually over medium heat for 10 to 12 minutes until cooked through. Remove to a plate with a slotted spoon and set aside.

Heat the olive oil remaining in the pan over medium heat; add the chopped onion, chile, ginger, and garlic. Stir-fry for 2 to 3 minutes or until the onions are slightly brown. Add the chopped tomatoes. Season with salt, pepper, and a little sugar. Increase the heat and cook, uncovered, for 4 to 5 minutes. Add the chopped amaranth and continue to cook for an additional 10 minutes; add the fried potatoes and continue to simmer until heated through. Season to taste. Add freshly squeezed lemon juice to taste if it needs to be perked up a little.

Scatter with lots of coarsely chopped cilantro and serve as a vegetable dish or with steamed rice.

Bengali Amaranth—Lal Shak Bhaja

Panch phoron, or Bengali five-spice powder, is a traditional spice mix used in Bengali cuisine that is usually a blend of five spices—cumin seeds, black mustard seeds, nigella seeds, fenugreek seeds, and fennel seeds. Bengalis love red spinach and have many recipes for this vegetable; it's considered part of daily meals with dal and rice and maybe some shrimp.

. . . .

SERVES 4

1 pound amaranth or red spinach leaves
2 tablespoons mustard or extra virgin olive oil
a pinch of panch phoron
4 garlic cloves, crushed
1 or 2 green chiles, chopped
1 teaspoon ground turmeric
salt and freshly ground black pepper
pinch of granulated sugar
⅓ cup roasted peanuts, coarsely chopped
steamed rice, for serving

Pull the leaves off the thicker amaranth stems and chop the leaves finely.

Heat the oil in a wok or sauté pan over high heat, add a pinch of *panch phoron*, stir for a few seconds, then add the garlic, chiles, and turmeric. Stir and cook for 1 to 2 minutes then add the chopped amaranth, salt, freshly ground pepper, and a pinch of sugar. Toss to coat with the masala spice mix, reduce the heat to medium, and continue to cook for 8 to 10 minutes, stirring regularly.

Season to taste, sprinkle with the peanuts, and serve with steamed rice.

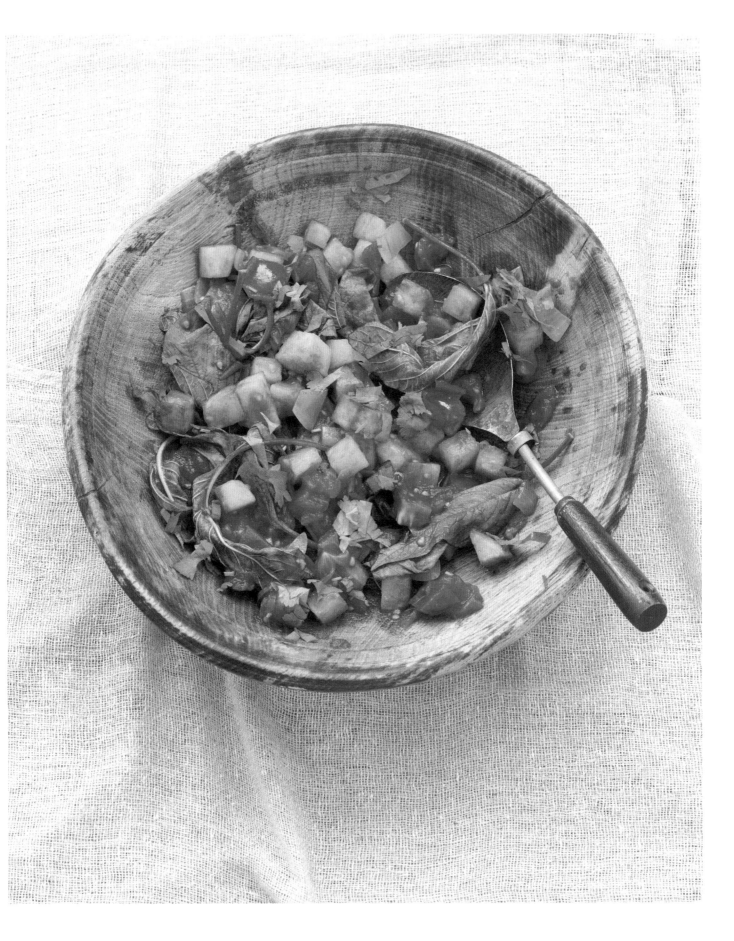

CELERY
Apium graveolens ANNUAL

Keep the ground clean and moist around young celery plants.

Celery was one of the very earliest vegetables grown in monastery gardens in Ireland, alongside leeks, onions and kale. Every provincial king in Celtic Ireland was apparently entitled to have "three condiments supplied for his nursing: honey, fresh garlic, and an unlimited amount of celery." I like to save the heart to use in a salad.

Celery was originally a marsh plant but it has been cultivated since antiquity. It's part of the Apiaceae family, a cousin of carrots, parsnips, fennel and parsley grown for its succulent stalks or petioles. Interestingly, many gardeners view celery as the ultimate challenge because it's quite difficult to grow successfully.

VARIETIES

There are two main types: trench and self-blanching. Trench celery is usually grown in trenches and is earthed up as it grows to blanch the stems, it is very hardy and has a longer growing season than the self-blanching type. The self-blanching type seems to have taken over entirely from trench celery, as there is less work involved because one doesn't have to earth it up to produce the same pale stems. However, it is not as hardy as the trench celery.

TRENCH CELERY VARIETIES

Giant Pascal—Heirloom trench variety, grows up to 3 feet tall—thick, pale yellow stems.
Octavius F1—Trench celery, juicy stems of good flavor.
Solid Pink—Large pink stems.

SELF-BLANCHING VARIETIES

Golden—produces thick, crisp and juicy stalks.
Tango—bright green tops on crunchy, non-stringy stalks.
Red Venture—Red stems and good, rich, nutty flavor.
Green Utah—Good disease resistance.

HOW TO GROW

Its origin in boggy marshland gives a clue to sort of soil conditions celery needs to thrive. The plant should never be allowed to dry out. When celery is allowed to grow naturally the stalks are green and more strongly flavored. Traditionally gardeners liked to grow it in trenches and "bank it up" with soil in order to blanch the stems, which were then paler in color and considerably milder in flavor.

Celery will grow in full sun but it prefers cooler weather and can tolerate light frost. It will crop until late winter.

In early spring, sow seeds in cells in potting compost. Make a little hole with your fingertip or a pencil in each one. The seeds are tiny so you may want to use tweezers to pop a seed into each cell. Lightly cover with potting soil. Water the cell tray evenly and don't allow to dry out while growing. Celery needs a humus rich soil that can hold water.

When the plants are about 4 inches high, harden them off for a couple of days. They will bolt and go to seed if they are planted out too early, or if they are not hardened off properly. We sow them in a "no-dig" bed. Celery needs nitrogen so we collect our coffee grinds and sprinkle them over the bed, which we lightly rake or fork in before planting.

Self-blanching celery is best planted in a block, with the plants 9 inches apart, so that the outside plants help to blanch the inside plants. Pop the plants out of the cell, dig a little hole, drop in the plant, fill and firm in with your hand level with the ground. Once they are planted, water in well, but it's vital they don't dry out at any stage during the growing season, otherwise they will bolt and become stringy and bitter.

CONTAINER GROWING

Celery can certainly be grown in a deep container. Keep well-watered and feed every 2 weeks with a balanced feed.

HARVESTING

When the celery matures into heads we use it as we need it.

PESTS AND DISEASES

Very few pests bother with celery but it can be attacked by Carrot Fly (see page 157). You can avoid this by growing a disease-resistant variety such as Green Utah. Slugs can be a problem early in their growing season and in trench celery they can be hidden inside the stems. If necessary, use an organic slug deterrent.

GOOD FOR YOU...

An excellent source of vitamins C, K, A, potassium, folate, B2, B6, phosphorous, magnesium and dietary fibre.

Celery lowers blood pressure, has a diuretic effect and helps to reduce cholesterol and inflammation. It also aids digestion and contains luteolin, a powerful flavonoid, shown to inhibit the growth of cancer cells.

It helps to prevent age-related degeneration of vision, plus it is low in calories, with just 10 calories per stalk.

WHAT TO DO WITH A GLUT

Celery doesn't freeze particularly well but if you have a glut it's still worth freezing it to use in stocks and soups. Prepare as though you were about to cook: string the outside stalks with a swivel-top peeler and cut it into the size

of pieces that you might use for stews, soup and stock. Blanch in boiling water in batches for 2 to 3 minutes. Scoop out and refresh in iced water. Drain well, freeze on baking-parchment-covered trays, then transfer to thick re-sealable bags when frozen. Label well. Celery will last for up to 9 months in the freezer, but use within 2 months if unblanched. Tight heads will last for 4 to 6 weeks in a fridge or cold room.

Celery soup is delicious, just make up the base, purée and freeze. The stock and creamy milk can be added before serving. Celery chutney is also worth experimenting with.

IN THE KITCHEN

Celery is a staple. We use it as a base flavor in many dishes, as an essential in stocks, and in the mirepoix of vegetables that adds flavor to so many stews. It adds a delicious crunch to salads and the leaves are surprisingly tasty in a tempura batter. Celery leaves are strongly flavored and not to everyone's taste, but they are pretty addictive when made into fritters. Heat about 1 inch of olive oil in a skillet and whisk an egg white until just fluffy. Dip the celery leaves into 1 tablespoon of well-seasoned flour and then lightly into the egg white. Fry briefly in the hot oil until pale golden. Drain on paper towels and serve as a garnish.

For many it is a forgotten vegetable, but our Christmas dinner certainly wouldn't be the same without a dish of creamy celery—this can also be served as a sauce and it's particularly delicious accompanying a poached turkey or chicken. To cook celery to serve 4 to 6, pull the stalks off the head of celery. If the outer stalks seem a bit tough, peel the strings off with a swivel-top peeler or simply save these tougher stalks for

Celery plants growing—the stalks and leaves are both visible above the ground.

the stockpot. Cut the celery into 1-inch chunks, preferably at an angle. Bring 2/3 cup water to a boil; add a little salt and the chopped celery. Cover and cook for 15 to 20 minutes or until a knife will go through the celery with ease. Drain, add the butter, and season with salt and freshly ground pepper. Sprinkle with lots of chopped parsley and serve.

For **Creamed Celery**, use the method above and remove the just-cooked celery to a dish with a slotted spoon. Thicken the remaining liquid with the roux (the quantity of roux will vary according to the amount of liquid). Add ½ to ¾ cup cream—enough to make sufficient sauce to coat the celery—and allow to bubble for a few minutes, then pour over the celery, sprinkle with curly parsley, and serve. This dish can be prepared ahead.

And there's **Celery Salt** to add to quail eggs. It's easy: just grind 1 tablespoon dried organic celery seeds in a spice grinder with 3 tablespoons flaky salt. Dry and store in a screw-top jar.

Crisp celery stalks are also delicious dipped in peanut butter or blue cheese.

Fennel, Celery, Raisin & Red Onion Salad

Somehow, I think of this as a winter salad—it's fresh tasting on its own but also good with ham or game. The fennel and celery add the crunch, while the plump raisins add sweetness, as do the onions—as well as a shocking pink color.

. . . .

SERVES 6

2 crisp fennel bulbs

3 or 4 stalks celery

1 medium red onion

freshly squeezed juice of 1 lime

⅓ cup raisins, plumped up in boiling water
    for 15 to 20 minutes, drained

a handful of fresh fennel sprigs or cilantro
    leaves

5 tablespoons extra virgin olive oil

2 tablespoons red wine vinegar

1 teaspoon honey

salt and freshly ground black pepper

Trim the fennel, cut the bulb in half lengthwise, and slice very thinly. Use a swivel-top peeler to remove the strings from the celery (toss them into the stockpot) then slice them thinly on the diagonal. Slice the red onion into very thin rings and sprinkle with the lime juice.

Combine the fennel, celery, onion, and drained raisins in a bowl; add the fennel sprigs or cilantro leaves. Season with salt and freshly ground pepper. Whisk the oil, vinegar, and honey together, drizzle over the salad, and toss. Season to taste and serve, or serve alongside a few slices of freshly cooked ham or bacon that has not been refrigerated. The salad is best enjoyed at room temperature rather than very cold.

Apple, Celery & Walnut Salad

One of the few mixed salad combinations that works really well. The tart combination of apple and celery makes it an excellent counterbalance to rich meats such as duck or pork, or it may be served as a first course on its own.

. . . .

SERVES 6

½ head of celery

½ pound green dessert apples

½ pound red dessert apples

approx. 2 tablespoons lemon juice

1 level teaspoon superfine sugar

⅔ cup mayonnaise (see page 196)

½ cup shelled fresh walnuts, plus extra
    to garnish

salt and freshly ground black pepper

sprigs of watercress and chopped fresh
    parsley, to garnish

Separate the celery stalks, wash them, and chop or julienne the stalks into 1½-inch lengths. Put them into a bowl of ice water for 15 to 30 minutes. Wash and core the apples and cut into ⅓-inch dice.

Make a dressing by mixing the lemon juice, sugar, and 1 tablespoon of the mayonnaise together. Toss the diced apple in the dressing and let it stand while you prepare the remaining ingredients.

Chop the walnuts roughly. Add the celery and the walnuts to the diced apple with the remaining mayonnaise and mix thoroughly. Season to taste.

Garnish with sprigs of watercress and scatter some chopped parsley and extra chopped walnuts over the center of the salad.

CELERIAC
Apium graveolens ANNUAL

I first came across celeriac when I was an au-pair in Besançon, in France, in my late teens, when Maman instructed me to collect some celeriac remoulade for supper from the local charcutier. We ate this as part of an hors d'oeuvre plate on a regular basis, but I had no idea what the vegetable looked like in real life until I eventually spotted it on a market stall. Its knobbly appearance doesn't inspire much excitement, but even though it wouldn't win any prizes in a beauty competition, it's a beautifully versatile winter vegetable. It's closely related to celery, with dark green stalks, jagged leaves, and a fat bulbous root—half of which grows above ground. They were bred from the same wild plant but celeriac is more disease resistant. The stalks became celery and the root was bred for celeriac. Christian Puglisi at Relæ, in Copenhagen, told me when I visited the restaurant that it's one of his all-time favorite vegetables and he works magic with a vegetable that many imagined was limited to soup, gratin or mash.

VARIETIES
Prinz—Early variety, with good flavor and nice smooth round roots. It resists bolting and leaf disease.
Mars—upright plants produce large, uniform roots.
Dia-mant—Large uniform roots, easy to clean and stores well. It has creamy white, delicately flavored flesh.
Alabaster—High-yielding variety that resists bolting.
Monarch AGM—Smooth-skinned with nice moist flesh.

HOW TO GROW
We sow the seeds in mid- to late spring into cells or pots in a greenhouse, under cloches or in a cold frame in shallow soil, because they need a little light to germinate. Germination can be erratic, so sow a few more than you need. When the seedlings are about 1/3 inch high, plant them into 3-inch pots at 55 to 60°F. Once all risk of frost has passed in late spring, plant them out into rich fertile soil in a sunny spot.

Celeriac was originally a bog plant so it does best in moist soil. It's a heavy feeder, so add well-rotted manure or compost to the soil before you plant. Give them plenty of space—12 inches between plants and 20 inches between rows. Celeriac takes 100 to 120 days to be ready for use. When you see the bulbs starting to swell, snip off some of the outer leaves to expose the crown of the bulb and allow it to develop fully.

CONTAINER GROWING
Not really suitable for container growing.

These celeriac plants started in trays (2 inches deep × 1½ inch wide) are ready to be transplanted.

PESTS AND DISEASES
You may be troubled by celery leaf miner, but it's less of a problem than on celery. Slugs can be a problem, see page 626 for deterrents.

HARVESTING
Harvest from autumn to early spring as needed; they can be used at any stage from tennis ball to a small football size. Like most root vegetables, a touch of frost adds to their sweetness. Resist the temptation to harvest too early, as they literally double in size in late autumn. If hard frost is a possibility in your area, cover the plants with straw. It's quite a business to unearth celeriac from the ground because of its densely matted root system. They can be lifted and stored in boxes of sand (known as clamps) or in a cool, dark place for 2 to 3 months. We also like to leave a few to flower, as they attract lots of hover flies and other beneficial insects.

Celery and celeriac are closely related so don't plant them in the same spot for several years, otherwise you may well get a build-up of fungal disease.

GOOD FOR YOU...
High in fibre, calcium, potassium and vitamin C and low in calories.

WHAT TO DO WITH A GLUT
Not usually a problem because it can be stored in the ground or in a sand or peat box, but it can be handy to freeze some blanched and refreshed cubes to add to stew or use for soup or purée.

IN THE KITCHEN
Celeriac can be used in the same ways as potato can but has far fewer calories. The root is terrifically versatile and can

be mashed, puréed, or made into fries. It works well in a gratin, interspersed with potato, and even parsnips, and is of course delicious added to stews or braises. Celeriac is also delicious baked. The leaves are very strongly flavored, as are the stalks, but the latter can be used to flavor stocks and broths.

Like Jerusalem artichokes, salsify, and scorzonera, celeriac discolors rapidly once it is peeled, so drop it into acidulated water, or blanch and refresh it quickly.

Celeriac can also be made into remoulade, a favorite winter salad when I was an au pair in France. To make this for 12 to 15 people, trim 1½ pounds celeriac with a knife and peel thickly, then grate coarsely. Stir 2 tablespoons of Dijon mustard and 4 tablespoons of French dressing into 1⅓ cups homemade mayonnaise and add some to the celeriac (reserve a little in case not all is needed). It should be saucy but not too sloppy. Add freshly squeezed lemon juice to taste and a little more seasoning if necessary. Scatter with chopped flat-leaf parsley. You may wish to use all mayonnaise but we like to add some French dressing for a less unctuous result.

Celeriac ready to harvest—the stalks can be used to flavor the stockpot.

Salt-Baked Celeriac with Olive Butter

I ate this in Manfreds in Copenhagen. I'm not sure exactly how they cooked it, but this version is very good. Slow roasting really intensifies the sweetness of the celeriac as well as tenderizing it. Mounting the olive paste with butter softens the flavor in a delicious way.

SERVES 4 AS A STARTER

1 celeriac, about ¾ to 1 pound
3 tablespoons extra virgin olive oil, plus extra for brushing
coarse rock or sea salt
3½ ounces Kalamata olives, pitted
2 tablespoons butter
sprigs of chervil or small basil leaves, to garnish

DID YOU KNOW?
Celeriac was referred to as *selinon* in Homer's *Odyssey*.

Preheat the oven to 325°F.

Scrub the celeriac well and dry carefully with a tea towel or paper towels. Brush with a little olive oil. Put in a deep ovenproof casserole or small roasting pan, sprinkle generously with salt and bake for 3 to 3½ hours until tender. Remove from the oven, let cool, then remove the celeriac and brush off the salt.

Meanwhile, purée the olives with the extra virgin olive oil in a blender to form a very smooth paste. Transfer the olive paste to a small saucepan over low heat and whisk in the butter.

Peel and slice the celeriac thickly and cut into uneven chunks. Spoon a couple of tablespoons of olive paste onto a small plate. Arrange 3 or 4 pieces of celeriac on top.

Drizzle with a couple of blobs of olive paste. Top with a few sprigs of chervil or small basil leaves and a few flakes of sea salt. Serve.

Lamb Breast with Gremolata & Celeriac & Potato Purée

Past student Jared Batson brought several of his friends from Chicago back to Ballymaloe, his old alma mater. They cooked a late-spring pop-up dinner in the Garden Café, much to the delight of the students, and this was the main course, which Jared kindly shared with us.

. . . .

SERVES 8

2 lamb breasts
sea salt and freshly ground black pepper
2¼ pounds purple sprouting broccoli,
    to serve (optional)

FOR THE GREMOLATA STUFFING

¼ cup extra virgin olive oil
½ onion, minced
1 garlic clove, minced
1 cup white bread crumbs
¼ cup chopped flat-leaf parsley
zest and juice of 1 lemon

FOR THE CELERIAC AND POTATO PURÉE

2 large celeriac (about 1½ pounds each)
1 pound potatoes
1 to 1½ cups (2 to 3 sticks) butter
1 to 2 tablespoons each chopped parsley
    and chervil
4 to 6 tablespoons cream
salt and freshly ground black pepper
freshly squeezed lemon juice, to taste
    (optional)

FOR THE WILD GARLIC SALSA VERDE

¾ cup wild garlic leaves, chopped
2 anchovy fillets, chopped
⅓ cup flat-leaf parsley, chopped
1 teaspoon white wine vinegar
¼ teaspoon Dijon mustard
olive oil, to loosen

Preheat the oven to 325°F.

Season the lamb breasts generously on both sides with salt and freshly ground black pepper. Lay skin-side up on a baking sheet and roast for 20 minutes, then reduce the temperature to 250°F and cook for 1½ hours until tender.

Meanwhile, make the gremolata stuffing. Heat the oil in a saucepan and sweat the onion and garlic for 5 to 6 minutes until soft but not colored. Add the white bread crumbs, chopped parsley, lemon zest, and lemon juice. Season with salt and freshly ground pepper. Cool, shape into two 1-inch rolls, and wrap in plastic wrap, twisting the ends, then freeze.

When the lamb is cooked, remove the tough outer skin and bones or cartilage. Shred the tender meat with the forks and chop it finely on a cutting board. Season with sea salt and freshly ground pepper.

Lay a sheet of plastic wrap on the work surface, spread the seasoned lamb evenly into a rectangle—a generous ½ inch thick. Lay the rolls of frozen gremolata down the middle, then use the plastic wrap to help wrap the lamb securely around the gremolata. Twist the ends tightly. Refrigerate overnight or up to 2 days ahead.

Make the celeriac purée. Quarter, peel, and cut the celeriac into 1-inch cubes. Cook in boiling salted water for about 15 minutes or until tender then drain well.

Meanwhile, scrub and boil the potatoes. Peel and put into a food processor together with the celeriac. Add the butter, chopped herbs, and cream. Season to taste. Taste and add a few drops of lemon juice if necessary.

To make the wild garlic salsa verde, process all the ingredients except the oil together in a food processor. Add the oil to loosen, then season to taste.

Preheat the oven to 325°F. Remove the lamb from the fridge and unwrap. Cut the roll crosswise into 1-inch-thick pieces. Arrange in a single layer on a baking sheet. Warm in the oven for 20 minutes until heated through.

To serve, cook the purple sprouting broccoli, if using, in boiling salted water for 3 to 4 minutes. Drain.

Put a dollop of celeriac purée onto each hot plate. Smear with a spoon. Pop two lamb breast roulades down the side. Lay a few pieces of purple sprouting broccoli on top and put a few dots of salsa verde along the side.

ASPARAGUS *Asparagus officinalis* PERENNIAL

Asparagus is one of nature's greatest gifts. In the early 1970s my father-in-law, Ivan Allen, planted five acres of Martha Washington asparagus in a sandy field close to Shanagarry strand—the flavor was superb. We would bring up baskets full of freshly cut spears and have them for supper. The children remember plates piled high with asparagus to eat with fresh toast and hollandaise sauce. There was so much that I combed through cookbooks for recipes to circle the changes and served it in every conceivable way: soup, with fish, chicken, lamb. Sadly, it was a bit too early, the market was too small at that time, so it was all grubbed out a few years later. Now we grow a smaller area and relish every precious spear.

I love perennial vegetables that just return year after year and keep on giving. Once again, this is a vegetable that has to be eaten within hours of being picked to really understand the magic. Spears that have travelled halfway round the globe to make it to your supermarket shelf aren't in any way worth the expense.

So, if you have the space, prepare a patch of soil carefully and plant an asparagus bed for posterity. A bed of 10 × 6 ½ feet will be big enough for 10 crowns. If you are short of space and desperate to have some asparagus, why not tuck a single plant here and there into a flower bed or herbaceous border? The delicate fern with its occasional red berries will be an attractive addition—but beware, the berries are poisonous.

VARIETIES

British and Irish asparagus is green whereas the French prefer white asparagus—interestingly, it's the same variety but to achieve the white color it's blanched when growing to exclude the light. We don't blanch our asparagus, as we don't feel that it's worth the extra work as it doesn't enhance the flavor. There are also some purple varieties.

Asparagus has male and female plants; males are favored since they won't waste energy making seed, instead diverting it into producing the asparagus shoots.

Martha Washington—Old trusted variety which we love, favored in the US with large spears and good flavor.
Connover's Colossal—Well-tried variety dating from the 1800s. It is early and produces lots of thick, chunky, well-flavored spears, which are bright green with purple tips.
Lucullus—All-male variety, it's a later cropper with a good yield of medium-sized spears. It has the reputation of being adaptable to various conditions.
Purple Passion—New variety with thick tender spears and no stringiness. Very mild and sweet flavor.
Jersey Knight—Matures quickly from seed and carries good disease resistance.

HOW TO GROW

Choose a sunny, open spot that's not too windy. Sandy soil is preferable, and dig in plenty of well-rotted manure or compost. Asparagus does best in soil with a pH of 6.5 to 7.5, so if your soil is acidic you may need to dig in some lime, too.

Plant the seeds in spring, about 2 inches apart in weed-free ground. Although we have grown from seed, I recommend planting crowns instead, about 3 feet apart, as it will save you 2 to 3 years of waiting before you can harvest.

Wait until late spring to plant crowns—if the weather is too cold they won't make any growth and may even die, and they need to be able to start growing immediately. Don't bury the crown, it should be just sticking out above the ground and the roots buried. Plant them a foot apart.

There's been a long tradition of sprinkling some cinders over the bed in winter to add potash. to the soil. If the weather is very dry over a prolonged period, the plants will benefit from a good watering.

It's vital to keep the bed free of all, particularly perennial, weeds. It's even worth waiting a year before planting to make sure that the bed is completely free of perennial weeds, or plant them through landscape fabric. Care is needed when weeding as careless hoeing will break the emerging spears, so hand-weeding is preferable.

Martha Washington is our favorite variety of asparagus.

Asparagus requires patience; it takes three years to get a good crop, because the plant needs to develop a good root system and store up enough energy, but it's certainly worth the wait and effort. Don't cut any in the first year, and if you can resist don't harvest in the second year either. In the third year you can have a feast—enjoy every morsel.

CONTAINER GROWING

One could grow a plant or two in a large trough. Again, it's vital to keep asparagus weed free, so we mulch with compost.

PESTS AND DISEASES

Aphids can appear on the spears, but just wash them off before cooking.

Asparagus beetle can sometimes be a problem. It can appear from early to late summer, the adults beetles are black with yellow spots on their wings and the larvae are grey. Both beetles and larvae can eat the foliage and also damage the stems. Be vigilant from late spring onwards and pick both the beetles and larvae from the plants, putting them into a bucket of soapy water to get rid of them. If you have had an infestation, at the end of the year remove and burn the old stems so the beetles can't overwinter in the plants.

HARVESTING

Asparagus is ready to harvest in early summer, but the season is short—4 to 6 weeks in total.

Choose thick stumpy spears with tight heads and cut them off with a sharp knife about 1 inch below the soil level. A really strong crown can produce ten or more spears in each season.

Stop harvesting after about 6 to 8 weeks to allow the crown to recover for next year's crop—picking for too long will result in thin spears the following year. The spears will grow into beautiful feathery ferns, and while it is tempting

to use these for flower arrangements, resist, or next year's yield will be drastically affected.

GOOD FOR YOU...

Asparagus contains high quantities of vitamins K, A, C, E, B1, B2, and niacin as well as minerals, such as zinc, potassium, iron and calcium. It is also a well-known diuretic and very rich in folic acid. Asparagus can be used to treat cystitis, gout and rheumatism, lower blood pressure and blood sugar, regulate and balance cholesterol.

WHAT TO DO WITH A GLUT?

If perchance you do, my advice would be to feast on it for every meal during the short season, and make a few batches of soup to freeze for later.

IN THE KITCHEN

A few boiled or steamed asparagus spears make delicious "posh soldiers" to dip into a soft-boiled egg, and simply served with butter they are divine. Asparagus on toast or grilled bread with hollandaise is particularly delicious with crab, mussels, flat fish, and sea bass. For 4 to 6 people, take 1½ to 2 pounds asparagus and hold each spear over your index finger down near the root end; it will snap at the

Try not to cut the asparagus fern, it's needed to feed the crop the following year.

point where it begins to get tough (use the woody ends for stock). Some people like to peel but we rarely do.

To boil: Tie similar-sized spears in bundles with twine. Choose a tall saucepan—there are specially designed tall asparagus pots with baskets. Cook in about 1 inch of boiling salted water (1 teaspoon salt to every 2½ cups water) for 2 to 3 minutes or until a knife tip will pierce the root end easily. Drain and serve immediately. If serving cold, refresh in cold water and drain again.

To steam: Stand the asparagus upright in a steamer and cook in boiling salted water for 4 to 5 minutes until almost tender, then drain and serve as desired.

To roast: Preheat the oven to 450°F. Drizzle the spears with a little olive oil. Toss gently to coat, season with sea salt, and roast in a pan for 5 to 8 minutes, depending on the thickness.

To grill: Heat a grill pan over a medium-high heat. Drizzle with extra virgin olive oil, then cook the asparagus for a couple of minutes, turning if necessary. Season as above.

Asparagus, Arugula & Wild Garlic Frittata

This is an example of how we incorporate seasonal ingredients into a frittata. Asparagus is an extra treat here; you can use any asparagus but I tend to use the thin, weedy, but still delicious spears in frittata and to add to scrambled eggs.

SERVES 6

½ pound thin asparagus

8 organic eggs

1 teaspoon sea salt and lots of freshly ground black pepper

1¾ ounces Parmesan

2 to 3 tablespoons roughly chopped wild garlic and arugula leaves

2 tablespoons olive oil

salad leaves, wild garlic, and arugula, to serve

Bring about 1 inch of water to a boil in an oval casserole. Trim the tough ends of the asparagus, add 1 teaspoon of salt, and blanch for 3 to 4 minutes until tender. Drain. Slice the spears on an angle, keeping 1½ inches at the top intact. Set aside.

Whisk the eggs together in a bowl. Add the blanched asparagus, except the tops, most of the Parmesan, and the wild garlic or arugula leaves. Season well.

Heat the oil in a skillet, add the egg mixture, and reduce the heat to the bare minimum—use a heat diffuser, if necessary. Arrange the asparagus tops over the frittata and sprinkle with the remaining Parmesan. Continue to cook over low heat until just set, about 15 minutes. Alternatively, after an initial 4 to 5 minutes on the stovetop, you can transfer the pan to the oven (this is my preferred option) preheated to 325°F for 10 to 15 minutes until just set.

Pop under the broiler for a few minutes, but make sure it is at least 5 inches from the heat source. The frittata should be set and slightly golden. Turn out onto a warm plate, cut into wedges, and serve immediately with a salad of organic leaves, including wild garlic and arugula. Garnish with wild garlic flowers, if available.

Nopa Asparagus with Dill Crème Fraîche & Lemon

Nopa is one of my favorite restaurants in San Francisco, and my visit coincided with the asparagus season.

SERVES 4

20 fat asparagus spears

4 lemon wedges, to serve

FOR THE BATTER

6 ounces chickpea flour or all-purpose flour

1 scant teaspoon sea salt

1 tablespoon olive oil

1 tablespoon freshly squeezed lemon juice

¾ to 1 cup ice water

vegetable oil, for deep-frying

FOR THE DILL CRÈME FRAÎCHE

2 tablespoons chopped fresh dill

½ cup plus 2 tablespoons crème fraîche

sea salt and freshly ground black pepper

Blanch the asparagus spears in boiling salted water for just 1 minute, refresh under cold water, drain, and cool.

To make the batter, put the chickpea flour and salt into a large bowl. Gradually whisk in the oil, lemon juice, and water until the batter is the consistency of thick cream.

Stir the dill into the crème fraîche, season with salt and freshly ground pepper.

Just before serving, heat the vegetable oil to 350°F in a deep skillet.

Dip the asparagus spears in the batter, one at a time, and cook a few at a time for 2 to 4 minutes, depending on thickness, in the hot oil.

Drain on paper towels, then pile 5 on each plate and serve immediately with a little bowl of dill crème fraîche and a wedge of lemon.

CHARD *Beta vulgaris* subsp. *cicla* ANNUAL

Chard is easy to grow—a great cut-and-come-again plant—delicious, nutritious, edible and ornamental. How about that for checking all the boxes? It's easier to grow than spinach and less likely to bolt in dry weather. We grow it indoors, outdoors, here and there in herbaceous borders, and edging vegetable beds.

A relative of chard and beet is perpetual spinach. It's also known as spinach beet but, despite its name, it's not spinach. This heirloom is one on my A-list. It's not exactly perpetual, but it's a cut-and-come-again vegetable that we wouldn't be without, a leafy green that keeps on giving. Remember to grow lots of it because it almost disappears in the cooking. Perfect for a small garden and less likely to bolt than summer spinach, plus you can cook the leaves and narrow stalks separately. In fact, we never waste the stalks because they are so good; two vegetables for the price of one.

VARIETIES

There are several varieties of chard, as well as the original Swiss chard with its thick white stems and robust greens. We love ruby chard and rainbow chard because so they look so attractive on the plate as well as in the garden.
Lucullus—Swiss chard, wide white stems.
Ruby Red—Red stems.
Bright Lights—Multicolored stems—white, ruby, yellow, orange. Looks spectacular in a flower border as well as in the vegetable garden or potager.

PERPETUAL SPINACH CHARD: (BETA VULGARIS VAR CICLA):
Erbette—Italian variety.
Giant Winter—Very hardy, large mid-green fleshy leaves. Stands up well.

TWO OTHER VARIETIES OF SPINACH WORTH GROWING
Tree Spinach—*Chenopodium giganteum*—Native to the mountainous areas of India and widely grown in Mexico, this is a pretty, decorative plant with magenta-splashed leaves. Plants will grow up to 49 inches tall, but it's best to snip the young leaves when they are no more than 8 inches high.
Strawberry Spinach—*Chenopodium capitatum*—A bushy plant with thin jagged leaves that can be used like spinach, it is mostly grown for its strawberry-like fruits. Children love them even though they are not particularly flavorful.

HOW TO GROW
If growing conditions are difficult you could plant this inside in cells or in gutters suspended in a greenhouse, if

Bright Lights.

space is limited. Outside, choose a sunny spot and well-drained, rich, fertile soil. Plant seed directly into the ground in early spring when all signs of frost are over—the soil temperature needs to be 60°F for the seed to germinate. We also do a midsummer sowing outside which will crop into the autumn.

For a late-summer crop, direct sow perpetual spinach in a 1/3-inch-deep drill in rich, moisture-retentive soil with lots of well-rotted manure or compost in mid-spring. Sow again in late spring for a maincrop which will produce continually throughout the summer and into the following year. Sow in autumn for a supply of leaves throughout the winter. Plant the rows 30 inches apart. Perpetual spinach doesn't bolt and run to seed as easily as summer spinach, but keep well watered and don't allow the plants to flower if possible. If the plant is covered with Reemay or plastic it will help to keep the leaves tender, and protect the crop from the elements.

CONTAINER GROWING
Chard can also be grown in a large container on a balcony, or in a herbaceous border. Perpetual spinach thrives in a large container or on a roof garden. We've even grown it in an old wheelbarrow. It's also shade tolerant and survives very cold weather. It can also be grown, like chard, brassicas, onions and garlic, throughout a flower garden.

PESTS
Chard is a host for blackfly. Like spinach it bolts very quickly and then blackfly lives in the soft tissue of the bolting shoot, so break it off and discard it. If there is overhead tree cover for birds they can be a problem, especially if there

isn't much else growing, but in the main growing season there are lots of other things to tempt them.

Slugs love the baby perpetual spinach leaves. In the greenhouse we have to take out our crops by midsummer because it gets covered with blackfly, which can spread to other crops. It is possible to spray with Pyrethrum but we haven't found it very effective. We have introduced the predator Aphidius colemani to control aphids in the greenhouse, and as well the predatory gall midge Aphidoletes aphidimyza.

You can also plant perpetual spinach near fava beans and strawberries to inhibit black- and green aphids. Perpetual spinach also benefits from being planted close to herbs such as rosemary, thyme, sage, mint, and hyssop. Later in the season, members of the Calendula (Compositae) and Ammi majus (Umbellifer) families are particularly good for attracting beneficial insects such as lacewing and ladybugs, whose larvae also eat aphids.

HARVESTING

Swiss chard can be harvested in 4 to 6 weeks, just as soon as the leaves are large enough to eat, about 3 to 4 inches long. They will grow much larger, but don't let them get bigger than 10 inches. Keep harvesting; the leaves continue to grow.

Chard is extremely frost tolerant and will sweeten in cold weather. Even if the outer leaves get frosted the inner leaves will be protected.

The leaves can be harvested individually or you can cut the entire plant in one go, but leave 4 to 6 inches of stem so the plant can resprout.

The glossy green leaves of perpetual spinach are tougher than those of summer spinach, the young leaves are most tender but the secret is to keep picking, a few at a time off each plant to encourage a constant supply. Even if

you can't keep up, keep on picking. Gift bunches to friends or put them onto your compost heap.

GOOD FOR YOU...

Low in calories, Swiss chard is rich in vitamins K, A, and C. It is also a source of magnesium, potassium, iron and fiber. Perpetual spinach is an excellent source of vitamins A, C, E, and K and magnesium, manganese, potassium, and iron and contains significant amounts of antioxidants such as phenolics and flavonoids.

WHAT TO DO WITH A GLUT

Trim, cook, purée, and freeze the leaves. Use as a side dish or as the base for soups, lasagna, curries, tarts, or quiches. Remember, spinach shrinks alarmingly in cooking, so grow lots and allow 1 pound raw spinach per person.

IN THE KITCHEN

Chard stems and leaves are edible; the stems of the red and rainbow varieties look gorgeous when cooked. Strip off the leaves, cook the stalks, then add the leaves at the end. Try tossing the stems in vinaigrette or olive oil and lemon juice.

To cook **Ruby or Swiss Chard with Butter** for 4 people, pull the leaves off 1 pound chard, wash, and drain. Cut the stalks into pieces about 2 inches long. Cook the stalks in boiling salted water (5 cups water and 2 teaspoons salt) for 2 to 3 minutes until they feel tender when pierced with the tip of a knife. Drain very well. Toss in a little melted butter or olive oil and serve immediately. I often add the greens to the cooking water for just a couple of minutes, until tender, then drain and anoint in butter or olive oil. Season with lots of freshly ground pepper and some freshly grated nutmeg.

For **Ruby Chard or Swiss Chard with Parmesan,** cut 1 pound chard stalks into 4-inch pieces and cook as above. Smear

Swiss chard.

a 9-inch square baking dish with a little butter, arrange some of the chard stalks in a single layer, and season with salt and freshly ground pepper. Sprinkle with about ¾ cup freshly grated Parmesan cheese and dot with a little butter. Repeat until the dish is full, then sprinkle the top layer generously with more cheese. Dot with a little butter. Bake in a preheated 400°F oven for 15 to 20 minutes or until golden. (This works well with sliced fennel bulbs.)

Chard stalks are also amazingly addictive chargrilled. Trim the leaves off the stalks and cut into 4 or 5 pieces. Preheat a pan-grill over high heat. Toss the stalks in extra virgin olive oil and season with salt and freshly ground pepper, then char-grill for a couple of minutes on each side. Serve immediately.

For a really easy way to cook spinach, you could use just the leaves, but I often cook the stalks also for a more rustic result. We add lots of other flavors too; chopped garlic can be sweated with the onions, or add fresh chile or chile flakes. A few chopped anchovies are delicious, as is a little diced chorizo or a dollop of cream. Use as a topping for grilled bread, with goat cheese, or rigatoni.

To serve 4 to 6, strip the leaves off 3 pounds perpetual spinach and chop the stalks into ¼-inch pieces. Chop the leaves and set aside. Heat 3 tablespoons extra virgin olive oil in a skillet, add 5 large shallots, thinly sliced, and cook until soft and slightly golden. Add the chopped spinach stalks and cook for 4 to 5 minutes. Season with salt and freshly ground pepper. Add the chopped spinach leaves and wilt down over high heat for 3 to 4 minutes. Season with salt and freshly ground black pepper and a

little freshly grated nutmeg.

People usually chuck out perpetual spinach stalks after they've strung the spinach, but they're delicious and it's a pity to waste them after all the hard work of growing them. Chop the spinach stalks into 1-inch pieces. Cook in boiling salted water—use 1 teaspoon salt for every 2½ cups water—for 3 to 4 minutes until tender. Drain well. Toss in a little butter or extra virgin olive oil. I sometimes toss in a few chile flakes and chopped fresh herbs. If you feel like an Asian flavor, substitute soy sauce or oyster sauce for the butter or olive oil.

We also love the cooked tender stalks and leaves folded into a creamy pasta or risotto just before eating. The leaves can also be used to make dolmades instead of vine leaves.

Swiss Chard with Tahini, Yogurt & Toasted Cashew Nuts

Chard is such a brilliant vegetable, it's another brassica that gives double value for money and keeps on giving. The currants, golden raisins, or raisins add an appealing sweetness. Spinach, plus the stalks, may be substituted in this recipe.

SERVES 4

3 pounds Swiss chard

2 tablespoons butter

2 tablespoons olive oil, plus extra to serve

⅓ cup cashews or almonds, roughly chopped

1 garlic clove, very thinly sliced

4 tablespoons currants, golden raisins, or raisins

sea salt and freshly ground black pepper

sweet paprika, to garnish

flatbread or pita, to serve

FOR THE TAHINI AND YOGURT SAUCE

¼ cup tahini

¼ cup plain full-fat yogurt

2 tablespoons lemon juice

1 garlic clove, crushed

a little honey, if necessary

First make the tahini and yogurt sauce. Place all the ingredients in a bowl with 2 tablespoons of water, season with a pinch of salt, and whisk until smooth. Taste and add a little honey, if necessary. Set aside.

Separate the green chard leaves from the white stalks. Cut both into ¾-inch-wide slices but keep them separate. Bring a large saucepan of well-salted water to a boil, add the chard stalks, simmer for 3 to 4 minutes, then add the leaves and cook for 2 to 3 minutes. Drain and squeeze the chard well until it is completely dry.

Next, put the butter and the olive oil in a large skillet over medium heat. Add the nuts and toss them in the pan until golden, about 2 minutes. Add the garlic and dried fruit and toss until they begin to turn golden. Return the chard to the pan and toss until warm. Season to taste.

Serve the chard with some of the tahini sauce on top. Drizzle with extra virgin olive oil and sprinkle with paprika. Serve with freshly cooked flatbread or pita.

Spinach, Feta & Sweet Potato Frittata

The basic frittata recipe here can be used as a basis for many herbs and vegetables in season, but we love this autumn version. We use blobs of Ardsallagh goat cheese in this recipe if we don't have feta.

SERVES 8

1 pound sweet potato or pumpkin, peeled and cut into ⅓-inch dice

3 tablespoons extra virgin olive oil, plus extra to serve

1 teaspoon flaky sea salt

lots of freshly ground black pepper

10 large organic eggs

2 tablespoons chopped marjoram

2 tablespoons chopped curly parsley

2 teaspoons chopped thyme leaves

5¼ ounces fresh spinach leaves, shredded into ⅓-inch-wide strips (about ¾ pound before destemming)

2½ ounces Gruyére cheese, grated

¾ ounce Parmesan cheese, finely grated

2 tablespoons butter

7 ounces feta or fresh goat cheese

arugula leaves and ¼ cup toasted pine nuts or cashews, to serve

Preheat the oven to 350°F.

Put the sweet potato or squash on a small baking sheet, drizzle with olive oil, and toss to coat. Season with ½ teaspoon of the flaky sea salt (the feta cheese will be salty so don't overdo the salt) and lots of freshly ground pepper, stir, and bake for 10 to 15 minutes or until cooked and tender. Remove from the oven.

Whisk the eggs in a bowl; add the remaining ½ teaspoon salt, freshly ground pepper, chopped herbs, shredded spinach, and grated cheese and whisk to combine. Melt the butter in an 9-inch nonstick skillet, and when it starts to foam, tip in the eggs. Sprinkle the roast sweet potato evenly over the surface, dot with the feta or goat cheese, and press in gently. Cook for 3 to 4 minutes over low heat.

Transfer to the middle rack of the oven and bake for 25 to 30 minutes. Switch the oven to broil and broil for a couple of minutes if color is needed. Let sit for 5 minutes before serving.

To serve, slide a metal spatula under the frittata to free it from the pan. Slide it onto a warm plate. Arrange some arugula leaves on top of the frittata, drizzle with extra virgin olive oil, and scatter with toasted pine nuts or coarsely chopped cashews and a few flakes of sea salt.

BEET *Beta vulgaris* ANNUAL

Boltardy beet—leaves, roots and stalks can all be eaten when young.

Beets are definitely one of my top ten vegetables to grow; few other vegetables deliver so much bang for your buck— three vegetables in one. We use the roots in myriad ways, but we also cook the young beet stalks and the tender leaves are delicious in salads or as a vegetable accompaniment. Each variety has a different color and flavor.

Beets are a perfect crop for a novice gardener to get started on, because they are fast growing and can be cultivated just about anywhere.

VARIETIES

Chioggia—Italian variety from an Adriatic coastal area, near the town of Chioggia. When cut it has alternating rings of pink and white, so it looks very attractive in a salad with a selection of beets. It loses its color when cooked but is tender and delicious with a more delicate flavor than Boltardy.

Boro F1—Beautiful candy-striped beet, delicious thinly sliced and eaten raw.

Bull's Blood—Beautiful crimson leaves to use in your salads, also striking grown in a border.

Sweet flavor and good late in the year.

Golden Detroit—Good maincrop variety, nice texture, and flavor, golden-yellow-colored flesh when cooked.

Detroit Dark Red—Very sweet beet with a silky texture; it doesn't get woody even when big.

Formanova Cylindra—Heirloom variety from Denmark, it has long cylindrical roots and is very good for slicing, sometimes known as "Butter Slicer" because of its texture.

Cheltenham Green Top—Dates back to 1880, grown extensively in market gardens around Cheltenham in the UK. It has long roots with deep red flesh and stores well.

Lutz Green Leaf—Heirloom variety— as its nickname "Winter Keeper" indicates, this is a good variety for storage.

HOW TO GROW

Beets will grow in any well-drained, fertile garden soil. It prefers neutral or slightly alkaline soil.

If you have a greenhouse or polytunnel, do a first sowing in early spring straight into the ground, which will be ready to harvest in early summer. Do a second sowing in late spring for a summer crop and a third in early summer for autumn and winter storage.

We sow the seeds of Boltardy spinach directly into the ground from late spring onwards. Plant the seeds in rows 12 inches apart. Sow them thinly—we don't thin the young seedlings but as they begin to swell, we pick them here and there, so the remaining beets will have room to grow. You can, of course, plant the seeds spaced out singly if you prefer.

In colder areas the young plants will need to be protected with fleece. For the seeds to germinate the soil needs to be at least 50°F and should not feel cold or soggy to the touch.

In the vegetable garden we like to interplant the beets with fennel (herb), calendula, cornflower and French marigold (African Fire Cracker), for extra visual impact.

CONTAINER GROWING

Beets can certainly be grown in containers—try pots, troughs, tubs or even in an old bathtub or wheelbarrow. The smaller globe-shaped and bolt-resistant varieties, such as Boltardy, Detroit Globe, and Rhonda F1 are more suitable for containers.

Beets are also very successful grown as a microgreens in seed trays; they are delicious in salads or as a garnish. Bull's Blood with its red leaves is particularly striking.

PESTS AND DISEASES

Reasonably trouble-free, but plant them away from fava beans as the black bean aphid may transfer onto them. Beets may bolt in temperature extremes, a cold spell or a drought. Seek out bolt-resistant varieties like Boltardy and Rhonda F1 and keep the soil moist.

HARVESTING

We are so impatient we can hardly wait for the young beets to be ready, so we harvest them from the time they are as big as a cherry belle radish, even smaller than a golf or table tennis ball. They quickly increase in size, but try not to allow them to become larger than a tennis ball as the texture will be woody, particularly in winter.

In milder climates, beets can be left in the ground and harvested throughout the winter, however, they get tougher and woodier so a better plan is to harvest them, trim the wilting leaves, and bury the roots in a deep box or a bin full of sand, preferably not touching each other, in a frost-free area. That way they'll keep for 3 to 4 months. We have also had success when we put them into paper potato sacks in a cold garden shed.

GOOD FOR YOU...

Beet greens are rich in calcium, iron and vitamins A and C. The roots contain folate, fibre, magnesium and potassium. Beet is recommended for lowering blood pressure.

WHAT TO DO WITH A GLUT

Beets pickle beautifully and I don't think you can ever have too many jars of home-pickled beet, it is so totally different from the vinegary concoction sold in jars that turns virtually everyone off beet. It's great for gifts, too, and we can't keep up with the demand for beet pickle and relishes from our farm shop and our farmers' market stall.

IN THE KITCHEN

Beets can be eaten raw or cooked, juiced, grated or sliced into salads, baked, roasted, boiled, or pickled. Beets can also be part of a kraut and made into chutneys, relishes, crisps, juices, beet cakes, and muffins. They make wonderful soup, both hot and chilled,

and are also a delicious hot vegetable.

Beets can be wrapped in foil and roasted or cooked in boiling salted water until the skin rubs off easily. The length of time they take to cook varies enormously, from 15 minutes for new season's beets to 2 hours for older ones, depending on their age. The young leaves are delicious in salad and more mature leaves can be cooked like spinach, added to soups or bean stews and curries. The chopped stalks can be used for a variety of cooked recipes and salads.

To prepare beet, leave 2-inch leaf stalks on top and the whole root on the "tail." Save the stalks and young leaves. Hold the beet under a running tap and wash off the mud with your palms, so that you don't damage the skin; otherwise the beet will bleed during cooking. Put in a saucepan, cover with cold water, and add a little salt and sugar. Cover, bring to a boil, and simmer on the stovetop (or transfer to the oven and bake) for 1 to 2 hours depending on size. Beet are usually cooked if the skin rubs off easily and if they dent when pressed with a finger. If in doubt, test with a skewer or the tip of a knife.

For **Roast Beets** for 4 people, prepare 12 baby beets (a mixture of red, golden and Chioggia would work well) and preheat the oven to 450°F. Wrap the beets in foil and roast for 1 hour, depending on size, until soft and cooked through. You'll know when they're cooked if there's a bit of give when you press the foil, or unwrap the beet and see if the skin will rub off. Rub off the skins, toss in extra virgin olive oil, and sprinkle with sea salt. Serve as a vegetable or as the basis of a warm or cold salad.

For **Beet Greens** for 4 people, take 1 pound fresh beet tops and, keeping

Chioggia beet looks like candy rock. We enjoy it both raw and cooked as well as the young leaves.

them separate, cut them into roughly 2 inch pieces. Cook the stalks in boiling salted water (7½ cups water to 1½ teaspoons salt) for 3 to 4 minutes or until tender. Then add the leaves and cook for an additional 2 to 3 minutes. Drain well, season and toss in a little butter or extra virgin olive oil. Serve immediately. For **Beet Tops and Cream with Pasta**, substitute 5 tablespoons to ½ cup heavy cream for olive oil. A little freshly grated nutmeg is also delicious. We love this over fettuccine with lots of grated Parmesan or pecorino.

Shaved Radish & Beet Salad

This is such a beautiful salad and is made in minutes—it also makes the growing number of raw food aficionados happy and is a super way to show off your beet crop.

. . . .

SERVES 4 AS A STARTER

8 French breakfast radishes
1 red beet, such as Boltardy
1 yellow beet, such as Golden Globe
1 Chioggia beet
a few sprigs of flat-leaf parsley, leaves
  picked
arugula leaves, golden marjoram, and
  chervil, to serve

FOR THE DRESSING

6 tablespoons extra virgin olive oil
2 tablespoons Forum Chardonnay white
  vinegar or white balsamic vinegar
sea salt and freshly ground black pepper

Mix the dressing ingredients together in a small bowl. Season to taste and set aside.

Just before serving, wash the radishes and beets. Shave each one into thin rounds on a mandoline. Toss the lot with the parsley and dress lightly with most of the dressing.

Arrange the slices of beet and radish on white plates, overlapping haphazardly. Drizzle over the remaining dressing and top with a few arugula leaves, golden marjoram, and chervil. (You may not need all the dressing depending on the size of the beets.)

Beet Kvass

My daughter-in-law Penny is an ardent and deeply knowledgeable fermenter, and this is one of her energy-boosting recipes. This is a slightly sour/salty tonic of a deep-red color known to help clean the liver and purify the blood. Drink a shot in the morning, or add it to cocktails, such as a Bloody Mary. Kvass has Eastern European origins, originally made from fermenting stale bread. The use of beet extract is also being studied in the treatment of certain cancers, such as pancreatic, breast, and prostate. Tolstoy relates that Russian soldiers took a ladle full of kvass before venturing onto the streets during a cholera epidemic, as it protected against infection and disease and was safer to drink than water. A ½ cup serving is usually enough for most people.

. . . .

MAKES ABOUT 1½ QUARTS

2 large beets
6 cups filtered or nonchlorinated water
2 teaspoons sea salt
3 tablespoons starter—this could be
  whey, water kefir, sauerkraut juice, or
  kombucha

Scrub the beets but do not peel them. Chop into small chunks—approx. ¾-inch cubes. Put them into a sterilized 2-quart jar with a lid. Add the water, sea salt, and starter, and secure the lid tightly. Let sit in a warm place, undisturbed, for about 5 days.

Bubbles will start to appear (a sure sign fermentation is happening). Taste it after 3 days and if it is to your liking, strain out the beet chunks (you could use these in a salad). Bottle and store in the fridge once it reaches the desired degree of sourness. It will keep for 4 to 5 days, maximum a week.

Beet, Blood Orange & Arugula Salad

The combination of citrus and beet is fresh tasting and delicious

. . . .

SERVES 6

1 pound baby beets
4 small handfuls of arugula leaves
seeds from ½ pomegranate
½ cup coarsely chopped pistachio nuts

FOR THE DRESSING
3 to 4 blood oranges
1 small shallot, minced
1 teaspoon balsamic vinegar
3 tablespoons extra virgin olive oil
sea salt and freshly ground black pepper

Roast the beets (see page 75), peel, and cut into wedges.

Meanwhile make the dressing. Grate the zest from 1 orange on the finest part of the grater. Put in a bowl with the shallot and squeeze in the juice of one orange. Whisk in the oil and vinegar. Season with salt and freshly ground pepper. It should taste nice and perky. Cut all the zest and peel off the remainder of the oranges and cut into thin slices.

To serve, divide the arugula leaves between four plates. Top with some beet wedges and blood orange slices rather haphazardly arranged. Scatter with the pomegranate seeds and chopped pistachios. Drizzle a little dressing over each salad and serve immediately.

Beet & Ginger Relish

A delicious combination, this relish complements goat's cheese, pâté de campagne and lots of other meats.

. . . .

MAKES APPROX. 2 CUPS

3 tablespoons butter
1 small onion, chopped
3 tablespoons sugar
1 pound beet, peeled and grated
2 teaspoons grated fresh ginger
2 tablespoons sherry vinegar
½ cup red wine
sea salt and freshly ground black pepper

Melt the butter in a skillet over medium–low heat. Add the onions and sweat slowly in the butter for 5 to 6 minutes until very soft. Add the remaining ingredients and cook gently for 30 minutes. Serve cold.

This relish is best eaten within 6 months.

Beet Soup with Chive Cream

This soup gets a rapturous reaction served either hot or chilled, but to have its magical sweetness the beets must be young. For Golden Beet Soup, use golden Chioggia here.

· ·

SERVES 8 TO 10

2 pounds young beets
2 tablespoons butter
½ pound onions, chopped
approx. 5 cups hot homemade chicken or
  vegetable stock
½ cup whole milk
sea salt and freshly ground black pepper
½ cup sour cream or crème fraîche and
  minced chives, to serve

Wash the beets carefully under cold running water. Don't scrub, simply rub off any dirt with your fingers. You don't want to damage the skin or cut off the top or tails because it will "bleed" in the cooking. Put the beets in a pan of cold water and simmer, covered, for anywhere from 20 minutes to 2 hours, depending on the size and age if the beets. The beets are cooked when the skins will rub off easily.

Meanwhile, in a skillet, melt the butter. Sweat the onions carefully and gently for about 10 minutes in the butter until they are cooked.

Chop the beets and add to the onions. Season with salt and freshly ground pepper. Put into a high-speed blender with the hot stock. Liquidize until quite smooth. Reheat, add some milk, taste, and adjust the seasoning—it may be necessary to add a little more stock or milk.

Serve garnished with little swirls of the sour cream or crème fraîche and a sprinkling of minced chives.

Beet & Raspberry Ice Cream

Sounds weird but this is a really delicious combination of flavors—ask your guests to guess the flavor!

· ·

SERVES 6

8 ounces fresh raspberries
¾ cup plus 2 tablespoons granulated
  sugar
1 teaspoon powdered gelatin
½ pound cooked ruby beet
2½ cups whipped cream
fresh raspberries and fresh mint leaves, to
  decorate

Purée the raspberries in a blender and push through a sieve.

Dissolve the sugar in ½ cup plus 2 tablespoons water in a saucepan over medium heat, then turn up the heat and boil for 2 minutes.

Sponge the gelatin in 1 tablespoon of water in a Pyrex jug and sit the jug in a saucepan of simmering water and stir until the gelatine is fully dissolved.

Purée the cooked beet with the sugar syrup and allow to cool. Once cool, add the raspberry purée—add a little to the gelatin and then mix the two together. Fold in the whipped cream and transfer to a freezerproof covered container. Put in the freezer for 3–4 hours.

To serve, scoop out the ice cream and serve on chilled plates. Decorate with fresh raspberries and mint leaves.

RUTABAGA *Brassica napus* ANNUAL

The humble rutabaga deserves to be better appreciated.

Rutabagas are often looked on as the poor relation of the vegetable world, but I'm very fond of this "homely" winter root that becomes sweeter after a few nights of frost, so don't dismiss the lowly rutabaga.

Rutabagas, also known as swede turnips came to us here in Ireland from Sweden recently enough—in the 1800s. They were a particularly welcome addition because they could be eaten by animals as well as be enjoyed by

people. Originally they were used as a winter food for livestock and had the advantage of being able to stay in the ground virtually throughout the winter. They tend to grow partly above ground so sheep can forage and graze on them in the field.

This humble and ridiculously inexpensive vegetable can cause considerable confusion. Here in Ireland we just call them turnips and they have pale yellow/orange flesh with thick purple skin, but there's also the white turnip, which is smaller and milder.

VARIETIES

Joan—sweet flavored yellow roots have purple tops; resistant to club root; stores well.
Helenor—Round, orange-fleshed bulb with a sweet flavor; high-yielding and develops early.
Laurentian—Pale, yellow-fleshed bulbs are sweet and mild.

HOW TO GROW

Rutabagas are a brassica, so factor that into your rotation. Rutabagas are not that fussy about soil type; as long as the ground is reasonably fertile they will thrive. They need the same soil conditions as other brassicas, ideally with a pH of 6 to 6.8.

For a winter crop, seeds can be sown directly into the ground in spring, but we also get excellent results when we start them in the nursery section of the greenhouse in late spring/early summer, in cell trays sowing each seed ¾ inch deep. They usually germinate within a week and after a month we harden them off and plant them outside in midsummer, spacing both plants and rows approximately 12 inches apart.

You can also sow them directly into the ground outside in midsummer.

CONTAINER GROWING

Rutabagas can be grown in a container, they need about 12 inches depth of soil, but I can certainly think of better uses for your container. Nonetheless, they are a very useful vegetable.

HARVESTING

In milder areas rutabagas can be left in the ground and harvested as and when you need them up to midwinter. Choose hardier varieties for colder areas. Rutabagas may be stored, too—dig or pull them up, trim the tops and store the roots in a dark shed, ideally buried in moist sand, or well covered with straw.

PESTS

Rutabagas can be susceptible to all brassica pests. Flea beetle can be a problem on seedlings, we don't tend to have it here, but if it's likely to be a problem the plants can be protected with horticultural netting (Bionet) like carrots.

Birds can be a problem both early and late in the season when there's not much other food around, so again you could protect with nets, which is easier when the plants are small. The young tender leaves are very tempting to them. Remove the net when the plants are well established.

GOOD FOR YOU...

Rutabagas are a good source of fibre, vitamins A and C, calcium and potassium.

WHAT TO DO WITH A GLUT

We use them in soups, braises, stews—

both meat and vegetable—mashes and purées, gratins and quiches. Rutabagas benefit from lots of butter and/or extra virgin olive oil, plus freshly cracked pepper and gratefully absorb the flavor of fresh herbs, chile and spices.

IN THE KITCHEN

Rutabagas are enormously versatile, filling and nourishing in a warm and wonderful way. The leaves can also be eaten as a vegetable. Rutabagas vary a little in size; they are usually about the size of a child's soccer ball and keep very well. You can use a half or a quarter and the remainder can be used up to several weeks later. Cubes of rutabaga can be added to meat or game stews, an inexpensive addition to increase yield.

Traditionally rutabaga were boiled in salted water or with bacon, which gives them a delicious flavor. However, they can also be roasted or layered up in a gratin. When they are mashed, it can be a smooth or chunky purée, and they lap up butter and/or extra virgin olive oil, and can be enhanced by a variety of fresh herbs and spices, such as thyme leaves, marjoram, cumin, coriander, mustard seed, and garam masala.

Rutabaga Soup with Pancetta & Parsley Oil

A poshed-up version of rutabaga soup, with some parsley oil dribbled on top and some crispy pancetta to nibble.

SERVES 6 TO 8

1 tablespoon sunflower oil or peanut oil
4 ounces onions, chopped
5¼ ounces potatoes, peeled and diced
¾ pound rutabaga, peeled and diced
3¾ cups homemade chicken stock
heavy cream or milk, to taste
sea salt and freshly ground black pepper
8 slices of pancetta, to garnish

FOR THE PARSLEY OIL

1 cup flat-leaf parsley, chopped
3 tablespoons extra virgin olive oil

First make the parsley oil. Combine the parsley with the olive oil in a blender and blend until smooth and green, then push through a fine mesh sieve.

Next, make the soup. Heat the oil in a saucepan and toss in the onions, potatoes, and rutabaga. Season with salt and freshly ground black pepper. Cover with parchment paper to keep in the steam and sweat over low heat for about 10 minutes until soft but not colored. Add the stock, bring to a boil, and simmer for about 10 minutes until the vegetables are fully cooked. Carefully transfer to a high-speed blender and blend until smooth. Taste and add a little cream or milk and some extra seasoning if necessary.

Preheat the broiler. Spread the slices of pancetta on a wire rack over a baking sheet. Broil for 1 to 2 minutes or until crisp.

Serve the soup in bowls; drizzle each with parsley oil and lay a slice of crispy pancetta on top.

Note: Those who dislike puréed soups or may not have access to a blender can serve this soup in its chunky form—also delicious.

Spicy Vegetable Stew with Yogurt

Fresh spices perk up the root vegetables here, and parsnips and/or celeriac can also be added. It makes a delicious meal served just with an accompanying green salad. Don't be put off by the long list of ingredients, most are just spices so it's just a question of adding a little of this and that.

. . . .

SERVES 6

2 pounds medium potatoes

1 pound rutabaga, peeled and cut into
    1-inch cubes

½ pound carrots

½ teaspoon sugar, plus a pinchr

1 tablespoon butter or ghee, plus extra
    for cooking

2½ teaspoons cumin seeds

1 tablespoon coriander seeds

1 inch cinnamon stick

1 teaspoon cardamom seeds

8 cloves

¼ teaspoon black peppercorns

½ pound onions, chopped

1 garlic clove, crushed

1½ ounces fresh ginger, peeled and
    crushed

¼ teaspoon grated nutmeg

½ teaspoon ground turmeric

1½ pounds very ripe tomatoes, peeled
    and chopped, or 1½ (14-ounce) cans
    chopped tomatoes

¾ cup plain yogurt

½ cup light cream or milk

sea salt

1 to 2 tablespoons fresh cilantro or flat-
    leaf parsley, chopped, plus sprigs to
    garnish

Boil the scrubbed but unpeeled potatoes until just cooked. Pull off the peel and cut into ⅓-inch-thick slices. Cook the rutabaga in boiling salted water for 30 to 40 minutes until tender.

Meanwhile, scrub the carrots; if they are small leave them whole, otherwise cut into slices about ⅓ inch thick. Cook in a covered saucepan in a very little boiling salted water with a pinch of salt and a pinch of sugar and a blob of butter until just tender.

Grind all the whole spices to a powder in a spice grinder or mortar and pestle.

Melt the butter in a wide heavy-bottomed saucepan, add the onions, and sweat for 10 minutes until tender and golden, then stir in the garlic, ginger, ground spices, nutmeg, turmeric, and the remaining ½ teaspoon sugar, cook for a minute or so, then add the chopped tomatoes and yogurt.

Add the sliced potatoes, cooked rutabaga, and carrots to this mixture and stir carefully to incorporate. Cover and simmer for 5 to 10 minutes until the vegetables have finished cooking. Remove the lid, then add the cream or milk and cook to reduce until the sauce is the consistency you like. Season to taste and stir in the chopped cilantro or parsley. Transfer to a hot serving dish and garnish with lots of fresh cilantro or parsley.

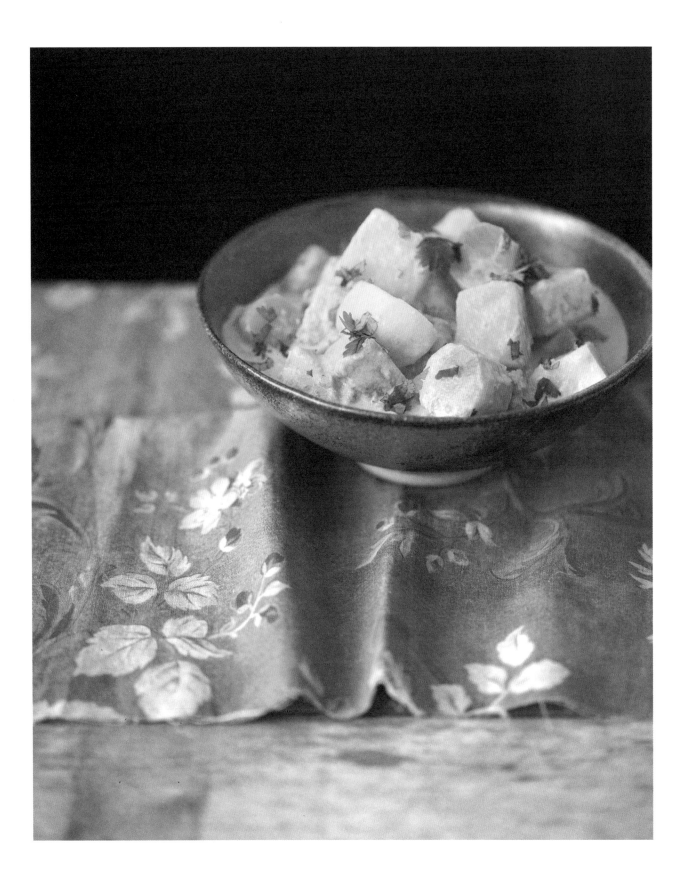

Rutabaga with Chorizo Crumbs & More

Rutabagas are best in winter and early spring, when a little frost has sweetened the flesh. The humble rutabaga is cheap and keeps for months and can be used in soups, stews, gratins and mashes.

. . . .

SERVES APPROX. 6

2 pounds rutabaga, peeled and cut into
¾-inch cubes
¼ to ½ cup (½ to 1 stick) butter
sea salt and lots of freshly ground black
pepper
minced flat-leaf or curly parsley, to garnish

FOR THE CHORIZO CRUMBS
¼ cup extra virgin olive oil
4½ ounces chorizo, casings removed, cut
into ¼-inch dice
1 cup coarse bread crumbs

Put the rutabaga cubes into a high-sided saucepan and cover with water. Add a good pinch of salt, bring to a boil and cook for 30 to 45 minutes until soft. Strain off the excess water, mash the rutabaga well and beat in the butter.

To make the chorizo crumbs, put the oil into a cool pan and add the diced chorizo. Toss over low heat until the oil starts to run and the chorizo begins to crisp. Be careful as it's easy to burn the chorizo. Remove the chorizo with a slotted spoon and set aside. Increase the heat, add the coarse bread crumbs, and toss in the chorizo oil until crisp and golden. Drain and add to the chorizo.

Taste and season with lots of freshly ground pepper and more salt if necessary. Garnish with parsley, sprinkle with the chorizo crumbs, and serve.

For Rutabaga with Wild Garlic Pesto, drizzle wild garlic pesto (see page 542) over the top, just before serving, and sprinkle with wild garlic flowers.

Rutabaga Purée with Olive Oil & Parmesan

Rory O'Connell's recipe for this flavorsome purée of the inexpensive root couldn't be simpler and is super-delicious as an accompanying vegetable with lamb, pork, or duck. Don't forget to save some of the cooking water to add to the purée. The purée can be prepared ahead of time and reheated later, in which case a little more of the cooking water can be added if necessary, but do not add the extra virgin olive oil and Parmesan until the very last minute.

. . . .

SERVES 4

1½ pounds peeled rutabaga, weighed
after peeling and cut into ¾-inch cubes
2 tablespoons butter
3 tablespoons finely grated Parmesan
cheese
3 tablespoons extra virgin olive oil
sea salt and freshly ground black pepper

Put the rutabaga in a saucepan, cover with 2 cups of cold water, and add a pinch of salt. Cook for 30 to 45 minutes or until the rutabaga is completely tender. If the rutabaga is not tender the purée will be lumpy.

Strain off the cooking water, reserving a little. Blend the rutabaga with the butter and enough of the cooking water to achieve a smooth purée. Season to taste.

Serve hot in a heated shallow serving dish so that the purée is no deeper than ¾ inch in the dish. Drizzle with the olive oil, sprinkle with the Parmesan, and serve immediately.

KALE *Brassica oleracea* ANNUAL

How wonderful it has been to watch the rise and rise of kale from cattle fodder to "superfood." We always grew kale in our kitchen garden in Cullohill when I was a child. I didn't love it then, as I found the flavor too strong, but Mum absolutely loved it and served it in many guises. She folded it through mashed potato to entice us to enjoy it. She talked about craving greens in the winter, baffling to me then but now that thought resonates—I long
for kale and would happily eat a little every day.

At Ballymaloe we grow 4 or 5 different varieties, as well as the curly kale or Scotch kale, Red Russian, Raggedy Jack, Cavalo Nero, and Asparagus Kale. My sister-in-law

Natasha recently introduced me to Ethiopian Kale (*Brassica carinata*), a delicious green that is very easy to grow. It's also known as Ethiopian mustard, African kale or Highland kale. The tender green leaves are delicious in salads, or served boiled or pickled.

It has a flavor of kale and mustard and is very nutritious.

When kale goes to flower in late spring, we use the yellow flowers abundantly in salads, but we also pick off the shoots that sprout out from the base and cook them quickly in boiling salted water; you can't imagine how delicious they are.

We have them for about 3 weeks and they are one of the highlights of the year before we pull out the plants to make room for a new crop— perhaps cucumbers.

Kales can also be grown throughout a herbaceous border, we particularly love Cavalo Nero, Red Winter, and Red Russian kale in the "hot border," side by side with the red dahlias, lobelia, love lies bleeding and sunflowers.

VARIETIES

Reflex F1—Our favorite organic curly kale variety because of its tenderness and good flavor.

Dwarf Green Curled—This old variety (1860s) is very reliable. It suits light soils, containers, and exposed sites, and produces short sturdy plants and attractive curled leaves. In our experience its more productive than Nero di Toscana.

Nero di Toscana—Produces long, dark green, blistered leaves.

Curly kale was once regarded as cattle feed—now it has reached "superfood" status.

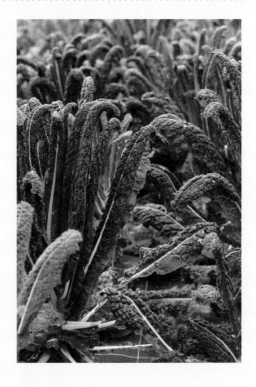

Cavolo nero, a black Tuscan kale, turns green from early spring.

Red Winter—Red frilly leaves on purple stems, sweeter than other kales, good to use as baby leaf when young.

Red Russian—An attractive blue-green kale with a purple tinge to the leaves. Can also be used as baby leaves.

Siberian—Its tender blue leaves are midly sweet.

Ethiopian Kale—Seeds are available from Madeleine McKeever's Brown Envelope Seeds, one of our seed-saving heroes here in Ireland.

HOW TO GROW

Kale needs the same conditions as other brassicas: rich, fertile, moisture-retentive soil. It can be grown pretty well all year round but I prefer it as a winter vegetable, because the frost sweetens and enhances the flavor.

To grow indoors, sow seed in midsummer in cell trays and transplant in early autumn. Allow 18 to 20 inches between plants and 2 feet between the rows. Even a little patch in a tunnel or greenhouse can be a boon in the winter.

Like cabbages, kale needs lots of nitrogen in the soil to grow well. To grow outdoors, sow the seed indoors in early spring, then plant out in midsummer. The crop lasts until late spring when the plants start to flower and bolt; we love to cook the tender shoots and sprinkle the yellow flowers on salads.

CONTAINER GROWING

Kale can also be grown in pots on a balcony. The larger the container, the more voluptuous the plant and the better it will crop.

PESTS

As with other brassicas, cabbage butterfly can be a problem and from seedling stage birds can also attack your crop. You may want to make a hoop frame over the plot and cover with netting. However, kale is less susceptible to clubroot and cabbage root fly than other brassicas.

HARVESTING

We continue to pick until late spring, having started harvesting in mid-autumn. Frost improves the flavor and sweetens the plant but some years the frost may not come until mid-winter or not at all, so you may prefer not to wait.

GOOD FOR YOU...

The leaves are rich in vitamins A, B6, B1 and B2, C and E. A source of brain-boosting phyto-nutrients, fibre, calcium and potassium, and omega-3

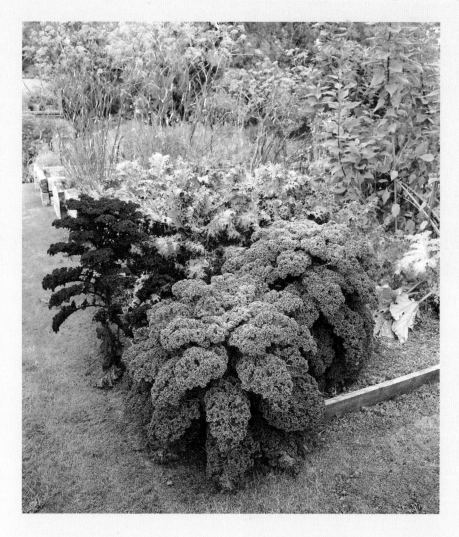

fatty acids, folate and niacin. Kale, like many other leafy greens, is high in antioxidants.

WHAT TO DO WITH A GLUT

Cook, purée, juice, and freeze; use as a vegetable or as a soup base.

IN THE KITCHEN

Some people love kale just wilted in the pan, but I prefer to cook it in a big pot of boiling salted water for 5 to 10 minutes or until soft and tender, then add a dollop of butter or a generous drizzle of extra virgin olive oil and lots of freshly ground pepper. It will also take on lots of other flavors, such as

Cavolo nero, Red Russian kale and curly kale with fennel in the background and Jerusalem artichoke foliage to the right.

chile, soy sauce, and sesame oil, to name a few.

I also love kale puréed or loosened to make a green sauce bursting with nutrients. We've got quite a repertoire of kale salads, too, and of course we add it to lots of scary green juices.

DID YOU KNOW?
The iron, protein and calcium content of kale rivals that of beef, and now its anti-inflammatory properties are being taken seriously.

Cottier's kale is propagated by slips rather than seed.

Braised Tuscan Kale with Pancetta & Caramelized Onions

Braising the kale long and slowly gives it a totally different sort of old-fashioned homey flavor that I find addictive.

SERVES 6

2¼ pounds Tuscan kale/cavalo nero, stemmed
2 tablespoons extra virgin olive oil
½ pound pancetta, cut into ¼-inch dice
2 sprigs of fresh thyme
1 bay leaf
2 sprigs of fresh flat-leaf parsley
¾ pound onions, minced
1 whole head garlic, cut in half crosswise
⅓ cup unsalted butter, cut into cubes
3 to 3¾ cups homemade chicken stock
sea salt and freshly ground black pepper

Preheat the oven to 350°F.

Blanch the kale in 7 quarts of boiling salted water (use 1 teaspoon salt per 1 quart water) for 2 to 3 minutes per batch. Drain well.

Warm the olive oil in an ovenproof pot, add the diced pancetta, and cook for 8 to 10 minutes until crisp, stirring occasionally. Transfer the pancetta to a plate with a slotted spoon and keep warm.

Make a bouquet garni with the thyme, bay leaf, and parsley. Put the onions and garlic into the pot and add the bouquet garni. Cook over medium heat for 5 to 6 minutes, stirring frequently, until the onions are golden brown and caramelized. Return the pancetta to the pot, add the butter, and stir until melted. Stir in the kale and add just enough stock to come halfway up the sides of the pot. Cover with a piece of parchment paper cut to fit the top of the pot and then the pot lid.

Transfer to the oven and braise for about 45 minutes, stirring once or twice, until the kale is very tender. Uncover the pot, then simmer on the stove for about 35 minutes, stirring occasionally, until almost all the liquid has evaporated but the kale is still moist and juicy. Fish out the bouquet garni and the garlic. Season to taste and serve.

Kale, Leek, Mushroom & Ricotta Strata

A strata is a savory bread and butter pudding. We do many delicious combinations but this one was inspired by Claire Ptak's version at Violet Bakery in London. A brilliant vegetarian main course.

. . . .

SERVES 8 TO 10

2 pounds stale white sourdough bread
butter, for spreading
green salad, to serve

FOR THE FILLING

3 large leeks, sliced ¾ inch thick (use
   white part only)
scant 1 tablespoon butter, plus extra for
   greasing
3 to 4 tablespoons extra virgin olive oil
2 tablespoons chopped fresh marjoram or
   rosemary
1 pound kale, such as cavalo nero, curly, or
   Red Russian kale
½ teaspoon Pul Biber chile flakes
   (Turkish)
9 ounces flat mushrooms, thinly sliced
4 ounces Gruyère cheese, freshly grated
¾ ounce Parmesan cheese, freshly grated
3½ ounces buffalo ricotta
sea salt and freshly ground black pepper

FOR THE SAVORY CUSTARD

8 organic eggs
5 tablespoons cream
1½ cups whole milk
freshly grated nutmeg

First, prepare the leeks—trim the green tops, wash and add to the stockpot. Wash and slice the blanched white ends. Heat the butter and 2 tablespoons of the olive oil in a sauté pan, and when it foams add the sliced leeks. Season with salt and freshly ground pepper and toss to coat. Add the chopped fresh herbs, cover, and sweat for 8 to 10 minutes until soft and not colored.

Strip the kale off the stalks and roughly chop the leaves. Cook the kale in boiling salted water (3 teaspoons of salt to 3½ quarts of water) for 5 to 6 minutes or until tender. Cook in batches if necessary. Drain very well. Season with salt, freshly ground pepper, and chile flakes. Add to the leeks.

Sauté the sliced mushrooms in the remaining olive oil in a hot pan, season each batch as you cook. Add to the leek and kale mixture.

Next, whisk the ingredients together for the savory custard. Add ½ teaspoon salt, lots of freshly ground pepper, and a generous grating of nutmeg.

Butter a 8 × 12-inch roasting pan or baking dish. Slice the bread thinly, butter lightly, and remove the crusts. Arrange a layer of bread on the base of the buttered roasting pan. Taste the kale mixture and correct the seasoning if necessary. Spread half of the kale mixture evenly over the bread followed by half the Gruyère, Parmesan, and ricotta. Top with another layer of bread, the remaining kale mixture, and most of the remaining cheese and ricotta, saving a little Parmesan to sprinkle over the top. Top with a layer of bread, buttered-side up.

Pour the custard evenly over the strata. Cover and refrigerate for at least an hour for the bread to absorb the custard, or overnight if possible.

Preheat the oven to 350°F.

Sprinkle the remaining Parmesan over the top. Bake for 50 minutes to 1 hour or until the top is golden and the custard has just set. Let sit for 5 to 10 minutes before cutting into portions. Serve warm with a good green salad.

Squash, Baby Kale & Goat Cheese Salad

Sarah Stegner, of Prairie Grass Café in Northbrook, Illinois, made this salad for a lunch in my honor at Mary Jo McMillin's house in Chicago—a delicious combination. The method below works with any variety of winter squash. I love the way she used baby kale in this recipe, but if your leaves are larger, just tear them into bite-sized pieces.

. . . .

SERVES 4

1½ to 2 pounds winter squash
extra virgin olive oil
sea salt and freshly ground black pepper
2 tablespoons honey
2 tablespoons butter, softened
1 large handful baby kale, stems trimmed
  or removed
1 red bell pepper, seeded and thinly sliced
20 very thin slices of soppressata
2 tablespoons toasted pumpkin seeds
4 tablespoons fresh goat cheese

FOR THE VINAIGRETTE

1 tablespoon apple cider vinegar
pinch of sea salt
½ teaspoon Dijon mustard
1 teaspoon honey
1 teaspoon olive oil

Preheat oven to 375°F.

Peel the squash, cut it in half, and remove the seeds. Cut the flesh into ¼-inch-thick wedges and cut in half again, creating 16 wedges. Toss the wedges in olive oil, salt, and pepper. Spread the squash out on a baking sheet and roast for 15 to 20 minutes or until the wedges begin to caramelize and they are golden brown.

Mix the honey and butter together. Coat the hot wedges with this mix and cook for an additional 10 minutes. Remove from the oven and let cool.

To make the vinaigrette, whisk together the ingredients in the order listed.

To serve, divide the squash among four plates. Toss the baby kale and bell pepper in the vinaigrette (you can leave it to sit in the vinaigrette for 5 to 10 minutes before serving. The vinaigrette "cooks" the kale and tenderizes it).

Toss the soppressata in a pan with 1 teaspoon of olive oil and sauté for about a minute until warm.

Spread the kale and peppers over the squash wedges, top each salad with a sprinkling of pumpkin seeds, 5 slices of the warmed soppressata, and a tablespoon of fresh goat cheese. Drizzle with any remaining juices from the squash and serve.

Nordic Kale Salad with Lemon & Cream

This is reminiscent of my grandmother's dressing for lettuce; it sounds a bit shocking but you are not going to eat the whole bowl yourself. Half the yogurt could be substituted for heavy cream. Don't alter the measurements, although it may sound scary, because the cream helps the body to absorb all the nutrients from the kale

. . . .

SERVES 10 TO 12

1 pound curly kale (½ pound stemmed)
1 lemon
2 tablespoons granulated sugar
1 cup heavy cream
sea salt

Strip the kale off the stalks, chop the leaves very finely, and massage well to release the juices. Toss in a bowl. Grate the zest of the lemon directly onto the salad. Squeeze the juice over the top and add the sugar and 1 teaspoon of sea salt. Toss, pour over the cream, and toss again.

Taste and add a little more sugar or salt if necessary—there needs to be a balance of zesty and sweet. Totally delicious and super nutritious.

All the Kales

Much as I love the winter roots—parsnip, celeriac, rutabaga, turnips—I also long for the clean sharp taste of greens in the late autumn and winter. Kale and the sprouting broccolis satisfy this need deliciously and in the case of kale, most decoratively. We grow several different varieties apart from curly kale; some of the leaves are serrated, others crinkly, others almost feathery, and they come in most beautiful shades from greeny gray, to blue, green, deep purple, cream, and yellow. Red Russian kale is one of our favorites and cavolo nero (black Tuscan kale or dinosaur kale) is another must-have. The sprouting shoots of kale are also delicious cooked as below.

. . . .

SERVES APPROX. 4

1 tablespoon salt, plus extra to taste
1 pound kale, stemmed (approx. 10 ounces stemmed)
freshly ground black pepper and a little freshly grated nutmeg (optional)
4 tablespoons (½ stick) butter
½ cup heavy cream

Put 3½ quarts of water and the salt in a large saucepan and bring to a boil. Add the kale and boil, uncovered, over high heat until tender; this can vary from 5 to 10 minutes depending on the variety.

Drain well, then chop coarsely or purée in a food processor, return to the saucepan, and season with salt, freshly ground pepper, and a little nutmeg, if you fancy. Add a nice lump of butter and some cream, bring to a simmer, and taste. Serve hot.

Kale Stir-Fry with Asian Flavors

Spinach, bok choy, or chard are also delicious cooked in this super-fast way; you could also add some coconut milk to soften the intensity if you wish.

. . . .

SERVES 6

¼ cup extra virgin olive oil
⅓ ounce fresh ginger, peeled and grated
1 garlic clove, minced
2 scallions, sliced
½ to 1 red or green chile, chopped
1 pound kale, stemmed and torn into small pieces
palm sugar
1 tablespoon dark or light soy sauce
2½ teaspoons toasted sesame oil
sea salt and freshly ground black pepper
1 tablespoon toasted sesame seeds

Heat the olive oil in a wok over medium heat; add the ginger, garlic, scallions, and chile. Cook for a minute or two, add the kale and a splash of water. Season with salt, freshly ground pepper and palm sugar, toss for 3 to 4 minutes or until wilted. Add the soy sauce and sesame oil, toss. Season to taste. Pile into a serving dish, sprinkle with toasted sesame seeds, and serve.

CAULIFLOWERS *Brassica oleracea* var. *botrytis Brassica* ANNUAL

Cauliflower probably won't be on your A list of crops to grow, but if you have the space and inclination it's definitely worth growing an heirloom variety. The flavor of cauliflower has suffered more than most from intensive production, and even though it could be argued that the leaves are the most flavorful part of the vegetable, they are normally trimmed of most of the stalks and tender leaves during harvesting, and then—a shame—the remainder is dumped by the cook. Another reason to grow your own, so you can enjoy every scrap.

VARIETIES

The white variety is the most familiar but there are also purple, yellow and green forms and cute little mini ones in a rainbow of colors. Choose a variety for the season in which you wish to harvest.
Purple Cape—Hardy variety that will overwinter and produce cauliflowers with purple florets from late winter to mid-spring. Looks gorgeous in the garden but loses its purple color in cooking and becomes muddy green, nonetheless it has lots of flavor.

Snowball—Popular all-season variety. It has dwarf compact plants which might suit a smaller space.
Medallion F1—Winter variety, sow at same time as spring cabbage for winter harvesting.
Cheddar—Heads mature to a bright orange color early in the season.

HOW TO GROW

Sow indoors in spring in cells and transplant for summer harvest or in autumn under glass, then plant out in mid-spring for an early summer crop.

Cauliflowers need a moisture-retentive, fertile soil with a pH of 6.5 to 7.5. Soil should be dug deeply. Space plants the same distance as cabbage, 18 inches apart and 18 inches between rows.

Our old gardener Pad used to fold the top leaves over the white curd near the end of the growing season to protect it from the elements.

CONTAINER GROWING

Cauliflowers may be grown in containers, choose a compact variety like Snowball. It's important not to let them dry out at any stage as the plants will be stunted and may not produce a decent curd.

PESTS

Cauliflower are subject to the same problems as other brassicas; strict rotation will help prevent club root. Slugs love them and the later varieties will be attacked by the cabbage butterfly, unless covered with a fine mesh. Cabbage root fly can also be a problem, as with all brassicas.

Grow your own and use all the green leaves as well as the florets.

HARVESTING

Harvesting will depend on the variety and sowing date. Cauliflower generally matures from mid-summer to early autumn. When the head swells, cut it off at the base with a sharp knife. Remove the stump from the ground and add to the compost heap.

If a few cauliflowers bolt at the end of the crop, pick off the florets and cook like broccoli, they will still be delicious.

GOOD FOR YOU...

Cauliflower is an excellent source of vitamins C, K and B6, folate, pantothenic acid, choline, dietary fiber, omega 3 fatty acids, manganese, phosphorus and biotin. It also contains vitamins B1 and B2, niacin and magnesium. Cauliflower is also low in calories—probably the reason for the current trend to substitute it for potatoes, pasta or rice in some dishes.

WHAT TO DO WITH A GLUT

This is a difficult one, cauliflower does freeze and also pickles deliciously. A couple of gratins and some soup tucked into the freezer could get you out of a "pickle" on a busy day. Otherwise, seek out a homeless shelter or food bank in your area.

IN THE KITCHEN

Cauliflower takes on extra flavors brilliantly and creative chefs are having fun roasting, pickling, slivering, drying. I'm not sure who came up with the idea of cauliflower rice, but I just love how one can use that as a staple and perk it up with Mediterranean, Middle Eastern, Mexican, and Thai flavors. To make **Cauliflower Rice** for 6 people, remove the outer leaves from a head of cauliflower (approx. 1¼ pounds) and save for another use (see below). Cut the head into quarters. Cut away the stalk and core and chop into smallish pieces. Put the core in a food processor and process for about 20 seconds. Add the florets, process for another 30 to 40 seconds until the cauliflower is about the size of grains of rice. You may need to do this in batches. Heat 2 tablespoons olive oil in a sauté pan. Add the cauliflower and toss for about 5 minutes until just tender. Season with salt and freshly ground pepper. Scatter with chopped parsley and serve. The cauliflower rice may also be cooked in boiling salted water for 1 to 2 minutes, drained well, and then tossed in extra virgin olive oil.

Or you can make a good old cauliflower cheese laced with mustard and plenty of aged cheddar. Leftover cauliflower cheese thinned out with homemade vegetable or chicken stock makes a delicious cauliflower cheese soup. We serve our dish with a garnish of crisp croutons mixed with some grated cheddar or chorizo crumbs.

It's sad to see the outer leaves and stalks of cauliflower discarded as they are delicious. Like sprouting broccoli, little florets of raw cauliflower are instantly appealing in a crudité selection. Thin slivers, too, add texture to a mixture of raw vegetables. Florets or a thick slice can be drizzled with extra virgin olive oil or a spicy marinade and roasted deliciously as a vegetable, a side, or the base of a robust salad.

Check out the new and heirloom varieties of cauliflower.

Cauliflower Steaks Infused with Ginger & Spices

This brilliant way of cooking cauliflower can be served plain or embellished in many ways. Terrific as a vegan or vegetarian main course, have fun dreaming up tasty toppings, such as chermoula (page 458), salmoriglio (page 502), labneh with harissa and coriander, spicy ground beef or ragu, roast tomatoes, and chimichurri or red pepper, tomato and olive salsa..

. . . .

SERVES 6 OR MORE

1 fresh cauliflower, weighing approx. 1½ pounds
1 teaspoon grated fresh ginger
1 garlic clove, crushed
1 teaspoon roasted and ground cumin seeds
1 teaspoon roasted and ground coriander seeds
½ teaspoon ground turmeric
½ teaspoon salt
7 tablespoons extra virgin olive oil
sea salt and freshly ground black pepper
fresh cilantro leaves and lemon wedges, to serve

Preheat the oven to 450°F.

Remove the leaves (save for a cauliflower cheese gratin), but just barely trim the bottom of the core. Cut the cauliflower head into ¾-inch-thick slices or "steaks" through the bottom, saving the two outer pieces for cauliflower rice or gratin.

Mix the ginger, garlic, spices, and salt with 5 tablespoons of the oil.

Heat the remaining oil in a wide skillet over high heat. Sear the cauliflower steaks for about 2 minutes on each side until nicely colored—use more oil if necessary. Transfer to a roasting pan and spoon the spicy oil over each steak; flip over and drizzle a little more over the other side. Roast for 20 to 25 minutes until the steaks feel tender when the stalk end is pierced with the tip of a knife and check after 15 minutes, it may need to be turned.

Serve along with lots of fresh cilantro and a wedge of lemon or as an accompaniment to a simple roast, lamb chop, or curry.

Roast Cauliflower Florets, Freekeh, Pistachio & Pomegranate

I first came across roast cauliflower in San Francisco about a decade ago and didn't love it, but I've grown accustomed to the taste and now I find it very appealing, particularly when dressed with a spicy Indian or Middle Eastern dressing.

SERVES 6 TO 8

1 pound freekeh or pearl barley

6 tablespoons extra virgin olive oil, plus extra for drizzling

1 small cauliflower, divided into small florets

3 tablespoons white wine vinegar

1 teaspoon ground turmeric

½ teaspoon harissa

2 teaspoons honey

seeds from 1 small pomegranate (dark red if possible)

1 tablespoon nigella seeds (optional)

scant 1 cup pistachios, coarsely chopped

6 to 8 tablespoons labneh (page 291) or thick natural yogurt

1 to 2 tablespoons sumac

lots of dill sprigs

sea salt and freshly ground black pepper

Put the freekeh into a saucepan with cold water, bring to a boil, and simmer for 20 minutes to 1 hour, depending on the freekeh (some are broken grains, others whole)—it should be soft but still slightly chewy. Drain, and while still warm, season with salt and drizzle with extra virgin olive oil and toss. Season to taste with pepper.

Meanwhile, preheat the oven to 400°F. Drizzle the cauliflower florets with the extra virgin olive oil and season with salt and freshly ground black pepper. Roast for 15 minutes or until slightly caramelized at the edges.

Meanwhile, whisk the 6 tablespoons of extra virgin olive oil, white wine vinegar, turmeric, harissa, and honey in a bowl. Spoon over the warm freekeh and toss gently; mix with the cauliflower florets and some of the pomegranate seeds, reserving some for sprinkling. Taste and adjust the seasoning if necessary. Add a few nigella seeds, if you like.

To serve, put a couple of tablespoons of the freekeh and cauliflower salad on each plate. Sprinkle with chopped pistachios. Put a dollop of labneh or thick natural yogurt on top. Scatter a few more pomegranate seeds, pistachio nuts, a pinch of sumac, and a few sprigs of dill over the labneh and serve immediately.

DID YOU KNOW?

Cauliflower is thought to have originated in Cyprus and is grown there in profusion. Earliest records go back to the sixth century.

Mark Twain rather amusingly described the cauliflower as "nothing but cabbage with a college education."

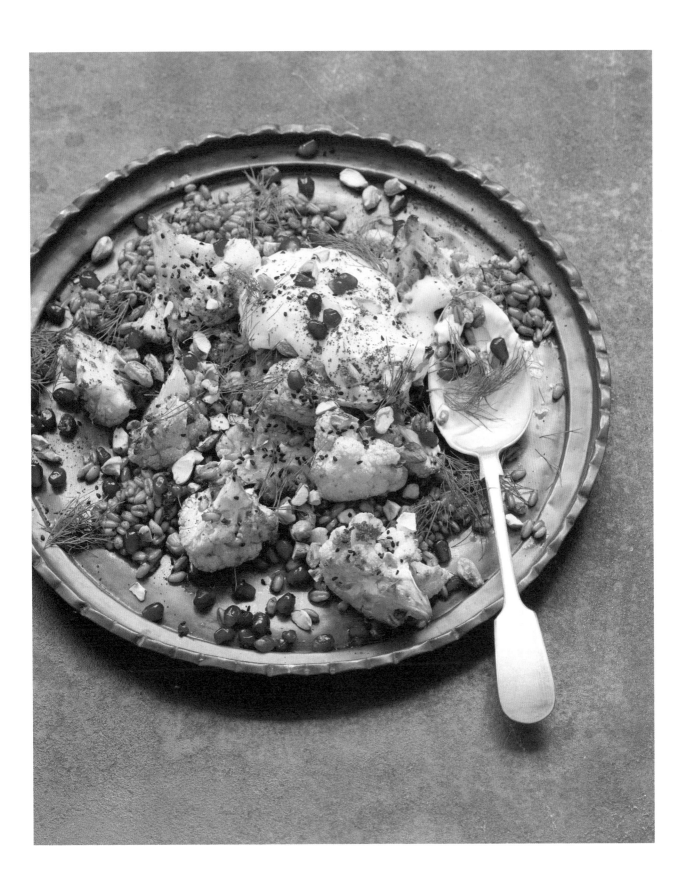

CABBAGE *Brassica oleracea* var. *capitata* BIENNIAL/ANNUAL

Rows of different varieties of cabbage growing alongside each other.

Cabbage has always been a much-loved vegetable in Ireland and part of a staple diet, particularly in rural areas. Traditionally, farmers grew a few drills of cabbage alongside the potatoes in a little kitchen garden near the house. In every parish there was somebody who grew cabbage plants, and they would often sell them in bundles at the local cattle mart or directly from their small gardens, before they became available in trays and cells in garden centers. Traditionally cabbage was cooked in the same pot with bacon or corned beef over the open fire.

VARIETIES

Careful selection of varieties provides cabbage throughout the year.

FOR SPRING HARVEST
Early Jersey Wakefield—3 to 4 pound heads mature in 60 to 75 days.

Pixie—Quick-to-mature pointy type.

FOR SUMMER HARVEST
Greyhound—Dwarf pointy type, with excellent flavor in early summer—plant seed early spring.

FOR WINTER HARVEST
January King—Red-tinged round cabbage cultivated since 1867; sow after midsummer.
Vertus—Savoy type, dark in color with good flavor.
Both of these can be harvested right through the winter.
Red Drumhead—Best round red cabbage—sow seed in early spring, it will tolerate frost.
Premium Late Flat Dutch—Blue-green heads with white interior weight up to 15 pounds
Mammoth Red—Solid, round heads reach up to 7 pounds. Very tasty.

HOW TO GROW

Cabbage needs a rich, fertile, moisture-retentive soil. If your soil is very acidic, add some lime before growing brassicas. Rake the soil before planting so it's nicely firm but not compacted. Cabbage should be planted firmly, so the plants won't rock and loosen in the wind. Cabbage is more tolerant of shade than many other vegetables, but it thrives in a sunny, sheltered spot.

Closer spacing gives smaller heads, so adjust to suit the space available. They can also be planted at half the required distance apart, thinning them out to this final distance and using the thinnings as "spring greens." We normally sow three rows of cabbages 20 inches apart in both directions. This way we can span the

hoops with nets over them to keep the birds and white butterflies off. When the cabbages start to mature, the leaves close in and weeding is no longer a problem.

If the roots take up too much moisture from the ground at the stage when the cabbage is mature and the head is firm, the head can split. It will then have to be used as quickly as possible before it spoils. In the past seasoned gardeners sometimes drove a spade down beside the root and cut off some of the roots, to restrict the uptake of moisture. Applying fertilizer too late in the growing season can also encourage splitting.

CONTAINER GROWING

Where space is a problem, cabbages may be grown in a container, but it's not ideal. The soil should have well-rotted manure added to provide nitrogen. It is difficult to protect cabbage in a container with a net, so it might be easier to grow kale or kohlrabi. Cabbage is hardy enough so there's no need to waste tunnel space, choose varieties to plant outside at different times of year.

PESTS

Cabbage root fly can affect seedlings. Planting them deeper can help, and this also provides anchorage for the plants as more roots will develop on the stem underground. A little mat tucked around the stem at planting can also help keep the root fly away from young plants.

The biggest problem is the cabbage butterfly, continuously laying eggs on the underside of leaves throughout summer and autumn. Hand-picking the caterpillars becomes tedious and time consuming, so you are better off covering them with nets (⅓ inch square mesh).

Only grow cabbages in the same ground every three years (minimum) because they are prone to attack by a fungal disease called club root that builds up in the soil if they are not rotated. This disease can survive in the same soil for 20 years. If your soil is acid it helps to add lime to reduce the acidity and lessen the risk of club root.

Before cabbage hearts up birds can strip the leaves off the stems, so it is best to keep them covered with netting.

HARVESTING

Harvest as the heads mature. After cutting a head make a cross in the stalk and you should get another four smaller heads.

GOOD FOR YOU...

Cabbage is a rich source of vitamins K, C and B6 and is also rich in manganese. It's high in antioxidants and a good source of fiber. Red cabbage has 10 times more vitamin A than green cabbage, while green cabbage has a higher vitamin K content. Red cabbage has a slightly higher vitamin C content and double the amount of iron.

WHAT TO DO WITH A GLUT

Share with your friends. Make cabbage salads and Sauerkraut (see overleaf).

IN THE KITCHEN

To retain its nutrients and green color, cabbage should be cooked quickly and not overcooked. It helps to slice it thinly. **Buttered Cabbage** takes only a few minutes to cook but first must be carefully sliced into fine shreds. For 4 to 6 people, remove the tough outer leaves from 1 pound Savoy cabbage. Divide into four, cut out the stalks, and thinly slice across the grain. Put 2 to 3 tablespoons of water into a wide saucepan with 2 to 4 tablespoons butter and a pinch of salt. Bring to a boil, add the cabbage, and toss constantly over high heat, then cover for a few minutes. Toss again and add some more salt, freshly ground pepper, and a knob of butter. It should be served the moment it is cooked. My daughter Emily adds lots of thyme leaves to the cabbage but you can also add ½ to 1 tablespoon of caraway seeds and toss constantly as above.

I find cabbage enormously versatile. We have numerous cabbage salads and little parcels made from the leaves. You can also eat it raw in coleslaw.

Red & Green Cabbage Slaw

Use both types of cabbage here. The end result is a juicy, nourishing salad.

. . . .

SERVES 10

¾ pound red cabbage, thinly sliced
¾ pound green cabbage, thinly sliced
2¼ ounces red onion, diced into ¼-inch dice, rinsed under cold water
1 or 2 cucumbers, diced into ¼-inch dice
1 or 2 apples, diced
2 tablespoons chopped fresh flat-leaf parsley
¼ cup coarsely chopped fresh mint
sea salt, freshly ground black pepper and honey, to taste
Ballymaloe French dressing (page 182)

Mix the salad ingredients together in a large bowl. Toss in enough Ballymaloe French dressing to make the leaves glisten. Season to taste. Sometimes a little honey is needed to add extra sweetness.

DID YOU KNOW?

Bacon and cabbage, and not Irish Stew, is traditionally thought to be the Irish national dish. However, Irish-Americans usually pair it with corned beef and eat it as a celebratory dish on St Patrick's Day.

Penny's (Sauerkraut) Kraut-Chi

My daughter-in-law Penny is an enthusiastic fermenter. This is her sauerkraut recipe, which she loves to share. At the most basic, sauerkraut is salted cabbage fermented in its own juice. It has existed in one form or another for thousands of years; sailors have carried it on ships to ward off scurvy because of its high vitamin C content. Any other vegetables in season can be added once they are finely sliced or chopped, but avoid potatoes, as they can become toxic when fermented. Weigh the vegetables after slicing and calculate the amount of salt needed (2 teaspoons Maldon sea salt for every pound).

. . . .

MAKES 1 QUART/ APPROX. 2 POUNDS

1 pound organic red or green cabbage or a
   mixture, finely sliced
5 ounces onion, finely sliced
2 green bell peppers, seeded and finely
   sliced
5 ounces carrots, coarsely grated
1 mild red chile, minced
4 teaspoons Maldon (or similar) sea salt

Mix all the ingredients together in a large bowl. Pack into a sterilized 1½-quart jar or crock. Pack a little at a time and press down hard using your fists (this packs the kraut tight and helps force water out of the vegetables).

Cover the kraut with a plate or some other lid that fits snugly inside the jar or crock. Place a clean weight on top (a jug or container filled with water works well). Cover the top with a light cloth to keep out flies and dust. Press down on the weight every few hours to help extract more liquid from. The liquid should rise above the vegetables. If it doesn't rise above the plate level by the next day, add some salt water (a basic brine is 2 teaspoons salt mixed in 2½ cups water) to bring the level above the plate.

Place in a cool area and let ferment for 4 to 5 days. At this stage the kraut is ready to eat. As you eat the kraut make sure the remainder is well covered in brine by pushing the vegetables under the brine and sealing well. It will keep for months; the flavor develops and matures over time.

Elsa's Red Cabbage

This recipe was given to my mother-in-law, Myrtle Allen, at Ballymaloe House over 30 years ago by our German neighbor Elsa Schiller—it's still the best. Some varieties of red cabbage are quite tough and don't seem to soften much, even with prolonged cooking. Our favorite variety, Red Drummond, gives best results. Serve with venison, duck, goose, or pork—the flavor is too strong to accompany fish and delicate meats.

. . . .

SERVES 4

1 pound red cabbage, such as Red
   Drummond
approx. 1 tablespoon wine vinegar
1 level teaspoon salt
2 heaping tablespoons granulated sugar
1 pound cooking apples, such as Rome,
   peeled, cored, and quartered

Remove any damaged outer leaves from the cabbage. Examine and clean it if necessary. Cut into quarters, remove the core, and slice the cabbage finely across the grain. Put the vinegar, ½ cup water, salt, and sugar into a cast-iron Dutch oven or stainless-steel saucepan. Add the cabbage and bring it to the boil.

Lay the apples on top of the cabbage, cover, and continue to cook gently for 30 to 50 minutes until the cabbage is tender. Season to taste and add more sugar if necessary. Serve in a warm serving dish.

It keeps brilliantly in the fridge for up to 2 weeks and freezes perfectly.

BRUSSELS SPROUTS

Brassica oleracea var. *gemmifera* ANNUAL

Brussels sprouts always put me in mind of Mr. McGregor's garden and that lovely Beatrix Potter watercolor of the Brussels sprouts in the snow and Flopsy, Mopsie, Cottontail, and Peter Rabbit.

Brussels sprouts as we know them were grown in Belgium as early as 1587, developed from a wild strain of cabbage. They are a winter vegetable and can withstand quite low temperatures. In fact, my husband always swore that he'd never grow Brussels sprouts commercially since he had to harvest sprouts for the Dublin market on bitterly cold frosty mornings when he was at agricultural college. The memory of the intense cold and frostbitten fingers meant he could never ask anyone else to harvest them either. Nowadays I expect that all the commercial sprouts are harvested mechanically by the stalk in one swift movement.

I know I'll have quite a job persuading the vitriolic Brussels sprouts bashers that sprouts are a wonderful winter

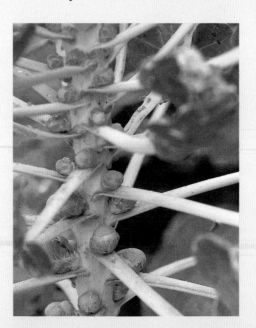

stalwart and totally delicious in many incarnations, and if not, it's the cook's fault. But before you write them off, taste freshly picked Brussels sprouts from your garden.

VARIETIES

Igor F1—Sow these seeds with summer cabbage in spring.

Groninger—Dark green sprout with a good flavor which improves after the first frost. Crops from late autumn to late winter.

Doric F1—Low growing, so suitable for exposed sites. Round buttons with good flavor.

Red Rubine—Red sprout, ornamental but better suited to a herbaceous border than the kitchen.

Diablo—very cold tolerant and well suited for a later crop.

Dagan—a good midseason variety. Srouts are often sold on the stalk.

Hestia—medium to small sprouts mature early and hold well in the garden.

Nautic—medium sized sprouts are very sweet. Plants are good for organic growing.

HOW TO GROW

Remember, sprouts are a brassica, so factor this in your rotation. Sow the seeds thinly in early spring, ¾ inch deep in a deep or shallow seed tray, placing two seeds in each hole. Transplant in early summer when the young plants are 4 to 6 inches high and have about 7 leaves. Plant as deeply as possible so they establish a good root system.

Any fertile well-drained garden soil is suitable, alkaline is perfect. The soil

Look how beautifully Brussels sprouts grow. These are ready to be picked.

needs to be well firmed so the plants can get a good grip and won't topple over. Choose a sheltered, sunny site, not exposed to strong winds or the plants may blow over.

Allow at least 2 feet between plants and 30 inches between rows. Water the plants before transplanting and water in well into their new position.

CONTAINER GROWING

Brussels sprouts have a very long growing season so may not be best use of your container space—a few salad crops would yield better value. Also, they grow very tall and could topple a pot. Ideally, one would need to net them to discourage the cabbage butterfly, so it wouldn't be an attractive container plant.

PESTS AND DISEASES

We have a problem with birds so we cover the plants with fine netting which inhibits both birds and butterflies. Like other members of the brassica family, sprouts can be affected by cabbage root fly, which often attacks at seedling stage. It helps to grow them under row cover.

Club root can affect all brassicas, but good drainage can help.

Caterpillars, especially of the white cabbage butterfly, will pay a visit. If you see the eggs on the back of the leaves you can squeeze them, or if they get as far as caterpillars it's possible to pick them off the plants if you don't have a huge area to cover.

In our experience, good crop rotation and planting at the correct time reduces the likelihood of disease.

HARVESTING

Sprouts taste best after they've had a touch of frost. We like to have Brussels sprouts ready to harvest at the end of autumn at the earliest. For ease of picking, remove the yellowing bottom leaves while harvesting. The crop will also be healthier for this.

Sprouts swell at the top of the stalk first, so home gardeners can harvest sprouts at the size they need. Nowadays, many commercial producers cut the entire stalk for ease of harvesting and consumers enjoy the variety of sizes.

GOOD FOR YOU...

Sprouts contain vitamins K, C, A, B6 and are high in folate and potassium. Of course, they must not be overcooked or much of this valuable content will be lost. Like other members of the cruciferous family they contain sulforaphane and there is ongoing research which may link this with cancer prevention.

WHAT TO DO WITH A GLUT

Like most green vegetables, Brussels sprouts are best eaten fresh, so enjoy them as often as possible when they are in season. Soup, salads and stir-fries will all be delicious.

IN THE KITCHEN

We enjoy the blowsy sprout tops cooked as greens, and when the crop starts to go to flower, soft tender shoots spring from the base, which are all beyond delicious. Finally there's the "famine food": peel the stalk and grate the tender interior, which tastes like kohlrabi, great in coleslaw- type salads. The pale yellow flowers can be sprinkled over salads. The outer leaves make a delicious sprout soup.

I had to include the secret of cooking Brussels sprouts here! Cut them into halves if small, quarters if medium or large and measure 1.2 liters of water into a saucepan. Add 3 teaspoons of salt, and when the water reaches a rolling boil, throw in the sprouts, return to a boil and cook uncovered for 3 to 4 minutes or until almost tender and still bright green. Drain, toss in extra virgin olive oil or a generous lump of melted butter and lots of freshly cracked pepper. Serve immediately and you'll convert even the most determined sprout haters. Shredded sprouts are also a revelation, sautéed or stir-fried in just a couple of minutes.

Salad of Aged Coolea or Parmesan, Brussels Sprouts & Celery shards

Skye Gyngell made this delicious fresh-tasting salad when she was a guest chef here at the school in 2007. She served it with slices of speck lard on top. We use Coolea farmhouse cheese from West Cork and have also added a little drizzle of honey. Another recipe to help redeem the image of the Brussels sprout.

SERVES 4

2 ounces Brussels sprouts (approx. 6)— trimmed, washed, and patted dry

5¼ ounces (approx. 3 stalks) celery, use inner stalks, keep the leaves and heart

4 ounces aged Coolea or Parmesan cheese

zest of 1 lemon and juice of ½ lemon

1 tablespoon chopped flat-leaf parsley

1 teaspoon honey

3 tablespoons new season extra virgin olive oil (we used Cappezana), plus extra to serve

12 slices of speck or prosciutto (optional)

sea salt and freshly ground pepper

Halve the sprouts and cut thinly crosswise.

Wash and dry the celery and cut it into long shards at an angle.

Slice the Coolea or Parmesan into odd slices—some fine, some slightly thicker— which makes it more interesting.

Place the sprouts, celery, and cheese splinters in a bowl, season with salt and freshly ground pepper, then add the lemon zest and juice, parsley, honey, and olive oil and toss well to combine.

Divide among four plates. Lay the speck or prosciutto on top, if using, but it's also delicious without it. Drizzle with a little more extra virgin olive oil and serve.

Brussels Sprouts with Thai Flavors

So you don't like sprouts? Well, try these—they are guaranteed to convert even the most ardent Brussels sprout haters.

. . . .

SERVES 4 TO 6

1⅔ cups coconut milk

1 tablespoon Thai green curry paste

1 green chile, pounded

¾ cup homemade chicken stock

1 pound Brussels sprouts, cut in half, blanched and refreshed in boiling salted water

2 kaffir lime leaves

½ tablespoon palm sugar or a little less of soft brown sugar

2 tablespoons fish sauce (nam pla)

20 basil leaves, preferably Thai basil leaves

1 large red chile, pounded

1 tablespoon Thai soy sauce (optional)

FOR THE STEAMED RICE

2 cups basmati rice

½ to 1 teaspoon salt

Measure the rice and wash gently in 2 or 3 changes of cold water. The final water should almost be clear. Drain the rice well in a sieve or fine strainer then tip it into a heavy-bottomed saucepan. Add an equal volume of water and the salt. Stir to mix. Bring to a boil, then reduce the heat to the absolute minimum—use a heat diffuser, if available. Cover with a tight-fitting lid—no steam must escape, so use foil under the lid if necessary. Steam the rice for 15 to 20 minutes, remove from the heat, and rest for 5 minutes. The rice will now be dry and fluffy but will keep warm for up to 30 minutes.

Meanwhile, heat a wok over low heat. Pour ⅓ cup of the coconut milk into the wok. Add the green curry paste and the green chile and mix well. Then add the stock, remainder of the coconut milk, Brussels sprouts, kaffir lime leaves, palm sugar, fish sauce, half the basil leaves, and the red chile. Stir constantly over medium heat for 5 minutes until the sauce boils and foams up. Reduce the heat and simmer, stirring constantly, otherwise the sauce may separate—it should be cooked in 10 to 12 minutes. Add the remaining basil leaves, season to taste, and add a dash of soy sauce if necessary.

Serve hot with the steamed rice.

Brussels Sprouts Masala

It was quite a surprise to discover Brussels sprouts in South India. Somehow I associated them only with these islands. This masala version, which I learned at a cookery class at the Bangala, tempts those who refuse to even taste Brussels sprouts.

. . . .

SERVES 4 TO 6

3½ teaspoons salt

1 pound Brussels sprouts

3 tablespoons vegetable oil

3½ ounces onions, minced

½ teaspoon ginger paste

1 teaspoon garlic paste

½ teaspoon ground turmeric

1 teaspoon mild red chile powder

½ cup fresh tomato purée

1 tablespoon chopped cilantro leaves

Put 5 cups of water and 3 teaspoons of the salt into a saucepan and bring to a boil. Quarter any larger sprouts. Add the sprouts to the boiling water and cook for 3 to 4 minutes. Drain in a colander and refresh in cold water.

Heat the oil in a wok over high heat. When the oil is hot but not smoking, add the onions and sauté for 1 to 2 minutes. Add the ginger and garlic pastes and the turmeric and chile powder. Stir and add the fresh tomato purée. Reduce the heat to low and cook for 5 to 6 minutes, stirring and scraping to ensure that nothing sticks to the bottom, adding a splash of water if necessary, until the oil separates around the edge, then add the sprouts to the masala. for 1 to 2 minutes. Season to taste.

Garnish with fresh cilantro leaves and serve as an accompaniment or with rice.

KOHLRABI *Brassica oleracea Gongylodes Group* ANNUAL

We need to net our kohlrabi to protect them from the birds.

These bizarre pale-green or purple-skinned vegetables look like sputniks with stalks and leaves projecting randomly from the sides. Kohlrabi is a member of the brassica family but tastes like a delicate sweet white turnip. It really deserves to be better known. They are so worth growing if you have space; both the leaves and bulbs are edible, plus kohlrabi is super nutritious. Enjoy it while it's young.

VARIETIES

Azur Star—An early variety which may be grown in a tunnel or outdoors. It has tender very striking purple/blue bulbs—white inside and resistant to bolting.

Kohlibri—Beautiful purple variety; the small bulbs have crisp, white flesh.

Winner—The 3 inch bulbs hold well in the garden without splitting; flavor is fresh and fruity.

HOW TO GROW

Kohlrabi requires the same growing conditions as other brassicas.

Sow in loam-based compost in cells in early spring and plant out about 4 weeks later. Kohlrabi likes fertile soil, and a sunny spot, but will tolerate partial shade. Once you get hooked you might want to sow every few weeks to get a succession of kohlrabi during the summer, they crop about 10 weeks after sowing.

CONTAINER GROWING

Kohlrabi can certainly be grown in troughs, half barrels or large pots with good drainage. Keep watered and feed with a general liquid fertilizer every 2 to 3 weeks.

Mini varieties like *Rolano, Logo, Korist F1* or *Kohlra* are best for containers.

HARVESTING

Harvest from golf-ball to tennis-ball size but no larger. Kohlrabi will continue to grow to almost grapefruit size, but they become increasingly woody in texture.

PESTS

Kohlrabi is subject to the same pests as other members of the brassica family, club root can be problem. Rotation is very important, kohlrabi should not be grown in the same ground immediately after another brassica crop, to prevent the build up of club root disease in the soil.

GOOD FOR YOU...

Kohlrabi is an excellent source of vitamin C and potassium, it also contains vitamin B6, folic acid, magnesium and copper.

> **DID YOU KNOW?**
> Kohlrabi is part of the *gongylodes* group of vegetables, which means rounded or swollen.
> Kohlrabi is much loved in India where it is called hot cabbage.

IN THE KITCHEN

Kohlrabi can be eaten raw or cooked. It's also delicious grated into salads or coleslaw. We love it in gratins and spicy Indian curry and Asian dishes. The leaves may also be used like spinach or kale. It's compact, so it's useful for cooking for small numbers or for one person.

Trim the outer leaves from the bulb, peel the distinct outer layer, and slice or dice. Melt a little butter in a sauté pan over medium heat, and when the butter foams add the kohlrabi. Season with salt and freshly ground pepper. Toss to coat. Cover with a piece of parchment paper cut to fit the top of the pan and then the lid of the pan and cook gently for 8 to 10 minutes until the kohlrabi is tender. I like to add some chopped marjoram but it will be delicious on its own. Substitute extra virgin olive oil for the butter if the kohlrabi is to be used for salad.

Kohlrabi, White Cabbage & Cranberry Slaw with Herbs & Sesame Seeds

I love this salad, which we borrowed from Yotam Ottolenghi who made it at a cooking class here at the school—the pickled ginger provides a zesty burst of flavor. White turnip can be substituted for kohlrabi in this recipe and dried cherries for cranberries, if you prefer.

. . . .

SERVES 4

3 or 4 kohlrabi bulbs
7 ounces white cabbage
½ cup flat-leaf parsley, chopped
½ cup dill, chopped
½ cup tarragon, chopped
½ cup dried cranberries
2 teaspoons pickled ginger (page 535), minced
1 tablespoon grated lemon zest
scant ½ cup lemon juice
2 tablespoons honey
¼ cup extra virgin olive oil
2 tablespoons sesame oil
¼ cup toasted white sesame seeds
2 tablespoons nigella seeds
sea salt and freshly ground black pepper

Peel the kohlrabi. Yotam peels them and slices them into matchsticks, but we grate it on the coarsest part of a box grater and it works very well.

Put into a large bowl, add the remaining ingredients, and mix well. Season with salt and freshly ground pepper, taste, and tweak if necessary.

Swedish Potato & Kohlrabi Salad

A simple salad but so good; I also love the way this recipe uses the green leaves so we get full value from the crop.

SERVES 4 TO 6

2 pounds potatoes
2 fresh kohlrabi
3 tablespoons extra virgin olive oil
2 tablespoons chopped fresh dill
flaky sea salt and freshly ground black
  pepper

Cook the potatoes in boiling salted water for 10 to 20 minutes until tender. Drain and set aside. Peel and cut into cubes or slices, depending on the size of the potato.

Meanwhile, peel and cut the kohlrabi into cubes, reserving the leaves. Heat the olive oil in a sauté pan over medium heat, add the kohlrabi, and toss to coat. Cover and cook over low heat for about 7 minutes until crisp but tender. Add the chopped kohlrabi leaves and continue to cook until they wilt and are soft. Add the potato and dill. Season with salt and freshly ground pepper. Stir gently to combine. Serve warm or at room temperature.

BROCCOLI *Brassica oleracea* ANNUAL

Freshly picked broccoli is an altogether different experience to those tired heads on the shelves in our supermarkets. It's not just the taste that's different, it's also the texture, plus it takes considerably longer to cook than storebought broccoli. The outer skin on the stalk is so tough that it really needs to be peeled off, otherwise all that part of the vegetable is wasted. I've seen people chop the thick stalk off altogether, even though the inner stalk is quite tender when cooked and can in fact be used in a slaw.

Your own fresh broccoli will be a revelation. Pick it smaller and the little florets will be tender in a way that commercial broccoli never becomes. It can be mushy but in a totally delicious way. It's particularly wonderful with pasta or risotto and you'll find yourself polishing off a whole bowlful, as will your children who have hitherto refused

Sprouting broccoli, the winter brassica that keeps on giving—a must-have.

point blank to eat it. I don't love al dente (half-raw) broccoli, but having said that I munch freshly picked florets with relish and am addicted to crudités with a bowl of aioli.

Although it is an Italian vegetable, I first came across broccoli raab (Cima di Rapa) in the US, where chefs and diners go crazy for it, but now many other home gardeners have discovered it. It's really worth knowing about this tender, slightly bitter, green-budded variety of sprouting broccoli as from the gardener's point of view it has the bonus of coming into production faster than purple sprouting broccoli, and is a valuable winter and spring green. Similar to kai-lan in China, it's related to both the broccoli and turnip family and tolerates light frost.

Romanesco is a stunning architectural broccoli which broke into our lives less than a decade ago. I was totally convinced this bizarre brassica must be a new-fangled hybrid vegetable, but I learnt that in fact it was first documented in Italy over 500 years ago. Broccoli Romanesco, in other words broccoli from Rome, looks like a cross between calabrese and cauliflower but is much more dramatically beautiful in appearance. It has a fractal patterned spiral head composed of lime-green conical florets. I'm often tempted to use it as part of the edible table arrangement. Romanesco is sweet and nutty and when broken up into florets it resembles Christmas trees, which our grandchildren gobble up with relish. If I could grow just one type of broccoli, this would be the one.

VARIETIES

Try to have succession by planting a selection of varieties which mature at different times.

Traditionally we have always looked forward to **Purple Sprouting Early** in early spring and **Purple Sprouting Late**, cropping from a few weeks later for several weeks, but you could sow a variety like **Rudolph** in late spring, for purple spears in December.

Also try a new variety called **Santee F1** to produce spears from midsummer to early winter, from sowing in succession from mid-spring to early summer.

BROCCOLI RAAB
Sessantina Grosso—Best for early crop as it has a short harvest window.
Spring Raab—Best for main season as it has bigger plants, relatively late. Goes well with olive oil and pasta.

ROMANESCO
F1 Veronica—Spiralled heads with creamy curds. Mild nutty flavor, good for eating raw as crudités or in salads. Originated in Northern Italy.
Romanesco—Beautiful lime-green heads, sometimes called Broccoflower, its flavor is a combination of broccoli and cauliflower. Also of Italian origin.

HOW TO GROW
Sprouting broccoli are great to fill the "hungry gap" period in late spring, but they do take up even more space than cabbages. Sow the seed at the same time as winter cabbages in early summer, then harvest in early spring. Allow 24 to 30 inches between the plants and 12 inches between rows.

Broccoli likes moist fertile soil in full sun. Plant deeply in firm soil, to avoid the plant rocking as it gets taller.

Grow broccoli raab in fertile, well-drained soil, full sun or partial shade. Sow mid-spring to early summer. Early sowings can be done in seed trays in a hotbed in early spring and then transplanted. Later sowings can be made directly in the ground, 10 to 12 seeds per 12 inches and the rows 18 inches apart. They do best in a polytunnel or a greenhouse. Keep weed-free.

Romanesco does best in alkaline soil; if you don't have the perfect spot you may want to add a little lime to your soil. Be careful not to plant it where any of the cabbage family have been growing the previous season, but it loves to follow peas or beans which will have fixed extra nitrogen from the air into the soil through the root nodules.

We start them off in cells in the greenhouse in late spring or early summer. Plant out 3 feet apart with 2 feet between rows.

CONTAINER GROWING
Broccoli needs a lot of space and is in the ground for a long time, so it may not be the best use of your container garden, particularly if space is limited. A few broccoli raab plants could be grown in a trough, as it grows 10 to 16 inches tall. You can plant romanesco in containers, particularly troughs or scattered through a flower bed.

PESTS AND DISEASES
Similar to other brassicas, it suffers from cabbage root fly, cabbage butterfly, and caterpillars. We put hoops over the beds and lay netting on top to discourage the cabbage butterfly.

All brassicas need to be rotated as club root can persist in the soil for a very long time. Ideally allow a three-year gap before brassicas are grown again in the same area.

Club root is a fungal disease to which all brassicas are susceptible (cabbages, broccoli and all their relations, including oriental salad greens). It builds up in the soil, so it's vitally important to rotate brassica crops. It can persist in the soil for up to 20 years. The symptoms of this disease are that above ground the growth will be stunted and in hot weather may wilt, and the leaves may get a purplish tinge. Underground the root will be swollen and the finer roots will die. Generally the plants will look unhealthy and the yield will be affected, so it is best to remove and destroy it—don't put it on the compost heap.

Prevention is the best option—rotation and adding lime to the soil, particularly if your soil is acid. Brassicas like slightly limey soil anyway. Planting your brassicas deeply and firmly will encourage strong secure plants, lots of fine side roots will develop and the plants will be healthier and better able to withstand disease.

HARVESTING
When grown inside broccoli is in season during autumn and winter. Cut the leading florets with a little stem on each as this will encourage more side shoots to sprout over a longer period.

Harvest broccoli raab in early to late autumn, 90 to 100 days after sowing. As with sprouting broccoli, harvest carefully and they will re-sprout over and over. Peak season is autumn to spring.

With Romanesco, we allow the main shoot to head up before we cut it, then other side shoots emerge. Cut the heads with a sharp knife as you need them, leave the plants in the ground and they may well sprout again.

GOOD FOR YOU...
Broccoli is a source of a wide range of vitamins and minerals, including calcium, iron, magnesium, manganese, potassium, riboflavin, folate and vitamins A, C, E, K and B6, but it is of course vital not to overcook it, so as not to destroy them.

Broccoli raab is rich in antioxidants and also a good source of calcium, potassium, iron, vitamins K, C and A.

Romanesco is very easily digested because it contains fewer of the substances in other brassicas that can cause flatulence in some people. It contains easily digested fiber and is naturally anti-inflammatory and antioxidant. It is a rich source of vitamin C, also contains vitamins A and K, along with carotene, folate, manganese, zinc, omega 3 fatty acids and iron.

WHAT TO DO WITH A GLUT
You can blanch and freeze the florets, but broccoli is really best enjoyed fresh. Broccoli soup can be frozen but, as with all green soups, care needs to be taken to keep it fresh and green. We feast on broccoli every day during the season.

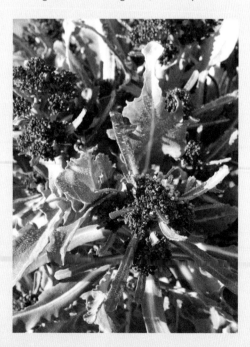

Sprouting Rudolph broccoli.

Stir-fry, use it in salad, give presents to friends. The leaves make a delicious soup or can be cooked as other greens.

IN THE KITCHEN

Purple varieties turn green when cooked. Steaming can help retain the color and it is less likely to overcook. Don't waste the stalks, they can be peeled and grated and are tasty used in coleslaw and also delicious eaten raw as crudités. For broccoli raab, boil or steam in well-salted water. Also delicious braised or fried in extra virgin olive oil. We love the flowers and tender leaves, which are delicious in salad and crudités. As with sprouting broccoli it is enhanced by other flavors—chile flakes, garlic, ginger, anchovies, pancetta, chorizo and sesame oil.

We also love broccoli in soup, even the larger leaves make a super-tasty winter soup, or cook them with a smoked ham hock. I love it piled onto a slice of pan-grilled bread, on its own or with a poached egg, and most of all I love to see my grandchildren eating it straight from the plant or squabbling over the last little florets in the bowl.

Asian flavors are a perfect match for these greens. To serve 6 to 8, boil or steam 2 pounds sprouting broccoli or Calabrese (use 1 tablespoon salt to every 5 cups water) for 4 to 6 minutes depending on size. Mix 1 tablespoon sunflower oil, 1 teaspoon toasted sesame oil, 3 tablespoons oyster sauce, and 1 tablespoon dark soy sauce together in a little saucepan and warm gently. Drizzle the well-drained vegetables with the dressing. Season to taste.

Broccoli (or Cauliflower) Salad is not an obvious choice but it is surprisingly delicious. The secret, as is the case with many salads, is to dip the florets in a good dressing while still warm so that they really absorb the flavors. Green broccoli (Calabrese), purple, or white sprouting broccoli can all be cooked this way and a mixture of all three looks and tastes wonderful. To serve 6, take 1 small head of broccoli (or cauliflower) with the leaves on and trim off the damaged ones. Wash and shred the remaining leaves and stalk, and split the broccoli into small florets so it will cook evenly. Take a saucepan that fits the broccoli exactly and boil 1 inch of water in it. Add a little salt, put in the shredded leaves in and sit the broccoli on top, stems down, and cover closely. Control the heat so that it does not boil dry. Remove from the pot when the stalks are barely tender. Divide into florets. Dip each into ½ cup Ballymaloe French dressing (see page 182) while they are still warm and arrange like a wheel on a round plate. Build layers to re-form the broccoli head. This looks good and tastes delicious as part of a cold buffet.

Romanesco can be eaten raw; its crunchy florets are delicious. Like cauliflower or Calabrese they can be

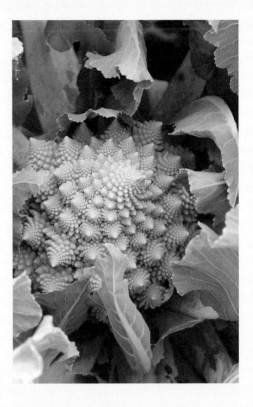

Romanesco—if you only have space for one variety it ought to be romanesco.

boiled, steamed, or roasted and when boiled will take on other flavors happily. However, it's hard to beat freshly picked romanesco boiled in well-salted water until just tender, then doused in really good extra virgin olive oil or butter. We love it with pasta or in the Sicilian way with olives and chile, or maybe pine nuts and raisins. Although good, Italian pine nuts are so expensive these days I think it has to be cashew nuts or almonds instead. It sounds very decadent, but I also love it on toast with hollandaise sauce. I also love **Christmas Trees with Aioli** (serves 6), remove the outer leaves of 1 head of romanesco and divide into florets or "Christmas trees." Serve raw on a plate with a bowl of aioli.

DID YOU KNOW?

Broccoli was first introduced to the United States by Italian immigrants but did not become really popular until the 1920s. The first commercial planting of broccoli took place on a trial basis by two Italian immigrant brothers in San Jose in California in 1922. They sent a few crates to Boston where there was a thriving Italian community, and it took off from there.

In Naples broccoli raab is known as *friarielli*, in Rome *broccoletti*, in Puglia *cimi de rape* and in Portugal and Spain *grelos di rape*.

Broccoli Salad with Anchovies & a Hen's Egg

Calabrese or other types of broccoli may be used in this salad and are particularly delicious with Caesar dressing.

SERVES 4

¾ pound fresh sprouting broccoli florets

1 tablespoon salt

2 organic eggs, preferably Araucuna eggs

12 anchovy fillets

FOR THE CAESAR DRESSING

1 (1¾-ounce/50g) tin anchovies

2 organic egg yolks

1 garlic clove, crushed

2 tablespoons lemon juice

a generous pinch of English mustard powder

½ teaspoon salt

½ to 1 tablespoon Worcestershire sauce

½ to 1 tablespoon Tabasco sauce

¾ cup sunflower oil

3 tablespoons extra virgin olive oil

3 tablespoons cold water

sea salt and freshly ground black pepper

First make the Caesar dressing. I make it in a food processor but it can also be made very quickly by hand. Drain the anchovies and crush lightly with a fork. Put into a bowl with the egg yolks and add the garlic, lemon juice, mustard powder, salt, Worcestershire, and Tabasco. Whisk all the ingredients together. As you whisk, add the oils slowly at first, then a little faster as the emulsion forms. Finally whisk in the water to make a spreadable consistency. Season to taste—this dressing should be highly flavored.

Trim the florets if necessary. Bring 2½ cups of water to a boil; add salt. In another saucepan of boiling water, hard-boil the eggs for 8 minutes. Remove from the water and dip into cold water. The yolk should still be soft in the center. Peel the eggs when they are cool enough to handle. Plunge the broccoli florets into the boiling, well-salted water. Bring back to a boil and cook for 3 to 4 minutes or until just cooked but still slightly al dente. Drain and refresh under cold water.

To serve, divide the florets among 4 plates, making a little stack interleaved with anchovy strips. Drizzle with Caesar dressing and pop a half egg on top. Sprinkle with a little freshly cracked pepper and a few flakes of sea salt.

Romanesco, Broccoli, or Cauliflower Pakoras

Romanesco, Calabrese, or cauliflower florets work perfectly in this recipe, so moist, and children love them too.

SERVES 4

1 Romanesco, calabrese, or cauliflower

sunflower oil, for deep-frying

Pomegranate & Grape Raita (page 110)

FOR THE BATTER

1 teaspoon cumin seeds

2½ cups chickpea flour

½ teaspoon chile powder

1 teaspoon ground turmeric

1 teaspoon salt

Trim the Romanesco or calabrese florets if necessary. Divide the cauliflower into florets, blanch, refresh, and drain.

Heat a dry skillet over medium heat, add the cumin seeds, and cook, stirring, for 3 to 4 minutes or until nicely toasted and slightly browned.

Sift the flour into a bowl. Add the chile, turmeric, and freshly roasted cumin seeds and ½ teaspoon of the salt. Whisk in enough water to make a batter with a light coating consistency—we use about 1¼ cups.

Heat the oil in a deep-fryer. Dip one floret into the batter, shake off the excess, and cook in the hot oil for about 4 minutes until crisp and golden. Taste and add more seasoning or spice to the batter if necessary. Drain on paper towels and cook the remaining pakoras in the same way. Serve with a bowl of raita.

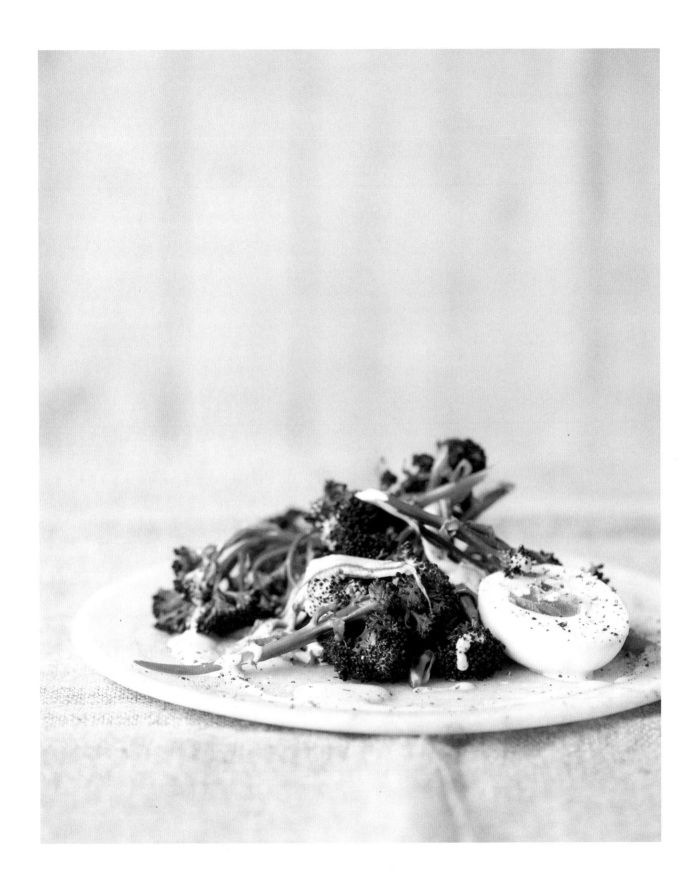

Pad Thai

Romanesco or broccoli florets are a delicious and nutritious addition to this Pad Thai, the famous Thai noodle dish. Use organic ingredients where possible.

. . . .

SERVES 4 TO 6

8 ounces rice noodles

1 tablespoon tamarind paste

2 tablespoons fish sauce (nam pla)

1½ tablespoons light brown sugar

2 tablespoons freshly squeezed lime juice

¼ pound Romanesco or broccoli florets

¼ pound carrots, cut into julienne

⅓ cup vegetable oil

2 teaspoons crushed garlic (about 5 cloves)

1 teaspoon grated fresh ginger

16 large wild shrimp, cooked and peeled

2 organic eggs, beaten

3 or 4 spring onions or scallions, sliced at an angle

2½ ounces fresh bean sprouts

3 tablespoons salted peanuts, roughly chopped

TO GARNISH

3 tablespoons chopped fresh cilantro

lime wedges

1 tablespoon sesame seeds

red pepper flakes (optional)

FOR THE CRISPY ONIONS

4 to 6 small onions or shallots

sunflower oil, for frying

Put the noodles in a bowl, cover with water, and leave for about an hour.

To make the crispy onions, peel and slice the onions or shallots very thinly. Separate the rings and allow to dry for several hours.

Meanwhile, whisk the tamarind paste, fish sauce, sugar, lime juice, and 3 tablespoons of water in a bowl.

Blanch and refresh the Romanesco or broccoli florets and carrots in boiling salted water—3 minutes for the broccoli, 2 minutes for the carrots—until al dente.

To make the crispy onions, heat the oil to 350°F in a wok or deep-fat fryer. Deep-fry for 2 to 3 minutes until golden. Spread them out on paper towels in a single layer and let cool.

Drain the noodles.

Heat a wok over high heat, add the oil, and continue to heat until almost smoking. Add the garlic and ginger, toss quickly, then add the peeled shrimp and cook for 1 to 2 minutes. Transfer to a plate.

Add the noodles to the wok and stir-fry for a minute. Pour in three-quarters of the tamarind paste and fish sauce. Toss to coat the noodles, push to the side of the wok, and add the whisked eggs. Stir to scramble a little then add the shrimp, Romanesco or broccoli florets, carrots, spring onions, bean sprouts, and half of the salted peanuts. Add the remainder of the tamarind/fish sauce. Toss, taste, and correct the seasoning with more fish sauce and lime juice if necessary.

Divide among four shallow hot plates. Garnish with the remaining peanuts, cilantro sprigs, and a sprinkle of sesame seeds.

Serve each with a lime wedge and a sprinkling of crispy onions and red pepper flakes if you crave some extra oomph. Enjoy.

TURNIPS

Brassica campestris/ B. rapa ANNUAL

Don't forget white turnips (*Brassica rapa*), they are "little dotes" and another oft-forgotten vegetable that goes on giving. As a family, turnips are easy to grow.

One may not think of eating white turnips like apples, but the variety we grow, Snowball, is deliciously crunchy. We just trim the leaves, run them under the tap, put them into a bowl on the table for everyone, including the grandchildren, to enjoy.

We eat both the leaves and roots, which are edible at all stages—from tiny radish-size roots to almost tennis-ball size. For me they are worth growing for one dish alone, the classic French braised duck with turnips, an old Ballymaloe favorite originally inspired by a recipe in *Mastering the Art of French Cooking* by Julia Child, Simone Beck, and Louisette Bertholle.

VARIETIES

Snowball—Early variety, will be ready to harvest after 5 to 6 weeks when they are 2½ to 4 inches in diameter. Delicate flavor.

White Globe—Traditional variety with smooth skin and bright purple top. Extremely tender. Overwinters well.

Purple Top Milan—Quick-maturing variety suitable for sowing in succession.

Market Express—Crops within 30 days, also suitable for sowing in succession.

HOW TO GROW

You may be surprised to learn that turnips are part of the brassica family, so factor that into your rotation. They thrive best in fertile soil that's rich in organic matter, they are fairly hardy so not too fussy about aspect. Sow in succession from early spring to midsummer.

For early turnips the seed can be planted under cloches in early spring, using a suitable variety. They will be ready to harvest in early summer.

Alternatively, sow directly into the soil, in early to midsummer, then thin them once, as soon as the leaves fill out and start competing with each other. Use the leaves from the first thinning in salads.

Turnips prefer cooler, moister weather rather than summer heat. It's important that they grow quickly and don't dry out, otherwise the texture becomes woody—but even these can be used for the stockpot.

If you thin them a second time, it may be possible to eat the tiny turnips as baby turnips. The remaining crop can then be allowed to grow on to tennis-ball size.

We usually do two sowings outdoors, but you could do three if you wish. Turnips are also useful for inter-cropping because they mature quickly. For example, if you have space between broccoli or spring cabbage, crops that will be in the ground for a long time, you can plant turnip in-between them.

CONTAINER GROWING

Turnips can be grown in a large container. Keep them well-watered, otherwise they will dry out and become woody.

PESTS

Turnips are susceptible to many of the same challenges as cabbage. Slugs are partial to the young foliage.

Snowball and Purple Top Milan turnips.

Club root can be a problem, though we haven't experienced it. Seek out club root-resistant seed varieties and be vigilant about rotation.

HARVESTING

One can begin to harvest the greens once the plants are about 4 inches high. After the foliage is cut they will re-sprout. Turnips can tolerate mild frost, which sweetens them. They are best harvested at about table-tennis-ball size, but not larger than a tennis ball....

We don't store white turnips.

GOOD FOR YOU...

The green tops of turnips are rich in vitamins and minerals—vitamins A, C and K, B-complex and carotenoid. The roots are low-calorie and a good source of dietary fibre and vitamin C and rich in minerals and antioxidants.

WHAT TO DO WITH A GLUT

Store like other roots in a sandbox or clamp. They can also be frozen—peel, cube and freeze in good-quality freezer bags. Use in the stock pot, pickle, etc....

IN THE KITCHEN

Turnip greens are delicious raw or cooked, and are much loved, particularly in Italy. Cook the stemmed and sliced greens in well-boiling salted water as you would kale. Add lots of butter or extra virgin olive oil and chile or any other seasoning you may fancy. Cooked turnip greens add extra oomph to potato dishes, and I've also enjoyed them in a risotto or served with polenta.

I love the delicacy of white turnips; cook them gently in a covered casserole with a little butter and 2 teaspoons water. Use olive oil instead if you plan to use them in a salad. Marjoram and white turnips are a match made in heaven, but of course a little tarragon and parsley work, too. If the roots get woody, use them for the stockpot.

For **Braised White Turnips** with Marjoram to serve 4 to 6, wash and peel 1 pound small white turnips and cut into ¼-inch-thick slices or wedges. Melt 2 tablespoons butter in a heavy-bottomed casserole. Add the sliced turnips, season with salt and freshly ground pepper, and add 1 tablespoon water and 2½ teaspoons chopped marjoram. Cover and cook over low heat for 8 to 10 minutes until the turnip is just tender. Season to taste, add a little more chopped fresh marjoram and serve immediately.

Lamb, Turnip, Onion & Butter Bean Stew

A virtually white lamb stew, delicate in flavor, which I first tasted in a taverna in Athens. The addition of turnips to this recipe bulks out the stew in an altogether appealing way.

SERVES 6

½ pound dried butter beans
2 tablespoons olive oil
2½ pounds shoulder of lamb, cut in 1½-inch cubes
1½ pounds baby onions, peeled
1 pound white turnips, peeled and quartered
6 whole garlic cloves, peeled
2 bay leaves
generous sprig of thyme
1¾ to 2¼ cups homemade lamb or chicken stock
1 teaspoon salt
freshly ground black pepper
lots of coarsely chopped flat-leaf parsley, to serve

Cover the butter beans with plenty of cold water and let soak overnight.

The following day, drain the butter beans, transfer to a pan, cover with fresh water, and cook for 10 to 15 minutes while you prepare the meat and vegetables.

Heat the olive oil in a skillet, lightly brown the meat, onions, white turnips, and garlic in the hot pan in batches, and transfer to a casserole. Drain the butter beans and add with the bay leaves and a large sprig of thyme. Pour in the stock; it should come about halfway up the meat. Add the salt and lots of freshly ground pepper. Bring to a boil and simmer for about 1 hour or until all the ingredients are tender. Fish out the bay leaves and sprig of thyme.

Taste—it may need more seasoning. The stew ought to be nice and juicy but if there is more juice than is necessary, pour it into a wide uncovered pan and reduce to the required strength and quantity. Return the reduced sauce to the casserole, reheat, and season to taste. Sprinkle with lots of parsley and serve

Duck with Turnips

This is a French classic. It may seem unusual to braise duck but the result is sensational; the turnips are infused with juices from the duck. Quite sublime. The combination of duck and turnips is a memorable one and is a flavor combination that I love to share.

. . . .

SERVES 4 TO 6

1 (5-pound) free-range duck
sea salt and freshly ground black pepper
1 sprig of thyme
1 bay leaf
3 or 4 flat-leaf parsley sprigs, plus extra
   to serve
2 pounds white turnips

Season the duck inside and out with salt and freshly ground pepper. Trim off excess fat and render it down in a casserole (reserve the precious surplus duck fat for roast or fried potatoes). Prick the skin gently on the breast and legs. Put the duck breast-side down into an oval casserole and brown slowly over low heat on all sides in a little of the duck fat. Stuff the cavity with the herbs, add a little more salt, cover the casserole, and cook very gently on the stovetop or, better still, in a preheat 300°F oven for 50 minutes to 1 hour. Originally this would have been cooked in a pot oven beside the open fire.

While the duck is cooking, peel the turnips and cut into quarters or large dice. Bring a saucepan of salted water to a boil, add the turnips, return to a boil, and cook for 5 to 6 minutes. Drain.

When the duck has been roasting for about 50 minutes, pour off most of the fat from the pot and save as before, but keep the juices in the casserole. Tuck the turnip around the duck, cover, and return to the heat (or put back in the oven). Cook for 30 to 40 minutes more, or until both the duck and turnips are tender.

Serve the duck (breast side up) on a hot dish surrounded by the turnips, which by now will have absorbed the duck cooking juices and be tender and succulent. Scatter with snipped parsley and serve immediately.

Southern Turnip Greens with Salt Pork

A gutsy, comforting, winter stew with a fine robust flavor. This is a traditional way to use turnip greens in some of the Southern United States.

. . . .

SERVES 6

4½ pounds turnip greens
1 tablespoon lard
1 pound salt pork or bacon, cut into
   ¼-inch lardons
1 large onion, chopped
½ teaspoon freshly ground black pepper
1 teaspoon sugar
½ teaspoon dried chile flakes
cornbread, to serve

Stem the greens and wash, drain, and coarsely chop the leaves.

Heat the lard in a casserole over medium heat, add the salt pork or bacon, and cook for 5 to 6 minutes until the fat runs and the meat is crisp and golden. Add the onion, cook for a couple of minutes, then toss in the coarsely cut greens. Stir to coat with fat, then season with the pepper, sugar and some chile flakes. Add 1½ cups of water. Bring to a boil, skimming the surface if necessary, reduce the heat and simmer for 40 to 45 minutes or until the salt pork or bacon is fully cooked and the turnip greens are tender.

Season to taste and serve with cornbread.

CHILE PEPPERS *Capsicum annuum* ANNUAL

Chiles are native to Mexico and Central America. Archaeological evidence suggests that chiles have been growing in Mexico since 7000BC, but it appears that they have been grown since 5000BC.

The first chiles were brought to Europe by Diego Álvarez Chanca, who was a physician on Christopher Columbus's voyage to the West Indies. When they were introduced to Spain in 1493, they were soon embraced enthusiastically by society.

The Portuguese brought them to the West Indies and they spread like wildfire from there. I found it fascinating to learn that there were no chiles in Indian, Chinese or Asian cooking until a few hundred years ago, and now we have all embraced the chile enthusiastically. Here at Ballymaloe Cookery School we grow

eight or ten varieties every year and dry them for later use.

Chiles come in a variety of shapes and colors from green, yellow, orange, red and black. Capsaicin is the volatile oil that gives chiles their heat, and this is measured on the organoleptic Scoville Scale, developed by American pharmacist Wilbur Scoville in 1912. It measures the combination of capsaicin from 0 for a sweet red pepper to a record 2,200,000 for *Carolina Reaper*, the hottest chiles so far recorded, followed in second place by the *Trinidad Moruga Scorpion* at 2,009,231.

VARIETIES

There are over 200 varieties, from mild to very fiery. They range in shape, color and size, and as a general rule the smaller they are the hotter they are, so the warier you need to be! It's also worth noting that the heat of the chiles can vary significantly, even on the same plant. The heat increases with the maturity of the fruit. As a rough guide: Anaheim are moderately hot chiles, Jalapeño medium-hot to hot and Serrano are hot.

Long Red Marconi—Long, red, sweet pepper with a mild flavor.

Ring O Fire—Cayenne type, good crop of long, thin, pointed pods ripening from green to red—not very hot.

Hungarian Hot Wax—Old heritage variety, large and mild to medium hot, can be eaten fresh, roast, stuffed or pickled. Green, orange, red, yellow.

Tabasco Habanero—Very attractive looking and reported to be one of the hottest peppers in the world—between 200,000 and 350,000 units on the Scoville scale.

Scotch Bonnet Red—Habanero type, fiery hot. Popular in Caribbean cooking.

Royal Black—Tall, elegant, bushy plant with dark purple foliage and almost black stems, bullet-shaped chiles. Medium hot.

Ancho Giantea—a medium hot ancho pepper, ripening from green to red

Orange AJ1—Also known as Peruvian Hot Pepper.

A few new varieties we are also growing this year **Serrano Tampiqueno**, **Piment de Especetie**, **Trinidadian Perfume**.

HOW TO GROW

Chiles are another fun crop and are surprisingly easy to grow. We plant 8 to 10 varieties every year in the greenhouse and outside, but in a cool climate they are best grown indoors.

We propagate from seed, however, if you would rather have several varieties but just one plant of each, pick up a few sturdy plants at a good garden center.

Sow from early spring in a seed tray or into 3-inch pots. Germination time varies significantly depending on the variety—anything from 1 to 3 weeks for Jalapeno and Serrano, whereas Harbanero or Scotch Bonnet can take up to 6 weeks or longer.

Sow in their final spot when they are about 4 inches high. The plants can be hardened off and planted out after all threat of frost has passed. Space dwarf varieties 12 inches apart and standard varieties 15 to 18 inches apart.

CONTAINER GROWING

Chiles can be grown very successfully in containers and potted up into 10 inches pots if they are being used as individual plants, or bigger, depending on the variety and the size of the plant. Feed every second week with liquid seaweed.

We grow them in terracotta pots and

Ring O Fire.

Palladio sweet pepper.

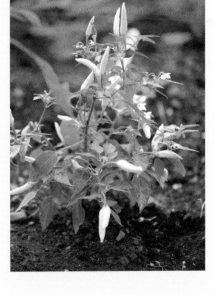

Basket of Fire—super hot on the Scoville scale.

large recycled tomato tins on the south-facing windowsills in the Ballymaloe Cookery School, as an ornamental plant so students can become familiar with the varieties.

Mini Bell Orange—Compact variety for container growing, it produces small, square, bright orange fruits, very hot, grows up to 2 feet tall.

Monkey Face—Similar to jalapeño, medium hot, grows 20 inches tall, suitable for container.

Glow—Grows to 28 to 32 inches, good for pots.

PESTS AND DISEASES

Red spider mite can be a nuisance in some seasons, but we control it with biological control in the greenhouse.

HARVESTING AND STORING

Chiles can be picked at many stages: while still green, when they ripen fully and turn red, or when they shrivel and dry on the plant in the sunlight. We harvest them in the autumn and store them in baskets and jute bags. We thread some on cotton string and hang them from the shelves in the cooking school, to make them fun, decorative and functional.

GOOD FOR YOU...

Chile peppers have a high beta-carotene content and have antioxidant properties, as well as being a source of vitamins C, B6, K1, A and potassium, iron, manganese and magnesium.

Capsaicin has anti-bacterial, anti-carcinogenic, analgesic and anti-diabetic properties, it has also been found to reduce LDL cholesterol levels in obese people.

WHAT TO DO WITH A GLUT

Chiles dry successfully and in Mexico many chiles are also smoked, which increases the flavor profile. We hang them up all over the school and loop them from shelves so they can be accessed easily to add to a dish.

IN THE KITCHEN

Chiles are a brilliant flavor note in the cook's armory, to be used in a vast number of ways to gently perk up a dish or enliven otherwise mundane ingredients, or to add a blast of heat that can bring tears to the eyes of even the most hardened aficionados.

Breeders continue to produce even hotter varieties by cross-breeding, and the accolade for the hottest chile in the world continues to change. Remember that the seeds and the membrane are the hottest part of the chile, so include or discard those, depending on the dish and your personal taste.

Capsaicin is fat soluble so the most effective antidotes to hot chile are dairy products such as yogurt raita. Starchy foods like rice and bread also assist in absorbing the heat. Milk is a help but water seems to exacerbate the problem.

Remember, the smaller they are, the warier you need to be—some of the tiny Asian chiles can be like a "scud missile," so tread carefully. Many a macho guy has been reduced to whimpers by a super-hot chile—it's not just hot, it's real pain.

Be super careful when handling fresh chiles, don't rub your eyes or any other sensitive part of your body, the burning sensation can last for quite a time, wash with water to relieve it.

Thai Pork or Chicken with Basil & Chiles

In a Thai version this would be super hot but I have reduced the chile—do increase the amount if you crave the authentic version. Serve this stir-fry with noodles; if Thai basil is not available use ordinary basil.

. . . .

SERVES 3

2 tablespoons vegetable oil

1½ pounds lean pork or 2 skinless chicken breasts, cut into strips

1 fresh Thai green chile, seeded if you want a milder flavor and minced

2 garlic cloves, cut into shreds

1 tablespoon sesame oil

1 medium red bell pepper, seeded and diced into ⅓-inch pieces

3 scallions, cut into ¼-inch strips

1 teaspoon freshly roasted and ground coriander

1 tablespoon brown sugar

1 teaspoon cornstarch

2 tablespoons fish sauce (nam pla)

1 tablespoon light soy sauce

¼ cup fresh Thai basil, shredded

sea salt and freshly ground black pepper

plain boiled rice and lots of chopped fresh cilantro, to serve

Heat 1 tablespoon of the vegetable oil in a wok or in a large skillet over high heat; toss in the pork or chicken strips. Add the green chile and garlic and stir-fry for about 5 minutes or until the pork or chicken changes color. We fry the meat in two batches, about 3 minutes for each batch.

Sprinkle with some of the sesame oil. Remove to a plate. Put the remaining 1 tablespoon vegetable oil in the pan. Add the bell pepper, scallions, ground coriander, and brown sugar, stir-fry for 2 minutes, then add the pork.

Mix the cornstarch with the fish sauce and soy sauce until smooth, then pour the mixture into the pan, stirring constantly until the juices thicken a little, about 1 minute. Sprinkle with the remaining sesame oil. Toss in the shredded basil, season to taste, then remove from the heat and serve immediately with noodles tossed in sesame oil or just simply with rice and lots of cilantro.

DID YOU KNOW?

At first, chiles just seem hot in varying degrees but soon we begin to appreciate that different varieties of chiles have different intriguingly flavor profiles as well.

Friggitelli—Roast Sweet Chile Peppers

We grow several varieties of large sweet chile peppers, such as Marconi, Rossa, Hungarian Wax, Atris F1, a little brown one called Mini Chocolate, and Mini Bell Orange. They are fantastically delicious and can also be stuffed or added to piperonata or tomato fondue.

SERVES 4 TO 6

1 pound sweet chile peppers, green, orange or red
¼ cup extra virgin olive oil
sea salt

Preheat the oven to 400°F.

Toss the peppers in extra virgin olive oil and sprinle with salt. Roast in the oven for 20 to 30 minutes or until soft and tender.

Serve with meat or fish dishes. I particularly love them with thin slices of rare sirloin or hanger steak and maybe a drizzle of béarnaise sauce.

Dried Shrimp Relish with Chiles & Lime

This relish epitomizes the four intense flavors of Thai food: the saltiness of dried shrimp and fish sauce, the punch of fiery chiles, the soothing sweetness of sugar, and the clear, sour bite of lime. It is terrific as a condiment or sprinkled over steaming jasmine rice.

SERVES 4 TO 6

1¾ ounces dried shrimp
5 tablespoons freshly squeezed lime juice
2 tablespoons fish sauce
scant ⅓ cup palm sugar
2 tablespoons thinly sliced shallot (sliced crosswise)
2 teaspoons thinly sliced fresh Thai chile or serrano chile (sliced crosswise)

Put the dried shrimp in a bowl and add enough hot water to cover. Let soak for 5 minutes. Drain.

Pound the shrimp lightly in a mortar, or coarsely chop them until they begin to break down. Combine the shrimp with all the remaining ingredients in a small bowl and stir well.

Keep in a fridge in a screw-top glass jar—it will keep for 2 to 3 months or more.

Stuffed Chile Peppers

It's not essential to peel the chile but I prefer the result—it's sweeter. I love the combination of roasted pepper with salty anchovy and creamy mozzarella.

. . . .

SERVES 4 TO 6

8 to 12 mixed red, orange, and yellow
  Hungarian wax chiles
½ to ¾ pound mozzarella or salted ricotta
2 tablespoons coarsely chopped marjoram
8 to 12 canned anchovies
sea salt and freshly ground black pepper
vegetable oil, for frying
cilantro springs, to serve

FOR THE BATTER
1¼ cups all-purpose flour
2 tablespoons extra virgin olive oil
1 to 1½ organic egg whites

Roast the peppers a couple at a time, directly over a medium gas flame until charred on all sides. Put them into a bowl and cover with plastic wrap or put them directly into a plastic bag and twist the top. This will create a steamy atmosphere which will make it easier to peel the chiles.

Rub off the blackened skin, slit down the side, and scoop out the seeds. Keep the stem intact. Slice the mozzarella into strips and season with salt and freshly ground pepper. Insert a piece or pieces of cheese into each chile or stuff with salted ricotta. Add a couple of marjoram leaves and an anchovy, press to seal, cover, and chill until ready to cook.

Meanwhile, make the batter. Sift the flour into a bowl and make a well in the center. Pour in the olive oil and stir. Gradually add enough water, about ¾ cup, to make a batter about the consistency of heavy cream. Let stand for at least 1 hour. Just before frying, whisk the egg whites until stiff peaks form and fold into the batter, adding a good pinch of sea salt.

To cook, heat the oil in a deep fryer to 400°F, dip the chiles, one at a time, into the batter, and cook in the hot oil for 4 to 5 minutes until crisp. Drain on paper towels. Serve 2 or 3 per person right away, with some sprigs of cilantro.

Tomato & Chile Jam

This zingy jam is great with everything from fried eggs to cold meat. Terrific on a piece of chicken breast or fish or spread on bruschetta with goat cheese and arugula leaves.

. . . .

MAKES TWO 12-OUNCE OR FOUR
½-PINT JARS

2¼ pounds very ripe tomatoes
4 to 8 red chiles
8 garlic cloves, peeled
2-inch piece of fresh ginger, peeled and
  roughly chopped
3 tablespoons fish sauce (nam pla)
2½ cups golden superfine sugar
¾ cup plus 1 tablespoon red wine vinegar

Peel the tomatoes and chop into ⅓-inch dice. Purée the chiles, garlic, ginger, and fish sauce in a blender. Put the purée, sugar, and vinegar into a stainless-steel saucepan, add the tomatoes, and bring to a boil slowly, stirring occasionally. Cook gently for 30 to 40 minutes, stirring every now and then to prevent sticking.

When cooked, pour into warmed, sterilized glass jars. Let cool. It will keep for 6 months in the fridge. Use within 2 weeks of opening.

CHICKPEAS *Cicer arietinum* ANNUAL

Chickpeas are so cheap to buy that it wouldn't even have occurred to me to grow them before I tasted fresh green chickpeas at a market in Maharastra in India. They seem to be in season there in early spring and are sold in bunches, still in their pods, fresh, green and delicious and packed with nutrients. Chickpeas are surprisingly easy to grow and very attractive with ferny silver leaves, growing to about 30 inches tall. They are best grown as a summer crop in the Northern Hemisphere, as they like full sun. The plant produces pods in abundance, the young chickpeas may be eaten like small green beans or petits pois, and others left to mature in the sun into chickpeas for drying.

Chickpeas are known as gram (see note at end) in India and are in fact one of the world's oldest cultivated crops. They are also called Garbanzo beans in the US and Canada, or Ceci beans, and are native to South Eastern Turkey, North Africa, and India. An uncommon black chickpea is grown in South-eastern Italy—ceci neri. On a recent trip to Burma I found fresh chickpea leaves

for sale at the market, apparently used for salad, and as a cooked vegetable and often mixed with potato.

VARIETIES

We grow **Principe**—a white-skinned variety which is reputed to have a better flavor. The seed comes from Italy; the varieties grown around the Mediterranean have a smooth skin.

The Indian cultivars have a wrinkled skin, among those are Annegri and **Bheema**, we haven't tried those yet.

HOW TO GROW

As ever, provenance of the seed is important, otherwise there will be poor germination. Chickpeas have a long growing season, they take about 100 days from seed to harvest in full sun.

The chickpea is a bushy plant with feathery green leaves and white flowers, some have a bluish/purple tinge, and seedpods containing one or occasionally two chickpeas. They grow between 8 to 30 inches tall and, like other legumes, fix nitrogen in the soil.

In spring, we sow the seed in 3 ½-inch pots in potting compost in our growing room, they take about two weeks to germinate. Transfer to the greenhouse or tunnel when they are 2 to 3 inches tall. After another 2 to 2½ weeks, transfer into larger pots (10 to 12 inches), or transplant into the ground 2 feet apart in all directions.

They are fairly tolerant of drought but at the flowering stage and when the peas are forming, watering can help swell the pods.

Chickpeas grow inside a slightly furry pod and are delicious and super nutritious both fresh and dried.

CONTAINER GROWING

We grow chickpeas in large recycled tomato tins on the wide windows in the cooking school. They look cool in tin cans, but a 15-liter pot, or a galvanized bucket with drainage holes is better. They need the space. You can feed them with a little comfrey tea or tomato feed, once they begin to produce pods, but our fresh chickpeas get eaten so fast they scarcely get time to mature.

PESTS AND DISEAES

We haven't encountered any problems so far, commercially grown chickpeas may be subject to blight.

HARVESTING

The fresh chickpeas are ready to harvest in mid- to late summer or early autumn. Cut the branches and enjoy the green chickpeas—sweet and crunchy and packed with goodness. They need to be used as quickly as possible after cutting, as they deteriorate quite quickly.

To dry the peas for storage, leave them until the leaves and pods begin to turn brown, but before the pods split, otherwise you will lose some of your precious crop. Tie the branches in bundles and hang them upside down in a warm dry place. As soon as they are dry the chickpeas can be collected.

GOOD FOR YOU...

Chickpeas are a brilliant low GI food with a high fiber content. They help to lower LDL cholesterol and triglycerides

DID YOU KNOW?

In India the husks are used as animal feed; they can be fed to hens.

and reduce heart disease. They are an excellent and inexpensive source of protein—20 per cent protein, 5 per cent fat, 55 per cent carbohydrate.

They are actually a complete protein: a serving of chickpeas provides all the amino acids the body requires every day.

A good source of vitamins, particularly B vitamins and minerals like potassium and phosphorus.

WHAT TO DO WITH A GLUT

Unlikely, but dried they keep for years, decades, even centuries—some were even found in the Pyramids.

IN THE KITCHEN

Chickpeas are immensely versatile; they can be eaten when they are fresh or dried and cooked, then used in a wide variety of soups, stews, salads, and, of course, puréed and mixed with tahini for Hummus Bi Tahina. They are also irresistible when roasted as a snack and some varieties are popped like popcorn.

For Spiced Chickpeas for 6 to 8 people to nibble, soak ⅔ cup dried chickpeas overnight in plenty of cold water. Drain, cover with fresh water, and cook for 20 minutes, then drain well. Preheat the oven to 400°F. Mix 2 tablespoons extra virgin olive oil with 2 plump crushed garlic cloves, add the chickpeas, and toss to coat. Spread on a rimmed baking sheet. Bake for about 15 minutes. Shake the sheet occasionally so they cook evenly. Pour onto paper towels, then toss while still warm with a mixture of 1 teaspoon paprika, 1 teaspoon ground cumin, ½ teaspoon salt, and freshly ground pepper. Enjoy hot or store in an airtight container for a few days.

The fresh young leaves can be eaten in salads; you can pick off the chickpea tips to help thicken up the plants and cook them in boiling salted water for 5 to 6 minutes until tender. Drain well. Toss in melted butter or extra virgin olive oil.

When you cook chickpeas, cook twice the quantity you need. Cover generously with cold water, soak overnight, and drain. Cover with fresh water and cook for 40 to 50 minutes, or until soft and tender. If time allows, leave in the water to cool and they will swell even further. Drain and freeze so they are ready to use as needed. Save the cooking water as a vegetarian stock for soups and stews.

Hummus Bi Tahina

I think it was the lovely Claudia Roden who first introduced us to Hummus Bi Tahina, when she taught here at the Ballymaloe Cookery School in 1985. For us it was quite exotic then but it has since become a much-loved basic. Use as a dip, starter, or as part of a plate of mezze. Brands of tahini vary considerably; we find the less expensive brands best. How about a plate with moutabal (see page 243), roast peppers (see page 580), tzatziki, hummus, a few olives, and some flatbread.

SERVES 4 TO 8 (DEPENDING ON HOW IT IS SERVED)

1 cup dried chickpeas, soaked overnight
freshly squeezed juice of 2 or 3 lemons, or to taste
2 or 3 large or small garlic cloves, crushed
½ cup plus 2 tablespoons tahini
1 teaspoon freshly roasted and ground cumin seeds
sea salt
pita bread or crusty white bread, to serve

Drain the chickpeas, place in a saucepan, cover with fresh water and cook for about 20 minutes until tender. Drain the chickpeas and save the cooking liquid.

Put the chickpeas in a food processor with the lemon juice, crushed garlic, tahini, cumin, and salt to taste. Blend to a soft creamy paste, adding a little of the cooking liquid, if necessary. Taste and continue to add lemon juice and salt until you are happy with the flavor.

Serve with pita bread or crusty white bread for dipping.

Aracena Chicken with Chickpeas, Peppers & Rice Pilaf

A favorite chicken dish at Finca Buenvino in Andalucia, Spain. Chickpeas are used in myriad dishes in Spanish cuisine.

SERVES 6 TO 8

1 free-range, organic chicken, weighing approx. 4½ pounds

2 tablespoons extra virgin olive oil

1 onion, sliced

1 garlic clove, crushed

2 red bell peppers, seeded and sliced

2 green bell peppers, seeded and sliced

6 large tomatoes (dark red and very ripe) or 1 (14-ounce) can of chopped tomatoes

pinch of granulated sugar

½ teaspoon saffron

5 cups homemade chicken stock

1 cup dried chickpeas, soaked overnight and cooked in fresh water until fully tender, or 2 (14-ounce) cans chickpeas, drained

2 to 3 tablespoons chopped fresh marjoram

sea salt and freshly ground black pepper

fresh cilantro leaves, to garnish

green salad, to serve

FOR THE PILAF

2½ tablespoons butter

2 tablespoons minced onion or shallot

2 cups long-grain rice (preferably basmati)

4 cups homemade chicken stock

2 tablespoons chopped fresh herbs, such as parsley, thyme, chives (optional)

First cut the chicken into serving pieces: Take three pieces from the leg—one drumstick plus two pieces from the thigh. Divide the breast in two and detach the inner fillet: three pieces from the breast, two pieces from the wing.

Heat the olive oil in a sauté pan and sauté the chicken pieces for about 5 minutes in batches until golden on all sides. Season with salt and freshly ground pepper, remove from the pan and set aside.

Add the onion and garlic to the pan, cover, and sweat for 5 to 6 minutes until soft but not colored. Add the peppers to the onion, toss, cover, and continue to cook.

Meanwhile, peel the fresh tomatoes, if using —scald them in boiling water for 10 seconds, pour off the water, and peel immediately. Slice the tomatoes and add to the pan; season with salt, freshly ground pepper, and sugar.

Soak the saffron in a few tablespoons of warm chicken stock for 5 to 6 minutes. Add the chicken to the pan with the onion mixture, then add the saffron and the remainder of the stock. Bring back to a boil and continue to cook, covered, over low heat for 15 to 20 minutes. Add the drained chickpeas and lots of marjoram. Simmer for an additional 10 to 15 minutes or until fully cooked. Season to taste.

To make the pilaf, melt the butter in a casserole, add the minced onion or shallot, and sweat for 2 to 3 minutes. Add the rice and toss for a minute or two, just long enough for the grains to change color. Season with salt and freshly ground pepper, add the chicken stock, cover, and bring to a boil. Reduce the heat to low (or transfer to a preheated 325°F oven) and cook for about 10 minutes. By then the rice should be just cooked and all the water absorbed. (Basmati rice cooks quite quickly; other types of rice may take up to 15 minutes.) Just before serving stir in the fresh herbs, if using.

Serve in a large wide serving bowl or deep soup plates with the rice pilaf and lots of cilantro. Follow with a green salad.

CHICORY or Belgian Endive *Cichorium intybus var. sativum* PERENNIAL

When I write about chicory I am referring to Belgian endive, or witloof chicory, rather than frisée, the bitter greens so beloved of the French for winter salads. There's much confusion about the name because in France and Belgium, chicory is called endive. I grow both and though entirely different I love them equally, and of course enjoy them in different ways. It is perennial, but usually grown as an annual.

It takes considerably more effort and skill and may well not result in the plump, tightly packed, pale cream chicons we buy in the greengrocers, but nonetheless they will be delicious, and for me it's certainly worth the effort.

VARIETIES

Witloof de Brussels—Belgian chicory, traditional variety for forcing.
Perseo—Early variety with red and white leaves.
Bel Fiore—Lovely old variety with red, white and green leaves.

Wallonne—Robust traditional variety which resists the first frosts and can be grown outside in autumn. It's a strong grower that hearts up well.
Leonardo—lovely shades of maroon for spring nad fall harvest.

HOW TO GROW

There are two main types of *C.intylus*—curly endive or frisée (var. crispum). Both are cold-weather vegetables and both are usually blanched to give them a paler appearance and a milder, less bitter flavor.

Escarole, a broad-leaved endive (var. *latifolia*) is also called Batavian endive. It will have a paler green center if covered with a 7- to 10-inch plastic pot or a light saucepan lid to exclude the light, from two or three weeks before harvesting. The edges will be darker green and more curled.

Sow endive and or escarole in mid- to late spring before the last frost (difficult to predict in these days of climate change). Sow the seeds ¼ inch deep and 1 to 2 inches apart. Thin the seedlings to 8 to 12 inches apart, they need lots of room, and allow 18 to 24 inches between rows.

Both crops need rich, fertile, well-drained soil and full sun, ideally, with soil with a pH of 5 to 6.8. Add aged compost or humus to the soil before planting.

To produce—start as above, but Belgian endive needs to be forced to produce the blanched chicons we know as chicory. Although this can be done while the plants are still in the ground, by cutting off the leaves and earthing up the stumps, we achieve better results by digging them up in late autumn or early winter and bringing them indoors. Cut off all the leaves about 1 inch above the crown, then chop off the end of the root to leave about 15 to 8 inches. Pack them flat into a sandbox, so you can take out a few at a time to force. That way you won't have to worry about a glut.

Plant 3 to 5 in a 10-inch pot in moist potting compost, so the corms are just showing above the soil. Cover with an inverted pot. Black out any drainage holes with tape and keep in a warm dark place. The blanched chicons should be ready to harvest in 3 to 4 weeks.

CONTAINER GROWING

Both can be grown in containers or individually in 6 to 8 inch pots.

PESTS

Chicory seems very hardy but occasionally slugs and snails like to nibble the young leaves. Trap in the usual way—see page 626. Slugs, snails,

Far left: *Chicory ready for forcing.*
Left: *Chicory in prime condition for harvesting.*

aphids and cutworms can attack curly endive and escarole. If cutworms are a problem, put a collar around each plant to discourage an attack.

HARVESTING

Plants will be ready to harvest 50 to 100 days after planting. Harvest when they are 5 to 6 inches long. Cut 1 inch from the crown, just above soil level, and cover as before, they will re-sprout and reward you with a second harvest. You can also just snip off a few leaves at a time, rather than harvesting the whole plant.

GOOD FOR YOU...

Both curly endive and escarole contain vitamins C, E, folate, and beta-carotene and potassium. It is rich in protocatechuic acid, which has been shown to protect against atherosclerosis. It also contains other medicinally important compounds such as inulin,

bitter substances, coumarins and flavonoids. Although most of the health benefits are attributed to the root of the chicory plant, the leaves have been shown to have anti-helminthic and gastroprotective activities.

WHAT TO DO WITH A GLUT

I've never had a glut, but perhaps one could make a few gratins to freeze and use lots in winter salads. They keep well in a cold pantry or fridge, provided light is fully excluded.

IN THE KITCHEN

Chicory and Belgian endive must be stored in the dark, otherwise the light will cause the edges of the leaves to turn green and become extra bitter.

Belgian endive or chicory is also delicious in salad. I also love it braised slowly and in gratins. When I was an au-pair in France many years ago, Maman would wrap the boiled chicory in cooked

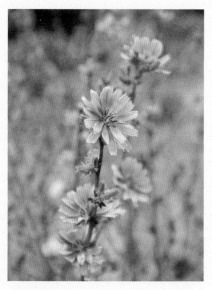

The pretty purply-blue flowers of chicory are an added bonus.

ham, then gratinate it in a bubbly cheese sauce with lots of Gruyère and Parmesan. Sooo good....

Braised Chicory

Slow gentle cooking in butter transforms the chicory into something melting and delicious—one of my absolute favorite winter vegetables.

SERVES 6

6 heads of chicory (Belgian endive—tightly closed with no trace of green at the tips)

2 teaspoons salt

1 teaspoon granulated sugar

good squeeze of lemon juice

1 to 2 tablespoons butter

chopped fresh flat-leaf parsley, to garnish

Remove a thin slice from the root end of each chicory. Remove the center root with the tip of a sharp knife if you find it too bitter. Bring 5 cups of water to a boil in a large saucepan, add the salt, sugar, and a good squeeze of lemon juice, then add the chicory and cook for about 45 minutes to 1 hour. Remove the chicory when it is tender and a knife tip will pierce the root end without resistance. Drain well and then squeeze out all excess water (I do this in a clean dishtowel).

Melt the butter in a wide sauté pan, put in the chicory in a single layer, and cook over very low heat, turning occasionally, until golden on all sides, about 45 minutes. Serve in a hot serving dish sprinkled with a little chopped parsley.

Chicory, Puy Lentils, Spring Onion, Avocado, Walnut & Pomegranate Salad

A delicious winter salad—perfect for a light but sustaining lunch.

SERVES 6 TO 8

¾ pound Puy lentils

¼ cup extra virgin olive oil

1 red or green chile, minced (perhaps a
   Hungarian Wax chile)

¼ cup freshly squeezed lemon juice

1 head of chicory (Belgian endive), sliced
   thinly across the grain

1 pomegranate, cut in half and seeds
   removed

4 spring onions, sliced on the diagonal

2 ripe Hass avocados, pitted, peeled, and
   diced

12 walnuts, shelled and toasted

lots of flat parsley and/or wild arugula
   leaves

sea salt and freshly ground black pepper

Cook the lentils in boiling salted water for 15 to 20 minutes or until just tender, drain, and toss in the extra virgin olive oil, chile, and freshly squeezed lemon juice. Season with salt and freshly ground pepper and taste—it should be highly flavored. Let cool.

Add the chicory, pomegranate seeds, spring onions, and avocado to the lentils. Toss, and season to taste. Scatter with the toasted walnuts and lots of parsley or wild arugula leaves.

Broiled Chicory or Radicchio

I like to serve this on a plate of antipasto, which might include some broiled peppers with basil, a crumbled slice of speck or prosciutto, a few black olives, and a slice of grilled bread.

SERVES 6

6 perfect plump heads of chicory (Belgian
   endive) or radicchio Trevisano, trimmed
   and cut in half lengthwise

extra virgin olive oil

sea salt and freshly ground black pepper

Preheat the broiler.

Make little cuts in the root part of the chicory so that the heat and oil can penetrate. Arrange the halves cut-side up in a broiler pan and paint with olive oil. Sprinkle with salt and pepper and put under the hot broiler. After 7 to 8 minutes turn the chicory over and brush the top sides with oil. Cook for an additional 7 to 8 minutes, and then turn again, basting with the oil in the pan and adding more if necessary. You may need to cook for an additional 5 to 8 minutes depending on size. It is cooked when the root end can be pierced easily with the tip of a knife.

Serve hot or lukewarm, as an accompanying vegetable or as part of a starter. Crumbled blue cheese melting over the top makes a memorable supper.

Chicory Tarte Tatin

This delicious chicory tart has converted even the most determined chicory hater. I like to serve it with a watercress salad scattered with a few little crumbles of blue cheese and toasted walnuts.

SERVES 6

6 or 7 heads of chicory (Belgian endive—tightly closed with no trace of green)

2 teaspoons salt

1 teaspoon granulated sugar, plus 2 tablespoons

good squeeze of lemon juice

1/4 to 1/3 cup butter

9 ounces Puff Pastry (see below)

FOR THE PUFF PASTRY

1 pound chilled flour (use bread flour if possible), plus extra for dusting

pinch of salt

1 to 1 1/4 cups cold water, depending on the flour

squeeze of lemon juice (optional)

1 pound butter, firm but pliable

To make the puff pastry, sift the flour and salt into a bowl and mix to a firm dough with water and a squeeze of lemon juice, if using. This dough is called detrempe. Cover tightly with parchment paper or plastic wrap and chill for 30 minutes.

Roll the detrempe into a square about 1/3 inch thick. Shape the butter into a slab roughly 3/4 inch thick, place in the center of the dough and fold the dough over the edges of the butter to make a neat parcel. Make sure your work surface is well floured, then flatten the dough with a rolling pin, and roll out into a rectangle about 18 inches long and 6 inches wide. Fold like an envelope neatly into three with the sides as accurately aligned as possible. Seal the edges with a rolling pin.

Give the dough a one-quarter turn (90 degrees), it should now be on your work surface as though it was a book with the open ends facing north/south. Roll out again, fold in three, and seal the edges with the rolling pin. Cover with plastic wrap or parchment paper and chill for 30 minutes.

The pastry has now had two rolls or "turns". Repeat the rolling process another two times giving the dough six rolls in total with a 30 minute rest in the fridge between every two turns. In hot weather it may be necessary to rest the pastry for longer between rollings. Chill for at least 30 minutes before using.

Remove a thin slice from the root end of each chicory. Remove the center root with the tip of a sharp knife if you find it too bitter. Bring 5 cups of water to a boil, add the salt, sugar, and a good squeeze of lemon juice, add the chicory, and cook for 30 to 45 minutes or until almost completely tender. Remove the chicory when it is tender and a knife tip will pierce the root end without resistance. Drain well then squeeze out all excess water (I do this in a clean dishtowel).

Melt 1 to 2 tablespoons of the butter in an ovenproof skillet, put in the chicory in a single layer, and cook over low heat for 20 minutes, turning occasionally.

Melt 4 tablespoons of the butter with the sugar in an 8-inch sauté pan and stir over medium heat until it is almost caramelized. Arrange the chicons on top in a single layer and continue to cook gently to caramelize a little more.

Preheat the oven to 425°F. Meanwhile, roll the chilled pastry into a round, slightly larger than the pan (about 2 3/4 inches), a scant 1/3 inch thick, and lay it on top of the chicory. Tuck in the edges and prick with a fork.

Put the skillet in the oven for 25 to 30 minutes until the pastry is cooked and the chicory is tender. Reduce the temperature to 400°F after 10 minutes. Remove from the oven and rest for 5 to 10 minutes, or longer if you like. Put a plate over the top of the saucepan and flip the tart on to a serving plate. Reshape the tart if necessary. Serve warm.

SEA KALE   *Crambe maritima* PERENNIAL, ZONES 4–9

Another of our all-time favorites, sea kale is a brassica which grows naturally around the coasts of the British Isles as well as on the shores of the North Atlantic, although it has become quite rare. Sea kale is an exquisite vegetable, delicate and rarely found in the shops, so for that reason alone, it's worth trying to find a space for this hardy perennial.

VARIETIES
You may find some plants in a specialist garden center, otherwise grow from seed.

HOW TO GROW
Not surprisingly, sea kale likes sandy soil. We grow from seed but, if you can, buy plants (known as thongs or crowns) as it speeds the process by several years.

Allow to harden off and then transplant into the permanent position. Plant 3 or 4 clumps in a sandy loam about 20 to 24 inches apart. Don't pick the first year and take just a few stalks in

It's best to stop sea kale from flowering to strengthen the plant for following years.

year two to allow the plant to establish.

It will have lots of pretty white flowers in the summer followed by bobbly seed heads which are decorative in themselves. However, it's best not to let the flowers develop as too much energy will be taken from the plant, so we cut them off before they open. The green leaves are edible but fairly tough.

In early spring, just before the sea kale starts to sprout, cover the plants to start the blanching. There's a choice of beautiful lidded terracotta pots or black plastic bins which look ugly but work brilliantly—top with a heavy concrete block to keep from blowing away.

We mulch sea kale with seaweed and compost which also helps to keep the covers and bins tight. The expensive terracotta pots are ideal because they not only look good, but are also practical as you can lift easily to take a peek at the progress of the plant.

The spears blanch to the palest yellow when all the light is excluded and are delicate, tender and delicious.

We mulch around the covers with cinders from the coal fire in the winter, as this helps to add potash to the soil.

CONTAINER GROWING
It is possible to grow sea kale in containers; we planted in large terracotta pots as more ornamental than functional plants outside the School entrance.

HARVESTING
Harvest in late spring and early summer. Use a sharp knife to harvest the sea kale with a clean cut into the stump. Resist the temptation to cut all the stalks, leave

A sea kale plant that wasn't fully covered, but the leaves are also edible.

at least a quarter to feed the plant for the following year. Then remove the cover to allow the plant to recover and build up strength for the following year.

PESTS AND DISEASES
Watch out for slugs, though they don't do much damage. Sea kale is disease- and cabbage moth–resistant.

GOOD FOR YOU...
Sea kale is high in vitamin C, so the Romans preserved it in barrels for sea voyages as it helped to prevent scurvy.

WHAT TO DO WITH A GLUT?
One can never have enough, feast on sea kale when it's in season.

IN THE KITCHEN
To serve 4 to 6, trim 1 pound sea kale into lengths about 4 inches. Pop into boiling salted water to cover and cook for 5 to 15 minutes until tender. Just as soon as a knife will pierce the sea kale easily, drain and serve on hot plates with ¼ to ⅓ cup melted butter and perhaps a few small triangles of toast.

Sea Kale on Toast with Shrimp & Hollandaise

The cooking time depends on the freshness of the sea kale, as you can imagine. Cooked mussels are also delicious here.

. . . .

SERVES 4 TO 6

1 pound sea kale
1 teaspoon salt
2½ tablespoons butter
18 large shrimp, cooked and peeled
6 slices of toast, buttered
small bunch of chervil, to garnish

FOR THE HOLLANDAISE SAUCE
2 organic egg yolks
2½ teaspoons cold water
½ cup (1 stick) butter, cut into cubes
approx. 1 teaspoon freshly squeezed
   lemon juice

Wash the sea kale gently and trim into manageable lengths—about 4 inches. Bring 2½ cups of water to a fast boil and add the salt. Add the sea kale, cover, and boil for 4 to 5 minutes until tender. The cooking time depends on the freshness of the sea kale. Just as soon as a knife will pierce the sea kale easily, drain it.

Meanwhile, melt the butter in a pan over low heat and toss in the shrimp to warm through.

To make the hollandaise, put the egg yolks in a heavy stainless-steel saucepan over low heat, or in a bowl over a saucepan of barely simmering water. Add the water and whisk thoroughly. Add the butter bit by bit, whisking all the time. As soon as one piece melts, add the next piece. The mixture will gradually thicken, but if it shows signs of becoming too thick or slightly scrambling, remove from the heat immediately and add a little cold water if necessary. Do not leave the pan or stop whisking until the sauce is made. Finally, add the lemon juice to taste.

Serve the sea kale with the shrimp on hot buttered toast, and drizzle generously with hollandaise sauce. Pop a little bunch of chervil on top of each toast and serve immediately.

Sea Kale Tempura with Chervil Mayonnaise

I love vegetables dipped in a tempura batter. If you have a surplus of sea kale this recipe is another way to enjoy this precious and sublime vegetable.

. . . .

SERVES 6 TO 8 AS A STARTER

2 tablespoons cornstarch
1 cup iced water
scant 1 cup all-purpose flour
1 pound sea kale
sunflower oil, for frying
8 ounces homemade mayonnaise
lots of finely chopped chervil
pinch of flaky sea salt

First prepare the batter. Mix the cornstarch into the water. Put the flour in a bowl and add the water gradually, stirring with chopsticks; it will be a bit lumpy at first but it will eventually be a light creamy texture. You may need to add a drop more water or flour to get a thin even coating batter. Season with salt.

Heat the oil in a deep-fryer to 350°F.

Trim the sea kale and cut into 4- to 4½-inch pieces. Dip one piece into the batter and fry for a couple of minutes or until crisp but not brown. Taste for seasoning and adjust the batter if necessary. Continue to cook the remaining mixture in the same way and drain the fritters on paper towels.

Thin the mayonnaise with a little water to a dip-like consistency. Add lots of finely chopped chervil and a nice sprinkling of flaky sea salt.

Serve the crisp tempura immediately with a little bowl of chervil mayonnaise.

CUCUMBERS *Cucumis sativus* ANNUAL

Cucumbers are just as easy to grow as tomatoes and the texture and the flavor bears no resemblance to the watery version we are subjected to for most of the year in the shops. They are members of the huge Cucurbit family, which includes squashes, pumpkins, melons, and gourds. They are mostly large-leaved and thrive in the heat, needing at least 65°F to grow, and none is frost-hardy. The modern greenhouse varieties don't need pollinating, but some of the very old varieties might.

VARIETIES

Both indoor and outdoor varieties are available. Choose those that suit your situation; I particularly love the flavor of small Lebanese cucumbers, 5 to 6 inches long, green-skinned with white flesh. Sometimes known as Oriental cucumbers, the skin is tender so doesn't need peeling.

INDOOR
Katrina—High-yielding early to midseason crop.

Izniko—Miniature variety and a prolific cropper. It's ready to eat in early summer, a couple of weeks before the main crop. They are a perfect size to tuck into children's lunchboxes.

OUTDOOR
The traditional cucumbers were "ridge" varieties, while the modern ones have a smoother skin.
Lemon—A yellow-colored cucumber. Not my favorite as I find the skin quite tough, but others love it.
Minature White—Small, mild, white-skinned variety, sweet tasting, low in acid and easy to digest.
Diva—exceptionally flavorful, tender, and sweet. High resistance to scab.

HOW TO GROW

Sow seeds individually on their sides in late spring into 3 ½-inch pots in the greenhouse or indoors. Cucumbers need fertile, well-drained soil in full sun because they are vigorous growers. We prepare the ground by putting a layer of humus on the surface and then rotavate it in. We also sprinkle chicken manure pellets on the ground to balance the nutrients. Transfer the plants into the ground, 18 to 24 inches apart, after all danger of frost has passed, which can be into early summer. Keep well-watered. Water around the base of the plants rather than on the leaves.

Outdoor varieties may be planted directly into the warm, fertile soil in early summer, 18 inches apart and the same between rows, or they can be planted in tepee fashion. They like full sun and a sheltered site. Train up string, wire or bamboo poles and twist clockwise around the support. When the plant reaches the top of the wire, stop it by pinching out the top, and leave the side shoots to grow. Feed the cucumbers every 10 to 14 days with a balanced liquid organic fertilizer—we use liquid seaweed. We only grow cucumbers in the greenhouse.

CONTAINER GROWING

Cucumbers can also be grown in pots or growbags. The miniature variety Piccolino works particularly well.

PESTS

Red spider mite is by far the biggest problem. Avoid that by growing your own plants from seed, rather than buying plants which may harbor red spider.

Winter hygiene is incredibly important for disease control. We power hose the greenhouse meticulously, knowing that if you are less than vigilant, bugs like red spider mite and whitefly can over-winter in cracks and crevices.

Cucumbers fattening on the vine.

Bury the string underneath the plant to anchor it and act as a support to climb up.

HARVESTING

Pick when fully mature, the end of the cucumber will be rounded rather than pointed.

Snip or cut *Piccolino* off the plant when it is 4 to 5 inches long, or 7 to 9 inches for larger varieties, when they are crisp and delicious. This will encourage the plant to produce more and more. Even if you have a glut, don't leave them on the plant, they just swell and the skin toughens. They become more watery and will lower the plant's productivity.

GOOD FOR YOU...

Cucumbers contain several B vitamins—B1, B5 (pantothenic acid) and B7 (biotin), also copper, potassium, manganese, phosphorus and magnesium, as well as vitamin C. They also contain silica, which helps promote healthy nail growth.

WHAT TO DO WITH A GLUT

Make cucumber, chile and mustard seed pickle, soup or cucumber lemonade.

IN THE KITCHEN

Dainty cucumber sandwiches were always a traditional part of afternoon tea. Many people eat cucumbers raw in salads, sandwiches, or soups. We love to cook them in lots of different ways. They are delicate, as you can imagine, but they absorb different flavors deliciously. One of the simplest and tastiest ways to cook either sliced or diced cucumbers is in a covered saucepan or casserole, tossed in a very little melted butter or extra virgin olive oil. Season well with salt and freshly ground pepper, cover, and cook over low heat for 5 to 6 minutes until just knife tender and juicy. A little snipped fennel, dill, tarragon, thyme, or chives can be added.

This delicate vegetable complements fish deliciously. **Cucumber Neapolitana** is another of my all-time favorites. The flowers and shoots are also edible and leaves can be cooked down like spinach, but you'd need to be hungry to enjoy their slightly acrid flavor.

To use up a glut, make **Nordic Cucumber Pickle** to serve 8 to 10. Combine 2¼ pounds unpeeled, sliced cucumbers, and 3 small thinly sliced onions in a large bowl. Mix 1 cup sugar, 2 level tablespoons of pure salt and 1 cup apple cider vinegar together and pour over the cucumbers. Place in a tightly covered container in the fridge and leave for at least 4 to 5 hours or overnight before using. This keeps well for up to a week in the fridge. (When we have our home-grown organic cucumbers we find that we need to reduce the sugar by ¼ cup or more.)

A **Cooler of Cucumber Sandwiches** is a long tradition in the Allen family, used for posh afternoon teas, children's tea, and picnics. To serve approx. 8, insert a long sharp knife into the side just above the bottom crust of a 2-pound pan-baked bread or a round country loaf. Push it through until it reaches, but does not go through, the crust on the far side. Without making any bigger the cut through which the knife was inserted, work the knife in a fan shape as far forward as possible, then pull it out. Do the same from the opposite end of the loaf. The bread should now be cut away from the bottom crust inside without a noticeable mark on the exterior of the loaf. Next, cut through the top of the loaf to make a lid, carefully leaving one long side uncut, as a hinge. With the lid open, cut the bread away from the sides. Ease out carefully, you should have a solid brick or round, with an empty case.

Mash 2 or 3 anchovies finely (this is optional) and mix with approx. ¼ cup butter. Anchovy butter gives a delicious saltiness to the cucumber sandwiches.

Cut it into slices—long horizontal ones, square vertical ones, or rounds, depending on the shape of the loaf. Carefully stack them, then butter each slice. Use a cheese slicer to cut long strands of cucumber; lay them side by side on the bread. Season with sea salt and freshly ground black pepper; top with another slice of bread. Continue with the remainder. Press together firmly, cut into finger sandwiches, and put them back, in order, into the loaf.

Pan-Grilled Fish with Vietnamese Cucumbers

This cucumber salad is quite delicious and can also be served with chicken or lamb or smoked fish. Pan-grilling is one of my favorite ways to cook fish, meat, and vegetables.

. . . .

SERVES 8 TO 10

8 (6-ounce) very fresh fish fillets, such as
  mackerel, gray sea mullet, cod, sea bass,
  or haddock
seasoned flour
small knob of butter (soft)

FOR THE VIETNAMESE CUCUMBERS

4 cucumbers
a little fish sauce (nam pla)
1-inch piece of fresh ginger, peeled and
  cut into fine julienne
2 tablespoons palm sugar
1 o 2 serrano, jalapeño, or fresh Thai chiles
juice of 2 to 3 limes
a handful of fresh mint, roughly chopped
a handful of basil, roughly chopped
thinly sliced scallions
sea salt and freshly ground black pepper

To make the Vietnamese cucumbers, peel the cucumbers, cut them lengthwise in half, and remove the seeds with a spoon if they are large. Slice the cucumbers into thickish half-moons and put them in a large bowl. Season with salt and pepper, sprinkle lightly with fish sauce, then add the ginger and palm sugar. Toss well, and leave the cucumbers to sit for 5 minutes or so.

Add a good spoonful of the chopped serrano or jalapeño chiles (seeds removed, if desired) or finely slivered Thai chiles. Squeeze over the juice of 2 limes and toss again, then cover and refrigerate until ready to serve.

Heat a grill pan. Dry the fish fillets well. Just before cooking, but not earlier, dip the fish fillets in flour which has been well seasoned with salt and freshly ground pepper. Pass the floured fillet between the palms of your hands to shake off the excess flour and then spread a little soft butter evenly over the entire surface of the flesh side, as though you were buttering a slice of bread rather thinly. When the grill is hot but not smoking, place the fish fillets butter-side down on the grill; the fish should sizzle as soon as they touch the pan. Reduce the heat slightly and cook for 4 to 5 minutes (time depends on the thickness of the fish). Turn over and cook on the other side for 2 to 3 minutes until crisp and golden. (Be sure to wash and dry the grill pan each time between batches.)

Just before serving, add a fistful of roughly chopped mint and basil leaves and some spring onions to the cucumbers. Taste and add more lime juice or seasoning if necessary. Serve the fish on a hot plate with the Vietnamese cucumbers.

Cucumber Limeade

A great way to use up a glut of cucumbers—fresh-tasting and tangy.

. . . .

MAKES 6 CUPS/SERVES APPROX. 6

2 large cucumbers, coarsely chopped
juice of 4 lemons and 2 limes or 5 lemons
a handful of fresh mint leaves, plus extra
  to garnish
1¼ cups simple syrup (page 290)
2½ cups still or sparkling water
lots of ice

Combine all the ingredients, except the ice, in a blender or food processor and blend until smooth. Strain through a nylon or stainless-steel sieve. Pour into a pitcher over ice and serve garnished with fresh mint leaves.

PUMPKIN, SQUASH & ZUCCHINI *Cucurbitaceae* ANNUAL

Everyone loves pumpkins and squashes, they bring out the inner child and I can hardly bear to harvest them. The seeds are large, so these are the perfect plants to sow with children who love to watch their seedlings emerge, and then there's the anticipation of Hallowe'en pumpkin carving.

Of all the families of fruit and vegetables, pumpkins and squashes must surely be the most confusing. Not only are there hundreds of varieties but some go by a multitude of names.

Roughly they seem to divide into three categories, depending on when they ripen.

Botanically speaking they are all members of the Cucurbitaceae family, a huge family of 965 species which also includes cucumbers, melons and decorative gourds. The majority of the summer squash are native to Central America and Mexico, while many of the winter squash originated in the Argentine Andes. We grow a selection every year, not just for cooking and carving, but for their "wow" factor when people walk through the vegetable garden into the greenhouse, where they sprawl in all directions. They clamber up the supports and look like an enchanted forest.

VARIETIES

They fall into three main categories: summer squashes and pumpkins; winter squashes and pumpkins; and edible gourds.

SUMMER SQUASH—*CUCURBITA PEPO*

It also includes the bright orange pumpkins that are often used for carving at Halloween, as well as many of the recognizable varieties like spaghetti and yellow summer squashes.

Tromboncino—Italian heirloom variety, also known as zuccheta, mainly used as a summer squash. Grows as a vine. It's a cultivar of Cucurbita moschata (butternut squash), while most summer squash come from Cucurbita pepo.

Lebanese white bush squash—Originated in Lebanon, it's sometimes known as "Lubnani" squash. Sweet and mild flavor.

Little Gem—Dark green/black tasty little squash the size of a cricket ball, matures in early/ late summer and can be stored until early winter. The deep yellow flesh is moist and sweet. They can be boiled whole and eaten with butter and cinnamon. Very popular in South Africa.

Zucchini are also part of this family—they come in green, yellow, and striped forms.

Cocozelle—Striped zucchini with a superior flavor, often seen in Mediterranean markets.

Dunja F1—New variety that produces good crops of dark zucchini, it has good disease and mildew resistance.

Partenon F1—Good for early sowing, high-yielding, dark green glossy zucchini.

Nero di Milano—Medium early, dark green, almost black zucchini.

Gold Rush—Lovely yellow-skinned zucchini, good texture and flavor, high yielding.

Spaghetti squash—Oval-shaped pale yellow squash with flesh that forms long spaghetti-like strands when cooked. Bake or boil, then serve with a gutsy Bolognese-type sauce or a garlic and parsley butter.

WINTER SQUASH

So-called not because they grow through the winter but because they survive through the winter as they have a hard rind.

Cucurbita moschata—This group includes the "cheese" pumpkin which is used for canned pumpkin. The Crookneck squashes and the familiar butternut squash fall into this category, too. These pumpkins may be eaten young but can also be stored.

Cucurbita maxima—As the name hints, the monster pumpkins fall into this

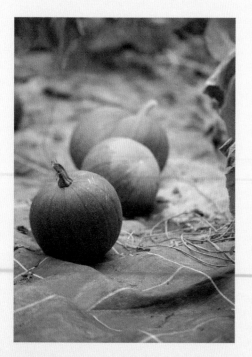

Small sugar squash on the floor of the greenhouse.

category. They can weigh over 100lb. They usually have thick skin and keep well.

Calabash is a vine grown for its fruits; when it's harvested young the shoots and fruit can be eaten. It can also be left to mature and dried out as a container, like a gourd.

Acorn—Named for its shape, dark green skin is most common but it also comes in shades of orange and cream, with a sweet, pale yellow flesh.

Hubbard—An old favorite, shaped a bit like a spinning top, pale green to bluey-grey with dull orange flesh. Good for baking, roasting, soups or add chunks into winter stews.

Delicata—Another of my favorites, with green, cream, yellow and orange stripes. Try to find small ones for their dry, sweet-tasting flesh—great for baking and stuffing.

Turk's Turban—Very decorative and easy to recognise, so beautiful you'll be reluctant to cook this vividly colored, striped squash. The flesh is bland and stringy and certainly not as tasty as some of the other varieties, but artists love to paint it.

Butternut squash—Smooth, pale-tan skin, longish neck, excellent flavor and texture.

HOW TO GROW

Squash comes in both bush and vine forms, both are easy to grow and a few plants will provide you with enough squash to share with all your family and friends.

Plant seeds indoors in late spring and plant out in early summer. They need fertile, well-manured and moisture-retentive soil. Avoid planting in shade. Space the plants 3 feet apart each way, overcrowding the plants may contribute to the development of powdery mildew. They are thirsty plants, so water regularly during dry spells, but avoid

overhead watering. Don't let them dry out. Mulching around the plants also helps but be careful not to put the mulch directly in contact with the stems.

Trailing varieties can be supported with netting, or planted adjacent to runner beans or corn which will help to support them. All pumpkins will trail upwards, but because of their weight they need support—we use sheepwire for this.

The Curcubitaceae family—melons, gourds, cucumber, squash and pumpkin—is fascinating for many reasons, not just the variety but because, unlike a tomato plant, for example, that has male and female parts in each flower, it carries separate male and female flowers on the same plant, but only the female flower will form fruit. They have a poor reputation for pollination.

In an optimum situation bees and other pollinating insects will transfer pollen from the stamens of the male flower to the stigma of the female flower, but how do you recognise a male and female flower? The male flower grows on a stalk and has a pistil inside;

Potimarron squash.

the female flower grows from the swollen ovary (looks like a small fruit) and has a stigma with three little ? Both flowers are yellow. If you have just a few plants, to ensure pollination in an area where there is a dearth of pollinating insects, hand pollination can be the solution.

Pick off a male flower. Carefully remove the petals from the base to expose the pestil or anther brush. Identify a female flower, then gently apply the "brush" to stigma of the female flower.

After pollination the ovary will begin to swell and the fruit will develop. If fertilization doesn't happen the ovary will just wither away. Alternatively, one can use a small paint brush or cotton buds to transfer the pollen. This is a fun thing to do, particularly when you have just a few plants—children are fascinated by the process too, and it's a simple way to explain about the birds and the bees!

Gold Rush yellow summer squash—brilliant and flavorsome yields.

CONTAINER GROWING
The moderately vigorous squash, pumpkins, and zucchini can be grown in growbags and roomy containers in rich soil. Keep them well-watered and hand-pollinate for a bountiful crop.

PESTS AND DISEASES
Young plants can be susceptible to attack from slugs and snails. Aphids can sometimes lodge in the soft growth at the tips, so be vigilant. Red spider mite and whitefly can be problem on indoor plants in tunnels and greenhouses, but not usually on plants grown outdoors in our climate. Powdery mildew can attack plants that are suffering stress from drought, so when planting incorporate some compost or well-rotted manure to help retain moisture.

HARVESTING
All parts of the squash family are edible; you may not fancy the leaves, but don't miss out on the flowers. It's usually better to harvest the male blossoms (the females have the fruit on the end), but be sure to leave a few on the plant to ensure pollination.

Harvest zucchini and summer squash when they are young and tender, so cut them when they are 4 to 5 inches long. Harvest pumpkins and winter squash from late summer onwards, but for optimum flavor don't harvest winter squash until there's been a cold snap, as a touch of frost enhances their sugar content. Winter squash harvested unblemished will keep in a cool, dark place, such as a garage or garden shed, for up to 6 months, or in some cases over a year.

DID YOU KNOW?
Squashes originated in the Andes and are believed to be some of the oldest crops on Earth, their origins can be traced back 10,000 years to MesoAmerica, when they arrived in Europe in the sixteenth century, soon after the discovery of the New World. The seeds were also pounded with oatmeal and applied to the skin to bleach freckles....

They are one of the three legendary crops, which, together with beans and corn (referred to as the three sisters) were traditionally grown by the Native Americans, who eventually shared them with the European settlers.

The loofah or luffa is also a member of the *Cucurbitaceae* family.

GOOD FOR YOU...
Somehow I'd always supposed that squash and pumpkins weren't up to much nutritionally but, on the contrary, apparently a study done at the University of Davis in California, found winter squash to be among the most nutritious vegetables, rivalling cabbage, carrots, spinach and potatoes. They are a tasty source of complex carbohydrates and fiber and provide iron, niacin and potassium. The orange flesh is high in beta carotene, a rich source of vitamin A, and the more orange the flesh the higher the content. Understandably, different types of squash have varying nutritional content but all are impressively nourishing. The skin of summer squash is particularly rich in antioxidants, so for maximum benefit, it's best not to peel.

WHAT TO DO WITH A GLUT
Smaller zucchini are best eaten young and tender; if you let them grow into "marrows" they will keep in a cold shed for months, but not as long as pumpkins. The true vegetable is a separate variety, which lovers of marrow and ginger jam insist on using as the best option. Zucchini can be frozen in slices for a winter vegetable, but honestly this isn't worth doing.

A glut of pumpkins can be used as gifts and for decoration at Hallowe'en. You can, of course, make pumpkin soup with some of them and freeze it, or make chutney. Pumpkins will keep until at least mid-winter in a frost-free shed. Unlike winter squash, summer squash cannot be stored for long periods of time.

IN THE KITCHEN
We pile pumpkins, squash, and zucchini up on the windows, in the conservatory, and on the ledges in the school in autumn, and we incorporate them into our meals in myriad ways almost every day—roasted, stuffed, steamed, and pickled, and in stews, casseroles, soups (using the hollowed-out pumpkin as a container), pies, gratins, muffins, and jams. They gratefully take a variety of flavors, spices, and herbs, and are perhaps the most versatile and beautiful plants we grow.

For **Whole Baked Pumpkin or Squash** to serve a soup or stew in, slice a nice lid off the top, preferably with the stalk attached. Scoop out the seeds and then most of the flesh, being careful not to damage the outer wall and rind. Drizzle a little oil inside and season with salt and freshly ground pepper. Preheat the oven to 350°F. Put the pumpkin on a baking sheet. Cook for 5 to 10 minutes, just enough to heat through to serve a soup inside. If, however, you would like to fill it with a stew, cook for 35 to 40 minutes or until the flesh is tender, then carefully transfer to a serving plate. Fill with hot stew or tagine. Garnish with flat-leaf parsley and serve immediately with a salad of organic leaves.

Roast Pumpkin Seeds with salt or sugar and add them to breakfast cereals, breads, or salads, or simply nibble on them to your heart's content. (Alternatively, dry the seeds and save for next year's crop.) Split the pumpkin, scoop out the seeds, and wash off the fibers. Bring the pumpkin seeds to a boil in a saucepan of salted water (1 teaspoon salt for every 5 cups water). Simmer for 10 minutes. Preheat the oven to 250°F. Drain the seeds, dry, and toss in a tiny amount of oil—½ to 1 teaspoon is enough for 1 pumpkin. Sprinkle lightly with sea salt and toss again. Spread in a single layer on a baking sheet. Dry roast for 30 to 35 minutes, then check after 30 minutes; they should be nice and crunchy. Cool and store in an airtight jar; they will keep up to 3 months at room temperature and longer in the fridge. They can also be tossed in a mixture of spices, such as cumin and coriander, or a mixture of sugar and cinnamon or ginger before roasting.

For a simple **Zucchini Salad** for 4 to 6, separate the flowers from 8 small

Squash thriving happily in an old drum.

zucchini (4 to 6 inches long). Remove the stamens and little thorns from the base of the flowers. Plunge the whole zucchini into boiling salted water and poach them for 4 to 5 minutes until barely tender. Remove from the pot and let cool slightly. While still warm, slice them at an angle to yield six slices from each zucchini. Season the zucchini slices with flaky sea salt and freshly ground pepper and then sprinkle with extra virgin olive oil. Toss gently and serve immediately, sprinkled with fresh basil leaves and surrounded by the torn zucchini flowers. Hot crusty bread is the only accompaniment needed.

The blossoms of all the Cucurbitaceae family are edible and delicious and are available in markets around the world. **Squash or Zucchini Blossoms** are also a favorite filling for quesadillas in Mexico, served with salsa. The golden petals look wonderfully exotic in green salads. For a really impressive first course, stuff each blossom with a little soft goat cheese or mozzarella and a dab of pesto and perhaps a morsel of anchovy or sun-blushed tomato.

We also love them in **Fritto Misto**— twist the tops of the petals together to seal, dip in a light batter, and deep-fry quickly in hot oil. Serve immediately while they are crisp and plump.

Zucchini Trifolati

Usually we are super careful not to overcook zucchini, but here the magic is in cooking them to meltingly tender. This favorite Italian method of cooking zucchini was taught to us by Gillian Hegarty, who cooked at The River Café, in London, for many years. It is delicious with fish, chicken, lamb, and shellfish.

SERVES 4

2 tablespoons extra virgin olive oil
6 medium green and yellow zucchini, cut at an angle into ¼-inch-thick pieces
2 garlic cloves, minced
1 teaspoon fennel seeds, toasted and ground
pinch of chile flakes
10 basil leaves
10 mint leaves
squash or zucchini blossoms (if available)
flaky sea salt and freshly ground black pepper

Choose a heavy-bottomed sauté pan that will hold the zucchini comfortably; they shouldn't come higher than 1½ inches up the side of the sauté pan. I like to slice the zucchini and put them in the pan first to check. If there are too many layers of zucchini in the pan they will stew and if there are not enough then the zucchini will dry out and burn.

Heat the pan over high heat and once it is hot, add the oil, quickly followed by the zucchini. Stir, making sure all the zucchini have been coated in the oil, and fry until golden brown. Then add the garlic, fennel, and chile flakes and continue to cook for 5 minutes over high heat. Season well with salt and pepper. If it's starting to stick to the pan at this stage, add a few tablespoons of water.

Reduce the heat to low, cover with a tight-fitting lid, and cook for 5 to 10 minutes. When the zucchini are soft and tender, tear in the mint and basil leaves and a few zucchini blossoms if you have them. Add 1 tablespoon of your best extra virgin olive oil. Season to taste. The zucchini should be soft, juicy, and full of flavor but not al dente.

Serve as an accompaniment to fish, chicken, lamb, or shellfish.

Zucchini Blossoms with Tuma & Anchovies

Zucchini flowers are widely enjoyed in Italian and Sicilian cooking, sometimes just dipped in batter and fried without any filling and served as part of a Fritto Misto—use the male flowers here rather than the female flowers, which produce the fruit. Tuma is a fresh sheep's milk cheese made by Sicilian shepherds, but buffalo mozzarella would make a good substitute. We also love a washed-rind cheese like an Irish Durrus or Gubbeen.

SERVES 6

2½ to 4 ounces Tuma or mozzarella
12 anchovies
12 freshly picked male zucchini blossoms
olive oil, for frying
FOR THE BATTER
1½ cups beer
1 cup semolina flour
good pinch of salt

Cut the cheese into little strips that will fit into the blossom and tuck an anchovy and a little strip of cheese into each flower.

Pour 1½ to 2 inches of oil into a deep skillet and heat to 350°F.

Meanwhile, make a simple batter by whisking beer into the durum flour until it's a light coating consistency. Add a good pinch of salt.

When the oil is hot, dip one flower at a time into the batter, twisting the ends as you slip it gently into the hot oil. Cook a few at a time, turning them over after a minute or two to crisp the other side, drain on paper towels, and serve immediately.

Roasted Stuffed Marrow

This recipe is best when made with a proper old-fashioned marrow, but if you can't get your hands on one, then it's the perfect way to make an entire meal of and add lots of badly needed flavor to an overblown zucchini. You can dream up all sorts of stuffings, but they should be tasty and well-seasoned; otherwise the end result can be exceedingly dull. Here I'm using a Duck Shepherd's Pie mix, but lamb or beef would, of course, be wonderfully comforting.

. . . .

SERVES 8 TO 10

1 marrow or very large zucchini, weighing approx. 5½ pounds

1 or 2 sprigs of marjoram (optional)

1¾ ounces cheddar cheese, grated

¾ ounce buttered crumbs (page 190)

sea salt and freshly ground black pepper

FOR THE STUFFING

2 tablespoons butter or 3 to 4 tablespoons extra virgin olive oil

6 ounces chopped onions

scant ¼ cup all-purpose flour

1¾ cups homemade lamb, chicken, or vegetable stock and leftover gravy

1 teaspoon tomato paste

1–2 tablespoons chopped chiles and/or sriracha sauce

2 teaspoons chopped curly parsley

1 teaspoon thyme leaves

1 pound minced cooked duck (including some crispy skin)

FOR THE MORNAY SAUCE

2½ cups milk

a few slices of carrot and onion

3 or 4 peppercorns

a sprig of thyme and parsley

approx. 3 tablespoons roux (page 267)

1¾ ounces Gruyère cheese, grated

½ ounce Parmesan cheese, grated

¼ teaspoon mustard, preferably Dijon

Preheat the oven to 350°F.

First make the stuffing. Melt the butter or extra virgin olive oil in a saucepan, add the onions, cover with a round of greased parchment paper cut to fit the pan, and cook over low heat for 5 minutes. Add the flour, stir well, and cook until slightly brown, 2 to 3 minutes. Add the tomato paste, chiles and/or sriracha, chopped parsley, thyme leaves, salt, and pepper and simmer for 5 minutes. Add the minced duck to the sauce and bring to a boil.

Split the marrow in half lengthwise and scoop out the seeds from one half. Cover the other half and save it for another recipe.

When the stuffing has reduced, season to taste—it should be intense and lively. Season the cavity of the marrow with salt and freshly ground pepper and a sprig or two of marjoram if you have it. Then fill it with the stuffing.

To make the Mornay sauce, put the cold milk into a saucepan with a few slices of carrot and onion, the peppercorns, and a sprig each of thyme and parsley. Bring to a boil, simmer for 4 to 5 minutes, remove from the heat, and let infuse for 10 minutes, if you have enough time.

Strain out the vegetables, bring the milk back to a boil, and thicken with the roux to a light coating consistency. Add the grated cheese and mustard. Season to taste.

Coat the stuffed marrow with the Mornay sauce and sprinkle the top generously with a mixture of grated cheese and buttered crumbs. Bake for about 1 hour until the marrow is very tender—it is cooked when a knife can pierce it without any resistance.

Note: We sometimes cut thick slices of marrow and fill the centre. Perfect for individual portions.

Spicy Butternut Squash or Pumpkin & Coconut Curry

A chunky stew with Asian flavors, also delicious with pumpkin. Squashes are a brilliant vegetable to soak up Asian flavors and bulk up curries.

. . . .

SERVES 8

2 tablespoons sunflower oil

1 large onion (approx. 6½ ounces), minced

3 stalks lemongrass, outer stalks removed and finely sliced

2 garlic cloves, crushed

5 large spring onions, chopped

grated zest and juice of 2 limes

2 kaffir lime leaves, shredded (use dried if fresh are unavailable)

2 teaspoons coriander seeds, roasted and ground

2 teaspoons roasted ground cumin

1½-inch piece fresh ginger, peeled and grated

1 to 3 small red chiles, seeded and thinly sliced

1 tablespoon fish sauce (nam pla)

1 tablespoon torn fresh basil

1 tablespoon roughly chopped fresh cilantro

1 tablespoon crunchy peanut butter

1 (14-ounce) can coconut milk

½ teaspoon salt

4½-pound butternut squash or pumpkin, seeded, skinned, and cut into 1½-inch chunks (3¼ pounds flesh after peeling and seeding)

TO SERVE

2 tablespoons toasted cashews

fresh cilantro leaves

jasmine rice

mango chutney

Preheat the oven to 400°F.

Heat a sauté pan over medium heat and add the oil. Stir-fry the onion for 1 to 2 minutes before adding the lemongrass and garlic. Add all the remaining ingredients. Stir gently. Bring to a boil, cover, and simmer for 15 minutes, stirring occasionally. Remove the lid 5 minutes before the end of the cooking time.

The coconut milk may separate but this won't affect the taste. Taste and add more fish sauce if necessart. Pour into a warm serving dish. Garnish with the toasted cashews and fresh cilantro leaves and serve with jasmine rice and mango chutney.

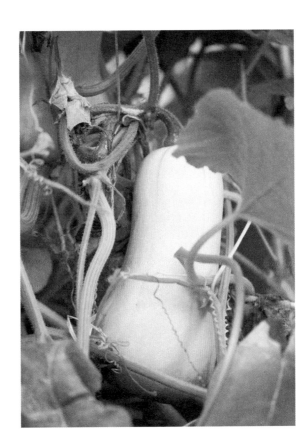

Squash Wedges with Cumin, Crème Fraîche & Chile Dill

Simple and delicious. I like to put a few arugula leaves on the plate underneath the squash when serving this as a starter. It can also be served as an accompaniment. It's best served while still warm or at room temperature, but it's also good cold. Choose a really flavorful pumpkin such as Red Kuri or Potimarron.

. . . .

SERVES 4

12 wedges squash, such as Red Kuri Potimarron, or 4 sweet potatoes, peeled and cut into wedges

approx. 4 tablespoons extra virgin olive oil, plus extra for drizzling

1 to 2 teaspoons cumin seeds, roasted and ground

4 tablespoons crème fraîche, labneh or thick yogurt

1 red chile, seeded and minced

lots of fresh dill sprigs

sea salt and freshly ground black pepper

Preheat the oven to 400°F.

Put the wedges into a bowl and drizzle with extra virgin olive oil. Sprinkle with cumin, sea salt, and freshly ground pepper and toss gently. Arrange in a single layer on a roasting pan. Bake for 15 to 20 minutes or until just tender.

Transfer to a serving dish or individual plates. Put a blob of crème fraîche, labneh, or yogurt on top of each wedge. Sprinkle with chopped chile and some dill sprigs. Drizzle with a little extra virgin olive oil and sprinkle with a few flakes of sea salt.

Beef & Pumpkin Stew

We love this simple winter stew. Lots of pumpkin and root vegetables help to "spin out" the rich stewing beef. Celeriac also works well here and the stew improves in flavor over several days. Serve with fluffy mashed potatoes or colcannon.

. . . .

SERVES 6

extra virgin olive oil

1½ pounds beef stew meat, cut into 1½-inch chunks

10½ ounces onions, chopped

¾ pound carrots, cut into 1-inch pieces

¾ pound pumpkin, cut into chunks

½ pound parsnips, cut into 1-inch pieces

1¼ cups beef stock (as a last resort, use water, and it will still taste pretty good)

pinch of chile flakes (optional)

sea salt and freshly ground black pepper

lots of coarsely chopped flat-leaf parsley or Gremolata (see page 513), to serve

Heat a little olive oil in a skillet, season the meat, and brown in batches in the hot pan. Transfer to a casserole, then toss the vegetables, one at a time, in the hot oil to caramelize slightly. Then add to the casserole. Season well with salt and pepper, and chile flakes, if using, add the beef stock, bring to a boil, and simmer gently for 45 minutes to 1 hour until the meat and vegetables are tender. Scatter with lots of chopped fresh parsley or drizzle with gremolata.

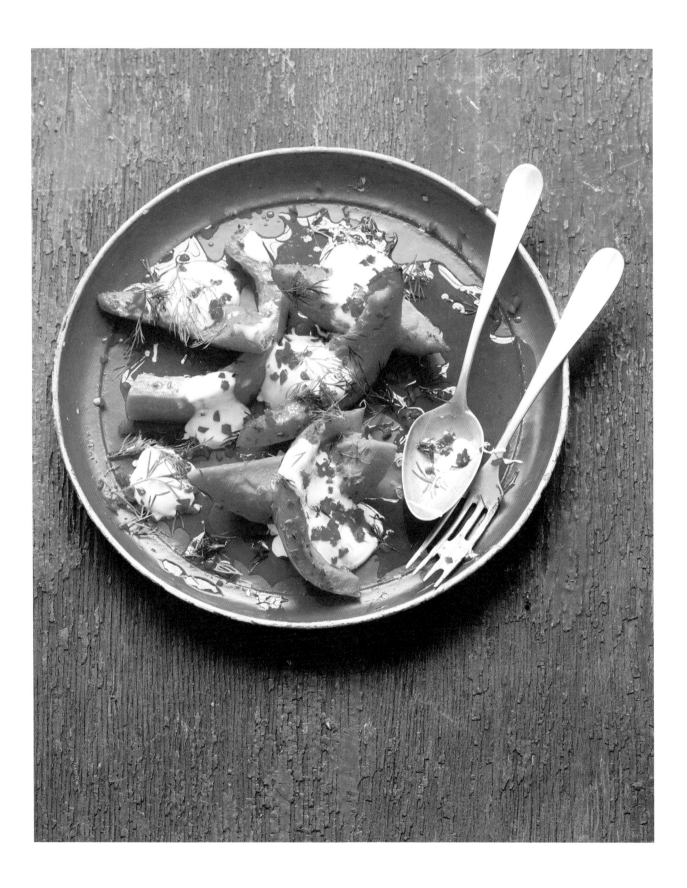

CARDOONS

Cynara cardunculus PERENNIAL, HARDY TO ZONE 6

Cardoons always remind me of the lovely Clarissa Dickson Wright, the highly irreverent cook who did more to tempt us all to try cardoons than any other food writer I know. They were her favorite vegetable and once you discover them you'll understand why.

Cardoons are a majestic member of the sunflower family, a relative of globe artichokes, but one eats the stem rather than the smaller cardoon flower head. The flavor is reminiscent of globe artichokes, loved by the Italians, French, and more recently by cool young chefs.

VARIETIES

You probably won't have much choice—look out for **Gigante di Romagna**, which will grow to about 98 inches tall, and has a fine flavor and taller stalks.

Other Italian varieties include Porto Spineless, **Cardoon Bianco Avorio** and **Cardoon Gobbo di Nizza**.

Some of the old varieties include Cardon de Tours, which is small and has a very good flavor. There is also a Spanish variety, **Cardo Cotnún**, which is less thorny.

HOW TO GROW

Some people like to grow cardoons as a hedge. Its dramatic, spiky, silvery grey leaves and purple thistle-like flowers can also add height and drama to a herbaceous border in midsummer. Our cardoons grow in a boxwood-edged bed in our formal herb garden, against a backdrop of the tall beech hedge.

Cardoons like light, well-drained soil in full sun. They are hardy and will grow

to about 98 inches high, with a spread of 35 inches.

Plant from seed from spring to early summer outdoors or indoors from early spring. Plants can also be divided in spring.

Better still, source strong plants from a specialist garden center.

Their pretty purple flowers emerge in midsummer and continue into early autumn. However, to maximize foliage, cut down flower stems as they emerge.

Cardoons grow much taller than globe artichokes and they have tiny flower heads in comparison.

CONTAINER GROWING

One could grow a couple of plants in large containers in suitable soil; water and feed regularly.

PESTS AND DISEASES

Cardoons are hardy perennials, and we haven't encountered any problems with disease. However, slugs can damage them when the plant is starting to shoot.

HARVESTING

We blanch the stems in early autumn by tying soft cardboard or a folded newspaper all around the base of the plant. This tenderizes the stalks and reduces the bitterness. They will be ready for cutting in late autumn.

GOOD FOR YOU...

Cardoons are a rich source of folic acid and minerals such as copper, calcium, potassium, iron, manganese and phosphorus.

WHAT TO DO WITH A GLUT

It is unlikely that you will have a glut when growing in an average garden. They can be brought indoors and stored in a cool, dry place if frost threatens.

IN THE KITCHEN

Recipes using cardoon stalks feature in traditional Christmas Eve dishes in Italy and other Mediterranean countries.

Cardoons are quite a mission to prepare but once you've tasted how good they are, you'll reckon it's worth it. Choose the lighter-colored cardoons; the darker green ones are more bitter. Separate the stalks from the heart and trim off the leaves and edges. Use a swivel-top peeler to peel the tough string off the outer stalks. Trim a sliver off the top and bottom of the stalks. Cut the stalks into 2- to 6-inch pieces, depending on the recipe. Drop into acidulated water if you don't plan to

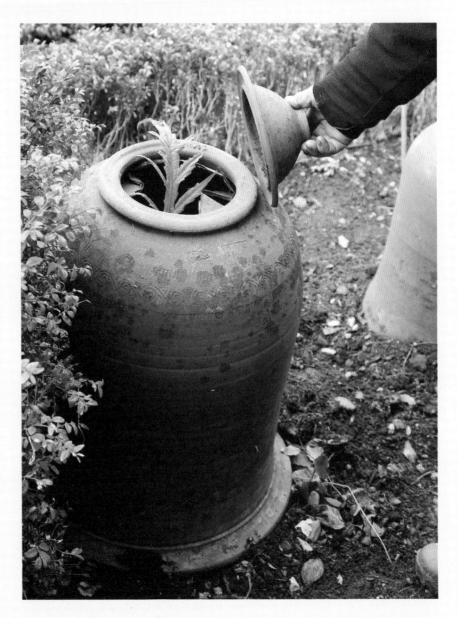

cook immediately. Cook in boiling salted water for about 30 minutes. Drain and use in your chosen recipe.

You can use a terracotta forcing pot to blanch the cardoon stems or wrap them in cardboard.

DID YOU KNOW?

Dried cardoon flowers are used as a substitute for rennet in Spain and some parts of South America. Cardoons were brought to the US originally by French Quaker emigrés early in the 1790s and were grown commercially around Philadelphia for this community. The French grew large quantities of cardoons in Provence, at Tours, and around Montpelier.

Cardoons with Bagna Cauda

I love this warm, oily, anchovy-and-garlic dip so beloved by the Italians; it makes a gorgeous dipping sauce for crisp raw or grilled vegetables and pan-grilled fish. *Bagna cauda* means "warm bath" in an Italian dialect.

SERVES 4

1 pound cardoons, blanched for 25–30 minutes until tender then cut into 3-inch pieces

FOR THE BAGNA CAUDA
5 finest anchovies, chopped
5 tablespoons butter, cubed
¼ cup extra virgin olive oil
3 garlic cloves, sliced very thinly
zest of 1 lemon
lots of freshly ground black pepper

Put the chopped anchovies in a heatproof bowl and sit it over a saucepan of simmering water. Add the butter, oil, garlic, lemon zest, and freshly ground black pepper. Heat gently until the butter melts into the olive oil. Taste—it may need a little salt.

Dip the cardoon pieces in the warm Bagna Cauda and enjoy.

GLOBE ARTICHOKES

Cynara scolymus PERENNIAL, HARDY TO ZONE 6

Not everyone will reckon that globe artichokes deserve a space in their garden, but I'm totally hooked on these majestic thistles.

There has been a stand of artichokes, about 130 feet (40 clumps) long in the walled garden at Ballymaloe House for over 70 years, and some plants are about 100 years old. The variety was brought from my mother-in-law Myrtle Allen's home in Monkstown.

If you don't want to give over space just for these plants you can scatter a few through your herbaceous border. The spectacular flowers really enhance the garden and are stunning in arrangements. In the formal herb garden we have planted a globe artichoke in several of the box-edged beds, to give height. We harvest some and allow others to flower.

VARIETIES
GREEN
Green Globe—Not totally hardy in cold areas, needs winter protection.

Imperial Star—very early maturing green variety that will produce from seed the first year.
LuLu Hybrid—good flaor and outstanding productivity.

PURPLE
Romanesco—Round, firm heads with a purple tinge and looks good in ornamental border. A good source of nectar for bees and other insects.
Violet de Provence—Early artichoke, great flavor, and very pretty.
Purple Sicilian—Small purple artichoke, while still young it's good to eat raw, but won't tolerate frost.
Colorado Star—Early maturing, grown as an annual from seed; purple heads.

HOW TO GROW
Globe artichokes will thrive in a variety of soils, but because they are a Mediterranean plant, they like lots of sun rather than a shaded position. They are easy to grow from seed, or alternatively, buy a few plants, but be careful to choose a really flavorful variety. Pot them out into their permanent position in spring when they are large enough to handle, allowing 30 to 40 inches between each plant. They will flower the following year. Divide the plants every 2 to 3 years to maintain health and vigor. They are hardy to zone 6 and warmer. Keep them weed-free and mulch with well-rotted manure or compost in late autumn to enrich the soil and protect from cold where necessary.

Grow as many artichokes as you have room for in a row. You can expect to get up to eight heads from each plant.

Globe artichokes look brilliant in a herbaceous border as well as a kitchen garden.

We seem to get a few days of strong wind each year in midsummer, so we need to stake them, otherwise those globe artichokes which grow to about 59 inches tall get flattened even in the sheltered herb garden.

Globe artichokes will cross-pollinate with each other and cardoons, so keep varieties well apart in the garden.

In the unlikely event of dry weather, the plants may need to be watered until established, but we find that if enough humus has been incorporated into the soil it will retain moisture.

CONTAINER GROWING
If space is a problem, grow a couple of artichokes in large terracotta pots. The huge silvery grey leaves make striking garden ornaments.

PESTS AND DISEASES
Plant well apart or they may develop mildew. Slugs and snails will demolish young seedlings, so protect them until they get established—use beer traps, crushed egg shells or copper tape. If you are fortunate enough to have a hedgehog in the garden, they love slugs. Once they get established these plants seem to be pest- and disease-free and go on forever.

HARVESTING
Allow the plants to establish for a year or two before harvesting all the artichokes. They will be ready to harvest from early summer. Use secateurs and cut them while still tightly shut and before they start to open. If you are lucky they will produce some secondary buds. Always harvest the first buds, even if small, or the plants will not produce as good a yield.

Beautiful globe artichoke in flower.

GOOD FOR YOU...

Artichokes have a high level of antioxidants and contain cynarin which lowers cholesterol. They are known to increase bile production in the liver, which is good for fat metabolism. They also contain significant levels of vitamin C, folic acid, potassium and fiber.

WHAT TO DO WITH A GLUT

The hearts can be cooked and preserved in olive oil.

IN THE KITCHEN

Globe artichokes, particularly the tiny ones, are delicious raw. I've enjoyed them in France served like little radishes with butter and salt, but I also love the Italian way of serving thinly sliced hearts with olive oil and flakes of Parmesan, or the Roman way alla Giudia, fried until crispy.

Globe artichokes discolor once cut, so drop them into acidulated water (water with freshly squeezed lemon) as you peel them to prevent this. To prepare artichoke hearts, choose large artichokes, then lay them on their side and slice the leaves off two-thirds of the way down. Pare all the remaining leaf remnants off the choke. It should look slightly concave. Then cook as desired.

For globe artichoke hearts braised in olive oil for 4 people, prepare 6 globe artichokes as described above. Heat 6 tablespoons olive oil in a wide pan, add 1 diced onion and 2 chopped garlic cloves, and sweat for a few minutes. Quarter the artichoke hearts, add to the pan with ¼ cup chopped flat-leaf parsley. Season and toss well. Add ¼ cup water, cover, and cook for 10 to 15 minutes until the artichokes are just tender.

Globe Artichokes with Melted Butter

Whole globe artichokes are quite fiddly to eat. Break off each petal, dip the base into a little melted butter with a few drops of lemon juice, vinaigrette, or hollandaise sauce (page 134), then draw off the soft fleshy base between your teeth. Continue until you reach the mound of small petals in the centre. Pinch those off and this will reveal the stringy immature flowers called the choke. Scrape this off with the round end of a knife or a spoon and cut the heart into manageable pieces, sprinkle with a little sea salt before you dip it into the remainder of your sauce. Simply delicious.

. . . .

SERVES 6

6 globe artichokes
approx. 2 teaspoons white wine vinegar
5 cups water
2 teaspoons salt

FOR THE MELTED BUTTER
¾ cup (1½ sticks) butter
freshly squeezed lemon juice, to taste

Trim the base just before cooking so the artichokes will sit steadily on the plate, and rub the cut end with lemon juice or vinegar to prevent it discoloring.

Have a large saucepan of boiling water ready, and add 2 teaspoons of vinegar and 2 teaspoons of salt to every 5 cups of water. Pop in the artichokes, and return to a boil. Simmer steadily for about 25 minutes. After about 20 minutes you could try testing to see if they are done. I do this by tugging off one of the larger leaves at the base—it should come away easily; if it doesn't, continue to cook for an additional 5 to 10 minutes. Remove and drain upside down on a plate.

Meanwhile, simply melt the butter and add the lemon juice to taste.

To serve, put each warm artichoke onto a hot serving plate and serve the melted butter in a little bowl beside it.

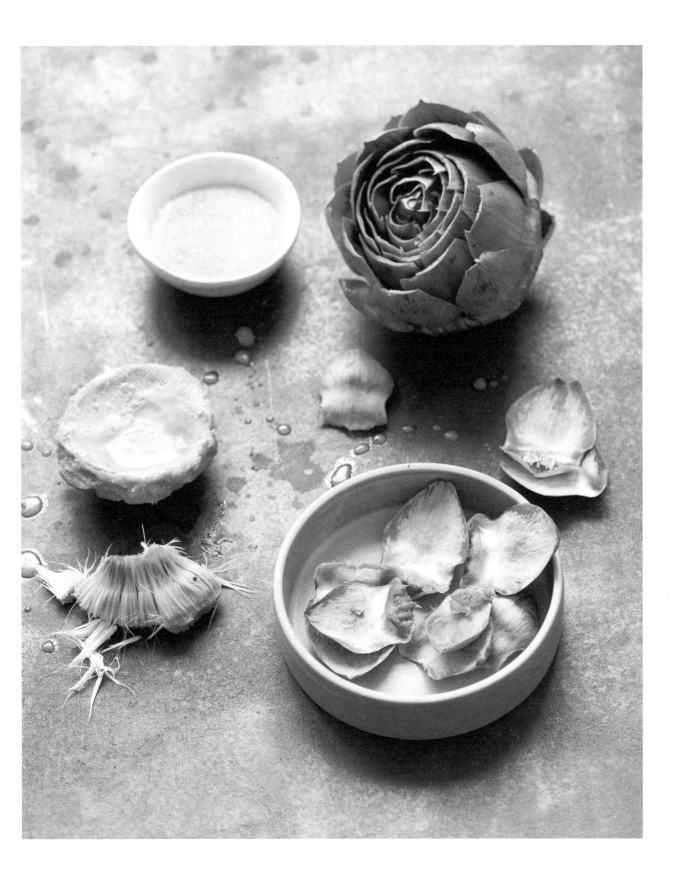

CARROTS

Daucus carota ANNUAL

White Satin F1, Cosmic Purple, and Miami F1 carrots.

Originally carrots were mostly purple but with occasional white and yellow mutations, but in the sixteenth century Dutch breeders created the orange version, quadrupling the vegetable's beta carotene content, which the body converts to vitamin A and is needed for good vision and to keep the eyes, skin and mucous membranes moist.

We grow carrots in the greenhouse and outdoors, also in containers and raised beds with the local kids who realize that there's nothing to compare with munching a sweet crunchy carrot straight from the ground.

VARIETIES

There is a dazzling array of carrot varieties available for the home gardener nowadays, a veritable rainbow of colors—red, yellow, purple, pink, white—and long, tall, thin, short, stubby. They cover the whole spectrum, each variety with its own visual and nutritional appeal. In fact, there are strong links between the color of carrots and their nutritional content. Like many vegetables, carrots come in early, maincrop or storage varieties.

EARLY

Nantes 2—Very versatile variety which can be sown in succession from early spring to early summer, giving a crop for quite a bit of the year.
Sugarsnax—Very sweet, early maturing, high in beta-carotene, one for the lunch box.

MAINCROP

Rodelika—Strong growing red/orange carrot, with a strong sweet flavor, good for juicing and stores well.
Miami F1—Top-class sweet carrot, for late summer and autumn, good for storage if sown in late summer, it can be eaten from winter into early spring.
Danvers Half-Long—An heirloom variety that produces uniform 8 inch long roots.

We also grow some colored varieties at the same time as the maincrop:
Yellow—Yellowstone—Excellent flavor.
White—White Satin F1—Very sweet, early, white carrot loved by children.
Dark—Purple Haze F1—Deep orange flesh with a smooth purple skin, rich in antioxidants and vitamin A, the flavor is best when eaten raw.
Kaleidoscope Mix—Multi-color mix of orange, red, purple and white.
Cosmic Purple—Purple on the outside, orange in the middle.

Thumbelina—Mini carrot with sweet taste and small core.

STORAGE VARIETIES
Autumn King, Rodelika, Chantenay, and **St Valery**
Of the colored varieties, **Miami** and **White Satin** store well too.

CARROT FLY RESISTANT VARIETIES
Flyaway and **Resistafly** have been bred for resistance, but it's worth the it still to cover with carrot fly netting.

HOW TO GROW

Carrots like a crumbly loam, free of stones, and a fine tilth. If they encounter an obstacle as they grow, they tend to fork, therefore slightly sandy soil is best.

If carrots are planted in freshly manured ground, this can also cause forking. Don't enrich the soil with too much nitrogen. Homemade compost or leaf mold will lighten heavy soil without adding too much nitrogen.

Plant early in spring, we find that the soil temperature needs to be at least 50°F before we can plant an early variety, even in the greenhouse. This also applies in a tunnel.

For outside planting, a soil temperature of 60 to 65°F is essential for carrots to germinate. A soil thermometer is a useful piece of equipment. Make a couple of drills, 12 inches apart. A good trick is to lay and press a brush handle into the fresh soil to make a nice straight drill (we do it in the greenhouse). Sprinkle the carrot seeds thinly along the drill, gently cover, and water evenly with a fine rose nozzle. The seedlings should appear within two weeks, depending on soil temperature. Once the seedlings emerge water only if the soil is dry. To have a succession you can sow in mid-spring, midsummer and late summer.

CONTAINER GROWING

If the soil is too heavy and wet the carrots will actually do better in a container, particularly a stubby variety like Parisian which needs less depth. The soil in the container should include some compost or leaf mould to lighten it.

Amsterdam Forcing—Early variety with a cylindrical root, good for container growing as the roots are quite shallow.

Bambino—Baby variety, early and sweet, best harvested at 4 to 6 inches.

Autumn King—High-yielding maincrop variety which also stores well.

PESTS AND DISEASES

Carrot root fly is the main pest that attacks carrots. Fear of being invaded by the dreaded carrot fly makes many home gardeners wary of growing carrots, but everything has changed since horticultural fleece and fine mesh net have become available.

To avoid carrot root fly:

1. Practice crop rotation.

2. Cover the crop with horticultural fleece or mesh net, pegging it down securely at the edges.

3. Seek out carrot varieties resistant to carrot fly.

4. Be meticulous about picking up thinnings or loose leaves.

5. Some gardeners find raised beds of at least 30 inches very successful, apparently carrot root fly can't fly higher than 2 feet.

HARVESTING

We harvest carrots from the greenhouse in early summer and greatly look forward to the first bunch.

Outside, we harvest from midsummer, depending on the weather and the size we want to harvest at. Dig them gently, and if you are using fleece or net to deter carrot fly, make sure to cover over the

Tender young carrot leaves make delicious tempura or carrot leaf pesto.

drill carefully once again.

We tuck the fleece into the soil completely at one side, so that the carrot root fly has no access. Weigh down the other side with sand bags, these are lifted when harvesting but replaced immediately. Keep covered as long as you have carrots in the ground. The early varieties in the greenhouse don't tend to get carrot root fly.

GOOD FOR YOU...

We all grew up being told to eat up

DID YOU KNOW?

I've just discovered that April 4th is International Carrot Day, now in its thirteenth year, which is enthusiastically celebrated in France, Sweden, Italy, Japan and Russia. Next year I'm determined to celebrate here in Ireland also.

Carrot cake has been made since the Middle Ages, when sugar and other sweeteners were rare and expensive, so people used sweet vegetables, such as carrot, parsnip, beet and pumpkin to flavor cake and puddings. The practice fell out of favor for several hundred years but re-emerged in the twentieth century. During World War II, the British Government rationed many household staples as well as luxury items, and promoted recipes for carrot pudding, cake and biscuits.

your carrots as "they will help you to see in the dark!". The scientific basis for this is that lutein, one of the hydroxyl carotenoids found in yellow and orange carrots, makes up the macular pigment of the human retina. Eating foods high in lutein may help increase the level of this pigment and reduce the risk of age-related eye diseases.

The health benefits of carrots are well established and span a wide range of conditions. They are known to be good for skin, hair, and immune systems as well as eyes. They can lower cholesterol because of their high antioxidant level, reduce risks of certain types of cancer and slow the effects of ageing.

Carrots are a rich source of vitamins C and E and are also a valuable source of beta-carotene, which converts to vitamin A.

Much of the nutrients are just beneath the skin of the carrot, so if you want to peel them, just do so very thinly.

While studies examining the health benefits of fruit and vegetables and the disease-preventing powers of the color pigments in plants are ongoing, there is some evidence from research at the University of Wisconsin-Madison suggesting that the pigments in more colorful carrots may help prevent heart disease and cancer, and reduce cholesterol.

WHAT TO DO WITH A GLUT

Carrots store well, even in a cool, dark garage or shed. Store the carrots in damp sand, either in boxes or in a heap against an inside wall in a frost-free shed. They can also be stored in an outside pit in a fairly sheltered spot in the garden. Build them up in a mound with the stalk end pointing outwards. Cover with a layer of soil at least 1-inch thick. Pat the soil down well with the spade so it doesn't wash off in the rain. Re-cover carefully as you take them out.

Be careful not to damage the root when digging. Trim the leaves to about 5cm from the top. Add the leaves to the compost heap.

Make lots of carrot soup and freeze it. Pickled carrots, carrot jam, and carrot marmalade (see page 162) are also delicious.

Carrots damaged by carrot fly can be trimmed and used in the stockpot.

Very small wispy leaves can be used in salad and carrot leaf pesto, but they must be young. They quickly become tougher and stronger in flavor as they get older.

IN THE KITCHEN

Carrots are definitely having their "moment" again. Every posh restaurant seems to have a carrot salad and/or carrots served in at least three ways on the menu. Who'd have thought that the humble carrot would be the basis for so many super exciting creations, other than supplying the base sweetness in myriad dishes, or just boiled, roasted, candied, caramelized, mashed, glazed, or juiced.

Only peel them if absolutely necessary. Very young carrots will only need a scrub and even older carrots, provided they are fresh, rarely need to be peeled. However, if you'd rather peel them, save the trimmings for the stockpot.

To make **Carrot Juice**, scrub the carrots and peel if necessary. Turn on a juice extractor to full power. Juice the carrot, cover, and chill.

For **Glazed Carrots** (serves 4 to 6), cut off the tops and tips of 1 pound carrots (Early Nantes and Autumn King have particularly good flavor) then scrub and peel thinly, if needed. Cut into ¼ inch slices, straight across or at an angle. Leave very young carrots whole. Put them in a saucepan with 1 tablespoon butter, ½ cup water, a pinch of salt, and

There's no need to peel carrots when they are this fresh, just wash off the earth.

a good pinch of superfine sugar. Bring to a boil, cover, and cook over gentle heat for 6 to 8 minutes until tender, by which time the liquid should have been absorbed into the carrots; if not, remove the lid and increase the heat until all the water has evaporated. Taste and correct the seasoning. Shake the saucepan so the carrots become coated with the buttery glaze. Serve in a hot vegetable dish sprinkled with chopped flat-leaf or curly parsley, or mint, or 1 to 2 teaspoons chopped tarragon. Extra virgin olive oil can, of course, be substituted for butter.

For **Mary Jo's Glazed Carrots** (serves 4), given to us by Mary Jo McMillin, cut 1 pound peeled carrots into 1-inch slightly angled slices. Put 1 tablespoon butter in a heavy-bottomed saucepan with a tight-fitting lid over a moderately brisk heat and add the carrots. Sprinkle with a pinch of salt and sugar, if needed. Cover and cook for 8–12 minutes.

Vietnamese Spring Rolls

These fresh spring rolls are the best fun to make and yummy to eat. The carrot julienne adds sweetness and texture and added nutrition to the finished spring rolls.

SERVES 4/MAKES APPROX. 8

1¾ ounces thin rice vermicelli noodles

1 carrot, peeled and cut into julienne or coarsely grated

pinch of sugar

¼ cucumber, cut into julienne

a little rice vinegar or white wine vinegar

8 tender lettuce leaves, such as butterhead

lots of fresh mint leaves

16 Chinese garlic chives (optional)

a handful of fresh cilantro leaves

8 large, cooked organic Pacific shrimp or tiger prawns or 32 Ballycotton shrimps, cooked and shelled

8 rice paper wrappers (banh trang), 8½ inches in diameter

sea salt, freshly ground black pepper

8 large lettuce leaves and sprigs of fresh mint, to serve

FOR THE VIETNAMESE DIPPING SAUCE

1 garlic clove, crushed

4 tablespoons fish sauce (*nam pla*)

4 tablespoons lime or lemon juice

3 tablespoons superfine sugar or less, to taste

3 or 4 hot red or green chiles

First make the dipping sauce. Mix the crushed garlic with the fish sauce, lime or lemon juice, sugar, and ¼ cup of water. Mix well and pour into 4 individual bowls. Cut the chiles crosswise into very thin rounds and divide among the bowls.

Soak the noodles in warm water for 15 to 20 minutes. Drain and set aside.

Put the julienned or shredded carrot into a bowl and sprinkle with sugar, salt, and freshly ground pepper; do the same with the cucumber in a separate bowl but also add a few drops of rice vinegar or white wine vinegar.

Put the lettuce, mint leaves, Chinese chives, and cilantro leaves on a plate. If the shrimp are large, cut them in half.

Have the dipping sauce or sauces ready in bowls. Assemble all the other ingredients on the table.

Fill a wide bowl with very hot water. Dip a rice paper wrapper into the hot water; it will begin to soften within a second. Remove, shake off excess moisture, and put onto a clean dishtowel where it will soften further. Lay a piece of lettuce over the bottom third of the rice paper, about a tablespoon of noodles, some cucumber, and carrot julienne on top and several fresh mint leaves. Roll the rice paper over halfway into a cylinder, then fold in the sides. Arrange 2 half shrimps or 3 or 4 small shrimp along the top with a few cilantro leaves, and add a couple of garlic chives, allowing them to peep out from one end. Continue to roll up and press to seal. Fresh spring rolls may be made several hours ahead, keep covered and chilled.

Dip the roll in the dipping sauce as you eat. Serve with lettuce leaves and sprigs of fresh mint. Some people like to wrap the spring rolls in lettuce leaves before dipping in the sauce.

Caramelized Carrot, Beetroot & Apple Salad

A couple of bocconcini make this caramelized carrot salad into a more substantial, and even tastier, dish.

SERVES 6

1⅓ pounds young carrots, with a little
  green top
2 teaspoons thyme leaves
extra virgin olive oil
honey
2 tablespoons pumpkin or sesame
  seeds, toasted
1 pound beet, cooked, peeled and cut into
  wedges or chunks
1–2 dessert apples
watercress, purslane and chickweed or a
  mixture of interesting leaves and 'weeds'
sea salt and freshly ground black pepper

FOR THE DRESSING

2 tablespoon freshly squeezed lemon juice
5 tablespoons extra virgin olive oil
1 tablespoon sesame oil
2 teaspoons honey
1–2 tablespoons chopped thyme leaves

Preheat the oven to 450°F.

Scrub the carrots, dry, split in half lengthwise, if too big. Put into a large bowl, add the thyme leaves, drizzle with the oil and honey, season with salt and freshly ground pepper, toss gently to coat. Spread out in a roasting tin. As soon as you put the trays into the oven reduce the temperature to 400°F. Roast for 10–15 minutes, turning occasionally until the carrots are almost tender and caramelized at the ends and edges. Remove from the oven and leave to cool.

To make the dressing, whisk the lemon juice, oils, and honey together, add the thyme leaves and set half the dressing aside. Grate the apple directly into the remaining dressing. Toss, taste and adjust the seasoning.

To serve, arrange a few sprigs of watercress, chickweed, and purslane on each plate. Whisk the dressing. Sprinkle over the carrot and beets. Taste, it should be nice and perky. Divide them between the plates. Spoon some grated apple here and there, sprinkle with toasted seeds, and serve with crusty bread.

Carrot Risotto

This is super delicious on its own or with a pan-grilled lamb chop and arugula salad.

SERVES 4

1¾ cups homemade chicken stock
1 cup fresh carrot juice (from 4 medium
  carrots, weighing approx. 14 ounces)
2 tablespoons butter
1¾ ounces onion, minced
1 teaspoon sea salt
1 teaspoon freshly ground black pepper
1 cup basmati rice
3 tablespoons dry white wine
1¾ ounces Parmesan cheese, finely grated
2 to 4 tablespoons chopped fresh flat-leaf
  or curly parsley

Put the chicken stock, carrot juice, and 1¾ cups of water in a saucepan, bring to a boil, and simmer over low heat.

Meanwhile, melt half the butter in a saucepan over medium heat, add the chopped onion, and cook gently for about 5 minutes until soft but not colored. Season with the salt and freshly ground pepper.

Increase the heat, add the rice, and stir for 2 to 3 minutes until all the grains are ranslucent. Add the wine, stir, and cook until all the wine is absorbed.

Add ½ cup of the simmering liquid and stir until most of the liquid is absorbed. Continue adding the broth, a small ladle at a time, until it is all incorporated and the rice is tender and is still a tiny bit al dente—this will take 25 to 30 minutes. Stir in the remaining butter and half the Parmesan. Season to taste and sprinkle with chopped parsley and freshly grated Parmesan and serve immediately.

Carrot Marmalade

We make this year round and find myriad ways to use it, including on scones with a dollop of cream, or drizzled over a dollop of labneh, or seasoned with salt and freshly ground pepper on a couple of crostini—then garnish with a few peppery arugula leaves. For a more tart marmalade, add an extra ½ to 1 lemon.

. . . .

MAKES 3 × ½-PINT JARS

1¼ pounds carrots, grated on the coarse
   side of a box grater
zest and juice of 2 organic oranges
zest and juice of 2 organic lemons
1½ cups water
2 cups granulated sugar

Preheat the oven to 350°F.

Put the grated carrots into a saucepan with the orange and lemon zests and juice. Add the water, bring to a boil, and simmer for 15 minutes.

Meanwhile, heat the sugar in the oven in a large pan for 5 to 10 minutes, then add to the carrots. Stir to dissolve, return to a boil, and continue to simmer until the marmalade reaches setting point or 220°C on a sugar thermometer, about 15 minutes.

Pour into sterilized ½-pint jars, cover, seal, and store in a cool, dark place. It will keep for a year or more, but, as ever, is best eaten sooner rather than later.

Carrot & Cardamom Cake

Light, tender, and delicious, this carrot cake is lovely for afternoon tea, but has also been much enjoyed for dessert. It will also keep really well for a week or more in an airtight container.

. . . .

SERVES 8 TO 10

3 tablespoons vegetable or sunflower oil,
   plus extra for brushing
1¼ cups all-purpose flour
1 teaspoon baking soda
½ teaspoon ground cardamom
pinch of salt
2 large organic eggs
scant ½ cup superfine sugar
¼ cup brown sugar
3 tablespoons plain yogurt
6 ounces carrots (approx. 1 large or 2
   medium), finely grated
dried food-grade rose petals (optional)
1 tablespoon pistachio nuts, coarsely
   chopped (optional)

FOR THE ICING
1¾ cups confectioners' sugar
2 tablespoons freshly squeezed lemon juice

Preheat the oven to 350°F. Brush a 8-inch round springform pan with oil and pop a round of parchment paper in the bottom.

Put the flour, baking soda, cardamom, and salt into a bowl. Whisk the eggs, sugars, yogurt, and oil together until smooth. Gently mix the egg mixture into the dry ingredients, add the carrots, and pour the mixture into the prapred pan. Bake for 40 minutes or until a skewer inserted into the center comes out clean. Turn out onto a wire rack and let cool completely while you make the icing.

Sift the confectioners' sugar into a bowl and add enough strained freshly squeezed lemon juice to make a thickish icing. Pour onto the top of the cold cake. Spread quickly with an offset spatula so it begins to dribble down over the sides of the cake. Sprinkle the surface with dried rose petals, and coarsely chopped pistachio nuts, if using.

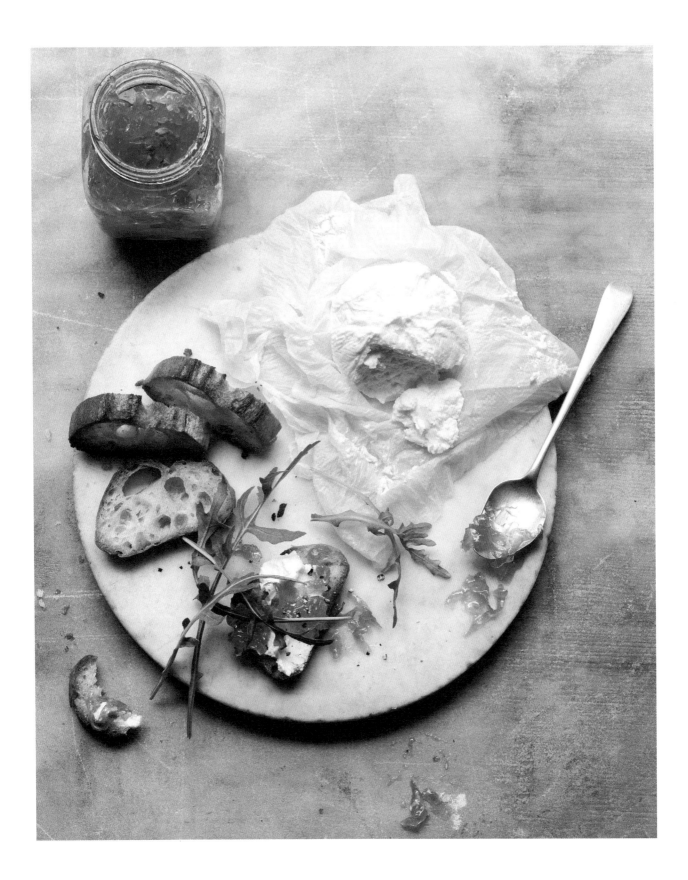

FLORENCE FENNEL

Foeniculum vulgare

SHORT-LIVED PERENNIAL, ZONES 4–9

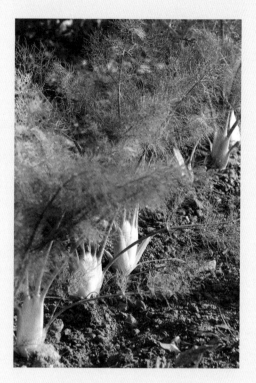

Use every scrap of fennel fronds as well as the crisp bulb.

Florence fennel is also known as Finocchio—particularly by the Italians, who love the swollen anise-flavored bulb and have many delicious ways to serve it, both raw and cooked. We have been growing this successfully for several years, as well as the herb fennel.

Florence fennel is "a selection" of the original, with a swollen bulb-like stem, sometimes called bulb fennel. It is usually grown as an annual but my friend Camilla Plum, from Fuglebjerggaard, outside Copenhagen, grows fennel as a perennial and tells me that lots of tender little bulbs grow from the base every year.

It is directly related to the plain *Foeniculum vulgare*.

VARIETIES

Finale—Excellent early variety with firm, uniform bulbs. It is bolt resistant.
Romanesco—"Sweet Florence" type suitable for later sowings. Big white bulbs.

HOW TO GROW

We do our first sowing in cells in the greenhouse in early spring, then later sowings in succession.

For outdoor plants we again start them in cells in the greenhouse in late spring and plant out from late spring into early summer. Wait till the weather warms up a bit as they will bolt if conditions aren't right. Choose a sunny spot. They don't come to much outside but we like to harvest them at tennis-ball size anyway.

Allow 6 inches between plants and 9 inches between rows.

The bulbs of Florence fennel can be harvested from 4 to 6 weeks after planting, depending on how big you like them to grow. We love them young and tender. In very dry weather they run to seed unless watered regularly. Don't allow them to flower or run to seed, otherwise the bulbs become tough and stringy.

CONTAINER GROWING

Unless you have a large zinc bath or something like that, it's not really worth doing, as it's not the best use of your container space.

PESTS AND DISEASES

We haven't had any problem with pests.

HARVESTING

The bulbs of Florence fennel can be harvested from 4–6 weeks after planting, depending on how big you like them. When you dig the bulb, trim off the stalks and fronds; save for salads and stock.

GOOD FOR YOU...

Fennel is rich in vitamin C and B9 (folate). Fennel bulbs have high levels of several minerals, particularly iron, calcium, potassium and magnesium.

WHAT TO DO WITH A GLUT

Pickle the bulbs, you can't imagine how delicious these are.

IN THE KITCHEN

Remove the outer layer if necessary and add to the stockpot. Fennel is deliciously fresh-tasting in a salad and can of course be cooked in many delicious ways. It takes well to slow braising.

Finnochio alla Giudia, from La Marche in Italy, is thought to have been introduced to that region by a Jewish family. The fennel bulbs are trimmed and washed, then cut in half and soaked in cold water with a pinch of salt for about 10 minutes. Drain the bulbs, cut in half, and arrange in a single layer in a sauté pan. Sprinkle with some crushed garlic and chopped parsley and season with salt and freshly ground pepper. Add a little water and a good splash of extra virgin olive oil. Bring to a boil on medium heat, cover, and then continue to cook over very low heat until fully cooked through and tender. Taste and correct the seasoning. Sprinkle with snipped flat-leaf parsley and serve hot or at room temperature.

For a salad or starter, slice the fennel thinly and crisp in ice water. Alternatively, brush the slices with extra virgin olive oil and crisp on both sides on a hot grill pan, which enhances the sweetness deliciously.

Camilla's Lamb with Fennel & Yogurt

My Danish friend Camilla Plum, organic gardener, seed saver, and original super cook, has created a Garden of Eden on her farm at Fuglebjerggaard, just north of Copenhagen. She cooked this gorgeous dish with our home-grown fennel for supper on a recent visit.

SERVES 8

7 lamb necks, each cut into 3 chops, weighing approx. 7 pounds in total
1 large onion, coarsely chopped
1 whole head of garlic, split in half horizontally
1½ tablespoons cumin seeds, slightly crushed
1½ tablespoons coriander seeds, slightly crushed
3⅓ cups homemade plain yogurt
7 medium fennel bulbs, quartered
1¼ cups lamb stock or water
zest of 3 lemons
¼ cup extra virgin olive oil
flaky sea salt
fresh spinach or chard, to serve

FOR THE GARNISH
¾ cup toasted whole almonds
1 cup fennel fronds
lots of fresh mint

Preheat the oven to 450°F.

In two roasting pans, mix the lamb neck chops with the chopped onion, garlic, and spices, and let marinate for 30 minutes to 1 hour.. Sprinkle with 2 teaspoons of salt and cook uncovered for about 30 minutes until browned. Turn regularly to make sure the spices don't burn.

Dollop on half of the yogurt and add the quartered fennel bulbs. Mix it around until everything is coated with the yogurt.

Put the lamb stock or water in the bottom of a deep roasting tin; add the lamb, fennel, lemon zest, and extra virgin olive oil. Reduce the oven temperature to 325°F. Cook for 2½ to 3 hours, then remove the lamb and fennel to a serving dish and keep warm. Transfer all the remaining juices to a saucepan, drain off excess fat, and reduce a little if necessary. The sauce should be thickish. Season to taste. Bit by bit, stir in the remaining yogurt, then pour over the lamb.

Garnish the dish with toasted whole almonds, fennel fronds, and fresh mint and serve with fresh chard or spinach.

Grill Fennel with Roast Red Peppers

Grilling sweetens the fennel deliciously. Add to Verdura Mista or this versatile combination. The fronds add a fresh licorice taste and the flowers a touch of anise.

SERVES 6

1 or 2 fennel bulbs

extra virgin olive oil

3 roasted red peppers, peeled, seeded, and sliced

1 teaspoon fennel seeds, slightly crushed

lots of fresh fennel fronds, coarsely chopped

fennel flowers (optional)

12 to 18 black Kalamata or Niçoise olives

sea salt and freshly ground black pepper

Heat a grill to high or heat a grill pan over high heat.

Slice the fennel very thinly, ⅛ inch thick, from top to bottom. Drizzle with extra virgin olive oil and season with sea salt and freshly ground pepper.

Grill until golden and slightly caramelized on each side. Arrange on a platter interspersed with warm roasted red pepper slices. Scatter some freshly roasted and slightly crushed fennel seeds over the top. Toss. Sprinkle over the chopped fresh fennel and a few fresh fennel flowers, if using, add a few black olives, and serve as an accompaniment to a pan-grilled fish or pork chop, or just as a starter.

Gillian Hegarty's Braised Fennel

The saucepan you choose for this dish is really important. A sauté pan is perfect. It should be big enough to fit just over one layer of fennel. If the saucepan is too big the fennel will burn and become dry. On the other hand if the saucepan is too small the fennel will boil and stew.

SERVES 6 TO 8

6 fresh fennel bulbs

3 tablespoons extra virgin olive oil, plus extra to serve

pinch of crushed chile

3 garlic cloves, thinly sliced

1 teaspoon ground fennel seeds

Maldon sea salt and freshly ground black pepper

2 tablespoons chopped fennel fronds, to serve

Remove the outer leaves from the fennel if stringy. Cut in half lengthwise and then cut each half into either 2 or 3 pieces depending on the size.

Heat a sauté pan over high heat until almost smoking. Add the olive oil and then the fennel. Season with Maldon sea salt and freshly ground black pepper. The pan should be hot enough so the fennel doesn't stew. Cook until it has a lovely golden brown color. Add the chile, garlic, and fennel seeds and fry for 3 to 4 minutes until the garlic reaches a light brown color. Cover with a lid and cook for 2 to 3 mnutes. You might have to add a few tablespoons of water at this stage. Season well.

To finish, drizzle with a good-quality extra virgin olive oil and sprinkle with the chopped fennel fronds.

JERUSALEM ARTICHOKES

Helianthus tuberosus PERENNIAL, ZONES 3–8

If I could only choose one winter vegetable it would have to be Jerusalem artichokes. They are the tuberous roots of a native North American plant and are nicknamed "fartichokes" for a very good reason. They contain a high level of inulin, which does cause bloating, particularly if eaten to excess. Jerusalem artichokes are the easiest and tastiest of the winter vegetabes we grow and the crop keeps on giving, plus they make the grandchildren giggle at their consequences. The variety we grow has been passed down through the family for generations and is particularly uneven, but it makes our grandchildren imagine all kinds of weird creatures. They love them best roasted and, of course, as chips. The petals of the flowers are also edible and we use the beautiful yellow flowers in large flower arrangements.

An old variety passed down through the family for generations with superb flavor.

VARIETIES

Jerusalem artichokes vary from white to pale brown, to slightly purple.

In the US, where there is a much greater range of cultivars grown, there are some red-skinned varieties available. When they are freshly dug there's usually no need to peel plus you have the bonus of the extra nutrients.

Stampede—extra early and high yielding; tuber up to ½ pound.

Dwarf Sunray—Long, smooth-skinned tubers. It doesn't grow as tall as the others—maybe 1 to 1.5m.

HOW TO GROW

Jerusalem artichokes are grown from tubers. Source from a friend or buy from a garden center or online. They will even grow from the artichoke tubers you buy as a vegetable. In spring, prepare the soil well and plant 4 to 6 inches deep, 12 inches apart. They enjoy a sunny spot. Draw up the soil around them as the stems grow, to help stabilize the plants and stop them toppling over. In an exposed area, it helps to cut them back in midsummer so they won't get loosened by the wind, or stake the foliage.

In autumn when leaves begin to wilt and turn brown, the stems can be cut back to about 3 inches. The stalks can be added to the compost heap; some people recommend putting them over the roots to keep the soil warm in very cold areas.

The foliage grows to 6 feet high, so it can double up as a hedge or windbreak, or to screen a compost heap. In a community garden, if space allows, they could make a good boundary fence. They have beautiful yellow flowers.

CONTAINER GROWING

Jerusalem artichokes won't thrive in a pot, or in a window box; they need space.

PESTS

Jerusalem artichokes are prone to attack from slugs, particularly young shoots. Try the various remedies for slugs: eggshells, beer-traps, sawdust. Pheasants also love eating them so many gamekeepers plant a plot of them for the birds.

HARVESTING

We start to dig artichokes as we need them, from early winter on. Like many root vegetables, they are sweeter after the first good frost. We continue to enjoy their sweet earthy flavor until late spring. They stay in the ground all winter, look like a knobbly potato and are a pain in the neck to peel, but are so worth the effort. We keep some tubers to plant in early spring for the following year.

GOOD FOR YOU...

Jerusalem artichokes are particularly high in inulin, which enhances our gut flora, highly beneficial now a growing number of people have gut problems. Inulin also helps break down fats and enables your metabolism to work more efficiently. They are useful after a course of antibiotics when the immune system has been depleted; the inulin helps to rebuild healthy gut bacteria.

WHAT TO DO WITH A GLUT

One Jerusalem artichoke will produce twelve tubers on average the following season. They spread like mad but will get weaker if they become overcrowded. Make lots of soup; it freezes very well.

IN THE KITCHEN

Jerusalem artichokes are delicious both raw and cooked. When freshly dug, the earth can be washed off in seconds so it's scarcely necessary to peel them. However, just like globe artichoke hearts, they oxidize quickly when you peel them, so pop them directly into a bowl of water acidulated with some lemon juice, or if you want them raw, toss in a little freshly squeezed lemon juice immediately.

They are delicious roasted, mashed, puréed, and in gratins, and have a real affinity with game, particularly pheasant, who also love to eat them in the garden

For **Roast Jerusalem Artichokes** for 4 to 6 people, preheat the oven to 425°F. Slice 1 pound well-scrubbed Jerusalem artichokes into ¼-inch rounds. Toss with 2 tablespoons extra virgin olive oil. Season well with salt. Arrange in a single layer on a lined baking sheet. Roast for 10 minutes until golden on one side then flip and cook on the other side. Test with the tip of a knife—they should be tender. Sprinkle with a little thyme or rosemary but they are perfectly delicious without any further embellishment. Season with freshly ground pepper and serve.

Scatter Jerusalem artichoke flowers into salads and use for flower arrangements.

Salad of Jerusalem Artichokes with Smoked Almonds & Preserved Lemon Dressing

The artichokes are raw and crunchy in this recipe, but roast artichokes (see above) could also be used. The almonds provide a smoky element, and the preserved lemon a perky note.

SERVES 4

¾ cup whole almonds
2 Jerusalem artichokes, scrubbed clean
a little freshly squeezed lemon juice
4 good handfuls of perky bitter lettuce
   and salad leaves
sea salt and freshly ground black pepper

FOR THE DRESSING
3 tablespoons extra virgin olive oil
1 tablespoon white wine vinegar
2 teaspoons honey
a good pinch of sea salt
½ preserved lemon, seeded and minced

To smoke the almonds, scatter 2 heaping tablespoons of applewood chips on the bottom of a flameproof roasting pan. Put a wire rack on top. Place the almonds on top of the wire rack and pop the pan on top of a gas flame on high until the wood chips start to smoke. Cover the pan and rack tightly so the smoke can't escape. Reduce the heat and smoke for 4 minutes. Remove from the heat and continue to smoke for an additional minute or two. Remove the almonds and let cool. Once cool, halve or coarsely chop them.

To make the dressing, whisk the oil, vinegar, honey, and salt together then add the preserved lemon.

Slice the Jerusalem artichokes thinly with a sharp knife. Squeeze a little lemon juice over the slices to prevent discoloring. Season with salt and freshly ground pepper.

Put the salad leaves into a bowl, add the artichoke slices and coarsely chopped almonds. Pour just enough dressing to coat the leaves. Season to taste and serve immediately.

Jerusalem Artichoke Soup with Crispy Croutons

This silky soup, delicious on its own, is also complemented by lots of garnishes. Jane Grigson suggested serving it with a few slices of fresh scallop. Cooked mussels and a few sprigs of chervil work equally well. We also serve it with Chorizo Crumbs (see page 84), or a few simple croutons mixed with some lardons of crisp bacon. For Jerusalem Artichoke Soup with Mussels and Chervil, add 32 to 40 cooked mussels and garnish with the warm mussels and snipped chervil. There's no need for potato in this soup; the artichokes produce enough body.

. . . .

SERVES 8 TO 10

4 tablespoons (½ stick) butter
1¼ pounds onions, chopped
2½ pounds Jerusalem artichokes, scrubbed, peeled if necessary, and chopped
4½ cups homemade chicken stock
approx. 2½ cups whole milk
sea salt and freshly ground black pepper
chopped fresh curly or flat-leaf parsley and crisp golden croutons, to garnish

Melt the butter in a heavy-bottomed saucepan; add the chopped onions and artichokes. Season with salt and freshly ground pepper. Toss to coat, cover, and sweat gently for about 10 minutes. Add the stock and cook for 3 to 5 minutes until the vegetables are soft.

Carefully transfer to a blender, blend until smooth, and return to the heat. Thin the soup to the required flavor and consistency with milk, and season to taste.

Serve in soup bowls or in a soup tureen. Garnish with chopped parsley and crisp golden croutons.

Fermented Jerusalem Artichokes

My daughter-in-law Penny Porteous-Allen is passionate about the importance of fermented food in our diet. She has developed many superb recipes of which this is one. Penny tells me it's particularly delicious with lamb and redcurrant jelly. Use organic ingredients where possible.

. . . .

SERVES 8–12

2 pounds Jerusalem artichokes, scrubbed clean but not peeled and cut into 0.5cm dice
5 level teaspoons sea salt
1 medium red onion
1 garlic clove
1 teaspoon winter savory, rosemary, or thyme
a few wild garlic leaves
gorse flowers (optional)
1 cup brine (made with 1 cup filtered water and 1 level tablespoon sea salt) (optional)

Put the Jerusalem artichokes in a large mixing bowl. Add the sea salt and mix well. While you prepare the remaining ingredients, the salt will begin to draw moisture out of the artichokes.

Thinly slice the red onion, finely chop the garlic and herb of your choice. Roughly chop the wild garlic, then add all these to the Jerusalem artichokes and mix well.

Take handfuls of the mixture and pack it into a 1.5-liter sterilized Kilner jar, pushing down with your fist every time. Once all the vegetables are in the jar, push down again. You want the liquid (brine) to come up and over the mixture. I usually find a jam jar fits snugly inside the bigger jar to use as a weight on top of the vegetables to keep them submerged. If needs be, add some or all of the extra brine. Successful fermentation takes place if all the ingredients are submerged under the liquid. Leave the on a work surface to ferment for 10 days. The resulting taste should be deliciously sweet, sour and savory with great crunch.

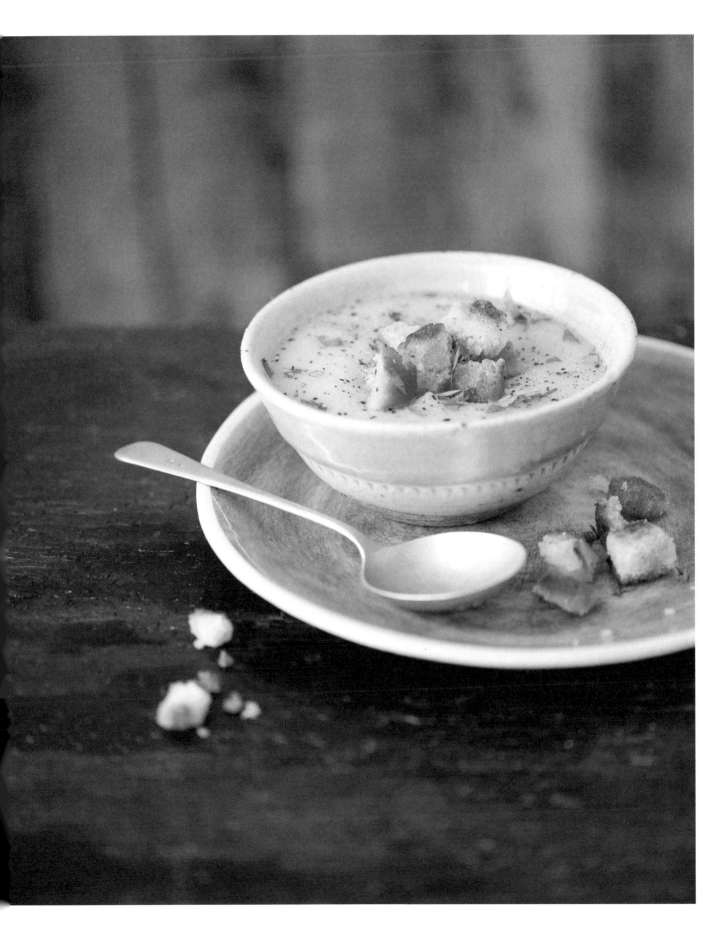

SWEET POTATOES *Ipomoea batatas* ANNUAL

In recent years we've become greatly enamoured with sweet potatoes. In many parts of Africa they are a staple, and in East Africa they were known as "Protector of Children" as often they were the only crop that saved them from starvation. We always bought them from our local greengrocer, but I kept wondering whether we could have a go at growing them in the greenhouses. They are essentially a tropical, or sub-tropical crop, but nowadays new hardier cultivars mean that we can in fact get bumper yields in our cooler climate.

Despite the name, sweet potatoes are not potatoes at all, they are a member of the Convolvulaceae family, the same genus as the beautiful Morning Glory. They have trumpet-shaped flowers and a vigorous growth habit. The leaves, shoots and tubers are edible.

VARIETIES

There are numerous varieties and a range of colors—from white, red, pink, violet, orange to purple. Choose cultivars suited to your local climate.
Beauregard Improved—Small tubers, salmon-orange flesh.
Georgia Jet—Gives good reliable results.
O'Henry—Tubers grow in clusters, which makes them easier to harvest.
Mahon Yam—pink skin and orange flesh; good yields of cylindrical tubers.

HOW TO GROW

Dig in well-rotted farmyard manure or compost before planting. You can try growing from the tubers that you can buy in the greengrocer but they are often tender varieties and are ill-suited to outdoor growing. So it's best to buy "slips" via mail-order from late spring. They don't usually have roots, although there may be signs of small roots starting to appear. They will look withered when they arrive from the seed company, but pop them into a vase of water for a couple of hours and they will perk up again. Plant them into large individual pots, in moist multi-purpose compost, with some vermiculite, perlite or sand. Put them in a warm, frost-free area for 3 to 4 weeks until they are nicely established.

When all risk of frost has passed, harden off and transplant them into fertile, well-drained, moisture-retentive soil in a warm, sunny spot. Slightly sandy soil suits them, with a pH of 5.5 to 6.5. They need a temperature of 70 to 79°F to thrive. Reemay or polythene will help warm the soil, fleece also helps.

Don't enrich the soil with too much nitrogen as this will result in too much leaf growth at the expense of tuber development.

Plant 12 inches apart and allow 30 inches between rows, make sure they are well watered and ventilated in full sun. Some gardeners like to plant them in ridges like potatoes which they feel results in a better yield.

CONTAINER GROWING

Sweet potatoes can be grown in large containers, 16 inches deep and at least 16 inches wide, a trough, or patio bags. You'll need to provide support.

You may wish to train the growth on to strings or a trellis. Outdoors the stems can just be spread across the ground but we pinch off the growing point of the stem at 20 feet, to encourage more lateral growth. They benefit from a high-potassium liquid feed every 2 to 3 weeks. Liquid comfrey is good.

Don't cut the vines back during the growing season or the tubers will suffer a setback.

HARVESTING

By late summer, 3 to 5 months after planting, the foliage will start to die back and wither so you can begin to dig your harvest as you need them, but be careful not to bruise the tubers. They can stay in the ground longer, but dig them out before the first frost.

They store well if the skins are cured. Lay them out in the sun in a single layer for a few hours after harvesting, then keep them indoors in a warm humid place for 10 days or so—a tunnel or greenhouse provides ideal conditions. Once the skins are "cured" they can be stored in cooler dry conditions for several months—up to a year at 55 to 60°F with 90 per cent relative humidity.

Once you have grown your own tubers, it is possible to take slips from them for the following year.

PESTS AND DISEASES

Sweet potato can be susceptible to red spider mite and whitefly when grown under cover, so provide plenty of ventilation and use biological control.

DID YOU KNOW?

Christopher Columbus brought the sweet potato to Spain from the New World and it was widely grown. Interesting to note that it predated the potato by the best part of half a century. It was considered to be an aphrodisiac by Sir John Falstaff in Shakespeare's *Merry Wives of Windsor*, first published in 1602.

Leaves can suffer from leaf spot and sooty mould. Brown rot can occur on stored tubers.

GOOD FOR YOU...

Sweet potato has been described as one of the world's healthiest foods. High in dietary fiber and carbohydrate content, vitamins A, B6, C and E as well as thiamine, niacin, riboflavin and carotenoids. They have fewer calories than potatoes but more natural sugar. But watch out, some varieties have been genetically modified, so ask when you are sourcing them.

Sweet potatoes are high in beta-carotene, a major antioxidant, which helps safeguard immune health. They aid digestion, reduce inflammation in stomach ulcers and aid circulation.

WHAT TO DO WITH A GLUT

Sweet potatoes store brilliantly. We dig them up and keep them in a cool dark shed, covered with sacks. Make lots of soup and purées and freeze until needed.

IN THE KITCHEN

Sweet potatoes are immensely versatile, as all parts are edible—leaves, shoots, and tubers. Sweet potatoes can be roasted, steamed, boiled, baked, deep-fried, mashed, puréed, dried...The leaves can be stir-fried, wilted, sautéed, or boiled. There are numerous recipes in Africa, Asia, New Zealand, North and South America, and Europe for both sweet and savory dishes based on sweet potato, so have fun experimenting.

Sweet potatoes are super nutritious—why not grow some yourself?

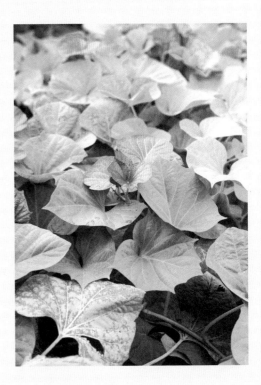

Roast Sweet Potato with Labneh, Chile & Sesame

This delicious combination can be served as a starter or a light lunch.

SERVES 4–6

2½ pounds sweet potatoes
1 tablespoon extra virgin olive oil, plus extra for drizzling
1¾ cups Labneh (page 291) or freshly dripped natural yogurt
1 small red onion
1 small clove garlic, crushed
1½–2 tablespoons fish sauce (*nam pla*)
1 tablespoon diced chile
2 tablespoons snipped flat-leaf parsley, plus sprigs to garnish
½–1 tablespoon freshly squeezed lemon juice
1 tablespoon toasted sesame seeds
flaky sea salt and freshly ground black pepper

Preheat the oven to 450°F.

Cut the sweet potatoes into quarters or sixths, depending on size, or 4cm- thick rounds—they need to be chunky. Toss in extra virgin olive oil and season with flaky sea salt and freshly ground pepper. Arrange in a single layer on a baking pan and roast for 20 minutes or until tender. Keep warm.

Meanwhile, mix the labneh or dripped yogurt with 1 tablespoon of extra virgin oil. Season with salt and freshly ground pepper.

Chop the red onion finely, put in a bowl with the garlic, fish sauce, diced chile, snipped parsley, and lemon juice and mix gently. Season to taste.

To serve, put a generous slick of labneh on each plate. Add three wedges or rounds of warm sweet potato. Spoon a little of the marinade on top. Sprinkle with toasted sesame seeds, flat-leaf parsley sprigs, a drizzle of extra virgin olive oil, and a few flakes of sea salt.

Monkfish, Sweet Potato & Coconut Stew

Another irresistible way to use sweet potato; there's no chile in the recipe but one could add a couple of whole chiles split down the side when adding the sweet potato. A little coconut butter could also be grated in if you would like.

. . . .

SERVES 4 TO 6

2 tablespoons extra virgin olive oil

5¼ ounces onion, minced

3 garlic cloves, minced

1-inch piece fresh ginger, peeled and finely grated

1 pound sweet potatoes, peeled and cut into 1-inch chunks

2½ cups hot fresh fish stock

¾ cup coconut milk

1 (14-ounce) can Italian tomatoes, chopped

1 pound monkfish or cod

2 tablespoons fish sauce (nam pla)

2 tablespoons lime juice

sea salt and freshly ground black pepper

fresh cilantro leaves, to garnish

Heat the oil in a sauté pan over medium heat, add the onion and sweat for 2 minutes. Add the garlic and ginger and cook gently for an additional 5 minutes.

Add the sweet potato to the casserole; season and stir gently to coat. Cook for 3 to 4 minutes, then add the hot fish stock and coconut milk. Add the chopped tomatoes and juice, season, bring to a boil and simmer, uncovered, for 10 minutes until both the sweet potato and tomato are just cooked.

Cut the monkfish into 1½-inch chunks, add to the pan, and cook gently for a couple of minutes until the fish turns opaque. Add the fish sauce and lime juice. Season to taste. Just before serving, sprinkle the fresh cilantro leaves over the stew. Serve with rice pilaf (see page 287).

Sweet Potato & Lemongrass Soup

Try this super-simple soup—it gives so much bang for your buck. Pumpkin or squash also works well with the combination of coconut milk and lemongrass.

. . . .

SERVES 4 TO 6

2 tablespoons butter

1 garlic clove, crushed

1 large onion (approx. ¾ pound), finely diced

3 medium sweet potatoes (approx. 2 pounds)

2 stalks lemongrass, cut into 1-inch pieces and bruised

2½ cups homemade chicken stock

1 (14-ounce) can coconut milk

sea salt and freshly ground black pepper

freshly squeezed lime juice (optional)

fresh cilantro leaves and lime wedges, to serve

Melt the butter over medium heat, add the garlic and onion and sweat for about 5 minutes until soft but not colored.

Meanwhile, peel the sweet potatoes, cut into ¼-inch cubes, and add to the pan.

Add the pieces of lemongrass and chicken stock to the pan. Bring to a boil, then reduce to a simmer and cook for 20 to 25 minutes until the sweet potato is soft.

Fish out the lemongrass and liquidize the soup until smooth.

Whisk in the coconut milk. Reheat and season to taste, adding some lime juice if necessary. Serve with fresh cilantro leaves and lime wedges.

SALAD GREENS

Salad leaves are a really good place to start your gardening adventure. It doesn't matter whether you live in downtown Manhattan or Ballyporeen, you can produce salad leaves the whole year round and growing them is a brilliant introduction to producing some of your own food.

All you need is a little soil or compost, preferably organic, a seed tray or recycled container, some seed, water and light and, hey presto, you can grow lots of delicious, nutritious salad greens on your windowsill, balcony or rooftop, even in an intensely populated urban area.

You might well say, why bother? Every shop now has little gas-flushed bags of salad leaf mixtures. So convenient, just slit the packet, toss into a bowl, add your favorite dressing. Well indeed, but those leaves are washed in a strong chlorine solution, which is unlikely to be beneficial to your gut flora, and I would be concerned about the effect on the nutritional value of the food.

Here at the Ballymaloe Cookery School, we grow a wide range of organic salad leaves in succession throughout the year. We cultivate them in tiny plots and harvest them on a cut-and-come basis. The salad bowl in the Blue dining room or the Garden Cafe here at the school is an absolute joy and changes throughout the seasons. I could write a book alone on the organic leaves, edible flowers and foraged greens we add to our salads.

TYPES
Salad Burnet
Golden Marjoram
Ice Plant – Also known as Brilliant Stonecrop. Succulent perennial with heads of small, star-shaped flowers in summer to autumn.
Komatsuna
Mizuna
Mibuna
Asian greens, such as **Bok Choi, Pak Choi, Tatsoi**. With all the Asian salads, the flavor gets more intense when they are about to bolt.
Mustard greens, red and green frills, mustard streaks – Birds don't enjoy these greens.
Claytonia
Summer purslane
Landcress – Comes in both green and red varieties.
Arugula – Sweet and wild. Wild arugula is a short-lived perennial that will fill the gap if you don't have sweet rocket at some point during the summer. If it runs to seed, pick off the flowers and use them in salad and the plant will produce some more leaves.
Red Orach

Red orach—an annual that re-seeds itself year after year.

Chop Suey Greens – Super fast growing Asian leafy greens.
Namenia – Also known as turnip greens or turnip tops. Mild yet tangy flavor and crunchy texture. Ideal for baby leaf salads. Very easy and fast to grow and ready to eat just a couple of weeks from sowing.
Lamb's Quarters – Also known as Mâche or Corn Salad. Best grown outdoors as it is susceptible to mildew in a greenhouse. It can withstand low temperatures, even extreme weather like snow.
Salad leaf mixes are also available, which often include a variety of colored and textured leaves and fresh herbs. Some combinations include spring onions and chervil, which hugely enhance the flavor. Try:
Winter greens mix
Baby leaf mix

FOR AUTUMN SOWING
These leaves are good options to sow in late autumn depending on how cold conditions are. They will give good value until spring. Keep as winter crops.
Mizuna
Mibuna
Komatsuna
Mustard frills – purple frills, golden frills
Lamb's Lettuce
Wintercress
Winter Purslane
Tatsoi
Namenia
Chop Suey Greens
Heart-forming lettuces – Butterhead, Oakleaf, Little Gem
Chinese cabbage, such as **Kaboko F1**
Pak Choi
Baby Choi – Half the size of a regular Savoy cabbage. Can be sown from late spring to early autumn.

China Choi – Strong-flavored dark green leaves, thick white stems. Sow from early autumn, good frost resistance.

LETTUCES
BUTTERHEAD
Roxy – Shiny red lettuce, slow to bolt, summer production. Will brighten up your salad bowl.

Marvel of Four Seasons – Red curly leaf variety, solid hearts with good flavor. Dates from 1880. Best sown in spring and autumn.

Buttercrunch – Bestseller and one of the best garden lettuces. Dark green, compact heads. Sow throughout the summer in succession, these stand well.

COS
Freckles – Bright green leaves with burgundy splashes, ideal for cut-and-come-again growing.

Parris Island Cos – Dates from 1883. Large cylindrical heads, great flavor.

Little Gem – Quick-maturing mini cos, reliable, suitable for containers.

CRISP HEADS
These take a little longer to mature than other lettuces.

Bedford – Sow spring, summer or autumn. Fresh green crunchy heads.

Webbs Wonderful – Dates from 1890, very popular, excellent quality.

LOOSE-LEAVED
These are quickest to crop; just pick off a few leaves as required.

Salad Bowl – Red and green classic. Attractive leaves, curly edges, stays in production for a long time. Gives lovely contrast in beds or containers.

Oakleaf – Large deeply-lobed leaves, dark green tinged with red, re-grows well after cutting and slow to bolt.

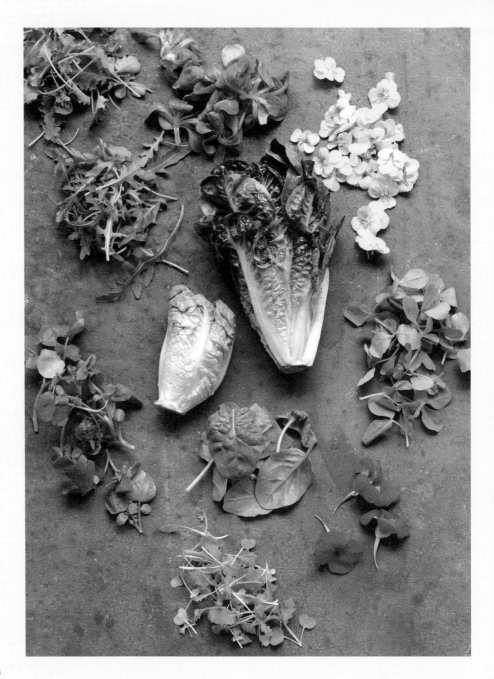

A selection of salad leaves including arugula, lamb's quarters, watercress, baby spinach, and little gem lettuce, plus edible flowers in the form of nasturtiums and yellow violets.

FOR A MORE FRIZZY LEAF – LOLLO ROSSA TYPE
Senorita – Good Lollo Rossa type.
Lollo Bionda – Good for borders or containers, resistant to mildew and bolting.

HIGHLY FRINGED RED LEAF
Red Fire – Very attractive, good flavor and slow to bolt.

FOR WINTER PRODUCTION
These are used for autumn sowings to harvest outdoors in autumn or winter – they will have an extended cropping season when grown indoors in a tunnel or greenhouse.

If you want an early spring sowing of lettuce, use a winter variety.
Mustard Red Giant – Color intensifies in cold weather.
Winter Density – Old variety (1800), semi-Cos type with dark green heads and crisp leaves. Outstanding hardiness which makes it very popular.
Rouge d'Hiver – Old French strain, upright semi-cos habit, striking red and green leaves, tender.
Lattughino – Loose-leaved, frilly red-tinged leaves, very productive and resistant to winter cold.
Neil – Tasty reliable winter butterhead, can be grown in tunnel or greenhouse.
Valdor – Attractive large green lettuce resistant to botyritis. Grow in greenhouse or in the open for early spring cutting.
May King – Mid-green with a slight red tinge, grow in a tunnel, frame, cold greenhouse or outdoors.

HOW TO GROW
To grow on a windowsill, fill a seed tray with organic seed compost and pat it with the palm of your hand to firm the seed bed. Sprinkle a mixture of salad leaf seeds evenly over the top – mibuna, mizuna, red and green mustards seeds, tatsoi – avoid arugula in this mix as it grows faster than the other leaves.

Use a watering can fitted with a rose nozzle to dampen the seeds. They should germinate on a warm windowsill in 7–10 days, depending on the temperature. Harvest from when the leaves are 2 to 3 inches in height. Keep the soil moist, you should get 2 to 3 harvests from the tray. Then return the soil to the compost heap. Sow every 2 weeks for a continuous supply of leaves.

Choose varieties that suit the season. Gardening books often advise to sow seed every 2 weeks – we find it easiest to sow into modular trays and then, when the plugs are big enough not to fall apart, we plant them out. Then you can do your next sowing.

There are new varieties of mixed leaves becoming available all the time to keep up with the demand, such as a multi-salad collection. Many of these are cut-and-come-again and suit small areas.

INDOORS
For a supply of greens from late summer to early winter, sow a variety or a mix directly into soil in a greenhouse in mid- to late summer. Nine square feet should be adequate for most families of four. Broadcast seed thinly over the prepared seed bed and rake in. Water lightly. The

Mizuna and mibuna. Mizuna is one of the many cut-and-come varieties we grow.

Red Oakleaf can be harvested leaf by leaf or allowed to form a head.

Wild arugula has a more robust, peppery flavor than the sweet variety.

Peppery Ruby Streaks mustard leaves add oomph to green salads and stir fries.

Red arach, a member of the amaranth family and an enthusiastic self-seeder.

A lush crop of Tatsoi greens—enjoy fresh or cooked.

seedlings can germinate within a week or two and be ready to harvest at 3 to 4 inches high in a further 3 to 4 weeks.

Treat as a "cut-and-come-again" crop. They can be overwintered and keep you supplied with salad and greens until they start to flower and bolt in late spring, by which time the new crop will be emerging.

At Ballymaloe Cookery School, we multi-seed in shallow module trays (77 to a tray) in seed compost. When the seedlings are about 1 inch high and, crucially, before the plants get pot-bound in the module, we transplant into Mypex-covered soil in the greenhouses. This will continue to produce salad leaves from late summer to early spring.

We also do a second sowing in the Growing Room in late autumn and transplant directly into the Mypex-covered soil in the cold greenhouse 3–4 weeks after germination. This crop will also continue to produce leaves until mid-spring because the growing season has slowed down.

OUTDOORS

Start indoors in modules in late spring and transplant into a cold frame or directly into a prepared bed in early summer. Protect from the birds with netting. Radishes and salad leaves are brilliant for inter-cropping between rows of corn.

Salad leaves can be grown throughout the year but you get best value by sowing in autumn to crop during cooler winter months. That way they will last longer before bolting.

Some types we like to have growing all the time for a constant supply – such as arugula and the frilly leaf mustards – so keep sowing them during the summer, too. In hot weather, grow them in shadier beds outside.

If sown in the greenhouse salad leaves will come quickly. Some of these self-seed if you allow them to flower and run to seed; flowers can be used in the salad bowl.

CONTAINER GROWING

A variety of salad leaves grow brilliantly in all manner of containers, seed trays, wooden fruit boxes, zinc basins, old wheelbarrows, even old drawers.

Bionda a Foglia Riccia – Good cut-and-come-again for all seasons.

Lattughino Verde – Sharply-serrated long green leaves, sometimes called finger leaves.

HARVESTING

Salad leaves are harvested as a cut-and-come-again crop. The more you cut the greater the yield. Don't allow the plants to go to seed.

It's possible to grow a supply of salad leaves throughout the year, even indoors on a south-facing kitchen windowsill (see Microgreens, page 184).

PESTS AND DISEASES

Slugs and snails love milder-flavored succulent leaves, but fortunately they are not keen on mustard greens, arugula and cress. To deter them, try the usual remedies (see page 626).

If growing mizuna and mibuna outdoors you may need to protect them from the birds using nets.

All brassica-type salad leaves are prone to get pinprick holes caused by the microscopic flea beetle, especially during dry conditions; to avoid, water during dry conditions.

Asian greens can also be attacked by flea beetles which nibble tiny holes in the leaves. We just live with it because they don't cause much damage and we don't want to spray.

Caterpillars can strip the leaves in double-quick time, particularly mizuna, pak choi and tatsoi. This is more of a problem outdoors, so grow under netting, one third of an inch square, to exclude white cabbage butterfly. Brassicas like Chinese Cabbage are susceptible to the white cabbage butterfly in late summer, caterpillars will damage the leaves.

GOOD FOR YOU...
Salad greens are high in fiber and low in calories. The darker loose-leaf types of lettuce contain more antioxidants and nutrients than the lighter-colored, tight-headed varieties. Red lettuce varieties are rich in vitamins A and K, while Romaine lettuce has a very high vitamin A content. Arugula, though not strictly a salad leaf, contains lots of nutrients and phyto-chemicals.

WHAT TO DO WITH A GLUT
It's vital to keep cutting, so stir-fry or use for melted greens and share with friends.

IN THE KITCHEN
It is such a joy to have a selection of fresh salad leaves to snip all year round. The flavor and texture is quite different to the intensively produced crops, many of which have been grown hydroponically – in water with added chemicals.

We serve a green salad with every lunch and dinner, both in the restaurant at Ballymaloe House, at Ballymaloe Cookery School and at home. Traditionally we enjoy green salad either eaten with or after our main course, which has a magical effect on one's digestion – it makes you feel less full and then one has room for dessert.

WINTER SALAD BOWL
Oriental salads, Lamb's lettuce, winter purslane – all crop best in cool conditions.

SUMMER SALAD BOWL
Summer lettuces come quickly and don't bolt as quickly. Keep succession going well. Depending on where you are gardening, you might like to start some summer lettuces inside, to get a head start, then plant later ones directly outside. Red Orach needs warmer summer conditions and adds a nice red colour to salads.

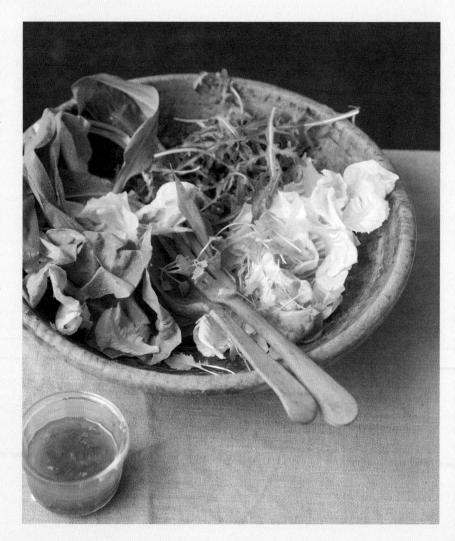

A Green Salad for Every Season

We serve a salad of lettuces, salad leaves, and edible flowers and occasionally foraged greens with every lunch and dinner at the cooking school. The content varies depending on the season. It is a total celebration in a bowl, a much-anticipated part of every meal. Students often tell us that they miss the beautiful green salad enormously when their course comes to an end. It is served in a huge hand-turned bowl of Irish elm, made for us by legendary Irish wood turner Keith Mosse. The beautiful salads are possibly the most photographed element of the cooking school.

FOR A SPRING GREEN SALAD

For this salad, use a selection of lettuces and salad leaves, such as butterhead, iceberg, radicchio, chicory, curly endive
Watercress
Leaf sorrel
Wild and sweet rocket leaves
Winter purslane or Claytonia
Wild garlic leaves and flowers
Navelworth
Mibuna
Mizuna
Salad burnet
Golden marjoram
Late spring—Broad bean tips, pea shoots, tiny carrot tops.

FOR A SUMMER GREEN SALAD

A selection of fresh lettuces and salad leaves, such as butterhead, oakleaf, iceberg, Lollo Rosso, frisée, Little Gem.
Mesclun or Saladisi
Red orach
Mizuna
Mibuna
Rocket
Edible chrysanthemum leaves
Green pea shoots or broad bean tips
Tiny chard and beetroot leaves
Wild sorrel leaves or buckler leaf sorrel
Salad burnet
Fresh herb leaves, such as lemon balm, mint, flat parsley, golden marjoram, annual marjoram, tiny sprigs of dill, tarragon, or mint.
Chive flowers
Calendula petals
Young nasturtium leaves and flowers
Borage or hyssop flowers
Courgette or squash blossoms
Chickweed
Yellow kale flowers
Watercress flowers
Garlic blossoms

FOR AN AUTUMN AND WINTER GREEN SALAD

A selection of autumn and winter lettuces, such as butterhead, oakleaf, Lollo, Lollo Rosso, radicchio, chicory, curly endive, Arctic Queen
Watercress
Leaf sorrel, lamb's tongue and wild sorrel leaves
Wild and sweet rocket leaves
Mache or lamb's lettuce
Tender leaves of kale
Winter purslane
Chickweed
Winter cress
Tips of purple sprouting broccoli are also delicious and if you feel like something more robust, use some finely shredded Savoy cabbage, maybe a few shreds of red cabbage, and some finely shredded stalks of fresh chard.

HOW TO MAKE A GREEN SALAD

A good green salad will have a contrast of texture, color, and flavor. The mixture of lettuce and salad leaves should ideally reflect the seasons. Seek out salad leaves that have been grown in rich, fertile soil rather than hydroponically, as they will have better flavor and be more nutritionally complex.

Wash and carefully dry the lettuce and salad leaves in a salad spinner. Leave whole or, if too large, tear into bite-sized pieces. Put into a deep salad bowl and add the herb sprigs and edible flowers. Toss, cover, and chill until further needed. Washed organic salad leaves keep perfectly in a plastic bag in the fridge for 4 to 5 days. Just before serving, toss the salad in just enough dressing to make the leaves glisten, taste, and add a little more seasoning if necessary.

Note: It is really worth investing in a good salad spinner to dry the leaves; otherwise the residual water will dilute the dressing and spoil the salad.

Salad Dressings

Dress a green salad just before serving, otherwise it can look tired and unappetising. The flavor of the dressing totally depends on the quality of the oil and vinegar. We use best-quality, cold-pressed oils and superb wine vinegars to dress the precious organic lettuce and salad leaves. The quantity one uses is so small it's really worth buying the best quality you can afford—it makes all the difference.

SIMPLE FRENCH DRESSING

MAKES ½ CUP, ENOUGH TO DRESS A SALAD FOR 4 PEOPLE

6 tablespoons cold-pressed extra virgin olive oil
2 tablespoons best-quality white or red wine vinegar
flaky sea salt and freshly ground black pepper

Whisk all the ingredients together just before the salad is to be eaten. Salad dressings are always best when freshly made but this one, which doesn't include raw garlic, shallot, or fresh herbs, will keep in a jar in the fridge for 3 or 4 days. Whisk to emulsify before using.

BALLYMALOE FRENCH DRESSING

MAKES APPROX. ½ CUP

½ cup extra virgin olive oil
2 teaspoons balsamic vinegar
1 teaspoon honey
1 garlic clove, crushed
½ teaspoon Dijon mustard
Maldon sea salt and freshly ground black pepper

Put all the ingredients into a small bowl or jam jar. Whisk with a fork until the dressing has emulsified. Preferably use fresh but it will keep in the fridge for a couple of days. Whisk to emulsify before using.

HONEY & WHOLE-GRAIN MUSTARD DRESSING

MAKES APPROX. 1 CUP

½ cup plus 2 tablespoons extra virgin olive oil or a mixture of olive and other oils, such as sunflower and peanut
3 tablespoons white wine vinegar
2 teaspoons honey
2 heaping teaspoons whole-grain honey mustard
2 garlic cloves, crushed
sea salt and freshly ground black pepper

Put all the ingredients into a small bowl or jam jar. Whisk with a fork until the dressing has emulsified. Season to taste. Preferably use fresh but it will keep in the fridge for a couple of days. Whisk to emulsify before using.

BUTTERMILK DRESSING

MAKES APPROX. 1 CUP

1 organic egg yolk
½ cup extra virgin olive oil
3 tablespoons buttermilk
3 tablespoons crème fraîche
1 tablespoon finely chopped shallot
1 tablespoon freshly squeezed lemon juice
salt and freshly ground black pepper

Put the egg yolk into a bowl. Whisk the oil in drip by drip to create an emulsion. Then add the buttermilk, crème fraîche, shallot and lemon juice and mix. Season with salt and freshly ground pepper.

POMEGRANATE MOLASSES SALAD DRESSING

MAKES A SCANT 1 CUP

2 garlic cloves, crushed
½ teaspoon ground cumin
½ teaspoon sugar, plus extra to taste
¼ cup pomegranate molasses
2 tablespoons lemon juice
½ cup extra virgin olive oil
sea salt and freshly ground black pepper

Mix the garlic, cumin, sugar, pomegranate molasses, and lemon juice in a bowl. Whisk in the olive oil. Season to taste with salt and pepper. Add a little extra sugar if you think it's a bit too sharp. Preferably use fresh but it will keep in the fridge for a couple of days. Whisk to emulsify before using.

YOGURT & MINT DRESSING

MAKES APPROX. ½ CUP

½ cup plain yogurt
1 tablespoon lime or lemon juice
1 tablespoon extra virgin olive oil
1 teaspoon honey
sea salt and freshly ground black pepper
1 tablespoon chopped fresh mint (optional)

Put all the ingredients into a small bowl or jam jar. Whisk with a fork until the dressing has emulsified. Season to taste. Preferably use fresh but it will keep in the fridge for a couple of days. Whisk to emulsify before using.

HERBED VINAIGRETTE

MAKES APPROX. 1 CUP

¾ cup extra virgin olive oil
¼ cup cider vinegar
1 teaspoon honey
1 garlic clove, crushed
2 tablespoons chopped fresh mixed
   herbs, such as parsley, chives, mint,
   thyme, watercress
sea salt and freshly ground black pepper

Put all the dressing ingredients
into a screw-top jar. Season to taste.
Shake well to emulsify before use,
otherwise process all the ingredients
in a food processor or blender for a
few seconds.

For a variation, use ¼ cup fresh
lemon juice or wine vinegar instead of
the cider vinegar. This dressing should
be served when freshly made, otherwise
the herbs will discolor. As a compromise
the dressing could be made a day or two
ahead without the herbs, then whisk and
add the fresh herbs just before serving.

ASIAN DRESSING

MAKES APPROX. 1¼ CUPS

2 Thai chiles, finely sliced
1 large garlic clove, crushed
3 tablespoons superfine sugar
¼ cup fish sauce (nam pla)
¼ cup lime juice
¼ cup rice vinegar
3 tablespoons extra virgin olive oil

Put all the ingredients in a screw-top jar
and shake well to dissolve the sugar. Best
fresh but will keep for 2 to 3 days in the
fridge.

VERJUICE AND HONEY VINAIGRETTE

MAKES APPROX. 1 CUP

3 tablespoons verjuice
1 tablespoon freshly squeezed lemon juice
¾ cup extra virgin olive oil
1 teaspoon honey
sea salt and freshly ground black pepper

Whisk all the ingredients together and
season to taste. Whisk to re-emulsify
before using.

ITALIAN SALAD DRESSING

MAKES ¼ CUP

1 tablespoon fresh lemon juice or balsamic
   vinegar
3 tablespoons extra virgin Tuscan olive oil
sea salt and freshly ground black pepper
granulated sugar, to taste (use only with
   lemon juice)

Combine the ingredients for the dressing.
Note: Italian lemons are much sweeter
and juicier than the imported fruit we
have access to, so it may be necessary to
add sugar to the dressing. Use fresh.

MICRO GREENS

Micro greens are so fun and easy to grow—vibrant little flavor bombs that have burst onto our plates in recent years. They might just be the little bit of magic that ignited your inner gardener. Micro greens are just that, tiny edible greens, a few days older than a shoot. At that stage they contain the concentrated essence of the fully grown plant. They are harvested after the first "true leaves" appear.

They can be grown year round, both outdoors and indoors, depending on the time of year, in all manner of containers, even recycled plastic fruit trays.

Many restaurants now grow micro-greens year round to garnish their dishes, but you can also grow them at home, on a less intensive basis, very easily.

VARIETIES

These are the ones we find best in terms of color, flavor, versatility and ease of growing.
Arugula
Red and green mizuna
Red and green mustard greens, red frills
Kale
Leaf beet
Ruby and rainbow chard
Cilantro
Dill, basil, fennel
Flat-leaf parsley
Cress
Celery
Radish Red Rioja
Red-veined sorrel
Amaranth
Opal basil
Purple kohlrabi

HOW TO GROW

You can sow these all year round. Fill a seed tray with sieved organic compost and level off the top—we use a piece of plywood that fits into the tray. Gently scatter the seeds thinly over the surface and water with a rose nozzle. Cover with a sheet of black plastic. For a "posh set-up" during cold times of the year, one can have a heat mat or warm bench at 60°F.

Lift off the plastic during the day and re-cover at night at first, but once the seeds have germinated, remove the plastic altogether. In 12 to 21 days, depending on the time of year, the micro greens will be ready to snip. If you wish to produce these in winter you will need a heat mat to rest the seed trays on and speed up growth.

No special seeds are needed but we seek out organic or untreated seeds. Micro greens are expensive to buy, as it takes more seeds to grow micro greens than seed crops, so it's well worth growing your own to add zing to your dishes.

PESTS AND DISEASES

We haven't had any problems. Fungal diseases like damping off or mould are possible so strict hygiene is essential—clean trays thoroughly between plantings. Spread seed evenly and don't plant too thickly. There will be a little bit of trial and error in knowing when to remove the black plastic cover, and how moist to keep the compost.

HARVESTING

Cut the micro greens with scissors just above the soil when they are less than 1 inch high, they will re-sprout once or twice more. If they get too big for micro greens, just add them to the salad bowl as baby greens. Put the compost back onto the garden.

GOOD FOR YOU...

Ongoing research has shown that micro greens can, depending on the variety, contain between 4 to 40 times more nutrients than their mature counterparts. Professor Qin Wang at the University of Maryland tested 25 different varieties and found consistently high levels of important nutrients like vitamins C, E, K, lutein and carotene. Researchers from the USDA agency were also astonished to find such high levels of nutrients which, as Dr Gene Lester says, are extremely important for skin, eyes and fighting cancer. They are especially high in nutrients when the soil is fortified with natural elements such as kelp.

IN THE KITCHEN

Micro greens became trendy several decades ago when Californian chefs started using, and in some cases growing, their own to add oomph to their starters and entrées. The pretty little micro greens can elevate a simple egg dish or a few sandwiches to new heights. They provide a whole palette of textures and flavors, from sweet to spicy, depending on the variety.

Clockwise from top: celery; red vein sorrel; red stem radish; mizuna; ruby chard; salad fennel and red amaranth.

TOMATOES

Lycopersicon esculentum ANNUAL

Even though the flavor of some tomatoes in supermarkets has greatly improved, there's still nothing to beat your own home-grown crop. The excitement, the anticipation as you watch the seedlings grow, the flowers set, the fruit start to ripen, the unmistakable smell when you pick and taste the first vine-ripened fruit at last, such a joy for gardeners and cooks.

Tomatoes are one of most popular choices for home growers because they are so versatile and feature in so many cuisines, from Indian to Italian. They are technically a fruit but I have included as a veggie because that's how cooks treat them. Us gardeners have the thrilling opportunity to grow lots of heirloom varieties when we grow our own.

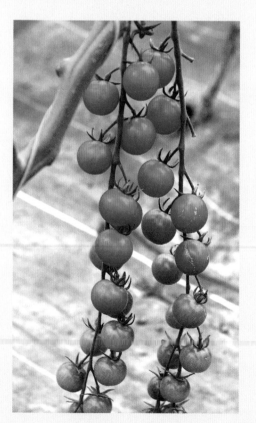

Tomatoes ripening from the top of the truss down to the tip.

VARIETIES

We grow more than 30 varieties of tomatoes every year, including many heirlooms, but if you have to choose just one variety it might have to be Sungold. Tomatoes come in many shapes and sizes—small cherry, traditional round, plum, irregular shapes—and colors—yellow, red, orange, black, purple.

SMALL-FRUIT TYPE

Sun Gold—Sweet, fruity tasting cherry tomato, early cropper.
Gardener's Delight—Very popular small cherry tomato, easy to grow, produces an abundance of sweet, flavorsome fruit.
Green Envy F1—Intensely flavored little gem with long-lingering sweetness.

LARGE-FRUIT TYPE

Brandywine—Heirloom, flavorsome large tomato with a lovely pink color.
Oxheart—Well-flavored, traditional Italian tomato with large, pink, heart-shaped fruits.

OTHER HEIRLOOM VARIETIES WHICH WE GROW AND LOVE:

Green Zebra
Black Zebra
Casady's Folly
Purple Calabar
Striped German
Green Prince
Black Russian
Black Cherry
Dancing with Smurfs
Blue Berries

HOW TO GROW

You'll need rich, fertile, well-draining soil. We start tomatoes from seed in 3 ½ -inch pots in the Growing Room in early spring and transplant into the greenhouse in late spring. We cover the ground with landscape fabric.

The seeds can be started in a propagator at 77°F in early spring, or on a windowsill. We start them in 3 ½-inch pots but if space is limited start them in cells and then transfer to 3 ½-inch pots. They can get leggy on the windowsill and the transition from the warm house to a cold greenhouse or tunnel can set the leaves turning purple.

It might be easier to buy a few plants of a variety you really like or a small selection of plants. When you are removing the side shoots of the growing plants, stick them into little pots of compost on the windowsill, they will root and catch up quite quickly with the parent plant.

Hang a string from the overhead wires to support plants. When the plant is 10 to 12 inches tall, make a hole 4 to 5 inches deep, place the string in the hole, leaving a little slack for twisting. Place the plant on the ground, firm into the ground and cover with soil. Carefully twist the string clockwise around the little plant, under the leaf and over the truss. Otherwise use a strong bamboo cane to support the plant. As it starts to grow, remove all side shoots which grow between the leaf stem and main stem. This encourages the plant to produce extra fruit rather than foliage, and continue to remove side shoots throughout the season.

Modern varieties are self-pollinating; once the first truss (flowers) has set, feed weekly throughout the season with organic tomato food.

There are a variety of training styles, but when the plant reaches the wire we pinch out the "leaders." The bottom trusses gradually ripen first, so remove the leaves from the bottom up as the tomatoes start to ripen. This allows more sunlight and improves air circulation, which helps to prevent botrytis.

CONTAINER GROWING

For outdoor tomatoes, choose a sheltered spot that has lots of light and sun. However, they do better inside in a greenhouse or tunnel, or even a glass porch. You can grow them in pots or grow bags or even hanging baskets in a rich loam-based compost. Water and feed regularly, particularly during hot weather. Bush varieties like *Tumbling Tom*, which is a prolific classic variety with bright red, sweet fruit, and *Losetto F1*, a patio cherry tomato resistant to late blight, grow brilliantly in containers.

HARVESTING

In a greenhouse or tunnel, depending on the weather and variety, one can expect the first tomatoes to ripen by mid- to late summer. As soon as the tomatoes ripen, pick with the calyx on—there's a natural joint where the tomato will snap off the truss, leaving the calyx intact.

PESTS AND DISEASES

Whitefly, red spider, and aphids can certainly be a problem. Be super vigilant to catch them early. We have had success with a biological control under cover, but it must be introduced early enough before the aphid gets established. It's advisable to order some biological control ahead as a preventative measure.

Whitefly can be the main problem, and though unsightly, it doesn't affect the tomato much. If there is a big infestation it will affect both the appearance and the yield by the

Tomatoes planted in landscaping cloth and ready to climb up their string.

end of season, and the leaves will be unpleasantly sticky. We start biological control a few weeks after planting.

Botrytis can also be a problem, air circulation is important, and don't over water. Red spider mite doesn't tend to attack tomatoes.

GOOD FOR YOU...

Tomatoes are naturally very low in saturated fat and cholesterol and high in fiber. They are a good source of vitamins E, B6, A, C and K and also contain thiamin, niacin, folate, magnesium, phosphorus and copper, potassium and manganese. The skin of the tomato is a good source of lycopene, which acts as an antioxidant in the body.

WHAT TO DO WITH A GLUT

We make lots of tomato purée to freeze and use during the winter. You can make tomato soup to freeze too, and tomato chutney is a great standby to have with cold meats and cheeses.

IN THE KITCHEN

Tomato salad made with various colors and shapes of tomatoes with fresh basil is one of the highlights of our summer. **Tomato Fondue** is a "great

Tomatoes can be grown well in containers such as these sacks.

convertible"—a delicious summer vegetable; a sauce for pasta, chicken breast, or fish; a filling for an omelet; a topping for pizza. Add a couple cans of beans and a few sausages and presto, a stew or cheat's cassoulet, and on and on. Just sweat 4 ounces sliced onions and 1 clove crushed garlic (optional) in 2½ teaspoons olive oil over a gentle heat—it is vital for the success of this dish that the onions are completely soft before the tomatoes are added. Remove the hard cores from 2 pounds very ripe tomatoes (you can also use half fresh tomatoes and half canned). Put them into a deep bowl and cover with boiling water. Count to 10 and then pour off the water immediately; peel, slice, and add to the onions. Season with salt, pepper, and sugar and add a generous sprinkling of chopped basil. Cook for 10 to 20 minutes more or until the tomato softens.

Fresh tomato juice is a revelation, yet it's made in minutes and is so worth making a part of your daily summer regime. A Bloody Mary becomes something quite different with fresh tomato juice, and if you whisk in a little natural yogurt and a whiff of crushed garlic, some mint, and a little extra salt you have a prized Persian cocktail.

Heirloom Tomato Salad

The Ballymaloe Cookery School stall at the Midleton Farmers' Market has a unique selection of organic heirloom tomatoes from the greenhouses in all shapes and sizes. Red, yellow, black, striped, round, pear-shaped, and oval. They make a divine tomato salad and are wonderful with lots of fresh basil and unctuous burrata made from the milk of the buffalo that graze on the lush pastures of West Cork.

· ·

SERVES 4

8 very ripe heirloom tomatoes, such as
    Oxheart, Dancing with Smurfs, Green
    Zebra, Brandywine, Purple Calabar, and
    Casady's Folly
3 tablespoons extra virgin olive oil
1 to 2 tablespoons lemon juice
approx. 2 teaspoons runny honey
2 teaspoons fresh basil leaves, torn
1 or 2 burrata or 2 to 4 fresh buffalo
    mozzarella (optional)
flaky sea salt and freshly ground black
    pepper
crusty sourdough bread, to serve

First make the tomato salad. Cut the tomatoes into haphazard ¼-inch-thick slices. Sprinkle with salt and pepper. Mix the oil, lemon juice, and honey together. Add the basil leaves, pour the mixture over the tomatoes, and toss gently. Taste and correct the seasoning if necessary.

To serve, tear a ball of burrata or buffalo mozzarella in half or apart depending on size. Add to the tomato salad. Drizzle with your very best extra virgin olive oil and add a few flakes of sea salt and a couple of fresh basil leaves.

Serve immediately with crusty sourdough bread.

Green Tomatoes with Wasabi Mayonnaise

Slices of tomato with a crisp green crust are a perfect foil for wasabi mayonnaise; the combination of juicy tomato, crunchy crust, silky mayo, and perky wasabi works brilliantly here. Try Green Zebra or Michael Pollan tomatoes for this recipe, if you grow those two green varieties; alternatively this is a terrific way to use tomatoes that haven't yet ripened at the end of the season.

· ·

SERVES 4

1¼ cups white bread crumbs
½ cup coarse cornmeal
extra virgin olive oil, for frying
4 large or 6 to 8 medium green tomatoes
sea salt and freshly ground black pepper
coarsely chopped flat-leaf parsley, to serve

FOR THE WASABI MAYONNAISE
½ cup homemade mayonnaise (see page
    196)
1 to 2 tablespoons wasabi paste, or to taste

Mix the bread crumbs and cornmeal on a plate and season well with salt and freshly ground black pepper.

To make the wasabi mayonnaise, mix the homemade mayonnaise and the wasabi paste together in a small bowl.

Heat a wide skillet and add a couple of tablespoons of extra virgin olive oil. Slice the tomatoes about ¼ inch thick, dip in the crumb mixture, and cook the tomato slices in batches for 2–3 minutes each side. Drain on paper towels.

Serve immediately with a dollop of wasabi mayonnaise and some coarsely chopped flat-leaf parsley.

Little Fish & Tomato Pots

We love these little pots of fresh fish, served with crunchy buttered crumbs on top, but of course other vegetables can be used; for instance, zucchini work well here. This is also a brilliant recipe to make a little fish go a long way. The little pots need to be saucy....

SERVES 8

3 or 4 ripe tomatoes
¾ to 1 pound super-fresh fish, such as
   haddock, hake, pollock or mackerel
½ quantity Béchamel Sauce (page 267)
chopped fresh flat-leaf parsley or dill
sea salt and freshly ground black pepper

FOR THE BUTTERED CRUMBS
2 tablespoons butter
1 cup fresh bread crumbs
1 to 1¾ ounces cheddar cheese or a
   mixture of cheddar and Parmesan, grated
   (optional)

Make the buttered crumbs. Melt the butter in a pan and stir in the bread crumbs. Remove from the heat immediately, let cool, and add the grated cheese, if using.

Slice the tomatoes into ¼-inch-thick rounds and season with salt and freshly ground black pepper.

Preheat the oven to 400°F.

To assemble, season the fish with salt and freshly ground pepper. Put a spoonful of well-flavored béchamel into the bottom of 8 ramekins (3½ inches wide × 1¾ inches deep, 6 ounces in volume) or shallow white eared dishes (we sometimes use large scallop shells). Top with a small piece of fish. Sprinkle with chopped parsley or dill and a slice or two of tomato, depending on size. Cover with another generous layer of béchamel. Scatter with the buttered crumbs. Cover and chill or pop straight into the oven and cook for 8 to 10 minutes or until the sauce is bubbling and the crumbs are crisp and golden.

Below left: *Dancing with Smurfs black cherry tomatoes.*
Below right: *Unripe Purple Calabash.*

"Sun-Dried" Tomatoes

Sun-dried tomatoes can be bought at considerable expense preserved in olive oil but you can make your own quite easily. I find this method of drying them in the coolest oven of my 4-door Aga quite successful. A convection oven works brilliantly also. Choose very ripe red tomatoes; the riper the tomatoes, the more intense the flavor.

. . . .

very ripe red tomatoes (any variety)

pinch of sea salt

pinch of sugar

extra virgin olive oil, for drizzling and storing

few basil leaves or a couple of sprigs of rosemary, thyme or annual marjoram (optional)

Cut the tomatoes in half crosswise, arrange in a single layer on a wire rack, season with sea salt and sugar, and drizzle with extra virgin olive oil. If you have a greenhouse you can sun-dry the tomatoes over a period of several days, but despite global warming, for most of us an oven is a more reliable alternative. I leave them in the coolest oven of my ancient 4-door Aga, or in a regular oven at the lowest temperature, until they are totally dried out and wizened, 8 to 12 hours depending on size (after about 8 hours, turn them upside down).

Store in sterilized jars covered with olive oil. A few basil leaves or a couple of sprigs of rosemary, thyme, or annual marjoram added to the oil makes them especially delicious. Cover and keep in a cool, dry, preferably dark place. for about a month. Use in salads or with pasta and enjoy sooner rather than later.

Penne with Sun-Dried Tomatoes & Chorizo

This is one of our favorite ways to use our "sun-dried" tomatoes. They burst onto the food scene in the 1980s like a new discovery but the Mediterraneans have been drying tomatoes in the summer to preserve them for the winter months for ever and ever.

. . . .

SERVES 6

salt and freshly ground black pepper

1 pound penne pasta

¼ pound fresh chorizo, diced

2 tablespoons extra virgin olive oil

¾ ounce Parmesan cheese, freshly grated

2 to 3 tablespoons coarsely chopped flat-leaf parsley

FOR THE SUN-DRIED TOMATO SAUCE

1 tablespoon olive oil

1 small onion, minced

2 garlic cloves, minced

4 ounces sun-dried tomatoes

1¾ ounces fresh chorizo, chopped

¾ cup heavy cream

First make the sun-dried tomato sauce. Heat the olive oil in a sauté pan. Add the chopped onion and garlic, stir, and cook for a few minutes over low heat until soft but not colored. Add the sun-dried tomatoes and chorizo. Cook for an additional 3 to 4 minutes and then add the cream. Bring the sauce to a boil and simmer for 3 to 4 minutes until it has reduced slightly.

Bring 1 gallon water to a boil in a large saucepan over high heat. When the water is boiling fast, add 2 tablespoons of salt and pasta. Stir well. Cook for 10 to 12 minutes.

Meanwhile, cook the diced chorizo in a little olive oil in a skillet until the fat runs and the chorizo begins to crisp.

When the pasta is cooked, drain and toss with the hot sauce and add the grated Parmesan. Toss again and check the seasoning. Sprinkle with the crispy chorizo and flat-leaf parsley and serve immediately.

Confit of Tomatoes

This method concentrates the flavor of the tomatoes deliciously. The oil absorbs the flavor of the tomatoes and will, of course, enhance dressings and salads. Serve on grilled bread, with pasta, mozzarella, and fish.

. . . .

MAKES APPROX. THREE 12-OUNCE JARS

2¼ pounds ripe small or cherry tomatoes
5 or 6 garlic cloves, slightly crushed
4 or 5 sprigs of fresh thyme
extra virgin olive oil, to cover
sea salt and freshly ground black pepper

Preheat the oven to 325°F.

Choose an ovenproof dish that will just fit the tomatoes in a single layer; remove the stems from the tomatoes and put the tomatoes in the dish. Tuck a few garlic cloves and the sprigs of thyme here and there among the tomatoes. Just cover with extra virgin olive oil and sprinkle with salt and freshly ground pepper. Bake for 1½ hours or until soft and tender.

Eat immediately or let cool then store in a sterilized jar covered in the confit oil and use within a week or so.

Roast Tomato Sauce

We love this sauce for pizza—roasting the tomatoes gives extra depth of flavor. Needless to say, it's also great as a basic pasta sauce.

. . . .

MAKES APPROX. 1¾ CUPS

1 pound very ripe tomatoes, halved (choose the sweetest and ripest you have access to)
6 garlic cloves, unpeeled
pinch of sugar
1 tablespoon cheap balsamic vinegar
2 tablespoons olive oil
flaky sea salt and freshly ground black pepper

Preheat the oven 465°F.

Put the tomatoes, cut-side up, and the garlic in a roasting pan in a single layer. Season with salt, freshly ground pepper, and sugar. Sprinkle over the balsamic vinegar and drizzle over the olive oil.

Roast for 15 to 20 minutes until the tomatoes are completely soft and slightly charred at the edges, and the garlic is soft and squishy (we cook them in a wood-burning oven). Run through a food mill or push through a sieve to remove all the skins and seeds. Season to taste.

This sauce will keep in a covered container in a fridge for 2 to 3 days. It can also be frozen but it loses its sweetness.

OCA *Oxalis tuberosa* TENDER PERENNIAL

Oca, originally from South America and sometimes known as the "lost crop of the Incas" or "South-American wood sorrel." It resembles wood sorrel (also an oxalis) and develops lovely yellow flowers in late autumn. Oca is an amazing crop, but unfortunately it still remains virtually unknown outside of the Andes mountains. In the last few years, however, it has gained in popularity in Europe. In New Zealand it's been commercially grown as New Zealand yam since the 1860s. The tubers, leaves and flowers are all edible.

Oca (also spelled Ocha) is a perennial pink-tinged tuber which looks very like pink fir apple potatoes, but has a variety of tastes, depending on how and when you use it. I've only come across pinkish oca but they can be white, yellow, orange/red and orange/purple. Freshly dug it tastes distinctly lemony, due to its high oxalic acid content. However, that dissipates and the sweetness comes

through if left for several days, resulting in two distinctly different flavors from one plant.

VARIETIES

I believe there are many varieties in South America where oca has been grown as a staple for centuries, but in the US for now you're likely to find only one generic variety.

HOW TO GROW

Oca thrives at altitudes too high for most other crops to thrive and yields well in poor soils. It likes a light, rich soil ideally, though. We started the oca off in pots and then transplanted them into the greenhouse in late spring. You could try this in a tunnel—allow at least 2 feet between plants.

The tubers can be planted outdoors directly into well-drained fertile soil in late spring, in much the same way as you would plant potatoes. Allow 12 inches between plants and 16 inches between rows. Earth up just like potatoes. Feed with an organic fertilizer. They should be watered during dry spells, a mulch of compost will help retain the moisture and encourage their growth.

CONTAINER GROWING

One can transfer the plants to a larger pot or a half barrel, but remember that like Jerusalem artichokes it will produce 20 to 24 tubers per plant so allow enough room and keep them well-watered during dry periods, especially in late summer and early autumn.

PESTS AND DISEASES

Oca has good disease and pest resistance and is also resistant to blight, in fact, for this reason some growers are planting it instead of potatoes. However, slugs can be a problem. Even if frost gets the leaves, the tubers will keep forming.

HARVESTING

The tubers don't seem to develop until early autumn, so the longer you leave them in the soil the better. They are not ready to harvest until after the first frosts of winter, by which time the foliage will have died down. Dig them carefully so as not to damage the tubers, dry them and store on a wire frames or trays in a cool shed. They don't need to be covered and can be eaten until they start to sprout again in the spring. Alternatively, they could be stored in boxes of sand in a cool frost-free shed. Save some of the best ones for replanting the following year.

GOOD FOR YOU...

Oca is a worthwhile source of carbohydrates, phosphorus, potassium, iron and vitamin C.

WHAT TO DO WITH A GLUT

Store for winter, save some for seed and store with flowers to encourage them to grow too. Make soup and freeze it.

IN THE KITCHEN

Oca can be fried, roasted, grilled, boiled, or steamed. It can be eaten raw in salads or cooked and then dressed; it takes 10 to 15 minutes to cook and the texture

The oca tubers growing.

is similar to a waxy potato. For **Roast Oca** for 4 to 6 people, preheat the oven to 400°F. Scrub 1 pound oca and slice into equal-sized pieces, so they all cook at a similar rate. Toss in extra virgin olive oil and 2 teaspoons thyme leaves. Spread out the oca in an even layer on a baking sheet. Season with salt and freshly ground pepper and roast for 15 to 20 minutes. Test, make sure they are cooked through. Pour into a hot serving dish and scatter with thyme flowers, if available.

The leaves, young shoots, and yellow trumpet flowers can also be added to salads.

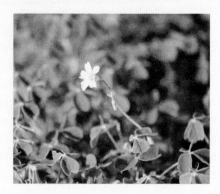

The delicate oca flower appears in late autumn and resembles wood sorrel.

Crudités with Aioli

One of my favorite starters, this can be served all year round and is the perfect way to showcase the raw vegetables from your garden. It fulfills all my criteria for a first course: small helpings of very crisp vegetables with a good homemade garlicky mayo. But to be really delicious one must choose very crisp and fresh vegetables. Cut the vegetables into bite-sized bits so they can be picked up easily. No need for knives and forks; they are usually eaten with fingers.

red cabbage, cut into strips
purple sprouting broccoli, broken into
  florets
calabrese, broken into florets
red or yellow chicory, split into leaves
very fresh Brussels sprouts, cut into
  halves or quarters
oca, peeled and sliced
celery, cut into 2-inch sticks
parsley, thyme, chives, or sprigs of
  watercress, to garnish

FOR THE AIOLI
2 organic egg yolks
1 to 4 garlic cloves, depending on size,
  crushed
pinch of English mustard powder or ¼
  teaspoon French mustard
¼ teaspoon salt
2½ teaspoons white wine vinegar
1 cup sunflower, peanut, or olive oil, or a
  mixture (we use ¾ cup peanut oil and
  ¼ cup olive oil)
2 teaspoons chopped flat-leaf parsley

First make the aioli. Put the egg yolks into a bowl with the crushed garlic, mustard, salt, and white wine vinegar (keep the egg whites to make meringues). Put the oil into a measuring cup. Take a whisk in one hand and the oil in the other and drip the oil onto the egg yolks, drop by drop, whisking at the same time. Within a minute you will notice that the mixture is beginning to thicken. When this happens you can add the oil a little faster, but don't get too cheeky or it will suddenly curdle because the egg yolks can only absorb the oil at a certain pace. Taste and add a little more seasoning and vinegar if necessary.

If the sauce curdles it will suddenly become quite thin, and if left sitting the oil will start to float to the top of the sauce. If this happens you can quite easily rectify the situation by putting another egg yolk or 1 to 2 tablespoons of boiling water into a clean bowl, then whisk in the curdled mixture, a half teaspoon at a time, until it emulsifies again. Finally, add the chopped parsley and taste for seasoning.

Wash and prepare the vegetables. Arrange on individual white side plates in contrasting colors, with a little blob of aioli in the center. Alternatively, arrange a large dish or basket for the center of the table. Arrange little heaps of each vegetable in contrasting colors. Put a bowl of aioli in the center and encourage your guests to help themselves.

For a summer variation you can use: whole cherry tomatoes or quartered ripe tomatoes, cauliflower florets, String beans or mangetout, carrots and cucumber cut into 5cm sticks, tiny spring onions, whole radishes, and thinly sliced fennel.

Oca, Chorizo, Scallion & Radish Salad

One of the many delicious ways to enjoy your oca and look how appetising it looks.

SERVES 8

2¼ pounds oca, boiled or roasted (page 195)

3 to 4 tablespoons Ballymaloe French Dressing (see page 182)

½ cup plus 2 tablespoons homemade mayonnaise (see below)

¼ pound cured chorizo, cut into ¼-inch dice, or crisp cooked bacon lardons

6 scallions, cut at an angle

lots of fresh radishes, cut in half

sea salt and freshly ground black pepper

FOR THE MAYONNAISE
(MAKES 1¼ CUPS)

2 organic egg yolks

pinch of English mustard powder or ¼ teaspoon French mustard

¼ teaspoon salt

2 teaspoons white wine vinegar

1 cup sunflower or olive oil or a mixture (we use ¾ cup sunflower oil and ¼ cup olive oil)

First make the mayonnaise. Put the egg yolks into a bowl with the mustard, salt, and white wine vinegar. Put the oil into a measure. Take a whisk in one hand and the oil in the other and drip the oil onto the egg yolks, drop by drop, whisking at the same time. Within a minute you will notice that the mixture is beginning to thicken. When this happens you can add the oil a little faster, but don't get too cheeky or it will suddenly curdle because the egg yolks can only absorb the oil at a certain rate. Taste and add a little more seasoning and vinegar if necessary.

If the mayonnaise curdles, it will suddenly become quite thin, and if left sitting the oil will start to float to the top of the sauce. If this happens you can quite easily rectify the situation by putting another egg yolk or 1 to 2 tablespoons of boiling water into a clean bowl and whisking in the curdled mayonnaise, a half-teaspoon at a time, until it emulsifies again.

While still warm, cut the cooked oca into ⅓-inch-thick slices. Toss gently in the French dressing.

Thin the mayonnaise with a little water if necessary. Sprinkle the chorizo or bacon and most of the scallions over the oca. Drizzle the mayonnaise over the top. Toss gently to coat. Taste and perk up the seasoning if necessary.

Sprinkle a few more slivers of spring onion and lots of radishes over the top.

> **DID YOU KNOW?**
> Oca is second only to the potato in agricultural importance in its homelands of Bolivia and Peru, Argentina, and Venezuela, so it's time for us to get acquainted.

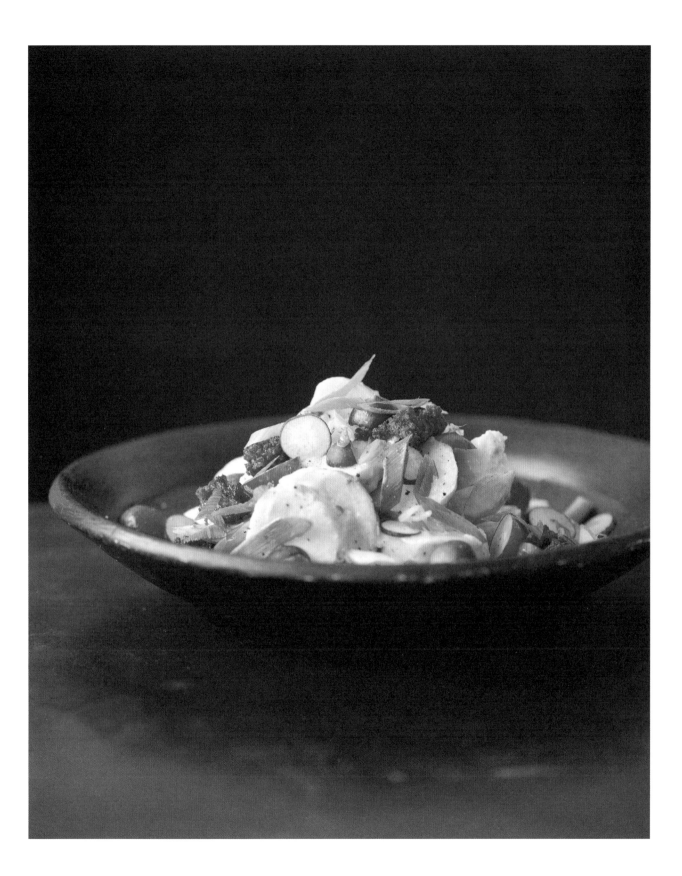

PARSNIPS

Pastinaca sativa BIENNIAL, USUALLY GROWN AS AN ANNUAL

Don't forget the humble parsnip, a fantastic winter friend which somehow lurks in the background and rarely stars as it should. After all, they are cheap and cheerful in the shops and farmers' markets, but with rare exceptions the parsnips in the shops have been in bleach to keep them white, so always buy unwashed roots if possible.

The ivory colored taproot is a great favorite in our family, not just for its sweet and nutty flavor but for its immense versatility. In the 1980s Jane Grigson gave the parsnip quite a boost when she published her recipe for Curried Parsnip Soup, which we all found terrifically exciting. It was a favorite at dinner parties all winter long.

VARIETIES

Halblange White—Flavorsome variety with a thick, short, pointed root, which does well in shallower soils. Frost hardy. **Lancer**—Large parsnip, with long roots and good flavor, with resistance to canker.

HOW TO GROW

Parsnips are easy to grow, we sow in mid-spring in rows. The seeds can take several weeks to germinate, but when they do appear, thin to 6 to 8 inches and then just sit back.

As with other root vegetables, it's best to avoid ground that has been manured during the previous two years, otherwise the roots are liable to fork if the soil is too rich.

CONTAINER GROWING

Parsnips aren't really suitable for containers because of the large, long root, and their slow growth; restricting their growth in a container won't help.

HARVESTING

We start to enjoy them from mid-autumn while they are still relatively small but so tender and delicious that they can be roasted whole and eaten in their entirety. Despite the general perception that they must be cooked, they are delicious raw, just freshly grated, tossed simply in freshly squeezed lemon juice and extra virgin olive oil. Older parsnips can have woody cores which are best discarded or added in moderation to the stockpot.

Like all root vegetables, a few nights of frost intensifies their sweetness, converting the starch into sugars.

PESTS AND DISEASES

Canker, the brown rot, is the main problem, which starts at the crown. Sowing later sometimes helps. Improve drainage, rotate crops, and sow canker-resistant varieties to help.

Parsnips can be attacked by the same

Freshly dug Tender and True parsnips—what an evocative name.

bugs as carrots, mainly carrot fly (see page 157 for how to prevent it).

GOOD FOR YOU...

Low in calories, high in fiber which helps with the management of blood sugar and cholesterol levels, obesity and constipation problems. Parsnips contain high levels of potassium, magnesium, phosphorus, zinc and iron, and an impressive range of vitamins—B, C, E and K and antioxidants.

WHAT TO DO WITH A GLUT

Provided the soil is well-drained, parsnips will happily remain in the ground throughout the winter. However, if you need to make space for other crops, dig up the remainder of your crop and store in a sand box in a cool, dark place or in a clamp. Do not wash the roots of parsnips, they keep better unwashed.

IN THE KITCHEN

Apart from the usual ways, cubes of parsnip bulk out a stew or casserole and add sweetness to a tray of roast vegetables, and silky parsnip mash is the perfect foil for the rich flavor of a haunch of venison, a roast duck, or squab.

To make **Potato and Parsnip Mash** to serve 8, scrub 2¾ pounds parsnips and 1 pound "old" potatoes, such as Golden

DID YOU KNOW?

Parsnips were originally used as animal fodder, and as a sweetener before sugar cane and sugar beet were introduced to Europe. Parsnip wine was widely drunk in Ireland.

Wonders or Kerr's Pinks, put them into a saucepan of cold water, add a good pinch of salt, and bring to a boil. When the potatoes are about half cooked (about 15 minutes for "old" potatoes), strain off two-thirds of the water, replace the lid on the saucepan, put over a gentle heat, and leave the potatoes to steam for 5 to 10 minutes or until they are cooked. Peel the parsnips and cut into chunks; cook for 15 to 30 minutes in boiling salted water until tender. Drain and mash; keep warm. When the potatoes are just cooked, bring 1¼ to 1½ cups whole milk to a boil. Pull the skin off the potatoes, mash the flesh quickly while they are still warm, and beat in enough boiling milk to make a fluffy mash. (If you have a large quantity, put the potatoes in the bowl of a stand mixer and beat with the paddle attachment.) Then stir in the mashed parsnip with about 4 tablespoons butter. Season to taste.

Parsnip Chips are beloved as a nibble and to pile high onto game salads.

Most of the flavor of parsnips is just beneath the skin, so don't overpeel them. Parsnips are closely related to carrots, parsley, and celery. The jury seems to be out on whether one can eat the leaves or not. I've nibbled the leaves of young parsnips without ill effect but in the absence of more scientific proof, it's best to be cautious.

Parsnip seedlings in a modular tray ready for transplanting.

Duck Shepherd's Pie with Potato & Parsnip Mash

We can't bear to waste a scrap of Nora Aherne's beautiful ducks, so we tear every single shred off the carcass to make this delicious duck shepherd's pie. The potato and parsnip mash is the perfect topping here but it's also delicious on its own.

SERVES 6

2 tablespoons butter or 3 to 4 tablespoons extra virgin olive oil
6 ounces chopped onions
scant ¼ cup all-purpose flour
1¾ cups duck stock and leftover gravy
2½ teaspoons mushroom ketchup (optional)
1 tablespoon chopped curly or flat-leaf parsley, plus extra to garnish
1 tablespoon chopped marjoram
1 teaspoon thyme leaves
1 pound ground cooked duck (include some crispy skin)
1 pound Potato and Parsnip Mash (see above)
sea salt and freshly ground black pepper
Garlic Butter (see page 47), to serve

Preheat the oven to 350°F.

Heat the butter or extra virgin olive oil in a pan, add the chopped onions, cover with a round of greased parchment paper, and cook over low heat for 5 minutes. Add the flour and cook until brown. Add the duck stock and gravy, bring to a boil, then skim. Add the mushroom ketchup, if using, then the chopped parsley, marjoram, thyme leaves, salt, and pepper, and simmer for 5 minutes.

Add the ground duck to the sauce and bring to a boil. Put in a 9-inch pie dish, cover with the potato and parsnip mash and score with a fork. Cook for about 30 minutes. Garnish with parsley and serve with garlic butter.

This pie can of course be refrigerated and reheated later. It also freezes well.

Parsnip & Maple Syrup Cake with Parsnip Crisps

A moist and delicious cake—this recipe uses parsnips in two ways; make extra crisps to nibble with drinks.

SERVES 8

¾ cup (1½ sticks) butter
6 tablespoons maple syrup
3 large organic eggs
2 cups self-rising flour
2 teaspoons baking powder
2 teaspoons pie spice mix
9 ounces parsnips, peeled and grated
1 apple, peeled, cored, and grated
½ cup pecans or hazelnuts, chopped
zest and juice of 1 small orange
edible flowers, to garnish (optional)

FOR THE PARSNIP CRISPS

1 large parsnip
sunflower oil or peanut oil, for frying
salt

FOR THE FILLING

10½ ounces cream cheese
2 tablespoons maple syrup

Preheat the oven to 350°F. Brush two 8-inch round cake pans with a little melted butter and line the bottoms with parchment paper.

Melt the butter and maple syrup in a pan over low heat, then cool slightly. Whisk the eggs into the mixture, then stir into the flour, baking powder, and pie spice mix. Add the parsnip, apple, chopped nuts, orange zest and juice. Divide the mixture between the two pans and bake for 35 to 40 minutes or until just starting to shrink from the sides of the pans. Cool on a wire rack.

Meanwhile, make the parsnip crisps. Scrub and peel the parsnip and either slice into wafer-thin rounds or peel off long slivers lengthwise with a swivel-top peeler. Let dry on paper towels.

Heat oil in a deep-fryer to 300°F. Drop a few slivers of parsnip at a time into the oil; they will color and crisp quickly. Drain on paper towels and sprinkle with salt.

To make the filling, mix the cream cheese and maple syrup together. Spread over the bottom of one cooled cake and the top of the other. Sandwich together. Decorate the top of the cake with parsnip crisps and edible flowers if available.

Luke's Parsnip Ice Cream

An unexpected use for parsnips, but they make gorgeous ice cream, plus the sliced parsnips can be cooked and made into a purée after they have been infused in the liquid. My friend Luke Dodd is a genial host and an adventurous cook.

SERVES 6

1 cup heavy cream
3 cups whole milk
9 ounces parsnips, peeled and thinly sliced
6 organic egg yolks
1 cup granulated sugar

FOR THE PEDRO XIMÉNEZ RAISINS

1¼ cups Muscatel or Lexia raisins
boiling water
1 cup Pedro Ximénez sherry, warmed

Pour the cream and milk into a heavy-bottomed saucepan, add the parsnips, and heat until just about to simmer. Remove from the heat and let infuse for several hours, or overnight. Strain out the parsnips and save for a purée or gratin.

Meanwhile, make the Pedro Ximénez raisins. Pour boiling water over the raisins; drain and let cool. When cold, put into a bowl with the warm sherry and let plump up for several hours. They will keep in a jar in the fridge for 4 to 5 days.

The next day, whisk the egg yolks and sugar together until pale and fluffy. Reheat the cream to the simmering point, then whisk it into the eggs, being careful not to let it curdle. Pour back into the pan and cook, stirring, over medium heat, until the mixture begins to thicken. Chill over ice, stirring regularly until cold. Pour into an ice cream maker and churn until thick and fluffy. Serve with a few Pedro Ximénez-soaked raisins scattered over the top.

Cod, Bacon & Parsnip Chowder

A chowder is a wonderfully substantial fish soup, or indeed it could almost be classified as a stew. It is certainly a meal in itself and there are lots of variations on the theme. A firm-fleshed fish like monkfish works best. The base can be prepared ahead. Some smoked haddock can be added but be careful not to add to much or it will be overpowering. The parsnip may seem like a surprise addition but it's so good.

. . . .

SERVES 8 TO 10

1 tablespoon olive or sunflower oil
¼ pound bacon, cut into ¼-inch dice
6 to 8 ounces onions, chopped
¼ cup all-purpose flour
1¾ cups milk
3¾ cups homemade fish stock or water
  as a last resort
bouquet garni made up of 6 parsley stalks,
  2 sprigs of thyme, and a bay leaf
¾ pound potatoes, such as Golden
  Wonders, peeled and cut into ¼-inch
  dice
½ pound parsnips, cut into ¼-inch dice
pinch of ground mace
pinch of cayenne pepper
1½ pounds haddock, monkfish, cod, or
  other firm white fish (or a mixture),
  skinned and deboned
½ cup plus 2 tablespoons light cream
sea salt and freshly ground black pepper
lots of coarsely chopped curly or flat-leaf
  parsley and chives, to garnish
hot crusty bread or hot crackers, to serve

Heat the oil in a stainless-steel saucepan and brown the bacon well for about 5 minutes until it is crisp and golden. Add the onions, cover, and sweat for a few minutes over low heat. Stir in the flour and cook for a couple of minutes more. Heat the milk. Add the fish stock or water gradually, then the hot milk, bouquet garni, potatoes, and parsnips. Season well with salt, pepper, mace, and cayenne. Cover and simmer for 5 to 6 minutes until the potatoes and parsnips are almost cooked.

Meanwhile, cut the fish into roughly 1-inch square pieces. Add the fish to the pot as soon as the tip of a knife will go through the potato. (Stir as little as possible once the fish has been added.) Simmer gently for 3 to 4 minutes, then stir in the cream. When the soup returns to a boil, remove from the heat. Remember that the fish will continue to cook in the heat of the chowder so it should not be overcooked. Season to taste and sprinkle with chopped fresh parsley and chives. Hot crusty white bread or hot crackers are usually served with a chowder.

SCARLET RUNNER BEANS *Phaseolus coccineus*
ANNUAL (IN THE TROPICS THEY ARE PERENNIAL)

These are gorgeous, kind of old-fashioned, but are so worth growing at least 5 or 6 to romp up a bamboo tepee in your garden. They can also be grown up a trellis to provide shelter or privacy—your very own fairy tale beanstalk. The hardy, vigorous vines grow to over 10 feet and are covered with clusters of scarlet flowers which produce a large volume of food for a relatively small area of ground space. Runner beans are hugely rewarding to grow and are more tolerant of cool conditions than green beans.

Some keen gardeners grow scarlet runners solely as an ornamental, but it's such a pity not to harvest the bean pods. Runner beans are very prolific, so don't worry if some beans get away on you, just let them grow until the beans swell inside. We enjoy them as shell beans—see below—or you can leave them on the plant even longer until the pods begin to dry and become wrinkly and slightly moldy, then collect them, dry and save for winter use in soups and stews. You can also save some of the beautiful, violet-purple mottled-black seeds for next year's crop. The pretty scarlet, white or purple flowers are also edible and beautiful in flower arrangements, but don't overdo the picking as each flower is a potential bean.

The "spent" plant is a worthwhile addition to the compost heap and, like all beans, they fix nitrogen in the soil. The runner bean is truly the plant that keeps on giving.

VARIETIES

Runner beans are also known as string beans, but now there are many stringless varieties, although we still love the following:

Painted Lady—Old favorite from 1855 with lovely red and white flowers.
Scarlet Emperor—Tall, well-known traditional early variety with scarlet flowers, dates back to 1906, reliable and popular as ever.
Lady Di—Dark green pods, bred to be completely stringless.
Celebration—Heavy cropper with lovely salmon-pink flowers and long straight pods.
White Emergo—Vigorous, well-flavored variety with attractive white flowers and cream-colored beans, similar to cannellini beans.
Hestia—Dwarf variety with red and white flowers, stringless.
Sunset—Unique peach-colored blossoms on 6 foot vines.
Blue Speckled Tepary—tan and blue spotted beans used in traditional Southwestern cooking.

HOW TO GROW

All beans enjoy fertile, well-drained soil and a sunny sheltered spot in the garden.

Runner beans are not frost tolerant and need a minimum temperature of 50°F to germinate.

You can get ahead by planting the seeds about 2 inches deep in a cool glasshouse in small pots of compost. Harden off the plants before planting outside a couple of weeks later. Then plant the seedlings 2 inches deep, 12 inches apart in rows 18 inches apart.

Seeds can also be planted directly in the ground outside in early summer, but mice love them and if the weather is very wet the seeds may rot in the ground.

You'll need to provide a tall support of bamboo canes, trellis or wire. Alternatively, choose the "three sisters method" which we use for corn, beans and squash. The corn provides a support for the bean to climb up, and in turn benefits from the nitrogen, as does the squash which also provides ground cover and helps to retain moisture in the soil. A brilliant symbiotic relationship—this method is practiced by the native American Indians and has worked brilliantly in our kitchen garden for years. It fascinates all who see it.

Sow 3 to 4 weeks apart for a continuous supply throughout the season. If you plant a row of sweet peas at the same time it will help pollination, as well as adding color and scent.

Runner beans climbing up a bamboo wigwam in the kitchen garden.

HARVESTING

Keep picking pods for a continuous supply of beans. Harvest from midsummer to mid-autumn.

Runner beans can be picked at many stages, from when the beans are 3 to 4 inches long up to 12 inches or more. However, some of our favorite varieties, like Painted Lady, get stringy and fibrous if allowed to grow too large. Bend the bean over your finger, if it snaps it's sure to be a bit tough, but the pliable beans will still be tender and delicious.

Trim the edges of the large beans with a paring knife to remove the strings.

Towards the end of the season, allow some of the beans in the large pods to swell. Harvest as fresh shell beans or cook as cranberry beans.

CONTAINER GROWING

They grow brilliantly in a large container or willow basket on a balcony or veranda. Make a wigwam with canes and tie securely at the top with strong string.

PESTS AND DISEASES

Birds can sometimes peck the flowers and damage them, so some scarecrows will help. Slugs may be a problem during initial growth stage but once they start climbing they are usually okay.

In a cold wet summer, lack of pollinating insects can be a problem in setting the flowers. This can improve later in the summer when earlier and

more attractive flowers like white clover are finished, so the bees will give more attention to the beans.

WHAT TO DO WITH A GLUT?

Freeze, salt or make **Runner Bean Chutney** (page 206)—yummy!

GOOD FOR YOU...

Runner beans are high in fiber and low in calories. They are also high in antioxidants and a good source of omega-3 fatty acids, also a source of iron, calcium, manganese and potassium.

IN THE KITCHEN

Runner beans are deliciously crunchy raw, when they are just an inch long. As they get a little longer, cook them whole in well-salted boiling water, and when larger but still pliable, string the edges and cut thinly at an angle.

Beans need a lot of salt in the cooking water to bring up the flavor. If you need to cook them ahead try this—the proportion of salt to water is vitally important for the flavor of the beans. To serve 8, choose 2 pounds beans of a similar size, and trim them. If they are small and thin leave them whole; if they are larger cut them into 1- to 1½-inch pieces at a long angle. Bring 5 cups water to a fast rolling boil, add 1 tablespoon salt, then toss in the beans. Boil very fast for 5 to 6 minutes or until just cooked (they should still retain a little bite). Drain immediately. (The beans may be refreshed under cold water at this point and kept aside for several hours.) Melt 2½ to 4 tablespoons butter or extra virgin olive oil in the saucepan, toss in the beans, taste, and season with freshly ground pepper and a little sea salt if necessary. To reheat, just before serving, plunge into boiling salted water for 30 to 60 seconds, drain, and toss in butter.

For **Runner Beans with Fresh Chile**, drain cooked beans well. Heat

Scarlet runner bean blossom—steal a couple of flowers to sprinkle over salads.

2 tablespoons olive oil in a wide sauté pan, add 1 chopped garlic clove and 1 or 2 chopped chiles, toss, season well with salt and freshly ground pepper, and add 1 tablespoon coarsely chopped curly or flat-leaf parsley. Toss, taste, and serve.

For **Runner Beans with Tomato Fondue**, cook the beans as in the above recipe and drain them. Mix with 1 quantity of the recipe of **Tomato Fondue** (see page 187). Heat through and serve. Add some chile flakes to the Tomato Fondue for extra zizz; a little chopped cured chorizo is also a yummy addition.

The leaves are also edible and can be eaten raw in salads or cooked as a "famine" green. Use the flowers in salads and to garnish both sweet and savory dishes.

Runner beans can be substituted in virtually all green bean recipes.

The roots can also be dug up at the end of the crop and cooked for yet another experience.

Scarlet Runner Beans with Tomato, Halloumi & Anchovies

Another interesting combination of flavors to showcase runner beans—sprinkle some of the scarlet flowers over the top.

. . . .

SERVES 4 TO 6

1 pound runner or green beans

3 tablespoons extra virgin olive oil

12 to 18 sweet cherry tomatoes

2 to 3 teaspoons honey

1 tablespoon lemon juice

4 to 8 ounces halloumi cheese

8 to 12 anchovies

fresh basil leaves

sea salt and freshly ground black pepper

a few scarlet flowers, to garnish (optional)

Prepare and cook the beans as per the method on page 204. Drain and drizzle with enough extra virgin olive oil to coat lightly.

Halve the tomatoes. Season with salt and pepper. Drizzle with a little honey. Sprinkle with lemon juice and extra virgin olive oil, toss gently, and taste.

Just before serving, heat a skillet over high heat and add a little extra virgin olive oil. Slice the halloumi and fry quickly for 2 to 3 minutes until golden. Transfer to hot plates.

Add some warm or room-temperature runner beans and a few pieces of tomato salad. Add the anchovies, a few basil leaves, some scarlet flowers, and a drizzle of extra virgin olive oil.

Green Bean Curry

This is one of my favorites Sri Lankan curries because of the clever combination of spices. Usually made with snake or yard-long beans, we use a variety of green beans, including runner beans and green beans, from the garden.

. . . .

SERVES 6 TO 8

2 tablespoons sunflower oil

2 teaspoons cumin seeds

4 shallots, finely sliced

4 green chiles, minced

4 garlic cloves, minced

20 curry leaves

1 teaspoon dried chile leaves (optional)

½ teaspoon ground turmeric

2 teaspoons fenugreek seeds, coarsely ground

2 teaspoons fennel seeds, coarsely ground

1 teaspoon salt

½ teaspoon granulated sugar

1½ pounds green beans, cut into 1-inch pieces

1 (14-ounce) can coconut milk

juice of 1 lime

sea salt and freshly ground black pepper

Heat the oil in a wok until hot, add the cumin seeds, then immediately add the shallots, chiles, garlic and curry leaves. Stir and cook for 2 to 3 minutes until the shallots have softened. Add the remaining spices, salt and sugar, stir for 30 seconds then add the green beans. Cook, stirring frequently, for 4 to 5 minutes. Pour in the coconut milk and simmer for 7 to 8 minutes or until it has thickened and the beans are tender. Add the lime juice and season to taste.

Serve as part of a selection of Sri Lankan curries or with rice—it is also delicious with a pan-grilled lamb chop.

Salade Niçoise

This is the quintessential French salad and makes a wonderful summer lunch. Some versions include crisp red and green peppers and some omit the potato for a less-substantial salad. All the many varieties of green beans can be included.

SERVES APPROX. 8

8 medium new potatoes, cooked but still
   warm
Ballymaloe French Dressing (page 182)
3 or 4 ripe tomatoes, peeled and quartered
4 ounces green beans, trimmed and cut
   into approx. 2-inch lengths, blanched, and
   refreshed
pinch of granulated sugar
2½ teaspoons chopped chives
2½ teaspoons chopped flat-leaf parsley
2½ teaspoons annual marjoram or thyme
1 crisp lettuce (optional)
3 hard-boiled organic eggs, quartered
12 black olives
1 teaspoon capers (optional)
2 (3½-ounce) cans tuna and/or 1 (2-ounce)
   tin anchovies
8 tiny scallions
sea salt and freshly ground black pepper

Slice the new potatoes into ¼-inch-thick slices and toss in some dressing while still warm. Season with salt and freshly ground pepper. Toss the tomatoes and beans in some more dressing, season with salt, pepper and sugar and sprinkle with some of the chopped herbs.

Line a shallow bowl with lettuce leaves, if using, and add the potatoes. Arrange the remaining ingredients appetisingly on top of the potatoes, finishing off with the olives, capers, if using, and chunks of tuna and/or the anchovies. Drizzle some more dressing over the top. Sprinkle over the remaining herbs and scallions and serve.

SALAD NIÇOISE WITH PAN-GRILLED OR GRILLED MACKEREL
Dry each fish fillet with a paper towel then dip them in well-seasoned flour. Spread a little soft butter on the flesh side of each fillet as though you were meanly buttering a slice of bread. Preheat a grill pan or grill. Cook the mackerel flesh-side down for 2 to 3 minutes then turn over and cook on the other side until the skin is crispy and golden. Serve 1 or 2 fillets of mackerel criss-crossed on top of each portion of salad.

Runner Bean Chutney

I first tasted this chutney at the gem that is Glebe Café near Baltimore, in West Cork. Jean Perry shared the recipe, which she originally found in an old treasured book—*The Complete Book of Preserving* by Mary Norwak.

MAKES EIGHT 12-OUNCE JARS

2¼ pounds runner beans, sliced into slivers
1½ pounds onions
3¼ cups vinegar
scant ¼ cup cornstarch
5 teaspoons ground turmeric
¼ cup mustard powder
1 pound demerara sugar

Cook the beans in boiling salted water for 8 to 10 minutes until tender then drain well. Cook the chopped onions in one-third of the vinegar for 15 minutes until tender.

Mix the cornstarch, turmeric, and mustard with a little vinegar into a smooth paste then put all the ingredients except the sugar in a large pan and cook for 10 to 15 minutes, stirring regularly. Add the sugar and boil for 15 minutes more.

Pour into sterilized jars, making sure there are no air bubbles, then seal.

They will keep unopened for 6 to 9 months, but are best enjoyed before that.

CRANBERRY BEANS

Phaseolus vulgaris ANNUAL

Even though I'm a passionate vegetable grower, few vegetables get me as excited as cranberry beans romping up the bean poles. They are so beautiful; the pale green, pink and red splattered pods are one of the most spectacular plants we grow in the garden. They are also called borlotti beans or Roman beans. I can't imagine a supper more satisfying than cranberry beans drizzled with a delicious extra virgin olive oil, served with some salted pork or streaky bacon. The only disappointment is that the speckled color fades during cooking, but the deeply satisfying flavor and texture more than compensate. We enjoy them both fresh as shelled beans and dried.

VARIETIES

We're very fond of **Lingua de Fuoco** (Tongue of fire), which grows to 79 inches high and is very reliable in our unpredictable climate.

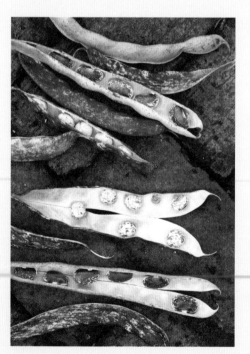

Lingua de Fuoco—*all the beans dry in the pods—so photogenic.*

HOW TO GROW

Cranberry beans like fertile, well-drained soil and a sunny sheltered spot. They are slightly more tender than runner beans. We start them off in the greenhouse, sowing the seed in deep seed trays or in toilet-roll tubes in early summer. When the seedlings are 6 inches high and all chance of frost is passed, we plant them directly into the ground. All beans and peas fix nitrogen in the soil. Plant them about 8 inches apart and keep a good eye out for slugs and snails.

If you are planting them directly into the soil outdoors, wait for another few weeks until all danger of frost has passed. Plant the seeds 5 inchs deep and 8 inches apart.

CONTAINER GROWING

Cranberry beans can be grown successfully in a large pot, but make sure there are lots of drainage holes. Plant three and make a bamboo wigwam for them to romp over. Keep well- watered and don't forget to mulch to retain moisture in summer.

Some dwarf varieties also suitable for container growing include: *Solista*, which reaches about 2 feet, *Cranberry Supremo Nano*, about 20 to 24 inches high, and *Splendido* which grows to 18 inches high.

PESTS AND DISEASES

Snails and slugs can decimate the young seedlings as they establish—see page 626 for how to discourage them. Try growing nasturtiums nearby to deter aphids. Mice can also be a problem at seed stage, so set traps to catch them.

Two stages of drying—the red pod is drying up and the yellow is just about to shrivel.

HARVESTING

Once again, one gets two bites of the cherry here. The fresh shell beans are ready to eat in mid- to late summer when the beans feel plump in the pods. Then you can dry the more mature beans for later use.

Let the pods dry naturally on the plants for as long as possible, the beans should rattle in the pods when they are ready to pick in late summer or early autumn. Leave them to dry out further inside, spread out on a wire rack or newspaper. Then remove the beans from

DID YOU KNOW?

The Iroquois American Indians believed that corn, squash and beans were three inseparable sisters who grow, support each other and thrive together.

the pods; they should be hard and dry. If in any doubt, leave them to dry further before storing in Kilner jars. They will keep for years. Put the pods onto the compost heap.

GOOD FOR YOU...

Cranberry beans are low GI and high in protein and contain all nine essential amino acids and B-complex vitamins.

WHAT TO DO WITH A GLUT?

Leave the beans to dry naturally for winter use. In early autumn when the pods begin to wither, just cut the plant and let it hang upside down from a wire or rafter, in a well-ventilated tunnel, greenhouse or shed until the pods are dry. Shell the beans, then dry for a few more days. We bring them into the kitchen and spread them on drying trays, then store in jars or baskets. They keep well, pretty much indefinitely, but gradually become drier. Dried beans can of course also be used for seed.

IN THE KITCHEN

Widely used in Italian cooking, especially hearty stews, they taste so good and are deeply sustaining.

To soak home-dried beans, cover with cold water, stir thoroughly with your hand—the loose bits will rise to the top—then pour off the water and repeat once or twice more until the water runs clear. Re-cover with cold water and let soak overnight.

Gillian's Cranberry Beans with Capezzana Extra Virgin Olive Oil

Gillian Hegarty cooked at the River Café for many years before coming to Ballymaloe House as head chef, and this is one of her favorite ways to enjoy cranberry beans. They can be used in soups or salads, or as an accompaniment with meat, fish, or risotto. If using dried cranberry beans, soak them overnight in lots of cold water.

. . . .

SERVES 6

1 pound fresh cranberry beans, shelled or
   ½ pound dried
2 tomatoes, cut in half
3 sprigs of sage
1 whole red or green chile
6 garlic cloves, peeled
Forum Cabernet Sauvignon red wine
   vinegar, to taste
⅓ cup extra virgin olive oil
flaky sea salt and freshly ground black
   pepper
arugula leaves, to serve (optional)

Put the first five ingredients into a large saucepan. Cover with roughly 3 times the volume of cold water. Bring to a boil then reduce the heat to a simmer and cook until soft but not mushy, approximately 20 to 30 minutes if fresh or 1 hour if dried. Each bean should still be perfectly intact. Fresh cranberry beans will take a lot less time to cook then dried beans.

When the beans are soft, drain off most of the liquid, leaving about 1 cup. Spread them out on a rimmed baking sheet so they are not squashed. Remove the sage and the skins from the tomatoes and discard. Pick out the garlic cloves, crush them, and add the flesh to the beans. Remove the seeds from the chile, chop the flesh, and add back to the saucepan. Season with flaky sea salt and freshly ground black pepper, a good-quality red wine vinegar such as Forum, and lots of extra virgin olive oil.

Serve hot or at room temperature with lots of fresh arugula leaves.

Duck Confit with Cranberry Beans & Chanterelles

We love the gutsy flavor of duck confit and chanterelles with cranberry beans. This is a superb winter dish. Use goose instead of duck if you prefer.

. . . .

SERVES 6

FOR THE DUCK CONFIT

6 free-range duck legs or 3 legs and 3
   breasts
7 garlic cloves, unpeeled
1 tablespoon sea salt
1 teaspoon freshly cracked black
   peppercorns
a few gratings of fresh nutmeg
1 teaspoon thyme leaves
1 crumbled bay leaf
2 pounds duck or goose fat
2 sprigs of thyme
2 sprigs of flat-leaf parsley, plus extra to
   serve

FOR THE CRANBERRY BEANS

1 pound fresh or dried cranberry beans
2 tablespoons extra virgin olive oil, plus
   extra for drizzling
1 large sprig of rosemary
2 sprigs of thyme
3 garlic cloves, minced
2 tablespoons butter
7 ounces chanterelles
sea salt and freshly ground black pepper

watercress and organic leaves, to serve

Rub the duck legs all over with 1 cut clove of the garlic. Mix the salt, pepper, nutmeg, thyme, and bay leaf together, sprinkle the duck legs sparingly with the salt mixture, and put into an earthenware dish. Cover and leave overnight in the fridge.

Preheat the oven to 225°F. If you have the carcasses, cut every scrap of fat from them and place in an ovenproof dish. Render slowly in the oven until the fat is liquid, then strain, and set aside. You will need about 2 pounds of fat, so add some from a jar if necessary.

Next day, melt the fat in a deep saucepan over low heat. Wash the cure off the duck legs, dry them, and put them into the fat—there should be enough to cover the duck pieces completely. Bring to a boil and add the herbs and remaining garlic cloves. Simmer over low heat until the duck is very tender, (1½ to 2 hours or when a bamboo skewer can go through the thickest part of the leg with no resistance).

Remove the duck legs from the fat. Strain it, leave it to rest for a few minutes, and then pour the fat off the meat juices. When the duck is cold, pack into a sterilized earthenware crock or jar and pour the cooled fat over so that the pieces are completely submerged. Store in the fridge until needed. (Leave for at least a week to mature. When needed, melt the fat to remove the confit.)

Cover the dried cranberry beans, if using, with plenty of cold water and soak overnight if possible.

Drain, transfer to a saucepan, and cover with fresh cold water. Add the extra oil, sprig of rosemary, thyme, and garlic cloves. Bring to a boil, reduce the heat, and simmer gently, covered, until the beans are soft, about 30 minutes if fresh and up to 1 hour if dried. Drain (save the cooking liquid for soup) and season with salt and freshly ground pepper. Drizzle with lots of extra virgin olive oil.

Heat a skillet over high heat. Melt the butter and toss the chanterelles in the foaming butter for 3 to 4 minutes. Season with salt and freshly ground black pepper and add to the cranberry beans with the parsley. Drizzle with extra virgin olive oil. Check the seasoning.

To serve, preheat the oven to 450°F. Put the duck confit on a baking sheet and cook for 10 to 12 minutes until warmed through and the skin is crisp. Put 3 to 4 tablespoons of the bean and chantrelle mixture onto a plate. Put a crispy skinned duck leg on top. Scatter with flat-leaf parsley sprigs and a few flakes of sea salt. Serve immediately.

STRING BEANS *Phaseolus vulgaris* ANNUAL

Purple Queen—looks attractive growing but turns a muddy green color when cooked.

String beans give so much bang for your buck, they keep giving all summer long. We grow several varieties every year, both round and flat pods, but if I had to choose, I'd opt for the latter. The flavor is super beany, the texture is soft and silky, they are cooked in a matter of minutes and lap up butter and extra virgin olive oil, fresh herbs, and spices and can, of course, be added to myriad other dishes.

VARIETIES

There are three types of string bean: dwarf, climbers and beans for drying. The dwarf type don't need support or staking, but the climbers do. For those with a small plot, the dwarf variety could be the best choice, they can yield up to 12 to 18 pounds (2 or 3 plants per station) if you keep picking.

DWARF

Royalty—Purple pods that turn green on cooking. Good cropper, stringless.
Slenderette—Maincrop variety, lovely waxy golden pods, good flavor, and crop over a long period. Freeze well.

CLIMBING

Helda—Medium early with flat pods, producing over long period.
Cobra—Tubular stringless pods, very productive, can be harvested over a long period, suitable for growing indoors or outdoors. Green pods with mauve flowers.
Fortex—Early and dependable; extra long round pods.

VARIETY BRED SPECIALLY FOR DRYING

Brown Dutch—Egg-shaped bean with a smooth texture and nutty flavor. If you are growing them to dry, the pods should not be picked until they are dry and crisp.
Light Red Kidney—early harvests of light red beans, perfect for chili and soup.

HOW TO GROW

String beans are easy to grow. Keep the ground weed-free and choose a warm, well-sheltered, sunny spot. Beans need rich, friable, fertile, moisture-retentive soil, so dig in plenty of compost in the winter. Like all members of the legume family, the root nodules have nitrogen-fixing bacteria which will benefit the soil and the follow-on crop, such as brassicas, so they don't need the addition of farmyard manure. The flowers are also pretty and vary in color depending on the variety, but are mostly mauve or white.

Beans need a minimum temperature of 65°F to germinate. In a greenhouse, tunnel, cold frame or cloche, sow in seed compost in spring in 3 ½-inch pots. Put 2 or 3 seeds into each pot to guarantee germination, and plant a few extra to allow for losses. Water with a fine rose nozzle, the seeds will germinate within a week. When 3 to 4 inches high, transplant into a prepared seed bed allowing 12 to 18 inches between plants and 30 to 39 inches between rows.

We train the beans up string in the greenhouse and sprinkle a little organic slug bait around the growing base. Water regularly in the morning, especially when they start to crop.

Wait until early summer to sow the seed outdoors or to transplant into prepared plot—they can be sown in the pots but not transplanted outdoors until early summer, as they need heat and must avoid late frosts. Plant the seed 8 to 9 inches apart. Water, and apply organic slug deterrent.

Climbers need the support of bamboo canes, twigs or a wigwam. They can be planted in a double row, allowing 2 feet between rows and 6 inches between plants. Even the bush variety can benefit from a little staking for extra support from wind and the weight of the crop.

CONTAINER GROWING

Dwarf beans work brilliantly in containers. Varieties such as **Speedy, Purple Queen** or **Violetta, Helios** or **Roquencourt** are easy to grow and produce well in large barrels, zinc buckets with holes, tubs or half barrels.

Climbers need a large container—half barrel, timber planter, timber apple box, large zinc bin, or even a plastic dustbin or grow bags. If the soil is rich in compost it will help retain moisture and reduce the need for watering. Feed with a little tomato food or liquid seaweed fortnightly.

PESTS AND DISEASES

Slugs and snails can wreak havoc on young seedlings in a wet season. Use some organic slug pellets to deter them and it's best to grow them on a raised platform and have a slug trap on the legs. Mice can also be a problem at seed stage.

Aphids can attack foliage and pods, more indoors than outdoors, but we don't have a problem with it. Ladybugs are the best biological control for greenfly. In wet years, root rot can be a problem in heavy soils. Plant in a drill so there would be water run-off.

Red spider mite can sometimes be a problem in greenhouses, but not outdoors.

HARVESTING

In our experience green beans yield more and have better flavor than purple or yellow varieties, which look great in the vegetable plot. As soon as the beans are about pencil thick, 8 to 12 weeks, we start to pick. It's essential to keep up with the harvesting to encourage extra yield. They

Flat pod string beans have superb flavor and can be eaten at every stage.

can be eaten at three different stages: small and tender, when the beans swell in the pod, at the end of the season when the seeds start to rattle in the dry pods. Harvest on a good day, spread on wire racks or mesh-lined crates in a dry shed, shell and dry for winter casseroles, or save for seed.

GOOD FOR YOU...

String beans are a rich source of dietary fiber, vitamins and minerals and are low in calories. They contain good levels of vitamin A and folates.

WHAT TO DO WITH A GLUT

Dry, pickle or freeze. The beans that get away can be left on the plant, then be harvested when they are dry and the beans rattle in the pods. Store in a dry place.

IN THE KITCHEN

Shell and cook fresh; toss in extra virgin olive oil. The secret to flavor, apart from freshness of course, is to cook the beans in plenty of boiling salted

Yellow round pod string beans.

water; for every 5 cups water, use 1 heaping tablespoon salt, and measure it religiously. Choose beans of a similar size. To serve 8, trim 2 pounds beans. If they are small and thin, leave them whole, if they are larger, cut them into 1- to 1½-inch pieces at a long angle. Bring the water to a fast rolling boil, add 1 tablespoon salt, then toss in the beans. Continue to boil very fast for 5 to 6 minutes or until just cooked (they should still retain a little bite). Drain immediately. The beans may be refreshed under cold water at this point and kept aside for several hours. Toss in 2½ to 4 tablespoons melted butter or extra virgin olive oil and season with lots of salt and freshly ground pepper.

Alternatively, once cooked, drain and refresh in plenty of cold water. Spread out on a baking sheet and let cool. To reheat later, just pop back into boiling salted water for a few seconds and dress as required.

Tender little raw green beans are irresistible to nibble on a plate of crudités. To judge whether they are still tender, bend a bean over your index finger. If pliable it's fine, but if it snaps it's sure to be a bit tough.

DID YOU KNOW?
All the *Phaseolus* species of cultivated beans originated in South and Central America and were grown by the Aztecs, but they have spread and naturalized worldwide. They were introduced to Europe and Asia by the Spaniards.

Green Bean Sodhi

There are many versions of this coconut milk vegetable stew in Tamil Nadu and Sri Lanka, but I particularly love this one made with green beans, which I tasted at The Bangala in Chettinad, South India.

SERVES 4

3 tablespoons vegetable oil

3 green cardamom pods

1-inch cinnamon stick or cassia

1¾ ounces onions, minced

2 fresh green chiles, slit along the side

¼ teaspoon ground turmeric

¾ cup thin coconut milk

1 teaspoon sea salt

5¼ ounces green beans, cut into ¾-inch pieces

¾ cup thick coconut milk

1 teaspoon or more of freshly squeezed lime juice

1 tablespoon cilantro leaves, to garnish

Heat the oil in a medium saucepan over high heat. When hot, add the cardamom pods and cinnamon or cassia; once the cardamom swells, about 30 seconds, add the chopped onions and green chiles, stir, and cook until the onion turns translucent. Add the turmeric, then add the thin coconut milk along with ½ cup water. Stir and cook for about 2 minutes before adding the salt.

Add the beans and bring to a boil, reduce the heat to low, cover, and simmer for 5 to 6 minutes. Add the thick coconut milk with ½ cup water or more if the stew seems too thick, stir, and continue to cook over low heat for 3 to 5 minutes; be careful not to let the sodhi come to a boil.

Add some lime juice and season to taste. Garnish with cilantro and serve in a warm bowl.

Green Bean Tempura with Asian Ginger Dip

This delicious recipe can be made with other fresh vegetables in season but is particularly good with green beans.

SERVES 6

sunflower oil, for deep frying

1 pound string beans, topped, tailed, and halved if necessary

FOR THE TEMPURA BATTER

1¼ cups rice flour

3 tablespoons cornstarch

1 teaspoon baking powder

½ teaspoon cayenne pepper

1 cup cold sparkling water

FOR THE ASIAN GINGER DIP

1 cup shoyu soy sauce

¼ cup sake

1 tablespoon finely grated fresh ginger

½ red or green chile, seeded and diced

1 tablespoon chopped fresh cilantro

First make the batter. Mix the dry ingredients in a bowl then stir in the sparkling water with a wooden spoon and keep in the fridge until needed.

To make the Asian ginger dip, mix the shoyu, sake, grated ginger, chile, and cilantro together in a bowl, then dilute with ¾ cup of water. Serve in little bowls.

Heat the oil to 375°F. Drop a few beans or prepared vegetables into the batter, lift them out with tongs, and shake off any excess batter. Lower them carefully into the hot oil. Cook for 2 to 3 minutes until the coating is crisp. Keep separate and turn when necessary. Remove with a slotted spoon and drain on paper towels.

Arrange on serving plates and serve immediately with the dip.

TOMATILLOS *Physalis philadelphica* ANNUAL

Tomatillos remind me of Mexico, one my absolute favorite countries, but we grow an abundance of them at Ballymaloe. Tomatillos look like green tomatoes or sometimes greeny purple ones with a papery husk on the outside, but they are not related. Tomatillos are part of the physalis family, related to deadly nightshade and the cape gooseberry. In Mexico they are also called the husk tomato and are an essential ingredient in both fresh and cooked sauces.

DID YOU KNOW?

Tomatillos are native to Mexico and were domesticated by the Aztecs around 800BC.

VARIETIES

Some varieties have a more purple skin than others.
Violet—Purple-skinned variety with excellent flavor.
Plaza Latina Giant—Large green fruit with a mild flavor, keeps well.

HOW TO GROW

Sow seed indoors in early spring; the soil temperature should be at least 60°F. They like a neutral or slightly acidic soil. Pot into 3½-inch pots. When risk of frost is past, transplant outside 40 to 50 inches apart, with as much between rows. They have a trailing habit so may need support; train 3 or 4 shoots on string or with bamboo. Regular watering and feeding is essential.

HARVESTING

They swell and eventually split the husk as they grow. When the husks are removed the tomatillos feel sticky, so give them a good wash before continuing with the recipe.

Harvest in late summer/early autumn when the fruit has swelled to the size of a medium tomato.

CONTAINER GROWING

Tomatillos grow well in containers. Plant in well-drained potting soil and keep moist but not soggy. Feed weekly with tomato food and look out for slugs (see page 626).

PESTS AND DISEASES

Whitefly may be a problem, but we haven't encountered it. The film which makes the tomatillo husks sticky contains a chemical called withamolides, which deters insects that dislike the taste, so they have their own in-built protection against insects.

GOOD FOR YOU...

Tomatillos are a good source of dietary fiber, niacin, potassium, and manganese. They also contain vitamins A, C, and E.

WHAT TO DO WITH A GLUT

Tomatillos freeze well, just like tomatoes. Make lots of tomatillo jam and salsas.

IN THE KITCHEN...

Tomatillos have a tart flavor similar to an unripe tomato, although the purple variety tends to be slightly sweeter. They have a high pectin content so are good for jams.

Tomatillos are easy to grow but difficult to find in shops.

Tomatillo Jam

This jam can also be made with green tomatoes.

. . . .

MAKES 2 × HALF PINT JARS

1 pound tomatillos
1½ cups granulated sugar
finely grated zest and juice of 1 lemon

Peel off the husks then wash and slice the tomatillos (no need to peel). Transfer to a stainless-steel saucepan with 1¾ cups water. Bring to a boil and continue to simmer, covered, for 50 minutes to 1 hour until tender. Add the remaining ingredients and dissolve the sugar over a gentle heat, stirring occasionally.

Boil rapidly for 10 to 12 minutes, uncovered, or until the setting point is reached. 450°F on a sugar thermometer. Pour into sterilized jars. It will keep unopened for 6 to 8 weeks but, as ever, best eaten fresh.

Huevos Divorciados—Divorced Eggs

Mexico has many memorable egg dishes, this one for Divorced Eggs, served with both a red and a green sauce, is both amusing and delicious. Sometimes a line of refried beans separates the two fried eggs on the plate. Serve with warm corn tortillas. The tomatillo salsa is much the best if made in a Mexican *molcajete*—a mortar and pestle made of lava rock. We have several in the school that we literally fight over. Alternatively, use a food processor, but the end result will be slightly watery. It is best on the day it's made.

SERVES 4

8 very fresh organic eggs

olive oil, for frying

warm corn tortillas, to serve

FOR THE SALSA DE JITOMATE (MAKES APPROX. 1 CUP)

2 tablespoons extra virgin olive oil

1 garlic clove, crushed

½ to 2 serrano or jalapeño chiles, chopped

1 (14-ounce) can chopped tomatoes

pinch of sugar

2 tablespoons chopped fresh cilantro (optional)

sea salt and freshly ground black pepper

FOR THE THE TOMATILLO SALSA (MAKES APPROX. 2 CUPS)

1 pound tomatillos

3 or 4 serrano chiles, minced

1 garlic clove, roughly chopped

2 tablespoons roughly chopped onion

flaky sea salt, to taste

½ cup loosely packed cilantro, roughly chopped

For the the salsa de jitomate, heat the oil in a sauté pan over medium heat. Add the crushed garlic and sizzle for a few minutes until pale golden. Add the chopped chile and the chopped tomatoes with their juices; season with salt, freshly ground pepper, and the sugar. Bring to a boil and cook for 5 to 6 minutes until the sauce breaks down. Add the cilantro, if you like, and simmer for a minute or two. Season to taste. Purée or serve as it is, hot or cold.

For the tomatillo salsa, peel the husks off the tomatillos and wash well as they can be slightly sticky on the outside. Put them in a small saucepan, barely cover with water, and bring to a boil. Simmer over low heat for about 5 minutes until soft but not falling apart, depending on the size. Drain, but reserve the cooking liquid.

If you have a molcajete, grind the chopped chiles, crushed garlic, chopped onion, and flaky salt together. Add the tomatillas, a few at a time; mash and grind well after each addition. Add a little of the cooking liquid to make a sauce of medium consistency.

If using a food processor, put ⅓ cup of the cooking water, the chiles, cilantro, crushed garlic, and chopped onion into the food processor; add a little more of the cooking liquid until you have a sauce of medium consistency. Add salt to taste.

Fry the eggs in hot oil in a skillet on one side.

Serve "sunny-side up," or flip one egg over and cook on the other side—"over easy." They should be plump and soft.

Serve two fried eggs per person on a warm plate with the warmed red salsa on one side and the green on the other. Serve with warm corn tortillas.

PEAS *Pisum sativum* ANNUAL

Ambassador—one of our favorite varieties.

You simply have to grow peas. For me, they are the essence of a vegetable garden. Peas give you so much pleasure— when the pea shoots are just 3 to 4 inches long, they are sweet and delicious in salads and as a garnish. As they grow, some of the tiny pods can be harvested as sugar peas, and then later when the peas start to swell inside they can be enjoyed as mangetout and finally you can pod the peas. Because the sugars turn to starch within a few hours of harvesting, you'll never get to taste the sweet, crunchy magic that is fresh shelled peas, unless you grow your own.

Peas are a big family—don't forget sugar snap, mangetout, petits pois. The difficult decision is which to grow if you are short of space.

VARIETIES

Although one can eat peas at every stage, for the sweeter, most tender, and succulent sugar peas or mangetout (snow peas), it is best to choose specific varieties. Choose from climbing and dwarf varieties.

Alderman—Old-fashioned variety grows to a height of about 1.5m, produces well-filled pods of sweet peas, goes on cropping all summer long.

Oregon Sugar Pod—High-yielding snow pea with sweet fleshy pods, 3 feet high. Resistant to powdery mildew.

Norli—A mangetout with small, deep green pods with delicious flavor, best picked 2 inches long, grows to 2 feet high. Resistant to fusarium wilt.

Sweet Horizon—High-yielding, late-maturing mangetout variety, pods 3 to 4 inches long, 28 inches high, resistant to powdery mildew.

Sugar Snap Large—Tall variety, over 5 feet high, resistant to fusarium wilt.

Maxigolt—a great, late variety that produces very large, sweet peas.

Premium—the tastiest early variety with medium sized peas.

HOW TO GROW

Peas will grow under glass or outdoors. Pea shoots can be grown in a seed tray on a windowsill and snipped to add to salad.

Last year, as an experiment, we soaked peas in cold water for 24 hours, then planted them and discovered that they germinated a little faster than those sown the traditional way.

Before sowing our early garden peas from the previous season in the glasshouse, we check them for germination. First we remove the peas from the pods that were allowed to ripen and dry on the plants, then we soak the dry shrivelled peas for about 12 hours until they swell and hopefully send out tiny shoots. We seem to have at least 90 per cent germination.

In early spring, peas may be sown directly into the soil, once the temperature is 45°F. Peas do best in well-drained fertile soil in a sunny spot; they'll tolerate partial shade but the yield will be reduced. Make a channel with the corner of a hoe and broadcast the seed along it at a nice even spacing, about 1 inch apart.

When the pea shoots emerge, cover immediately with fleece. Support growing shoots with bamboo poles placed 5 feet apart. Tie bio-degradable string along the poles at 70-inch intervals.

CONTAINER GROWING

Peas may be grown in a container or grow bag, but if so, it's best to choose a dwarf variety such as Norli so you won't have to do much staking. Pea shoots grow well in seed trays; scatter then water.

PESTS AND DISEASES

Birds and mice can steal the pea seeds from the soil before they have a chance to germinate. Peas can be subject to powdery mildew and fusarium wilt, so if you have come across either of these fungal diseases in your garden, look for resistant varieties of seed. Powdery mildew can develop in late summer, especially if conditions are very dry. There will be a dusty white coating on the leaves and stems. Fusarium-affected plants will be stunted and may discolor before shrivelling and dying.

HARVESTING

Harvest the peas every day to enjoy them at optimum size. Best picked in the morning when the dew has dried, they will be crisp and crunchy. Hold the vine with one hand and snip off the pod with the other, to avoid dislodging the vine.

Some can be left on the plant at the end of the crop to dry for seed or to use for winter soups and stews. The pea shoots will be ready in about 10 days.

GOOD FOR YOU...

Peas are low in calories but high in protein, vitamins, and fiber. An excellent source of folic acid, vitamins C, K, and A.

WHAT TO DO WITH A GLUT

Peas freeze well but must be blanched and frozen immediately after picking. We've never had a glut because we eat them in every possible way during the season.

IN THE KITCHEN

We love fresh peas, and fresh they need to be to enjoy the sweetness. The sugars turn to starch just hours after picking so the real magic evaporates quickly. Shelling peas should never be looked on as a chore; think of it as a delightful pastime to share with family and friends around the kitchen table with a glass of wine or cordial. We use the pods to make a pea pod soup or stock and then feed the remainder to the hens.

Peas take a very short cooking time, just 3 to 4 minutes in only a little boiling salted water (we use 1 teaspoon salt to ¾ cup of water for 1 pound peas), then anoint them with a nice lump of unsalted butter and serve immediately. I also like to remove one side of the pod or carefully split the pea pod lengthwise and serve them this way with a little minted crème fraîche. At Ballymaloe we love to put little bowls of freshly picked pods on the tables in the drawing room for the guests to nibble while they peruse the menu. Ambassador is the variety we grow. Sugar snaps, barely blanched, make another favorite pre-dinner nibble, which kids also love. Whole pea pods dipped in a tempura batter and served with a dip are also pretty irresistible, as is a purée of fresh peas with crispy fish and chips.

Chargrilled Peas (serves 4 to 6) are super delicious and totally addictive. Pop a grill pan on high. Toss 1 pound pea pods in a little extra virgin olive oil and some flaky sea salt. When the pan is very hot, add the pods in a single layer, allow to colour, flick over, and char on the other side. Add more salt if necessary.

Sweet Pea Guacamole on Warm Tortillas

I came across this combination in California served on tiny warm tortillas, but little pancakes are also very good and easier to make! Of course, guacamole is traditionally made with avocado, but the peas work brilliantly here. If you can't find little tortillas, cut large ones into triangles instead.

MAKES APPROX. 16

1 pound podded fresh or frozen peas
2 tablespoons extra virgin olive oil
2 tablespoons freshly squeezed lime juice
2 tablespoons minced cilantro
½ chile, seeded and minced
¼ teaspoon freshly ground cumin seeds
½ teaspoon ground coriander
2 tablespoons chopped flat-leaf parsley
about ½ teaspoon sea salt
16 warm (6-inch) corn tortillas
vegetable oil, for frying
crème fraîche or plain Greek yogurt (optional)
fresh cilantro sprigs and finely sliced red chiles, to garnish

Cook the peas in boiling salted water for 3 to 4 minutes. Refresh under cold water and drain. Combine the olive oil with the lime juice, cilantro and chile in a food processor and process for 1 minute. Add the peas, cumin, coriander, parsley, and salt, and blend until almost smooth. Season to taste, put into a bowl, and cover until needed.

Fry the tortillas or tortilla triangles in hot oil until crisp. Drain on paper towels.

Serve the sweet pea guacamole on tiny hot tortillas with a blob of crème fraîche or yogurt, if you like. Garnish each with a sprig of cilantro and thin slices of red chile. This pea guacamole even tastes delicious on a slice of hot crispy toast.

Pearl Barley with Peas, Radishes & Smoked Mackerel

A nice combination, fresh tasting yet sustaining, prompted by one of Nigel Slater's midweek dinners. I love the way Nigel tosses the peas in the spicy butter here—the end result is an exciting, nourishing blend of flavors.

SERVES 4

1 cup pearl barley

2 cups homemade vegetable or chicken stock

2 organic eggs

4 tablespoons (½ stick) butter

1 tablespoon curry powder or a mixture of roasted cumin and coriander

1 cup cooked peas

9 ounces smoked mackerel

4 radishes, 3 quartered and 1 sliced, keep the fresh leaves

sea salt and freshly ground black pepper

sprigs of flat-leaf parsley and lots of sprigs of fresh dill, to serve

Put the pearl barley into a saucepan with the vegetable or chicken stock. Bring to a boil, then reduce the heat and keep at a steady simmer for 20 to 25 minutes until all the stock is absorbed and the barley is tender.

Boil the eggs in salted water for 8 minutes, drain, and cover with water to cool.

Melt the butter in a skillet and add the curry powder. Stir and cook for a minute or two, then add the cooked peas. Stir gently to coat in the spiced butter and add to the warm pearl barley. Season to taste if necessary.

Tear the smoked mackerel into nice chunks and add to the barley. Add the radishes and their leaves. Shell the eggs and quarter them—they should be slightly soft in the center.

Pile into a dish and arrange the quartered eggs on the salad. Scatter with lots of flat-leaf parsley and dill sprigs and serve.

Pea & Cilantro Soup

This utterly delicious pea soup has a perky zing and is also good chilled, but be particularly careful not to overcook it—the texture should be smooth and silky, and the consistency should be thin, so add a little more stock if necessary. For Pea and Crab Soup, sprinkle a tablespoon of white crabmeat mixed with some snipped cilantro over each bowl of soup.

SERVES APPROX. 6

3¾ cups homemade chicken stock

4 tablespoons (½ stick) butter

5¼ ounces onions, minced

2 garlic cloves, chopped

1 green chile, seeded and minced

1 pound fresh or frozen peas

approx. 2 tablespoons chopped cilantro

pinch of granulated sugar

sea salt and freshly ground black pepper

softly whipped cream and fresh cilantro leaves, to garnish

Bring the chicken stock to a boil.

Melt the butter over low heat then add the onions, garlic, and chile. Season with salt and freshly ground pepper and sweat for 3 to 4 minutes. Cover with the hot stock. Bring to a boil with the lid off, add the peas, and cook for 3 to 4 minutes or until the peas are just tender. Add the cilantro and carefully transfer to a blender and blend until smooth. Season with salt, freshly ground pepper, and a pinch of sugar, which enhances the flavor even further.

Serve with a swirl of softly whipped cream and a few fresh cilantro leaves sprinkled over the top. Or place a few fresh peas and pea shoots into individual wide soup bowls and put the soup in a pitcher, then ask your guests to pour the soup into the bowl themselves.

Aloo Tikki (Potato & Pea Cutlet)

Our lives are enriched in so many ways by students who come from all over the world to the Ballymaloe Cookery School. They often share a favorite recipe with us—this came from Aarudhra Giri from Tamil Nadu, in India, who came to us in 2015 to do the 12-week Certificate Course. There are many versions of Aloo Tikki—you can also shape the dough into a larger patty, 10cm in diameter.

. . . .

SERVES 6/MAKES 18

5 ounces onions, minced

extra virgin olive oil, for frying

5 ounces fresh green peas (frozen are fine)

1 pound potatoes, boiled and peeled and
   still warm

½ to 1 green chile, minced

1½-inch piece fresh ginger, peeled and
   grated very finely

1 tablespoon chopped fresh cilantro

1 level teaspoon freshly ground cumin
   seeds

1 level teaspoon freshly ground coriander

½ to 1 level teaspoon chilli powder (you
   may prefer to use less)

1 level teaspoon salt

freshly ground black pepper

well-seasoned all-purpose flour, for dusting

3 tablespoons natural yogurt, to serve

lime wedges, to serve

FOR THE MINT AND CILANTRO CHUTNEY

½ cup fresh mint, chopped

¼ cup fresh cilantro, chopped

2 ounces red onions, chopped

1 green chile, chopped

juice of ½ lemon

1½ teaspoons mixed flower honey

salt

Fry the onions in a little extra virgin olive oil until golden.

Cook the peas in a pan of boiling salted water for 2 to 3 minutes. Drain.

Mash the cooked peas and potatoes together. Add the onions, chile, ginger, fresh cilantro, ground cumin, ground coriander, chile powder, salt, and freshly ground pepper. Mix well and season to taste.

Shape small balls of dough, roll in well-seasoned flour, flatten into discs, and lay them on a baking sheet lined with parchment paper. Cover with another sheet of parchment and keep in the fridge until you are ready to cook. There are many versions of Aloo Tikki—you can also shape the dough into a larger patty, 4 inches in diameter.

To make the mint and cilantro chutney, combine everything in a blender and blend until smooth. Season to taste. Keep chilled until ready to serve.

Just before serving, heat a few tablespoons of extra virgin olive oil in a skillet and shallow-fry the potato cakes (or as Aarudhra calls them, "cutlets") for 3 to 4 minutes until golden on both sides. Drain on paper towels. Continue to fry the "cutlets" in batches.

Serve 3 potato cakes per person with a little bowl of mint and cilantro chutney, a blob of yogurt, and a wedge of lime.

Alternatively, lay on a plate, top with a tablespoon of curd, plain Greek yogurt, some tamarind purée, and a generous spoonful of mint chutney. Sprinkle on some crispy sev (a deep-fried chickpea flour snack), a few mung bean sprouts, and finally some crispy onion. Tiny cubes of paneer (¼ inch) can also be added for extra nutrients.

RADISHES *Raphanus sativus* ANNUAL

Radishes, with their peppery flavor and crisp crunchy texture, are a brilliant place to start your gardening adventure—even if you've never sown a seed in your entire life you can certainly grow radishes. Surprise surprise, there's no comparison between what you grow and those you buy, plus you can enjoy the fresh leaves also. In summer they can crop in less than 30 days; just sprinkle the seeds onto a seed tray or into the ground and up they come.

VARIETIES

Radishes come in a wide range of shapes, sizes, colors and flavors. They can be white, red, pink, purple, black or champagne. There are two types: round and long. Radishes may be grown nearly all year round in a glasshouse or tunnel.

ROUND

Black Spanish—Black-skinned, globe-shaped with crisp white flesh.
Cherry Belle—Favorite for year-round production, scarlet, globe-shaped roots.

Celesta F1—Round, red radish suitable for indoor or outdoor growing.

AUTUMN/WINTER VARIETIES

Black Spanish Round—Black-skinned globe variety with white flesh. Sow in summer, directly into the ground, thinning to 4 inches apart.
China Rose—Long pink roots with firm, strong-flavored pure white flesh. Sow midsummer.
French Breakfast type—Popular variety, red skin with white tips, mild spicy flavor, quick growing.
Miyashige—this traditional daikon matures in fall producing high quality roots.

HOW TO GROW

In the greenhouse, we sow radish seed directly into the ground every two weeks throughout the summer, starting in mid-spring, to have a succession of small radishes through the season. Sow little and often for a year-round supply. Be careful not to sow the seed too thickly or the radishes will be overcrowded and won't swell. They also become woody if they are stressed or allowed to grow too large.

Outdoors, plant seeds directly into fine, rich, fertile soil from early summer onwards. For winter crops, choose varieties suited to the season (see above).

Radishes grow best in moist, cool conditions. In warmer weather grow them in a shadier spot and don't let them get dry. If conditions are too hot they might get attacked by flea beetle. From seed to munch in midsummer can be

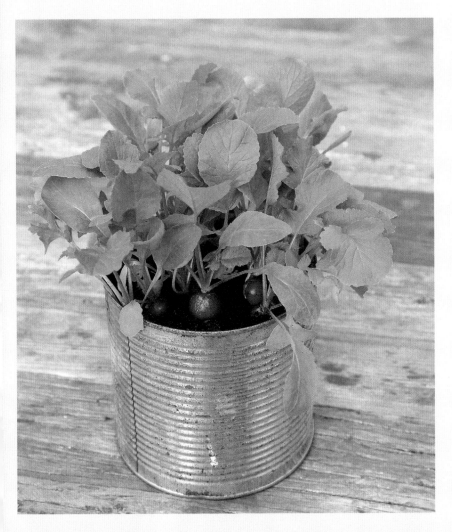

You don't need a garden to grow radishes, these are growing in a recycled tomato can on a windowsill.

as little as three weeks, both leaves and root are edible.

Keep them watered otherwise they will toughen and become woody.

CONTAINER GROWING

You don't even need a balcony, a seed tray or shallow box on a window sill with about 3 inches of soil or potting compost is all you need to get started. You could even recycle an old egg box.

PESTS AND DISEASES

Slugs are the biggest problem but radishes can also be attacked by flea beetle, which will make lots of tiny holes in the leaves. Companion planting with mustard can be effective in helping to deter flea beetle.

HARVESTING

Harvest radishes continuously, as they swell, otherwise they continue to swell and become woody. They are best from late spring to late summer.

GOOD FOR YOU...

A perfect little bomb of nutrients. Radishes are a rich source of calcium, iron and vitamin C. They help to eliminate toxins from the body, clear the sinuses, may help to protect against cancer and have a low glycaemic index.

WHAT TO DO WITH A GLUT

Just eat them as fast as you can, slice them into green salads, add to starter salads, nibble with drinks, pickle, add to stir-fries, crisp up in iced water. There are also several cooked radish recipes to enjoy with lots of freshly snipped herbs.

IN THE KITCHEN

As ever, the French have created one of the simplest and most delicious ways to enjoy fresh radishes. Serve them with a little pat of unsalted butter and a few flakes of sea salt. If the radishes are a little limp, pop them into a bowl of iced water to perk them up, and make them even crunchier. The peppery leaves of radishes are also edible and may be added to a green salad or made into a delicious radish leaf soup (see opposite).

We make sure we have an endless supply of radishes on a daily basis during the summer, so I use them in salads, sliced or whole. We slice them thinly, both crosswise for Cherry Belle and French Breakfast, and soak them in iced water so they crisp and curl—delicious added to salads, or even piled onto a slaw. Mix with flat-leaf parsley sprigs or little arugula leaves to serve atop roast chicken or even a chicken casserole or stew. They add a delicious crunch to so many dishes, particularly in a stir-fry, and are pretty good cooked or quickly roasted. Radish roses used to be all the rage in the 1960s and are still fun to make. Choose an even-shaped radish with no blemishes, cut off the root, and remove the green stem and leaves from the top. Slice from the root towards the stem end, not all the way through, about halfway. Place in a bowl of cold water for about half an hour and the "petals" will open out.

For **Buttered Radishes** to serve 6, wash and trim 1½ pounds red radishes, leaving a little of the green stem attached. Cut each radish in half lengthwise. Melt ⅓ cup butter in a wide sauté pan and toss in the radishes. Season with salt,

A selection of round and long radishes, each with a distinct flavor.

freshly ground pepper, and a little sugar. Add ¾ cup water, bring to a boil, cover, and simmer for about 5 minutes or until the radishes are soft but not mushy. Remove the lid and evaporate most of the remaining liquid. Toss in 3 tablespoons minced dill or fennel fronds and 1 tablespoon lemon juice.

DID YOU KNOW?

In Oaxaca, in Mexico, the Night of the Radishes, La Noche de los Rábanos, has been celebrated on 23 December every year since 1897. Huge radishes are carved into scenes from the Nativity, the Maji, the Flight into Egypt, Our Lady of Guadalupe....They are displayed around the Zócalo Central Square and the competition attracts thousands of visitors from around the world. There is also a category that uses corn husks and dried flowers. The radish sculptures are carved from oversized radishes using knives and toothpicks.

Daikon Curry

This recipe comes from Ahilya Fort in Maheshwar, where Kalyan Singh or Krishna Kumar Bhujel showed me how to make this simple daikon radish curry. He uses both the root and the leaves in it.

SERVES 10 TO 20

½ cup mustard oil or sunflower oil

2 bay leaves

1 teaspoon cumin seeds

10½ ounces onions, cut in ¼-inch dice

1 teaspoon garlic paste

1 teaspoon ginger paste

1 teaspoon freshly ground coriander seeds

1 teaspoon freshly ground cumin seeds

1 teaspoon ground turmeric

1 teaspoon garam masala

3 daikon radishes (3 pounds), peeled and cut into ⅓-inch dice

9 ounces daikon leaves, stalks removed and finely chopped into ⅓-inch pieces

sea salt and freshly ground black pepper

Heat the oil in a wok over medium heat and add the bay leaves. Stir and cook for 1 minute, then add the cumin seeds. A minute later, add the chopped onions and cook for 8 to 10 minutes until starting to brown. Then add the garlic and ginger pastes, stir, and continue to cook for 2 minutes. Add the salt, freshly ground coriander, cumin, turmeric, and garam masala. Stir and cook, then add 1 tablespoon water. Continue to cook for 5 to 8 minutes until the oil rises to the top of the masala (this is an important stage, otherwise the spices will taste slightly raw).

Add the diced daikon. Season with salt and freshly ground pepper. Stir and cook for 6 to 7 minutes or until tender; add another splash of water if it threatens to stick to the pan.

Add the finely chopped daikon leaves and cook, uncovered, tossing regularly, for 3 to 4 minutes or until wilted and soft. Season to taste. Serve as a vegetable or as part of a thali (a collection of dishes served on a platter).

Radish Leaf Soup with Chervil Cream

Many people have never tasted a radish leaf, but when you grow your own, the fresh leaves can be used in salads and this soup. The leaves are slightly peppery when fresh but become milder when cooked and a teensy bit prickly.

SERVES 4

3 tablespoons butter

5 ounces peeled and chopped potatoes

1 cup chopped onions

3¾ cups water or chicken or vegetable stock

1¼ cups whole milk

5¼ ounces radish leaves, chopped

sea salt and freshly ground black pepper

sliced radishes, to serve

FOR THE CHERVIL CREAM

1 cup full-fat crème fraîche

large bunch of chervil

Melt the butter in a heavy-bottomed saucepan, and when it foams, add the potatoes and onions and toss them until well coated. Sprinkle with salt and pepper. Cover and sweat over a gentle heat for 10 minutes.

Meanwhile, make the chervil cream. Place the crème fraîche into a bowl. Simply chop the chervil very finely and mix with the crème fraîche. Season to taste.

When the vegetables are almost soft but not colored, add the water or stock and milk, bring to a boil, and cook for about 10 minutes until the potatoes and onions are fully cooked. Add the radish leaves and boil with the lid off for 4 to 5 minutes. Do not overcook or the soup will lose its fresh green color. Purée the soup in a high-speed blender or food processor. Season to taste. Garnish with sliced radishes and a blob of chervil cream on top of each bowl.

Fish Taco with Salsa Verde & Radishes

These are pretty addictive and best when both the tortillas and fish are still warm and the radishes are fresh and crunchy. Tuck in the peppery leaves to add a little more zing to the taco.

· ·

SERVES 4

2 tablespoons lime juice
extra virgin olive oil
¼ pound radishes, sliced
4 small scallions, sliced at an angle
½ to 1 red or green chile, seeded and chopped
1½ pounds John Dory or sea bass, skinned
½ teaspoon coriander seeds, roasted and ground
12 (6-inch) corn tortillas
½ cucumber, halved, seeded and cut in long slivers at an angle
wedges of lime, to serve

FOR THE SALSA

1¼ cups fresh cilantro
2 tablespoons lime juice
2 tablespoons extra virgin olive oil
flaky sea salt and freshly ground pepper

Preheat the oven to 465°F.

First make the salsa. Combine the cilantro, 2 tablespoons of water, lime juice, extra virgin olive oil, and salt and freshly ground pepper in a food processor and process until smooth. Transfer to a small bowl, cover, and chill.

Mix the lime juice, 1 tablespoon of extra virgin olive oil, and the sliced radishes, scallions, and chile together. Season with salt and freshly ground pepper.

Brush a baking sheet with a little oil. Lay the skinned fish fillets on the baking sheet in a single layer. Season with salt, freshly ground pepper, and a sprinkling of ground coriander seeds. Roast for 3 to 4 minutes.

Meanwhile, hold the corn tortillas over a gas flame with a tongs for about 30 seconds to slightly crisp.

Fill each tortilla with a couple of chunks of fish, the radish, scallion, and chile salad, and a couple of pieces of cucumber. Drizzle with salsa, fold over, and repeat with the others.

Serve 3 per person with a wedge of lime.

French Breakfast Radishes with Anchoiade

This is a simple but completely irresistible way to enjoy fresh radishes and their leaves.

· ·

SERVES 6

approx. 30 French breakfast radishes

FOR THE ANCHOIADE

3.8 ounces canned anchovy fillets
1¼ cups olive oil
2 garlic cloves, chopped
½ teaspoon thyme leaves
1 tablespoon chopped basil
1 tablespoon Dijon mustard
1 tablespoon red wine vinegar
lots of freshly ground black pepper

Wash and snip the long wispy tails from the radishes but keep the leaves intact. Crisp the radishes in a bowl of iced water.

Whizz all the anchoiade ingredients except the oil together in a food processor. Add the oil gradually. Taste add a little more oil if necessary. When all the oil is incorporated you will have a lovely thick garlicky, anchovy emulsion. Store in a covered jar in the fridge.

To serve, arrange a few crisp chilled radishes on a plate, with a blob of anchoiade on the side for dipping—delicious! Remember to enjoy all the radish leaves as well. Any leftover anchoiade will keep very well covered in the fridge.

WATERCRESS *Nasturtium officinale* PERENNIAL

Watercress has virtually been a staple here at Ballymaloe for as long as I can remember. We're fortunate to be able to pick lush peppery watercress from several local, clean, fast-flowing streams almost year round, but it's something that you can easily cultivate at home.

Apparently watercress is one of the oldest leaf vegetables eaten by humans; it is related to mustard, cabbage and arugula. In Birr Castle in Co. Offaly, Lord and Lady Rosse still serve soup made with watercress gathered from around St Brendan's well, just below the castle walls.

HOW TO GROW

You don't need a local stream to grow watercress. If you don't have a clean, safe source of wild watercress, it's a cinch to grow at home in your backyard. In fact, you can even sprout a few sprigs of watercress from the greengrocer in a jam jar, they are the same variety. When the little white roots appear from the base of the stem, plant each one carefully in

Wild watercress flowers in summer.

moist potting compost and keep it well watered—best to put it sitting in a tank or trough that water regularly passes through.

HARVESTING

You can pick it all year round, but it's best up to the flowering stage in early summer. Cut it back then for re-growth. To help with identification in the wild, remember the top leaf is the biggest on a watercress sprig, as opposed to wild celery which always seems to grow alongside watercress in the wild—on that plant the bottom leaves are the largest. This is good to know because wild celery can be mildly toxic when eaten raw.

PESTS AND DISEASES

If you are picking wild watercress you need to make sure that the stream is not one where cattle or sheep drink as the water could be contaminated by the parasite that causes liver fluke. Be careful also that there is not too much nitrogen run-off from farmland going into the stream where you are picking fresh watercress. Whether you grow your own or forage it, the water must be clean otherwise the watercress will be contaminated.

DID YOU KNOW?

According to my hipster friends, watercress is the new arugula, well, how about that? It's replacing arugula on many of the coolest plates. I love both. *The top leaf of watercress is the largest (right) while the opposite applies to wild celery (left), which can be mildly toxic.*

GOOD FOR YOU...

Watercress contains large amounts of vitamins K, C and A, some vitamin E and B6. It also contains iron, calcium, manganese, potassium, thiamine, magnesium and phosphorus, so is quite a valuable source of nutrients.

WHAT TO DO WITH A GLUT

Watercress is available all year round but if you come across a patch that looks really good, pick a good basketful and make lots of soup and freeze it for the winter. Watercress can also be cooked as a vegetable, either wilted or boiled and well buttered up at the end.

IN THE KITCHEN

The peppery flavor of watercress enhances so many dishes, add some to smoothies for a real vitamin boost. We love it as a nibble, on the side of a plate, and, of course, in soup. As well as the leaves, the pretty white flowers are delicious in salads. It also makes a delicious green vegetable purée and is particularly good added to colcannon instead of cabbage or kale.

Watercress Smoothie

Watercress is super nutritious so this uncomplicated smoothie is a vitamin and mineral boost.

. . . .

SERVES 1

1 bunch of watercress, plus a sprig for
   garnish
1 cup plain yogurt
1 teaspoon honey (optional)

Strip the watercress off the fibrous main stalk. Chop coarsely. Blend with the other ingredients in a high-speed blender until smooth.

Pour into a glass and serve immediately with a sprig of watercress on top.

Scallion, Watercress & Fresh Herb Frittata Rolls

A superfast and tasty lunch or supper dish. Pack with fresh herbs and good things from your garden.

. . . .

SERVES 4 TO 6

8 organic eggs
4 scallions, finely sliced
¼ cup chopped watercress
2 tablespoons minced dill
2 tablespoons minced cilantro
2 tablespoons minced flat-leaf parsley
2 tablespoons minced marjoram
¼ cup minced chervil
2 tablespoons minced basil
¾ ounce Parmesan cheese, freshly grated
extra virgin olive oil, for frying
sea salt and freshly ground black pepper
radish, cucumber, and mint salad, to serve

TO SERVE
baby salad leaves
cherry tomatoes
fresh herbs

Whisk the eggs, add the scallions, herbs, and cheese and season well with salt and freshly ground black pepper.

Heat a small nonstick skillet over high heat. Add a tablespoon of extra virgin olive oil. Pour a sixth of the frittata mixture onto the pan, tilt, and cook as though making an omelet. Flip over and cook for a few seconds or pop under the broiler until almost set, then slide onto a plate. Cook the remaining mixture in the same way.

To serve, lay a thin frittata on a plate. Put a bunch of salad leaves, a few slices of seasoned cherry tomatoes, and some fresh herbs on top, roll up, and serve with a little radish, cucumber, and mint salad.

Watercress, Chicory, Apple, Pomegranate & Hazelnut Salad

A refreshing, clean-tasting autumn or winter salad. Just by reading this one can visualize how delicious this salad will taste, with lots of peppery watercress.

. . . .

SERVES 8

a handful of whole unblanched hazelnuts
2 bunches of watercress
1 bulb red chicory
4 medium dessert apples, such as
   Honeycrisp, Fuji, or Braeburn
seeds from 1 small or ½ large pomegranate
a small bunch of chives, cut into 1-inch
   lengths, to serve

FOR THE DRESSING
1 teaspoon honey
2 tablespoons cider vinegar
pinch of flaky sea salt
½ cup hazelnut oil or extra virgin olive oil

Preheat the oven to 400°F.

Arrange the hazelnuts on a baking tray in a single layer and toast for 8 to 10 minutes in the oven. Let cool. Rub off the skins and break the nuts into coarse pieces with a rolling pin or in a mortar and pestle.

Whisk the ingredients for the dressing in a large bowl.

Remove the more fibrous stalks from the watercress. Separate the leaves of the chicory. Cut the apples into quarters, remove the core with a sharp knife, and slice some into thin wedges and others into chunks.

Just before serving, gently toss the chicory, watercress, and apple in the dressing and season to taste. Transfer to a serving dish or individual serving plates. Sprinkle liberally with the toasted hazelnuts, a few pomegranate seeds, and chives.

Sorcha's Watercress Juice

A super-charged shot of nutrients to launch you into the day. Sorcha Moynihan is one of our super-charged lecturers.

. . . .

SERVES 1 OR 2

1 green apple (6½ ounces), chopped
½ cucumber (6 ounces), seeded and
   chopped
1 cup fresh watercress
1 teaspoon chopped fresh mint
1 teaspoon lime juice

Combine all the ingredients in a Nutribullet and blend until smooth. Alternatively, juice the chopped unpeeled apples, cucumber, watercress, and mint. Add the lime juice. Taste and serve.

AGRETTI *Salsola soda* PERENNIAL

To many of us, agretti is a new vegetable but in fact it's been around for a very long time, not as a vegetable but as a substance used in glassmaking; the famous clarity of sixteenth-century cristallo glass from Venice and Murano depended on the purity of the soda ash from Levantine agretti. It grows wild in coastal areas, and chefs in Rome get all excited and literally line up for this verdant Italian plant when it first appears in the market in late spring. I first came across it at Stevie Parle's Dock Kitchen, in London, a couple of years ago; I was desperate to get seeds but my first couple of attempts to grow it failed miserably. I now know that it's easy to grow but vital to have fresh, viable seed which, now that more people are growing it, is easier to find.

Agretti has several other enchanting

names, including Monk's beard, Friar's beard, Goat's beard and Russian thistle. Opposite-leaved Saltwort or Barilla plant are two others. In Japan, it's called Land seaweed. It looks a bit like a bush of grassy, willowy chives and grows about 2 feet tall, spreading about 12 inches wide, so it provides excellent ground cover. Agretti is related to spinach, quinoa, chard and beet and tastes slightly acidic and salty with a light minerally taste.

VARIETIES

Agretti/Roscano/Barbe Di Frate—When mature after 50 days or so they are a 12 inches wide and 2 feet tall bush that looks like a huge chive. Mild-flavored green with a little bitterness.

HOW TO GROW

Agretti is native to the Mediterranean basin. It's a halophyte—a salt-loving plant. Nonetheless, agretti doesn't necessarily need to grow by the sea, it's not too fussy but it thrives best in loose, rich, fertile soil with close to neutral pH. One can plant it any time from late February to the end of October. If you wish, it can be started in deep seed trays or cells in potting compost or, best of all, sow it directly into soil or a raised bed. The seed has a reputation for poor germination so it's worth sowing it thickly just in case. It has a short sowing window and the seeds won't keep.

In cells, sow the seed individually. Cover the seeds with ⅓ inch of soil, space 4 inches apart and allow 10 inches between the rows.

If the seed is viable it should germinate in 8 to 10 days. Thin out the seedlings and transplant into the ground in a bright, warm sunny spot.

CONTAINER GROWING

No problem growing in a container but choose a large pot, old trough or galvanized tub, a half barrel or a no-dig bed with a good base of well-rotted manure. Don't let it dry out but it doesn't need a lot of water.

PESTS AND DISEASES

None that I've encountered so far, once the plant becomes woody it's no longer edible.

HARVESTING

Once established, the plants will romp away and spread, which helps to suppress weeds. One can usually start to harvest the fine, succulent fronds after 5 to 6 weeks.

Start cutting the plants when they are 6 to 8 inches tall; cut the green tops or sections of the plant and it will then re-grow. Keep cutting otherwise the stems will start to get woody. Cut the plant about 1¼ inches from the ground with a sharp knife or scissors, it will look like long wispy chives. The more you cut it the more it grows.

NUTRITION

Agretti has detoxifying, laxative and anti-aging properties as well as lots of nutritional benefits. Excellent source of vitamins A, C, and K, and calcium, iron, chlorophyll, and beta-carotene.

DID YOU KNOW?

In ancient times, agretti was widely cultivated as a natural source of sodium carbonate which was extracted from the ashes and used in both glass and soap making.

WHAT TO DO WITH A GLUT

You may well have a glut if your agretti takes off, so keep on snipping to keep it tender. You may want to blanch, refresh and freeze some but I'd also introduce it to your friends and offer it to adventurous local chefs who may well be thrilled to buy it from you or sell it at your local farmers' market.

IN THE KITCHEN

Traditionally, agretti was blanched and dressed with olive oil and lemon and served as an accompanying vegetable, but there are so many delicious ways to serve it. It is great in omelets, with pasta, and on pizza. Cooks and chefs are having fun; I've even seen it used as a gluten-free substitute for pasta, and it's great with crab or rock shrimp and a pinch of chile flakes. Stevie Parle serves it with gnudi and peas.

Once established, agretti grows abundantly, keep cutting and it will continue to grow lush and tender.

Agretti with Butter & Bottarga

Love the saltiness of the bottarga here with the agretti; you may even wish to add a poached egg...

SERVES 4 TO 6

1 pound or 1 bunch of agretti

1 tablespoon sea salt

⅓ cup butter

¾ to 1¾ ounces bottarga, freshly grated

¼ cup extra virgin olive oil

Wash the agretti well and remove any woody stems if necessary. Bring 5 quarts of water to a boil in a large saucepan, and add the salt and the agretti. Stir well, cover, and cook for 6 to 8 minutes. Taste; it may need 2 to 3 minutes more. Drain.

Melt the butter in a wide pan and toss in the drained agretti. Sprinkle on some freshly grated bottarga, toss, and taste.

Drizzle with a little extra virgin olive oil and serve immediately.

Agretti Pasta with Anchovies & Chile

Wow, the reemergence of this almost-forgotten vegetable is really causing a stir. Last-season seeds were in really short supply but now agretti is more widely available. Perhaps because of its Italian origin, it pairs deliciously with pasta.

. . . .

SERVES 4 TO 6

1 pound or 1 bunch of agretti
1 pound spaghetti or linguine
¼ cup extra virgin olive oil
2 large garlic cloves, crushed
4 to 6 anchovy fillets
good pinch of red chile flakes
4 scallions, thinly sliced at an angle
sea salt and freshly ground black pepper
zest of 1 organic lemon, to serve

Wash the agretti well and remove any woody stems if necessary. Bring 5 quarts of water to the boil in a large saucepan and add 1 tablespoon of salt and the agretti. Blanch for a couple of minutes, then remove the agretti with a slotted spoon and refresh in cold water.

Bring the water back to a boil, add the pasta, and stir. Bring back to a boil, cover, and cook for 4 minutes. Remove from the heat and let sit in the water in the tightly covered pot for 8 to 10 minutes or until just al dente.

Meanwhile, heat the extra virgin olive oil in a skillet, add the garlic, and cook for a minute or two, then add the anchovies, mash slightly, and add the chile flakes and scallions. Cook for a couple of minutes, add the well-drained agretti, and continue to cook until tender but still with a bite—a minute or two.

Drain the pasta, add to the pan, and toss well. Drizzle with more olive oil. Season to taste, grate over some fresh lemon zest, and turn into a hot serving bowl. Grate over some more lemon zest and serve as soon as possible.

BLACK SALSIFY *Scorzonera hispanica* PERENNIAL

Black salsify, also known as scorzonera, is probably unfamiliar to many gardeners but sometimes it's fun to move out of your comfort zone. You are unlikely to find them in your local supermarket or in most farmers' markets. Do consider growing it for the delicate flavor of their roots and shoots—truly delicious.

Salsify's root is slim and has dark browning-black skin and white flesh. There is also white-skinned salsify, which is related but not quite the same.

Native to central and southern Europe it is grown and relished for its roots, which are said to have the flavor of Jerusalem artichokes, asparagus and oysters. The latter is a bit of a stretch but the flavor is definitely distinctive and delicate, well worth growing.

VARIETIES

Belstar Super—early and vigorous, thick 11 inch long roots, and edible flowers.

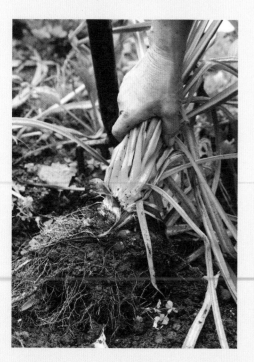

Enorma—Thich 11 inch long roots on vigorous plants; young leaves are edible.

HOW TO GROW

Sow the seeds in spring in drills ⅓ to ¾ inch deep, allowing about 6 inches between rows. They are not too fussy but they do best in light, well-drained, stone-free soil, not freshly manured as, like most root vegetables, they are prone to forking. Thin to 4 to 5 inches apart and then just let them grow, but keep the area as weed free as possible. They like full sun.

You could also try growing a piece of root from the greengrocer's, if you can get one.

The leaves resemble young leeks but salsify are deeper and has leaves a bit like those of a tall lily of the valley, though wider, with yellow flowers.

It can be left in the ground well into winter and dug as required. It can take at least 120 days to mature.

Digging salsify roots is quite a mission; use a fork and take it gently because the roots snap easily and are difficult to ease out of the ground. They benefit from being dug after a frost, because like other root vegetables and kale frost sweetens and tenderizes them. The starches turn to sugar after the frost.

CONTAINER GROWING

To grow in a container the soil would need to be at least 2 feet deep to provide enough space for the roots to go down.

PESTS AND DISEASES

Easy to grow and in my experience and aren't bothered by pests and diseases.

Lots of trimming to be done on the Russian Giant Black Salsify.

GOOD FOR YOU...

Black salsify is rich in iron and calcium, potassium, phosphorus and fiber, vitamins A, B, E and C and inulin. It is reputed to lower blood pressure and boost the immune system. High in iron and copper it also contains high levels of potassium, as much as bananas apparently.

WHAT TO DO WITH A GLUT

A glut is unlikely but they can be lifted and stored in boxes of damp sand in a root cellar or dark shed.

IN THE KITCHEN

To cook, scrub and trim. They can be cooked in their skins and peeled later; if you do peel them, immediately drop them into acidulated water because, like artichokes, they discolor quickly. Salsify exudes a sticky, milky liquid when cut, which is why it's better to cook whole.

Cook them in a little salted water in a covered pan. Whole salsify will take 10 to 30 minutes, depending on size. Refresh under cold water and discard the cooking water, which will be brown. Peel and slice; finish in whichever recipe you choose. They can be added to slow-cooked dishes or dipped in batter or bread crumbs to make delicious fritters or pakoras. Delicious with mussels, scallops, and oysters; in a fish soup or chowder; or in salad with shellfish.

DID YOU KNOW?

In the Middle Ages, salsify was considered a powerful tonic and a snakebite cure.

Ballymaloe Chicken & Black Salsify Pie

During the season, we love to add some black salsify to a chicken or pheasant pie. Salsify also works brilliantly but it has to be said that the pie with a layer of buttery puff pastry is delicious even without any further additions.

. . . .

SERVES 6–8

1 large free-range organic chicken
 (3 to 5 pounds)
2 large carrots, cut into chunks
2 large onions, roughly cut
2 celery stalks, cut into small chunks
5 black peppercorns
Bouquet garni and a sprig of tarragon
2–3 cups water or chicken stock

1 pound streaky bacon, cooked
16 button onions
16 button mushrooms
⅔ cup dry white wine
1 cup cream
salt, pepper
½ cup roux (see page 267)
1 pound puff pastry (see page 132)
½ pound cooked black salsify, cut into
 1 inch pieces
egg wash

Preheat the oven to 350°F.

Put 2 inches of water or chicken stock in a heavy ovenproof casserole and add the vegetables and bouquet garni. Lay the chicken on top. Add a sprig of tarragon if available and cover with a tight-fitting lid. Bring to the boil and cook in the oven for 1–2 hours, depending on the size of the bird. Watch that it does not boil dry. The water should be deliciously rich and may be a little fatty.

Meanwhile fry the mushrooms, season with salt and freshly ground pepper. Sweat the button onions over a low heat in butter in a covered casserole until soft. Cut the cooked bacon into cubes. Remove the chicken from the pot when fully cooked, carve the flesh. De-grease cooking liquid. Arrange the sliced chicken in layers in a deep pie dish, covering each layer with bacon, onions, mushrooms, and black salsify.

To make the sauce, bring 2 cups of the cooking liquid and the dry white wine to the boil and thicken with the roux. Cook until thick and smooth. Add the cream. Bring to the boil again. Season to taste. Leave to cool, cover with puff pastry. Chill until required.

Preheat the oven to 450°F. Just before cooking, brush the top with eggwash and cook for 10 minutes, then reduce the temperature to 400°F for a further 15–20 minutes or until golden brown.

Black Salsify & Parmesan Fritters

These crisp fritters are so moreish and irresistible with romesco sauce .

SERVES 6

6 sticks of black salsify or salsify

lemon juice

olive or sunflower oil, for deep frying

well-seasoned flour

1 egg, beaten

white bread crumbs or panko bread
  crumbs

¼ cup grated Parmesan

Aioli (page 195), to serve

FOR THE ROMESCO SAUCE (SERVES 12)

1 head of garlic

4–6 tablespoons extra virgin olive oil

2 slices of slightly stale country bread

75g almonds, preferably Marcona

3 large, very ripe tomatoes or 15 ripe
  cherry tomatoes

1 large or 2 small red peppers, halved or
  quartered and deseeded

freshly squeezed lemon juice, to taste

sea salt and freshly ground black pepper

To make the romesco sauce, preheat the oven to 200°C/gas mark 6. Trim the top off the head of garlic to expose the bulbs. Wrap in a little foil parcel but leave enough space to pour in a dessertspoon of extra virgin olive oil. Pinch the top of the foil to close. Cook for 30 minutes or until the garlic cloves are soft and squishy.

Cut the crusts off the bread and fry the bread in a little extra virgin olive oil until golden brown. Drain on kitchen paper and add to a food processor.

Fry the almonds in the remaining oil until golden, adding a little more oil if necessary. Add to the bread.

Halve the tomatoes around the equator, put in a bowl then add the peppers. Drizzle with extra virgin olive oil, season with flaky salt and freshly ground black pepper, spread in a single layer on a baking tray and roast for 30–40 minutes until the tomatoes are soft and peppers are catching at the edges. Leave to cool.

Add the tomatoes and peppers to the bread and almonds. When the garlic is soft, remove the skins and add to the mix. Whizz, season and add lemon juice to taste. Add enough water to thin to a soft consistency.

Peel the salsify and toss in lemon juice immediately to prevent any discoloration.

Place it in a pan of water and bring to a boil. Simmer until the salsify is tender, 3 to 4 minutes depending on size. Remove from the heat and let cool in the pot. Cut in 3-inch lengths.

Heat the oil in a deep fryer. Roll the pieces of salsify in well-seasoned flour, then dip in beaten egg, coat in bread crumbs, and finally roll in grated Parmesan. Cook a few at a time in the hot oil, drain on paper towels, and serve with Romesco Sauce or Aioli, if you like.

EGGPLANT *Solanum melongena* ANNUAL

I love eggplants and adore their smoky flavor, glossy skin, and the many different textures one can coax from exactly the same vegetable. The eggplant is part of the solanum (nightshade) family, so is related to the potato, tomato, sweet pepper, chile pepper, and cape gooseberry, and botanically speaking it is a fruit. It is a beautiful, bushy plant with pretty, star-shaped, purple flowers with a yellow center, native to the Mediterranean and South East Asia and brought from the East by traders. I'll admit it is not exactly the easiest plant to grow, particularly in our climate, but the difference in flavor between the large boring eggplants available on the supermarket shelves and the varieties one can grow is startling. In fact, the most readily available varieties, Black Magic and Classic, are probably the least flavorful of all.

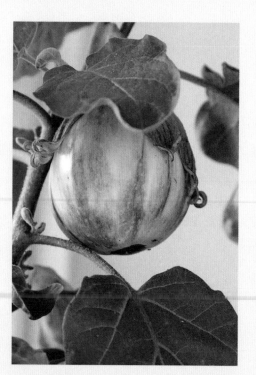

Rosa Bianca eggplant growing in the greenhouse.

VARIETIES

Eggplants come in many shapes, sizes and colors from deep purple to pink streaked green, and even white, hence the name eggplant.

Violetta di Firenze—Italian variety with unusual dark mauve fruits, needs warmth to ripen fully.

Violetta Lunga—Another Italian variety with long, curved, dark purple fruit.

Black Beauty—Produces 3 to 6 dark, glossy, violet eggplants per plant. Oval shape up to 5 inches in length, this variety was introduced in 1910 and has retained its popularity.

Long Purple—Good cropper—long, deep violet, pear-shaped fruit.

Rosa Bianca—An Italian heirloom cultivar, lovely delicate flavor, spherical fruits with rose-colored white-flecked skin. Popular with gardeners and cooks alike.

Slim Jim—Very pretty with purple-marked leaves, the sweet fruit is small, long and slender and grows in clusters. Good variety for growing outdoors in a sunny sheltered spot as it has a shorter ripening time.

Orient Express F1—Fast-growing and early maturing variety, it sets fruit in cooler weather than other cultivars, so is suitable for growers with cool or short growing seasons. Also does well in heat. Long slender fruit, deep purplish black.

Millionaire—Japanese variety, slender dark fruit with a good flavor, violet-tinged leaves.

HOW TO GROW

It's really important to choose a variety that suits your part of the world. Eggplants need similar growing conditions to tomatoes.

Eggplants take up to 6 months from sowing seed to harvesting. Sow seeds in 3 ½-inch pots in early spring. When the roots have filled the space, we transfer them into larger pots, 9 to 10 inches, or transplant them directly into the rich, fertile soil of the greenhouse in early summer. Rows need to be 2 feet apart. The temperature needs to be about 70°F. If you'd rather plant them outdoors, choose a warm, sheltered, sunny spot. Either way, support the plants with strong bamboo canes. Mist regularly with water to help the flowers to set and to discourage red spider mite.

When 5 or 6 flowers have set, use a high-potash fertilizer feed, liquid seaweed or tomato feed once a week as with tomatoes.

CONTAINER GROWING

Eggplants can also be cultivated in grow bags, two to a bag, or a large pot.

Choose a dwarf variety such as *Fairy Tale* which produces abundant long, sausage-shaped, purple- and white-striped fruit (10 to 12 small eggplants per plant). Other varieties suitable for growing in a container are **Patio Mixed F1 Hybrid**, **Listada de Gandia**, **Ophelia F1 Hybrid**, **Czech Early**, **Orlando F1**, and **Diamond**, which has long slim fruit.

PESTS AND DISESASES

Whitefly can be a problem. Use a biological control such as *Encarsia Formosa*—a parasitic wasp which comes impregnated on a piece of card that can be hung on the plant. The wasp hatches in the greenhouse and parasitises the whitefly. It should be introduced as soon as possible after the first adult whiteflies are seen. It needs a minimum night temperature of 50°F, and 65°F during the day.

Plant a few French calendulas close by to discourage whitefly and attract pollinating insects.

HARVESTING

Harvest from midsummer to mid-autumn. Use a knife or secateurs to snip the fruit off the plant and watch out for the soft prickles. Five or six fruit is a good yield for a large variety, although some plants produce more, particularly white Rosa Bianca.

> **DID YOU KNOW?**
> Eggplants are sometimes known as "Apple of Love" or "Poor Man's Caviar.".

GOOD FOR YOU...

Considered to be a powerful source of antioxidants, specifically nasunin, which help to lower cholesterol. They also contain phytonutrients as well as vitamins C and B and is a valuable source of potassium and folic acid.

However, people suffering from arthritis are advised to avoid the nightshade family as it is thought to aggravate the condition.

WHAT TO DO WITH A GLUT

You won't want to waste one of your precious eggplants. We rarely have a glut but when we have a few to spare I make Pickled Eggplants, a divine preserve recipe I got from Sam Chesterton from the lovely Finca Buenvino near Aracena, Andalucia.

Melanzane alla Parmigiana, a gratin of eggplants and tomatoes, is another gem of a recipe which can help to use a glut of both tomatoes and eggplants.

IN THE KITCHEN

Eggplants are incredibly versatile and take on other flavors. Many people like to salt them first to drain out the bitterness and firm them up, but that's largely unnecessary nowadays with modern varieties.

They can be roasted whole and the pulp used for moutabal or baba ganoush; sliced and pan-grilled, roasted, fried, or dipped in a light batter for fritters; layered in moussaka; added to stews or casseroles; steamed; or baked. Charring eggplants over a naked flame or charcoal gives the finished dish an irresistible smoky flavor. Eggplants guzzle oil, so make sure you use a really good-quality extra virgin olive oil.

Moutabal

This smoky eggplant dip was served on virtually every menu when I visited Syria. It was always slightly different but always delicious. I ate moutabal 14 times in a row, all in the name of research....Charring the eggplant over a gas flame or charcoal grill gives the dip a distinctive smoky flavor. Be careful not overdo the tahini; you only need a little to bring out the flavor of the eggplant.

SERVES 4

2 large eggplant (approx. 1½ pounds)
1¾ ounces tahini
1 tablespoon lemon juice
sea salt, to taste
extra virgin olive oil, for drizzling
1 tablespoon pomegranate seeds (optional)
pita bread, for serving

Char the eggplant directly over a gas flame, holding them with tongs, until the flesh is really soft and tender and the peel is black and charred. Peel carefully and discard the skins. Leave the eggplants to cool to room temperature.

Finely chop the eggplant flesh and place in a bowl. Add the tahini, lemon juice, and salt to taste and mix well. Drizzle a little extra virgin olive oil on top and sprinkle with pomegranate seeds, if using.

Serve with pita bread. Eat alone or as part of a Middle Eastern mezze.

Eggplant Fungetto with Scallops

Lughan Carr, a past student and super-talented chef, cooked this gutsy eggplant dish for me. It almost tastes of porcini, hence the name *fungetto*, which means "petit four in the shape of a mushroom" in Italian.

....

SERVES 6 OR 7 AS A STARTER

12 to 14 scallops, out of the shell with
   coral still attached
arugula leaves and lemon wedges, to serve

FOR THE FUNGETTO

2¼ pounds eggplant (approx. 3 large)
extra virgin olive oil, for frying
3 large garlic cloves, very thinly sliced
2 tablespoons capers in vinegar, rinsed and
   chopped
1 (2-ounce) tin anchovy fillets, chopped
4 ripe tomatoes, peeled, seeded, and
   chopped
1 (14-ounce) can whole plum tomatoes,
   drained, rinsed of their juice, and
   chopped
pinch of dried red chile flakes
1 tablespoon chopped fresh marjoram
sea salt and freshly ground black pepper

To make the fungetto, cut the eggplants lengthwise into 6 wedges, then cut each wedge into ¾-inch pieces.

Heat 1 inch of extra virgin olive oil in a pan over high heat. Fry the egglant in batches in the olive oil until golden and cooked through, 3 to 4 minutes per batch. Season lightly when cooked.

Heat 3 tablespoons olive oil in a wide pan. Fry the garlic gently for 3 to 4 minutes but do not let it burn. Add the capers, anchovies, tomatoes, and chile. Season with pepper only. Cook for 5 to 6 minutes, then add the eggplant. Stir to combine very gently, then cook for 5 to 6 minutes. Add the marjoram and season to taste.

Pan-fry the scallops in a hot dry pan for about 2 minutes on each side, depending on size. Add a generous tablespoonful of warm fungetto and serve with a few fresh arugula leaves and a wedge of lemon

Eggplant Fritters with Honey & Thyme Leaves

This dish also makes an irresistible starter plate—we love the combination of thyme, honey, and eggplant.

SERVES 6

1 pound eggplant, cut into ¼-inch-thick
slices
flaky sea salt
olive oil, for deep-frying
honey, for drizzling
thyme leaves, to serve

FOR THE BATTER

¾ cup plus 2 tablespoons all-purpose
flour
5 tablespoons olive oil
½ cup plus 2 tablespoons cold water
2 organic egg whites

Sprinkle the eggplant lightly with salt and set aside in a colander for 30 minutes, if you wish.

Meanwhile, make the batter. Sift the flour into a bowl, make a well in the center, and gradually whisk in the oil and water. Cover and set aside until needed.

Pat the eggplant pieces dry with paper towels. Heat the oil in a deep fryer or pour ½ inch of olive oil into a deep skillet and heat to 350°F. When you think that it should be ready, drop in a cube of bread; it should brown nicely in a minute; if it burns, the oil is too hot.

Whisk the egg whites to soft peaks in a clean bowl and fold into the batter, then add a pinch of salt. Dip the eggplant slices, a few at a time, into the batter, add them to the hot oil, and deep-fry for 1 minute on each side until golden. Drain briefly on paper towels and serve immediately while they are still hot and crisp, drizzled generously with honey and sprinkled with thyme leaves and sea salt.

Fish-Fragrant Eggplants

This Sichuanese dish doesn't contain any fish at all, but it is so-called because the same flavorings are often used in cooking fish in that area of China. Madhur Jaffrey introduced us to this delectable recipe and urged us to seek out the long slim variety of eggplants, so we use the Slim Jim variety that we love to grow in the greenhouses in the summer.

SERVES 4 TO 6

1½ pounds Slim Jim or Japanese eggplants
¼ teaspoon sea salt
3 tablespoons best-quality peanut butter
3 tablespoons Chinese light soy sauce
5 teaspoons Chinese Chinkiang red vinegar
1 tablespoon sugar
2 teaspoons Chinese rice wine
1 tablespoon toasted sesame oil
1 tablespoon garlic, minced
1 tablespoon fresh ginger, peeled and
minced
2 tablespoons minced cilantro, plus a few
extra sprigs to garnish

Quarter the eggplants lengthwise and then cut them into 3-inch-long fingers. Sprinkle lightly with salt and allow to drain in a colander.

Put a Chinese steamer over a wok, add the eggplant, and steam over high heat for 15 to 20 minutes or until tender.

Meanwhile, put all the remaining ingredients, except the cilantro, into a bowl and mix well.

When the eggplant batons are soft, lift them gently onto a serving plate. Stir the cilantro into the sauce, taste, and add a little more sugar if necessary. Spoon the sauce evenly over the eggplant. Serve warm or chilled, garnished with a few sprigs of fresh cilantro. Although we love this dish warm or at room temperature, it can in fact be prepared a few hours or even a day ahead, covered, then refrigerated.

Rajasthani-Spiced Eggplant with Roast Lamb Chops

Eggplant, or *bainagan* or *brinjal*, is an important vegetable in Indian food and there are so many recipes to choose from. Eggplant takes on spices brilliantly and is wonderfully versatile, as this Rajasthani recipe demonstrates. We use this irresistible eggplant mixture on canapés, starters, as a vegetarian main course, and as an accompaniment. The spiced eggplant mixture is also good served cold or at room temperature alongside hot or cold lamb or pork. Chump is the V-shaped joint between the loin and the leg, usually a perfect size for two people, but it can be enough for three, depending on the size of the lamb.

SERVES 6

2 or 3 lamb chops
freshly ground toasted cumin
1 pound eggplant
approx. 1 cup extra virgin olive oil
1-inch piece of fresh ginger, peeled and
  coarsely chopped
6 large garlic cloves, coarsely crushed
1 teaspoon fennel seeds
2 teaspoons cumin seeds
¾ pound very ripe tomatoes, peeled and
  finely chopped, or 1 (14-ounce) can
  tomatoes plus 1 teaspoon sugar
1 tablespoon freshly ground coriander
  seeds
¼ teaspoon ground turmeric
⅓ teaspoon cayenne pepper (more if you
  like)
⅓ cup raisins
sea salt and freshly ground black pepper
arugula leaves, to serve

Preheat the oven to 350°F.

First roast the lamb chops. Remove the bone if you prefer. Score the fat; season with salt, freshly ground pepper, and roasted and ground cumin. Roast for 30 to 45 minutes or until cooked to your taste.

Cut the eggplants into ¾-inch-thick slices. Sprinkle with salt and stand upright in an oven rack to drain. Heat a grill-pan over medium heat and add a layer of extra virgin olive oil. Dry the eggplant slices and pan-grill in batches until golden on each side and cooked through. Set aside.

Put the ginger, garlic, and 3 tablespoons of water into a food processor. Process until fairly smooth.

Heat 3 tablespoons of the oil in a sauté pan. When hot, add the fennel and cumin seeds (careful not to let them burn). Stir for just a few seconds then put in the chopped tomatoes, the ginger-garlic mixture, coriander, turmeric, cayenne, and salt. Simmer for 5 to 6 minutes, stirring occasionally, until the spice mixture thickens slightly.

Add the eggplant slices and raisins and coat gently with the spicy sauce. Cover the pan, reduce the heat to very low, and cook for an additional 3 to 4 minutes. Serve warm.

Serve with slices of pink roast lamb and a salad of arugula leaves. I love to sprinkle a little flaky sea salt over each delicious helping.

POTATOES *Solanum tuberosum* ANNUAL

The Spanish Conquistadors, having sailed across the oceans to Peru, in South America, in search of gold, brought the potato to Europe. From there it came to Ireland with Sir Walter Raleigh in 1589 and was first planted at his home, Myrtle Grove in Youghal, County Cork. After initial suspicion, the Irish quickly embraced the potato and realized its immense value as an easy-to-grow, easy-to-cook food crop. Unfortunately, they concentrated on a single high-yielding variety and the entire crop was wiped out with blight several years in a row, which led to the potato famines in the 1840s. Over a million people died and another million plus left Ireland, many packed aboard ships bound for America.

I'm often asked by wannabe vegetable growers where to start and which vegetables they should grow first. Apart from radishes, which in summer produce crunchy nibbles within a couple of weeks, early potatoes are definitely the way to go. You might wonder why you'd bother to

Colleen potato plant growing in a plastic bag. Keep topping up with compost.

grow potatoes when they are available to buy everywhere. It's not just the flavor, it's the magic of harvesting those beautiful earthy jewels from the potato seed you carefully planted about four months earlier. Underneath where you sowed just one seed potato, there will be virtually enough for a whole meal—it's like digging for hidden treasure! It doesn't matter whether you are a banker, a baker or a school child, it's a deeply moving, almost primeval experience.

Commercial potatoes are sprayed with a whole cocktail of pesticides, often up to once a week, to prevent blight, and they also get another spray to stop them sprouting in storage, so they are an altogether different product from your own home-grown potatoes.

VARIETIES

There are many tried-and-tested traditional varieties and lots of new ones, so get some seed catalogues, or ask other people in your locality what grows well in the soil. Do a bit of homework and choose the best-flavored varieties. It's worth putting your chef's hat on.

Ask yourself a few questions, would you like early, mid-crop or maincrop potatoes, or will you choose a succession of varieties to have a year-round supply. Will you use a lot of potatoes? Do you like floury or waxy potatoes, or a mixture?

If you are short of space, concentrate on growing earlies, as they will produce an abundant crop at the time when potatoes are most expensive in the shops.

The following are my favorite varieties for our soil and location; we live on the south coast of Ireland, so our soil is quite

a heavy clay but has a nearly neutral pH of about 6.5, just slightly acid, but you will need to rely on local knowledge for the best variety for you.

EARLIES

Purple Viking—tubers have striking purple and red skin with snow whiter flesh; stores well.
French Fingerling—prized for their flavor when boiled or roasted; oval tubers have red skin and yellow flesh.
Yukon Gold—Early, high yields of delicious yellow tubers; keeps well.
Charlotte—Second early, yellow skin, and creamy yellow waxy flesh, good flavor.
You can plant Colleen, an organic variety, if you have a greenhouse or tunnel, in late winter, in order to have potatoes in mid-spring. If you want to plant potatoes in a tunnel, then sow an early variety after Christmas and dig them out before the tunnel gets too hot in late spring.

MAINCROP

Kerr's Pink—Late-maturing "floury" potato with white to pink skin and eyes.
Pink Fir Apple—Fingerling type, super tasty waxy potato. Good for salads and keeps its shape brilliantly.

BLIGHT-RESISTANT VARIETIES

Satina—vigorous plants produce plenty of yellow skinned and fleshed tubers.
Strawberry Paw—High yields of round, red-skinned, white fleshed tubers. Plants are resitant ot blight and scab.
Kennebec—fast-growin gplants produce high yields of good sized, oblong tubers. Resistant to many dieseases.

HOW TO GROW

Prepare the soil carefully. Potatoes do

well in rich, fertile, well-drained soil that has been enriched with well-rotted manure or compost. After storms we also collect seaweed from our nearby strand as it makes a brilliant fertilizer and mulch both in the greenhouse and in the field. Don't spread it too thickly or it will not be broken down in time for planting. Seaweed provides nitrogen, phosphorus, potassium and other trace elements. Seaweed fertilizer from the garden center makes a good substitute.

Many books recommend chitting but this is not totally necessary. The idea is that it will encourage the potatoes to sprout before you plant them. Chitting would usually be done about six weeks before planting, to provide a head start. We haven't found a significant difference. Just cut the potato into a couple of pieces, each needs to incorporate an eye, as this will make the seed potatoes go further.

Here, in Ireland, for outside planting of early potatoes it's usual to wait until St Patrick's Day (early spring), but if the weather is good you can get them in earlier. Two weeks after that you can plant the second earlies. Then after a further two weeks the maincrop can go in. We find that it's best to get the maincrop in early to avoid blight, as we don't spray. We plant the earlies and maincrop at the same time to give the maincrop a head start against blight—being close to the south coast we have a relatively kind climate, but our summers can favor blight.

If the shoots have appeared above ground and frost threatens, you can cover them with horticultural fleece.

CONTAINER GROWING

Potatoes can be grown in all manner of containers: plastic shopping bags, tires (not sure about this, surely the chemicals in the rubber leach into the soil—some say yes, some say no, if you would still like to try this line with a plastic bag),

galvanized trash cans, barrels, terracotta pots, willow baskets, or sacks.

HARVESTING

Eileen, our gardener, has great fun showing our grandchildren and local kids how to plant potatoes in black bin bags, in which they gradually unfurl. When they are ready to harvest we slit the bottom of the bag and root out the potatoes a few at a time—you can't imagine the excitement!

Potatoes will flower before they are ready to harvest, then you can gently poke around under the plant with your hand or a trowel, in anticipation to see what has been produced. Gently dig around the stalk, you can usually remove the potatoes by hand into a bucket or basket. When digging be careful not to damage the potatoes with the sharp tines of the fork.

Potatoes should always be stored out of the light or they will turn green. This indicates the development of a toxic substance called solanine; it's best avoided, so discard any potatoes that are affected. For winter storage, potatoes can be stored in a clamp—(see page 23).

PESTS AND DISEASES

Potatoes are particularly susceptible to blight which is caused by the fungus *Phytophthora infestans*. Warm, humid, damp summer weather favors blight. As organic growers we focus on blight-resistant varieties and always buy certified virus-free seed. However, some of my favorite potatoes are not necessarily blight-resistant but, in a good year, if the weather is not too wet and humid, one can manage to get a decent crop.

If you do get blight, you will notice dark brown blotches on the tips and edges of the leaves, white spores will

Digging a potato plant and finding all these jewels underneath is magic.

develop in these areas and the stems will blacken. Cut off the affected stems and remove from the area, to prevent the spores spreading—they can spread by wind and rain. In Ireland the Meteorological Service issues blight warnings on radio and TV—that's how seriously we take our potatoes.

It is very important to rotate your vegetable crops so that potatoes are not grown in the same ground for a minimum of three years. This is because blight spores can lodge in the ground ready to attack next year's crop.

When buying seed, make sure it is healthy and also certified eelworm free. Eelworm is a very serious problem; if perchance you get an attack, lift potatoes immediately, burn them and forget about growing potatoes in that patch of ground for at least six years. Don't compost affected plants.

Slugs can also be a nuisance, particularly in wet weather when they can burrow into the tubers. Lift the crop as soon as possible and eat or store.

Wire worms, ¾- to 2-inch-long brown worms, burrow into the potatoes, rendering them unusable. This is not

Potato "eyes" turn into sprouts, which can be cut up and planted for the crop next year.

usually a problem where soil is well turned and exposed to weather and birds in the winter. Try to keep the crop weed free and lift them earlier than later.

Calendulas, corn and nasturtiums are also thought to distract aphids and some gardeners swear by the effectiveness of growing horseradish in sunken pots near potatoes, to curtail disease.

GOOD FOR YOU...

Potatoes are a good source of fiber and they also contain vitamins C, B1, B6, iron, folate, phosphorus, manganese, niacin and pantothenic acid. Vitamin C is higher in new potatoes than in more mature crops. They are low calorie, naturally fat free, sodium free, and low in sugar. Potatoes alone supply every vital nutrient except vitamins A and D. The easily grown plant has the ability to provide more nutritious food faster and on less land than any food crop and in almost any environment.

WHAT TO DO WITH A GLUT

Early and mid-crop potatoes are at their best when freshly dug. They deteriorate and lose flavor quickly and go green, so just dig enough for that meal. Maincrop potatoes store well in a pit or a dark cool shed, so a glut shouldn't cause a problem.

IN THE KITCHEN

Potatoes are immensely versatile; they can be boiled, baked, steamed, roast, fried, grilled, deep-fried, cooked in a bubbly gratin, or made into bread. They take on myriad flavors from herbs, spices, and chiles and are also good smoked. As the goodness is stored close to the skin, it's best to cook potatoes in their skins as much as possible.

There are many wonderful French potato gratins, but if I were forced to choose one it would have to be this sinfully rich **Gratin Dauphinoise**. This is a particularly good version of the classic recipe because it can be made ahead and reheated with great success. To serve 6 to 8, peel 3 pounds equal-sized potatoes with a peeler and slice them into very thin rounds. Don't wash them but dab them dry with a tea towel. Spread out on a worktop and season with salt and freshly ground black pepper, mixing it in with your hands. Pour 1⅔ cups milk into a saucepan, add the potatoes, stir gently, and bring to a boil. Cover, reduce the heat, and simmer gently for 10 minutes. Add 1½ cups heavy cream, 2 crushed small garlic cloves, and a generous grating of nutmeg and continue to simmer for 20 minutes, stirring occasionally so that the potatoes don't get an opportunity to stick to the saucepan. As soon as the potatoes are cooked, remove them with a slotted spoon and put them into a large gratin dish. Pour the creamy liquid over them (the gratin can be prepared ahead to this point). Reheat in a bain-marie in a preheated oven at 400°F for 10 to 20 minutes or until they are bubbly and golden on top. Sprinkle ½ cup grated Gruyère or Parmesan cheese on top before reheating in the oven. I sometimes add 2 or 3 bay leaves or a couple of sprigs of rosemary to the milk when poaching the potatoes, then remove them before transferring to the gratin dish.

It's vitally important for flavor to add salt to the water when cooking potatoes and new potatoes are particularly good cooked in seawater. To serve 4 or 5, bring 5 cups seawater (or 5 cups tap water plus 1 teaspoon salt) to a boil. Scrub 2 pounds new potatoes. Add a sprig of seaweed to the water, and then add the potatoes. Cover the saucepan, return to a boil, and cook for 15 to 25 minutes or until fully cooked, depending on size. Drain and serve immediately in a hot serving dish with good local butter.

A great way to use up leftover boiled potatoes is to make **Thrice-cooked French Fries**. To serve 4 to 6, cook 4 to 6 large potatoes, such as Golden Wonders or Kerr's Pinks, in boiling salted water until almost fully cooked. Peel and cut into fries of the desired size. Heat lard or good-quality oil to 325°F. Cook the fries in batches for 4 to 5 minutes until golden; drain well on paper towels. Do not crowd the pan, or the temperature of the fat will be lowered and consequently the fries will be greasy rather than crisp. Shake the pan once or twice, to separate the fries while cooking. To serve, heat the fat or oil to 375°F and fry once more until crisp and a deep golden color. Drain well on paper towels, sprinkle with a little salt and turn onto a hot serving dish.

Potato Soup

Most people have potatoes and onions in the house even if the cupboard is otherwise bare, so you can make this simply delicious soup at a moment's notice. For Potato and Fresh Herb Soup, add 1 to 2 tablespoons chopped fresh herbs, such as parsley, thyme, lemon balm, and chives, to the sweated vegetables with the stock, continue as below, and serve sprinkled with fresh herbs and flowers. Chorizo Crumbs (page 84) also make a delicious sprinkle to liven up a mild and silky potato soup.

. . . .

SERVES 6

4 tablespoons (½ stick) butter

1¼ pounds peeled potatoes, cut into ¼-inch dice

¼ pound onions, cut into ¼-inch dice

4 cups homemade chicken or vegetable stock

6 tablespoons whole milk

sea salt and freshly ground black pepper

chopped fresh herbs and herb flowers, such thyme or chives, to serve (optional)

Melt the butter in a heavy saucepan. When it foams, add the potatoes and onions and toss them in the butter until well coated. Sprinkle with salt and a few grinds of pepper. Cover with a round of parchment paper cut to fit the top of the pan and then the lid of the saucepan. Sweat over a gentle heat for about 10 minutes.

Meanwhile, bring the stock to a boil. When the vegetables are soft but not colored, add the stock and continue to cook for about 10 minutes until the vegetables are soft. Purée the soup in a blender or food processor. Season to taste. Thin with milk to the required consistency. Serve sprinkled with a few chopped fresh herbs and herb flowers, if available.

VARIATIONS

Potato & Roast Red Pepper Soup—Roast or broil 4 red bell peppers, peel and seedt them (save the sweet juices), and carefully purée the flesh with the juices. Season with salt and black pepper. Add a dash of balsamic vinegar and extra virgin olive oil if necessary. Season to taste. Make the soup as per the recipe above.

Just before serving, swirl the red pepper purée through the soup or simply drizzle on top of each bowl. Top with some chopped fresh flat-leaf parsley. You could also try adding one or two roast chiles for a little extra buzz—serrano and jalapeño are both good.

Potato & Parsley Soup—Add 2 to 3 tablespoons chopped fresh flat-leaf parsley to the soup before you purée it and omit the herbs in the master recipe.

Potato & Mint Soup—Add 2 to 3 tablespoons mint to the soup just before blending and omit the herbs in the master recipe.

Potato & Tarragon Soup—Add 1½ tablespoons of tarragon with the stock. Purée and finish as above. Sprinkle a little mint over the soup before serving.

Potato Soup with Harissa Oil—Drizzle a little harissa oil over the top to serve.

Potato, Chorizo, & Parsley Soup—Omit the herbs in the original recipe. Just before serving, cook 12 to 18 slices chorizo for a minute or two on each side on a nonstick pan, the oil will render out. Serve 3 slices chorizo on top of each bowl, sprinkle a few flat-leaf parsley sprigs on top, drizzle a little chorizo oil haphazardly over the soup, and serve immediately.

Potato & Melted Leek Soup—Serve a spoonful of melted leeks (see page 44) on top of each helping. Scatter with snipped chives and chive flowers in season.

Burmese Pork & Potato Curry

We found a version of this dish in virtually every local restaurant in Burma, and the pork was always fat and succulent. I learned this version at a cooking class at the Bagan Thiripyitsaya Sanctuary Resort in Myanmar. The chef used water and included a teaspoon of "chicken seasoning" but I have substituted some homemade chicken stock instead. I have also reduced the chili powder, but you can use the maximum quantity if you like it super hot. The sauce is packed with flavor, it reheats brilliantly and even a little will electrify a bowl of rice.

. . . .

SERVES 4 TO 6

1 pound heritage pork with rind on

¾ pound waxy potatoes, peeled and diced

1 tablespoon vegetable oil

¼ pound onions, chopped

2 garlic cloves, crushed

1-inch piece of fresh ginger, peeled and grated

1 large ripe tomato or 6 cherry tomatoes, chopped

½ teaspoon ground turmeric

½ to 1 teaspoon chili powder

1 tablespoon fish sauce (nam pla)

½ teaspoon Indian masala (see below)

5½ cups homemade chicken stock

sea salt and freshly ground black pepper

sticky or basmati rice, to serve

FOR THE INDIAN MASALA
(MAKES 2½ TEASPOONS)

2 bay leaves

1-inch piece of cinnamon stick

1 whole star anise

3 cloves, crushed

FOR THE PORK MARINADE

½ to 1 teaspoon chili powder

2 teaspoons fish sauce (nam pla)

½ teaspoon Indian masala

1 teaspoon vegetable oil

½ teaspoon sugar

FOR THE POTATO MARINADE

½ teaspoon ground turmeric

¼ teaspoon chili powder

1 teaspoon fish sauce (nam pla)

To make the Indian masala, combine the ingredients in a spice grinder and grind, or crush using a mortar and pestle and mix together.

Cut the pork into ¾-inch strips. Mix the pork marinade ingredients together and rub all over the pork with your fingers. Let marinate for 45 minutes to 1 hour.

Meanwhile, cut the potatoes into ¾-inch cubes. Transfer to a bowl and add the ingredients for the potato marinade. Toss to mix. The turmeric stops the potato from blackening.

Heat the oil in a wok or sauté pan. Add the chopped onions, cook for 3 to 4 minutes, add the crushed garlic, grated ginger, chopped tomatoes, turmeric, chili powder, fish sauce, and Indian masala. Stir well, add ½ cup of the chicken stock. Cook for 2 to 3 minutes until all the liquid has evaporated. Add the pork pieces and enough of the remaining chicken stock to almost cover. Bring to a boil, reduce the heat, cover, and simmer for 1½ hours until the pork is almost tender.

Remove the lid, add the cubed potatoes, and cook, uncovered, for an additional 20 to 30 minutes. Season to taste.

Serve with sticky or basmati rice.

Potato Gnocchi with Chile-Parsley Butter

Who doesn't love gnocchi? Floury potatoes are best here. The sauce can, of course, be varied but a simple chile and herb or sage butter makes a tasty accompaniment.

. . . .

SERVES 6

2¼ pounds floury potatoes, such as British Queens, Kerr's Pinks, or Golden Wonders, unpeeled

2 large organic egg yolks (keep the whites)

1¼ cups all-purpose flour

½ cup plus 1 tablespoon semolina

2 to 4 tablespoons chopped parsley

sea salt and freshly ground black pepper

FOR THE PARSLEY AND CHILE BUTTER

½ cup (1 stick) butter

¼ teaspoon chile flakes, or 1 fresh red or green chile, finely sliced, seeds included or discarded as you wish

2 tablespoons minced curly or flat-leaf parsley

Cook the potatoes in a large amount of boiling salted water for 15 to 30 minutes depending on freshness and variety. Drain and peel while hot.

Put the potatoes through a food mill or ricer into a bowl, or mash with a potato masher. Lightly fold in the egg yolks, flour, semolina, parsley, and salt, and work together quickly to make a dough. Add a little egg white if necessary.

Divide the gnocchi dough into four. On a clean surface, roll each piece of dough into a long roll shape a little fatter than your index finger. Cut into ¾-inch lengths. Roll each small piece in the palm of your hand with the tines of a fork. This will make indentations, which will catch a bit of the sauce.

To make the parsley and chile butter, melt the butter and when it foams add the chile and cook for a minute or so, then add the minced parsley.

Bring a large pan of salted water to a boil. Add the gnocchi and cook over high heat for 2 to 3 minutes or until they rise to the surface. Remove with a slotted spoon, letting the spoon rest on a clean folded cloth to drain off any excess water. Serve on hot plates with the parsley and chile butter.

Tortillitas à la Patata

Sam and Jeannie Chesterton of Finca Buenvino in Andalucia recently introduced me to this little gem. They are so easy to make and completely addictive—kids also love them and they make perfect little bites to nibble with a drink, preferably a glass of Fino or Manzanilla. This is a totally brilliant way to use up leftover boiled potatoes. The tortillitas are made in minutes and can be served as part of every meal from breakfast to supper.

. . . .

MAKES 26

4 organic eggs

½ pound cooked potatoes, cut into ¼-inch dice

½ teaspoon salt

¼ teaspoon freshly ground black pepper

3 tablespoons minced parsley and chives

extra virgin olive oil, for frying

Maldon sea salt, for sprinkling

Aioli (page 195), to serve

Whisk the eggs in a bowl, add the diced potatoes, season with the salt and pepper and add the herbs.

Heat about ¼ inch of extra virgin olive oil in the skillet over high heat. Cook a teaspoon of the mixture and taste for seasoning. Correct if necessary.

Continue to cook the mini tortillitas as needed, using a scant 2½ teaspoons of the mixture each time. Cook on one side for 1 to 2 minutes, flip over, and continue to cook on the other side for a similar length of time, or until slightly golden. Drain on paper towels and sprinkle with a few flakes of sea salt.

Serve hot, or at room temperature, with a blob of aioli.

SPINACH *Spinacia oleracea* ANNUAL

Rows of spinach—one of my top ten must-have vegetables.

Native to central and western Asia, spinach was first cultivated by the Persians as a medicinal plant; it was believed that raw spinach juice could be used to prevent any form of disease, such was its high concentration of vitamins and minerals. The leaves of the annual or summer spinach are more tender and less stringent in flavor than perpetual spinach or chard (see page 68). It is delicious both raw in salads and cooked in a variety of ways. It's a brilliant cut-and-come-again crop that can provide a non-stop harvest of tasty leaves throughout the summer and into the late autumn. Home-grown spinach tastes altogether different to the bags of little leaves you can buy in the supermarket. It's fresher and more delicious and, of course, it's immensely versatile.

VARIETIES

Bloomsdale—dark green, glossy, savoyed leaves are tender and tasty.
Corvair—smooth-leaved variety for early crops; dark green, uniform leaves on slow-bolting plants
Carmel—for baby leaves or full sized; grows fastl ideal for fall crops.
Bordeaux F1—Lovely red-veined variety, great in salads.

HOW TO GROW

Set seeds in compost-filled cells, water in, then pop one seed into each and cover with a thin layer of compost, 6 inches deep is good. Press down lightly. When the plant has about 4 leaves, transplant into a prepared bed, about 2 ¾ inches apart with 10 inches between rows for baby leaves, 6 inches for larger. Keep watered and watch out for slugs.

Sow summer crops in semi-shade to discourage bolting and snip off any flower heads. Spinach thrives in rich, fertile soil with a high nitrogen content. It benefits from plenty of humus or well-rotted manure. Don't let the soil dry out during dry spells otherwise annual spinach will bolt. Annual spinach can be grown indoors in a greenhouse or tunnel or directly into the soil. Sow late spring and early summer to have succession. It can also be grown as a filler plant and doesn't suffer from rotation problems. You can sow a winter variety in late summer or early autumn.

CONTAINER GROWING

Spinach grows well in containers or raised beds, even on a windowsill.

PESTS AND DISEASES

Downy mildew can also be a problem, particularly in warm humid conditions.

Some varieties are more resistant than others, such as *Palco F1*.

HARVESTING

Annual spinach should be ready to harvest about 6 weeks from sowing. There are two harvesting options, either snip off the outer leaves, or treat it as a cut-and-come-again crop—cut each plant down to about 2 inches above the ground, after 2 to 3 weeks the plant will have produced another cutting of young tender leaves. Constant harvesting helps to reduce the risk of bolting.

GOOD FOR YOU...

Thanks to Popeye, just about everyone knows that spinach is a good source of iron but it also has lots of vitamins, including A, C, E, K and antioxidants, lutein, lipoic acid, potassium and double the fiber of other greens. Spinach, home-grown in rich, fertile soil is likely to have lots more nutrients than intensively grown hydroponic spinach and far superior flavor.

Spinach is considered to be one of the world's healthiest vegetables—a powerhouse of nutrition. Apart from being an important source of iron, it's an excellent source of vitamins K, A, B, B6, E and C and manganese, folate, magnesium, copper, calcium and potassium.

It's also a good source of dietary fiber, phosphorous, B1, zinc, protein and choline, a very important antioxidant.

WHAT TO DO WITH A GLUT?

Make spinach soup, it freezes very well. Spinach can also be cooked down into a purée and frozen in a block, which makes a really useful standby.

IN THE KITCHEN

There are so many good things to do with spinach, from silky spinach soup to smoothies, to Persian kuku and frittata, to wilted spinach anointed with extra virgin olive oil, and myriad salad combinations benefit from a fistful of tender baby spinach leaves.

Spinach is fantastically versatile. Strip the leaves off the stalks and cook each separately. The latter can be chopped, then tossed into boiling salted water for 3 to 4 minutes, drained, then anointed with lots of butter or a good glug of extra virgin olive oil along with a few twists of pepper. Spinach has an extraordinary capacity to absorb butter and cream. I remember a recipe called Four-Day Spinach in Jane Grigson's *Good Things* that added more butter every day

for 4 days—even I balked at that! The stalks also lap up lots of other flavors, such as chile, fresh herbs, soy sauce....

The leaves can be simply wilted in butter or olive oil on the pan, then well-seasoned with salt and pepper and a good grating of nutmeg. But I'm a traditionalist and prefer to give them a quick wash in cold water and then cook them with just the droplets that adhere to the leaves. The spinach will exude lots of liquid, so just drain well and save the liquid—it's full of good things—then add lots of seasoning and good butter or extra virgin olive oil to the spinach. It also works well to throw the leaves into a large pot of boiling water for a few minutes until soft and tender, drain really well, and anoint as above.

Creamed spinach is particularly

delicious with a simple roast and, of course, with poached eggs, when it changes its name to *oeufs Florentine*. We often wilt spinach into bean stews just before serving, a delicious and nutritious addition, and then of course there's spinach and rosemary soup, spinach gnocchi....We also dip spinach leaves into a batter for pakoras, and of course a spinach soufflé or tart is also irresistible, so it's a must-have vegetable.

Indian cooking has myriad tempting ways to eat spinach: saag, paneer, palak, daal, crispy palak pakoras. A handful added to a vegetable stew just before serving is delicious and adds an extra nutritional element. Spinach is also now a must-have for a new generation of juicers, too.

Spinach & Rosemary Soup

Despite initial misgivings, everyone loves this recipe when we serve it, both at Ballymaloe House and at the cooking school. The trick with these green soups is to not add the greens until the last minute, otherwise they will overcook and the soup will lose its fresh taste and bright green color. For a simple spinach soup, omit the rosemary and add a little freshly grated nutmeg with the seasoning.

SERVES 6 TO 8

4 tablespoons (½ stick) butter

¼ pound onions, chopped

5¼ ounces potatoes, diced

2½ cups homemade chicken stock or vegetable stock, or water

scant ½ cup heavy cream

1¾ to 2½ cups whole milk

½ to ¾ pound spinach, stemmed and chopped

1 tablespoon chopped fresh rosemary

sea salt and freshly ground black pepper

2 tablespoons whipped cream and a sprig of rosemary or rosemary flowers, to garnish (optional)

Melt the butter in a heavy-bottomed saucepan. When it foams, add the chopped onions and potatoes and turn them until well coated. Sprinkle with salt and freshly ground pepper. Cover and sweat over low heat for about 10 minutes.

Meanwhile, bring the stock, cream, and milk to the boil in a saucepan over medium heat. Add the boiling liquid to the pan, return to a boil, and simmer until the potatoes and onions are fully cooked. Add the spinach and boil with the lid off for 3 to 5 minutes until the spinach is tender. Do not overcook or the soup will lose its fresh green color. Add the chopped rosemary.

Carefully transfer to a high-speed blender and blend until smooth. Taste and adjust the seasoning if necessary. Serve in warm bowls garnished with a blob of whipped cream, if you like, and a sprig of rosemary. If you have a rosemary bush in bloom, sprinkle a few pretty blue flowers over the top for extra pizzazz.

Spanakopita—Greek Spinach & Cheese Pie

The same mixture can be used to make one large flaky pie or a number of individual "snails." As you work with each sheet of pastry, keep the others covered with a damp cloth to prevent them drying out.

SERVES 6 TO 8

4 tablespoons extra virgin olive oil
½ pound onion, minced
4 scallions with greens, finely sliced
2 pounds stemmed fresh spinach
freshly grated nutmeg
4 tablespoons chopped flat-leaf parsley
3 to 4 tablespoons chopped dill
8 ounces feta cheese, crumbled (or
   5 ounces feta, crumbled, and 2 ounces
   Parmesan, freshly grated)
1 organic egg, beaten
12 to 14 sheets of phyllo dough
1 cup (2 sticks) butter, melted, or 1 cup
   olive oil
sea salt and freshly ground black pepper

Preheat the oven to 350°F.

Heat the extra virgin olive oil in a sauté pan and add the minced onion and scallions. Stir, cover, and sweat over low heat until soft but not colored. Increase the heat, add the spinach, and toss; season with salt, freshly ground pepper, and nutmeg. Add the chopped parsley and dill and continue to cook for 4 to 5 minutes or until the spinach is tender.

Turn into a colander and drain and cool. Mix the crumbled feta into the beaten egg. Add the well-drained spinach and season to taste. Purée in a food processor for a smooth texture; otherwise use immediately as a more robust filling.

Brush an 11-inch shallow pan with melted butter, then line with 6 to 7 sheets of phyllo dough, brushing each sheet with butter before laying the next on top. Spread the filling into the tin, then arrange another 6 to 7 sheets of dough on top, buttering each as you go and scrunching up the top layers for extra crunch. Brush the pastry with egg wash, then with melted butter and bake for about 45 minutes until crisp and golden. Serve warm.

VARIATION

The same filling can be used to make individual "snails." Halve the quantity of filling and use 6 to 8 sheets of phyllo dough. Lay one sheet of dough on your work surface and brush with melted butter. Lay a strip of filling along one side, about 1 inch in from the edge. Roll into a long sausage, the coil into a snail and place on a greased baking sheet. Repeat with the other snails and brush with egg wash and then with melted butter. Bake for about 30 minutes or until crisp and golden.

> **DID YOU KNOW?**
> In French classical cooking any dish with Florentine in the title will include spinach. The area around Florence was particularly famous for the flavor of its spinach.

Lasagna with Mushroom & Spinach

Lasagna is basically a formula—once I realized that simple fact I started to play around with it and now we make many versions with meat, fish, and vegetables. The end result needs to be bubbly and juicy with lots of filling. Zucchini with marjoram or basil, eggplant, roast red pepper and basil or wild garlic pesto, pumpkin, chard, goat cheese...

. . . .

SERVES 12

1 pound lasagna pasta

7 cups milk made into well-seasoned Béchamel Sauce (page 267)

1 recipe Piperonata (see page 000)

1 recipe Buttered Spinach or Chard (see page 257)

8 ounces Parmesan or mature cheddar cheese, grated, or a mix

sea salt and freshly ground black pepper

green salad, to serve

FOR THE MUSHROOM A LA CRÈME

2 to 4 tablespoons butter

1 cup finely chopped onions

16 ounces mushrooms, sliced

a squeeze of lemon juice

¾ cup double cream

chopped fresh flat-leaf parsley

1 tablespoon chopped chives (optional)

To make the Mushroom a la Crème, melt the butter in a heavy saucepan until it foams. Add the chopped onions, cover, and sweat over a gentle heat for 5 to 10 minutes or until quite soft but not colored; remove the onions to a bowl and set aside.

Meanwhile cook the sliced mushrooms in a little butter, in a hot frying pan, in batches if necessary. Season each batch with salt, freshly ground pepper and a tiny squeeze of lemon juice. Add the onions to the saucepan, then add the cream and allow to bubble for a few minutes. Season to taste and add the parsley and chives, if using. Mushroom a la Crème keeps well in the fridge for 4–5 days and freezes perfectly.

Preheat the oven to 350°F.

First taste each component and make sure they are all delicious and well seasoned.

Blanch the lasagna noodles as directed on the package; some "easy cook" lasagna may be used without blanching. Lay the noodles on a dishtowel or paper towels.

Spread a little béchamel sauce over the bottom of a 9 × 13-inch baking dish (or use two smaller dishes), cover with a layer of noodles, and then a layer of piperonata. Next put on another layer of noodles. Spread with béchamel sauce, sprinkle with half the grated cheese, and add a layer of buttered spinach. Cover with another layer of noodles, then the mushroom, and top with a layer of noodles. Carefully spread béchamel sauce over the lot (make sure all the pasta is under the sauce) and finally sprinkle liberally with the remaining grated cheese.

Bake for 10 to 15 minutes, or until golden and bubbly on top. If possible, let stand for 10 to 15 minutes before cutting to allow the layers to compact. Serve with a good green salad.

Gnudi with Spinach & Goat's Curd

Don't confuse these little ricotta dumplings with gnocchi, which are made using wheat flour and potatoes. They are super simple to make and take just a few minutes to cook. This is a variation on the delicious recipe that Clare Lattin and Tom Hill from Duck Soup in London shared with us when they did a guest chef slot at the Ballymaloe Cookery School during Litfest 2017 – they used wild watercress instead of spinach – also delicious.

SERVES 6–8

FOR THE GNUDI
18 ounces buffalo ricotta
1 organic egg yolk
¼ cup '00' flour
⅓ cup freshly grated Parmesan
zest of 1 lemon
11 cups semolina flour, for dusting
salt and freshly ground black pepper

FOR THE SAUCE
⅓ cup butter
½ cup extra virgin olive oil, plus extra for
    drizzling
16 ounces spinach, stalks removed
5½ ounces goat's curd or a good-quality
    cottage cheese, preferably made with
    raw milk
zest of 1 lemon

Mix the ricotta, egg yolk, '00' flour and Parmesan together in a bowl, then add the lemon zest and salt and pepper and mix again.

In a wide, deep baking tray or plastic container, spread out a generous layer of semolina flour, one-fifth of an inch thick.

Roll the gnudi mixture into 18–24 balls and then lay each one on the semolina flour in a single layer, making sure they do not touch each other.

When you have used up all the mixture, completely cover the gnudi with the remaining semolina flour and chill in the fridge for 24 hours. By then, the semolina will have formed a crust on the gnudi – this helps the dumplings hold their shape.

When you're ready to cook the gnudi, bring a large pan of salted water to the boil, dust off the excess semolina flour (any excess semolina flour can be kept in the fridge and used again) and boil the gnudi for about 3 minutes, in batches, until they rise to the top of the saucepan, reserving some of the cooking water.

To serve, heat the butter and extra virgin olive oil in a large saucepan over a medium heat until the butter begins to foam. Add the spinach leaves and a couple of small ladles of the gnudi cooking water and stir gently. As soon as the spinach starts to wilt, add the goat's curd or cottage cheese and give it another stir (you may need to add a little more of the gnudi water to thin the sauce slightly).

Drain the gnudi and add to the sauce. Stir very gently – careful not to break the gnudi. Divide the gnudi and sauce between 6–8 bowls, finish each bowl with a grating of lemon zest, a good drizzle of extra virgin olive oil and a few twists of black pepper.

CROSNES *Stachys affinis Lamiaceae* ANNUAL

Crosnes look like little coiled springs and reappear every year.

A few years ago I got a present of a few tiny curvaceous knobbly roots from a botanist in Cork. I popped them into a bed at the top of the Kitchen Garden and almost forgot about them. I've now got a patch 5 feet square, enough to feast on, and wow are they delicious! Crosnes, also called Chinese artichokes, look like beautiful turreted shells. They take careful washing because of their curves, but the flavor is well worth the effort—a winter vegetable definitely worth growing as the yield increases every year.

In Asia they are also called *chorogi* and are part of the Osechi celebrations for Japanese New Year. The French name *crosnes* is pronounced "crone," as in wizened old woman. Crosnes are called *kamulu* in China, meaning "gentle dew." Chinese poets have referred to them as strings of white jade beads.

HOW TO GROW

Plant the tubers in early spring in rich, fertile soil in full sun, they will spread and provide ground cover. Space them 10 inches apart in rows 18 inches apart.

CONTAINER GROWING

Not the best use of a container, though they would grow in a trough or barrel.

PESTS AND DISEASES

They are not bothered by pests or diseases.

HARVESTING

Harvest in late autumn, early winter, and until late spring when they are about 2 inches in length and ⅓ inch in diameter. The plants can yield about 1 pound Jerusalem artichoke-flavored tubers.

GOOD FOR YOU....

High in natural sugars and carbohydrates. Rich in protein and betaine.

WHAT TO DO WITH A GLUT

Crosnes, like Jerusalem artichokes, remain in the ground until needed, but if you do have a glut, share with friends.

IN THE KITCHEN

Chefs have recently rediscovered crosnes so they are being touted as one of the hot new foods. They love the flavor, reminiscent of Jerusalem artichokes, and the crisp texture of the crunchy tubers. Just like artichokes, they can be roasted, braised, or puréed. They make a delicious soup and intriguing salads.

Pickled Crosnes

The wine-colored perilla leaves will dye the crosnes red; a few slices of beet will do the same, but neither are essential.

SERVES 4

1 pound crosnes (Chinese artichokes)
1 cup cider or white wine vinegar
½ cup sugar
½ teaspoon chile flakes
1 teaspoon coriander seeds
½ teaspoon fennel seeds
4 red shiso or perilla leaves (optional)

Scrub the freshly dug crosnes meticulously, trim them, rinse well, and put in a sterilized 1-quart jar.

Bring the vinegar, sugar, spices, and perilla to a boil for 2 minutes. Pour over the crosnes, cool, refrigerate, and let mellow for a few days before eating.

Alternatively, pack into jars, cover with the brine and seal tightly. Store in a cool, dark place, and consume with cold meats, cheese, and in salads. They will keep for several months but are better eaten sooner rather than later.

Chinese Artichoke & Shrimp Salad

Just like Jerusalem artichokes, crosnes (or Chinese artichokes) really complement shellfish—mussels, cockles, prawns, and shrimp.

SERVES 6 TO 8

2 pounds crosnes (Chinese artichokes)
extra virgin olive oil, for frying
Ballymaloe French Dressing (page 182)
6 to 8 ounces cooked and peeled shrimp
sea salt and freshly ground black pepper
freshly snipped flat-leaf parsley, to garnish
crusty bread, to serve

Scrub the freshly dug artichokes with a soft brush under running water. Trim—there's no need to peel.

Heat a little olive oil in a heavy saucepan. Toss in the artichokes and season well with salt and freshly ground pepper. Cover with a round of parchment paper cut to fit the pan and then the lid of the saucepan. Cook over low heat for 8 to 10 minutes until tender. They cook unevenly so be careful to test a few.

When the crosnes are cooked, toss in the dressing while still warm. Then gently toss in the cooked shrimp or mussels.

Serve while still warm with a sprinkling of snipped flat-leaf parsley and some crusty bread.

SALSIFY

Tragopogon porrifolius BIENNIAL

Salsify is a hardy biennial, a member of the dandelion tribe, within the daisy family. It is probably unfamiliar to many gardeners but do consider growing this for the delicate flavor of its roots and shoots—truly delicious in late autumn and winter. It has skin not unlike a parsnip but is stubbier and is covered with whiskery roots, which gives it its other names of goat's beard and vegetable oyster.

You are unlikely to find salsify in your local supermarket or in most farmers' markets, which in itself earns it a place in your kitchen garden.

It can be used for soups, stews, gratins or served in a creamy sauce. If you leave the plants in the ground you will be rewarded with a delicious crop of shoots and flower heads in spring, the taste of which is reminiscent of asparagus – they are delicious in salads.

VARIETIES

Mammoth Sandwich Island—an improved variety—they grow to about 10 inches with a long, tapered root. **Gammel Gotlandsk**—very thin roots with pure white flesh.

HOW TO GROW

Sow the seeds in spring in drills ⅓ to ¾ inch deep, allowing about 6 inches between rows. They are not too fussy but do best in light, well-drained, stone-free soil, not freshly manured because, like most root vegetables, they are prone to forking. Thin to 4 to 5 inches apart and then just let them grow, but keep the area as weed free as possible. They like full sun.

You could also try growing a piece of root from the greengrocer's.

The leaves resemble young leeks but salsify has blue-purple flowers (see right).

Salsify is hardy and can be left in the ground well into winter and dug as required. It takes at least 120 days to mature.

CONTAINER GROWING

To grow in a container the soil would need to be at least 2 feet deep to provide enough space for the roots to go down.

PESTS AND DISEASES

Salsify is easy to grow and in my experience isn't bothered by pests and diseases.

GOOD FOR YOU...

Salsify is rich in iron and calcium, potassium, phosphorus and fiber, vitamins B and C and inulin.

WHAT TO DO WITH A GLUT

A glut is unlikely but they can be lifted and stored in boxes of damp sand in a root cellar or dark shed.

IN THE KITCHEN

To cook, scrub and trim. Salsify can be cooked in their skins and peeled later, but if you do peel them, drop them immediately into acidulated water because, like artichokes, they discolor quickly. They exude a sort of sticky, milky liquid when cut, which is why it's better to cook them whole.

Cook them in a little salted water in a covered pan. If they are whole they will take 10 to 30 minutes, depending on size. Refresh under cold water and discard the cooking water, which will be brown. Peel and then slice and finish in whichever recipe you choose. They can be added to slow-cooked dishes or dipped in batter or bread crumbs to make delicious fritters or pakoras.

Salsify is delicious with mussels, scallops, and oysters, in a fish soup or

---

DID YOU KNOW?

Up until the 1500s, black salsify was often used in treating the plague as it was belived to help rid the body of toxins. It is also hown as the oyster plant or vegetable oyster because of its oyster flavour.

chowder, or in salad with shellfish. We find that the fresh salsify leaves taste better than black salsify leaves. Use them in salads or wilted.

Left: *Wash the roots of salsify well, then peel and immediately pop into acidulated water to prevent discoloration.*
Right: *The pretty blue-purple flowers of salsify are an extra bonus and attract beneficial insects to the garden.*

Salsify or Asparagus in Phyllo

Fans of the irrepressible Jeremy Lee's Quo Vadis in London's Dean Street will recognize this recipe, which is quintessential Jeremy. He serves salsify, black salsify, and new season's asparagus in filo like this. Jeremy sweetly shared the recipe for this delicious bite with me. Try using parsnip in this recipe if you can't source salsify or black salsify, it doesn't sound as posh, but you'll be surprised at how delicious they taste here.

SERVES 12

12 sticks of salsify or asparagus spears, in season
juice of 1 lemon
extra virgin olive oil (optional)
12 sheets of phyllo dough
¾ cup (1½ sticks) unsalted butter, melted
5¼ ounces Parmesan cheese, finely grated, plus extra to serve
sea salt and freshly ground black pepper

Peel the salsify and toss in the lemon juice immediately to prevent discoloring. Put in a saucepan of boiling salted water, just enough to cover, return to a boil and simmer for 3 to 4 minutes until the salsify is tender. Remove from the heat, drain, and let cool. Cut into 4- to 5-inch-long pieces.

(If you are using asparagus, trim the ends, cook as above, or toss in a little extra virgin olive oil and cook in a grill pan over high heat for 3 to 4 minutes; it should retain a nice bite.)

Lay a sheet of phyllo on your work surface, cut crosswise into 4 pieces, and brush with melted butter. Sprinkle it evenly with finely grated Parmesan and season with salt and pepper. Place one salsify stick or asparagus spear in the middle. Tuck in the edges and roll up tightly. Arrange in a single layer on a baking sheet, brush with melted butter, and sprinkle with a dusting of Parmesan. Repeat with all the remaining ingredients, then chill.

Preheat the oven to 400°F.

Bake for 8 to 10 minutes—you may need to turn them over once or twice so that they are crisp and golden all over.

Serve piping hot, sprinkled with a little more Parmesan.

Salsify Gratin

Both salsify and black salsify lend themselves well to a gratin recipe. In fact, one can use both in many root vegetable recipes. They also take on Asian, Mediterranean, and Middle Eastern flavors deliciously.

SERVES 6

10 to 12 sticks of salsify or black salsify
juice of 1 or 2 lemons
1 teaspoon Dijon mustard
4 ounces Gruyère cheese, grated
1¾ ounces Parmesan cheese, grated

FOR THE ROUX
½ cup (1 stick) butter
¾ cup plus 2 tablespoons flour

FOR THE BÉCHAMEL SAUCE
1¼ cups cold milk
a few slices of carrot
a few slices of onion
3 peppercorns
1 small sprig of thyme
1 small sprig of parsley
3 tablespoons roux (see above)
sea salt and freshly ground black pepper

FOR THE BUTTERED CRUMBS
4 tablespoons (½ stick) butter
4 ounces fresh bread crumbs

To make the roux, melt the butter and cook the flour in it for 2 minutes over low heat, stirring occasionally. Use as required. (Roux can prepared ahead and used when needed or it can be made up on the spot if preferred. It will keep for at least 2 weeks in the fridge.)

To make the buttered crumbs, melt the butter in a pan and stir in the bread crumbs. Remove from the heat immediately and let cool.

Peel the salsify or black salsify and toss in the lemon juice to prevent discoloring. Put in a saucepan of boiling water, just enough to cover, return to a boil, and simmer for 3 to 4 minutes until tender. Remove from the heat, drain, and let cool. Cut into 4- to 5-inch pieces.

Meanwhile, make the béchamel sauce. (This is a marvelous quick way of making béchamel sauce if you already have roux made.) Put the cold milk into a saucepan with the carrot, onion, peppercorns, thyme, and parsley. Bring to a boil, simmer for 4 to 5 minutes, remove from the heat, and let infuse for 10 minutes. Strain out the vegetables, return the milk to a boil, and thicken with the roux to a light coating consistency. Season to taste. Add the Dijon mustard and three-quarters of the cheese. Season to taste.

Spread a little sauce over the bottom of a gratin dish. Add the just-cooked salsify or black salsify. Cover with another layer of sauce. Sprinkle with a mixture of the remaining cheese and the buttered crumbs. Let cool and chill until later if needed.

Reheat in a preheated 350°F oven for 20 to 25 minutes until bubbling with a crisp golden crust on top.

FAVA BEANS *Vicia faba Fabaceae* ANNUAL

Ah fava beans, definitely one of my all-time favorite vegetables. The magic is in the freshness so it's best to grow your own so you can enjoy them super fresh. Like peas, the natural sugars in the beans turn to starch within 5 hours. The first of the fava beans nestled in their furry cases create terrific excitement. For weeks before they are mature enough to harvest, my grandchildren search impatiently along the fava rows hoping to find a pod that's big enough to pluck. They love to take the beans out of their fluffy pod and gobble them up both raw and cooked. What a joy for me to watch. As with many other homegrown vegetables, when you cultivate your own you get double or triple value from the plant. The plants fix nitrogen naturally in the soil, so follow them with brassicas in your crop rotation.

VARIETIES

With careful selection of varieties one can have a succession of fava beans from late spring to early autumn.

Windsor—The classic English variety, 6-inch pods each with 3 to 5 large beans

Vroma—Heat-tolerant, produces 7-inch pods with up to 5 seeds in each.

Super Aquadulce—Hardy, high-yielding, suitable for autumn or spring sowing.

Crimson Flowered—Heritage variety that dates back to the 1700s with beautifully scented crimson flowers. It looks very attractive in the vegetable garden, planted near alliums or red orach, which we use in salads. We plant chives close by, the purple flowers enhance the color scheme and attract pollinators.

HOW TO GROW

For indoor growing, sow directly into the soil in a tunnel or greenhouse in early spring. Plant 2 seeds in each hole, 1½ to 2 inches deep. We plant them in double rows with 18 inches between the rows. When they are about 3 ½ inches high, put a cane behind each pair of shoots for support, being careful not to damage the roots. When the plants are about 6 inches high, tie them to the canes, allowing for the stems to thicken.

Fava beans should be ready to harvest in late spring and early summer.

Fava beans are very hardy, so unless you want a very early crop it's not necessary to grow them indoors. Nonetheless, if you have space in the tunnel or greenhouse, use it and get ahead. We sow indoors in cell trays (or pots) 2 inches deep in mid-spring. Harden off before planting outside.

Plant them 8 inches apart in a double staggered row with 8 inches between the rows. However, seeds can be sown

Fava beans ready at last—try to eat home-grown beans within 30 minutes of picking.

directly into the ground once the soil temperature reaches 41°F. Plant in succession for a continuous supply. They will need support with bamboo canes.

CONTAINER GROWING

Fava beans can be grown in a large container. We start the seeds indoors, in compost, in empty toilet rolls and then plant maybe three plants to each container; this way the roots will not be disturbed when transplanting and the cardboard will disintegrate in the soil. Don't overcrowd the container and don't allow them to dry out. Fava beans generally do better in containers early in the growing season, rather than later.

The Sutton is a dwarf variety suitable for growing in containers and can be over-wintered, even in an exposed site. The Crimson-flowered heritage variety looks very attractive in containers.

PESTS AND DISEASES

Blackfly can be a problem and are off-putting to look at. In the greenhouse we pinch out the growing point when the plants are about shoulder high and the first beans are starting to form. This discourages blackfly. If you have just a few plants you can just rub off the fly or spray with diluted liquid soap. Planting summer savory beside the beans also helps to control blackfly.

If you are fortunate to have ladybugss in your garden they will help deter greenfly. We love ladybugs and collect them to increase the population in the greenhouses.

Rust and chocolate spot can sometimes attack fava beans, but vigorous well-grown plants are far less susceptible to disease.

Plants in containers are more likely to

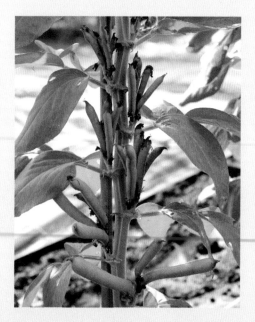

suffer stress. Plant in moisture-retentive compost so they won't dry out too quickly and keep them watered.

HARVESTING

Fava beans are in season from late spring to early autumn, depending on the variety. They can be eaten at many stages; the tiny pods can be harvested when they are 3½ to 4 inches long and actually cooked whole, but you'd need to wait until the pods are larger, about 6 inches, for the beans to swell inside. We pick some of the side shoots for salads Keep picking the pods, but if some get too large, particularly at the end of the crop, let them dry and save for seed.

GOOD FOR YOU...

Favas are a rich source of protein and fiber, antioxidants, folate, vitamins E and C, minerals and plant sterols. They are a valuable source of iron, copper,

manganese, calcium and magnesium, as well as potassium.

WHAT TO DO WITH A GLUT

If a few pods get away on you, larger beans can be made into soup, or make a decision to leave them on the plant until the pods start to swell, then pod and dry thoroughly and enjoy with smoked pork or bacon in winter. Dried beans are a staple in many Middle Eastern countries for wonderful soups.

IN THE KITCHEN

When favas are young and tender, there's no need to peel them, but when they become larger, most people prefer to pop them out of their skins. Definitely a bit of extra bother, but the work is forgotten when you taste the first forkful. To feed 6, bring 2½ cups water to a boil in a medium saucepan and add 1 teaspoon salt and 1 or 2 sprigs of summer

Add fava bean tops to salad and steal a few flowers to sprinkle over the top.

savory, if you like. Add 1½ pounds shelled fava beans, return to a boil, and cook for 2 to 5 minutes, until tender. Drain and quickly toss in a little butter or olive oil and lots of freshly ground pepper. If the beans are larger, drain and refresh under the cold tap until cool enough to handle. Pop each bean out of its skin and toss in hot butter or olive oil.

Fava Beans on Pan-Grilled Sourdough

We love young fava beans on warm grilled bread. I sometimes serve this as a nibble with an aperitif but it also makes a wonderful first course. Be careful not to cut the bread too thickly or the proportions will be affected.

. . . .

SERVES 2 AS A FIRST COURSE OR 4 WITH AN APERITIF

¼ pound shelled really fresh small fava beans

2 garlic cloves, peeled

a squeeze of lemon juice

6 to 8 fresh mint leaves

6 to 8 fresh basil leaves

a generous tablespoon of freshly grated Parmesan cheese, plus extra to serve

¼ cup extra virgin olive oil, plus extra to serve

4 slices sourdough bread, cut ⅓ inch thick

sea salt, to taste

Blanch the fava beans in boiling salted water for 1 to 2 minutes (1 teaspoon salt to 2½ cups water). Drain and refresh under cold running water. Slip the beans out of their skins and discard the skins.

To make the topping, pound 1 garlic clove with a little sea salt using a mortar and pestle. Add the fava beans and continue to pound to a coarse purée. Add the mint and basil leaves and continue to pound until they are incorporated. Finally, add the Parmesan and extra virgin olive oil. Season to taste.

Heat a grill pan over high heat until very hot. Grill the bread on both sides. Rub each side with the remaining garlic clove and drizzle with a little extra virgin olive oil. Spread some of the crushed fava beans over the hot grilled bread, grate a dusting of Parmesan on top, and serve immediately.

Pappardelle with Double Fava Beans & Arugula

Pappardelle is a wide pasta, usually homemade, which works beautifully with fava beans. We use this purée in many ways—you can imagine how good it is with ham or bacon, duck, summer plaice, or John Dory.

. . . .

SERVES 4

½ pound shelled fava beans
1 pound pappardelle
approx. ¼ cup extra virgin olive oil
a handful of arugula leaves
sea salt and freshly ground black pepper
grated Parmesan or pecorino cheese, to
   serve

FOR THE FAVA BEAN PURÉE

1 teaspoon sea salt
1 pound shelled fava beans
sprig of summer savory, plus 1 to
   2 teaspoons chopped fresh summer
   savory
approx. 2 tablespoons butter
2 to 3 tablespoons heavy cream

To make the fava bean purée, bring 2 cups of water to a rolling boil; add the sea salt, fava beans, and summer savory. Boil very fast for 3 to 4 minutes or until just cooked. Drain immediately.

Melt the butter in the saucepan, toss in the fava beans, and season with freshly ground pepper. Taste and add the chopped savory and a little salt if necessary. Add the cream, and purée. Check the seasoning and keep warm.

Cook and peel the remaining ½ pound fava beans and keep warm (see page 269).

Cook the pappardelle until al dente in plenty of boiling salted water. Drain quickly. Add a little extra virgin olive oil to the pan; add the fava beans, pasta, and arugula leaves and toss well. Season with lots of pepper and some sea salt. Put 2 tablespoons of the warm fava bean purée onto each plate. Put a portion of the pasta on top, sprinkle with freshly grated Parmesan or pecorino, and serve immediately.

DID YOU KNOW?
Fava beans are thought to have originated in the Mediterranean and some have been dated back to 6800BC. Stewed fava beans—*ful medames*—is the traditional Egyptian breakfast as well as being Egypt's national dish.

An Arab saying still reminds us that "Beans have satisfied the Pharaohs." What good taste they had!

Double-Cut Lamb Chops with Sumac, Fava Beans, Melted Cherry Tomatoes & Cilantro Flowers

Great with a green salad and some freekeh, farro, or even a pearl barley pilaf. The fava beans are particularly delicious in this summery combination.

....

SERVES 8

8 double-cut bone-in lamb chops
2 to 3 tablespoons sumac, plus extra to serve
extra virgin olive oil, for drizzling
½ to ¾ pound shelled fava beans
sea salt and freshly ground black pepper
fresh cilantro flowers or shredded mint, to garnish (optional)

FOR THE TZATZIKI

1 crisp cucumber, peeled and cut into ¼- to ⅓-inch dice
1 or 2 garlic cloves, crushed
dash of wine vinegar or lemon juice
1¾ cups plain Greek yogurt or best-quality yogurt
¼ cup heavy cream
1 heaping tablespoon chopped fresh mint
pinch of sugar, to taste (optional)

FOR THE MELTED CHERRY TOMATOES

40 ripe red firm sweet cherry tomatoes
3 tablespoons butter or extra virgin olive oil
3 to 4 tablespoons chopped fresh mint
1 to 2 tablespoons chopped fresh rosemary
pinch of sugar, to taste (optional)

To make the tzatziki, put the cucumber into a sieve, sprinkle with salt, and let drain for about 30 minutes. Dry the cucumber on paper towels, put into a bowl, and mix with garlic, a dash of wine vinegar or lemon juice, and the yogurt and cream. Stir in the mint and taste; it may need a little salt and freshly ground pepper, or even a pinch of sugar.

Preheat the oven to 450°F.

Score the fat of the chops. Sprinkle each one with sumac, rubbing it well into the fat and flesh. Season with Maldon sea salt and freshly ground pepper. Transfer to a roasting pan. Drizzle with extra virgin olive oil. Roast for 15 minutes, turn off the heat, and let rest.

Meanwhile, cook and slice the fava beans and keep warm (see page 269).

Just before serving, cook the cherry tomatoes. Scald the tomatoes in boiling water for 10 seconds, drain, and pop out of their skins. Heat the butter in a skillet large enough to take all the tomatoes in a single layer until it bubbles, or use oil. Toss in the tomatoes and roll gently over medium heat until just warmed through. Sprinkle with the herbs and salt, pepper, and maybe a little sugar.

To serve, lay each double lamb chop on a hot plate. Spoon some melted cherry tomatoes around the edge. Sprinkle with fava beans and cilantro flowers, if available. Alternatively, use some shredded mint leaves. Sprinkle with a pinch of sumac and a few flakes of sea salt and drizzle with extra virgin olive oil.

Serve the tzatziki as an accompaniment.

WASABI *Eutrema Japonicum Brassicaceae* PERENNIAL

Wasabi plants ready to pot up, keep out of direct sunlight.

Wasabi is unlikely to be on your list of essential vegetables, but it's fun to have a go at growing some more unusual, and in this case, super delicious plants from time to time. Wasabi is a member of the brassica family and is also referred to as Japanese horseradish, and although horseradish is also from the brassica family, it's a different species.

Sushi lovers will be familiar with wasabi which, with pickled ginger and soy sauce, is one of the holy trinity of accompaniments, but you may not be aware that the little blob of green wasabi paste is unlike to be pure, more probably a mixture of horseradish, mustard, dye and possibly as little as 15 per cent wasabi.

Wasabi is one of the world's most expensive rhizomes, fetching up to $300 a kilo. This famously pungent stem is native to Japan, Taiwan, North Korea, and New Zealand, but more recently it has been grown with considerable success in the US and along the Oregon coast in the Pacific South West and in parts of the Blue Ridge Mountains in North Carolina.

In Devon, a watercress farmer diversified into wasabi in 2012 and is now supplying a number of eager top chefs in the UK and selling plants (offshoots) to keen gardeners. The general perception is that it's difficult to grow wasabi. We've been growing it for 3 to 4 years; I managed to kill one beautiful healthy plant which our gardener Eileen had proudly grown in a big pot to show the students in the cooking school. I think I may have watered it with syrup by mistake, plus I now know it doesn't like to be in full sun on the windowsill in the demo area.

VARIETIES

The two main varieties are **Daruma** and **Mazuma**.
Mazuma tends to be hotter.
There are other species of wasabi also grown for their spicy root: **wasabi koreana** and **wasabi tetsuigi.**

HOW TO GROW

Wasabi is a semi-aquatic plant. It grows naturally in a moist, shady spot, under a canopy of trees at between 46 and 68°F, but it can survive temperatures as low as 23°F. So choose a shady site away from direct sunlight. It thrives in a dull, cloudy Irish summer.

Keep watered but it doesn't like to be left sitting in water, so moist gravelly soil is best.

If you plan to start wasabi from seed, soak the seeds overnight in distilled water. The next day, plant them about ⅓ inch deep and 1 to 2 inches apart.

If you allow them to flower you can save the seed for the following year. Alternatively, order some offshoots and plant them directly into gravelly soil at the beginning of autumn.

The plant grows to a height of about 2 feet with long stalks (petioles) and large, heart-shaped leaves. It takes a minimum of 2 years and up to 4 years for the plant to mature, depending on the conditions.

CONTAINER GROWING

Our plants have grown very successfully in large—12 inches—pots.

HARVESTING

The whole wasabi plant is edible—the leaves, stalks and, of course, the stem, which becomes more pungent as it matures. Trim the stalks off the stem and then grate and use as desired.

PESTS AND DISEASES

We only have a few plants and we haven't had any difficulty so far, but I understand that some varieties can be susceptible to soft rot and black leg. Keeping the area surrounding your wasabi plant clear of weeds and cleaning up any dead leaves will give a healthier growing environment and discourage slugs and snails.

DID YOU KNOW?
Inhaling the pungent vapor from wasabi has an effect similar to smelling salts; this property is being used in research to make a smoke alarm for deaf people.

GOOD FOR YOU...

Wasabi contains potassium and magnesium and is high in vitamins C and B6 and iron. It's a powerful antioxidant, helps to guard against bacterial infections and boosts the body's immune system. Wasabi has natural cancer-fighting isothiocyanates. It's known to kill harmful food-borne bacteria, hence its value with sushi and sashimi. It's naturally antibacterial, antiviral and antimicrobial.

WHAT TO DO WITH A GLUT?

So far I've never had a glut.

IN THE KITCHEN

Fresh wasabi is an eye opener in every sense of the word. It's worth investing in a little wasabi grater so you can grate it as you need to make a wasabi paste to serve with sushi. Traditionally the Japanese use sharkskin (*samegawa*) or a copper *oroshigane* grater and a little brush to extract every morsel from the grater. These graters ensure the wasabi is grated to the perfect texture. If you have gone to all the trouble of growing and enduring the anticipation, then it's a pity not to enjoy wasabi at the optimum peak of perfection. A Japanese student showed me how to hold the peeled root at a 45-degree angle to the surface of the grater and grate in a circular movement to achieve the perfect balance of grating and mixing. Grate it only as you need it, as it loses flavor within 15 minutes; in really fancy sushi restaurants they grate it at the table and sushi chefs sandwich it between the fish and the rice to seal in the flavor.

You will find all sorts of delicious pairings. A wasabi root will keep covered in the fridge for a month or two, but rather than keeping it for too long, try drying it, then grind to a powder and store in an airtight container. As needed, mix with water to make a soft paste.

To make **Wasabi Butter** to serve with grilled steaks or fish, cream ½ cup butter; add 1 tablespoon grated wasabi and 2½ teaspoons minced parsley. Season with lots of pepper and a few drops of lemon juice. Form into a roll with parchment paper and keep chilled. Use within 2 to 3 days.

Mackerel Gravlax with Wasabi & Dill Mayonnaise

This basic Nordic pickling technique can be used for many fish—salmon, haddock, mackerel....I've substituted wasabi for French mustard with delicious results. We are all addicted to this pickled salmon gravlax, which keeps for up to a week. Fresh dill is essential.

. . . .

SERVES 12 TO 16 AS A STARTER

4 to 6 mackerel
1 heaping tablespoon sea salt
1 heaping tablespoon sugar
1 teaspoon freshly ground black pepper
2 tablespoons fresh dill, minced
dark brown bread and butter, to serve

FOR THE WASABI AND DILL MAYONNAISE
1 large organic egg yolk
1 to 1½ tablespoons grated wasabi
1 tablespoon sugar
150ml peanut oil or sunflower oil
1 tablespoon white wine vinegar
1 tablespoon fresh dill, minced
sea salt and white pepper

Fillet the mackerel and remove all the bones. Mix the salt, sugar, pepper, and dill together in a bowl. Line the gratin dish with a piece of plastic wrap. Sprinkle some cure on the bottom of the gratin dish and lay the mackerel fillets on top, skin-side down. Sprinkle more cure on top, add another layer of mackerel, and finish with a layer of cure. Wrap tightly with plastic wrap, weight it down slightly, and chill for at least 1 hour and up to 2 hours, depending on size.

To make the wasabi and dill mayonnaise, whisk the egg yolk with the wasabi and sugar. Drip in the oil drop by drop, whisking all the time, then add the vinegar and fresh dill. Season with salt and white pepper.

To serve, wipe the cure off the fish and slice thinly. Arrange on a plate. Drizzle with the wasabi and dill mayonnaise and serve with dark brown bread and butter.

CORN *Zea mays* ANNUAL

A freshly picked ear of corn, rushed to the kitchen, cooked within minutes, slathered with butter, then sprinkled with a few grains of sea salt is a total revelation. If anything can persuade a doubting Thomas of the value of growing your own, it's the first juicy mouthful of fresh corn kernels. As with peas, you'll never taste corn in all its sweet intensity unless you grow your own. The sugars start to turn into starches within minutes of being picked and have lost up to 40 per cent of their sweetness within 6 hours.

On the first morning of the Summer Certificate Course, we give our students from all over the world a corn to plant into the rich soil in the greenhouses. They mark it with a lollipop stick with their name and then wait impatiently for the whole 12 weeks for it to be ready to eat. Each plant will produce 3 or 4 cobs; they watch them gradually swell and when at last the tassels turn brown they

are ready to harvest. So on the last day we have a corn fest, they are cooked in boiling salted water for just 3 minutes and rushed to the dining room, no cutlery needed just lots of butter, sea salt, and a fine napkin to catch the drips. A last memorable blast of flavor which reinforces their resolve to start to grow some of their own food.

VARIETIES

There are literally hundreds of types, much of the commercial corn is genetically modified but that seed is not available to home gardeners. There are excellent traditional varieties and also super-sweet hybrids which contain up to twice as much sugar.

Golden Bantam—Heirloom variety, nice and sweet, must be harvested in time and eaten fresh as it will go over quickly.
Black Aztec—Black and navy blue seeds, this variety can be eaten fresh or dried.
Silver Queen—late season variety produces large, tender, pure-white kernels.
Sugar Buns—This sugary-enhanced (se) corn matures early in the season on compact plants with some disease resistance.

HOW TO GROW

In our unpredictable Irish climate, corn is best grown in a greenhouse or tunnel, although in a rare good summer they have matured in the kitchen garden. Corn can be successfully grown outdoors throughout America. Sow individual seeds in 1½- to 2-inch pots or seed trays, 1 inch deep, in late spring. Because it is wind pollinated, corn is best grown in blocks, as

When corn is ready to harvest, the tassels on top will brown. Peep inside the husk—the cob should be covered with corn.

this allows the fruit to get better set.

Corn likes rich, fertile soil, enriched with compost or well-rotted manure.

To grow outdoors, choose a sheltered sunny spot and mulch with compost or organic matter to suppress weeds and conserve moisture. Water well in dry weather. Take care when hoeing as the roots are shallow.

Poor pollination results in sparsely filled cobs, so to help with pollination we have bumble bees in the greenhouse.

Corn grows about 6 feet high and can also be used to provide shelter and privacy. Corn is one of the "three sisters" regularly planted together in South America—beans and squash are the other two (see page 203).

CONTAINER GROWING

Corn may be grown in a container, choose a shorter-stalked variety such as **Mirai 003 F1 Hybrid**. Choose a pot at least 12 inches wide and 12 inches deep, which will hold four plants. Fill the pot with fertile soil enriched with compost. A warm sheltered site is best.

PESTS AND DISEASES

Slugs and birds can polish off young seedlings, the slugs eat the stems so you may want to scatter some organic slug pellets. (See page 626.)

DID YOU KNOW?

Corn, a member of the grass family, was first cultivated in Mexico in 7000BC, and introduced to Europe in 1779 when corn kernels were first given to the settlers by the Native American Iroquois.

HARVESTING

Corn are ready to harvest when the tassels turn brown and the cob is well filled. Squeeze a kernel between your thumb and fingernail, if liquid squirts out it's not yet ripe; if it's creamy it's good. Twist off the cob and head for the kitchen at speed with the freshly harvested corn.

GOOD FOR YOU...

Corn is a valuable source of dietary fiber, carbohydrate, folic acid, and iron. It also contains the antioxidant ferulic acid, another known to have anti-inflammatory and anti-cancer properties. Cornmeal, polenta ground from dried corn kernels, is gluten free, so is suitable for celiacs. Corn also has significant amounts of zinc, magnesium, copper, iron and manganese.

WHAT TO DO WITH A GLUT?

Just enjoy it and share with your friends. Corn also freezes well if blanched and refreshed first, and of course you can dry some corn and save the seeds for planting the following year and for popcorn.

IN THE KITCHEN

Rush fresh sweetcorn to the kitchen, peel off the leaves and silks and drop it into a pot of boiling salted water for just 3–4 minutes. Drain, slather it with butter and a few flakes of sea salt and enjoy. Barbecued sweetcorn is also delicious.

For **Fettuccine with Sweetcorn and Marjoram** (serves 6), bring 4 quarts water to a rolling boil in a large saucepan and add 1 tablespoon of salt. Add 5½½ cups fettuccine, cook for 2 minutes if fresh pasta or 10–12 minutes if dried. Peel 6 ears of corn, trim both ends, drop into the water. Cover the saucepan and return to the boil, then cook for 3 minutes. Drain, leave to cool, then slice the kernels off the cob. Melt 3 tablespoons butter in a saucepan, add the corn and ½ cup double cream. Season with salt and freshly ground black pepper, add 2 tablespoons of chopped annual marjoram, bubble for 1–2 minutes, stir once or twice. Drain the pasta, drizzle with extra virgin olive oil, toss with the corn. Season to taste. Serve immediately.

Grilled Corn on the Cob with Chile Butter

In Istanbul carts selling corn are at virtually every street corner. It's the same in Mexico and India, where they often dip a piece of lime in chile salad and run it up the cob for an extra perky flavor. The corn can be boiled and refreshed, even a day ahead—keep refrigerated and grill as needed.

SERVES 4

4 ears of fresh corn
flaky sea salt
lime wedges

FOR THE CHILE BUTTER
½ cup (1 stick) butter, softened
1 to 2 tablespoons minced flat-leaf parsley
½ to 1 red chile, seeded and chopped
½ to 1 tablespoon lime juice
2 teaspoons freshly ground black pepper

To make the chile butter, process all the ingredients in a food processor to combine. Use parchment paper to form into a roll and wrap in the paper, or put into a bowl, cover, and chill until needed. Let come to room temperature before using

Heat a grill to medium or heat a grill pan over medium heat.

Cook the corn in boiling salted water for 2 minutes. Scoop out and refresh in cold water. Brush with soft chile butter. Grill for about 5 minutes, turning frequently, until lightly charred. Sprinkle with flaky sea salt. Serve with a slice of chile butter and a wedge of lime.

Corn & Scallion Pancakes with Roast Tomatoes, Bacon & Avocado Salsa

A yummy combination for brunch or supper. The sweetness of the corn pancake is irresistible with the bacon and tomato—one of my favorite brunch dishes.

. . . .

MAKES 12/SERVES 6

¾ cup plus 2 tablespoons all-purpose flour
1½ teaspoons sugar
1 teaspoon baking powder
¼ teaspoon salt
½ teaspoon sweet paprika
2 organic eggs
⅓ cup milk
¼ pound scallions, sliced
10½ ounces fresh corn kernels or drained canned corn kernels
2 tablespoons chopped cilantro
2 tablespoons chopped flat-leaf parsley
2 tablespoons chopped marjoram
4 tablespoons olive oil, plus extra to serve

FOR THE ROAST TOMATOES

4 ripe tomatoes, sliced in half lengthwise
¼ cup extra virgin olive oil
sea salt and freshly ground black pepper

FOR THE AVOCADO SALSA

2 ripe avocados, pitted and diced
⅓ cup cilantro leaves
2 tablespoons minced scallion
½ to 1 chopped minced green Serrano or Jalapeño chile (optional)
2 tablespoons freshly squeezed lime or lemon juice
sea salt and freshly ground black pepper

TO SERVE

1 bunch fresh arugula leaves
4 freshly cooked bacon slices

Preheat the oven to 350°F.

To make the roast tomatoes, place the tomatoes on a baking sheet, cut-side up, and drizzle with olive oil. Sprinkle liberally with some thyme leaves with sea salt and pepper. Roast for 15 to 20 minutes or until soft and slightly shriveled.

To make the salsa, mix all the ingredients gently together in a bowl, taste, and correct the seasoning.

Sift the flour, sugar, baking powder, salt, and paprika into a large bowl. Whisk the eggs and milk together and gradually whisk into the dry ingredients until you have a smooth, thickish batter. Mix the scallions, corn, and chopped fresh herbs in a large bowl and add the batter.

Heat 1 tablespoon of the olive oil in a heavy skillet over medium heat—cook a little of the mixture to test for seasoning and adjust if necessary. Spoon 1 tablespoon of the batter onto the hot pan—you should be able to make 4 pancakes at a time. Cook for 3 to 4 minutes or until the underside of each pancake is golden. Flip over and cook on the other side for a similar length of time. Transfer to a plate and keep warm while cooking the remaining batter.

To serve, pop a corn and scallion pancake onto each warm plate. Top each with a couple of roast tomatoes, a small handful of arugula, and a crisp slice of bacon. Add another pancake and a dollop of avocado salsa, drizzle with extra virgin olive oil, and serve immediately.

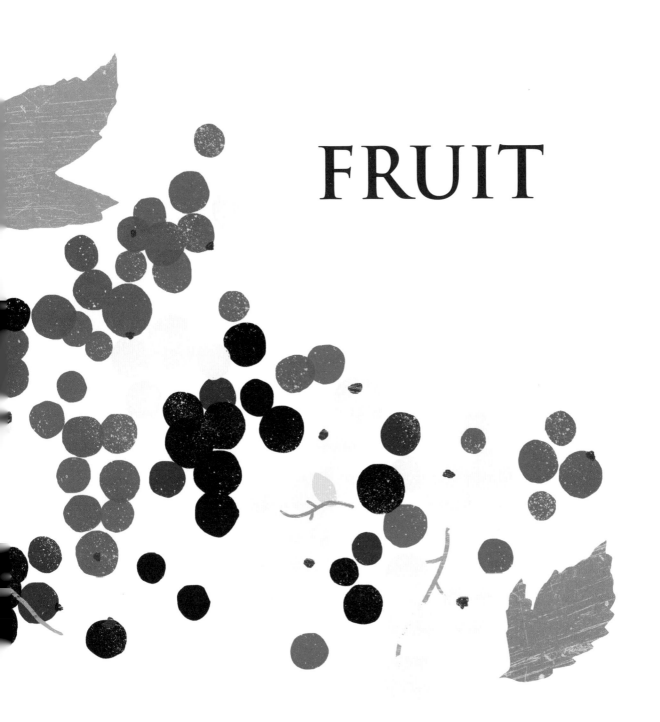

FRUIT

KIWI *Actinidia chinensis/deliciosa* DECIDUOUS, ZONES 3–10

Those who like to grow some unusual plants might like to consider kiwi fruit or Chinese gooseberry as it also known. We planted several in the greenhouse a few years ago, not expecting much, but they settled in brilliantly and now romp away up the dollies (metal supports) and along the central path. There were lots of leaves but nothing else for a year or two, but then suddenly they were covered with small fragrant, off-white, rose-like flowers, and eventually a fantastic crop of small, furry brown fruit. The first crops were much smaller than the average supermarket fruit, nonetheless, they are delicious. They sit happily on

Hayward kiwi growing in the greenhouse in late spring. A kiwi can be very productive in a greenhouse or tunnel but allow enough space and prune yearly, otherwise it can take over.

the vine right through winter in our unheated greenhouse, so the Spring 12-week students can taste them.

VARIETIES

A number are available and it's best to plant several for good pollination. Some modern varieties are self-fertile.

We planted **Hayward**—an early female variety and the most easily available, large well-flavored fruit that keeps well. One male plant is required for up to six female plants.

Ken's Red Hardy—large, smooth with red skin and red flesh. Very sweet.

Geneva—very early and produce. Large fruit is very sweet.

SELF-FERTILE VARIETIES
Blake—High-yielder—over 100 pounds of fruit is promised.
Issai—large green fruit on super productive plants.

HOW TO GROW

In this part of the world where the climate is cooler and more unpredictable, if this is to be a productive exercise, kiwis must be planted in a tunnel or greenhouse. However, they will grow outside, depending on variety, throughout the United States. They like similar conditions to tomatoes. They need lots of space but we have trained them over the central path so they don't

climb over anything else. If space is not a problem, they are worth it for the wow factor alone. The plants will come potted and are best planted in spring or fall. Plant in rich, loamy soil and provide strong support. We grow them up the metal support in the greenhouse, but any sturdy pole would work well. The fruits form on the side shoots, so careful pruning is needed to tame what can become an unruly climber, without affecting the harvest. Don't remove the side shoots but they can be cut back to a few leaves beyond where the fruit is carried, chop back to one or two buds, so they don't twist into each other and become a mess. They can also be grown flat against a wall inside or outside.

CONTAINER GROWING

Not suitable for container growing. Kiwis are a vigorous plant that can grow up to 33 feet or more so are difficult to contain in a pot and won't produce much fruit in restricted conditions.

PESTS AND DISEASES

They seem quite hardy in the greenhouse, but you may need to provide some extra winter protection in very cold areas, perhaps cover with fleece.

HARVESTING

Harvest gradually after the leaves fall as they ripen in late autumn/early winter,

DID YOU KNOW?
Despite perhaps being named after the flightless fuzzy brown kiwi bird, kiwis are not native to New Zealand. They were introduced there from China and East Asia in the early twentieth century by the Christian missionaries. Then, the commercial growers seized upon this new crop as an alternative to growing tomatoes, as this market was getting flooded.

but they sit happily on the vine into the first months of the new year and have sensational flavor.

GOOD FOR YOU...

Organic kiwis are a powerhouse of nutrients. They are an excellent source of vitamin C, and contain good amounts of vitamins A, E, and K, plus lots of potassium, calcium, magnesium, and dietary fiber. Kiwis have a low glycemic index, so are suitable for diabetics.

They are a good source of antioxidants, help to build a strong immune system, excellent for cardiovascular health; provide serotonin..

WHAT TO DO WITH A GLUT

Unlikely, kiwis seem to sit on our plants until we are ready to eat them.

IN THE KITCHEN

Kiwis are best served fresh rather than cooked. They are best peeled, by cutting off the ends, then sliding a tablespoon underneath the thin furry skin. Kiwis make an instant dessert, peeled and sliced, with a little lemon juice, a drizzle of honey, and some shredded mint. They pair deliciously with other fruits in a salad or in fruit kebabs.

Lovers of meringue or pavlova know how well that combination works; pineapple and mango complete the trio of complementary flavors. A kiwi is really good added to smoothies and a kiwi fruit granita can be paired with lots of other fruit, particularly raspberries. Kiwi fruit contains an enzyme that breaks down gelatin, so it doesn't work in dessert gelatins.

We get an excellent crop of kiwi fruit in the greenhouse—the fruits last on the plants until late winter.

Kiwi Fruit Granita with Sugared Summer Berries

My brother Rory loves to make this simple and lovely ice with our furry crop of kiwi fruit, it's a delicious fresh tasting way to use them.

SERVES 6 TO 8

½ cup superfine sugar plus extra for the berries, depending on sweetness

zest and juice of 1 lime

3¼ pounds kiwi fruit (approx. 9 fruit)

1 pound raspberries, loganberries, boysenberries, tayberries, or jostaberries, to serve

fresh mint leaves, shredded

Put the sugar in a bowl and add the zest and juice of the lime. Peel the kiwi fruit using a swivel-top peeler and make sure to remove the woody piece from the stalk end of the fruit. Chop the peeled kiwis coarsely and add to the sugar and lime. Blend briefly until smooth in a juicer or with an immersion blender. If you over-blend them, the little black seeds may be crushed in which case the granita may become a bit peppery and the color will be spoiled. Place the bowl in the freezer to freeze and set.

When the mixture is semi-frozen or slushy looking, remove and whisk it vigorously to break up the large crystals. Return the mixture to the freezer and repeat the process three more times. By then the ice should be a granita and ready to serve when you are ready.

Serve the granita in coarse shards with any of the sugared summer berries—raspberries, loganberries, boysenberries, tayberries, or jostaberries, and a little shredded mint.

Avocado, Kiwi, Apple, Toasted Almond & Watercress Salad

This is a delicious fresh-tasting combination—a perfect little appetizer and a slightly unusual way to enjoy the juicy fruitiness of kiwi.

SERVES 4

2 ripe Hass avocados

freshly squeezed juice of 1 lemon

2 to 4 kiwi fruit, depending on size

2 sweet apples, such as Golden Delicious

a little granulated sugar

1 bunch of watercress, enough for four plates

extra virgin olive oil

honey, to taste

sea salt flakes, to taste

⅓ cup toasted almonds, halved

Halve the avocados and remove the pits. Peel and cut into wedges. Put in a shallow bowl with some of the lemon juice. Peel the kiwis and cut into quarters or sixths, depending on size, then add to the avocado.

Peel, core, and cut the apple into ¼-inch dice, toss in a little freshly squeezed lemon juice and a very light sprinkle of sugar, and add to the bowl.

Pick the watercress sprigs, chop half of them coarsely, and leave the rest whole.

Sprinkle the chopped watercress over the avocado, kiwi, and apple. Drizzle with a little extra virgin olive oil and toss gently. Taste and add a little drizzle of honey if necessary and a sprinkle of sea salt.

To serve, scatter a few whole watercress leaves on individual plates and arrange a portion of salad on top. Scatter with toasted almonds and serve.

BARBERRIES *Berberis* PERENNIAL, ZONES 4–8

An excellent crop of barberries—berries can be red or blue/black.

Berberis is a hardy, prickly shrub that can grow to a height of 13 feet. The leaves are small and shiny and serrated at the edges and the yellow flowers appear in late spring. The fruit, which the birds also love, has a sharp flavor and is high in pectin.

VARIETIES

Berberis fendleri—Native to New Mexico and Colorado, can tolerate shade, with fragrant yellow flowers.
Mahonia aquifolium—Yellow flowers and prickly leaves with strong lily-of-the-valley scent in early spring. Blue/black berries.

HOW TO GROW

An easy plant to grow in most gardens, berberis is tolerant of most soils unless waterlogged or parched. In fact it grows wild in many parts of Central and Southern Europe.

It is very prickly so be careful where you plant it; in New Zealand it is often used as a hedge and can be used to advantage in certain situations, to deter both animals and humans. Order a plant from a specialty nursery. Dig a hole large enough to accommodate the roots and fill in with soil around it. Water it in to settle the soil around the roots. If you are planting it during the growing season, you may need to water occasionally if the weather is dry.

PESTS AND DISEASES

Berberis can harbor wheat rust, which is hugely damaging to crops, so avoid planting them if your garden is near grain-growing land.

Barberries are an important ingredient in Syrian and Middle Eastern cooking and one I only recently discovered thanks to Yotam Ottolenghi and Sami Tamimi. I'm now hooked the tart sour berries. They are red and wrinkled and taste like lemony currants. But the best bit of news is that they are in fact the dried fruit of the common berberis that grows widely around Ireland, not least in my own garden. Fancy that, there I was, buying Iranian barberries from Middle Eastern grocers, not realizing I already had them.

It should be noted that some barberries contain a compound that can be toxic if consumed in large quantities. So it's best to use barberries as an accent in dishes, not as the central component. The Japanese barberry (*Berberis thunbergii*) is terribly invasive and should not be planted, although some nurseries do still sell it as an ornamental.

HARVESTING

The barberry fruit from *Berberis vulgaris* is an oblong berry about ¼ to ⅓-inch long and ⅒ to ¼ inch wide. It ripens in late summer or early autumn. The very tart red berries are edible and high in pectin.

CONTAINER GROWING

Several varieties of berberis can be grown satisfactorily in containers provided the receptacle is large enough. Keep pruned and watered.

WHAT TO DO WITH A GLUT

The barberries can be dried and included in salads and pilafs to add a refreshing sour note.

GOOD FOR YOU...

Rich in vitamin C it is valued for treating heartburn, kidney stones, and gallstones and is valuable as a tonic.

IN THE KITCHEN

The dried berries need to be rehydrated for 10 minutes in cold water before adding to stuffings, pilafs, or fillings. In Iran the berries are an important ingredient, used instead of currants in a rice pilaf. You'll find them in Middle Eastern grocers or you can buy online.

Rice Pilaf with Chicken & Barberries

Although a risotto can be made in 20 minutes, it entails 20 minutes of pretty constant stirring which makes it feel rather laborious. A pilaf on the other hand looks after itself once the initial cooking is underway. The pilaf is versatile—serve it as a staple or add whatever tasty bits you have on hand. Beware, however, of using pilaf as a garbage can; all additions should be carefully seasoned and balanced.

SERVES 8

2 tablespoons butter

2 tablespoons finely chopped onion or shallot

2 cups long-grain rice (preferably Basmati)

salt and freshly ground black pepper

4 cups homemade chicken stock

8 to 12 ounces cooked chicken, warmed in a light chicken stock

½ cup barberries

2 tablespoons chopped fresh herbs, such as parsley, thyme, chives: optional

Melt the butter in a large Dutch oven, add the finely chopped onion, and sweat for 2 to 3 minutes. Add the rice and toss for a minute or two, just long enough for the grains to change color. Season with salt and freshly ground pepper, add the chicken stock, cover, and bring to a boil. Reduce the heat to low and then simmer on top of the stove or in the oven at 325°F for about 10 minutes. By then the rice should be just cooked and all the liquid absorbed. (Basmati rice cooks quite quickly; if using other types of rice this may take up to 15 minutes.)

Just before serving, stir in the warmed chicken, barberries, and fresh herbs, if using. Serve immediately in deep wide soup bowls.

Kuku Sabzi—Persian Frittata with Barberries

One of the many delicious ways to use your dried barberries.

SERVES 6

1 tablespoon olive oil
8 large organic eggs
1 large garlic clove, finely chopped
2 tablespoons all-purpose flour
½ teaspoon ground turmeric
1 teaspoon salt
freshly ground black pepper
½ cup scallions, finely sliced
2 tablespoons finely chopped dill
2 tablespoons finely chopped marjoram
2 tablespoons finely chopped flat parsley
¼ cup coarsely chopped walnuts
¼ cup barberries
a salad of organic leaves and plain yogurt,
  to serve

Preheat oven to 325°F. Heat the oil in an 8-inch frying pan.

Whisk the eggs with the garlic, flour, turmeric, salt, pepper, scallions, herbs, walnuts, and barberries. Pour into the frying pan. Cook over low heat for 3 to 4 minutes. Transfer to the oven for 7 to 8 minutes or until just set. Flash under a broiler if necessary for a couple of minutes.

Serve with a salad of organic leaves and a blob of plain yogurt.

CITRUS FRUIT

Citrus spp. Lemon, lime, and kumquat, ZONES 7–10

Citrus fruits do not grow naturally in Ireland. They need a much warmer, ideally tropical, climate. However, they can be grown successfully in southern and western parts of the United States. It's possible to buy many citrus fruits in garden centers around the country. Of course I succumbed to the irresistible perfume of the blossom, and so we have several types of lemons, lime, kumquats, and calamondin. It's such a joy for the students to see these grown in the greenhouse and window sills.

SPECIES

They are many, but **Citrus Aurantifolia** is the easiest to come by, and the hardiest for a greenhouse.

Citrus meyeri is a beautiful fragrant lemon. The Meyer lemons are delicious, the zest fresh and citrusy. It's serious one-upmanship to offer a friend a gin and tonic and wander nonchalantly over to the tree to pluck a home-grown lemon, to pop in the glass......

We have several types of lime, but I confess I admire more than use them; they are more decorative than delicious.

However, I'm very proud of my kumquat tree, **Citrus japonica**, and we have picked the fruit for a kumquat compote and for kumquat marmalade, my favorite marmalade of all. We keep it indoors in winter, but it flourishes outside in summer. Like all citrus, it does not like to be under glass all year round.

We've also grown **Calamondin** which look a little like kumquats, but are a round shape and can be used in the same way.

Bergamot, **Citrus bergamia**, looks like a smooth orange, but is bright yellow in color and makes a super marmalade. Bergamot has the sweet citrus scent that is used as a flavoring in Earl Grey tea.

Juvenile lemon which will ripen to yellow.

The flavor of a freshly picked lemon is incomparable to even the best money can buy.

HOW TO GROW

Citrus are ideal for container-growing, and can be moved out into the garden in summer and indoors for winter protection. Grow your citrus in large terracotta pots. They need rich, loose, well-drained soil. When well looked after, they can be quite long-lived. Old country house gardeners reckoned that diluted fresh urine was the best feed for citrus.

It is not recommended to grow outdoors in soil all year round in a cool and unpredictable climate. Prune and feed with a seaweed solution and move outdoors in spring. Keep outside throughout the summer and autumn, continuing to feed weekly with the seaweed solution. We just mulch them with seaweed from the nearby beach at Ballinamona. Prune again in winter, pick fruits, and move indoors.

CONTAINER GROWING

We grow a wide variety of citrus in containers, their blossom has a wonderful heady scent which fills the greenhouse and conservatory. Choose terracotta pots or half barrels or containers large enough for your citrus plant.

PESTS AND DISEASES

When citrus plants are outdoors in summer, there should be few problems. If there is an attack of mold or scale insect, wash the leaves with dish soap or water.

HARVESTING

Pick the fruits as they ripen. Fortunately, they do not ripen all at once, but continue over several weeks, which can be both an advantage, or disadvantage, depending on how many of each variety you have.

GOOD FOR YOU...

All citrus fruits are rich in vitamin C, but also folate, thiamine, calcium, niacin, vitamin B6, and dietary fiber. They also contain pectin—a type of soluble fiber that aids digestion—which is in pith, so eating whole fruits is better than drinking just the juice. They also contain many beneficial phytochemicals, including flavonoid and hesperidin which is thought to have an anti-inflammatory effect.

WHAT TO DO WITH A GLUT

Make lots of marmalade and candied peel. Kumquat compote is one of the most useful items to have in your fridge.

IN THE KITCHEN

The flowers of all citrus have a wonderful scent that fills the house in early summer. They are edible and can be used to make orange blossom water or they can be crystallized to decorate cakes or buns. We make copious amounts of candied peel to add to cakes, salads, and to garnish cakes and cookies. Surplus citrus peels are dried for kindling or used as slug traps.

Lemon juice is indispensable in the kitchen—it lifts many a mediocre dish.

Kumquats—the baby of the citrus fruit family.

Homemade Limeade or Limonada

Homemade lemonades are easy to make, refreshing, and delicious, and a rewarding alternative for the designated driver. A good way to use up a glut because it uses lots of juice. We use a variety of citrus juices to keep it interesting.

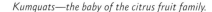

SERVES 6 TO 8

freshly squeezed juice from 5 limes or
   lemons
1 cup sugar syrup (see below)
6½ cups sparkling or still water
mint ice cubes (see below)

FOR THE SIMPLE SYRUP
makes 3½ cups

1¾ cups granulated white sugar

Mix the lime juice with the sugar syrup and water in a large pitcher and stir well. Taste and add more syrup or lime juice or water if needed. Cover and chill.

Serve in tall glasses with mint ice cubes.

SIMPLE SYRUP

Flavored syrups are such an obvious thing to do that I can't imagine why people don't have some in their pantry all the time. We make many different ones and use them not only for homemade lemonades but also for fruit salads and compotes. Sweet geranium, lemongrass, and lemon verbena syrups are particularly good for poaching fruits. They keep for months in a fridge, or a shorter time if unrefrigerated.

To make the simple syrup: Dissolve the sugar in 2½ cups water and bring to a boil. Boil for 2 minutes, then let it cool. Store in the fridge until needed.

MINT ICE CUBES

Put a couple of fresh mint leaves into each ice cube cavity. Fill with still or sparkling water and freeze.

Kumquat Compote with Labneh

We are never without kumquat compote during the winter season. A gem of a recipe, this compote can be served as a dessert or as an accompaniment to roast duck, goose or glazed ham. It is super versatile and delicious served with Labneh (see below), goat's cheese, vanilla ice cream or yogurt or even with dices of chorizo.

. . . .

SERVES 6 TO 20 DEPENDING ON HOW
IT IS SERVED

½ pound kumquats
½ cup granulated sugar
grated dark chocolate, to serve

FOR THE LABNEH (MAKES 1 POUND)
4 cups plain yogurt

To make the labneh, line a strainer with a double thickness of sterilized cheesecloth. Place it over a bowl. Pour in the yogurt. Tie the four corners of the cheesecloth to make a loose bundle and suspend the bag of yogurt over a bowl. Leave it in a cool place to drip into the bowl for 8 hours. Then remove the cheesecloth and put the labneh in a bowl. Refrigerate overnight, and store until needed in a covered glass or plastic container. The liquid whey that has drained off can be fed to pigs or hens or used for fermented dishes and in whey lemonade.

To make the kumquat compote, slice the kumquats into 4 to 5 rounds depending on size, and remove the seeds. Put the kumquats into a saucepan with ¾ cup of water and the sugar and let them cook very gently, covered, for 30 minutes or until tender. If it accidentally overcooks or becomes too dry, add a little water and bring back to a boil for a minute—it should be juicy.

Serve warm or cold. This compote keeps for weeks, even months in the fridge.

To serve, spoon a little compote over the labneh and sprinkle with grated dark chocolate.

Kumquat Marmalade

Kumquats are expensive and can be difficult to slice, but this is so worth making for the exquisite flavor. I adore marmalade and if I could only have one, this recipe that I first tasted in Sydney would have to be it. Store in small jars. Since Ireland has switched over to cane sugar (after our last factory producing sugar from sugar beet closed in 2006), which appears to be more intensely sweet, we have reduced the sugar to 5 cups. The intensity of sugar varies in different countries.

. . . .

MAKES 5 TO 6 × ½ PINT JARS

2¼ pounds kumquats

5 cups granulated white sugar

Slice the kumquats thinly crosswise. Collect the seeds and put into a small bowl with 1 cup water. Put the kumquats into a larger bowl with 6½ cups water and cover. Let both stand overnight.

The next day, strain the seeds and reserve the liquid (this now contains the precious pectin, which contributes to the setting of the marmalade). Discard the seeds. Put the kumquat mixture into a large saucepan with the reserved liquid from the seeds. Bring to a boil, reduce the heat, and simmer, covered, for 10 minutes or until the kumquats are very tender. Remove the lid and reduce the liquid to about half the original volume.

Meanwhile, warm the sugar in the oven at 350°F for 8 to 10 minutes.

Add this to the fruit and stir until it is fully dissolved. (The mixture should not be more than 2 inches deep.) Bring the mixture back to a boil and cook rapidly with the lid off for about 15 minutes. Remove the pan from the heat while testing for a set by putting a teaspoon of the mixture on a cold saucer—it should barely wrinkle when pressed with a finger (or 425°F on a sugar thermometer).

Pour into sterilized jars. Cover, seal, and store in a cool, dry place for 3 to 4 months. Serve on toast, pan-grilled sourdough, or with goat cheese or labneh (page 291).

Portuguese Chicken Soup with Mint & Lemon

A great little soup, food for the soul!

. . . .

SERVES 6

7 cups homemade chicken stock

2 organic, free-range skinless chicken breasts

freshly squeezed juice and zest of 1 lemon

1 cup basmati rice or orzo

1 to 2 tablespoons chopped fresh mint

sea salt and freshly ground black pepper

chopped fresh flat-leaf parsley, to garnish (optional)

Put the stock in a saucepan and add the chicken breasts and lemon zest. Bring slowly to a boil and simmer for 5 minutes. Remove the chicken, cool, and slice into thin shreds.

Meanwhile add the rice, lemon juice, and mint and season with salt and freshly ground pepper. Return to a boil and simmer for 6 to 8 minutes until the rice is cooked; orzo will take 8 to 10 minutes. Add the chicken as soon as it is shredded.

Season to taste and add more lemon juice if necessary. Serve immediately. A little chopped fresh parsley is good scattered over the top.

Lemon Tart with Lemon Ice Cream & Candied Lemon Peel

All elements of this dessert are delicious, but eaten together are sublime. The clean fresh taste comes through in the ice cream, an excellent accompaniment to the classic lemon tart.

. . . .

SERVES 10 TO 12

FOR THE CANDIED LEMON PEEL

2 lemons
simple syrup made with ¾ cup sugar
  and ¾ cup water, cooked together
  for 2 minutes (see page 290)
mint or lemon balm leaves

FOR THE SWEET SHORTCRUST DOUGH

1⅓ cups all-purpose flour
5 tablespoons butter
2 teaspoons of superfine or
  confectioners' sugar
large beaten egg, to bind

FOR THE FILLING

3 large organic eggs and 1 large organic
  egg yolk
zest of 2 lemons (washed well)
juice of 3 lemons (¾ cup)
juice of 1 orange (⅔ cup)
⅔ cup heavy cream
½ cup granulated sugar

FOR THE LEMON ICE CREAM

1 large organic egg
1 cup milk
½ cup superfine sugar
freshly squeezed juice and finely grated
zest of 1 good-sized lemon

To make the candied lemon peel, peel two lemons very thinly with a swivel top peeler, being careful not to include the white pith, and cut the strips into a fine julienne. Put in a saucepan with 2 cups cold water and simmer for 5 minutes. Remove from the pot, refresh in cold water, and repeat the process again. Put the julienne in a saucepan with the syrup and cook gently for 5 to 8 minutes until the lemon julienne looks translucent. Remove with a slotted spoon and let cool on parchment paper or a cake rack. When cold, sprinkle with superfine sugar. This can be stored in a jar or airtight container for weeks or even months.

To make the dough, in a food processor, pulse together the butter, sugar, and flour to give coarse, "flat" bread crumb texture. Add the egg and pulse again until the dough comes together. Transfer to a sheet of plastic wrap, form into a flat round, and chill for at least 30 minutes or 1 hour, if possible.

Preheat the oven to 350°F.

First line a 9-inch tart pan. Roll the dough out on a floured work surface, under a sheet of plastic wrap. Slip the base of the tart pan under the dough, lift into the pan, and mold into the ring. Cover with plastic wrap and let rest in the fridge for 30 minutes or freeze until needed.

Bake blind with baking beans for 20 to 25 minutes until the dough is pale golden and almost fully cooked. Remove the beans, paint the base with a little beaten egg or egg white, and return to the oven for 2 to 3 minutes. When it is cooked, let it cool while the filling is prepared. Reduce the oven temperature to 325°F.

Whisk all the ingredients for the tart filling together. When the mixture is nice and frothy, pour it into the tart crust. The mixture needs to come right to the top. Bake the until the filling has become firm, about 35 minutes. Check by giving the pan a little shake. When the tart is lukewarm, remove the tart from the pan and leave it on a wire rack to cool (it's best eaten on the day it's made).

Meanwhile, make the ice cream. Separate the egg, whisk the yolk with the milk, and keep the white aside. Gradually mix in the sugar. Add the lemon zest and juice to the liquid. Whisk the egg white until quite stiff and fold into the other ingredients. Freeze in an ice-cream maker according to the manufacturer's instructions or put in the freezer in a covered plastic container. When the mixture starts to freeze, remove from the freezer and whisk again, or break up in a food processor. Then return to the freezer until it is frozen completely.

To serve, arrange a slice of lemon tart on a plate with a scoop of lemon ice cream either directly on the plate or in a little bowl. Garnish with candied lemon peel and fresh mint or lemon balm leaves.

MELONS *Cucumis melo* ANNUAL

Melons can be grown horizontally as above or trained on wires or supports.

The melons we all know and love are tender plants. However, they can be grown outdoors throughout the U.S. We grow a few melons but it has to be said, due to our unpredictable climate, without spectacular success! They like the same conditions as cucumbers, warm and humid but, whereas a cucumber plant may produce up to two dozen fruit, we're lucky to get four or five from a melon. Nonetheless, if you can afford the space, it's totally worth the effort. We watch them like a hawk and try to catch them at the peak of juicy perfection. The plants look unruly as they grow but the little yellow flowers are pretty and the scent of ripening melons is intoxicating.

VARIETIES

There are hundreds of varieties, but they divide in three main groups:

CANTALOUPE

With orange colored and broadly ribbed skin, often smooth, but sometimes rough and scaly, these are best varieties to grow. **Ogen**—Israeli strain with sweet, juicy, aromatic flesh, and yellow-green rind. **Divergent**—disease resistant hybrid with good flavor. **Musk Melons**—Sweet, greeny-orange flesh and coarse netted yellow-green rind. (Actually a type of melon, not a variety.) **Charentais**—Type of cantaloupe— **Orange Sherbert**—netted skinned, oval shaped with orange flesh. **Alvaro** is another **Charentais**, smooth pale yellow fruit with green stripes and very aromatic. Juicy and tender salmon-colored flesh—will ripen outdoors— harvest late summer. **Edonis** is another flavorsome charentais type.

HONEYDEW

is a winter melon, oval-shaped with yellow skin, pale flesh, and a not very distinguished flavor, so I wouldn't recommend growing it. **Galia**—Cross between a cantaloupe and a honeydew—the outer skin is like a cantaloupe and the flesh is light like a honeydew. Outdoor wonder is a Galia type which produces tennis-ball-sized, pale green–fleshed melons and has good mildew resistance.

WATERMELON

Crimson Sweet—blocky fruit up to 25 pounds, bright red, sweet flesh.

Sugar Baby—the standard by which all small watermelons are measured; black, crack resistant rinds over delicious flesh. **Sunshine**—juicy, very sweet, bright-yellow fruit in an icebox-sized melon.

HOW TO GROW

Melons need rich, fertile, well-drained soil and high humidity—the same environment as cucumbers. A couple of weeks before picking, dig some well-rotted compost into the soil.

We start them in 3½-inch pots in the growing room and treat them pretty much like cucumbers. When they reach the four-leaf stage, we transfer to our cold greenhouse, harden off for 10 to 14 days and transplant into the ground 2 feet apart with 3 feet between rows. In the U.S. they can be planted outdoors after all threat of a spring frost has passed. They need to be supported, so make a hole large enough for the plant, lay the string underneath, put the plant on top, cover with loose soil, and firm into position. Tie the string to the overhead wire. Train the plant clockwise on the string as it grows, we do this for tomatoes too as their leaves grow clockwise. When the growth reaches the top of the wire (about 70 inches) we pinch out the growing point—the melons will form on the side shoots. Keep well-watered and the air moist, like cucumbers.

Melons can be grown on the ground like pumpkins but they take up a lot of space. Feed once a week with seaweed fertilizer, the same as cucumbers and tomatoes. Watermelons need less humid conditions, but copious amounts of water. Good ventilation is important, particularly when the melon is in flower, to ensure good pollination.

You'll need to net the fruit to support them as they swell.

DID YOU KNOW?

When Christopher Columbus returned to the New World, he found lots of melons growing where his previous expeditions had landed and discarded the seeds from the melons they'd eaten.

CONTAINER GROWING

Melons can be grown quite successfully in a large pot in the same soil conditions as above. Keep well watered and fed.

PESTS AND DISEASES

Provided the growing conditions are good, you shouldn't have too many problems. It's terribly important to provide a humid atmosphere as stressed earlier, but if there are any signs of red spider mite or white fly, introduce a general purpose predator. This biological control is widely available now, but is only really effective if introduced early enough.

HARVESTING

The major bonus of growing our own melons is being able to allow them to ripen to glorious, perfumed perfection on the plant. Commercial melons are usually picked under-ripe to allow for transit.

WHAT TO DO WITH A GLUT

You can freeze the flesh.

GOOD FOR YOU...

Melons are rich in vitamins A, C, and K, as well as niacin, magnesium, and potassium. Watermelons also contain iron. Melons are high in fiber but low in calories. The seeds of the Cantaloupe melon are a source of omega 3 in the form of alpha-linolenic acid.

IN THE KITCHEN

A perfectly ripe melon will perfume your whole kitchen deliciously. Chill in the fridge before eating. We love to bring melons on a summer picnic, nestled into a cooler. Serve them in wedges with nothing more than slice of lemon or lime. **Melon Granita** or sorbet

Canteloupe melon supported by string.

is super refreshing; we serve it as a light and tingling appetizer or put a spoonful in an elderflower cocktail. Chunks of juicy melon are also delicious in both sweet and savory salads, and don't forget the delicious marriage of melon and prosciutto which sounds like a cliché, but with a sweet juicy Ogen or Galia melon at the peak of ripeness plus a slice of paper thin, but fatty prosciutto is heavenly.

Raspberry, Nectarine & Melon Salad

A tasty and refreshing combination—summer on a plate. These ingredients work brilliantly together, one of best ways to use deliciously ripe melons.

SERVES 6

2 ripe peaches or nectarines
1 to 1½ cups fresh raspberries
1 Ogen melon, or 2 bananas
superfine sugar
freshly squeezed juice of 1 to 2 lemons
chopped fresh mint, to garnish

Just before serving, slice and peel the peaches or simply slice the nectarines into ¼-inch thick slices. Put into a bowl with the raspberries. Scoop the melon flesh into balls or cut into ½-inch dice and add a good sprinkling of superfine sugar and the lemon juice. If using bananas, slice and add to the salad just before serving. Add a little chopped mint to wake it up and make it even more delicious.

Melon Granita with Lime Syrup

This sorbet or granita is only as delicious as the melon, so make sure you use a ripe Charentais, Ogen, or Galia melon. The granita is a refreshing way to use up a ripe melon.

SERVES 6 TO 8

1 ripe Charentais, Ogen, or Galia melon (not honeydew), weighing about 1¼ pounds
zest and juice of 2 limes or 1 small lemon
¼ cup superfine or confectioners' sugar
1 cup sugar syrup (page 290)
salt
1 small ripe Charentais, Ogen, or Galia melon, weighing about 1¼ pounds and fresh mint or lemon balm leaves, to serve

Cut the first melon in half horizontally. Remove the seeds and then scoop out the flesh with a tablespoon. Purée the melon flesh in a juicer, then strain it into a bowl through a fine sieve or strainer. Add half the lime zest and juice, the sugar, and a tiny pinch of salt and whisk to dissolve the sugar. Transfer to an ice-cream maker and freeze. Alternatively, just pour into a plastic container or stainless steel bowl and freeze. After a couple of hours, use a whisk to dissolve the frozen edges into the center. Repeat several times so the texture is granular. Alternatively, scrape out with the tines of a fork just before serving.

To make the syrup, add the remaining lime zest and juice to the syrup, then add the juice of half the lime.

To serve, peel and cut the melon in quarters, remove the seeds, and slice into thin slices or dice. Put a scoop of granita onto each chilled plate or into a chilled glass. Spoon a little syrup and zest over the top and garnish with melon and fresh mint or lemon balm leaves.

Melon in Lovage Syrup

A beautiful ripe melon needs little embellishment, but even a mediocre melon is greatly enhanced by the haunting flavor of lovage syrup.

SERVES 4

FOR THE LOVAGE SYRUP (MAKES 1½ CUPS)

¾ cup granulated sugar
1 ounce lovage leaves

FOR THE MELON

1 ripe Galia, Charentais, or Ogen melon
2 tablespoons shredded mint leaves

To make the lovage syrup, put the sugar and 1 cup of water in a saucepan and add the lovage leaves. Bring to a boil, stirring until the sugar dissolves. Remove from the heat. Leave to infuse for 1 to 2 hours. Taste.

Strain the syrup, discard the lovage leaves. Store in a sterilized glass bottle in the fridge. It will keep for several months.

Slice or cube the ripe melon. Put in a large bowl. Drizzle with the lovage syrup. Toss gently and let marinate in the fridge for an hour or so.

Before serving, toss the melon with the shredded mint leaves.

Divide among four chilled plates and serve immediately.

QUINCE
Cydonia oblonga DECIDUOUS, ZONES 5–9

Beautiful ripe quince—aromatic and furry.

I wish I could grow quince here in Shanagarry, but for some reason, despite my best efforts, they do not love our soil. However, in West Cork, I have two trees that seem to be flourishing on granite and acidic soil. Nonetheless, don't let that put you off because many gardening books seem to reassure us that quince are easy to grow, easy to care for, and not prone to many of the common fruit diseases.

I adore quince; they have pretty pink and white blossom in spring, and the beautiful, slightly fuzzy, canary yellow fruits ripen in late autumn and fill the house with their sweet fragrance. The hard fruits resemble knobbly apples or pears. Even when ripe, they never soften. Most varieties are inedible when raw, but if you can find Isfahan, Shams, or Iranian quince they do eventually soften and sweeten and can be eaten fresh. The others cook magnificently and make delicious compotes, jellies, and of course membrillo. A bowl of quince perfumes my kitchen in autumn, and gradually ripens in the heat of my ancient Aga.

Quince apparently originated in the foothills of the Caucus Mountains, which stretch from Iran in the east to Turkistan. Can you imagine how beautiful and fragrant it must have been when they flowered in spring, and how spectacular when covered with fruit in late autumn?

Flowering Japonese quince, *Chaenomeles*, are also worth growing; the fruits are hard and green, and much smaller, but they make a delicious Japonica jelly to serve with game.

VARIETIES

It's difficult to know why quince are not more widely grown, or even known. Perhaps it's because they don't offer instant gratification, and in our climate really need to be cooked to be enjoyed. However, newer varieties have been developed that can be eaten fresh.

Meech's prolific—Ripens mid-autumn; golden yellow fruits with good flavor.

Orange—small, compact tree produces large, golden-yellow fruit.

Portugal—vigorous, round, bright yellow fruit in early autumn.

Smyrna—very large fragrant fruit, perfect for preserves. Also keeps well.

Toho Nishiki—Japanese quince with small fruits high in pectin.

HOW TO GROW

Although many gardeners will say that quince will tolerate any soil type, I believe they do best in neutral to mildly acidic, fertile soil in a sheltered, sunny location.

You'll have a choice of many sizes from large, spreading specimen trees to half-standards that are perfect for smaller gardens. Free-standing trees can be grown up to 20 feet high. Quince are self-fertile, but it's best to plant two for even better pollination.

They can also be trained into a fan shape on a south- or west-facing wall. Mulch with compost in spring, and keep plants watered if there is a dry spell during summer.

Quince are grafted onto a semi-dwarfing quince A or dwarfing rootstock quince C. Feed with a general organic fertilizer.

CONTAINER GROWING

Some dwarf varieties grown on a C rooting stock, can grow and fruit in a large (2 feet) pot.

PESTS AND DISEASES

We haven't encountered any, neither do the birds seem to have any interest in the fruit. However, they can be susceptible to quince leaf blight which affects fruit

DID YOU KNOW?

Jewish folklore tells us that Adam tempted Eve with a quince rather than an apple. Quince have been a feature of Persian food, both sweet and savory, for over 2,500 years, Morabba Beh is a traditional quince jam and Chorosht'e Be, a veal and quince stew.

There are 19 varieties of quince in the Brogdale Orchard in Kent, part of the UK National Collection. They are under-planted with wildflowers, how beautiful that must be in late spring.

production and disfigures the tree. It's more likely to develop in wet conditions, so select resistant varieties and plant in an open airy site.

Brown rot is also a possibility, common to many other fruits. Caused by a fungus in wet summers, remove and destroy affected fruit.

HARVESTING

Quince need a long growing season—the fruit takes until late autumn to ripen. They will be bright yellow in color and aromatic but still unyielding.

Store in a cool, dry place on shallow or compressed paper trays—not touching. They will keeps for up to three months.

GOOD FOR YOU...

Quince is a good source of vitamin C, zinc, potassium, copper, iron, and dietary fiber, it also has other phytonutrients and has anti-inflammatory properties.

WHAT TO DO WITH A GLUT?

Make membrillo and Quince jam (page 302).

IN THE KITCHEN

First, we make several batches of quince jelly or membrillo. It takes time, but everyone loves it. We serve it with cheese, and add to sauces and salads throughout the year. Quince are also delicious in savory dishes with pork or veal stews.

Quince flowers are also edible, as are the pink, red, and orange flowers of Japonica, the Japanese flowering quince. Use them in salads or to decorate cakes, but I prefer to let as many as possible develop into fruit.

Membrillo—Quince Paste Jelly

This recipe alone is reason enough to grow a quince tree. The resulting paste will keep for over a year if you can manage to resist nibbling it. Serve it with cheese—it's particularly good with Manchego, Cheddar, goat, or blue cheese.

as many quinces as you can lay your
  hands on
¾ of that weight of granulated sugar

Preheat the oven to 225°F.

Use a cloth to rub the down off the skins of as many quinces as you can pack into a large earthenware jar. Do not add any water. Cover the pot and place in a low oven for about 4 hours until the fruit is easily pierced with a skewer. Quarter the fruit, remove the cores and any blemishes, and put the pieces through a Mouli grater, using the biggest disc. (If you do not have one, buy one!)

Weigh the quince pulp and add 3 parts of sugar to every 4 parts of pulp. Cook the mixture in a preserving pan over medium heat for 10 to 12 minutes stirring continuously with a wooden spatula until the mixture becomes a russet color and stops running together again when the spatula is drawn through the mixture.

Line the base and sides of 2 × 9-inch × 12-inch Swiss roll pans (with high sides) with parchment paper or silicone paper. Spread evenly with the paste and leave overnight to cool and solidify.

The following day, dry the pans of quince paste out in a low oven (225°F) for about 4 hours until it is quite firm. I do it overnight in the coolest oven of my ancient Aga. Check to see if it is ready by lifting a corner of the paste: it should be solid all the way through. When the paste has cooled, cut into 4 strips, wrap in parchment paper, and store in an airtight container. It will keep for at least 4 months, but is best eaten freshly made. Cut into 1-inch squares to serve.

Pork with Quince

A slightly fatter pork shoulder gives extra succulence to this delicious stew. Quince is often added to stews in Greece and many of the Middle Eastern countries where quince trees dot the landscape and the fruit is plentiful. If quince are not available, try adding underripe pears—you will be surprised how delicious they are.

SERVES 6

2¾-pound organic pork shoulder, cut into 1½-inch cubes

sea salt and freshly ground black pepper

extra virgin olive oil

1 pound onions, sliced

2-inch cinnamon stick

1 generous teaspoon grated fresh ginger

½ teaspoon saffron, crushed and soaked in 1 tablespoon warm water

light chicken stock or water

1½ pounds quince

1½ to 2 tablespoons honey, mixed flower or apple blossom

juice of ½ lemon

lots of flat-leaf parsley

Season the pork pieces with salt and freshly ground pepper. Heat a little oil in a Dutch oven over medium heat, add the pork a few pieces at a time, and toss until the meat is lightly browned. Do this in batches, if necessary. Remove the meat from the pan and set aside.

Spoon a little more oil into the pot, then add the onions, cinnamon, ginger, saffron, and its soaking water. Sprinkle in a teaspoon of salt and cook for 4 to 5 minutes, stirring occasionally to make sure it doesn't stick. Return the pork to the pan. Pour in enough chicken stock or water to come about halfway up the meat. Cover and simmer gently for about 1¼ hours until the meat is almost tender. Alternatively, transfer the casserole to the oven and cook at 325°F.

While the pork is cooking, rub any fuzz from the outside of the quince, (don't peel—the skin adds to the flavor and texture of the stew). Wash and cut each quince into 8 wedges. Remove the cores and cut each piece in half. Drop into lightly acidulated water to prevent them from discoloring.

When the pork is almost cooked, season to taste. Add the quince with the honey and lemon juice, cover, and simmer for another 20 to 40 minutes until both the pork and quince are tender but still keeping their shape. (Add a little more stock when adding the quince if necessary.) Taste and serve with rice or a simple couscous and scatter with flat-leaf parsley.

Quince Jam

Another great way to use up your quince. Monitor the sugar—the quantity can be reduced if the quince are very ripe but be careful not to decrease too much or the jam won't keep as well. Serve with cheese or coarse pâtes.

MAKES 7 × HALF-PINT JARS

2¼ pounds quince (about 5 to 6), grated or finely diced

juice and zest of 1 large lemon

3¼ to 3¾ cups granulated sugar

Put the quince into a stainless steel saucepan with 3½ cups of water, bring to a boil, then add the lemon juice and zest. Continue to cook over low heat for about 20 minutes until the quince softens.

Add the sugar, return to a boil, and stir until the sugar is fully dissolved. Continue to cook, uncovered, for 40 to 50 minutes until the quince thickens and the color deepens to a rich amber.

Pour into sterilized jars, cover, and store in a cool, dry place for up to a year.

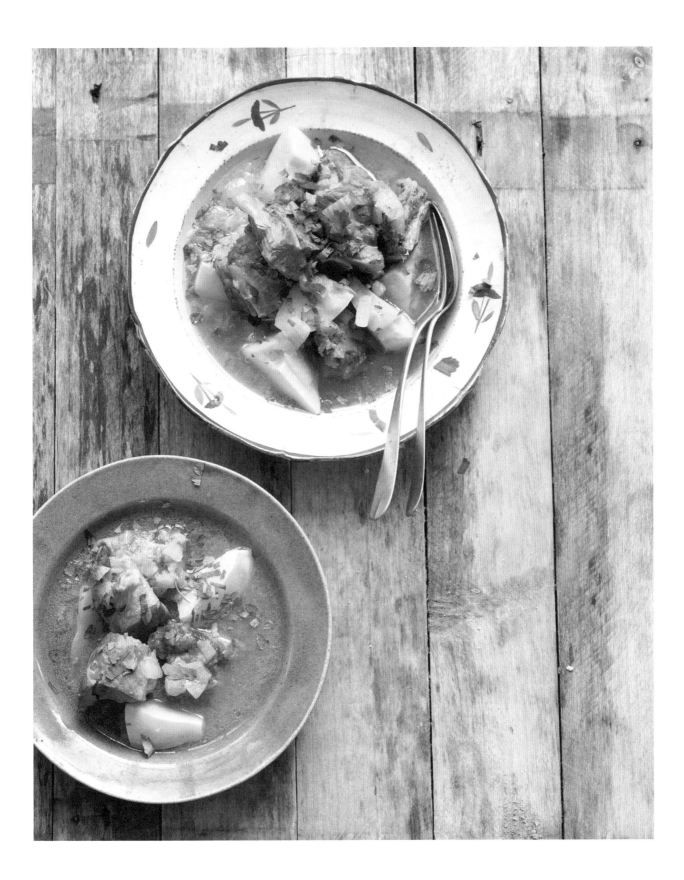

FIGS *Ficus carica* PERENNIAL, ZONES 6–10

Figs ripen at different stages. Use the leaves to wrap fish or cheese for pan-grilling.

We grow figs both outdoors on a sunny wall and in the greenhouse. In a good year some figs ripen in the fruit garden at the Cookery School, but the fig trees along the east end of the greenhouse are by far the most productive. We get 2 to 3 flushes during the summer, from early summer right through to late autumn.

But it's not just the fruits we enjoy, we also use the fig leaves under cheese on the cheeseboard. We love to use the fig leaves to wrap fish and cheese parcels to roast on the barbecue. The leaves impart a distinctive coconut-y flavor.

Fig leaves have had their uses since the time of Adam and Eve!

VARIETIES

There are 600 fig species and many different varieties, our favorites are:

Brown Turkey—My favorite, reliable and a prolific cropper.
Brunswick—Good cropper, flavorful greenish white fruit with pink centers.
Violette Dauphine—One of most frost-resistant varieties, up to -4°F. Large, tasty red fruit.

HOW TO GROW

Figs are self-fertile, the traditional advice was to curtail the roots, much like mint, to encourage a higher yield of fruit, we put them in old washing machine drums to restrict them, the light fibrous roots can get out but not the heavy roots. Don't over-feed with too much nitrogen which just promotes lots of unnecessary foliage.

Make a generous hole. It's advised to plant figs deeply to protect the roots from frost, and to encourage them to develop a good root base. Figs are often grown against a wall, this provides some support and shelter. It was thought that this would encourage more fruit to develop, but if they are not overfed with nitrogen they should fruit anyway.

CONTAINER GROWING

A fig can grow happily in a large pot. In a warm porch, tunnel or greenhouse they will produce lots of fruit, provided they are well cared for, pruned, and watered regularly. They also make a decorative and pleasing houseplant.

PESTS AND DISEASES

We got an attack of woolly aphid that came in on another plant and had quite a challenge getting rid of it. We are using biological control and are hopeful. Be super vigilant when you buy in plants.

Usually, birds and wasps are the only

A bowl of voluptuous ripe Brown Turkey figs.

problem when the fruit are ripe, so pick daily so they don't get a chance. They have unerring judgment and always spot the figs that are at the peak of perfection.

HARVESTING

In the greenhouse the first ripe figs usually appear in early summer. We keep an eagle eye out for them so the blackbirds don't get there first. We check every day because, like many fruits, they ripen a few at a time so we try to get each one at the peak of perfection. We get a second late flush of fruit in the mid-to-late autumn. Figs grown outdoors tend not to ripen until the autumn but the reality in our climate is that some do not ever fully ripen.

GOOD FOR YOU...

Figs are known to be a laxative and are rich in minerals including potassium, calcium, magnesium, iron, and copper and are a good source of antioxidant vitamins A, E, and K.

IN THE KITCHEN

Most of our figs get eaten raw because they are so irresistible when they are ripe and freshly picked, but we do have many tarts, pies, and salads, both sweet and savory, that we embellish with them.

We also infuse them, use the leaves to make a fig leaf syrup, and leave them to macerate in alcohol to make fig leaf gin or vodka. A fig leaf panna cotta was also a success, as was fig leaf ice cream, particularly when we served it with ripe figs and fresh raspberry sauce.

A fig leaf also makes a perfect base on which to serve a piece of beautiful fresh cheese with a few homemade crackers alongside, and do try using them to wrap fish and cheese. The little parcels can be cooked on the barbecue or on a grill pan or in the oven.

Fresh Figs with Fig Leaf Ice Cream, Fresh Raspberries & Raspberry Sauce

This is a sublime combination of flavors when both the figs and raspberries are freshly picked—it will be a sad disappointment if made with underripe out-of-season fruit. This recipe both fruit and leaves. Although I associate this ice cream with summer and love to serve it alongside some fresh raspberries, we have made fig leaf ice cream as late as mid-December and served it with kumquat or quince compote.

. . . .

MAKES 8/SERVES 4

FOR THE FIG LEAF ICE CREAM
(MAKES 2 CUPS)
6 large fig leaves
¾ cup heavy cream
¾ cup whole milk
4 large organic egg yolks
¼ cup superfine sugar

FOR THE RASPBERRY COULIS
3 to 6 tablespoons superfine sugar
2 cups raspberries
lemon juice (optional)

TO SERVE
8 freshly picked ripe figs and leaves
1½ to 2 cups fresh raspberries
½ cup whipped cream, slightly sweetened
    with confectioners' sugar and flavored
    with a little vanilla extract
fresh mint or lemon balm

To make the ice cream, destalk and coarsely chop the fig leaves and place them in a heavy saucepan with the cream. Heat to the shivery stage, remove from the heat, and set aside to infuse until cool.

Warm the milk until just below boiling point. Whisk the egg yolks in a bowl with the sugar and add in the warm milk gradually. Return to a clean saucepan and cook over low heat, stirring constantly, for 7 to 8 minutes until the custard coats the back of a spoon (around 325°F). Strain the cream into a bowl, stir in the custard, mix well, and chill thoroughly.

Freeze according to the directions of your ice-cream maker.

To make the raspberry coulis, make a syrup with sugar and water: Dissolve the sugar in 8 tablespoons of water and bring to a boil. Boil for 2 minutes then allow it to cool. When cool, add to the raspberries. Liquidize and strain through a nylon sieve, taste, and sharpen with lemon juice if necessary. Store in a fridge. It will keep, covered, for 4 to 5 days.

Just before serving, trim the stalk in cut a cross in each fig, cutting down almost to the base. Gently open out the fruit to resemble a flower unfurling. If you'd rather peel them, make a nick just under the stalk and peel off the skin in strips.

Lay a fig leaf on each plate, pop a fig on top, then put a little dollop of cream in the center. Spoon a little raspberry coulis over the top and serve the remainder in a bowl. Decorate with a few fresh raspberries and a sprig of mint or lemon balm. Eat immediately.

Goat Cheese Salad with Arugula, Figs & Pomegranates

If the figs aren't ripe, it's best to use soft dried Turkish figs here. Plump dried figs are best cut into slices rather than wedges and scattered over the salad. Figs and pomegranates grow in a similar climate—the combination of flavors makes a delicious light appetizer salad.

. . . .

SERVES 8

1 fresh pomegranate

32 fresh walnut halves

enough arugula for 8 helpings and perhaps
   a few leaves of radicchio

4 small fresh goat cheese wedges

8 to 12 fresh figs or plump dried figs
   (try to find the Turkish ones on a raffia
   string)

crusty bread, to serve

FOR THE DRESSING

½ cup extra virgin olive oil

2 to 3 tablespoons freshly squeezed
   lemon juice

½ to 1 teaspoon wildflower honey

sea salt and freshly ground black pepper

Cut the pomegranate in half around the equator, break each side open, and flick the glistening jewellike seeds out into a bowl, avoiding the bitter yellowy pith. Alternatively, if you are in a hurry, put the cut-side down on the palm of your hand over a bowl and bash the skin-side firmly with the back of a wooden spoon; the seeds will drop into the bowl between your fingers—this works really well but it tends to be a bit messy, so be sure to protect your clothes with an apron as pomegranate juice really stains.

Next make the dressing—just whisk the oil, lemon juice, and honey together in a bowl. Season well.

Toast the walnut halves in a dry pan over medium heat for about 5 minutes until they smell sweet and nutty. Do not allow to burn.

Just before serving, toss the arugula and radicchio in a deep bowl with a little dressing. Divide between eight large white plates. Cut each cheese into 6 pieces.

Cut the figs into quarters from the top, keeping each one still attached at the base. Press gently to open. Divide the cheese between the plates, three pieces on each, and place a fig in the center. Sprinkle with pomegranate seeds and freshly roasted walnuts. Drizzle with a little extra dressing and serve immediately with crusty bread.

> **DID YOU KNOW?**
> Figs are indigenous to Asia Minor and were one of the first fruits to be cultivated. They were brought to Europe by the Romans. The India rubber plant is also a member of the Moraceae family (*Ficus elastica*).

STRAWBERRIES *Fragaria* PERENNIAL, ZONES 3–10

Strawberries all year round? What can I say? Most young people have absolutely no idea when strawberries are in season, and only the vaguest idea of what a real strawberry tastes like. Their only experience being variations one of the mass-produced, super-size, watery offerings now available. Every year strawberries seem to get larger and more innocuous and are one of the very worst foods for retaining pesticide residue.

Commercial strawberries, with a few rare exceptions, are by now such a pale imitation of the original. They now seem to be grown solely for size, so I keep hoping that we will soon have a consumer revolt that will invite a response similar to what happened when the tomato got so unbearably tasteless that eventually the horticultural industry recognized the crisis and we were offered tomatoes grown for flavor.

Most of the the flavor is bred out in favor of size and visual impact. Understandably, these fruit are unlikely to have either the flavor or nutrient content of a heritage berry grown in rich, fertile soil. So the reality is if you want to taste berries that will blow your mind, you need to grow your own.

We grow several varieties, the fruits are smaller and less uniform. But even though they wouldn't win any prizes in a beauty competition, and certainly wouldn't pass muster on a supermarket shelf, they are intensely flavored and super-delicious.

VARIETIES

There are numerous varieties, all derived from *F.chiloensis,* but can be categorized into two main types: traditional varieties that fruit in summer and perpetual or ever-bearers that continue to produce fruit right into autumn. So you may want to order a few plants from each category for a succession of strawberries.

Hood—large June-ripeneing fruits with great flavor. Perfect for fresh eating or freezing or preserves

Puget—large, dark red berries on late bearing plants.

Albion—a day-neutral overbearing strawberry with good disease resistance. Produces a good crop of conical fruit.

Jewel—mid-season produce of a large crop of good tasting fruit.

Mara des Bois—this French overbearing variety produces a continues crop of delicious fruit from June until frost.

Earliglow—the earliest variety; produces a large crop of deep red, firm fruit.

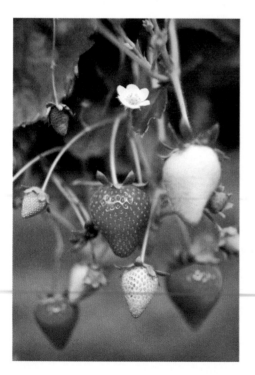

Grow your own and remember what strawberries should taste like.

HOW TO GROW

Strawberries, whether June bearing or ever bearing varieties, need rich, fertile soil, good drainage, and lots of sun. Slightly acidic to neutral soil is best. So choose the sunniest spot in your garden for maximum flavor. Dig in plenty of well-rotted manure or compost. Leave enough space—2 feet each way—between plants at least, better still 3 feet between rows. Avoid a site where potatoes or tomatoes have recently grown as these plants suffer from the same diseases. Water in, but be careful not to over-water, this dilutes the flavor of the berries.

Although strawberries prefer to be outdoors, growing indoors in a greenhouse or tunnel, provides many bonuses—earlier crops, protection from inclement weather and pesky birds which can decimate a crop.

Strawberry plants are best replaced every three or four years. Older plants develop viruses, so are best discarded.

One can even grow from seed but runners or virus-free plants are preferable and easily available. Harvest the first runners and prune the rest to keep the plant vigorous. So take the first "plantlet" from an early runner of a vigorous plant. Peg it into the ground by pinning it down on either side. We use bent wires, better still sink a small pot filled with potting compost into the ground and pin the plantlet into that. When it's rooted, snip the runner at either side and you've got a plant ready to plant into a new site. Plant in autumn for the following year. It's important not to plant into old ground and is a fun thing to do with children.

We mulch the plants with seaweed to feed, and lay a layer of straw to keep the fruit off the soil and for ease of picking. Many gardeners plant through black polythene or landscape fabric which suppress the weeds. Keep removing the runners unless you want to propagate more plants.

Strawberries start to flower in early to mid-spring so can be damaged by late frost. Keep an eye on the weather forecast and cover with fleece overnight if necessary.

A feed of liquid comfrey every couple of weeks before fruiting benefits the plants and enhances the flavor.

CONTAINER GROWING

Strawberries can be grown in a wide variety of containers, from window boxes and hanging baskets to large recycled tomato tins or even an old tea pot. They need regular watering and feeding. Possibly the least successful containers are the terracotta pots or towers sold specifically for growing strawberries as there's not usually enough room for the roots to expand and watering can be challenging.

Grow bags work well—four plants to a bag. Strawberries are great to grow with children, give them their own plants to look after and it just could be the start of a lifelong love of growing.

PESTS AND DISEASES

Botrytis is a grey mould which can appear on strawberries. Cloudy, wet weather, and cool temperatures suit botrytis. Remove dead leaves and

having enough space between plants to encourage aeration can help.

Powdery mildew can appear on the leaves and fruit. It thrives in warm, dry weather, and can sometimes overwinter on plants.

Verticillium wilt is a fungus which penetrates into the plant causing them to gradually fail and die back. Affected plants should be removed and destroyed. Burning is probably the best option.

HARVESTING

On a dry, sunny day, pick or better still snip off fruit as they ripen; always pick with the calyx attached. Strawberries are perishable so use within a couple of days and keep cool. I prefer not to keep them in the fridge, but if you do, cover everything, because strawberries can taint other foods.

GOOD FOR YOU...

Strawberries are a brilliant source of vitamin C with smaller amounts of vitamins K, B6, and E and some iron. They are a good source of folic acid and fiber. They have high levels of manganese, some magnesium, phosphorus, potassium, and calcium. Several studies suggest that organically grown fruit have significantly higher antioxidant levels, including vitamin C.

WHAT TO DO WITH A GLUT

Strawberries freeze well, and having tried various methods, we now pick into small pints, blast freeze in the pints, and

then when fully frozen, transfer them into quart bags ready for smoothies and jam making. That way there is minimum handling so less bruising. We remove the calyx just before using with the pointed top of a potato peeler.

Strawberry purée mixed with sugar syrup also freezes well and can be used as a base for ice creams and drinks.

IN THE KITCHEN

It's difficult to beat strawberries and cream. I serve them piled up, calyx still attached, in a Shanagarry Pottery bowl, with a bowl of cream and superfine sugar. Strawberries sliced and sprinkled with lemon juice, honey, and shredded mint are particularly fresh or zingy. Add a few drops of aged balsamic vinegar to a bowl of sliced strawberries, toss gently, and marvel at the intensity of flavor. The transformation is magic even if the strawberries are a little underripe. Freshly ground black pepper also enhances the flavor.

Homemade strawberry ice cream, granitas, and ice pops are so easy to make and just blow your mind with their yumminess. Strawberry lemonade and daiquiris are also pretty irresistible, and then of course strawberry meringue or pavlova or roulade, strawberry shortcake, a feather light sponge oozing with strawberries and cream, Eton Mess....

Frozen berries have got me out of a pickle on several occasions when I was short on dessert. Put equal volume of sugar and cold water into a saucepan— I use 2½ cups and add 5 to 6 sweet geranium leaves (not essential). When the syrup comes to a boil, pour over the frozen berries in a bowl. The hot syrup defrosts the frozen berries in double quick time and they in turn cool down the syrup but remain plump—hey presto, a delicious dessert! Just add some heavy cream.

Strawberry Shortcake

Strawberry Shortcake is made with shortbread on this side of the world, but I like the American version made instead with what we'd call sweet scones. Don't skimp on the strawberries and sprinkle them with sugar.

. . . .

MAKES 10

1 × basic scone recipe (page 402)
1 pint strawberries, plus 6 to 8 to garnish
2 teaspoons superfine sugar
1¼ cups cream
2 teaspoons confectioners' sugar
¼ teaspoon vanilla extract

Prepare the scones according to the recipe on page 402, omitting the blueberries. While they are baking, hull the strawberries and cut into quarters. Sprinkle with the superfine sugar and a few drops of freshly squeezed lemon juice, toss gently, and set aside.

Shortly before serving, whip the cream softly with the confectioners' sugar and add the vanilla extract. Split the cooled scones and top the bottom half with a blob of sweetened cream and lots of sugared strawberries and a little lemon zest. Add the tops, dust with a little confectioners' sugar, and decorate with whole or halved strawberries and fresh mint or strawberry leaves.

Strawberry Lemonade

Thirst-quenching and delicious but also a terrific way to use up a glut of strawberries.

. . . .

MAKES APPROX. 3 QUARTS

simple syrup made with 1¾ cups
   granulated sugar and 2½ cups water
   (page 290)
FOR THE LEMONADE
6 lemons
approx. 1½ cups sugar syrup
approx. 6 cups still or sparkling water
1 pound strawberries, hulled and puréed
fresh mint leaves
ice cubes

Measure the correct amount of syrup carefully for the lemonade. It is not necessary to use the all the syrup made; this quantity is enough for several batches of lemonade and can be stored in the fridge until needed.

Juice the lemons and mix with the simple syrup, adding still or sparkling water to taste.

Add the smooth strawberry purée to the lemonade. Taste and add a little more syrup or lemon juice as needed. Serve over ice with a sprig of fresh mint in each glass.

Fresh Strawberry Ice Pops

We make these ice pops from fresh fruit purées all year round, ostensibly for the children, but the grown-ups snatch them up too. So fun to serve after a dinner party or at a barbecue.

. . . .

MAKES 16 OUNCES OR 6 × 2½-OUNCE
ICE POPS

14 ounces fresh strawberries
freshly squeezed juice of ½ to 1 lemon
⅔ cup simple syrup (see page 290)

Clean and hull the strawberries, put into a juicer or food processor, and blend. Strain through a nylon sieve, taste, and add freshly squeezed lemon juice and simple syrup to taste.

Pour into 2½-ounce ice pop molds and freeze for 3 to 4 hours.

ALPINE STRAWBERRIES

or frais du bois *Fragaria vesca* PERENNIAL, ZONES 5–9

You simply must have alpine or wood strawberries, these hardy little perennial plants will grow everywhere and anywhere. The more you pick these fragrant and dimunitive strawberries the more they produce, and a packet of seeds will give you the best part of 200 plants, so choose the variety carefully and spread them around.

They can be planted in the vegetable garden or through the herbaceous border, but they edge a garden path prettily and romp away through fine gravel or make an excellent ground

Another gem, frais du bois pop up year after year.

cover. They even settle in cracks between stones, slabs or a patio.

One of the highlights of recent years was a visit in early summer to the Carpathian Mountains in Transylvania to walk in the wildflower meadows. They were indescribably beautiful and dense with exquisitely flavored wild strawberries—I long to return.

VARIETIES

Mignonette—Considered to be the most delicious of all the varieties with large sweet fruit, although Sarah Raven favors Alexandria.

Yellow wonder—Yellow fruiting strawberry with excellent flavor.

Alexandria—vigorous plants produce sweet, thimble-size fruit.

HOW TO GROW

Likes most well-drained soils but prefers an alkaline pH and a little well-rotted manure dug in before planting will improve yield. A feed of comfrey tea every couple of weeks boosts both flavor and yield. They grow in sun but also thrive in dappled shade.

They fruit in the first season and for 3 to 4 years afterwards.

CONTAINER GROWING

Wild strawberries will grow happily in a hanging basket, window box, in strawberry pots and all manner of containers.

PESTS AND DISEASES

Birds adore them but otherwise these hardy perennials are not troubled much by pests and diseases.

HARVESTING

You will be able to start picking them in late spring and carry on well into the autumn.

DID YOU KNOW?
In Bavaria farm folk used to make offerings to the elves in the form of baskets of wild strawberries tied to the horns of their cattle in the hope that the elves would enjoy them and in return endow them with lots of calves and a good supply of milk.

It's difficult to find any specific references but they have similar nutritional value to strawberries.

WHAT TO DO WITH A GLUT
You're unlikely to have a glut of these jewellike fruit, but if you do, make Alpine strawberry jam, pour it into small jars, and share with your best friends.

IN THE KITCHEN
Alpine strawberries also freeze, but honestly why would you? Just enjoy them with a sprinkling of superfine sugar and cream, or pop a few in your Prosecco.

The berries are so, so precious. Sprinkle them sparingly onto the top of fruit salad, and use them often as a garnish, still attached to the stalk, with a flower and a maybe a leaf, for crème caramel, panna cotta, or vanilla bean ice cream.

Aunt Lil's Wild Strawberry Sponge Cake

When I was a little girl I spent a few weeks of my summer holiday every year on my great-aunt and uncle's farm in Ireland. Noard was a working farm. One of my favorite haunts was the long boreen down to the bog where I picked wild strawberries into a little tin "ponnie." I still remember the desperate inner struggle to prevent myself from eating too many of the exquisite wild berries so that Aunt Lil would have enough to sprinkle over her tender sheet of sponge cake.

. . . .

SERVES 6 TO 8

melted butter, for greasing
1¼ cups all-purpose flour, plus extra
　for dusting
⅔ cup superfine sugar, plus extra for
　dusting
5 large organic eggs

FOR THE FILLING
1½ cups heavy cream
12 ounces to 1 pound wild strawberries
superfine sugar, for sprinkling

Preheat the oven to 375°F. Line the bottom and sides of a 9 × 12-inch Swiss roll pan with parchment paper. Brush the paper with melted butter and dust with flour and superfine sugar.

Put the eggs and superfine sugar in a heatproof bowl (not stainless steel) set over a saucepan of simmering water. Whisk the mixture until it is light and fluffy. Remove it from the heat and continue to whisk until the mixture is cool again. (If you use an electric mixer, no heat is required.) Sift in about one-third of the flour at a time and fold it into the mousse using a large spatula or metal spoon. Pour the mixture gently into the pan. Bake for 12 to 15 minutes. It is cooked when it feels firm to the touch in the center. The edges will have shrunk in slightly from the sides of the pan.

Lay a piece of parchment paper on the work top and sprinkle it evenly with superfine sugar. Turn the hot cake onto the sheet of parchment paper. Remove the pan and parchment paper from the bottom of the cake and let cool.

Meanwhile, whisk the cold cream until softly whipped. When the cake is cold, spread softly whipped cream over the top, cover with wild strawberries, sprinkle with superfine sugar, and serve.

GOJI BERRIES
Lycium barbarum/Lycium Chinense DECIDUOUS, ZONES 6–9

Also called wolfberries. You can probably live your life without a goji berry plant, but it's fast and easy to grow and the shiny red berries can be eaten fresh off the bush or dried and added to cereals. They've got a mildly liquorice flavor. Plants can grow up to 8 feet tall and have been a major Chinese tonic herb for the best part of 2,000 years.

VARIETIES
Look for the Tibetan goji berry **Lycium chinense**—which flowers from early to late summer, with mauve flowers and red berries. This too, will grow into a big bush 8 × 6½ feet but is quite hardy and will grow near the sea.

HOW TO GROW
One plant is probably enough unless you are a goji berry fanatic—they are self-pollinating and prefer alkaline soil with at least a ph of 7. Dig a hole and plant it at same level as it was in the pot. Goji berries can also be propagated from cuttings. Prefers sun or dappled shade. It takes 2 to 3 years for a plant to produce berries. They become thorny in the second year.

CONTAINER GROWING
It will grow happily in a good-sized tub in a sunny spot, despite originating in the Himalayas and China. Keep pruned to a manageable size.

I bet you didn't know you could grow your own goji berries? They will flourish in a pot and can be nibbled fresh or dried.

PESTS AND DISEASES
More or less pest free. Birds love the ripe berries so cover with netting to make sure you get your fair share.

HARVESTING
The berries will be ripe from midsummer to late autumn and become a deeper red as they ripen.

You can eat the highly nutritious leaves when young as well as the berries—add to salad or use the leaves to make an infusion.

GOOD FOR YOU...
The goji berry was hailed as a "superfood" a couple of years ago. They are very high in vitamins C and iron, boost your immune system and cleanse impurities. Touted as a powerful antioxidant and recommended for re-alignment of blood pressure and diabetes. Goji berries have been used for centuries in China to benefit eyesight, protect the liver, and promote longevity. In China they are added to broths and are also used in East Asian food and medicine.

WHAT TO DO WITH A GLUT
Unlikely, but they can be dried for best flavor or frozen.

IN THE KITCHEN
Goji berries have a tangy, bittersweet flavor and can be used to make tea, added to granola, biscotti, or muffins, on chocolate, or with quinoa or tabbouleh. To make an infusion, simply pour boiling water over some fresh leaves and allow to brew for a couple of minutes.

DID YOU KNOW?
In Ningxia, China's main goji berry growing region, the crop is planted to help prevent erosion of the three deserts that border the area.

Almond, Pistachio & Goji Berry Mendiants

Mendiants are a perfect base for all types of nuts and berries—goji and myrtle berries, hazelnuts, currants...

MAKES 25 TO 30

8 ounces dark chocolate (approx.
  62 percent cocoa solids)
approx. 1 tablespoon unblanched almonds
approx. 1 tablespoon pistachio nuts
approx. 1 tablespoon goji berries

Break up the chocolate and pop into a Pyrex bowl. Place the bowl over a saucepan of water, bring almost to a boil, turn off the heat immediately, and leave the chocolate to melt gently in the residual heat.

Meanwhile, sliver the almonds and chop the pistachio nuts and almonds coarsely.

Cover a baking sheet with parchment paper, spoon little blobs of chocolate well apart, then sprinkle each one with a mixture of almonds, pistachio, and goji berries.

Set aside to cool then peel off the parchment.

Serve as a petit four with a cup of espresso.

APPLES *Malus domestica,* ZONES 3–8

I simply don't know where to start with apples, it's just the hugest family. There are over 5,000 named varieties and that's probably the tip of the iceberg. Yet here we can get only, at most, a dozen in the shops. But in America there are many more available through plant and seed catalogs. Songs have been sung, poems have been written and a myriad of books, many scholarly tomes, have been written about apples. It's time we taught our children there's more to apples than Red Delicious and Granny Smith.

We've had orchards in Shanagarry since the 1930s and 65 acres of commercial orchards up to the 1980s when sadly we had to face the reality that the orchards were no longer viable at our scale, and it was impossible to compete with cheaper imports. Nonetheless, we still have over 30 varieties of both dessert and cooking apples. With careful planning you can grow varieties that provide fruit year-round, including some varieties that

ripen slowly and store well. It's also worth grafting to include some old Irish or British varieties, and certainly choose from the many superb old apple varieties that cannot be found in the shops. Sadly, much of the energy put into developing new varieties has resulted in apples that fulfill all the criteria for the retail trade but rarely deliver the wow factor in taste terms in the way the old varieties do. The superlative Cox's Orange Pippin has been diluted in a way that makes it scarcely recognizable to those of us who know and love the original.

So, if you've got space in your garden, flower border or even in your lawn, consider planting at least one cooker and one sweet apple tree. It will thrill you throughout the year from the first fresh, green leaves to the apple blossom, and then the joy of watching the fruit gradually ripening to perfection, and of course, your very own apples for a juicy bitter-sweet apple pie. If you decide to give over some precious space in your garden, make sure to seek out reputable nurseries that can offer old varieties.

If space is limited then the apple trees can be trained in espalier fashion, against a wall or fence; choose the varieties carefully as apples from some rootstocks will be more suitable than others.

There are good and bad apple years, depending on the weather during apple blossom time.

VARIETIES

DESSERT

Here are some of my favorite dessert eating apples:

An arch of Egremont Russet apple blossom frames the black mulberry in the fruit garden.

EARLY

Irish Peach—Good eaten straight from tree, pale creamy flesh, doesn't keep, good disease resistance, originating in Ireland possibly in 1820s.
Honey Crisp—cold-hardy plants produce aromatic and sweet fruit.

MID-SEASON

Worcester Pearmain—Medium-sized, juicy, crisp apple with a strawberry flavor.
Egremont Russet—Real English russet apple, nutty flavor, and crisp flesh.
Golden Delicious—cold-hardy, heat-tolerant, and self-pollinating trees produce crisp aromatic fruit.

LATE SEASON

Pitmaston Pineapple—Another English russet apple, golf-ball sized with a distinct pineapple flavor.
Cox's Orange Pippin—This mid-to-late, much-loved apple has yellow skin with a red blush, juicy, firm flesh, great flavor, and best picked when fully ripe or else pick picked slightly under-ripe and stored for a few weeks.
Little Jewel—French variety producing very sweet, small, think-skinned fruit.

These are some of the other eating apple varieties we have planted in our orchard here at the Cookery School:
James Grieve
Miller's Seedling
Allen's Everlasting
Allington Pippin
Ard Cairn Russet
Ben's Red
Blenheim Orange
Ellinson's Orange 1911
George Cave
Ashmead's Kernel

Orlean's Reinette 1776
Crispin
Rosemary Russet
Ross Nonpareil

COOKERS
A codling was a name given to cooking apples that cook down quickly and become soft and tender with very little cooking.
Liberty—similar to McIntosh, but trees have multiple resistances; good for cooking and storing.

And some of my other favorite cooking apples:

EARLY
Grenadier—Pale green cooker that cooks down into a fluff, but doesn't keep very long.

MID-SEASON
Golden Russet

LATE
Bramley Seedling—Reliable and delicious later apple, good to keep—familiar variety which one sees in the shops as a cooking apple.
Wolf River—an antique variety from the upper midwest, with very large tree on trees carrying multiple resitances.

CIDER APPLES
Dabinett
Crimson King
Tremlett's Bitter
Calville Blanc

DUAL PURPOSE
Some varieties are sharp at first but then mellow as they ripen and may be initially used as cooking apples and then dessert when they have ripened more.
Pig's Snout
Allington Pippin
Orleans Reinette

Cortland
Grimes Golden
Snow Apple

MINIATURE
Coronet—A dessert apple developed specially for growing in small gardens or balconies. It crops in the first year and remains miniature.

HOW TO GROW
Apples are best grown outdoors in rich, fertile, well-drained soil; but, having said that, they seem to grow almost anywhere, although they won't thrive under glass. Neither will they grow if the ground is water-logged, parched, or in a frost pocket. It is also essential to get expert advice on mutually compatible varieties that pollinate each other. It is best to buy healthy, young apple trees from a reputable source, grafted onto the appropriate rootstock for your situation. Half standards or M25 rootstocks are best. Some cultivars grow to about 60 inches high. Allow 1 to 8 yards between trees. Apples can be grown from a seed but rarely resemble the original.

Bare rooted varieties are planted during the dormant season (late autum to early spring).

Bare-rooted trees are generally cheaper and if you are planting a lot of apple trees this is the time to do it as they won't need watering and won't cost as much. Also you can source a better selection from specialist sources.

Potted apple trees may be planted any time, they will need to be watered if they are planted during the growing season, until they become established.

Apple trees may be trained over arches—up walls, as espaliers, fan-trained. All need careful pruning, so arm yourself with a good manual. Some varieties are more suitable than others for training, generally trees that spur on the main stem rather than the tip,

Bramley apple blossom.

do better, eg Egremont Russet or Arthur Turner. Trained apples will take up much less space and are suitable for smaller gardens or restricted spaces.

They can form a nice division between a vegetable and flower garden.

In early spring, the dormant season, dig a generous sized hole so the roots can spread, and firm in well and mulch in the spring. They can grow in grazed meadows and are happy to have grass growing underneath.

CONTAINER GROWING
Apples, particularly dwarf varieties Coronet are best for growing in larger pots or barrels. They need hard pruning in winter unless they are specific miniature varieties. Container would need to be at least 7-gallon capacity.

PESTS AND DISEASES
There are many, codling moth and apple sawfly are the more common pests, but they can be prevented by rigorous hygiene. Caterpillars from the codling moth hatch and tunnel into the maturing fruit, they are very off-putting and the apples won't keep. Pheromone traps will catch many male moths and they are

Cox's Orange Pippin.

Beauty of Bath.

hung on the tree from late spring until late summer.

Apple sawfly cause damage similar to the codling moth but it happens earlier in the season and will cause a lot of immature fruit to drop early. Some of the fruit which does go on to mature may have some scarring and distortion. To prevent, pick up all fallen fruitlets in early summer, as a last resort some permitted sprays may be used after the flowers have set.

Canker is caused by damage to the wood. Cut back to healthy wood. Trees recover from canker.

Apple scab is an airborne fungus which shows as black or grey lesions on the leaves and fruit—the fruit can still be used, cutting away damaged parts. The spores over-winter on fallen leaves so it is important to gather them up and burn.

Hens can be an asset in an orchard, they forage for pests and are beneficial in that they will also eat up diseased apples on the ground. Keeping the soil healthy and in good condition is vital in fighting disease and pests.

HARVESTING

Early apples are best picked ripe and eaten directly off the tree. Mid-season varieties are also best eaten freshly picked. They will keep sometimes for several weeks but do deteriorate in a short time.

Later ripening varieties are best left on the tree as long as possible until hard frosts are imminent, then carefully picked and stored, not touching each other, in a single layer. We recycle thick moulded papier maché trays from our greengrocer, or lay them in timber trays in shredded paper. They are stored in a cold, dark rodent-proof shed where they keep for up to six months. We also put unblemished Bramleys into large apple boxes and store them well off the ground in a cold shed. They usually last until late spring, by which time they have all been used up.

We monitor them carefully and pick out and discard any that are deteriorating. We use prunings for firewood and the apple wood sawdust for both hot and cold smoking.

GOOD FOR YOU...

Choose organic apples to avoid the cocktail of pesticides that conventionally grown apples often receive. Apples are one of the worst fruits for containing pesticide residues.

Apples are rich in many different phytochemicals such as flavonols procyanidin, quercetin, and catechin and chlorogenic acid (phenol). Good source of soluble fiber. Useful amounts of vitamin C and potassium.

Most phytochemicals and much of the fiber are contained in the skin so they are best eaten unpeeled.

WHAT TO DO WITH A GLUT

In good years, many people will have a glut of apples, so gifting your neighbors and friends may not be an option. However, later varieties keep particularly well and you can make copious quantities of apple jelly with cookers, or a mixture of cookers, windfalls, and crab apples, and the many fruits of the hedgerows—sloes, damsons, medlars, rowan berries, haws, and elderberries. Fresh herbs and spices also add intriguing flavors. If you have a glut of dessert apples, it is worth buying a centrifuge (juice extractor) to make fresh apple juices. One could pasteurise it for longer storage, but this definitely affects the flavor. We prefer to freeze the fresh juice in quart containers, but we also send several bins of our organic apples to the Apple Farm in Tipperary to be made into apple juice for the school. A couple of dozen small tubs of apple sauce or purée are also a brilliant asset to have in the freezer. Some people peel, core and chop cooking apples and freeze them raw for making pies, you need to work quickly before they start to brown and it saves having to blanch them.

The lads also experiment with a few batches of cider every year—the result is sometimes amazing, occasionally questionable, but always fun and surprising, and we get some unexpected cider vinegar.

IN THE KITCHEN

What would we do without this most versatile fruit in our kitchen? No apple pies, sauce, jelly, roasted or baked apples...

or stewed apples, my special comfort food.

I use them in both sweet and savory dishes and love crunchy apples in salads. Crab apples, cookers, and windfalls make delicious sweet and savory jellies.

Apple and horseradish sauce is delicious—served with spiced beef, pickled or smoked ox tongue, and

should you wish to indulge in one of my occasional favorites, pig's head and brawn, or fromage de tête, you'll find it's a happy marriage of flavors also.

Apple & Custard Pie

This is one of our favorite fall and winter desserts, a windfall apple pie with built-in custard—completely irresistible. Apples and custard are one of those time honored combinations that bring us back to childhood and this is a French take on the favorite pairing. Here we use a shortcrust pastry dough, but it's also good with puff or flaky pastry dough.

SERVES 4

FOR THE BREAK-ALL-THE-RULES
SHORTCRUST PASTRY DOUGH
8 tablespoons butter (1 stick)
2 tablespoons superfine sugar, plus extra
    for sprinkling
1 large organic egg
1⅓ cups all-purpose flour
egg wash, to glaze

FOR THE PIE
2 pounds apples, such as McIntosh,
    Golden Delicious, or Braeburn
½ cup granulated sugar
2 to 3 cloves (optional)

FOR THE CUSTARD
1 extra large organic egg
1 tablespoon superfine sugar
⅔ cup cream
½ teaspoon vanilla extract
softly whipped cream

Preheat the oven to 350°F.

First make the shortcrust pastry dough. Cream the butter and sugar together by hand or in a food mixer. Add the egg and beat for several minutes. Reduce the speed and mix in the flour. Chill for at least 1 hour, otherwise it is difficult to handle.

Peel and core the apples and chop into chunks. Put into the base of an 8-inch pie dish, sprinkle with the sugar, and add the cloves, if using.

Roll the dough into a sheet ⅛-inch thick and cut several strips to fit around the rim of your pie dish. Brush the rim of the dish with cold water and press the strips of dough firmly in place. Cut a circle of dough to form a lid, brush the dough rim with cold water, and press the top firmly down onto the edges. Trim off the excess dough. Flute the edges and scallop with the back of a knife. Brush the pie with beaten egg. Cut some leaves from the excess dough and use to decorate the pie. Cut a hole in the center. Brush with eggwash again.

Bake for 30 minutes until the apple is almost cooked; test with a skewer to make sure the apple is tender (the skewer should pierce it easily).

Meanwhile, make the custard filling. Whisk the egg and sugar together in a bowl, then mix in the cream and vanilla extract. Open up the hole in the center of the pie if necessary and pour in the custard mixture from a jug. Put the pie back into the oven for another 25 to 30 minutes or until the custard has set. Sprinkle the crust with a little superfine sugar and serve with lots of softly wipped cream.

Tarte Tatin

The ultimate French apple tart. The Tatin sisters ran a restaurant at Lamotte-Beuvron in Sologne at the beginning of the century. They created this tart, some say accidentally, but however it came about it is a triumph—soft, buttery caramelized apples (or you can also use pears) with crusty golden crust underneath. It is unquestionably my favorite French tart! You can even buy a special copper tatin especially for this tart.

. . . .

SERVES 6 TO 8

6 ounces Puff Pastry (page 132), rich Sweet Shortcrust Pastry Dough (page 294)

approx. 2¾ pounds Golden Delicious, Granny Smith, or McIntosh apples

8 tablespoons (1 stick) butter

1 cup superfine sugar

softly whipped cream, to serve

Preheat the oven to 425°F for puff pastry dough or 350°F for shortcrust dough.

First, roll out the dough into a round slightly larger than a heavy 8-inch tatin mold or copper or stainless steel sauté pan with low sides. Prick it all over with a fork and chill until needed.

Peel, halve, and core the apples. Melt the butter in the saucepan, add the sugar, and cook over medium heat for 4 to 5 minutes until it turns golden—fudge color. Put the apple halves in upright, packing them in very tightly side by side. (The apple halves have been arranged flat rather than upright in the photograph—another option.) Replace the pan over low heat and cook for about 30 minutes until the sugar and juice are a dark caramel color. Hold your nerve otherwise it will be too pale. Put into the oven for about 15 minutes.

Cover the apples with the dough and tuck in the edges. Put the pan into the oven for 25 to 30 minutes until the dough is cooked and the apples are soft. For puff pastry, reduce the temperature to 400°F after 10 minutes.

Remove from the oven and set aside to rest for 5 to 10 minutes or longer if you like. Put a plate over the top of the pan and flip the tart onto a deep serving plate. Watch out—this is a rather tricky operation because the hot caramel and juice can ooze out. Reshape the tart if necessary and serve warm with softly whipped cream.

DID YOU KNOW?

Apples have been growing in the wild since prehistoric times and were well known to the Phoenicians. They have been tempting us since the time of Adam and Eve.

Doctors and dentists no longer recommend an apple a day, because many of the modern cultivars are so sweet that they are considered injurious rather than beneficial to our teeth and overall health.

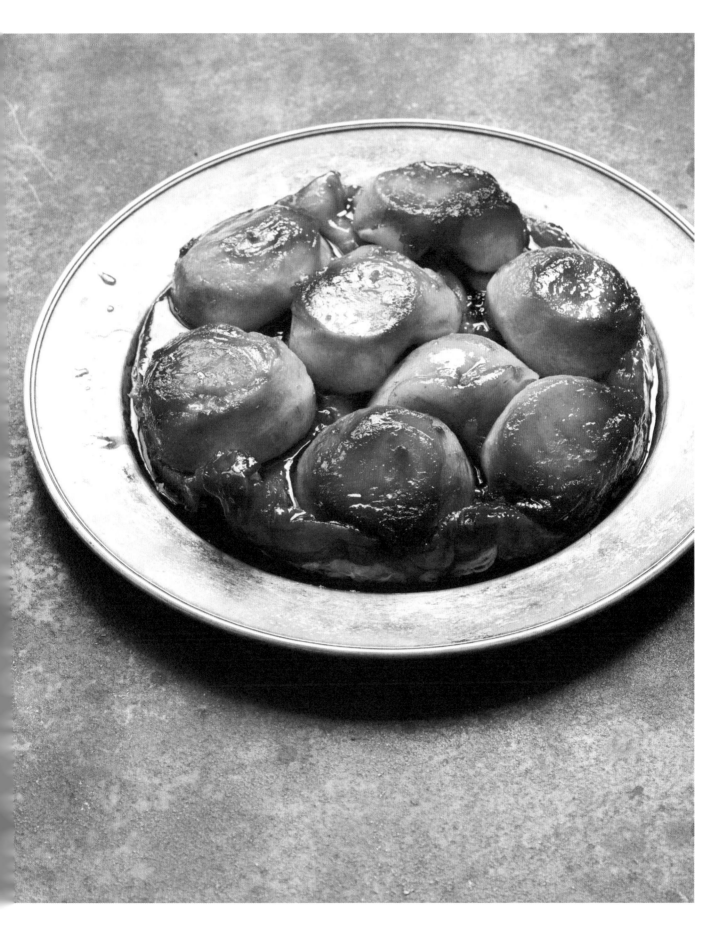

Casserole of Roast Pheasant with Apple & Calvados

This recipe smacks of the 1970s, but don't let that deter you—it's always a winner. It comes originally from Vallée d'Auge in Normandy, France where they have wonderful rich cream and delicious apples, an irresistible combination with gamey pheasant. Chicken or a guinea fowl also work really well in this recipe.

. . . .

SERVES 4

1 plump young pheasant, weighing approx. 1¾ to 2¼ pounds
sea salt and freshly ground black pepper
3 tablespoons butter
¼ cup Calvados
1 cup cream or ½ cup cream and ½ cup homemade chicken stock
Roux (page 267—optional)
3 to 4 sweet apples, such as Golden Delicious or McIntosh, peeled and cut into ¼-inch dice
watercress salad or sprigs of chervil, to garnish

Preheat the oven to 350°F.

Choose a Dutch oven or heavy pan with a lid, preferably oval, just large enough to fit the bird. Season the cavity, spread 3 teaspoons butter over the breast and legs of the pheasant, and place breast-side down in the dish. Leave it to brown over low heat for 5 to 6 minutes, turn over, and sprinkle with salt and freshly ground pepper. Cover with a tight-fitting lid and cook for 40 to 45 minutes. Check to see that the pheasant is cooked (there should be no trace of pink between the leg and the breast). Transfer the pheasant to a serving dish and keep warm in a low oven.

Carefully strain and degrease the juices in the dish. Bring to a boil, add the Calvados, and ignite with a match. Shake the pan and when the flames have subsided, add the cream or stock and cream. Reduce until the sauce thickens, stirring occasionally; season to taste. Cook the peeled and diced apple in the remaining butter over medium heat, stirring regularly for 4 to 5 minutes or until golden. Carve the pheasant and arrange on a hot serving dish or individual plates with the sauce and a watercress salad or a bunch of chervil.

Bramley Apple Snow

This is a simple, traditional featherlight pudding that I absolutely love. It's great with shortbread cookies or even Lady Fingers, and amazingly delicious for little effort. Windfall apples or can be used, just discard any bruised bits. This recipe has come down from my mother-in-law Myrtle Allen's family.

. . . .

SERVES 6

1 pound Bramley, Cortland, or Baldwin apples
approx. ¼ cup granulated sugar
1 to 2 tablespoons water
2 organic egg whites
cream, brown sugar, and shortbread cookies or Lady Fingers, to serve

Peel and core the apples, cut into chunks, and put into a saucepan. Add the sugar and water, cover, and cook over low heat for 8 to 10 minutes, stirring every now and then until the apples dissolve into a fluff. Rub through a nylon sieve or liquidize in a juicer or blender. Bramley apples can be very sour at the beginning of the season, so taste and add a little more sugar if it seems too tart.

Whisk the egg whites until stiffly whipped, then fold in gently. Pour into a pretty glass bowl, pop into the fridge, and serve well-chilled with cream and brown sugar and shortbread cookies.

Blood Sausage with Golden Delicious Applesauce

Irish black pudding is entirely different to traditional French blood sausage, but also marries well with both pommes purée or Golden Delicious sauce, plus maybe a drizzle of grainy mustard and cream. The combination of flavors has become a favorite.

. . . .

SERVES 4

extra virgin olive oil
4 pieces of blood sausage, approx.
  4 to 5 inches long
a little chopped flat-leaf parsley, to garnish

FOR THE GOLDEN DELICIOUS APPLE
SAUCE
1 pound Golden Delicious apples
approx. 2 tablespoons sugar

FOR THE POMMES DE TERRE PURÉE
1 pound floury potatoes
approx. ½ cup hot milk
3 tablespoons butter
1 to 2 organic egg whites
sea salt and freshly ground black pepper

First make the Golden Delicious Applesauce. Peel, quarter, and core the apples; cut the pieces into two and put them in a stainless steel or cast-iron saucepan with 1 to 2 tablespoons of water and sugar. Cover and cook over very low heat for 5 to 8 minutes until the apples break down into a fluff. Stir and taste for sweetness.

To make the Pommes de Terre Purée, boil the potatoes still in their jackets in a little boiling salted water. Peel immediately while hot, put through a ricer, then beat in the milk, egg whites, and butter. Season with salt and freshly ground black pepper. The purée should be light and fluffy.

Brush the slices of sausage with extra virgin olive oil. Cook gently in a pan over low to medium heat for 6 to 8 minutes, turning constantly until heated through.

To serve, spoon a generous helping of hot, pommes de terre purée onto a hot plate, and top with a piece of sausage and a dollop of hot Golden Delicious Sauce and maybe sprinkled with a little chopped parsley.

Raw Apple Muesli

This is right up there with oatmeal as the best and most nourishing breakfast ever. It's also super-delicious and can be made in minutes, even when you are semi-comatose in the morning. Choose ripe eating apples for this recipe—the proportion of apple to oatmeal should be equal. Taste and adjust as you wish. During the soft fruit season we crush strawberries, raspberries, loganberries, or tayberries and fold into the oatmeal instead of grated almonds. A few blackberries are delicious.

. . . .

SERVES 4

3 heaping tablespoons organic rolled oats
1 small sweet apple, such as Empire
approx. 1 teaspoon honey, depending on
  the tartness of the fruit
half-and-half and brown sugar, to serve

Measure out 6 tablespoons of water into a bowl and sprinkle the oatmeal on top. Let the oatmeal soak up the water while you grate the apple. A stainless steel grater is best for this job—use the largest side and grate the apple coarsely, skin and all. I grate through the core, but watch your fingers when you are coming close to the end. Be sure to pick out the dark seeds and discard.

Stir the honey into the oatmeal and then stir in the grated apple, taste, and add a little more honey if necessary. This will depend on how heavy you were on the oatmeal and how sweet the fruit is. Serve with half-and-half and soft brown sugar.

MEDLAR
Mespilus germanica DECIDUOUS, ZONES 4–9

Old-fashioned and utterly charming, many people won't even have heard of this delightful small deciduous tree, popular in mediaeval times. In my opinion it's well worth considering even for a suburban garden. You're unlikely to find these fruit on a supermarket shelf because they are too difficult to handle and virtually unknown to all but a handful of gourmet gardeners and cooks. A bowl of medlars looks so beautiful on the kitchen or dining room table and is always a subject of conversation. A member of the rose family it grows to about ten feet tall and gives me joy throughout the year. The leaves emerge in late spring, followed by pale pinkish flowers, reminiscent of dog roses which the bees seem to love. Bizarre, sputnik-shaped fruit, rosy rust to dusty brown in color, appear in early summer and ripen in autumn. We use them to make medlar butter or with crab apples to make jelly, both good with game. The leaves color divinely in autumn, red, orange, and bright crimson, so it certainly earns its place in my garden. It has a semi-weeping habit, so it provides a sheltered den for children to play in.

VARIETIES

Royal—Another popular variety with excellent flavor if smaller fruit.
Breda Giant—produces large fruit riepening in fall.
Sultan—large fruiting, heavy bearing tree, producing in spring.
Macrocarpa—large fruit growing on compact trees.

HOW TO GROW

Medlars are self-fertile so you only need one tree.

Plant in autumn. Allow 14½ to 20 feet between each tree, but one will be enough for most households. Mulch with well-rotted manure in mid-spring. Medlars tolerate most soils but do best in deep, fertile, well-drained soil. They like a warm, sheltered area, will tolerate some shade but a sunny spot is preferable. The medlar tree has a straggly habit and forms a droopy umbrella shape, but can be pruned to suit the space—the fruit resembles a flattened rosehip in appearance. Medlars really need pruning every year to maintain their shape. Mine has got very straggly, but do be careful because mature trees

My medlar tree is straggly but you can keep it pruned into a more pleasurable shape.

do not respond well to heavy pruning, so you need to prune them back gradually and be aware that they fruit on the ends of the branches.

PESTS AND DISEASES

Generally trouble-free, but the leaves may sometimes be attacked by caterpillars, if caught in time you can pick them off, at least on the lower branches. Sometimes they may get Hawthorn Leaf Spot which shows as multiple brown or purple spots, in which case gather up and burn affected leaves. Don't plant the tree in a crowded area, allow plenty of air circulation.

HARVESTING

Harvest in late autumn. The fruit is best eaten when it has softened, have turned brown and appear over-ripe—the term used is "bletted" from the French bletter "to make soft." There's a narrow window of opportunity here, so you'll need to harvest regularly or they go over and become too soft and rotten. To ripen, pick while firm, lay in a single layer in a timber box and leave to soften slowly over a couple of weeks, in a cool, dark shed.

GOOD FOR YOU...

In the Middle Ages, a syrup made from bletted medlars was used to treat intestinal disorders.

Women were recommended to eat them to prevent hemorrhages after childbirth.

DID YOU KNOW?

Medlars have a leathery russeted skin with an open calyx, which earns them their popular name in Ireland, "dog's arse." In France they seem to have come to the same conclusion where they are known as *cul de chien*—how funny is that?

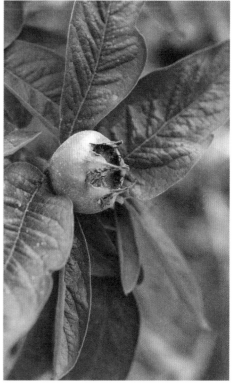

Beautiful flowers in spring and exotic fruit in the autumn mean that medlar deserves its space in the garden.

WHAT TO DO WITH A GLUT

We enjoy them most in jellies or preserves—medlar jelly alone is good if you have an abundance of fruit but we also love medlar and crab apple jelly or medlar cheese.

IN THE KITCHEN

Medlars have a curious flavor, and the ripest can be eaten when they are generally quite small, about the size of a flattened walnut. However, it depends on the variety, and some fruit can be larger. We use them in cooked preserves. A little medlar jelly is delicious whisked into a gravy for mutton or lamb and served with game or a fine roast of mutton.

The shape of the fruit earns medlar the popular name "dogs arse."

Windfall Apple & Medlar Butter

Serve with goose, duck, pork, or game or on scones or toast. Apples and medlar work well together. They are in season at the same time, and since you may only have a small quantity of medlars, the apples will make them go further.

MAKES 7 × 8-OUNCE JARS

4¼ cups sweet cider
2¼ pounds apples (perfect to use up windfalls)
2¼ pounds medlars
2½ cups granulated sugar
1 teaspoon ground cinnamon
¼ teaspoon ground cloves
½ teaspoon ground ginger
¼ teaspoon ground nutmeg

Put the cider in a large saucepan. Bring to a boil and reduce by half. Core the apples and chop into ½-inch dice. Quarter the medlars, then add both to the saucepan.

Bring back to a boil, cover, and simmer for about 30 minutes until the apples and medlars are completely soft. Purée through a food mill or press through a strainer. Return this purée to the saucepan. Add the sugar, cinnamon, cloves, ginger, and nutmeg. Bring to a boil and simmer for 35 to 40 minutes until thickened. Pour into sterilized jars immediately. Store for 4 to 5 months in a cool, dry pantry.

Roast Pheasant with Medlar & Crab Apple Jelly

This is a good way to use medlars when they are firm rather than bletted. Serve this delicious jelly with pheasant, grouse, pork, or coarse patés or goat cheese.

. . . .

SERVES 4

1 young, plump pheasant—we leave feet
   on but they can be removed
3 tablespoons butter
gravy made from 1¼ cups game or
   chicken stock
roast potatoes and buttered cabbage with
   thyme leaves, to serve

FOR THE MEDLAR AND CRAB APPLE JELLY
3 pounds medlars (firm not bletted)
1 pound crab or Granny Smith apples
2¼ cups granulated sugar (possibly more)
2 strips of lemon and juice of 1 lemon
1-inch piece of cinnamon stick
2 cloves

FOR THE FRESH HERB STUFFING
3 tablespoons butter
½ cup chopped onions
½ cup soft white bread crumbs
1 tablespoon chopped fresh herbs, such as
   parsley, thyme, chives, or marjoram
sea salt and freshly ground black pepper

To make the medlar and crab apple jelly, cut the medlar and the apples into similar sized pieces (no need to peel) and put in a stainless steel saucepan. Barely cover with water, bring to a boil, and cook for 15 to 20 minutes until soft. Pour into a jelly bag and leave to drip overnight. Don't squeeze the jelly through the bag or the juice will be cloudy.

The next day, measure the juice and allow 2¼ cups sugar for every 1¼ cups juice. Heat the sugar and add to the hot juice, then stir until dissolved. Add the strips of lemon and lemon juice. Add the spices and boil for 8 to 10 minutes until setting point is reached (see page 391). Remove the spices, pour into hot sterilized jars, and cover immediately. Makes 10 × 12-ounce jars. Keeps for at least 6 months, in a cool dry place.

Gut the pheasant if necessary and remove the "crop," which is at the neck end; wash and dry well.

To make the stuffing, melt the butter and cook the onions for 5 to 10 minutes until soft but not colored, then remove from the heat. Stir in the bread crumbs and herbs and season to taste. Unless you are about to cook the bird right away, let the stuffing cool completely before putting it into the bird.

Preheat the oven to 375°F.

Season the cavity with salt and freshly ground pepper and stuff the pheasant loosely. Truss with cotton string. Sprinkle the breast with salt and freshly ground pepper. Melt the butter and soak a square of cheesecloth in it. Wrap the pheasant completely in the cheesecloth. It will brown under the cheesecloth. Alternatively, just slather the legs and breast with soft butter.

Roast for about 1 ¼ hours. Test by pricking the leg at the highest point—the juices should just run clear. Remove the cheesecloth from the pheasant and keep warm on a serving dish while you make the gravy.

Serve with a little bowl of Medlar and Apple jelly, lots of gravy, some cabbage with thyme leaves, and roast potatoes.

MULBERRY *Morus* DECIDUOUS, ZONES 5-9

Ever since I came upon a mulberry tree in the garden of St Anthony's College in Oxford during the Oxford Food Symposium in the 1990s, I longed to plant a mulberry tree. The long, slim fruit are one of the most delicious things you'll ever taste, the flavor is a cross between a raspberry and blackcurrant. It's rare to find mulberries for sale even in a farm shop or at a farmers' market so it's worth planting if you have the space for this deciduous tree. We grow both black and white mulberries in the fruit garden.

VARIETIES

It's self-fertile so a single tree will be fine. There are three species: black—*morus nigra*, red—*morus rubra*, white—*morus alba*.

Look out for **Illinois Ever-bearing**, which produces delicious, almost seedless

Plant a mulberry bush so you can dance around it in spring and enjoy the sublime fruit in autumn.

fruit within three years.

Wellington is fairly readily available in good nurseries.

Carman, a cross between white and red has particularly delicious fruit.

HOW TO GROW

The mulberry likes a sheltered site and full sun. Plant it right away as it takes at least three years to produce fruit and some varieties take up to ten years, so choose very carefully, but it's worth waiting for.

PESTS AND DISEASES

Birds love mulberry fruits, so you may need to net or cover them. Slugs love them and can also strip the leaves. Use the usual deterrents (see page 626).

HARVESTING

Pick in late summer. Depending on variety, the fruit ripen over a couple of weeks, they are fragile and bleed easily and the juice stains, so do protect your clothes.

GOOD FOR YOU...

Mulberries are rich in phytonutrients. Studies have shown that consumption of mulberries has potential health benefits against cancer, some ageing and neurological diseases, inflammation, diabetes, and bacterial infections. They are a rich source of vitamin C and also contain small amounts of vitamins A and E. They are also a source of iron and other minerals like potassium, manganese, and magnesium and contain vitamins B and B6, niacin, riboflavin, and folic acid. The nutrients vary from one species to another but they are all highly nutritious.

WHAT TO DO WITH A GLUT

When the tree is established, you may well have a glut, can you imagine such a divine problem? They freeze well but you can also make jam, mulberry gin or vodka.

IN THE KITCHEN

Mulberries are sublime eaten freshly picked off the tree with cream just like raspberries, strawberries, loganberries, or blackberries. They can be substituted for all those berries in smoothies and virtually any recipe. They are also delicious with panna cotta, in crumbles or cobblers, and in salads. They make wonderful pies, jams, ice cream, sorbets, fools, and clafoutis.

DID YOU KNOW?

Silkworms feed on the leaves of the white variety—*Morus alba*. Black mulberries are thought to have the best flavor. In Turkey, I found delicious dried white mulberries in all the markets.

Mulberry Vodka or Gin

Save these boozy mulberries to serve with homemade ice cream or alongside roast duck or pigeon, so you get double value for this delicious fruit. We've had excellent results with both gin and vodka so use whichever one you have on hand.

. . . .

MAKES ABOUT 1 QUART

1¼ pounds black mulberries

3 cups superfine sugar

2½ cups vodka or gin

3 sweet geranium leaves (optional)

Put all the ingredients into a large mason jar for 3 to 4 months. Shake occasionally for the first week or two. Strain. Enjoy in small glasses.

Plums, blackberries, sloes, haws, or myrtle berries also make delicious liqueurs.

A Feather-light Sponge Cake with Mulberries

The addition of a little baking powder to this classic recipe results in the tenderest of sponge cakes. It will become a family favorite.

. . . .

SERVES 8 TO 10

butter, for greasing

3 large organic eggs

1 cup superfine sugar, plus extra to decorate

⅓ cup warm water

1¼ cups all-purpose flour, plus extra for dusting

1 teaspoon baking powder

FOR THE FILLING

12 ounces fresh mulberries: or sliced fresh strawberries, raspberries, loganberries, and maybe frosted redcurrants or kumquats or Green Gooseberry and Elderflower Compote (page 390) or homemade jam

1 cup softly whipped cream

Preheat the oven to 375°F. Grease and flour 2 × 8-inch round cake pans.

Separate the egg yolks from the whites. In a food mixer, whisk the yolks with the superfine sugar for 2 minutes and then add the warm water. Whisk until light and fluffy—this will take about 20 to 30 minutes. The mixture will have greatly increased in volume and should hold a figure of eight for a few seconds.

Sift the flour and baking powder into the mousse in batches and gently fold in. Whisk the egg whites until they hold a stiff peak. Fold them in very gently.

Divide the mixture between the pans and bake for 20 minutes. Remove from the pans and cool on a wire rack.

When cool, sandwich the two together with the mulberries, or the fruit of your choice, and whipped cream.

Sprinkle superfine sugar or confectioners' sugar over the top before serving.

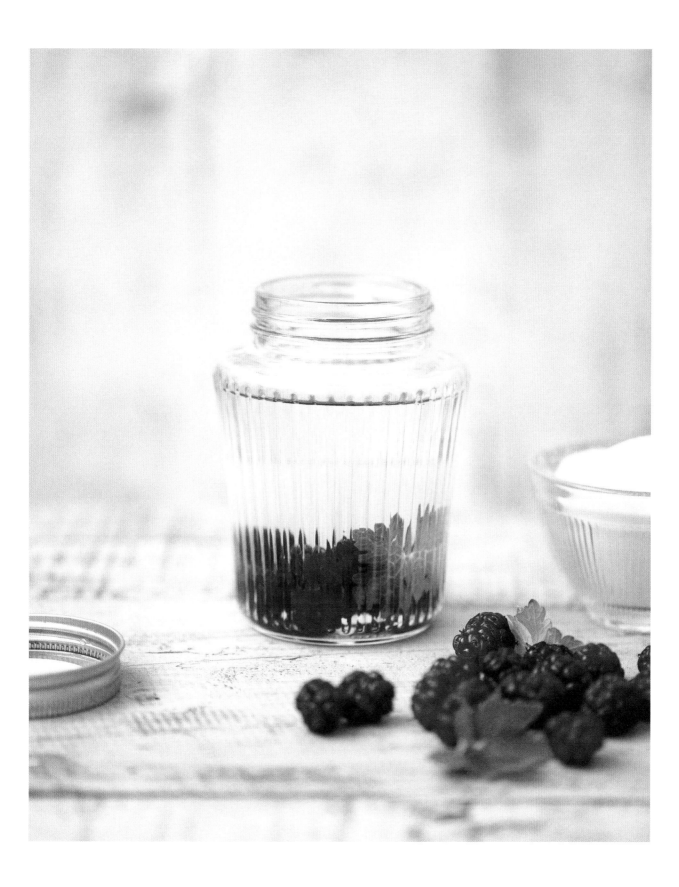

CHILEAN GUAVA

Myrtus ugni (Myrtle Berry, New Zealand cranberry), ZONES 6–10

I discovered this delightful and delicious evergreen shrub with cranberry-sized, dark red berries quite by accident in 1986. I had planted what I thought was a *Myrtus luma* in a boxwood circle in the center of the formal herb garden at Kinoith, in honor of my inspirational mother-in-law Myrtle Allen.

It sort of sat there not doing much for a couple of years but suddenly in late spring it was covered with a profusion of fragrant pale pink and white flowers shaped like Lily of the Valley. My gardener friend Jim Reynolds identified it as *Myrtus ugni*. I loved that by mistake I had a shrub that also has the most delicious wine-colored berries in autumn and early winter. I now know that it's called Chilean guava and is native to Chile and neighboring countries. Everyone should grow at least one *Myrtus ugni*. I've planted several more, both in the garden and in large terracotta pots around the school so the students can nibble on the berries and pick them in autumn to add, often till after Christmas, to salads. They fruit in winter, are delicious with game and the birds don't seem to bother them.

VARIETIES

Myrtus ugni is sold as a generic variety, but there is also a variegated form called Flambeau which is equally delicious and slightly hardier.

It's now being grown commercially again in Australia where it has been renamed Tazziberries, whereas in New Zealand they are called New Zealand cranberries, so watch out for tiny punnets of berries flown from the other side of the planet.

HOW TO GROW

Chilean guava needs moist, well-drained soil in a sheltered, sunny spot. They can be planted individually or as an edible hedge. They are self-fertile and can tolerate temperatures below -50°F. Keep pruned or allow to grow naturally untamed. You can grow from seed but it's best to buy a healthy specimen in a garden center.

CONTAINER GROWING

Choose a large pot (at least 4 gallons to start with) as you may want to transfer it into the ground after 5 to 6 years to prevent it becoming pot bound as then the berrying will be diminished.

Myrtus ugni in flower. We grow them in large terracotta pots around the school.

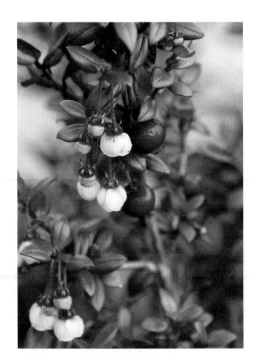

PESTS AND DISEASES

We haven't had a problem, birds are sort of interested but seem to prefer the haws and other berries available at the same time of year.

HARVESTING

The winey-red berries, $\frac{1}{3}$ to 2 inch diameter, can be picked over a two month period or longer, from the start of autumn and by a happy coincidence are in season with game.

GOOD FOR YOU...

The essential oil derived from the leaves is sometimes used for respiratory conditions as it clears congestion of the nasal tract and can help to relieve coughs and breathing troubles. It is also valued as an antioxidant, anti-cancer, anti-diabetic, anti-viral, anti-bacteria, anti-fungal. It is reputed to protect the liver and nervous system and also promotes thyroid health. It has been used traditionally in the treatment of malaria and to deter mosquitoes. A diluted chilean guava oil has been tested successfully in washing fruit and vegetables to reduce bacteria, instead of using chlorine or synthetic products.

WHAT TO DO WITH A GLUT

I've never had a glut because the berries can be picked over a two month period. I'm planning to grow an edible hedge, so perhaps I'll have a glut before too long. Apparently they make a delicious jam but I've never had enough to test a recipe, but do save some to make some chilean guava gin.

IN THE KITCHEN

The berries are tasty both raw and cooked. They are totally delicious fresh off the plant. We love them in salads, particularly with pheasant or guinea fowl. If you have enough they can also be used in a similar way to cranberries or blueberries. Add them to a fruit compote or make a cranberry-like sauce to accompany roast poultry or game. Leaves can be used to make tea and the dried, roasted seeds, can be used as a coffee substitute, depending on how desperate you are! The fresh or dried berries can of course be added to muffins (see below). The berries are also adorable on top of little buns with lemon glacé icing. One of our 12-week students decorated a Walnut Cake with Frosting with the berries, which made it look very festive for Christmas.

Everyone should have a Chilean guava plant—the berries are addictive and last for 2 to 3 months.

Chilean Guava Muffins

My sister, Blanaid Bergin, makes the yummiest muffins—seemingly in minutes. She usually makes them with blueberries but chilean guavas make a nice surprise.

MAKES 8

1¾ cups all-purpose flour
½ teaspoon salt
1 level tablespoon baking powder
⅔ cup superfine sugar
5 tablespoons butter
1 large organic egg, beaten
½ teaspoon vanilla extract
¾ cup milk
¾ cup chilean guavas, blueberries, or raspberries
confectioners' sugar, for dusting

Preheat the oven to 400°F and line a 8-hole muffin pan with muffin liners.

Sift the flour, salt, and baking powder into a bowl. Stir in the sugar. Rub in the butter until it looks like bread crumbs. Combine the beaten egg, vanilla extract, and milk and add to the dry mixture. Combine with a fork to give a wet consistency. Fold in the fruit gently. Spoon into the muffin liners. Bake for 20 to 25 minutes until well-risen and golden. Cool on a wire rack and dust with confectioners' sugar. Best eaten fresh, otherwise store in an airtight container and enjoy sooner rather than later.

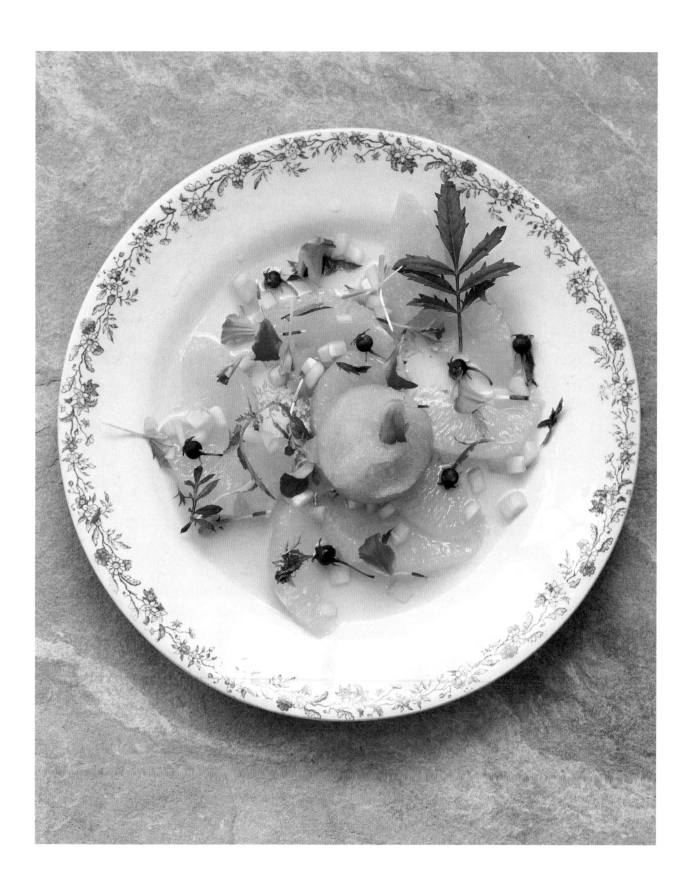

Salad of Oranges, Cucumber, Marigolds & Chilean Guavas with Lemon Verbena Granita

Another magical combination dreamed up by my brother Rory, it looks divinely pretty and each mouthful just flits across the tongue. We use *Tagetes Tenufolia—Red Gem*, delicate leaves, and pretty little flowers..

SERVES 4

4 oranges, carefully segmented and
    seeds removed
2 tablespoons peeled and very finely
    diced cucumber, discarding seeds
2 teaspoons honey
2 to 4 teaspoons lemon juice
1 tablespoon tiny marigold leaves
1 tablespoon chilean guavas
 2 teaspoons marigold petals

FOR THE LEMON VERBENA GRANITA
3 handfuls of lemon verbena leaves
1 cup granulated sugar
1 pint cold water
freshly squeezed juice of 3 lemons

To make the Lemon Verbena Granita, put the lemon verbena leaves, sugar and cold water in a pan. Place over a moderate heat. Stir occasionally to dissolve the sugar and bring it to a simmer. Simmer gently for 2 minutes. Remove from the heat and leave to cool completely. You will end up with a pale green syrup.

Add the freshly squeezed lemon juice to the syrup and right before your eyes you will see the green tinge leaving your syrup. Strain out the leaves through a sieve pressing on the leaves to extract as much flavour as possible.

Place the strained syrup in a wide container and freeze until set. Remove from the freezer and break up the ice with a fork. It will look like a slushy mess. Refreeze and repeat the process twice more, three times if you can bear it, and eventually you will end with the distinctive shard-like consistency of a granita. Refreeze, covered, until you are ready to serve it.

Place the orange segments and diced cucumber in a bowl and add the honey and lemon juice. Stir very gently to mix. Be careful not to break up the orange segments. Taste and correct the sweetness if necessary with a few more drops of lemon juice. Add the marigold leaves and chilean guavas to the bowl, mixing them in gently. Cover and chill until ready to serve.

To serve, divide the orange mixture and its juices between 4 chilled shallow bowls or plates. Place 2 teaspoons of granita on top of the fruit and finally sprinkle with the marigold petals. Serve immediately.

PASSION FRUIT *Passiflora* PERENNIAL, ZONES **10–12**

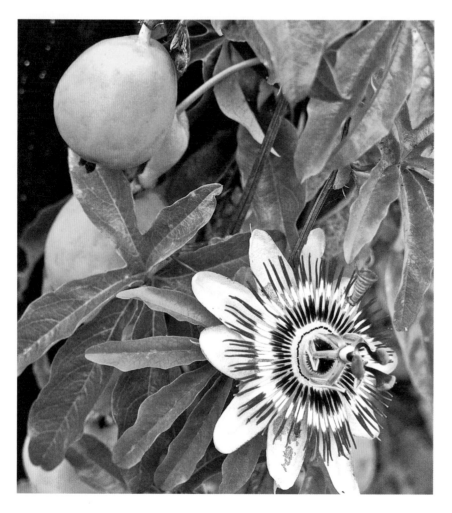

Passiflora caerulea—*double bonus giving fruit and spectacular passion flowers.*

Passiflora caerulea—Produces orange oval-shaped fruit, juicy and delicious but not nearly as good as the imported passiflora edulis which one buys in a market.

Passiflora alata—medium sized orange-to-yellow fruit.

HOW TO GROW

Although passion fruit can grow and fruit outside, they will do better in a greenhouse, tunnel or conservatory. Of course you can grow from seed but it's easier to source a healthy organic plant from a specialist nursery.

Passion flower is not too fussy about soil. Moderately fertile, well-drained is good. It likes full sun but will also survive in dappled shade. Mulch well to protect the roots and keep moist. Prune off surplus or dead growth at the end of the season.

CONTAINER GROWING

You can indeed grow a *passiflora caerulea* in a large pot with humus-rich soil on a terrace or roof garden. Provide a strong support for the plant's tendrils to to climb up. Feed every few weeks and keep well-watered. If you are growing passion fruit in a conservatory it's best to put it outside for the summer. Bring indoors in late autumn and winter.

PESTS AND DISEASES

If you buy a plant check it carefully for any pests or diseases before you bring it home. Watch your passion fruit plants during the year, particularly indoors, as they can develop cucumber mosaic virus. If they do develop this disease, it's best to

I've grown passion fruit both inside the greenhouse and outside on an east-facing courtyard wall. It's a climbing vine so give it plenty of support or plant beside a fence, on an arch or allow it to romp over a garden shed.

Passion fruit comes from a large family that includes several hundred species, many native to South and Central America, Mexico, Brazil, and the West Indies, but there are also some species that are native to Australia. The Spanish were the first to bring them to Europe.

The passion fruit originally got its name from the sixteenth-century missionaries in South America who used the spectacular flower to tell the story of the passion of Christ. The flowers have three stigmas which represent nails; five anthers—the wounds; the corona—a crown of thorns; the petals around the outer rim—the disciples and apostles.

SPECIES

Passiflora edulis—Tropical plant that needs heat with white and purple flowers, will grow in a greenhouse.

dispose of them by burning. Passion fruit can be attacked by red spider mite, white fly, and mealy bug, we use biological controls for these pests indoors.

HARVESTING

Pick the fruit when bright orange or green—depending on the variety—and tender to the touch, when they will detach easily from the plant. The flavor is best when they are slightly wrinkled.

GOOD FOR YOU...

A powerhouse of nutrients, passion fruit is high in vitamins A and C and rich in potassium, calcium, iron, and magnesium.

It has been, and is still is, used as an herbal medicine by indigenous tribes in Latin America, as the leaves make a calming sedative. The fruit was used as a heart tonic and to make *maracuja grande*, a favorite drink used to treat asthma, bronchitis, and whooping cough. In other areas like Peru, the juice is used to treat urinary infections and as a diuretic.

IN THE KITCHEN

We add the fragrant seeds of passion fruit to mousses, ice cream, frostings, fruit salads, and lemonades or just scoop them out of the skins with a spoon to enjoy their perfumed flavor. Passion

fruit and mango are a marriage made in heaven and the favorite topping for a pavlova in Australia and New Zealand.

The reality is that *Passiflora caerulea* is much less flavorful than *passiflora edulis*, best when the skin is wrinkly rather than smooth. Nonetheless it is fun to grow the Passiflora vine even if only for the beautiful flowers.

To make **Passion Fruit and Mango Compote** for 4 to 6, peel 2 ripe mangoes and slice or chop the flesh. Put in a bowl, add the seeds and juice of 2 passion fruit, 2 to 3 tablespoons of fresh lime juice, and sugar to taste. Delicious on its own with ice cream or softly whipped cream.

Meringue Roulade with Passion Fruit & Mango

Roulade was definitely the "hot dessert" of the 90s. It's brilliantly versatile, it can be filled with a myriad of fruit, ripe berries, kiwi, and even lemon curd. Rhubarb or blackcurrants are particularly good because they cut the sweetness.

SERVES 10

4 organic egg whites
1 cup superfine sugar
confectioners' sugar
sweet cicely, to garnish (optional)

FOR THE MANGO AND PASSION FRUIT SAUCE

1 large ripe mango
4 passion fruit
1 to 2 tablespoons freshly squeezed lime juice
1 to 2 tablespoons superfine sugar

FOR THE FILLING

1 large ripe mango, peeled and thinly sliced
2 passion fruit
1¼ cups whipped cream

First make the roulade. Preheat the oven to 350°F.

Put the egg whites in the spotlessly clean bowl of a food mixer. Break up with the clean, dry whisk and then add all the superfine sugar in one go. Whisk at full speed for 4 to 5 minutes until the meringue holds a stiff peak.

Line an 8 × 12-inch Swiss roll pan with foil. Brush lightly with a non scented oil such as sunflower or arachide. Spread the meringue gently over the pan with a palette knife (it should be quite thick and bouncy). Bake for 15 to 20 minutes.

Put a sheet of foil on the work surface and turn the roulade onto it. Remove the base foil and leave the meringue to cool.

Now make the mango and passion fruit sauce. Peel the mango, chop the flesh, and purée in a food processor. Put into a bowl, add the passion fruit seeds and juice, then add freshly squeezed lime juice and sugar to taste. Cover and chill.

Put the sliced mango and passion fruit seeds and juice into a bowl, and toss gently.

To assemble, turn the roulade onto a sheet of silicone paper dusted with confectioners' sugar. Spread two-thirds of the cream over the roulade, cover with a layer of fruit, but keep a little for decoration. Tightly roll up the roulade and tansfer carefully onto a serving dish. Top with piped rosettes of cream and the reserved fruit. Garnish with sweet cicely, dredge with confectioners' sugar and serve.

Lemon Polenta Cake with Passion Fruit Curd & Crème Frâiche (Gluten-Free)

This is a delicious, moist, and fresh tasting cake that keeps really well. It is Californian in origin and is great served as an afternoon snack or as a dessert served with a few fresh summer berries and a blob of crème fraîche. You can also slather the passion fruit curd over scones or brioche. The passion fruit curd is a super recipe to use your own passion fruit—but expensive if you have to buy the fruit.

. . . .

SERVES 8 TO 10

16 tablespoons butter (2 sticks), softened, plus extra for greasing
rice flour, for dusting
1 cup superfine sugar
2 cups ground almonds
1 teaspoon vanilla extract
3 large organic eggs, lightly beaten
grated zest of 2 lemons and juice of 1
1 cup fine cornmeal (polenta)
1 teaspoon gluten-free baking powder
pinch of salt
softly whipped cream or crème frâiche, to serve

FOR THE PASSION FRUIT CURD (MAKES 1½ × 8-OUNCE SMALL JARS)

10 ripe passion fruit
2 large organic eggs, plus 2 large organic egg yolks
¼ cup superfine sugar—amount of sugar can vary depending on sweetness of the passion fruit
7 tablespoons butter

Preheat the oven to 325°F. Brush a 9-inch springform cake pan with a little melted butter and flour the pan with rice flour. Cut out a round of parchment paper for the base of the pan.

In a large mixing bowl, beat the butter until pale and soft. Add the superfine sugar and beat until light and creamy. Stir in the ground almonds and vanilla extract. Add the eggs, a little at a time, beating thoroughly before adding the next bit. Fold in the lemon zest and lemon juice, polenta, gluten-free baking powder, and salt. Pour the mixture into the prepared pan and bake for 50 minutes or until deep golden and a skewer comes out clean. Let cool on a wire rack.

Meanwhile, make the passion fruit curd. Halve the passion fruit, scoop out the seeds, put into a food processor, and blend for a few seconds. Strain through a nylon sieve.

Whisk the eggs and egg yolks. Put the butter into a saucepan over very low heat with the sugar, then gently whisk in the eggs and passion fruit juice. Stir until the mixture thickens.

Pour into sterilized jars. Store in the fridge for up to 2 weeks.

Split the cake in half with a sharp serrated knife, spread with a little passion fruit curd, and sandwich the bases of the cake together.

Serve cut into slices with a blob of softly whipped cream or crème frâiche.

PHYSALIS
Physalis peruviana ANNUAL (CAN ALSO BE PERENNIAL)

Fun and easy to grow, cape gooseberries are not a kitchen essential but hugely decorative with pretty yellow flowers with a black center, and surprisingly delicious when home grown. They are also known by several other names including inca berry, physalis, and ground or winter cherry.

We've been growing them successfully in the greenhouse for years. They grow about 3 feet tall and have straw-colored, papery husks as opposed to their bright orange relatives, the Chinese lanterns. From the *Solanaceae* family they are also cousins of the tomatillo (see page 216) which come from Mexico and produce much larger green and purply fruit—*Physalis ixocarpa*.

VARIETIES

We grow just one type which doesn't have a name apart from Cape Gooseberry.

HOW TO GROW

They aren't particularly hardy so we find they grow best under glass. We treat them similarly to tomatoes, sow at the same time, and only get a decent drop when sown in the greenhouse. We start them in 3½-inch pots as with the tomatoes. You may want to provide support as they have a straggly growing habit, we find that training them up strings like tomatoes works well, the plant can be fanned out onto a few strings, remove some shoots. Give at least 3 feet of space. They will grow quite successfully in pots in the conservatory during the winter.

CONTAINER GROWING

You may want to provide a little bamboo frame to support the plant which can become quite straggly.

PESTS AND DISEASES

We find that they are pretty pest resistant and disease free.

HARVESTING

They are ready for harvesting in late summer, when the yellow fruit has swollen inside and the papery husks have changed from green to the color of fresh straw. Snip off the fruit, they keep well for several weeks in their sheaths which are inedible.

Home-grown physalis berries will be deliciously bittersweet, unlike the cape

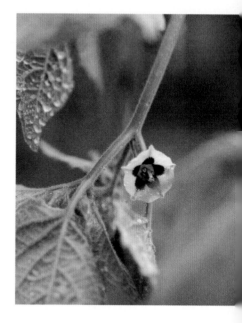

The pretty flowers are yet another reason to grow physalis.

gooseberries you can buy which are often completely tasteless. We get a prolific crop in the greenhouse which continues to yield fruit into early winter.

WHAT TO DO WITH A GLUT

If you have a glut, and we sometimes do because they crop brilliantly in the greenhouse, make jam or jelly, which is called Tippari. The fruit can also be dried.

DID YOU KNOW?

The *solanaceae* family is related to the potato. Physalis is native to South America but it has been cultivated in England since the late eighteenth century, and in the region of the Cape of Good Hope in South Africa since the early nineteenth century, where it was grown by the early settlers. The French call it *amour en cage*, love in a cage, how cute is that?

IN THE KITCHEN

Cape gooseberries are so pretty, we use them in lots of ways, in both sweet and savory dishes. Remove the husks and pop into salads, either whole or halved, in the same way as tomatoes.

We also peel back the papery husks and twist them above the fruit, then dip them in a pale caramel, so they have a crackly exterior, or in white fondant or dark chocolate. They make delightful decorations on cakes or can be served as a petit four to serve with a cup of expresso to round off a special meal. They also make a delicious (if seedy!) simple sauce to serve with ice cream. Just remove the husk and stew with a very little water and freshly squeezed lemon juice.

You'll need to provide some support for the physalis vines to grow.

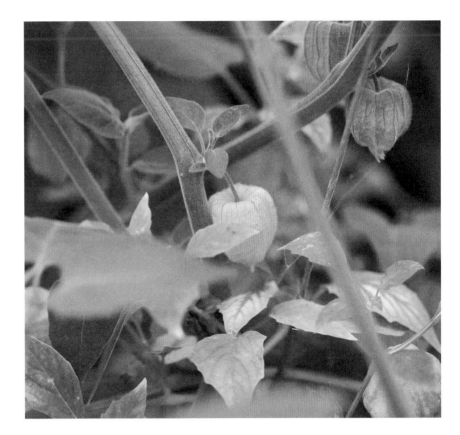

Physalis Jelly

This is called Tippari in South Africa, where they make copious amounts of both jam and jelly from the abundant fruit.

2¼ pounds physalis—or whatever quantity you can manage
juice of 2 lemons
about 5 cups granulated sugar

Remove the husks and halve the fruit. Barely cover with water in a stainless steel saucepan and cook for 5 to 6 minutes until soft. Strain through a nylon sieve and measure the juice.

Add the lemon juice and 2¼ cups sugar to every 2¼ cups juice. Return to a boil and cook for 5 to 6 minutes until set.

Pour into sterilized jars, cover, and store in a cool place for up to three months.. Enjoy with goat cheese or whatever else you fancy.

Cucumber, Physalis & Mint Salad

A super recipe to use your physalis, the sweetness of the fruit is delicious with the cucumber and fresh mint.

SERVES 4 TO 6

1 cucumber
sea salt flakes and freshly ground black
    pepper
15 physalis/cape gooseberries
2 tablespoons freshly squeezed lemon
    juice
1 tablespoon honey, mixed flower
fresh spearmint leaves, shredded, plus
    whole leaves to garnish

Halve the cucumber lengthwise. Scoop out the seeds and cut one half at an angle. Cut the other half lengthwise and slice into ¼-inch thick pieces at an angle. Put into a bowl. Season with sea salt flakes and freshly ground pepper.

Dehusk and halve the physalis, then add to the bowl.

Mix the lemon juice and honey together. Drizzle over the cucumber and physalis. Add some shredded mint and season to taste.

Sprinkle with whole mint leaves and serve.

Almond Cake with Physalis & Angelica

We serve tiny slices of this delicious moist cake with a cup of China tea or espresso coffee.

SERVES 10

½ cup melted butter, plus extra for
    greasing
⅔ cup all-purpose flour, plus extra
    for dusting
1 cup ground almonds
1 cup confectioners' sugar
3 large organic egg yolks
10 physalis
4½ to 5½ ounces Candied Angelica
    (page 429), cut into little diamonds

FOR THE ICING

1½ cups confectioners' sugar
1½ tablespoons freshly squeezed lemon
    juice

Preheat the oven to 350°F. Grease a 7-inch round pan with shallow sides evenly with melted butter and dust with a little flour (a pop-up base is handy but is not essential).

Mix the ground almonds, confectioners' sugar, and flour into a bowl. Make a well in the center, add the egg yolks and the cooled melted butter, and stir until all the ingredients are thoroughly mixed. Spread the cake evenly in the prepared pan, make a little hollow in the center, and tap on the worktop to release any large air bubbles. Bake for 20 minutes. It should still be moist but cooked through. Let it sit in the pan for 5 to 6 minutes before unmolding turning onto a wire rack. Set aside to cool.

To make the icing, sift the confectioners' sugar into a bowl, then mix to a thickish smooth icing with the strained lemon juice. Pile onto the cake using a palette knife dipped in the boiling water and dried to spread it gently over the top and sides of the cake.

Twist the papery skin husks of the physalis upward to expose the fruit. Decorate with the physalis and little diamonds of angelica.

APRICOTS

Prunus armeniaca PERENNIAL, ZONES 4–9

As it becomes increasingly difficult to find perfectly ripe fruit at the peak of perfection in our supermarkets, it's really worth considering planting a few "semi-exotics" in your garden or greenhouse. Apricots, like pretty much all stone fruit, do best in a greenhouse or tunnel in our cool UK climate, although they can fruit on a sheltered south-facing, preferably brick, wall. They can easily be grown outdoors throughout most of the United States. When you pick the fruit straight from the trees on a warm summer's day, you'll remember what an apricot should and can taste like—juicy and sublime. Choose the cultivar really carefully, many varieties have been bred specially to crop reliably in cooler climates. As a tree they can grow between 85 to 130 feet tall.

VARIETIES

Alfred—Traditional hardy variety with medium fruits and juicy orange flesh. Self-fertile, doesn't need a pollinator.
Tomcot—Good for a cool climate, crops early midsummer and produces large orange apricots with a crimson blush.
Moorpark—Another late cropper.
Wilson Delicious—consistantly large yields of sweet yellow fruit.

DWARF

Garden Annie—self-fertile genetic dwarf, medium-to-large fruit with bright yellow skin.

HOW TO GROW

Choose both the cultivar and the situation carefully. The variety should be suited to your local climate. One can grow from a seed, but my recommendation is to buy a few healthy saplings that will have been grafted onto a rootstock from a good garden center.

In our climate, apricots do best in a greenhouse.

They flourish best in deep, rich, fertile soil, preferably slightly alkaline (pH 6 to 7) and well drained. Dig in a bucket of well-rotted farmyard manure or humus a few weeks before planting.

Plant during the dormant season in autumn or early spring. Ours are planted in a greenhouse, as apricots flower very early (with pale pinkish blossom), so are susceptible to frost. Cover with fleece or polythene to protect the flowers, but remove during the day to allow bees and pollinating insects to reach the flowers. This may sound daunting but in fact it's very simple and rewarding. Find a soft artist's or child's paintbrush, a cotton wool bud will also work. Choose a warm sunny day, best around noon.

When the fruits are the size of a hazelnut, remove any misshapen fruit or anything growing too close to the wire or wall, and allow 40 to 50 inches between each plant so they develop freely.

Keep well-watered and mulch with well-rotted manure or compost in spring. Feed with a general purpose compost in spring. Plants grown in pots or on dwarf rootstocks may need the addition of some pelleted chicken manure. Train, depending on the shape you desire.

PESTS AND DISEASES

Compared to peaches, apricots are less susceptible to leaf curl. They can suffer from die-back of branches in summer, caused by the fungus Entypa lata, which can be caused by a wound from pruning, so that large branches can suddenly die. Avoid winter pruning, prune when the sap is flowing and the buds are swelling.

HARVESTING

Depending on the variety, the fruit will be ready to harvest individually from midsummer onwards. Pick carefully to avoid bruising and enjoy straight from the tree.

GOOD FOR YOU...

Apricots have vitamins E, C, and B6. They are high in fiber. They are known to relieve constipation.

WHAT TO DO WITH A GLUT

We make sublime apricot jam and pies from damaged or misshapen fruit. We have also dried some successfully both in a dehydrator and on wire racks in the greenhouse. They are darker in color than the commercial apricots which are treated with sulphur dioxide.

IN THE KITCHEN

The apricots one buys are so often a disappointment, but even if underripe they can be transformed into something

DID YOU KNOW?

Apricots are thought to have originated in Armenia—indeed the Greeks referred to them as the "Armeniam plum"—but there seems to be some confusion as others say they originated in China. The Italian liqueur Amaretto and Amaretti biscotti are flavored with extract of apricot kernels. The FSA have issued a warning advising people to avoid apricot kernels, because large quantities can be fatal, but there have also been reports of people experiencing cyanide-like side effects from smaller amounts.

We loved driving through the apricot orchards of Cappadocia in Turkey—the largest producer of apricots in the world.

delicious by poaching in a sweet geranium syrup. For 1 pound apricots, use 1 cup sugar to ¼ cup water and 4 to 6 large leaves of *Pelargonium graveolens*. Poach the pitted fruit for 3 to 4 minutes until soft. The compote will keep for several weeks in your fridge. Delicious for breakfast with plain yogurt, as a dessert, or along with vanilla ice cream.

Apricots also roast brilliantly—just sprinkle the halves with sugar and roast in a hot 250°F oven for 15 to 20 minutes or until beginning to stick at the edges.

Apricots are super versatile and are a wonderful addition to many sweet and savory dishes. If you have enough, add a few pieces of ripe apricot to appetizer salads in summer, particularly those with mozzarella and some toasted hazelnuts. Dried apricots are gorgeous in stews and tagines, or stuffed with sweet or savory fillings. Don't waste a single one of your precious crop—even slightly bruised fruit can be used in apricot jam.

Spiced Fruit Preserve

This spiced fruit preserve keeps for months. You'll find lots of ways to use it. We find it perks up oatmeal, rice, and is delicious with cold hams or bacon. Serve a little alongside a rich chocolate cake.

MAKES 2 CUPS

½ cup golden raisins
½ cup muscatel raisins
½ cup currants
½ cup dried apricots, sliced into pieces
¾ cup granulated sugar
1 Ceylon cinnamon stick
1 star anise
4 cardamom pods
1 ounce candied peel (page 294), chopped

Cover the dried fruit with warm water. Let soak and plump up for 3 to 4 hours.

Put the sugar and ¾ cup of water into a saucepan, then add the cinnamon, star anise, and cracked cardamom pods. Bring to a boil and simmer for 4 to 5 minutes or until the syrup thickens. Drain the fruit, then add to the syrup with the chopped candied peel. Simmer gently for 2 to 3 minutes. Keeps for 6 months or more.

Chicken & Apricot Stew with Gentle Spices

We use chicken thighs for this recipe, but of course white meat could also be used. Children also love this mildly spiced curry. The apricots add a fruity sweetness that lifts the stew deliciously.

. . . .

SERVES 6

1¼ cups dried apricots

½ to ¾ teaspoon dried chile flakes or Aleppo pepper

1 teaspoon ground cumin

1 teaspoon ground coriander

4 cloves

4 green cardamom pods, lightly crushed

1 tablespoon garlic, crushed

¼ cup water

1 tablespoon grated fresh ginger

¼ cup sunflower oil

2-inch cinnamon stick

1½ cups finely chopped onions

1½ teaspoons salt

2¾ pounds boneless, skinless chicken thighs, diced into ½-inch pieces

10 cherry tomatoes, peeled and quartered

2 tablespoons concentrated tomato paste mixed with ½ cup water

3 tablespoons coarsely chopped cilantro

Rice Pilaf (page 287), to serve

Soak the apricots overnight in 2 cups cold water, or if you are in a hurry soak them in hot water for 2 to 3 hours.

To make the masala, combine the pepper flakes, cumin, coriander, cloves, cardamom, garlic, and ginger in a small bowl. Add ¼ cup of water and stir to make a spice paste.

Heat the oil in a large sauté pan over medium heat and add the cinnamon. Add the chopped onions and salt. Cover and cook for 4 to 5 minutes until the onion is a little soft. Stir in the spice masala. Add the chicken, toss to coat, and cook for 4 to 5 minutes. Add the apricots with their soaking liquid, quartered cherry tomatoes, and tomato paste.

Cover and simmer for about 30 minutes until the chicken is cooked through. You may need to reduce the liquid by removing the lid halfway through the cooking.

Season to taste. Serve in a warm bowl, sprinkled with lots of chopped fresh cilantro. We serve it with rice pilaf and a green salad.

CHERRIES
prunus avium DECIDUOUS, ZONES 4–9

What bliss to have a couple of cherry trees. If you have the space, plant several, a mixture of dessert and cooking varieties so you can enjoy them fresh and cooked, in a cherry pie or jam. They are beautiful in blossom and a joy to behold when covered with fruit. They can be fan-trained as a cordon, against a west, southwest or even north-facing wall.

VARIETIES

There are many to choose from and it is crucial to choose varieties that will pollinate or are self-pollinating. Sour cherries are all self-fertile, producing fruit from a single tree.

SWEET (*PRUNUS AVIUM*) DESSERT
May Duke—Fruits early, even on a north wall, though not as early as the name suggests, usually mid-summer. Partly self-fertile.
Bing—Mid-season, another dark red

bittersweet cherry in season from early to late summer. Not self-fertile.
Stella—Dark red fruit, fruits in summer. Self-fertile.

SOUR (*PRUNUS CERASUS*) COOKING
Morello—Dark red color, bittersweet flavor. Ripens mid to late summer. Self-fertile.
Montmorency— Well-known variety of sour cherry lighter red in color. Used widely in the US and Canada for cherry pies. Self-fertile.
North Star—sturdy trees produce heavy crops of bright red fruit.

HOW TO GROW

Choose suitable varieties for your area, and order healthy plants on Colt or Mahaleb rootstock from a good nursery. Some sweet cherries need pollinating partners others are self-fertile. Plant from winter to late spring. Cherries flourish

in deep, fertile, well-drained soil with a pH of 6.5 to 6.7. They will not thrive in sandy, shallow soil and prefer full sun, although they can tolerate some shade.

The tart or sour varieties tend to be smaller in size, but hardier and less susceptible to disease. Allow enough space between trees—13 feet between dwarf trees—and at least twice that between standard trees.

Before you plant a fan-trained tree, install the necessary support. Allow 14 to 18 feet between fan-trained trees.

Mulch the trees to help retain moisture should you get a good summer!

Cherries flower early in mid-to-late spring and are susceptible to wind and cold, so you might want to cover them with fleece at night, but uncover during the day so the insects can pollinate the blossoms. If you have a poly tunnel and can allow the space for a 10-foot tall tree, you will be rewarded with a bumper crop virtually every year.

PESTS AND DISEASES

Birds are the main problem, they LOVE cherries, so you will need to net the tree unless you have enough to share.

Bacterial Canker and silver leaf are the two main problems—to avoid these we prune them the trees in early spring, just as the sap is starting to flow and when the buds are swelling, rather than in the dormant season. The pruning cuts heal more quickly and there's less chance for disease to set in.

Heavy rain at harvesting times usually results in fruit splitting. Watch the weather forecast so harvest as soon as possible. Split fruit can be used in jams and pies.

A profusion of blossom on a Morello cherry tree.

Stella is self-fertile and will produce lots of dark red fruit in summer.

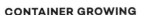
A tempting crop of cherries ready for picking.

CONTAINER GROWING

A cherry tree can grow happily in a large pot or half-barrel in well prepared soil. Choose a dwarf variety like *Stella* (compact, self-fertile).

HARVESTING

Pick the cherries as they ripen; it's best to snip off with scissors. They will keep for a week or more. Don't pile them too high or they will bruise. Store in a fridge or cold room.

Standard trees can produce 28 to 48 pounds of cherries in a good year, so it is well worthwhile making space for a sweet cherry.

GOOD FOR YOU...

Sweet and sour cherries are bursting with goodness. They are low in calories and an excellent source of potassium, manganese, significant amounts of iron and phosphorus, minerals, and calcium.

Sour cherries in particular are an excellent source of vitamins C and K, B6, and pantothenic acid (B5), a good source of thiamine and riboflavin, and a little niacin, folate, and some vitamin A.

Cherry juice contains melatonin, helps with jet lag and enhances the immune system.

They are high in antioxidants, like anthocyanins and cyanidin, plus useful amounts of soluble fiber. Recent research has shown that they may play a role in protection against cancer, also heart disease, diabetes, and Alzheimer's.

Research shows they have anti-inflammatory properties—which may be why cherries and cherry juice are used as a natural remedy for gout.

WHAT TO DO WITH A GLUT

What bliss to have a glut. A basket of fresh cherries will enchant your friends and gain you new ones. Make lots of cherry jam from the bitter varieties. Cherries freeze well for pies, sauces, and, of course, jams and jellies. Unripe, bitter cherries can also be frozen and cooked later. Pickled cherries are also really worthwhile, as is cherry liqueur.

IN THE KITCHEN

Sweet cherries are best eaten raw, but choose the tart cherries for pieces, sauces, tarts, cakes, jams, jellies, liqueurs, and pickling. You'll need to remove the pits from the cherries for some recipes so here's a tip: Find a paper clip, insert into the stalk end of the cherry, rotate, and lift out the seed. You can also do this by pushing up with a straw from the base. If you do it over the top of a bottle, the seeds will fall into the bottle. The latter is a little more wasteful, but also works well.

During cherry season I substitute cherries in several of our staple recipes: Lemon Squares, Tuscan Plum Tart, in crumbles, and add them to apple pies, or go all out and make a cherry pie. You'll need to add a little cornstarch with the sugar to thicken the juices somewhat. Black Forest Gateau is probably the most famous, or infamous, cherry cake, depending on how or when it is made, but it can be totally delicious. You may like to add some kirsch to the custard.

Cherries also add a delicious note to salads or what could be cuter than a whole cherry on an frosted cupcake?

Morello Cherry Pie

This pie dough is made by the creaming method so people who are convinced that they suffer from "hot hands" don't have to worry about rubbing in the butter. We like to cook the cherries whole so there will be lots of pits to play "he loves me, he loves me not..."

SERVES 8 TO 12

FOR THE BREAK-ALL-THE-RULES
PASTRY DOUGH

16 tablespoons butter (2 sticks)

¼ cup superfine sugar

2 large organic eggs

2½ cups all-purpose flour, preferably
   unbleached

FOR THE FILLING

2 to 2¾ pounds fresh Morello or
   Montmorency cherries, depending on
   how much fruit you'd enjoy

1 to 2 tablespoons Kirsch (optional)

¾ cup granulated sugar

1 tablespoon ground almonds

1 tablespoon cornstarch

egg wash, to glaze

superfine sugar, for sprinkling

softly whipped cream, to serve

Preheat the oven to 350°F.

First make the dough. Cream the butter and sugar together by hand or in an electric food mixer (no need to over cream). Add the eggs and beat for several minutes. Reduce the speed and mix in the flour. Turn onto a piece of floured parchment paper, flatten into a round wrap, and chill. This dough needs to be chilled for at least 2 hours, otherwise it is difficult to handle.

To make the pie, roll out the dough approx. ¼-inch thick and use about a little more than half of it to line a 9-inch round pan, 1-inch deep. Destalk the cherries and fill the tart pan. Sprinkle with Kirsch, if using, then cover with a mixture of sugar, ground almonds, and cornstarch. Cover with a lid of dough, seal the edges, then decorate with cherry shapes and dough leaves. Brush with eggwash and bake for 45 minutes to 1 hour until the cherries are tender.

When cooked, sprinkle lightly with superfine sugar and serve with softly whipped cream.

DID YOU KNOW?
Cherry pits were found in the several Stone Age caves in Europe and have been enjoyed since ancient times in Rome, Greece, and China; the Romans brought them on their routes of conquest. They share the same family as plums and peaches.

Labneh with Cherries, Olive Oil & Mint

Labneh is so versatile—it can be served as a sweet or savory dish using seasonal fruits. This simple combo is particularly good, but it may need a little drizzle of honey depending on the sweetness of the cherries. The bittersweet cherries are a delicious foil to the silky labneh.

. . . .

SERVES 6

30 ripe cherries
2 tablespoons superfine sugar
1 pound labneh (page 291)
3 tablespoons extra virgin olive oil
¼ cup cream
zest of 1 lemon
some fresh mint leaves

Halve the cherries and discard the pits. Sweeten them to taste with some of the superfine sugar. Set aside to macerate for at least 15 minutes to draw some of the juices out of the cherries and for the sugar to dissolve.

Divide the labneh between 4 plates and sweeten lightly with a sprinkling of superfine sugar. Scatter the cherries over and around the labneh. Drizzle with a little olive oil, cream, and any juice remaining from the cherries. Finally zest the lemon over each and scatter with a little shredded mint leaves.

Cherry & Pistachio Squares

A gorgeous dessert that makes an irresistible treat to nibble with a cup of tea or coffee. I like to leave the stalks on some of the cherries, but you may need to warn your guests to look out for pits. This combination of pistachio and cherries is a very happy one.

. . . .

MAKES 24

12 tablespoons butter, softened
¾ cup superfine sugar
2 large organic eggs
1¼ cups self-rising flour
¼ cup ground almonds
1 pound fresh cherries, stoned
½ cup pistachios, coarsely chopped

Preheat the oven to 350°F. Line a 10 × 7-inch Swiss roll pan with parchment paper, leaving an overhanging piece at each end.

Put the butter, superfine sugar, eggs, self-rising flour, and ground almonds into a food processor. Pulse for a few seconds to amalgamate. Spread evenly in the prepared pan.

Sprinkle the cherries over the top, allowing a little space between the fruit. I like to leave some whole, but you can pit them all (see page 347 for a nifty trick). Sprinkle some coarsely chopped pistachios between the cherries.

Bake for 20 to 25 minutes or until golden brown and well-risen. Cut into squares.

Pickled Cherries

This pickle is delicious with game, cold meats and particularly duck. The pickled cherries also keep well and are a super little store cupboard standby.

. . . .

MAKES 10 × HALF-PINT JARS

2 pounds cherries

1 quart white wine vinegar

1¾ cup granulated sugar

4 cloves

6 peppercorns

1 allspice berry

Check the cherries carefully to ensure they are unblemished; otherwise the pickle won't keep. Put the vinegar, sugar, cloves, peppercorns, and allspice into a stainless-steel saucepan. Bring to the boil for 3 to 4 minutes. Add the cherries, bring back to the boil and simmer for a further 2 minutes.

Fill into sterilized jars, cover, and seal. Store in a cool, dark cupboard for at least a month before eating.

Cherries in Brandy

Infusing fruit in a spirit is such an easy way to preserve the essence of the flavor. This recipe can be used for other fruit and gin or vodka subsituted for the brandy.

. . . .

MAKES 1 PINT

1 pound bitter cherries

about ½ cup granulated sugar

brandy

Prick each cherry in 3 to 4 places with a sterilized darning needle. Then fill a sterilized jar almost to the top with the cherries. Add enough sugar to come about one third of the way up the jar. Fill to the top with brandy.

Seal well and store in a cool, dark place until winter, if you can wait that long. Shake occasionally and drink in small glasses or add to a cocktail.

PLUMS *(prunus domestica)* & GREENGAGES *(prunus italicus),*
DECIDUOUS, ZONES 5–9

I can't wait for the plump Victoria plums to ripen on the tree next to the garden gate each year. They are definitely best eaten warm and plump, right off the tree.

There are more cultivars than virtually any other fruit. All are descended from less than twenty wild species. They are predominantly hybrids of Prunus cerasifera, the myrobalan plum or cherry plum and the sloe, Prunus spinosa. I definitely think a plum tree merits a space, even in a small garden.

Our plum trees are erratic, every 3 to 4 years the tree is so laden with fruit that we need to support some of the branches. In other years the crop can be non-existent, or very spare. Nonetheless

I think it's so worth making space, particularly as nowadays one can choose a cultivar suitable even for the smallest garden, or a large pot.

Greengages are like green plums but with golden aromatic flesh.

VARIETIES

There are over 2,000 varieties and many colors. Plums can be grown as standards, fans or pyramids.

Coe's Golden Drop—Golden yellow, light cropper, apricot like flavor, late season, not self-fertile.

Shiro—the best of all yellow plums, cluseters of bright yellow fruit with juicy flesh; heat tolerant

Santa Rosa—a prolific variety developed by Luther Burbank; fruit is large and sweet; trees are heat tolerant.

Fellenberg—large oval blue plums are great for fresh eating, canning, or drying

GREENGAGE

Greengage—old-world plum; very sweet and juicy green to yellow fruit, widley adapted to many climates.

Bavays Green Gage—an old variety that is still considered to be the ideal desert fruit in Europe

Cambridge Gage—An improvement on Old Gage, excellent flavor, juicy, ripens mid–late autumn, partially self-fertile.

HOW TO GROW

Plums and greengages do best in rich, well-drained soil. They do need quite a bit of moisture but will not thrive in a waterlogged area. If the soil is light, add some humus before planting. They do best when planted bare-rooted during the dormant season and if the weather is dry, they will need some water to get established. Mulch with well-rotted farmyard manure in spring. If possible choose a sunny, sheltered spot. They are the earliest fruit to blossom so it's best to avoid a windy area to give the blossom time to develop. Frost can also harm the developing fruit. Pruning is best done in spring or early summer to lessen the chance of silver leaf disease developing.

CONTAINER GROWING

Ensure the pot is large enough, choose a variety that has been grafted onto a dwarfing rootstock, such as **Pixy**. The pot would need to be at least 1½ feet.

Plums growing on a tree at Ballymaloe.

PESTS AND DISEASES

PLUMS

Plums are subject to silver leaf disease. Avoid this by pruning only in late spring and early summer, and only in dry weather. Wasps can also attack the ripe fruit, I have no magic formula to keep them away apart from wasp traps.

GREENGAGES

Birds and wasps enjoy the sweet greengages. Keep an eye on them and try to pick them as soon as they are ripe.

HARVESTING

Pick the fruit as they ripen. The fruit will yield to the touch when ripe; don't waste a single one. Under-ripe and slightly wasp damaged fruit can be used for preserves.

GOOD FOR YOU...

Prunes, the dried version of plums, are justly famous for their laxative effect but fresh plums can also relieve constipation.

They are a good source of vitamins C, K, and A. Plums are also rich in potassium, magnesium, and iron.

They are an excellent source of beta carotene and contain high levels of chlorogenic acid, a polyphenol that is most concentrated in the skin; dark-skinned plums contain more than lighter ones.

WHAT TO DO WITH A GLUT

Plums and greengages freeze well and can be used for compotes, jams, and chutneys.

Bottled plums are also really useful and plum tarts or plum and apple make a really good combo.

We've also had several goes at drying them to make our own prunes but they were pretty chewy and nothing like as good as the Agen Prunes, so I think I'll leave that to the experts, and we'll enjoy as many fresh ones as we can during the short season.

IN THE KITCHEN

We feast on plums and greengages for the few weeks when they are in season, making pies, tarts, fools, sauces, and salsa. We also love them added to salads and roasted.

Top: *Greengage harvests are pretty erratic so good harvests are cause for celebration.*
Bottom: *Beautiful Victoria plum blossom, but the crop depends on pollination and crucially frost-free mornings.*

Roasted Plums with Buffalo Mozzarella & Mint

Roasting the plums intensifies the flavor, and I put them together with some tender fresh mozzarella—so simple but it gets a terrific reaction. I serve it as an appetizer but it could be tweaked and served as a dessert with a drizzle of honey.

SERVES 4

arugula leaves
2 × 4½ to 5½-ounce balls buffalo mozzarella
10 plums, pitted and roasted (see recipe below)
extra virgin olive oil
sea salt flakes
fresh mint leaves, shredded
grilled sourdough bread, to serve

Lay the arugula on a plate.

Tear a ball of mozzarella in half and then tear again into three pieces and arrange on top of the leaves. Spoon a few pieces of roasted plum over the cheese. Drizzle with extra virgin olive oil. Sprinkle with a few sea salt flakes and shredded mint.

Serve with grilled sourdough bread.

Duck Breast with Roasted Beets & Plums

Plums and beets are a surprisingly good combination—they complement the duck deliciously.

SERVES 4 TO 6

4 to 6 beets
4 to 6 plums
granulated sugar
4 duck breasts
extra virgin olive oil
red wine vinegar
mint, marjoram, or flat-leaf parsley sprigs
balsamic vinegar
sea salt flake

Preheat the oven to 450°F.

Wrap the beets in foil and roast for 1 hour until soft and cooked through.

To roast the plums, pit the fruit, sprinkle with sugar, and toss. Arrange in a single layer in an ovenproof dish or nonreactive roasting pan. Roast for 10 to 15 minutes or until soft and slightly caramelized at the edges.

Fifteen minutes or so before cooking, score the fat on the duck breasts in a criss-cross pattern. Season on both sides with salt and let sit on a wire rack.

Dry the duck breasts with a clean kitchen towel or paper towels. Put skin-side down on a cold grill pan, turn the heat to low, and cook slowly for 15 to 20 minutes or until the fat has rendered and the duck skin is crisp and golden. Flip over and cook for a couple of minutes, or transfer to a preheated 350°F oven for 5 to 10 minutes. Set aside to rest for at least 5 minutes.

Remove the skins from the beets, cut into quarters, and warm if necessary. Drizzle with extra virgin olive oil and a dash of red wine vinegar. Warm the plums also.

Divide the beets and roasted plums among the plates. Thinly slice the duck breasts and arrange or scatter on top. Sprinkle with sprigs of flat-leaf parsley and annual marjoram or shredded mint. Add a few drops of aged balsamic vinegar and a few sea salt flakes.

Plum or Apricot Tart

This tart looks like it came straight from a French patisserie. Try to allow the edges of the fruit to scorch.

. . . .

SERVES 10 TO 12

MAKES 1 × 11-INCH OR 2 × 7-INCH TARTS

FOR THE PASTRY DOUGH
1¾ cups all-purpose flour
8 tablespoons (1 stick) butter
2 tablespoons confectioners' sugar
1 large organic egg

FOR THE FILLING
18 to 20 plums or apricots
2 tablespoons butter
3 to 4 tablespoons superfine sugar

Redcurrant Jelly (page 384) or Apricot
   Glaze (page 407) (optional)
softly whipped cream, to serve

Make the pastry dough in the usual way. Sift the flour onto a work surface and rub in the butter. Add the sugar. Make a well in the center and break in the egg, adding a little water if necessary. Use your fingertips to rub in, pulling in more flour mixture from the outside as you work. Knead with the heel of your hand, making three turns. You should end up with a silky smooth ball of dough. Wrap in plastic wrap and leave in the fridge for at least 1 hour before using. It will keep for a week in the fridge and also freezes well.

Preheat the oven to 350°F.

Roll out the dough, drape into one 11-inch tart pan or 2 × 7-inch tart pans, line with parchment paper and fill with dried beans, and bake blind for 20 to 25 minutes. Remove the beans and parchment.

Cut the plums in half, discard the pits, and arrange cut-side up on the tart, packing them in quite tightly at an angle because they will shrink during cooking. Sprinkle with superfine sugar and dot with butter. Cook for 30 to 45 minutes until the fruit is really soft and slightly scorched. Serve the tart warm just as it is with some softly whipped cream or paint with redcurrant jelly (for plums) or apricot glaze (for apricots) thinned out with some of the juices.

Plum Puddings

A cute way to serve a plum pudding. These remind me of Eve's Pudding, one of our favorite childhood desserts served with homemade custard. Apricots, raspberries, blueberries, or even a bunch of bananas also work well.

. . . .

SERVES 4

8 tablespoons (1 stick) butter
½ cup superfine sugar
2 large organic eggs
1 cup ground almonds
⅓ cup all-purpose flour
2 teaspoons vanilla extract
4 Satsuma or blood plums
confectioners' sugar, for dusting
softly whipped cream, to serve

Preheat the oven to 400°F.

Chop the butter into cubes, put into the bowl of a food processor with the superfine sugar, process for a few seconds, then add the eggs, ground almonds, flour, and vanilla extract. Process until the mixture is just combined.

Carefully remove the pits from the plums. Slit around the sides, and press together again when the pit has been removed. Put the plums in 4 small ovenproof bowls or ovenproof cups.

Divide the frangipane mixture between the four ovenproof bowls. Bake for 15 to 20 minutes depending on the depth of the bowl or cup. When golden and puffed up, dredge with confectioners sugar and serve with softly whipped cream.

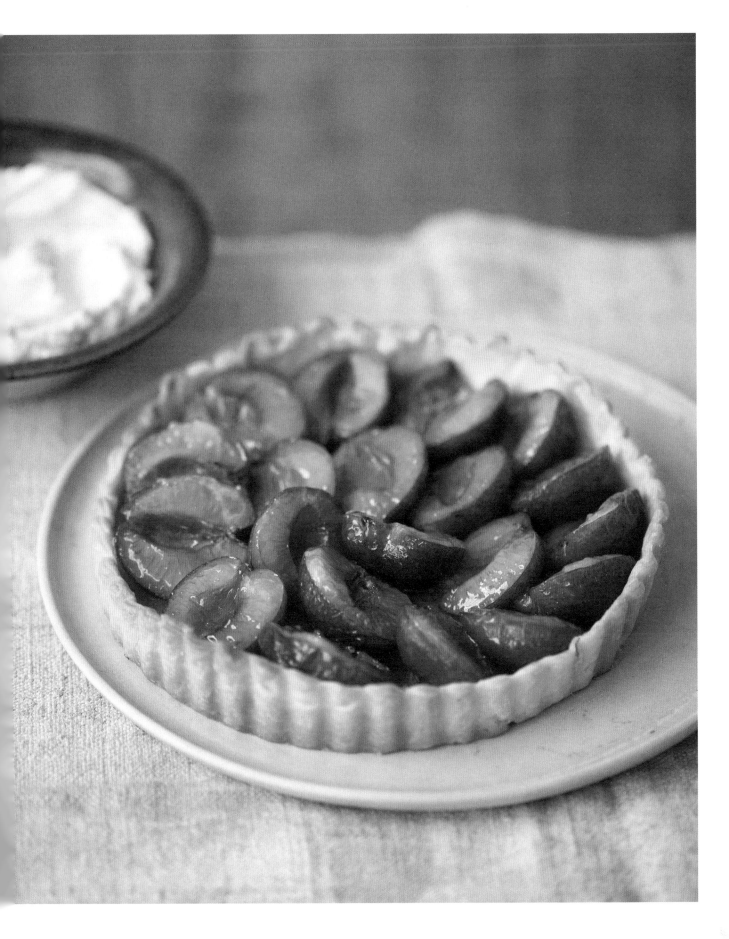

PEACHES, NECTARINES & FLAT PEACHES

Prunus persica DECIDUOUS, ZONES 5–8

When did you last taste a perfect peach? Peaches are yet another fruit that have been compromised beyond recognition. At present, doughnut peaches seem to have a better flavor than the poor diminished peach itself, which is very good reason to consider growing your own.

Commercial peaches and nectarines also get a ton of chemicals and are especially bad for retaining pesticide residues, so apart from the deliciousness of growing your own, that's certainly another consideration.

Stone fruit seem very exotic here in Ireland, but we've certainly had modest but worthwhile success both growing in the greenhouse and outside. We've been growing the white peach **Peregrine** on the south facing wall of the Blue Dining Room overlooking the Fruit Garden for many years now. It's a warm and sheltered spot and it seems to produce abundant fruit every year. It flowers in early spring with beautiful purple–pink blossom which sets by late spring/early summer.

VARIETIES

PEACH

Peregrine—Reliable variety which produces good crops of large, juicy, red-skinned fruit in late summer/early autumn.

Rochester—Similar flavor to Peregrine with a yellow skin flushed with red. It flowers later in spring which is an advantage for colder gardens where the frost comes later.

Red Haven—Heavy-bearing, easy-to-grow tree produces bushels of sweet fruit.

NECTARINE

Royal Giant—Big, sweet, and juicy fruit, ripening in mid-August.

HOW TO GROW

Peach trees are fussy about soil; they like it well-drained and moisture retaining. Peaches can be planted as a stand-alone tree or trained in a fan-shape on a south-facing wall. They need sun to ripen. Remember to water regularly and use an organic liquid fertilizer or comfrey tea once a fortnight. They need a period of dormancy each year. We knock up a few protective timber and plastic screens and cover the outdoor peach trees in early spring, and then we remove in late spring/early summer, once all danger of frost has passed. This protects the plants and helps to deter peach leaf curl.

CONTAINER GROWING

Both peaches and nectarines can be grown in large pots on a sunny balcony or veranda, choose dwarf varieties. There are a number of compact peach tree varieties which may be grown in containers—they will reach 50 to 60 inches tall. The fruit are full size but there are usually less of them—**Pixzee** and **Bonanza** are suitable varieties. Nonetheless they are so worth considering for the pale pink blossom in early spring, and the joy and anticipation of watching the fruit gradually ripen to perfection.

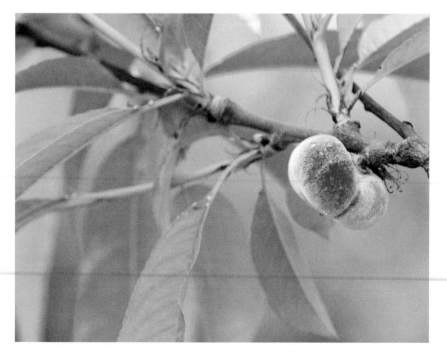

Doughnut peaches are a relatively new arrival on the fruit scene and invariably have more flavor than store-bought peaches.

358 GROW, COOK, NOURISH

PESTS AND DISEASES

Trees may get the disease known as peach leaf curl which causes the young leaves to blister and pucker, turning red or purple. The spores of this disease become active early in the year and rain will spread it onto the buds. To avoid this we cover the peaches with plastic, allowing ventilation at the bottom and sides where the bumble bees can enter for pollination. The blossoms will appear in early spring and the plastic will protect them from the spores. When the leaves come out in late spring we remove the plastic. It has the added bonus of producing the blossom early and we get a bumper crop of fruit.

If you are unlucky enough to get peach leaf curl any infected leaves should be removed and burned. We also plant garlic around the base of the plants to deter this disease, I'm not completely sure that it makes any difference, but many gardeners swear by its effectiveness.

HARVESTING

White peaches are divinely juicy but very difficult to pick at the peak of perfection without bruising, we just cut out the bruised area and enjoy the rest.

The peach leaves add a delicious almondy flavor to crème brulée, crème Anglaise or panna cotta.

The flowers are both pretty and delicious sprinkled over salad, but remember each flower is a potential peach.

GOOD FOR YOU...

Peaches and nectarines contain all the essential amino acids in a good ratio; they are rich in protein compared to other fruit and have vitamins A, C, and E.

WHAT TO DO WITH A GLUT?

Sounds unlikely but even if you have just one tree they can all ripen more or less simultaneously. Peach jam is good and it's also possible to dry peaches, though we haven't had great success with them. Poached peaches freeze very well.

To dry peaches, halve and pit the fruit, spread on wire racks, and either sun dry in the greenhouse or conservatory or in a dehydrator.

Make peach juice—add lemon juice to stop discoloration and freeze.

IN THE KITCHEN

Home-grown peaches rarely look perfect or uniform. Slightly damaged or bruised peaches can be puréed—just remove the pits, process, then press through a fine nylon strainer. Use immediately for Bellinis or add a little lemon juice, taste, and freeze. For a Bellini to rival those invented by Guiseppe Cipriani at Harry's Bar in Venice in 1948, add three parts Prosecco to one part white peach purée. Having said that, yellow peach purée is equally delicious.

I also love peaches poached in lemon verbena syrup—they keep in the fridge for weeks and also freeze really well.

We use nectarines in fruit salads, a delicious cobbler, or this summer salad with prosciutto and mozzarella.

Top: *Peregrine peach growing in the greenhouse.*
Bottom: *Fantasia nectarine.*

DID YOU KNOW?

I didn't know until recently that peaches and nectarines are virtually identical except for a single gene that causes nectarines to be smooth and peaches to be fuzzy. Both can have white or yellow flesh.

Peach, Gorgonzola & Watercress Salad

A gorgeous summer appetizer salad—made in minutes. A super way to use really ripe peaches, I find the combination of peaches and watercress irresistible. Here, one also has the saltiness of the blue cheese and freshness of the scallions—delicious.

SERVES 8

FOR THE DRESSING

2 tablespoons white wine vinegar
6 tablespoons walnut oil
1 teaspoon whole-grain mustard
1 teaspoon wildflower honey
sea salt and freshly ground black pepper

FOR THE SALAD

4 ripe peaches or nectarines
2 to 3 tablespoons freshly squeezed lemon
    juice and a little honey, sprinkled over the
    peaches to keep them from discoloring
small watercress or arugula leaves
8 ounces Gorgonzola or other blue cheese
1 cup walnut halves, coarsely chopped
4 scallions, thinly sliced

First make the dressing: Whisk all the ingredients together in a little bowl with a fork. Season to taste.

Choose perfectly ripe peaches or nectarines, slice in 6 to 8 pieces, and sprinkle with freshly squeezed lemon juice and honey if not serving immediately. Scatter a few watercress sprigs or arugula leaves on each plate, tuck a few peach slices in here and there, and crumble some Gorgonzola or other blue cheese over the top. Drizzle a little dressing over the salad and sprinkle some toasted walnuts and thinly sliced scallions over the top. Serve immediately.

Nectarine, Prosciutto, Mozzarella & Spearmint Salad

We are inordinately proud of our home-grown peaches and nectarines. Not all look picture perfect so we use those in salads like this one. Add some prosciutto to make it more substantial, but a meat-free combination is also gorgeous.

SERVES 8

4 ripe nectarines or peaches
arugula leaves
12 slices of prosciutto or Serrano ham
    (optional)
3 fresh buffalo mozzarella
sea salt and freshly ground black pepper
approx. 30 spearmint leaves
extra virgin olive oil
mixed flower honey

Halve the ripe nectarines or peaches and remove the pits. Slice each into half again.

Scatter a few arugula leaves on each plate. Put 3 pieces of fruit on each serving. Add some prosciutto or serrano ham, if using. Tear the mozzarella and tuck a few pieces here and there. Season with sea salt flakes and freshly ground pepper. Scatter with torn spearmint leaves. Drizzle with extra virgin olive oil, add a little honey, and serve.

Rory's Peach Sorbet with Raspberry Cream

This recipe sounds too good to be true, but if you have really ripe peaches, the resulting sorbet is delicious. The sorbet is best frozen in an ice-cream machine, but excellent results can be achieved in a normal deep-freeze and this mixture can also be turned into a granita or ice. Serve it just as it is or with a peach and blueberry salad. I sometimes like to combine it with a raspberry cream and a crisp, buttery, nutty cookie.

SERVES 6

1½ pounds ripe peaches
¾ cup superfine sugar
3 tablespoons lemon juice
small mint leaves, to serve

FOR THE RASPBERRY CREAM
1¾ cups raspberries
⅓ to ⅔ cup superfine sugar
1¼ cups whipped cream, quite stiff

Begin by peeling the peaches: Score the peaches top and bottom with a small cross and place in a deep bowl. Pour in boiling water and keep them immersed for 10 seconds. Strain immediately and cool in iced water. Drain again and peel off the skins. Slice the flesh off the pits and place in a blender with the sugar and lemon juice. Purée until the fruit is smooth and silky and the sugar is dissolved. Freeze in an ice-cream machine until quite frozen. Place in a bowl, smooth the top, cover, and keep in the freezer until ready to serve.

To make the raspberry cream, sprinkle the raspberries with the superfine sugar and let sit for 30 minutes. Crush the berries and sugar coarsely, not rendering them into a purée. Fold in the whipped cream to create a streaked effect.

Serve in neat scoops with the raspberry cream or a sugared peach and blueberry salad and a few small and tender mint leaves if available.

PEACH GRANITA

If you don't have a machine for freezing the mixture you can proceed as follows and make a granita: Cover and freeze the puréed mixture from the peach sorbet recipe in a shallow bowl. When partially frozen, remove and break up with a fork to attain shards of peach ice. Replace in the freezer and repeat the process twice more. Serve as above.

PEACH ICE

If you don't have an ice-cream machine, you can also make peach ice. Freeze the mixture until completely frozen.

Remove from the freezer and break up thoroughly with a whisk or in a food processor. Beat 2 egg whites to a soft peak. Add 1 tablespoon of superfine sugar and continue beating to a stiff peak. Fold into the mixture and refreeze. The resulting texture will be halfway between a sorbet and a granita. Serve as above.

Nectarine Cobbler

Cobblers, like crumbles, always produce a nostalgic response and are so easy to make with whatever fruit you have in season. We love nectarine or peaches and raspberry or loganberry or green gooseberry and elderflower.

. . . .

SERVES 6 TO 8

1½ pounds fresh nectarines, peaches, or apricots, or a mixture, pitted and cut into wedges (keep the juice)

5 tablespoons granulated sugar

1 tablespoon all-purpose flour or cornstarch

freshly grated zest of ½ lemon (optional)

crème fraîche or softly whipped cream, to serve

FOR THE COBBLER

¾ cup all-purpose flour

¾ teaspoon baking powder

¼ teaspoon baking soda

1 tablespoon superfine sugar, plus 1 tablespoon for sprinkling

2 tablespoons butter, cubed

½ cup buttermilk (2 tablespoons cream if the buttermilk is low-fat)

Put the sliced fruit in a bowl, add the sugar, flour, lemon zest, and a tablespoon of juice, toss well, and transfer to a 9-inch Pyrex pie dish.

Preheat the oven to 400°F.

Next make the topping: Sift the flour, baking powder, and bread soda into a bowl and add the superfine sugar. Rub in the butter and bind with rich buttermilk until the mixture just comes together. Drop tablespoons of the dough over the filling—it doesn't matter if there are spaces, the dough will expand as it cooks. Sprinkle with another tablespoon of sugar. Bake for 30 to 45 minutes or until puffed and golden.

Serve warm with crème fraîche or softly whipped cream.

POMEGRANATE

Punica granatum DECIDUOUS, ZONES **7–11**

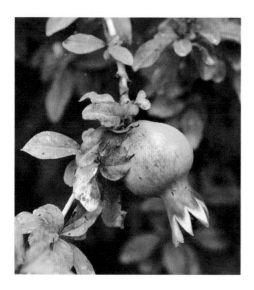

Our very own home-grown pomegranate in East Cork.

We have one pomegranate tree in the greenhouse of which we are inordinately proud. It's planted on the south side and produced one pomegranate after two years. We were beyond excited and it was certainly the most admired and photographed pomegranate in these islands. We couldn't bear to pick it and eventually it split to reveal pale colored seeds inside, not particularly tasty. Since then it has become more productive every year. It was covered in beautiful, orange, bell-like flowers among glossy green leaves from early summer to autumn this year and it looks like we will have an impressive crop of fruit. They are self-fertile so you will only need one. Pomegranate trees can grow up to 15 feet tall in ideal conditions.

Pomegranates are one of the oldest fruit in cultivation. Not surprisingly, with all those jewel-like seeds inside, they are considered to be a symbol of fertility both in the arts and religion. They are sometimes referred to as wine apples. Pomegranate seeds stain so be careful not to splash some on your clothes.

VARIETIES

Wonderful—Excellent flavor, 6 to 8 inches tall.
Favorite—From Russia, excellent flavor.
Parfianka—Sweet, tart juice, great flavor.

HOW TO GROW

It's easy to grow a pomegranate plant from seeds. Select a few whole seeds, dab off the juice on paper towels and then wash under the cold tap to remove all flesh.

Dry the seeds or sow right away. Fill a small pot with a little gravel. Top up with moist compost. Sow about ¼ inch deep, cover and put into a clear plastic bag. Find a warm spot, 70°F is ideal, or put on a rack over a radiator. The seeds should germinate in 6 to 10 days.

Once they have sprouted, remove the plastic bag and transfer the pot to a sunny window sill. Keep moist, transplant when the seedlings are about 4 inches tall, either into a larger pot or outdoors into well-drained soil.

Best to start indoors in winter to plant outdoors in spring against a south-facing wall, it needs to be tied in and supported.

It's worth noting that most, if not all of the pomegranates that you buy in your supermarket are hybrids, so the seeds are unlikely to produce identical fruits to the original.

Pomegranates like a loamy well-drained soil with some stones and grit. Keep watered but they don't like to sit in water. Pomegranates fruit on new wood,

Even the flowers of the pomegranate are stunningly beautiful.

prune out any dead wood and suckers and snip back lightly.

CONTAINER GROWING

A pomegranate bush can grow happily in a large pot or container on your sunny terrace or veranda, in well-drained soil. It is surprisingly hardy. You can choose a dwarf variety like Nana—Plant in a 3-foot pot or a full size cultivar, depending on your needs and space. They are also beautiful in a courtyard and even if they don't fruit, the flowers will give pleasure all summer long. Bonsai enthusiasts can also train a pomegranate.

PESTS AND DISEASES

Pomegranates may be attacked by aphids, ours haven't as yet. Spray with horticultural soap and water. Planting calendulas underneath may help to distract the aphids.

WHAT TO DO WITH A GLUT

Unlikely, but juice and reduce in a wide stainless steel sauté pan to make your very own pomegranate molasses, better than anything you can buy. I've never

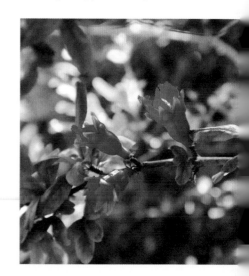

had enough of my own to do this but we have made it very successfully with bought pomegranates. Use the fruits in flower arrangements and garlands.

GOOD FOR YOU...

Pomegranates have antioxidant, antiviral, and anti-tumor properties. They are a natural cholesterol buster and a good source of vitamins A, C, E, and folic acid, in fact they have three times as many antioxidants as green tea.

IN THE KITCHEN

We use the ruby-like seeds of this super versatile fruit in salads, game dishes, pilafs, cakes, desserts, and even stews, and drinks.

To remove the seeds cut in half around the equator, lay the cut side on the palm of your hand, then tap with the back of a wooden spoon. The seeds will fall into the bowl. Pick out any little pieces of membrane.

Duck Cooked with Pomegranate from the Kashmir Dogra Court

How exotic does this sound? This is one of the house specialities at Ahilya Fort in Maheshwar in India, one of my favorite places in the world to unwind.

SERVES 4

3 tablespoons mustard oil

2 cloves

1 teaspoon fenugreek seeds

2 green cardamom pods

4 duck thighs, bone removed (approx. 1¼ pounds meat), skinned and diced into 1-inch pieces

1 bay leaf

2 onions, cut into rings ¼-inch thick

1 teaspoon ground ginger

1 teaspoon garlic, crushed

1 teaspoon kashmiri chili powder

1 teaspoon ground cumin seeds, not toasted

¼ teaspoon ground turmeric

1 cup pomegranate juice

½ cup plain yogurt, homemade if possible

1 tablespoon palm sugar or jaggery

3 tablespoons tamarind water

salt

2 tablespoons lemon or lime juice

pomegranate seeds, 1 teaspoon chopped mint leaves, and fresh lemon wedges, to serve

Heat the mustard oil in a wok over high heat, add the whole spices, stir for 1 to 2 minutes, and then add the duck. After 5 minutes, remove the meat from the oil and set aside.

Strain the oil and reheat over medium heat, then add the bay leaf and onion rings. When the onion is half-cooked, add the ginger and garlic. Cook for 2 to 3 minutes, add the kashmiri chili powder, cumin, turmeric, and the duck. Stir and cook for a minute, then add the pomegranate juice and bring to a simmer. Gradually stir in the yogurt, palm sugar, tamarind water, and salt. Cook over low heat for about 45 minutes. Taste, add freshly squeezed lime or lemon juice, and I like to scatter a few fresh pomegranate seeds over the top with lots of fresh mint leaves. Serve with a wedge of lemon.

Pomegranate & Rosewater Tartlets

Exquisite little mouthfuls of pomegranate seeds perfumed with rosewater in crispy tart crusts.

. . . .

MAKES 20

20 tiny frozen tartlet shells or JR's cream
    pastry dough (page 388)
1 pomegranate (but you will only need
    about half)
superfine sugar
rosewater (available from many Asian
    supermarkets)
freshly squeezed lemon juice
confectioners' sugar, for dusting

Preheat oven to 350°F.

If you're using JR's cream pastry dough, roll it out very thinly, line the tartlet pans, and fill with parchment paper and baking beans.

Bake for 5 to 6 minutes, remove the beans from each pan, continue to cook until the tartlets are cooked through, and cool on a wire rack.

Meanwhile, cut the pomegranate in half around the equator, open out, and flick out the seeds, (keep the other half for a fruit salad). Sprinkle with a little superfine sugar and a few drops of rosewater and a squeeze of lemon juice. Taste.

Not long before serving, arrange the tartlets on a large plate, dust with confectioners' sugar, then fill each tartlet with pomegranate seeds. If by any chance you have a pink rose around, scatter a few small petals over the top.

Green Salad with Pomegranate Molasses Dressing

Pomegranate molasses is a versatile dressing, delicious with salad leaves, but also with grilled fish, grilled chicken, and grilled vegetables. You can make your own, otherwise it is available from some specialty grocery stores.

. . . .

SERVES 10 TO 12

3½ cups freshly squeezed pomegranate
    juice (1 × 28-ounce bottle)
¼ to ⅓ cup granulated sugar (optional)
4 tablespoons lemon juice
2 garlic cloves, crushed
½ teaspoon ground cumin
½ teaspoon superfine sugar
8 tablespoons olive oil
8 to 10 handfuls of lettuces and salad
    leaves, such as butterhead, iceberg,
    radicchio, endive, chicory, watercress,
    buckler leaf sorrel, arugula, and winter
    purslane
sea salt and freshly ground black pepper
a few fresh pomegranate seeds (optional)

To make 1 cup pomegranate molasses, pour the pomegranate juice into a wide sauté pan, and add the sugar, if using. (I usually make this without sugar, but occasionally one can have a batch of particularly bitter fruit, so taste and decide.) Bring to a boil, stirring occasionally. Simmer for about 30 minutes until thick and syrupy. Add 2 tablespoons of lemon juice to taste. Simmer for 2 to 3 minutes; it should be bittersweet. Pour into sterilized bottles and store in a cool place—it should keep for 6 months or more.

Mix the garlic, cumin, sugar, ¼ cup of pomegranate molasses, and the remaining lemon juice in a bowl. Whisk in the olive oil. Season to taste. Add a little extra sugar if you think it's a bit too sharp.

Wash and dry the lettuces and other leaves very carefully in a large sink of cold water. If large, tear into bite-sized pieces and put in a deep salad bowl. Cover with plastic wrap and refrigerate if not to be served immediately. Just before serving, toss with a little dressing—just enough to make the leaves glisten. Serve immediately with a few pomegranate seeds sprinkled over the top.

PEARS *Pyrus communis* DECIDUOUS, ZONES 5–7

Somehow it doesn't occur to as many people to grow pears as apples, but it's really worth considering, for exactly the same much-repeated reason—it's really difficult to find a really super pear that makes you stop in your tracks and cause you to go wow! Commercially produced pears can also contain pesticide residues.

Yet these pears exist if you choose the variety carefully, thanks to several dedicated breeders in France and Spain who selected most modern varieties.

In our climate they thrive, espaliered, on a warm south-facing wall, so take up little space in your garden and are long-lived. We also grow two Asian pear trees (Nashi) in the Fruit Garden by the school. These crunchy, russeted fruit look more like an apple than a pear. The flavor is a bit insipid, but they are crisp and juicy and are super easy to grow, and seem to produce a terrific crop every year.

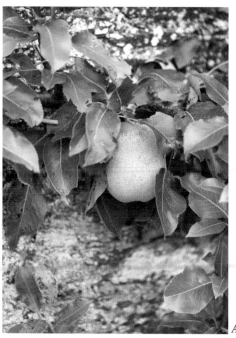

A pear ripe for picking.

VARIETIES

Over 3,000 varieties of pear are recorded. Some of our favorites include:

Beurre hardy—russeted fruit with delcious yellow flesh; ripens in autum, scab resistant

Conference—Early ripener, scab resistant, yields and stores well, good for cooking.

Doyenne du Comice—Delicious flavor, ripens late autumn and can be stored into winter.

Bartlett—good for canning, but also an excellent table fruit.

Choose varieties for purpose, eating, cooking or making pear wine.

FOR PEAR WINE (PERRY)

Huffcap and **Barnet** are dual purpose, they can be eaten ripe or made into perry. Pear trees are grafted onto a rootstock which determines their size. It's crucially important to choose the correct rootstock for your situation.

Quince A—Can be used for bush or espalier trees.

Quince C—More suitable for cordons, but can also be used for bush and espalier, but is slightly less vigorous.

HOW TO GROW

Pears need rich, fertile, well-drained soil. Choose a sunny, sheltered site away from any possible frost pockets. Pears don't like wind, apples are more tolerant. Choose relatively hardy varieties or make sure to espalier against a south or west facing wall. If not growing as an espalier, space the trees 15 foot apart.

Bare-root and potted plants should be planted in late to early autumn. Lift the sod, put it aside, take out nearly a square yard of top soil, loosen the subsoil, put in the sod back into the hole upside down and chop it up, put a stake in the ground, 2 feet high. Use a flexible tie to attach the tree to the stake, in a figure of 8 shape, if the stake isn't too tall it will allow the top of the tree to have some movement, this strengthens the tree, but the roots will be supported. The stake should be place on the windward side of the tree. Place the tree gently in position, don't cover the graft, and then cover the roots with fine soil. Firm gently into position. (This method can be used for all fruit trees.)

Water in and during dry spells mulch. Mulch with a seaweed fertilizer and prune once a year. Compost well in winter. Pears can tolerate, and benefit from, heavy pruning in winter and some summer pruning. They can be trained into a myriad of shapes and there used to be much rivalry between country house gardeners to see who could produce the best crop and create the best espaliers.

CONTAINER GROWING

Pears can grow happily in a really large terracotta pot or half barrel. Chose an appropriate variety. It can be fun to grow three different pears on one rootstock. Keep them pruned so they don't outgrow the pot.

PESTS AND DISEASES

Pears tend to be hardier than apples. Scab and canker can be a problem in wet climates, and for that reason don't plant into compacted or very wet soil. They are difficult to control, winter pruning can help, but seek out resistant varieties. Beurre Hardy is scab resistant and Concorde is canker resistant. Burn any infected pruning material. Pears can sometimes get mildew in the summer months, but we don't find it a problem.

Provided the blossom is not affected by frost, you should have a good crop.

HARVESTING

Watch the tree and pick the pears slightly underripe then leave to ripen to perfection in your kitchen or in a cooler place if you want to slow them down. They become woolly if left on the tree. Store in a cool dark shed, not touching, and use as they ripen.

For late ripening varieties like Doyenne de Comice, pick the crop as soon as the birds start to attack and leave to ripen gradually in a cool pantry or garage—don't allow them to touch each other because if one starts to rot it will infect the adjacent ones.

Asian pears are picked off in early autumn and, unlike European pears, they remain crisp.

GOOD FOR YOU...

Pears are a good source of dietary fiber and antioxidants. They contain vitamins C, A, B1, B2, and B6. They are also a good source of minerals, copper, iron, potassium, manganese, and magnesium. Pears are frequently recommended as weaning food for babies and people with food allergies as they are easy to digest.

IN THE KITCHEN

A beautifully ripe, juicy pear is a delicious fruit to enjoy after dinner. Look out for an old variety and savor it slowly. A bowl or mason jar of poached pears is one of my favorite stand-bys and my go-to for a delicious compote for breakfast or for a simple dessert after a light lunch or dinner. Add some homemade vanilla ice cream, a dribble of chocolate sauce, and some toasted almond slices, and you have the legendary and much-loved Poire Belle Helene.

Pears take on other flavors deliciously, and I love the tart flavor of pears and blackcurrants. They also pair well with

Asian pear.

loganberries, boysenberries, tayberries, or the more familiar raspberries.

Even dull, underripe pears benefit greatly from being poached in a sweet geranium or lemon verbena syrup, to give them a haunting lemony flavor.

Pear trained as an espalier against a brick wall.

DID YOU KNOW?
The Chinese called the pear "li" and considered it a symbol of immortality.

A Salad of Blue Cheese with Grilled Pears & Spiced Candied Nuts

A salad of many contrasts—warm grilled pears, spicy nuts, salty blue cheese, and a few little leaves. These flavors work so well together in this French-inspired fall salad.

. . . .

SERVES 8

selection of salad leaves, ideally curly
  endive and watercress
3 to 4 ripe pears, such as Bartlet or Anjou
sunflower oil
3 to 3½ ounces ripe blue cheese, such as
  Stilton, Gorgonzola, or Crozier Blue
chervil sprigs, to garnish

FOR THE SPICED CANDIED NUTS

1 cup walnut halves
⅓ cup granulated sugar
¼ teaspoon freshly ground cinnamon
¼ teaspoon freshly ground coriander
1 pinch freshly ground star anise

FOR THE DRESSING

2 tablespoons red wine vinegar
6 tablespoons extra virgin olive oil
sea salt and freshly ground black pepper

Preheat the oven to 350°F. Arrange the walnuts in a single layer on a baking sheet and toast them for 4 to 5 minutes just until they smell rich and nutty.

Meanwhile, mix the sugar with the spices. Spread over the base of a frying pan in an even layer. Scatter the walnut halves on top. Cook over medium heat until the sugar melts and stars to color. Carefully rotate the pan until the walnuts are completely coated with the amber-colored, spicy caramel. Turn onto a Silpat mat or silicone paper or a greased baking pan. Set aside to cool and harden. (Store in an airtight container—they keep for several days but are best used fresh.)

Whisk all the dressing ingredients together, pour into a mason jar, and cover.

Heat a grill pan over high heat. Peel, quarter, and core the pears. Toss in a little sunflower oil, grill on both sides, and then on the rounded side for 3 to 4 minutes.

Cut the cheese into cubes or small wedges. Sprinkle the salad leaves with the dressing and toss gently until the leaves glisten. Season to taste.

Divide the salad between the plates making a little mound in the center. Slice each grilled pear in half lengthwise and tuck 3 pieces in between the leaves. Scatter with a few cubes of the cheese and some spiced candied walnuts. Sprinkle with a few sprigs of chervil and serve.

Pear or Asian Pear Chutney with Lemon Verbena

A good way to use up a glut of pears or Asian pears and a delicious accompaniment to serve with pheasant, chicken, or pork.

. . . .

MAKES 4 × 7-OUNCE JARS

2 large onions, chopped
1 lemon, quartered and thinly sliced
1 teaspoon fennel seeds
¾ cup granulated sugar
2 garlic cloves, chopped
¾ cup white wine vinegar
6 Conference or Asian pears, peeled,
  cored, and cut into ¼-inch dice
½ cup golden raisins
1 tablespoon lemon verbena

Put the onions in a stainless steel saucepan, then add the lemon, fennel seeds, sugar, garlic, and vinegar.

Peel, core, and chop the pears and add to the saucepan with the golden raisins. Bring to a boil and simmer gently for about 25 minutes, (Nashi will take longer to cook), stirring occasionally, until reduced by more than half its original volume. Add the lemon verbena and continue to cook for another 4 to 5 minutes. Pour into sterilized jars and seal with the lids.

If you can resist, set aside to mellow in a cool, dry place for 2 weeks before serving. It will keep for 6 months or more.

RHUBARB

Rheum hybridum PERENNIAL, ZONES 3–8

Rhubarb originated in Asia over 5,000 years ago and was originally cultivated for its medicinal uses. It is believed to have a balancing effect on the digestive system and is widely used in Chinese medicine. Rhubarb is technically a vegetable rather than a fruit but I have put it in this section because for culinary purposes it is treated much more like a fruit. For me rhubarb is a must-have fruit, of all the fruits we grow, if I could only choose one, it would have to be rhubarb. It's great to have a few perennials that pop up every year.

We keep dreaming up new ways to use it in both sweet and savory dishes. We also enjoy the stalks as a flower arrangement in late spring.

VARIETIES

I personally don't love "forced" rhubarb because the flavor seems so flaccid to me. The idea behind forcing rhubarb is to have an early crop—traditionally a few crowns were covered with an upturned bucket or blanching pot covered with straw, light is excluded and the stalks will be protected from the elements and mature earlier than the rest of the crop. Even just covering with straw or strawy manure will encourage some early stalks. Forcing is practiced on a commercial scale and this extends the rhubarb season. I grow and recommend the following:

Victoria—Late variety which yields well, the stalks are green but if making juice, it will turn pink.

Crimson Red—bright red, plump, tender stalks develop quickly in spring.

Starkrimson—Cold hardy and heat tolerant plants produce sweet, low acid stalks.

HOW TO GROW

Buy three or four crowns from a reputable source, (ample for a family of four), although that also depends on your growing space. Plant into rich but well-drained, fertile soil in an open site that gets lots of sun. However, in a cooler, shadier spot it won't dry out so quickly. Rhubarb will tolerate a pH level as low as 5, but ideally it should be 6 to 6.8 to achieve good yields (slightly acidic to neutral). It doesn't like to be disturbed, so try to plant it somewhere permanent. The stools can be divided if they become too big.

Plant in spring or autumn, depending on the conditions, the soil needs to be reasonably warm and moist, but not waterlogged, so postpone planting if the weather is too wet. Dig a large hole, 10 inches wide and 12 inches deep. Plant the crowns about 50 inches apart with 40 to 80 inches between rows and the nose just sticking up above soil. Allow the crowns to establish for a year to let the plants build up vigor before you start to harvest.

Rhubarb is a hungry plant, so it needs, and benefits from, a good dressing of well-rotted farmyard manure or compost in winter or early spring. The manure is best put around the crown, not directly on top, otherwise it may damage the fresh young growth.

Sometimes during a dry season the rhubarb can go to flower, if this happens, cut off the flowers immediately because they will draw from the plant, to the detriment of the stalks. In my experience if a rhubarb goes to flower, it's best to dig it out and discard because it will most likely do the same the following season.

CONTAINER GROWING

Rhubarb can survive in a half-barrel in a backyard, providing there is good depth of soil and plenty of moisture. Don't expect the same yield as from rhubarb grown in rich, fertile soil in the garden. It will not thrive if the pot is less than 2 feet wide.

Choose a variety like **Fulton's Strawberry Surprise**, which can be grown in borders or large containers. This variety is recommended for its unusual bittersweet flavor.

PESTS AND DISEASES

None that we have encountered; rhubarb seems to be quite resistant to pests and disease.

HARVESTING

You should be able to harvest a few pink spears in early Spring and it will continue to produce until midsummer, by which time it will be getting coarse and the leaves will start to die back.

No house should be without rhubarb. It can even grow in a large pot on a balcony.

When harvesting, twist the base of the stalk and pull from the base until it pops out of the socket. Don't cut because there is a danger that the remaining piece of stalk will rot. The rhubarb stalk will slip out of the plant so another can grow in its place. Trim off the stalk, but don't waste the pale red base as it's the most delicate part of the stalk (no need to peel).

Rhubarb leaves are considered to be poisonous, they do contain high levels of oxalic acid, but the jury is certainly out, so it's best to follow the precautionary principle here. However, perhaps surprisingly, they can be added to the compost heap or used to make an organic insecticide which you can spray on cabbage caterpillars and aphids. Boil up the leaves in water for 15 to 20 minutes. When cool, strain into a container, then add some soap flakes, stir until dissolved and use as a spray.

GOOD FOR YOU...

Rhubarb is believed to have a balancing effect on the digestive system and is widely used in Chinese medicine. The roots are dried and used in treating ailments such as constipation, poor circulation, and problems of the liver and gall bladder.

The stalks are rich in several B-complex vitamins such as folates, riboflavin, niacin, vitamin B-6 and thiamine. Recent research has identified 40 polyphenol compounds in rhubarb and confirmed its medicinal use by identifying several beneficial compounds that fight cancer, lower cholesterol, reduce inflammation, lower blood pressure and protect eye and brain health. Rhubarb is high in both oxalic acid and malic acid but this can be counteracted by eating it with cream, crème fraîche, yogurt or ice cream.

The redder varieties are rich in anthocyanin which boosts the immune system and also contain more vitamin A than the green varieties.

WHAT TO DO WITH A GLUT?

Make rhubarb jam or give bundles to your friends. We find it freezes brilliantly, cut it into 1-inch pieces and pop it into quart bags, ready for winter tarts, jams and compotes.

IN THE KITCHEN

Despite popular belief, there's no need to peel rhubarb—it removes many of the vitamins and in fact it will be far less flavorful if you do. Just give the stalks a quick wipe with a damp cloth.

A little chopped angelica stalk or leaves added to rhubarb intensifies the flavor and reduces the need for sugar. The redder the stalks, the sweeter the rhubarb; it can also be eaten raw. A little sauce of stewed rhubarb cuts the richness of pork, duck, homemade sausages, chicken, and some fish. Rhubarb and strawberry is a favorite combo, but try rhubarb and raspberry or rhubarb and banana.

One needs to be super careful not to let the rhubarb overcook when poaching, otherwise it dissolves into a mush in minutes so, when poaching, just cover the rhubarb in cold syrup in a stainless steel saucepan and bring slowly to a boil. Turn off the heat, cover tightly, and let sit for 20 to 30 minutes until the rhubarb is tender but still intact. Delicious, warm or cold. Swirl softly whipped cream into the compote for a delicious rhubarb fool, or serve with simple shortbread cookies. A little rosewater adds a haunting flavor

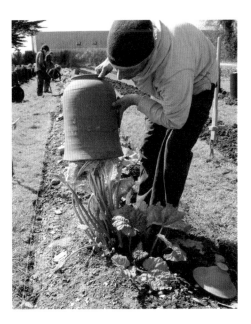

Aidan Walsh carefully lifts a cloche off a plant of tender forced rhubarb in early spring.

to a rhubarb compote or you may like to add it to the accompanying whipped cream.

Roasting is a great way to cook rhubarb and intensify the flavor. To serve six, preheat the oven to 400°F. Slice 2 pounds rhubarb into 1-inch pieces and arrange in a single layer in a medium-sized ovenproof dish. Scatter 1 cup granulated sugar over the rhubarb and let macerate for 30 minutes. Roast for 20 to 30 minutes depending on size, until the rhubarb is just tender. Serve alone or with cream, ice cream, panna cotta, or labneh (page 291).

DID YOU KNOW?

In West Yorkshire in the UK there is an area known as the "Rhubarb Triangle" between the towns of Wakefield, Morley, and Rothwell, famous for its forced rhubarb. It covers an area of 9 square miles and at its peak it stretched to 30 square miles. In 2010 Yorkshire Forced Rhubarb was awarded a PDO (Protected Designation of Origin) by the EU.

At the height of the textile industry, some of the low grade textile waste from the mills was used as fertilizer, along with horse manure and sludge. The cold wet climate of Yorkshire suited the production of rhubarb.

Cinnamon Sugar Beignets with Roasted Rhubarb Compote

The flavor of roasted rhubarb is a relatively recent revelation—it intensifies the flavor and is so much easier to cook this way as one does not have to worry about it dissolving into a mush. It would matter here.

. . . .

MAKES APPROX. 40

FOR THE CHOUX PASTRY DOUGH
1 cup bread flour
pinch of salt
7 tablespoons butter, cut into ½-inch
  cubes
3 to 5 large organic eggs, depending
  on size

FOR THE ROASTED RHUBARB COMPOTE
1 pound rhubarb
¾ cup granulated sugar
2 teaspoons rosewater

FOR THE CINNAMON SUGAR
½ teaspoon ground cinnamon
½ cup superfine sugar

olive oil, for deep-frying

First make the choux pastry dough: Sift the flour with the salt onto a piece of silicone paper. Heat 1 cup of water and butter in a high-sided saucepan until the butter is melted. Bring to a fast rolling boil, then remove from the heat. (Prolonged boiling evaporates the water and changes the proportions of the dough.) Immediately add all the flour at once and beat vigorously with a wooden spoon for a few seconds until the mixture is smooth and pulls away from the sides of the saucepan to form a ball. Return the saucepan to low heat and stir for 30 seconds to 1 minute or until the mixture starts to furr the bottom of the saucepan. Remove from the heat and cool for a few minutes.

Meanwhile, set aside one egg, break it, and whisk it in a bowl. Add the remaining eggs to the dough, one by one, with a wooden spoon, beating thoroughly after each addition. Make sure the dough comes back to the same texture each time before you add another egg. When it will no longer form a ball in the center of the saucepan, add the beaten egg little by little. Use just enough to make a mixture that is very shiny and just drops reluctantly from the spoon in a sheet.

To make the roasted rhubarb compote, preheat the oven to 400°F.

Slice the rhubarb into 1-inch pieces and arrange in a single layer in a medium-sized ovenproof dish. Scatter the sugar over the rhubarb and let macerate for at least 45 minutes or 1 hour, if possible, until the juice starts to run. Cover with a sheet of parchment paper for 10 minutes. Remove and continue to roast for 15 to 25 minutes, depending on size, until the rhubarb is tender. Purée and add rosewater to taste—just a little to give a haunting flavor.

To cook the beignets, mix the sugar and cinnamon in a bowl.

Heat the oil in a deep-fry to 400°F. Drop teaspoons of the choux dough into the hot oil and cook for 2 to 3 minutes or until puffed and golden. Toss in the cinnamon sugar.

Serve immediately, allowing 5 per person, with a little bowl of roasted rhubarb purée for dipping.

Lughan's Mackerel with Roasted Pickled Rhubarb

Lughan Carr, a past student and teacher, cooked this inspired combination one day when we had an abundance of fresh mackerel and extra rhubarb from the garden.

. . . .

SERVES 4 AS AN APPETIZER

FOR THE ROASTED PICKLED RHUBARB
8 ounces rhubarb, cut into small, even
  chunks (about 1¾ cups)
¼ cup granulated sugar
1½ tablespoons red wine vinegar
a pinch of salt

FOR THE MACKEREL
2 fresh mackerel—4 fillets
seasoned all-purpose flour
2 tablespoons butter
chervil sprigs

Preheat the oven to 250°F.

To make the pickled rhubarb, mix the rhubarb with the sugar, half the vinegar, and a pinch of salt. Spread on a parchment-lined baking sheet and roast, uncovered, for 15 to 20 minutes. The rhubarb should be just tender. Cool slightly, then mix in a bowl with the remaining vinegar.

To pan-grill the mackerel, heat the grill pan. Dip the fish fillets in the seasoned flour. Shake off the excess flour and then spread a little butter with a knife on the flesh side, as though you were buttering a slice of bread rather aggressively. When the grill is quite hot but not smoking, place the fish fillets butter-side down on the grill; the fish should sizzle as soon as they touch the pan. Reduce the heat slightly and cook for 4 to 5 minutes on that side before you turn them over. Continue to cook on the other side until crisp and golden.

Split the mackerel fillets lengthwise and serve two pieces per person on warmed plates. Serve some roasted pickled rhubarb alongside and garnish with chervil sprigs.

Rhubarb Soda

Deliciously fresh tasting and a cool way to use the rhubarb syrup saved from rhubarb compote (see page 374). When angelica is in season, I add some fresh young leaves to the rhubarb when making the syrup.

. . . .

MAKES APPROX. 1½ LITERS
1¾ cups rhubarb syrup (page 373)
juice of 2 lemons
3½ to 5 cups sparkling water
ice

Put the rhubarb syrup into a pitcher. Add the freshly squeezed lemon juice.

Just before serving, add sparkling water and ice to taste.

VARIATION

Rhubarb Mimosa—Fill the champagne flutes one-third full with rhubarb syrup. Top off with champagne or sparkling wine.

Polenta Muffins with Roasted Rhubarb

This was inspired by a Roasted Rhubarb Muffin at Violet Cakes in London. The owner, Claire Ptak, says that this mixture can also be cooked in a 9-inch springform cake pan for 50 minutes. We top these muffins with slices of peach, apricot, plum, or figs as the season progresses. This recipe also has the advantage of being gluten-free provided you use gluten-free baking powder.

MAKES 18

8 ounces rhubarb
⅔ cup superfine sugar
8 tablespoons (1 stick) butter, softened
1 cup ground almonds
½ teaspoon vanilla extract
2 medium organic eggs
grated zest of 1 lemon
freshly squeezed juice of ½ lemon
⅓ cup medium fine cornmeal (polenta)
½ teaspoon gluten-free baking powder
pinch of salt
crème fraîche, to serve (optional but
  gorgeous)

Preheat the oven to 400°F.

Slice the rhubarb into 1-inch lengths and arrange in a a single layer in a medium ovenproof dish. Scatter half the sugar over the rhubarb and leave to macerate for an hour or more until the juice starts to run. Cover with a sheet of baking parchment and roast for 20 to 30 minutes until the rhubarb is just tender. Leave to cool.

Line a muffin pan (or pans) with paper liners.

Cream the butter. Add the remaining sugar and continue to beat until light and creamy. Stir in the ground almonds and vanilla extract. Add the eggs, a little at a time, beating thoroughly before adding the next bit. Fold in the lemon zest and lemon juice, polenta, gluten-free baking powder, and salt. Spoon the mixture into the paper liners and lay a couple of pieces of roasted rhubarb (or ripe peach or nectarine) on top of each muffin and bake for 30 to 35 minutes or until deep golden and a skewer comes out clean. Let cool on a wire rack.

Enjoy with crème fraîche, but they are totally delicious on their own.

Raw Rhubarb, Cucumber & Mint Salad

Do try this fresh-tasting combination, you'll be surprised how delicious it is. Use tender young stalks of rhubarb. My friend Camilla Plum first introduced me to raw rhubarb salads, and we've had fun experimenting ever since.

SERVES 4

2 to 3 stalks of young rhubarb
½ crisp cucumber, peeled
1 tablespoon sea salt
2 handfuls of arugula leaves
1 tablespoon freshly squeezed lemon juice
local wildflower honey or sugar, to taste
a handful of shredded mint leaves

Using a vegetable slicer such as a mandolin or a thin-bladed knife, cut the rhubarb slightly on an angle into very thin slices. Repeat with the peeled cucumber.

Toss the rhubarb and cucumber in a bowl with the sea salt and set aside for 10 minutes; rinse and drain.

Toss the rhubarb and cucumber with the arugula leaves in a salad bowl. Drizzle with lemon juice and a little honey or sugar to taste. Scatter the mint leaves over the top and toss gently. It should be fresh tasting.

Serve with pan-grilled salmon or sea bass.

CURRANTS *Ribes* PERENNIAL, ZONES 3–8

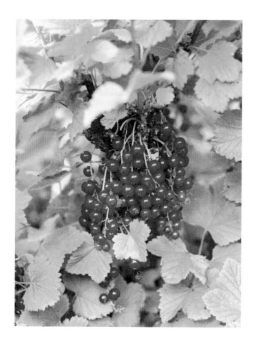

A bumper crop of Jonkheer van Tets red currants.

It's so worth growing some currants—black and white currants are particularly difficult to find unless you grow your own or have a farm shop close by. The bittersweet burst of flavor when you first taste them is so distinctive and different from other summer berries. Even for beginners, currants are easy to grow, they are hardy and not too demanding.

BLACK CURRANTS—*RIBES NIGRUM*

You simply must plant at least one black currant bush, and better still three that fruit in succession, if you are fortunate enough to have the space.

For very little effort you will be rewarded with an abundant harvest every year for more than two decades.

Plant not just for the fruit, but also for the fragrant young leaves that perfume lemonades and sorbets in late spring, and then in summer there's all that fruit from a virtually trouble-free bush; bunches of gleaming black currants, hanging like ringlets from the stems. The fruit is bursting with juicy goodness and flavor and presents a myriad of possibilities for the creative cook.

VARIETIES

Ben Sarek—This is a very early variety with good disease resistance.
Ben Connan—Early variety, compact bush, very heavy cropper with good disease resistance.
Ben Hope—Good cropper, large berries, good disease resistance and tolerance of most soil conditions but does better in a sheltered site.
Wellington—vigorous four-foot-tall bushes, large hanging clusters of fruit.

RED CURRANTS—*RIBES RUBRUM*

May not be on your A-list but let me make a case for you to plant at least one bush—it will last up to 20 years. The shiny red berries grow in clusters of 3 to 10 on little branches or racemes. They are super high in pectin, their bittersweet flavor makes a gorgeous jelly that complements not only lamb, ham and game but makes the perfect glaze for red summer berries in open tarts.

VARIETIES

Jonkheer van Tets—Heavy cropper, large berries on long trusses, ripens early in mid-summer.
Red Start—A good choice to follow an early variety, crops later in summer with a high yield.
Red Lake—Disease-resistant and a heavy cropper.
Rovatta—Disease-resistant bushes produce loads of dark red fruit.

WHITE CURRANTS—*RIBES GLANDULOSUM*

Perhaps the least known of the currant family but I love them to bits. The hardy shrub is actually a version of the red currant (*ribes rubrum*)—an albino variant, with translucent white fruits and a slightly sweeter but still deliciously tart flavor.

VARIETIES

White Versailles—Good crop of large, sweet-tasting berries.
Blanka—High-yielding, large berries.
White Pearl—Highly recommended with superb fruit.

HOW TO GROW

For all currants, choose a sheltered spot and even though they prefer full sun which produces riper sweeter

---

DID YOU KNOW?

Black currants have been grown in the British Isles for over 800 years and variety breeding and selection is run from the world famous Scottish Crop Research Institute at Invergowrie near Dundee. Ben Lomond was the first of the Ben varieties and was released in 1975 and led the way in modern black currant growing.

The town of Bar-le-Duc in France has long been famous for its white currant jelly, also referred to as Lorraine jelly which can sell for €18 for a 3-ounce jar.

currants, they will tolerate dappled shade. All currants will grow in any well-managed garden soil and will tolerate a moister soil than other fruit. They thrive in potash rich soil.

If you have the space, I suggest three black currant bushes, two red currant and one white currant. They require little attention, apart from a little feeding in spring, a nice mulch of compost or well-rotted farmyard manure or horse manure if available, enough to feed them as well as acting as a mulch, watering if there is a dry spell in summer when the fruit is starting to swell, and a bit of judicious pruning in autumn.

Black currants, red currants and white currants are pruned in slightly different ways—red and white currants in a fashion similar to gooseberries.

CONTAINER GROWING

Even though they make a big bush, currants may be grown in a large pot—it needs to be at least 2 feet wide and 20 inches deep—and filled with well-drained soil, which has been enriched with plenty of well-rotted manure or humus. You will need to be vigilant about pruning them, keep 4 to 5 branches, otherwise they will become too large for the pot and will be top heavy. Regular watering during the growing season is essential, particularly when the fruit is swelling.

Ben Lomond—Black currant suitable for container growing, it flowers relatively late in spring and therefore can miss some of the effects of frost.

Rovada—Good choice of red currant for pots. Heavy cropper, good flavor.

HARVESTING

We use the fresh young leaves in spring and early summer to make a refreshing tea, lemonade, jelly, sorbet and granita.

Currants will be ready for picking from mid to late summer. Wait until they are fully ripe and snip off one string at a time. Strip them off the strings over a bowl, grip the stalk at the top and sweep a fork down the length, making sure that the stalk is between the tines so they'll pop off.

PESTS AND DISEASES

Birds love all currants, so either grow them in a fruit cage or cover with netting before ripe. Aphids may attack currants, in particular the currant blister aphid. It looks nasty, the leaves pucker with red and yellow blotches, but interestingly it doesn't really affect the crop.

Big bud is another disease common to currants, mainly black, and attacks the bushes in late winter, although Ben Hope is said to be resistant to it. It is caused by a mite that lives in the dormant buds during the winter; in spring the buds will look enlarged and round rather than conical as they would normally look before opening in the spring. The best way to avoid this is to purchase the bushes from certified stock in a nursery. If your bushes get a light attack, pick off the infected buds during the winter and burn them. The only cure for a bad infestation is to dig up the infected bushes and replace with new ones in the autumn, particularly if they are old. Plant clean stock in a new area of ground to ensure that there's no residue of disease remaining in the soil.

Powdery mildew can also attack the currant bushes, seek out mildew-resistant varieties. Plant in a well ventilated area, space them well, and prune them carefully.

In the early 1900s, growing currants and gooseberries was banned in the U.S. to prevent the spread of white pine blister rust. The federal ban was lifted in 1966, but some states still prohibit currant

White currant in blossom—indicating a bumper crop ahead.

growing. Concert, Cursader, and Titania varieties are resistant to the rust fungus.

GOOD FOR YOU...

Black currants are very rich in vitamin C, they are much the best source in terms of fruit, especially when raw and all currants are rich in antioxidants and minerals. They also have high concentrations of potassium, magnesium, iron, calcium, and vitamins A and B. Red currants have similar nutritional value and also contain vitamin K. White currants also contain vitamin C and potassium (though not as high as black currants) and are a source of bioflavonoids and proanthocyanidins.

WHAT TO DO WITH A GLUT

All currants freeze perfectly. There is no need to destalk before freezing, just shake the bag when frozen to detach the stalks. Use for desserts or to make jam or jelly during the winter. Black currants can be dried and used in scones, muffins, and granolas. Make lots of homemade black currant cordial and crème de cassis.

Shaken currants, a Scandinavian tradition, is a beautiful way to preserve red currants or white currants in the short term. Take 2 pounds currants, rinse if necessary, remove the stems, put them into a container with a lid, add 2¼ cups granulated sugar, and mix gently. Leave at room temperature for 3 days, shaking now and again to make sure the sugar is dissolved. Then transfer to the fridge, where it will keep for several weeks. Delicious for breakfast with yogurt or oatmeal, or with ice cream or even as an accompaniment to fish or chicken.

IN THE KITCHEN

We love black currant compotes, summer fruit salads, cakes, pies, and ice creams. Black currant jam, delicious as it is, benefits from the addition of rose geranium or lemon verbena.

The bittersweet flavor of red- and white currants enhances both sweet and savory dishes, and they can be frosted with egg white and superfine sugar. No commercial red currant or white currant jelly will be nearly as delicious as the red currant jelly you can make in eight minutes, see page 384. White currant jelly is rarer and arguably more delicious than the more well known red currant version. Red currants are very high in pectin, so some red currant juice added to strawberry or blackberry jam will add a tart note and help the jam set. To make 1¾ cups Red currant Juice, put 1 pound red currants (fresh or frozen) into a stainless-steel saucepan with ¾ cup water. Bring to a boil and simmer for about 20 minutes. Strain through a fine sieve. Freeze for use later if necessary.

Ripe black currants ready to pick—get there quickly before the birds.

Black Currant Leaf Granita on a Black Currant Leaf

Black currant leaves have a distinctly black currant flavor. Use only the young leaves in spring and early summer—when the bushes begin to flower the leaves lose their intense flavor. We also use this recipe to make an elderflower sorbet—substitute 4 to 5 elderflower heads in full bloom.

. . . .

SERVES 6 TO 8

2 large handfuls of young black currant leaves
2½ cups cold water
1 cup granulated sugar
juice of 3 lemons
1 organic egg white (optional)
large black currant leaves, to serve
violet or viola flowers (optional)

Crush the black currant leaves tightly in your hand and put into a stainless steel saucepan with the cold water and sugar. Stir to dissolve the sugar and bring slowly to a boil. Simmer for 2 to 3 minutes. Let cool completely. Add the lemon juice. Strain and freeze for 20 to 25 minutes in an ice-cream maker or sorbetiere.

If you do not have a sorbetiere, simply freeze the sorbet in a dish in the freezer. When it is semi-frozen, whisk until smooth and return to the freezer again Whisk again when almost frozen and fold in one stiffly beaten egg white. Keep in the freezer until needed.

If you have access to a food processor, freeze the sorbet completely in a pan, then break up and pulse for a few seconds in the processor, add 1 slightly beaten egg white, pulse, and freeze again. Serve.

Serve in chilled glasses or chilled white china bowls or on pretty plates lined with frosted blackcurrant leaves (painted with egg white and dusted with caster sugar). Sprinkle a few violet or viola flowers on top.

Frosted Black Currant Parfait

So simple and so good with an intensely black currant flavor. Friends are mightily impressed when I serve this parfait drizzled with black currant sauce for a dinner party.

SERVES 6

¾ pound fresh or frozen black currants
¾ cup simple syrup (page 290)
granulated sugar (optional)
2½ cups very softly whipped heavy cream

FOR THE BLACK CURRANT SAUCE
½ pound black currants
1 cup simple syrup (page 290)
½ to ⅔ cup water

lemon balm leaves, to garnish

Double-line a 5 × 8-inch loaf pan with plastic wrap and parchment paper.

Cover the black currants with simple syrup. Bring to a boil and cook for 4 to 5 minutes until the fruit bursts. Liquidize and strain or purée the fruit and syrup and measure out ¾ cup. Taste—you may need to add extra sugar. Frozen black currants tend to be less sweet. When the purée has cooled, add the very softly whipped cream. (You can make the recipe to this point and serve as Black Currant Fool.)

An alternative presentation is to layer the purée and softly whipped cream in tall sundae glasses, ending with a drizzle of thin purée over the top.

Pour into the lined pan, cover with a piece of parchment paper, and wrap the pan in plastic wrap to seal. Freeze.

To make the black currant sauce, pour the syrup over the black currants and bring to a boil, then cook for 3 to 5 minutes until the black currants burst. Liquidize and pour through a nylon strainer. Let cool. Add ½ to ¾ cup water and then mix to loosen.

To serve, cut the parfait into ½-inch thick slices. Serve on chilled plates with a drizzle of black currant sauce. Garnish with lemon balm leaves.

Black Currant Leaf Lemonade

We make this fresh tasting lemonade in late spring and early summer while the leaves are still super fragrant. We use the leaves to flavor granitas, syrups, and custards.

SERVES ABOUT 6

2 large handfuls of young black currant
  leaves
1 cup granulated sugar
freshly squeezed juice of 3 lemons
3 to 3¾ cups still or sparkling water
ice cubes

Crush the black currant leaves tightly in your hand, then put them into a stainless-steel saucepan with 2½ cups of water and the sugar. Stir to dissolve the sugar and bring to a boil slowly. Simmer for 2 to 3 minutes, then set aside to cool completely.

Add 3 cups water, taste, and add more water if necessary. Serve chilled with lots of ice.

Fresh Red Currant Soda

A deliciously refreshing summer drink with a bittersweet flavor with lots of spritz.

. . . .

MAKES 3 CUPS

1 pound fresh red currants
1¼ cups simple syrup (page 290)
juice of 1 lemon
soda or sparkling water, or to taste
mint ice cubes (see page 290)

Process the berries with the syrup and lemon juice in a blender. Strain through a nylon sieve and press gently. Store in a dark colored glass, screw-top bottle in the fridge but use within 3 to 4 days.

To serve, shake the bottle, pour a little into a glass to taste, and top off with soda water or sparkling water. We use between a third and half red currant purée. Or make up a pitcher of Red currant Soda with 3 cups red currant syrup to 4 cups soda water. Add some mint ice cubes.

Crème de Cassis

This is so worth making—can you imagine having your own homemade crème de cassis that's better than anything you can buy? And it's the perfect base for a Kir Royale or Cardinal (made with red rather than white wine). A little crème de cassis is delicious added to whipped cream or used to make cocktails.

. . . .

MAKES 9 × 8-OUNCE BOTTLES

2¼ pounds fresh organic black currants, strings removed
1 liter good-quality red wine, a Burgundy would be most appropriate
approx. 6½ cups superfine sugar
approx. 3½ cups gin or vodka (28 ounces)

Put the black currants and red wine into a stainless steel or stoneware crock bowl and let macerate overnight.

The next day, liquidize the wine and currants and pour through a fine nylon sieve into a stainless steel saucepan. Measure and add 5 cups superfine sugar for every 4 cups of black currant liquid. Stir over medium heat for 4 to 5 minutes until the sugar dissolves, then leave over low to medium heat for about 2 hours, by which time the liquid will be slightly syrupy. Do not allow to boil or the flavor will taste more like jam.

Mix 1 part vodka or gin to 3 parts of cool black currant syrup. Store in vodka or gin bottles, seal, and allow to mature for at least a week before using. Crème de cassis keeps well but use before the new season's crop.

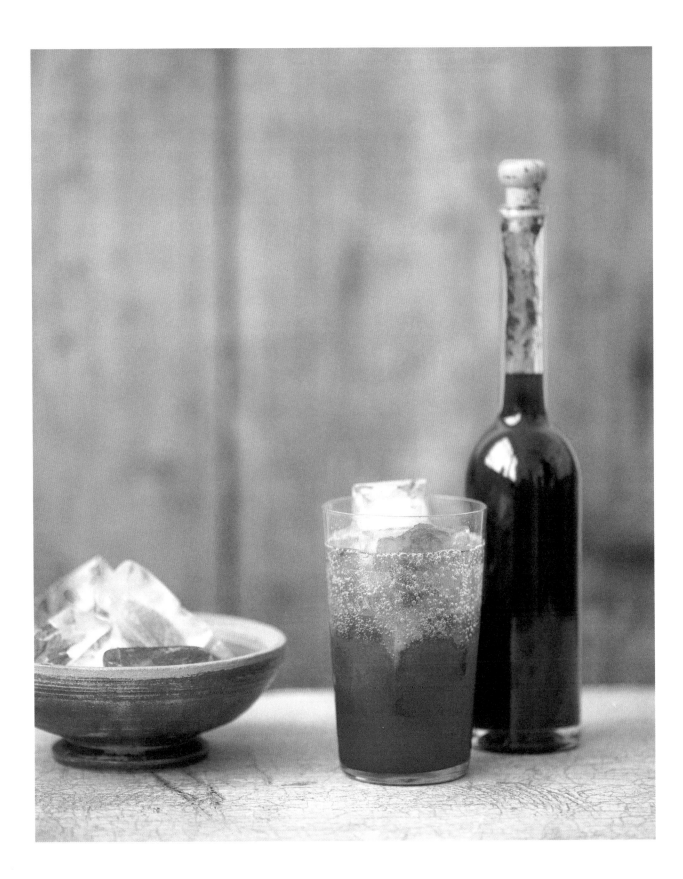

Red Currant or White Currant Jelly

This version is made in just eight minutes and the resulting currant pulp can be used as a tart filling, added to strawberry jam to increase the pectin, or as a basis of a sauce to serve with ice cream. Unlike other fruit jelly recipes, no water is needed. Red currant jelly can be used like a jam on bread or scones, or served as an accompaniment to roasted lamb, bacon, or ham. It is also good with some coarse pâtés and game. It is invaluable as a glaze for red fruit tarts. You can also use white currants for a version that is wonderful with cream cheese or the perfect accompaniment to lamb or pork.

. . . .

MAKES 3 × 8-OUNCE OR 4 × 6-OUNCE JARS

2 pounds red currants or white currants
4 cups granulated sugar

Remove the strings from the red currants either by hand or with a fork. Discard. Put the red currants and sugar into a stainless steel saucepan and stir continuously until the sugar dissolves. Boil for exactly 8 minutes, stirring only if the currants appear to be sticking to the bottom. Skim carefully.

Pour through a nylon strainer and allow to drip through. Don't push the pulp through or the jelly may be cloudy. Stir in gently once or twice just to free the bottom of the strainer of pulp. This will only take a few minutes.

Pour the jelly into sterilized jars immediately. Red- and white currants are very high in pectin so the jelly will begin to set at once. Cover and store in a cool, dry place. It will keep for 6 to 12 months, and once opened, at least a month in the fridge, or even longer if the berries are organic.

Save the red currant pulp to serve in a tart or with plain yogurt, or add a little water and use as a sauce with roasted chicken or pheasant, or add a little Kirsch to the red currants and serve with ice cream.

Black Currant Pastilles

These tiny treats are utterly delicious. They taste intensely of black currant, so cut them into little bites to savor slowly.

. . . .

MAKES 25 × 1½-INCH SQUARES

2¼ pounds fresh or frozen black currants
2½ cups granulated sugar, plus extra for dusting
⅓ cup corn syrup
¼ cup liquid pectin

Line an 8-inch square pan with parchment paper.

Put the black currants into a large stainless steel saucepan over low heat. Cook gently for 8 to 10 minutes until the fruit bursts and there's lots of juice. Push the fruit through a nylon strainer until just the pulp remains and discard.

Return the juice to the saucepan and add the sugar, corn syrup, and liquid pectin. Heat gently until the sugar dissolves, increase the heat, and boil, stirring constantly, for 12 to 15 minutes until the mixture thickens. When it reads 225°F on a sugar thermometer, pour into the pan. Allow to set for several hours. Turn onto a clean cutting board, cut into squares, and toss gently in granulated sugar. Let dry, then pack into pretty boxes. They will keep for months but are best eaten within a few weeks.

GOOSEBERRIES

Ribes uva-crispa (Ribes grossularia)

Gooseberries are a gardener's must-have in my book because they are rarely found on supermarket shelves, although they do occasionally pop up in good markets and farmers' markets. So don't leave it to chance, plant a few carefully chosen varieties in your garden. With a little judicious pruning they'll fruit for years and produce an abundance of berries for tarts, pies, fools, ice creams, jams, compotes and sauces. They are hardy and work well in any climate and have a wonderful flavor when freshly picked. The large number of varieties available means you can choose some for cooking, but allow others to ripen to enjoy later when they are plump and juicy.

VARIETIES

COOKING VARIETIES

Invicta—Relatively new variety which dates from 1960, a heavy cropper with

Gooseberry bush grown as a cordon.

excellent mildew resistance.
Pixwell—Large, productive plants produce, mild, dependable fruit.

DESSERT VARIETIES

Dessert varieties are eaten raw, so allowed to ripen on the plant until soft and juicy, but of course can be cooked when they are still unripe.
Black Velvet—Vigorous grower, mildew resistant and strong against sawfly.
Hinnonmaki Red—Excellent flavor, very sweet, good cropping, good mildew resistance.
Hinnonmaki Yellow—Sweet, thin-skinned, greenish yellow berries that ripen in midsummer.
Captivator—Red-skinned, sweet and juicy.
Jeanne—a new variety resistant to powdery mildew and blister rust. Good desert quality fruit.

HOW TO GROW

Gooseberries are easy to grow in any fertile well-drained soil. If you buy bare-rooted bushes, plant them during the dormant season—later winter to early spring. Bushes purchased in pots can be planted any time, but will need to be watered if the weather is dry.

If space allows plant them 80 inches apart. It will give you more room to pick them, they need lots of space and benefit from good air circulation, so they aren't stressed and hence more susceptible to disease.

They don't need full sun but some sun will encourage a heavier, riper crop. We prune them in midsummer before fruiting, it opens up the bush and helps

air circulation which discourages mildew and make it easier to see if the bush is being attacked by sawfly. We prune again in the winter.

There are several good books on pruning, for example *The Fruit Tree Handbook* by Ben Pike, *The Fruit Garden Displayed* (RHS) by Harry Baker.

CONTAINER GROWING

Standard gooseberries make excellent plants for a large tub. The container needs to be 14 inches deep and filled with a loam-based compost; you can use a bigger pot for larger plants. Regular bushes can also be trained as a single cordon supported by a cane or tied to a trellis when space is at a premium. You could plant a number of different varieties this way even with limited space.

PESTS AND DISEASES

Sawfly larvae which look like tiny caterpillars can strip the leaves off the plant in record time. Gooseberry bushes planted well apart seem less susceptible and we seem to have almost eliminated this pest by mulching with humus.

Mildew can definitely be a problem in some varieties, but once again enough space and good pruning helps. Choose mildew-resistant varieties where possible. A well-ventilated area and summer pruning will help by removing the tips of the branches where mildew is likely to lodge, but in my experience you're better to cut your losses and dig out and discard the bush because the chances of another attack in the following year is very probable. The fruit will develop little brown furry spots if mildew is present.

HARVESTING

Pick green cooking varieties in early summer. Gooseberry branches are prickly so you may want to wear gloves for extra protection. Dessert gooseberries may be picked as they ripen during the summer, you may have to cover with a net to keep the birds from eating them.

GOOD FOR YOU...

Gooseberries are a source of antioxidants, especially flavones and anthocyanins, both of which are thought to have positive effects against inflammation, and neurological diseases. They are low in calories, are a rich source of vitamin C, and contain a small amount of vitamin A.

WHAT TO DO WITH A GLUT

Gooseberries freeze really well. If you have time, trim them first but that can also be done while they are still frozen, though it's a bit messier. You can make jam, jellies, chutney, and cordials to store. You could also try making Gooseberry Wine, and very good it is too.

IN THE KITCHEN

By a happy accident of nature, green gooseberries and elderflower are in season at the same time—a marriage made in heaven. I love gooseberries in tarts, pies, compotes, fools, crumbles, chutneys, and cordials. They make a delicious sauce with barbecued mackerel or roasted pork. Simply stew the gooseberries in a little simple syrup until they burst—simple but delicious. It's important to allow the gooseberries, particularly the green ones, to burst while cooking, so the sugar can penetrate into the tart fruit, otherwise they will look perfect but be mouth puckeringly bitter.

Green Goosegog Crumble

When I was little we always called gooseberries goosegogs. Crumbles are a quintessential British comfort food and this is a brilliant master recipe—just vary the fruit according to the season. Tart green gooseberries work really well here, contrasting deliciously with the crumble.

SERVES 6 TO 8

1½ pounds green gooseberries
3 to 4 tablespoons dark brown sugar

FOR THE CRUMBLE
3 tablespoons butter
¾ cup all-purpose flour, preferably
 unbleached
¼ cup superfine sugar
¼ cup sliced almonds

FOR THE ELDERFLOWER CREAM
1 tablespoon elderflower cordial
1¼ cups whipped cream

Preheat the oven to 350°F.

First stew the gooseberries gently with the sugar and 1 to 2 tablespoons of water in a covered casserole or stainless steel saucepan until the fruit bursts. Taste and add more sugar if necessary. Turn into a 9-inch pie dish. Let cool while you make the crumble.

Rub the butter into the flour just until the mixture resembles *really coarse* bread crumbs, then add the sugar. Sprinkle this mixture over the gooseberries in the pie dish. Scatter the sliced almonds evenly over the top. Bake for 30 to 45 minutes or until the topping is cooked and golden.

Add the elderflower cordial to the cream and whisk lightly; it should be very softly whipped.

Serve with elderflower cream or just softly whipped cream and brown sugar.

VARIATIONS

Gooseberry & Elderflower: Stew the gooseberries with white sugar, add 2 elderflower heads tied in cheesecloth while stewing, remove the elderflowers, and proceed as above.

Crumble Variations: ¼ cup oats or sliced hazelnuts or almonds can be good

JR's Green Gooseberry Tartlets

JR Ryall is the passionate young pastry chef at Ballymaloe House who creates the sweet treats for which Ballymaloe is justly famous. His Green Gooseberry Tartlets are truly delicious, best served warm for afternoon tea or dessert. The dough is scarily rich and is best made the day before, but it is gorgeously flaky without the rolling and folding involved in puff pastry. Use green gooseberries at the beginning of the crop, when they are still hard and tart.

MAKES APPROX. 36 TARTLETS

FOR THE COLD CREAM PASTRY DOUGH
¾ cup all-purpose flour
8 tablespoons (1 stick) cold salted butter
⅔ cup cold cream

FOR THE FILLING
1 pound tart green gooseberries, trimmed
superfine sugar

To make the dough, sift the flour into the bowl of an electric food mixer. Cut the butter into small cubes and rub into the flour using the paddle attachment until the mixture forms a coarse texture (slow speed and then a little faster). DO NOT overmix; if you do the mixture will form a shortbread-like ball! Pour the cold cream into the coarse mixture and mix on low speed until a smooth dough forms. Wrap the dough in parchment paper and chill overnight. This dough keeps in the fridge for up to six days.

Preheat oven to 375°F.

Always roll cream pastry dough straight from the fridge. If the dough comes to room temperature, it will be too soft to handle. Using plenty of flour, roll the cold dough to a thickness of 1/16-inch. Cut the dough with a 3-inch round cutter and use the discs of dough to line three standard shallow bun pans.

Cut the gooseberries in half and arrange 6 to 7 halves, cut-side upward, on each disc of dough. Spread a rounded teaspoon of superfine sugar on top of the fruit in each tartlet. Bake for 15 to 20 minutes or until the sugar begins to caramelize and the dough is a golden brown color. Use a palette knife to remove the tartlets from the bun pan while still hot. Place on parchment paper that has been sprinkled with superfine sugar.

VARIATIONS
Open Apple Tartlets: Replace the gooseberries with thinly sliced apple.

Open Rhubarb Tartlets: Replace the gooseberries with thinly sliced pink rhubarb.

> **DID YOU KNOW?**
> The cooling properties of the gooseberry were used in the treatment of fever during the Middle Ages. North American Indians used the leaves, branches, and inner bark to treat colds and diarrhea.

Green Gooseberry & Elderflower Trifle

Our repertoire of trifles continues to grow—this green gooseberry and elderflower one is a fairly recent addition—delicious, the combination of green gooseberry and elderflower with custard and sponge cake, what's not to like?

. . . .

SERVES 16 TO 20/ MAKES 1 × 2-QUART OR 2 × 1-QUART GLASS BOWLS

FOR THE SPONGE CAKE

9 tablespoons (1 stick + 1 tablespoon) butter, plus extra for greasing
1⅓ cups all-purpose flour, plus extra for dusting
¾ cup superfine sugar
3 large organic eggs
1 teaspoon baking powder
1 tablespoon milk

FOR THE GREEN GOOSEBERRY AND ELDERFLOWER COMPOTE

2 pounds green gooseberries
3 to 4 elderflower heads
2½ cups cold water
2 cups granulated sugar

FOR THE CUSTARD

1¾ cups milk
⅔ cup heavy cream
1 vanilla bean, split
3 large organic whole eggs, plus 3 yolks
¼ cup superfine sugar
⅔ cup elderflower cordial

2½ cups softly whipped cream
gooseberries and leaves or pink sweet geranium flowers, to garnish

Preheat the oven to 375°F.

First make the sponge cake. Grease 2 × 7-inch round cake pans with melted butter, dust with flour, and line the base of each with a round of parchment paper. Cream the butter and gradually add the superfine sugar, then beat until soft and light and quite pale in color. Add the eggs one at a time and beat well between each addition. (If the butter and sugar are not creamed properly and if you add the eggs too fast, the mixture will curdle, resulting in a cake with a heavier texture.) Sift the flour and baking powder into the mixture and stir in gradually. Mix all together lightly and use the milk to moisten.

Divide the mixture evenly between the pans, hollowing it slightly in the center. Bake for 20 to 25 minutes or until cooked—the cake will shrink in slightly from the edge of the pan when it is cooked, and the center should feel exactly the same texture as the edge. Alternatively, a skewer should come out clean when inserted into the center of the cake. Turn onto a wire rack and let cool.

Meanwhile, make the compote: First trim the green gooseberries. Tie the elderflower heads in a little square of cheesecloth or just put them directly into a stainless steel or enameled saucepan, add the sugar, and cover with cold water. Bring slowly to a boil and continue to boil for 2 minutes. Add the gooseberries and simmer just until the fruit bursts. The tart green gooseberries must actually burst, otherwise the compote of fruit will be too bitter. Let cool completely.

Next make the custard: Heat the milk and cream with the vanilla bean until barely simmering. Whisk the eggs with the sugar. Add the milk to the egg mixture, whisking all the time. Put into a heavy saucepan and stir over low heat for 5 to 6 minutes until the custard coats the back of the wooden spoon lightly. Don't let it boil or it will curdle. Pour into a cold bowl and stir as it cools. Remove the vanilla bean.

To assemble, take two trifle bowls. Put a little custard in the base of each and top with some green gooseberry compote. Split the cakes in half, put a layer of cake on top of the compote, drizzle with elderflower cordial, follow with another layer of custard, green gooseberry, and elderflower compote, more cake, elderflower cordial, gooseberry compote, and finally a layer of custard.

Cover each bowl and let settle in the fridge for at least 2 hours or overnight, if possible.

To serve, spoon a layer of softly whipped cream over the top. Pipe a ruff of cream around the edge and decorate with gooseberry leaves and sweet geranium flowers or simply fresh mint and elderflowers.

Red Gooseberry Jam

Somehow this jam brings childhood memories flooding back—it's surprisingly rare in these days of raspberry and strawberry jam ad nauseam. Gooseberry jam made from the ripe summer gooseberries is a quite different flavor to the green gooseberries, but also super delicious.

MAKES 10 × 5-OUNCE JARS

2¼ pounds red gooseberries

freshly squeezed juice of 1 lemon

3¾ to 5 cups granulated sugar, heated in a moderate oven (page 396)

Top and tail the gooseberries. Put into a wide, stainless-steel saucepan with the lemon juice. Cook for 5 to 6 minutes until the fruit bursts.

Add the hot sugar. Stir until the sugar is dissolved. Return to the boil and cook for about 30 minutes until setting point is reached. If you have a sugar thermometer, the jam will set when it reaches 390°F. Otherwise put a spoon of jam onto a cold plate, leave it to sit for a minute or two, then push the jam with your index finger. If it wrinkles, the jam will definitely set. Pour into dry, sterilized jars. Cover immediately and store in a dark, dry place.

This jam will, of course, keep for months, but why would you not tuck in and enjoy as soon as possible.

Green Gooseberry & Elderflower Jam

It's worth growing a gooseberry bush just to make this jam alone. The gooseberries should be green and tart and hard as hailstones—as soon as the elderflowers are in bloom in the hedgerows, search for the gooseberries under the prickly bushes or seek them out in your local greengrocer or farmers' market.

MAKES 6 × PINT JARS

3½ pounds tart green gooseberries

freshly squeezed juice of 2 lemons, mixed with enough water to measure 1¼ cups in total

5 to 6 elderflower heads

4½ cups granulated sugar

Preheat the oven to 320°F.

Trim the gooseberries and put into a wide stainless-steel saucepan or preserving pan with the lemon water and the elderflowers tied in muslin. Simmer for about 30 minutes until the gooseberries are soft and burst.

Warm the sugar in a bowl in the preheated oven for about 10 minutes.

Remove the elderflowers and add the warm sugar, stirring until it has completely dissolved. Boil rapidly for about 10 minutes until setting point is reached (390°F on a jam thermometer) or put a teaspoonful on a cold plate, leave in a cool place for a few minutes, if the jam wrinkles when pushed with the finger it has reached setting point. This jam should be a fresh green color, so be careful not to overcook it.

Pour into hot clean sterilized jars, cover, and store in a dry, airy cupboard. It will keep for 6 to 12 months but is best enjoyed when it's fresh.

RASPBERRIES *Rubus Idaeus* PERENNIAL, ZONES 3–9

The flavor of raspberries has suffered less deterioration than commercial strawberries. Summer raspberries are undoubtedly a little tricky to grow. We grow both main crop for summer fruiting and autumn varieties. The latter are by far the most worthwhile. The berries are less fragile and less perishable. They fruit on new season's wood and continue to yield berries into the late autumn. As a grandmother, one of my greatest joys is to see my grandchildren bounding out to the raspberry patch to eat their "pudding" straight off the bushes. The older ones put a raspberry on the toddlers' fingertips so they can nibble them off one by one.

Raspberries are particularly disease-prone so are often heavily sprayed, another pertinent reason to grow your own, although your home grown fruit are unlikely to look as large and beautiful as the "perfect" commercial fruit.

Summer-fruiting raspberry canes that have been pruned and tied in.

VARIETIES

Seek out old cultivars for maximum flavor and nutrition. There are summer and autumn fruiting varieties, so choose what's best for your particular situation. There are red, yellow, white, and even some black varieties.

SUMMER
Early
Killarney—medium-sized fruit on tall upright plants.
TulaMagic—Large, firm, sweet, light red berries
Prelude—produces big, firm, delicious red berries.
Caroline—produces two crops of red berries, in early summer and fall.

MID-SEASON
Bristol—Heirloom black raspberry with outstanding flavor.
Jewel—Large, glossy, black fruit, great for jams and jellies.
Latham—Honored, old-time variety with dependable crops of red fruit.

LATE SUMMER
Royalty—Very productive, the most popular purple variety.
Encore—Large, vigorous canes produce good crops of sweet fruit

AUTUMN
Autumn Bliss—The original autumn raspberry, excellent large succulent fruit. Good resistance to root rot.
All Gold—Sweeter than Autumn Bliss, well flavored yellow berries.
Fall Gold—Yellow-fruited variety.

Joan J—Big berries, superb flavor, spine-free canes.
Polka—Good disease resistance, very big fruit, with a long fruiting season from summer to the first frost.

HOW TO GROW

Raspberries prefer a damp climate and a rich neutral or acidic soil. We use copious amounts of compost and thick mulches. Surprisingly, summer varieties can thrive in semi-shade but the autumn fruiters yield best when we have a hot, dry summer and a moist autumn.

Raspberries can be grown undercover, but it's not necessary, however netting or a cage affords protection from birds who can polish off copious amounts of berries.

It is essential to provide strong support for raspberry canes. It's best to provide three double strands of wires so the canes can be restrained between them. Tie in to the support as they grow. They can also be trained up a tripod. Summer raspberries are pruned in autumn, cut out the old canes to allow room for new growth—consult a good manual.

Autumn raspberries are so easy, we just cut everything to the ground in late winter and use the canes for kindling.

Keep the plants well mulched to suppress weeds and avoid damaging the shallow roots while weeding.

CONTAINER GROWING

Raspberries do not grow or yield satisfactorily in containers.

PESTS AND DISEASES

Viral disease can cause stunting on canes and loss in yields, most likely to occur in mid to late summer. There will be spots and blotching on the leaves. Remove the canes and destroy.

Spur blight can affect raspberries as well as loganberries and other hybrids.

It is a fungus, which usually appears in late summer, causing the canes will to be stunted and weakened and the buds killed. More common in wet summers. Remove diseased canes and destroy. Choose varieties which have some resistance to spur blight like Glen Moy and Malling Admiral.

Raspberry beetle, like most pests, can be controlled by good hygiene. Rake back the mulch in winter to allow birds and poultry if you have them to hoover up the pupae. The grubs of raspberry beetle will damage the fruit, it shows as dried up patches. There are a number of permitted sprays that can be used such as pyrethrum and seaweed solution sprays with magnesium sulphate added, or as a soon as most of the blossom has fallen.

Autumn varieties seem to be more resistant to disease and pests. Birds are the greatest challenge, so cover if feasible and we also concoct a variety of bird scarers, including an inflatable battery-operated "man" that pops up randomly every 8 to 15 minutes. However, the birds definitely get used to that by the end of the season. Noisy bird scarers work well but certainly won't endear you to your neighbors. Put them on a timer switch so they turn off at night.

Tansy, garlic or calendulas planted close by deter pests and look pretty in the garden. We have left grass paths between rows for ease of mowing.

HARVESTING

Summer raspberry varieties are particularly fragile, so pick them as they ripen and carefully pull off the stalk on a dry day, into small punnets or bowls, so they don't get crushed. Cover and store raspberries in the fridge and eat as soon as possible. But bring back to

All Gold—attractive fruits but not quite as flavorful as some of the red varieties.

room temperature to enjoy them at their best. Raspberries are very perishable, use within a day or so or freeze immediately.

GOOD FOR YOU...

Raspberries are high in vitamin C and antioxidants. They are also good sources of riboflavin and niacin, magnesium, manganese, folic acid and dietary fiber and help regulate blood sugar levels.

WHAT TO DO WITH A GLUT

Raspberries freeze well and are perfect for jam. We also make raspberry vinegars, shrubs (drinking vinegars), and a probiotic, water kefir.

IN THE KITCHEN

Raspberry jam is one of the quickest and easiest jams to make, even if you don't have a lot of raspberries. It can be made in small quantities, even just enough to top sponge cake or eat with scones. To make 3 × 16-ounce jars of **Raspberry Jam**, preheat the oven to 350°F. Spread 2¼ pounds freshly picked raspberries on a baking sheet and put 3¾ cups

Polka—excellent variety—disease resistant with a long growing season.

superfine sugar into a heatproof (Pyrex) bowl. Heat until they are both hot. When the berries are really hot and are just beginning to bubble at the edges, scatter with the hot sugar and stir until the sugar is dissolved. Use a spatula to transfer back into Pyrex bowl and stir again. Pour into sterilized jars. Dip 3 parchment discs into brandy or kirsch and lay one on top of the jam in each jar. Cover with a screw-top lid, cool, and store in a fridge if possible. Enjoy within 3 to 4 months and use quickly once the jar is opened.

In summer I can scarcely get past putting freshly picked raspberries into a bowl and enjoying them with sugar and cream, but there are a myriad of ways to enjoy them. Add them to muesli and granolas for brunch, add to berry and fruit salads, or slice in half lengthwise to garnish both appetizer and dessert plates. We also love raspberry ice cream and sorbet—the intensely fresh berry flavor.

Danish Raspberry Shortbread

Every time I'm in Copenhagen I make a beeline for a little stall in Torvehallerne called Café Rosa. There the Japanese owner who was inspired by Pippi Longstocking makes a range of homemade pastries and Danish cinnamon buns that look refreshingly unprofessional but each and every item tastes sublime. I end up buying far more than I can eat, but everyone is willing to share. This is one of my favorites; Meyers Bageri also makes a delicious version.

. . . .

MAKES 12 × 3-INCH SQUARES

2½ cups all-purpose flour, sifted

½ cup confectioners' sugar, sifted

14 tablespoons (1 stick + 6 tablespoons)
  butter, chilled

2 organic egg yolks

rice flour, for dusting

¼ cup raspberry jam (page 396)

confectioners' sugar, for dusting

Put the flour and confectioners' sugar in a bowl and grate in the butter on a box grater. Rub in until the mixture resembles bread crumbs, add the egg yolks, and bring together with your hands, but don't knead. Wrap in parchment paper and chill for 1 hour.

Preheat the oven to 400°F.

Sprinkle a sheet of parchment paper with rice flour. Divide the dough in half, then roll out separately to make two squares, 10-inch × 9-inch × ¼-inch thick. Still attached to the paper, transfer to two baking sheets and cook for 10 minutes until pale golden in color.

Spread raspberry jam evenly on one of the squares, while still warm. When the other square is cool, lay on top and peel off the paper. Press gently. This is a super short, but really delicious dough, however it's a nightmare to cut evenly. Do your best to cut it in squares or rectangles. Dust with confectioners' sugar and enjoy as soon as possible. Best on the day it's made but I've certainly enjoyed it the next day.

Beet, Raspberry, Honey & Mint Salad

This is a surprising but delicious combination of raspberries and beets that I first came across in a restaurant in London. Now we use this bizarre sounding duo in several salads and in ice cream to rave reviews. My brother Rory likes to add a few teaspoons of thick yogurt or labneh when serving.

. . . .

SERVES 4

2 cooked beets, peeled and very thinly
  sliced on a mandolin

24 raspberries

sea salt and cracked black pepper

mixed flower honey

lemon juice

extra virgin olive oil

16 small mint leaves

Divide the sliced beets between 4 white plates

Cut some of the raspberries in half lengthwise and some in cross-section slices, and scatter over the beets. Season with salt and freshly cracked black pepper.

Dress the salads with a drizzle of honey, a squeeze of lemon juice, and a drizzle of olive oil. Sprinkle with the tiny mint leaves and serve.

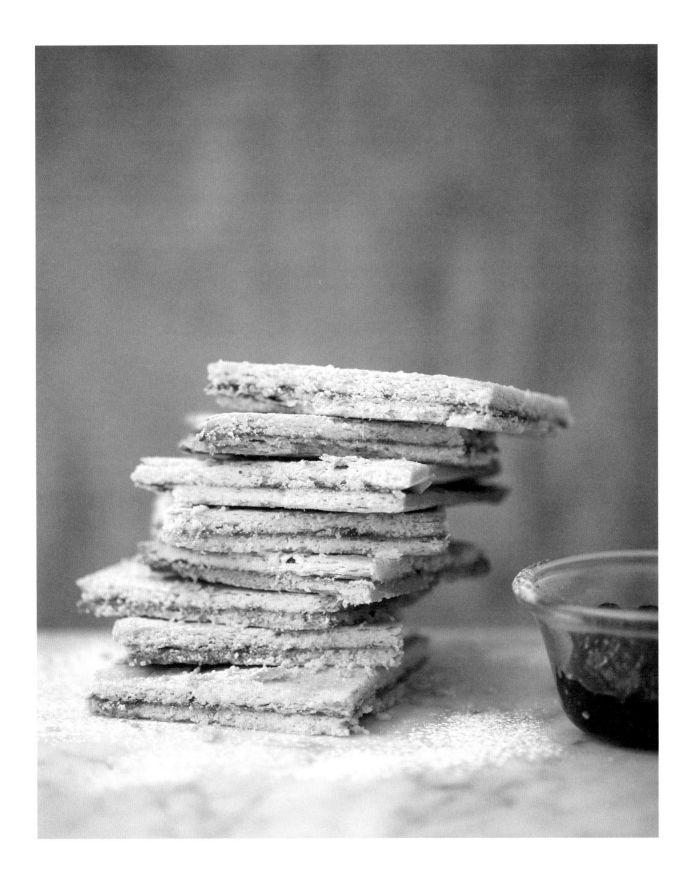

Papanasi with Jam & Smetana

Possibly the best loved of all Transylvanian desserts—one bite and you'll understand why. Smetana is a Romanian sour cream. Lightly crushed fresh raspberries are delicious on the papanasi but jam is more traditional.

SERVES 6 TO 8

1½ cups ricotta
⅓ cup all-purpose flour
2 large organic eggs
½ teaspoon salt
3 tablespoons superfine sugar
1 teaspoon baking soda
zest of 1 lemon
vegetable oil
granulated sugar, for dusting
¾ cup smetana or sour cream
raspberry jam (see below), to serve

Mix the ricotta, flour, eggs, salt, sugar, baking soda, and lemon zest together in a bowl. Mix thoroughly until smooth. Lay a sheet of oiled parchment paper on a baking sheet. Scoop out a little blob of the dough enough to make a ball about 2 inches in diameter. Lay on the sheet, flatten a little, and poke a hole in the center to resemble a donut. Continue with the remainder of the dough.

Heat a deep fry pan to 350°F. Lower a couple of papanasi gently into the oil and fry them for 3 to 4 minutes on each side. Remove and drain on paper towels, then toss in sugar.

Serve immediately with a dollop of smetana and a blob of raspberry jam on top.

Quick Raspberry Jam

Raspberry jam is the easiest and quickest of all jams to make, and one of the most delicious. Loganberries, boysenberries, or tayberries may also be used in this recipe.

MAKES 3 PINT JARS

2 pounds fresh raspberries
4 cups granulated sugar

Wash, dry, and sterilize the jars in a preheated 350°F oven for 15 minutes, then heat the sugar in the oven for 5 to 10 minutes.

Put the raspberries in a wide stainless steel saucepan and cook for 3 to 4 minutes until the juice begins to run, and then add the hot sugar and stir over low heat until fully dissolved. Increase the heat and boil steadily for about 5 minutes, stirring frequently.

Test for a set by putting about a teaspoon of jam on a cold plate, leaving it for a few minutes in a cool place. It should wrinkle when pressed with a finger. Remove from the heat immediately. Skim and pour into the sterilized jam jars and seal immediately with a lid.

Hide the jam in a cool place or else put on a shelf in your kitchen so you can feel great every time you look at it! It will keep for up to a year.

VARIATION
Raspberry & Cassis Preserve: Make the jam as above and add ¼ cup of cassis to the jam just before sealing. Store as above.

LOGANBERRIES, BOYSENBERRIES & TAYBERRIES

Rubus hybrids PERENNIAL, ZONES 6–9

Loganberry is a hybrid of a raspberry and American blackberry. Supposedly discovered by accident in California in the 1880s by a Judge JH Logan. It is a long, bittersweet berry of considerable deliciousness. It needs to be very ripe to be eaten raw and has a solid center like a blackberry.

Boysenberries were thought to be a hybrid between blackberries and raspberries, but it is more likely a cross between a youngberry and loganberry, which resulted in large, winey, black berries with a sweet, tangy flavor. They are delicious berries and well worth growing if you have space. Grow and

Left: *Loganberriess—resist picking until the fruit is dark red and fully ripe.*
Middle: *Boysenberries—large, purple, raspberry-like fruits which ripen midsummer.*
Right: *Tayberries make the best soft fruit jam of all.*

support in the same way as raspberries. A bush can produce up to 10 pounds of fruit in a good season, and continue to produce fruit for up to 15 years when carefully pruned and mulched.

Tayberries are a cross between a red raspberry and a blackberry and are named after the River Tay in Scotland where they were bred and patented in 1979. If you have space for one hybrid berry, try to grow one or several tayberries. The large, dark maroon-colored berries have a bittersweet flavor, a divine perfume and a central plug like blackberries. Many people rate tayberries more highly than loganberries which, although delicious, are smaller and less aromatic. They are vigorous plants and prolific fruiters. Like boysenberries they are long-lived and go on fruiting for up to 25 years.

Don't pick the fruit until fully ripe, a dark reddish purple color, rather than red.

Prune by cutting off the old wood

that has produced fruit, and be careful not to cut out the new growth that will produce fruit the following season.

VARIETIES

LOGANBERRY
Thorned loganberry LY59—Excellent flavor, long berries.
Thornless loganberry L654—Very healthy stock if one can get it.

BOYSENBERRY
Large red fruits which turn purplish as they ripen.
Thornless—Good flavor, heavy cropping, good for jam and freezing.

TAYBERRY
Tayberries have large sweet fruit, more aromatic than loganberries. The are quite vigorous growers and prickly.

HOW TO GROW

They all thrive best in rich fertile well-drained moisture-retentive soil. If planting bare-rooted bushes plant in the dormant season, potted bushes may be planted at any time of year, but make sure they don't dry out after planting.

CONTAINER GROWING

I wouldn't recommend growing any of them in a container, as they are hungry plants and wouldn't thrive.

PESTS AND DISEASES

All the berries suffer from similar pests. Raspberry beetle can be a problem but birds are the main challenge, you will need to net the bushes to get your fair share.

Cane spot and spur blight can also occur.

HARVESTING

Pick the fruit as it ripens, it needs to be dark red.

GOOD FOR YOU...

Boysenberries contain manganese, iron, potassium, calcium, folate, vitamin C and fiber. They are also a source of anthocyanins and natural antioxidants which help to maintain healthy brain cells.

WHAT TO DO WITH A GLUT

One can never have too many. Make lots of jam or jellies. All these berries freeze well so we add to fools, pies, or popsicles in winter or apple tarts. Our grandchildren also love them crushed into Bircher Muesli for their breakfast before they run off to spend a busy day at school.

IN THE KITCHEN

Enjoy boysenberries in the same way as raspberries, loganberries, and tayberries in pies, jams, and crumbles. Savor tayberries as you would other berries, but they are best eaten warm off the bushes with heavy cream and a sprinkling of sugar. They freeze well.

DID YOU KNOW?

Scotland is famous for raspberry growing and in the 1950s, when the fruit was brought to the London market by train, it became known as The Raspberry Special.

Loganberry Fool

It's not at all the thing to mash one's berries in polite company. I must confess to doing just that behind closed doors, because somehow they taste much more delicious that way. Compromise, and serve the berries as Fool and then you have the best of both worlds.

SERVES 8 TO 10

1 pound fresh loganberries, boysenberries, tayberries, blueberries, strawberries or raspberries

½ to 1 cup sugar

2½ cups softly whipped cream

Crush the berries with a fork and sprinkle with sugar.

Whip the chilled cream to soft peaks, and fold gently through the fruit to get an irresistible streaky fool.

Serve as soon as possible, well chilled, with a thin shortbread cookie.

Ballymaloe Loganberry & Hazelnut Meringue

We use this All-In-One meringue recipe for birthdays, anniversaries, Valentine's Day, or simply for a special dessert. Fresh raspberries, tayberries, or boysenberries are also irresistible in this recipe. Loganberries need to be dark and fully ripe, otherwise they can be very bitter. This version has three layers, but you can make 4 × 7-inch discs instead.

SERVES 8 TO 10

⅔ cup fresh hazelnuts, chopped
2 cups confectioners' sugar, sifted
4 organic egg whites
sprigs of mint or lemon balm, to garnish

FOR THE FILLING

1¾ to 2½ cups whipped cream
1 pound raspberries, loganberries, tayberries, or boysenberries

Preheat the oven to 350°F.

Spread the hazelnuts on a baking sheet. Roast for 10 to 15 minutes or until the skins loosen. Put into a kitchen towel and rub off the skins. Cool and chop coarsely.

Reduce the oven temperature to 300°F.

Check that the bowl and whisk are dry, spotlessly clean, and free from grease or any residue of detergent. Mark 3 × 8-inch circles on parchment paper.

Put the confectioners' sugar into the bowl with the egg whites. Whisk for about 8 minutes until the mixture forms stiff dry peaks. Fold in the cooled hazelnuts. Divide the mixture between the three circles and spread evenly with a palette knife, keeping the edges rounded rather than flat.

Bake immediately for 45 minutes or until set and crisp. Turn off the oven. Let cool in the oven if possible and then transfer to a wire rack. The meringue should peel easily off the parchment paper. (The meringue discs will keep for several weeks in a pan.)

To assemble, sandwich the meringue layers together with the fruit and the softly whipped cream. (Proportion is really important here, and each layer of filling should not be thicker than a disc of meringue.) If you chill for an hour before serving it will be easier to cut.

Decorate with rosettes of whipped cream and fresh loganberries. Garnish with little sprigs of mint or lemon balm.

BLUEBERRIES

Vaccinium corybosum PERENNIAL, ZONES 4–7

Blueberries are ridiculously easy to grow if you have acid soil, if however your soil is limey they are really not worth considering—it will be an uphill battle to get a decent yield. They are native to North America and we have a little plot of blueberry bushes in West Cork where the soil is naturally acidic, which yield a phenomenal crop of juicy, bittersweet blueberries almost every year. Blueberries have pretty white flowers in spring and the foliage also colors beautifully in autumn so it's worth growing for aesthetics as well as the flavor and nutritional value of the fruit.

VARIETIES

Earliblue—One of the first varieties to ripen in midsummer.

Duke—A slightly later variety.

Chandler—Late summer variety.

Nelson—Mid-to-late variety and self-fertile.

Top Hat—Heavy-cropping, self-fertile dwarf variety, so could be considered for growing in a container.

HOW TO GROW

Blueberries hate lime and only thrive in acid soil. Soil acidity can be measured with a pH meter which you can buy from a DIY shop or garden center. Blueberries need the same type of soil as rhododendrons or azaleas. The pH needs to be 5.5 or lower for blueberries to flourish. They need to be kept well-watered, but use rain rather than tap water which is usually alkaline and will raise the pH level.

You won't need to prune for the first 2 to 3 years, but after that remove the old wood to encourage new growth.

Grow in a sunny or sheltered spot. You'll need to grow at least two bushes unless you are growing a self-pollinating variety.

CONTAINER GROWING

Blueberries grow perfectly in a large pot in ericaceous compost (you will need a self-fertile variety if you are just growing one).

If growing in a container, choose a specimen that is at least 12 inches diameter, then transfer into a larger pot (18 to 20 inches in diameter) when it outgrows the smaller one, keep moist with rainwater.

PESTS AND DISEASES

Blueberries are resistant to most pests. However, birds love blueberries and will polish off the lot as soon as they ripen unless you protect them with a net or a

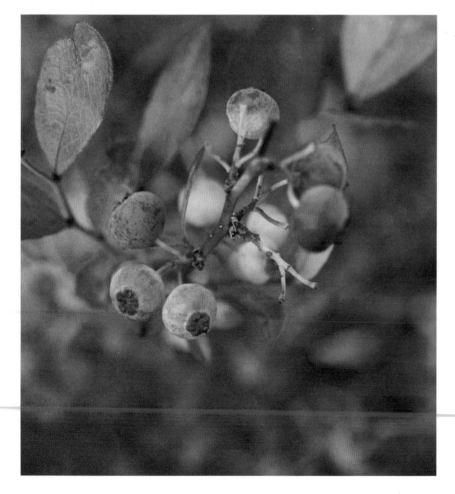

Blueberries are very productive. You can expect to yet 7 to 9 pounds per bush.

simple fruit cage. When planted in acid soil they are relatively problem free but powdery mildew can be a problem if the plant is allowed to dry out (see page 627 for ways to prevent it).

HARVESTING

Blueberries are quick and easy to harvest, no prickles. They are in season from midsummer to early autumn and are ready to pick when they turn a deep, cloudy navy blue.

You can expect to get 7 ½ to 9 pounds of fruit from one bush after a couple of years.

GOOD FOR YOU...

Blueberries are very high in antioxidants, vitamins C, A, and E, iron, zinc, phosphorus, and calcium. They are low in calories, considered by many to be a superfood, decrease the risk of heart disease, help prevent cancer, and improve mental health and digestion. Best eaten raw.

WHAT TO DO WITH A GLUT

Blueberries freeze very well but can also be dried very successfully in a dehydrator or at the lowest setting in a convection oven. Apple and blueberry jam is delicious as is blueberry cordial.

IN THE KITCHEN

Blueberries can be eaten fresh or cooked, or they can be preserved in jams or pickles. They don't need any pitting or peeling or trimming. We use them in both sweet and savory dishes, blueberry muffins, and scones. Try tossing them into salads.

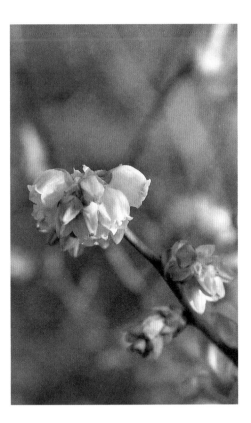

Blueberry blossom.

Blueberry Cake

A simple cake that showcases blueberries enjoyed with a cup of coffee or can be served for dessert.

. . . .

SERVES 9

10 tablespoons (1 stick + 2 tablespoons) butter, softened
½ cup superfine sugar
3 large organic eggs, separated
finely grated zest of 1 lime
⅔ cup all-purpose flour
½ cup cornstarch
1½ cups blueberries, plus extra to serve
softly whipped cream, confectioners' sugar, and fresh mint sprigs, to serve

Preheat the oven to 350°F. Line the bottom and sides of a 9-inch square pan with parchment paper.

Cream the butter and ½ cup superfine sugar until pale and fluffy. Beat in the egg yolks and lime zest.

Whisk the egg whites until softly whipped, add the remaining ¼ cup superfine sugar, and whisk until it reaches a really stiff peak. Sift the flour and cornstarch together and fold into the creamed mixture, alternating with the whisked egg whites. Finally, fold the blueberries in gently.

Pour the mixture into the lined pan. Bake in the center of the oven for 45 minutes or until well-risen and golden and just firm to the touch. Let cool in the pan.

Cut into nine squares and serve with a dollop of whipped cream, a dusting of confectioners' sugar, some extra blueberries, and a sprig of mint.

Salad of Warm Smoked Fish with Blueberries, Avocado, Walnuts & Greens

Sounds like an odd combination but try it—it's surprisingly delicious and the chia seeds add extra crunch.

SERVES 4

FOR THE HONEY CHIA DRESSING
3 tablespoons extra virgin olive oil
1 tablespoon white wine vinegar
1 teaspoon mixed flower honey
1 tablespoon chia seeds
good pinch of salt

FOR THE SALAD
2 handfuls of arugula, baby spinach leaves, and baby kale, washed and dried
1 small red onion, halved and thinly sliced
¾ cup blueberries
1 avocado, diced
½ pound warm smoked salmon, flaked, or hot-smoked mullet
12 walnuts, halved, toasted, and coarsely chopped
edible flowers, calendula petals, chives, or wild garlic flowers, to garnish (optional)

Whisk the ingredients for the dressing together.

Put the greens into a bowl. Sprinkle with dressing. Add the onion and blueberries and toss gently to coat. Pile onto a serving plate, then sprinkle with avocado, warm smoked fish, and walnuts on top. Fork up gently.

Garnish with edible flowers, if available.

Blueberry Scones

Fresh fruit are an interesting addition to scones and strawberries or raspberries work equally well here.

MAKES 18 TO 20 × 2¾-INCH SCONES
7½ cups all-purpose flour
pinch of salt
⅔ cup sugar
3 heaped teaspoons baking powder
4 ounces blueberries, chopped
12 tablespoons butter
3 organic eggs
approx. 2 cups milk
eggwash, made with 1 beaten egg and a pinch of salt
demerara sugar, for sprinkling

Preheat the oven to 465°F.

Sift all the dry ingredients together in a large wide bowl. Cut the butter into cubes, toss in the flour, and rub in the butter; add the blueberries. Make a well in the center. Whisk the eggs with the milk, add to the dry ingredients, and mix to a soft dough. Turn out onto a floured board. Don't knead but shape just enough to make a round. Roll out to about 1 inch thick and cut with a biscuit cutter. Put onto a baking sheet—no need to grease. Brush the tops with egg wash and dip each one in demerara sugar. Bake for 10 to 12 minutes until golden brown on top. Cool on a wire rack.

Serve with a blob of whipped cream.

CRANBERRIES

Vaccinium oxycoccos PERENNIAL, ZONES 3–6

How cool is it to be able to make cranberry sauce from your very own homegrown cranberries, the flavor and texture are far superior. This bushy creeping, evergreen plant won't thrive in limey conditions, it needs an acid, peaty soil and so grows well in the same marshy terrain as blueberries, bilberries and lingonberries—moist, boggy, humus-rich soil—they seem to be a less popular choice to grow than other berries. In the US, huge acres of them are grown and the fields are flooded to harvest them. If you are a keen gardener and have the space why not try them? They have pretty, rosy-pink flowers in early summer, followed by the tart red berries.

VARIETIES

Vaccinium macrocarpon—Large berries. Excellent flavor, a North American species of cranberry.

Viburnun occulus americanus (**Highbush cranberry**) plants grow to 15 feet tall and produce cluster of small fruit.

HOW TO GROW

Unless you have the correct soil conditions, don't bother to grow cranberries. They need a low pH and lots of organic matter. Buy a plant, or several, from a good garden center, plant in moist acidic soil in autumn or late spring, firm well and allow 2 to 3 feet between the

plants and rows. Cranberries are self-fertile.

Keep weed free and well-watered, but don't saturate. They send out runners and provide ground cover.

We haven't grown them indoors.

CONTAINER GROWING

Choose a large pot or container. Fill it with a mixture of peat compost, sand and leaf-mold (ericaceous compost). Plant one seedling, firm and water regularly

Wild cranberries grow in the Bog of Allen— they need acid soil.

with rainwater rather than tap water. If you are in a limey area, as we are here in Shanagarry, such plants generally need to be replaced every three to four years, unlike those grown in a garden.

PESTS AND DISEASES

Not much on a garden scale. Plants will need to have runners snipped back after a couple of years.

HARVESTING

Harvest the dark red berries from autumn to early winter. Cranberry plants do not produce fruit until their third or fourth year, so you have a "head start." Commercial growers harvest by flooding the fields, cranberries float and are therefore easier to scoop up or rake

---

DID YOU KNOW?

Cranberries have been grown successfully on a commercial basis in the Bog of Allen in Co. Kildare for a number of years. They are called mónog in Irish, and are also referred to as bogberry or mossberry after a pilot conducted by Bord na Móna (originally established in Ireland as The Turf Development Board). In the US they are a major commercial crop in Wisconsin, Massachusetts and less so in Oregon, Washington, and New Jersey.

off, but we simply pick off the ripened berries by hand before they get hit by frost.

GOOD FOR YOU...

Cranberries seem to be a powerhouse of nutrients. We all know that cranberry juice relieves urinary tract infections, but they are lauded as one of the world's healthiest foods, and you can bet your bottom dollar that your own home-grown berries will be super-high in antioxidants. There is a growing body of research to suggest that cranberries have anti-cancer properties. They also boost the immune system. High in vitamins C, E, K, manganese, fiber and pantothenic acid.

WHAT TO DO WITH A GLUT

Unlikely, but fresh cranberries not only keep well—for up to two months in the fridge—but freeze perfectly and keep for a year or more. You can make copious amounts of cranberry sauce, but I prefer to make it fresh from chilled or frozen berries. They contain a large amount of benzoic acid, which is a natural preservative. If you have a dehydrator, it's a simple matter to make your own dried cranberries. They will keep for at least six months and up to a year.

IN THE KITCHEN

Terrifically versatile, cranberries' tart, fruity flavor is great in sauces, pies, tarts, crumbles and crisps, cakes, juices, and chutneys. The astringent taste cuts the sweetness of meringues and pavlovas. They also work in punches and cocktails. We scatter a few into our favorite salads and sprinkle them over pancakes in the same way as blueberries or black currants. Remember sugar toughens the skin of cranberries, so cook them first and then stir in the sugar.

The tart berries are also delicious added to scones, or sugared or frosted to decorate cakes, particularly for the festive season. We also love an apple and cranberry crumble.

Don't forget to add them to salads, particularly cabbage or kale salad, or to a winter tabbouleh. Make your own fresh cranberry or cranberry and apple juice in a centrifuge (juice extractor). Dried cranberries have a special flavor—you find yourself popping them into ice cube trays, adding them to scones, cupcakes, fruit loaves and a myriad of other dishes.

Cranberry Sauce

Cranberry sauce is delicious served with roasted turkey, game, and some coarse pâtés and terrines. We enjoy this simple version best and it keeps in the fridge for 7 to 10 days. It's also great with white chocolate mousse or in a meringue roulade as it cuts through the sweetness. We like to use local cranberries but this recipe also works well with store-bought cranberries.

SERVES APPROX. 6

2 cups fresh cranberries
⅓ cup granulated sugar

Put the fresh cranberries in a small heavy-bottomed stainless steel or cast-iron saucepan with ¼ cup of water—don't add the sugar yet as it tends to toughen the skins. Bring to a boil, cover, and simmer for about 7 minutes until the cranberries pop and soften. Remove from the heat and stir in the sugar until dissolved. Serve warm or cold.

VARIATIONS

Cranberry & Orange—Use freshly squeezed orange juice instead of water and add the rind of ½ organic orange.

Cranberry & Apple—Mix Cranberry Sauce made as above with half quantity of homemade Apple Sauce (page 323). It's delicious!

Festive Cranberry & Pear Tart

This tart is mighty. It is wonderful served warm but is also very good cold and it keeps for several days. Splash in a little kirsch if you are using pears (Calvados would be better with apples). I've used both fresh and dried cranberries in this recipe, both are good. The cranberries make the tart look festive.

SERVES 8 TO 10

FOR THE SHORTCRUST PASTRY DOUGH
1⅔ cups all-purpose flour
pinch of salt
8 tablespoons (1 stick) butter, cold
1 organic egg yolk
3 to 4 tablespoons cold water

FOR THE POACHED PEARS
1 cup granulated sugar
2½ cups water
a couple of strips of lemon peel and juice of ½ lemon
6 pears

FOR THE FRANGIPANE
7 tablespoons butter
½ cup superfine sugar
1 organic egg, beaten
1 organic egg yolk
1 cup whole blanched almonds, ground
3 tablespoons all-purpose flour
2 tablespoons kirsch, if using pears

FOR THE APRICOT GLAZE
(MAKES 1¼ CUPS)
12 ounces apricot jam
juice of ½ to 1 lemon

approx. 1 cup cranberries
softlt whipped cream, to serve

First make the shortcrust pastry dough: Sift the flour and salt into a bowl, cut the butter into cubes, and rub into the flour with your fingertips. When the mixture looks like coarse bread crumbs, stop. Whisk the egg yolk and add the water.

Take a fork or knife and add just enough liquid to bring the dough together, then discard the fork and collect the dough into a ball with your hands. This way you can judge more accurately if you need a few more drops of liquid. The drier and more difficult-to-handle dough will give a crisper crust. Cover the dough with plastic wrap and transfer to the fridge to rest for at least 15 minutes or 30 minutes if possible. This will make the dough much less elastic and easier to roll.

Next poach the pears: Bring the sugar and water to a boil with the strips of lemon peel in a nonreactive (stainless-steel) saucepan.

Meanwhile, peel the pears thinly, cut in half, and core carefully with a melon baller or a teaspoon, keeping a good shape. Put the pear halves into the syrup, cut-side uppermost, add the lemon juice, cover with a parchment-paper lid, and the lid of the saucepan. Bring to a boil and simmer for 15 to 20 minutes until the pears are just soft. Let cool.

Preheat the oven to 350°F. Roll out the dough, line a 9-inch diameter tart pan with a removable bottom, prick lightly with a fork, flute the edges, and chill for about 10 minutes until firm. Bake blind for 15 to 20 minutes.

Next make the frangipane: Cream the butter, gradually beat in the sugar, and continue beating until the mixture is light and soft. Gradually add the egg and egg yolk, beating well after each addition. Stir in the almonds and flour and then add the Kirsch or calvados. Pour the frangipane into the crust, spreading it evenly. Drain the pears well and when they are cold, cut them crosswise into very thin slices, then arrange the sliced pears around the tart on the frangipane pointed ends toward the center. Fill in all the spaces with the cranberries.

Increase the oven temperature to 400°F. Bake the tart for 10 to 15 minutes until the dough is beginning to brown. Reduce the oven temperature to 350°F and cook for another 20 to 30 minutes or until the fruit is tender and the frangipane is set in the center and nicely golden.

Meanwhile, make the apricot glaze: In a small saucepan (not aluminum), melt the apricot jam with the lemon juice and enough water to make a glaze that can be poured. Push the hot jam through a nylon strainer and store in an airtight jar. Reheat the glaze to melt it before using.

When the tart is fully cooked, paint generously with half the apricot glaze, remove from the pan, and serve warm or cold with a bowl of softly whipped cream.

GRAPES *Vitis vinefera* DECIDUOUS, ZONES 3–8

Ballymaloe House, like many other country houses with walled gardens, has several ancient vines growing in the lean-to greenhouses on the south side. The Victorians perfected table grape cultivation and made it into a fine art, in heated greenhouses and with lots of gardeners. We're not sure who planted the Black Hamburg vine at Ballymaloe. It now has a thick gnarled stem, but each year we are eternally grateful as it produces copious bunches of plump blue-black grapes that remind us of how grapes should taste. Many people have forgotten (or never knew) what grapes even look like. Only last year when we were selling some beautiful home-grown grapes at our local farmers' market, a lady complained that the grapes she'd bought the previous week, had "nearly choked her child" because they had seeds in them—can you imagine! She was absolutely serious and had apparently never come across a grape with seeds before—time for a revolution.

Having said that, it's fun to grow a grape vine, even outdoors on a south-facing wall; it will at least produce vine leaves and may even produce some grapes. But the reality is that for dessert grapes you'll need to grow the vines under glass in this part of the world. They will grow without protect throughout the U.S. as long as the proper variety is chosen.

Colm McCan, our consultant sommelier at Ballymaloe House, and wine tutor here at the Ballymaloe Cookery School, ordered some vines. We planted them both in the greenhouse and outdoors—one on a sheltered wall in the courtyard and the rest in the currant and berry garden, as an experiment. We intend to make some wine with the Autumn 12 week students. Maybe we'll prove once and for all that you can't make a premier cru in Ireland....

VARIETIES FOR EATING
BLACK
Black Hamburg—Superb old variety with large bunches of fat, juicy black grapes. They can be exceedingly long-lived. Also used for winemaking.
Blue Muscat—large bunches of dark blue, seedless fruit, well distributed on the vine.

Mars Seedless—an improved Concord grape, ripening in late summer.

WHITE
Hope Seedless—Huge harvest of sweet green fruit

RED
Reliance —Seedless red dessert grape, with tender skin and exceptional flavor.

FOR WINE MAKING
Here are some of the varieties we planted, most of these are varieties more suited for cold climate vine growing areas, and with the exception of Pinot Noir, most would not be household names on a wine list.
WINE GRAPES
Orion
Bacchus
Solaris
Rondo
Pinot Noir
LaCrescent—makes sweet white wine.
Marquette—for a rich, robust red wine.
Swenson Red—can make a floral white wine.
St. Croix—for a Burgundy style wine.

HOW TO GROW
Vines will grow in most soils, acid or alkali, inside or out. Much better cultivated inside unless it's a really hot spot. If growing inside put the roots outside to get all the moisture they need, which will make them less prone to powdery mildew. We plant root outside and train through a hole in the greenhouse wall. The vines will need to be supported on wires.

Black Hamburg.

COMPANION PLANTING

In France roses are often grown at the end of the row of vines to attract pollinating insects. The rose bushes will also be an indicator to the grower if there is a problem with mildew and the vines might need to be sprayed. French calendulas planted underneath the vines will deter white fly.

CONTAINER GROWING

Vines can certainly be grown in large containers. They prefer not to be confined but when carefully pruned and judiciously watered, they can work well and can look good on a terrace.

PESTS AND DISEASES

Grapes are susceptible to many insects and diseases—mealy bug, mildew, red spider, use biological control (see page 627). Keep well-watered and ventilated. Birds love ripe grapes so net them unless you have lots to spare but we find that we have so many other crops in the greenhouse ripe at the same time that the grapes aren't the biggest attraction.

HARVESTING

As they ripen snip off the bunches with a piece of stalk attached being careful not to bruise. We've harvested grapes up to the end of November, still sweet and delicious.

GOOD FOR YOU...

Grapes are rich in vitamins A, C, B6, and folate. One of best sources of potassium, they also contain calcium, iron, phosphorus, magnesium, and selenium.

Resveratrol which is found in red and purple grapes, has the ability to dilate blood vessels, helping with heart health. Studies have also linked it with brain-protecting ability, and research is ongoing as well as looking at its benefits for prostate and colon cancer.

WHAT TO DO WITH A GLUT

Make a sourdough starter. Home-grown organic grapes have lots of wild yeast on the skin, which make an active sourdough starter. Make wine....

We dry bunches of small grapes to make raisins. The dehydrator works well but I simply put them on the shelf over the Aga and allow them to frizzle up gradually, or put them on a wire rack near a radiator. They taste delicious but are a nuisance to seed, however I now serve them on the branch with cheese, so guests can enjoy removing the seeds themselves!

IN THE KITCHEN

One of our favorite appetizers on Christmas Day is **Grape, Melon**, and **Mint** salad—it's fresh, fruity, and light.

Black Hamburg growing on a vine in the greenhouse.

It's a great 70s-style and much-loved family recipe. Just a combination of ripe melon, peeled and seeded green grapes, a little freshly squeezed orange and lemon juice, and lots of fresh mint. You might be thinking that life is too short to peel and seed a grape, but it really makes a difference in a fruit salad. The flavors combine deliciously. Another US friend serves fresh grapes tossed in just enough a little sour cream and a sprinkling of superfine sugar—you can't imagine how delicious.

For **Iced Grapes**, snip the grapes into small bunches. Freeze in a single layer and fun and delicious to serve with cheese.

Quail, Grape & Jerusalem Artichoke Salad

A gorgeous light little salad that can make a tasty start to a meal, or a light main course.

SERVES 4

4 quail

4 generous teaspoons mixed flower or
  apple blossom honey

20 black or green grapes

¼ cup chopped thick-cut bacon

1 tablespoon extra virgin olive oil

4 handfuls of lettuce and salad leaves

3 to 4 Jerusalem artichokes, sliced and
  roasted (page 169)

sprigs of chervil

sea salt and freshly ground black pepper

FOR THE HAZELNUT OIL DRESSING

3 tablespoons hazelnut oil

1 tablespoon sunflower oil

1 tablespoon white wine vinegar

¼ teaspoon Dijon mustard

Preheat the oven to 350°F.

Brush each quail with 1 teaspoon of honey and season with sea salt and pepper. Place in a roasting pan and cook for 20 to 30 minutes depending on the size of the bird. Baste the quail while cooking and check for doneness as you would a chicken.

Whisk the ingredients for the dressing together.

While the quail are cooking, halve if black, or peel and seed the green grapes. Toss in 1 tablespoon of the hazelnut oil dressing. Blanch the bacon and keep hot for later. When the quail are cooked, break them down by removing the drumstick and thigh in one portion and the breasts in one portion each, thereby ending up with 4 cuts from each bird. Keep the quail warm.

Sauté the bacon in hot olive oil and keep warm.

To serve, arrange the grapes around each plate and toss the lettuces carefully in the hazelnut oil dressing and place in the center of the plates. Hide a few slices of warm roasted artichokes in between the leaves. Sprinkle with the warm bacon and finally put the warm quail on top of the lettuces, add a few sprigs of chervil, and serve immediately.

Pomegranate & Grape Raita

I ate this pomegranate raita at the Bangala in Karaikudi in Tamil Nadu, South India. It's called Thayir Mathulampazham, or Thayir Pachadi there, and is just one of a whole range of raitas that Meenakshi Meyyappan serves with her curries. I loved the combination of pomegranate and grape here but one can, of course, omit the grapes also.

SERVES 4 TO 6

1 fresh pomegranate

12 green grapes, seeded and cut in half

1¼ cups plain yogurt

pinch of freshly roasted cumin seeds

2 to 3 tablespoons coarsely chopped
  cilantro

a little honey

sea salt and freshly ground black pepper

Split the pomegranate in half around the equator, and place it cut-side down on the palm of your hand. Hold over a container and tap vigorously with a wooden spoon—the seeds will dislodge and fall into the receptacle. Add the halved green grapes, yogurt, a good pinch of freshly roasted cumin seeds and coarsely chopped cilantro, and season with salt and freshly ground pepper. Taste, as it may need some sugar or honey, depending on the yogurt. Serve with hot spicy dishes or mild madras curry.

HERBS

CHIVES *Allium schoenoprasum* PERENNIAL

A member of the vast onion family and an indispensable herb, chives are a perennial friend that re-emerges cheekily from the earth in early spring. I can't help but feel a jolt of excitement when I see the first tender green spears tentatively peeping out of the ground, a definite harbinger of spring.

Chives are among the herbs that go on giving—the more you cut them, the more they come. They also make a pretty edging for flower or herb beds and we also use them to encourage beneficial insects to help with pollination.

VARIETIES

We grow many varieties of allium, several beauties whose pompom flower heads enhance the flower beds and borders, including *Allium giganticum, Allium hollandicum* 'Purple Sensation' and *Allium sphaerocephalon*. But for culinary use we have just three favorites:

Allium schoenoprasum (zones 4–8)— Common chives, hardy perennial. Grows to about 1 foot tall, with hollow, tubular, green, spear-like leaves and round, purple flower heads throughout early and midsummer. There's also a fine-leaved form and a delicate white form that grows to a height of about 8 inches. They, too, have cylindrical leaves and purple and white globular flowers respectively. All are good for eating and cooking.

Allium tuberosum(zones 3–9)—Garlic chives, also known as Chinese chives and flowering chives or leeks. Hardy perennial that grows about 16 inches high. Flat leaves and white flowers that appear in late summer, but are not as bulbous as the other varieties. The leaves have a distinctly garlic flavor and become coarser as the season progresses.

Allium tulbaghia violacea (zones 7–10)— South African, a wild garlic. Also called social garlic because it never makes your breath smell. Glaucous, grey, flat leaves and pretty pale purple flowers. We love it from early summer until late autumn.

HOW TO GROW

Chives are not too fussy, but they appreciate rich, fertile soil and a fairly sunny position. Garlic chives are happiest in a sunny spot, but will also grow in semi-shade.

Add well-rotted manure or compost to the soil if necessary. They can be grown from seed, but need a temperature of 66˚F to germinate. Plant in early spring in deep seed trays in a propagator with bottom heat for best results. We sow about 2 to 3 seeds into each plug, then

Chive flowers in full bloom in early summer with forget-me-nots and variegated lemon balm.

transplant out into the garden when the soil warms up in late spring. Big clumps of established chives can be divided into clusters of 10 to 12 little bulbs and planted about 6 inches apart. Chives die back when temperatures drop in late autumn and early winter

Plant some close to the kitchen door so you can snip without getting your feet wet. We plant chives at the base of apple trees and in the currant and berry garden to protect against disease and a variety of aphids.

CONTAINER GROWING

Chives grow well in containers of all sizes and shapes, even recycled tin cans or windowboxes with drainage holes. Keep watered and feed occasionally with tomato feed.

PESTS AND DISEASES

Fairly disease free outdoors, but they may be attacked by greenfly indoors, particularly if the pot is too small or if not watered regularly during dry spells. Wash thoroughly with a liquid horticultural soap.

Chives can suffer from rust, a serious virus that needs to be eradicated. Dig up the plant and dispose of it immediately—not in the compost heap.

DID YOU KNOW?

Chives are a deterrent to other insects in the garden, but bees love them as they are attracted to the flowers, so it's good to leave some to go to seed for that reason. Chives are one of the *fines herbs* in French cuisine, along with tarragon, chervil and parsley.

HARVESTING

Always cut chives with a scissors or sharp knife about 1 ¼ inches above soil level. The flowering stalks are tougher than the other leaves so avoid those for chopping. We use them in cut-flower arrangements as well as scattered into salads and as a garnish.

GOOD FOR YOU...

Like many of the Allium genus, chives are highly nutritious. They include vitamins A, B6, C, K and small amounts of vitamin E, plus minerals such as calcium, copper, iron, manganese, magnesium, phosphorous, potassium, selenium and zinc. They are also an excellent source of dietary fiber and folic acid. The leaves are mildly antiseptic and are said to simulate appetite and aid digestion.

WHAT TO DO WITH A GLUT

Freeze in ice cubes or dry freeze; also add to breadcrumbs and freeze for stuffings and gratins.

IN THE KITCHEN

We snip the soft, fresh leaves into countless dishes, but you need to use them judiciously. Despite their reputation for having a mild flavor, they are stronger than you might think and it's very easy to overdo it and spoil a dish. Add lots to potato salads, mashed potatoes, and potato cakes. Scatter over salads, into sauces, fold through soft cheese or plain yogurt for a simple dip or a cooler to serve with a spicy dish. Occasionally we add a little sprinkle to scrambled eggs, omelets, frittatas, or kuku (a Middle Eastern frittata); in fact, chives enhance almost all egg dishes.

The pretty pinky-purple pompom flowers are invaluable as a garnish or broken up into individual florets to disperse over salads.

Cut the leaves at a long angle to add to Asian dishes and use the unopened flower heads of the garlic or Chinese chives in stir-fries and peeping out of spring rolls.

Garlic chives flower later in summer.

Stir-fried Eggs with Garlic Chives & Shrimp

A favorite Cantonese family recipe. If garlic chives are not available, you could substitute common chives, but use less— about half the amount.

. . . .

SERVES 2 TO 4

4 large organic eggs
1 tablespoon milk
salt and freshly ground black pepper
2 tablespoons vegetable oil
4 ounces cooked shrimp, peeled
1 large or 2 small fresh garlic cloves, crushed
1 teaspoon peeled fresh ginger, freshly grated
1½ to 2 ounces garlic chives, cut into ¾-inch pieces
fresh garlic flowers (optional)
dark or light soy sauce, to serve

Whisk the eggs with the milk, then season with salt and pepper.

Heat 1 tablespoon of oil in a wok until almost smoking. Add the shrimp, then toss for 30 seconds to 1 minute. Add the garlic and ginger and continue to toss for another minute or so. Add the garlic chives, toss once or twice, and turn onto a plate.

Add the remaining tablespoon of oil to the wok and allow to heat again. Add the beaten egg mixture and cook, stirring, until the eggs start to scramble and form soft folds. Add the shrimp mixture, then stir for a minute or two. Season to taste. Turn onto a serving plate and scatter with a few fresh garlic chive flowers, if using.

Serve while still warm, drizzled with soy sauce.

Aged Cheddar Cheese & Chive Soufflé

Many are convinced that making a soufflé is far beyond them—not at all. If you can master a white sauce, whisk egg whites stiffly into a fluffy mass, and fold them gently, then you can make a soufflé that will draw gasps of admiration from your family and friends. Cheddar cheese soufflé does not rise to quite the heights of a Gruyère and Parmesan soufflé, but it is nonetheless a very tasty dinner dish or a delicious appetizer. Be careful not to overdo the chives. Cheddar and chives are such a good combination, but if you don't love chives just omit them; the soufflé will still be delicious. We sometimes bake these in ovenproof tea cups and serve them on a saucer with a teaspoon.

. . . .

SERVES 6 TO 8

2 tablespoons butter, plus extra for
  greasing
approx. ½ cup toasted fine bread crumbs
  (optional)
2 tablespoons all-purpose flour
1¼ cups milk
3 organic egg yolks
1 level teaspoon salt
½ teaspoon Dijon mustard
1 tablespoon finely chopped chives
1½ cups aged cheddar cheese, grated
4 organic egg whites
green salad, to serve

Preheat the oven to 400°F for one large soufflé or 350°F for smaller soufflés. Grease and crumb one large (2½-cup) soufflé dish or 6 to 8 individual soufflé dishes.

Melt the butter in a heavy-bottomed pot. When it has stopped foaming, add the flour and stir well. Cook gently for 2 minutes. Remove the saucepan from the heat, slowly whisk in the milk, return to the heat, and cook until the sauce boils and thickens. Remove from the heat once more and beat in the egg yolks one by one. Then add the salt, mustard, chives, and all but 2 tablespoons of the cheese (set aside to sprinkle over the top). (The soufflé can be prepared ahead to this stage, but the base mixture must be warmed gently before the egg whites are folded in.)

Whisk the egg whites until they reach a stiff peak. (The egg whites must not be whisked until you are ready to cook the soufflé, otherwise they will lose volume.) Stir about one-third of the egg whites into the cheese mixture and fold in the remainder very carefully. Put into the prepared soufflé dish or individual soufflé dishes.

Sprinkle the remaining grated cheese on top and bake for 9 to 10 minutes for individual soufflés or for 25 to 30 minutes for a large soufflé. They should be well risen and golden on top, yet slightly soft in the center.

Serve immediately on hot plates with a salad of organic leaves.

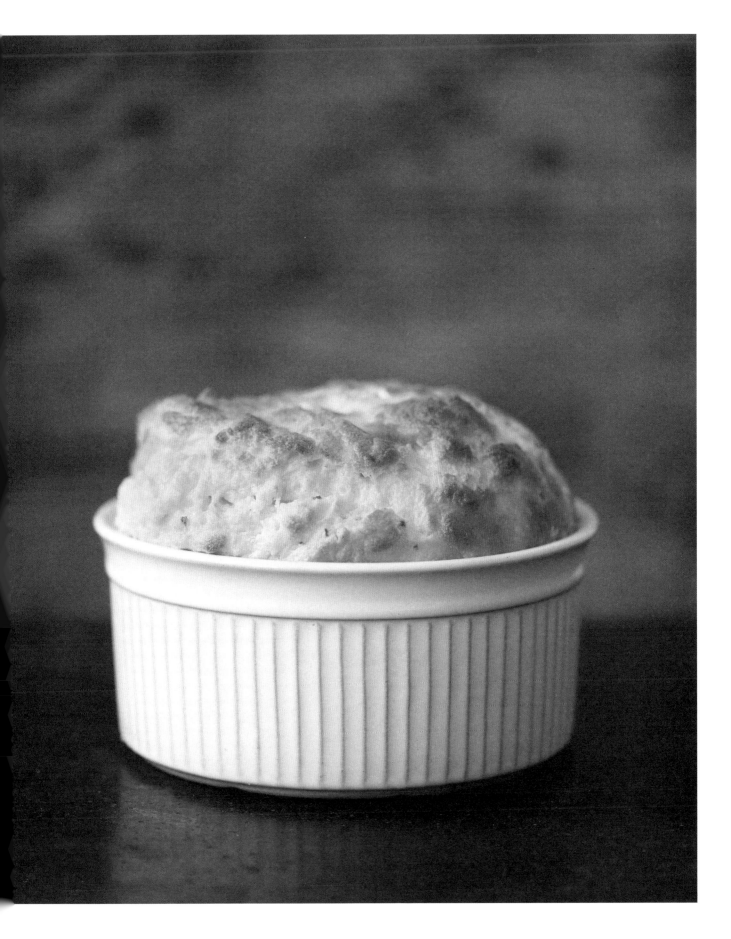

LEMON VERBENA

Aloysia triphylla PERENNIAL, ZONES 8–10

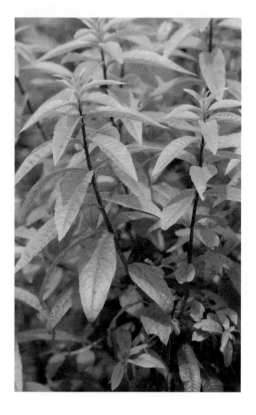

A tender perennial with an evocative lemon flavor and many health-giving attributes.

A divine perennial herb with a souped-up citrus scent and flavor. It's so worth growing lemon verbena. Apart from it being a lovely shrub with little sprays of pretty white flowers, I love being able to snip off a few leaves to make a lemon verbena tisane at a moment's notice. It was first brought to Europe by the Spaniards in the seventeenth and eighteenth centuries to be used in the perfume and cologne industry, but it has a myriad of culinary and medicinal uses. It's called verbena or citronelle in French and is native to Chile and Argentina.

VARIETIES

Aloysia triphylla *(Lippia citriodora)*—

Half-hardy, deciduous perennial, grows up to 10 feet high. Tiny white flowers tinged with lilac in early summer. Strongly lemon-scented leaves.

HOW TO GROW

Buy a healthy plant at a good garden center. Take semi-hardwood cuttings in early autumn, pot them up quickly and put them out when two years old and well established. Lemon verbena likes light, free-draining soil and lots of sun and shelter. Protect from frost in winter and, if you garden anywhere cooler than zone 8, it would be prudent to bring indoors. It re-sprouts late in spring so don't panic if it looks lifeless.

CONTAINER GROWING

Even though I live in a mild area with few frosts, I grow several lemon verbenas in large pots as an insurance. We keep them outdoors in summer, but move them indoors into an unheated greenhouse in winter.

PESTS AND DISEASES

It can suffer from whitefly, so it's a good idea to leave it out during the summer if it's in a pot.

HARVESTING

Pick or snip the leaves as needed.

> ### DID YOU KNOW?
> Lemon verbena is an excellent fly repellent—hang a bunch in your kitchen in the summer to discourage flies and all manner of insects.

GOOD FOR YOU...

Lemon verbena has been used for medicinal purposes such as reducing fever, as a sedative, and for preventing spasms. It is known to boost the immune system and help with digestion, soothe frazzled nerves, and help alleviate congestion. It is also claimed to be effective for weight loss; lemon verbena tea helps to maximize the metabolic system.

WHAT TO DO WITH A GLUT

Lemon verbena is one of the few herbs we dry. Leaves dry quickly and keep their color and aromas very well for us in lemon verbena tea or pot pourris.

IN THE KITCHEN

Just crush a lemon verbena leaf between your fingers and the citrussy smell will immediately suggest a ton of ideas. Lemon verbena granita is so deliciously fresh and lemony, it just flits across the tongue. Lemon verbena ice cream is another favorite, alone or with poached apricots. Add a few leaves to a syrup, or tuck a few under a madeira cake and maybe add a few frosted leaves on top. It makes delicious homemade lemonade, cute little ice cubes, and flavored sugar to sprinkle over tarts, cakes, and fruit salads. To make 2¼ cups **Lemon Verbena Sugar**, process 2¼ cups granulated or superfine sugar with 1 cup chopped lemon verbena leaves in a food processor, in one or two batches. Spread on a baking sheet to dry for several hours or speed up the process in a convection oven at 175°F. Store in sealed glass or mason jars. All the above are delicious, but if you never do anything more than make tea or an infusion from the leaves, it's still worth having a lemon verbena in your garden.

Honey Mousse with Lemon Verbena Peaches

We use our new season's honey for this light mousse and pair it with some of our precious homegrown peaches. Try to find local honey if you don't have your own bees. A delightful combination of delicate summer flavors.

. . . .

SERVES 6 TO 8

2 large organic eggs
3 teaspoons gelatin
3 tablespoons cold water
½ cup best-quality honey
2½ cups heavy whipping cream
1 tablespoon Grand Marnier, or to taste

FOR THE LEMON VERBENA PEACHES
4 large ripe and juicy peaches
1 tablespoon superfine sugar
1 tablespoon finely chopped lemon
  verbena or lemon thyme leaves
1 tablespoon lemon juice

First, make the honey mousse: Beat the eggs in a small bowl until the mixture froths slightly.

Sponge the gelatin in the cold water and then dissolve gently in a small saucepan over low heat. Add the honey to the dissolved gelatin and stir until smooth, if necessary keeping the gelatin over low heat. Cool this mixture until it starts to thicken slightly.

Add the beaten egg to the cream and then mix with the honey mixture. Finally, add the Grand Marnier to taste. Chill for a couple of hours to set.

Shortly before serving, peel the peaches: put the peaches into a Pyrex bowl, fill another bowl with iced water, cover the peaches with boiling water, and leave for 30 seconds, then remove and drop into the iced water. The skins should now peel away easily. Halve them, remove the pits, and cut the flesh into thin slices. Put them into a bowl with the sugar, lemon verbena or thyme, and lemon juice and mix together gently. Leave to macerate for at least 15 to 20 minutes.

Serve the peaches with the honey mousse.

Lemon Verbena Lemonade

A delicious thirst-quenching lemonade with a grown-up flavor! If you keep some chilled Simple Syrup (page 209) made up in your fridge, fresh fruit drinks are simplicity themselves to make. They contain no preservatives so they should be served within a few hours of being made. Many different types of citrus fruit may be used.

. . . .

MAKES 4 TO 6 GLASSES

freshly squeezed juice of 3 lemons
1 cup Lemon Verbena Syrup (page 420)

Mix the lemon juice with the Lemon Verbena Syrup and 2¾ cups of water. Taste and add more syrup if necessary.

Summer Fruit Salad with Lemon Verbena Leaves

I discovered this recipe, which has now become a perennial favorite, quite by accident a few summers ago as I raced to make a dessert in a hurry with the ingredients I had at that moment. Fresh mint or sweet geranium leaves may be substituted for lemon verbena in this recipe.

. . . .

SERVES 8 TO 10

FOR THE LEMON VERBENA ICE CREAM

2 cups cream

¾ cup superfine sugar

10 to 15 lemon verbena leaves, coarsely
   chopped

1 cup whole milk

FOR THE FRUIT SALAD

¾ cup raspberries

¾ cup loganberries

¾ cup redcurrants

¾ cup blackcurrants

¾ cup small strawberries, halved

¾ cup blueberries

¾ cup fraises du bois or wild strawberries

¾ cup blackberries

FOR THE LEMON VERBENA SYRUP

1½ cups granulated sugar

2 cups water

8 to 10 lemon verbena leaves, plus extra
   to decorate

To make the lemon verbena ice cream, put the cream, sugar, and lemon verbena into a saucepan and heat gently. When it reaches the "shivery" stage, remove from the heat, cover, and let infuse for 30 minutes. Strain, discard the lemon verbena, and add the milk. Chill. When the mixture is completely cold, churn the mixture in an ice-cream maker. Pour into a container, cover with a lid, and freeze until firm.

Put all the berries into a white china or glass bowl.

To make the lemon verbena syrup, put the sugar, water, and lemon verbena into a stainless-steel saucepan and bring slowly to a boil, stirring until the sugar has dissolved. Boil for just 2 minutes, then cool for 4 to 5 minutes.

Pour the hot syrup over the fruit and let macerate for several hours. Remove the lemon verbena.

Serve the fruit salad chilled with the lemon verbena ice cream. You can also serve the fruit salad with softly whipped cream or vanilla ice cream or simply by itself. Decorate with a few fresh lemon verbena leaves.

GALANGAL

Alpinia galanga SIAMESE GINGER, ZONES 11–12

How much fun is it to grow your own fresh galangal? An essential ingredient in Thai and Asian cuisine, it's not that easy to buy fresh unless you live close to an Asian shop. Like ginger, it's a rhizome and a member of the Zingiberaceae family. It has a smoother, paler skin than ginger and a more pronounced flavor. Native to South-east Asia, it is widely cultivated in Malaysia, Laos, and Thailand and is also known as blue ginger, Thai ginger, or Laos root.

VARIETIES

There are four plants known as galangal. *Alpinia galanga* (Greater galangal)—The culinary species widely used throughout southeast Asia.
Alpinia officinarum (Lesser galangal)—Native of China and used extensively in South China.

HOW TO GROW

In our climate you need to grow galangal in a tunnel or greenhouse. Buy some fresh galangal rhizomes, preferably organic, otherwise they may have been sprayed with anti-sprouting powder.

Soak the galangal in a bowl of cold water until the sprouts emerge in 1 to 2 days. Then plant in a 12 to 16-inch pot. Wait for the shoots to appear. Wait a few weeks for the shoots to appear. It likes moist but not too wet soil and needs protection from frost.

CONTAINER GROWING

Galangal is best grown in a large pot. It makes an attractive conservatory plant.

PESTS AND DISEASES

Spider mite might attack plants under cover but we haven't experienced any problems.

HARVESTING

Galangal can be harvested most of the year. Wait for a year before harvesting from new plants; give them time to get established and just remove bits from the sides of the plant.

GOOD FOR YOU...

Galangal has anti-inflammatory properties, it's an antioxidant and fights free radicals in the body. It also inhibits the growth of fatty acids and is used in the treatment of nausea, flatulence and indigestion. The dried root is used in Chinese medicine to treat stomach problems and also helps circulation in the hands and feet. It is sometimes used like snuff to fight nasal infections.

Galangal plant about to flower, but it's the rhizomes that we eat.

WHAT TO DO WITH A GLUT

You are unlikely to have a glut, but galangal root can be dried or frozen. The latter produces a spongy result, but nonetheless it is useful in many dishes if you don't have access to the fresh rhizome.

IN THE KITCHEN

Peel and grate or mince to use in stir-fries. If using whole slices of galangal in a dish, they can be a bit stringy so it is best to remove them before serving. Galangal is also available in powdered form in Asian food shops. You can buy very good Thai curry paste in many supermarkets, but it is never quite the same as making it yourself. Emer Fitzgerald is one of our senior teachers and recipe testers at the Ballymaloe Cookery School. To make **Emer's Thai Green Curry Paste** (approx. 13½ ounces), grind 8 chopped shallots, 6 chopped garlic cloves, 3 chopped stalks of lemongrass, 12 roughly chopped green chiles, 8 tablespoons of chopped cilantro, 1 tablespoon of peeled and chopped fresh galangal or ginger, 2 teaspoons of ground coriander, 1 teaspoon of ground cumin, 1 teaspoon of ground white pepper, 6 roughly chopped lime leaves, 3 teaspoons of shrimp paste and 2 teaspoons of sea salt flakes together in a mortar and pestle or blend together in a food processor. This paste keeps well in a sealed jar in the fridge for 2 weeks and freezes perfectly.

DID YOU KNOW?

Galangal's origins can be traced back to China; it found its way to Europe in the 800s AD through the spice trade with the East.

Thai Chicken, Galangal & Cilantro Soup

A particularly delicious example of how fast and easy a Thai soup can be. We serve it in blue and white Chinese porcelain bowls. The kaffir lime leaves and galangal are served, but not eaten. The chile may, of course, be nibbled. Shrimp can be substituted for chicken in this recipe with equally delicious results. We usually use one red Thai chile, but the number depends on your taste and how hot the chiles are. Fresh lime leaves are not available in every store so buy them any time you spot them and pop them into a bag in your freezer. Blanched and refreshed rice noodles are also delicious added to this soup—hey presto, you have a main course. Serve in wide pasta bowls with lots of fresh cilantro scattered over the top.

SERVES 8

3¾ cups homemade chicken stock

4 kaffir lime leaves

2-inch piece of galangal, peeled and sliced
(if using fresh ginger, use a third less)

¼ cup fish sauce (*nam pla*)

6 tablespoons freshly squeezed lemon
juice

8 ounces free-range, organic chicken
breast, very finely sliced

1 cup coconut milk

1 to 3 Thai red chiles

approx. 5 tablespoons cilantro leaves

Put the chicken stock, lime leaves, galangal or ginger, fish sauce, and lemon juice into a saucepan. Bring to a boil, stirring all the time, then add the chicken and coconut milk. Continue to cook over high heat for 1 to 2 minutes until the chicken is just cooked. Crush the chiles with a knife or Chinese chopper and add to the soup with the cilantro and cook for just a few seconds.

Ladle into hot bowls and serve immediately.

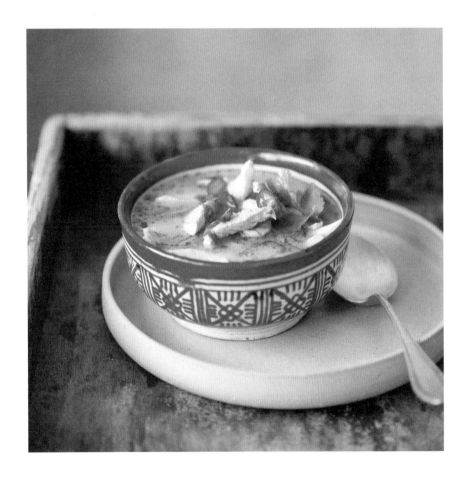

DILL *Anethum graveolens* ANNUAL

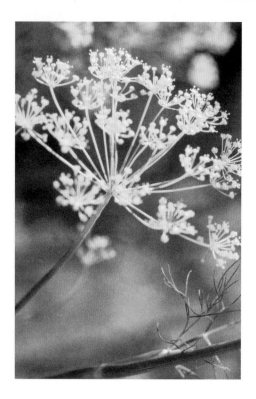

Use anise-flavored dill flowers as a garnish or add to salad—so flavorful.

An annual well worth making space for, this beautiful feathery herb always reminds me of my Danish friend Camilla Plum. She puts fistfuls of it into a myriad of dishes in her wonderfully generous way. Dill is a herb that can often be a little forgotten, but plant lots and you too will discover the joy of being able to use it with gay abandon.

It looks very similar to the fennel herb and its wispy leaves perplex the students at the school until they become familiar with the difference in flavor and subtle difference in appearance.

VARIETIES

Anethum graveolens—Grows to a height of 2 to 5 feet with feathery green leaves and clusters of yellow flowers in flattened umbelliferous flower heads.

HOW TO GROW

Sow seeds in plugs or pots indoors in early spring. Avoid seed trays; dill dislikes being transplanted. It bolts quickly if its roots are disrupted. Germination takes 3 to 4 weeks.

Harden off and plant out 11 inches apart when they are 3 to 4 inches tall, and all threat of frost has passed. We wait until midsummer. They like full sun and will do well on poor, well-drained soil as long as it's in a sheltered spot. Be careful not to plant near fennel or they will cross-pollinate.

You can sow directly into the ground in mid-spring. Thin if necessary, leaving enough room for each plant. Sow in succession to ensure a plentiful supply throughout the season. The seeds are viable for three years, so it can reseed and live up to its other name: dill weed. This can be looked on as a bonus, depending on your situation.

CONTAINER GROWING

Dill will happily grow outdoors in pots, tubs or any roomy container. It needs sun and shelter. Keeping it watered and constant snipping will promote new growth, but dill is fairly short-lived so plant three containers to "see" you through the season.

PESTS AND DISEASES

Slugs love dill, so take the usual precautions (see page 626) to protect the small plants.

Greenfly can be a problem if dill plants are planted too close together. If there's a problem, treat with a liquid horticultural soap.

HARVESTING

Allow the plants to establish, then snip the leaves as needed. It wilts quickly so store in damp kitchen paper or in water; either way it won't keep fresh for more than 2 to 3 days.

The flowers are also delicious and the seeds can also be dried and harvested for use in cooking and pickling or for next year's crop. Store in sealed glass jars in a cool, dark place.

DID YOU KNOW?

The word dill is said to be derived from the Anglo-Saxon dylle or the Norse dilla, meaning "to soothe or heal," one of its many attributes. Remember gripe water which contained dill and soothed babies with wind or colic for generations? In the Middle Ages dill was considered to be a protection against witchcraft. Magicians used it in their spells and added it to wine to "enhance passion." Dill was mentioned in the Bible in the Gospel of St Matthew and was used by Egyptian doctors as a soothing medicine for indigestion more than three thousand years ago.

GOOD FOR YOU...

Dill is another powerhouse of nutrients and its many health benefits have been known and valued since ancient times. Earliest references were in Egypt five thousand years ago, when it was referred to as a 'soothing herb'. The health benefits are derived from its organic compounds, vitamins and minerals, which include powerful monoterpenes— limonene, carvone and anethofuran—as well as flavonoids like vicenin and kaempferol. It contains signficant amounts of vitamins B6, B12, A and C, as well as minerals, iron, manganese and folate. Dill has anti-inflammatory and antibacterial properties.

WHAT TO DO WITH A GLUT

Dill can be frozen and works brilliantly chopped and frozen in ice cubes; use for soups and stews.

IN THE KITCHEN

Dill is enjoyed all over the world; it is native to the Mediterranean, southern Russia, and western Africa, and is also widely used in India and the Middle East. Dill enhances the appetite and improves the digestion, but quite apart from all that, dill adds to the enjoyment of so many of our dishes. I love to add it to potato, cucumber, and beet salads. Snip some fronds into a green salad or try the **Greek Green Salad** (page 434) in which it's used lavishly. Chop lots of fresh dill into cream cheese to slather on bagels, add it to tzatziki as an accompaniment to lamb or as part of a mezze platter, or stir into mayonnaise, crème fraîche, yogurt, labneh, or kefir for an instant sauce or dip to enhance another repast. Add it to fish pies, omelets, frittatas, risottos, ceviche, and, of course, gravlax.

To make **Dill Oil** (¼ cup), process ½ cup chopped dill stalks, ½ cup light extra virgin olive oil or ¼ cup extra virgin olive oil and ¼ cup sunflower oil with a pinch of salt in a blender and drip through a fine sieve (do not push through). The solid material can be processed with 3 tablespoons butter to make a dill butter—a delicious accompaniment to a piece of broiled fish.

Mackerel & Dill Soup

This soup may sound most unlikely, but I was delighted to find this Scandinavian recipe. It is quite delicious and very inexpensive to make. Use very fresh, whole mackerel—the bones are essential to the flavor of the soup, but it will be dire if the fish are stale.

. . . .

SERVES APPROX. 10

2 large or 3 medium very fresh mackerel

6 cups water

2 to 4 tablespoons finely chopped dill, plus the stalks

1 to 2 teaspoons salt

10 whole white peppercorns

¼ cup cream

freshly squeezed juice of 1 lemon

2 organic egg yolks

crusty white bread, to serve

Gut the mackerel, wash well, and remove the heads. Cut into 1-inch pieces. Put the mackerel into a saucepan with the water, dill stalks, salt, and peppercorns. Bring to a boil, simmer for 5 minutes, and strain. Discard the peppercorns and dill stalks then carefully remove the mackerel flesh from the bones.

Return the flesh to the saucepan with the strained broth, add the chopped dill, half the cream, and half the lemon juice. Simmer for a few minutes, then mix the remainder of the cream with the egg yolks. Whisk a little of the simmering liquid into the egg and cream mixture, then stir into the soup. Season to taste and add more lemon juice if necessary.

Serve hot with crusty white bread.

Transylvanian Crêpes with Ricotta & Dill

We ate two versions of these dill pancakes in Transylvania, one at the Herb Garden in SzentÁbrahámi where Emese Csiko makes a selection of exceptionally good herb teas from the freshly dried herbs grown on her farm. Emese added egg yolks to the ricotta, but a Mosna version without egg was also delicious.

. . . .

MAKES 12 CRÊPES/SERVES 6

FOR THE CRÊPE BATTER
1⅓ cups all-purpose flour
good pinch of salt
2 extra large organic eggs and 1 to
   2 organic egg yolks, lightly beaten
2 cups milk, or for very crisp, light delicate
   crêpes, half milk and half water
1 to 2 tablespoons melted butter

FOR THE FILLING
¾ to 1 cup Urdu or fresh ricotta
superfine sugar, to taste
1 to 2 tablespoons dill, chopped
4 to 5 tablespoons dill flowers and sprigs,
   if available
lemon wedges, to serve

First make the batter: Sift the flour and salt into a bowl, make a well in the center, and drop in the beaten eggs. With a whisk or wooden spoon, starting in the center, mix the eggs and gradually bring in the flour. Add the liquid slowly and beat until the batter is covered with bubbles. Cover and let sit in a cold place for an hour or so—longer will do no harm. Just before you cook the crêpes, stir in the melted butter. This will make all the difference to the flavor and texture of the crêpes and will make it possible to cook them without greasing the pan each time.

Meanwhile, mix the ricotta with sugar to taste and stir in the chopped dill.

Heat an 11-inch heavy cast-iron crêpe pan or a nonstick pan until very hot, then pour in just enough batter to cover the base of the pan thinly. Loosen the crêpe around the edge, flip over with a spatula, cook for a second or two on the other side, and slide off the pan onto a plate. Repeat until you have used up all the batter.

To serve, spread the ricotta and dill filling onto a crêpe, leaving a ¼-inch border around the edge. Lay another crêpe on top. Press down gently and cut into quarters. Decorate with dill flowers and sprigs (if using) and serve at room temperature. Alternatively, spread each crêpe with the ricotta and dill filling, fold into quarters, garnish, and serve with lemon wedges.

Greek Green Salad

The dill sprigs transform this fresh-tasting salad, which was served to us with some simple pan-grilled fish in a little café on the island of Aegina just off Athens. We've been enjoying it ever since.

. . . .

SERVES 4 TO 6

romaine lettuce or 3 Little Gem lettuce
3 to 4 scallions, sliced
lots of small sprigs of dill
¼ cup Greek extra virgin olive oil
1 to 2 tablespoons lemon juice
a little honey (optional)
sea salt flakes and freshly ground black
   pepper

Wash, drain, and chill the lettuce. Slice across the grain about 1-inch thick. Put into a bowl, then sprinkle with the scallions and lots and lots of tiny sprigs of dill.

Just before serving, whisk the oil with the lemon juice and perhaps a little honey if the lemons are very tart. Sprinkle over the salad, season with a little salt and pepper, toss, and serve immediately. We particularly enjoy this salad with moussaka.

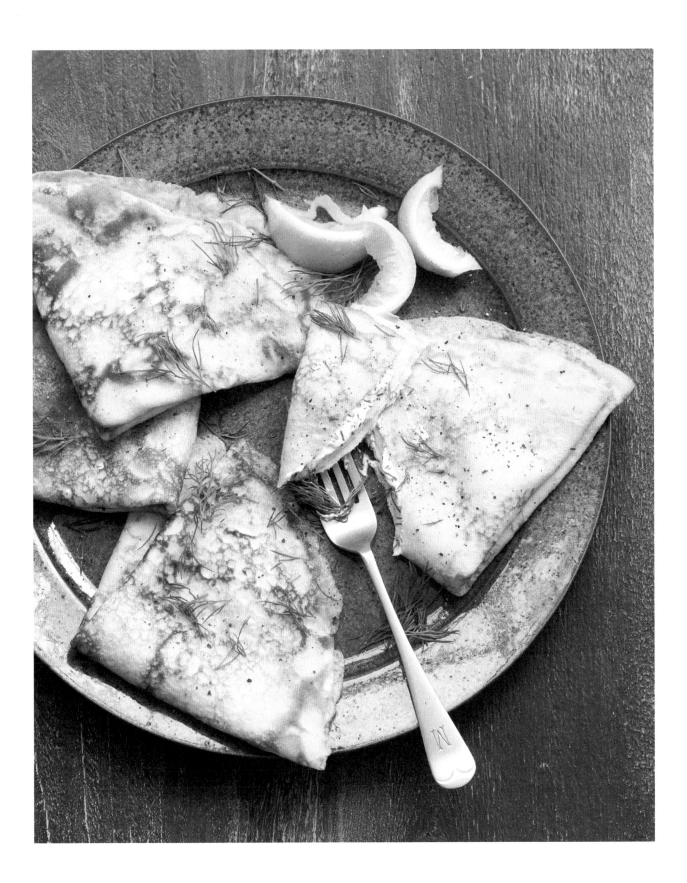

ANGELICA

Angelica archangelica BIENNIAL, ZONES 5–7

Oh, how can I persuade you to consider giving this tall, elegant biennial plant a place in your garden? Its impressive stature could be used to add height to your herbaceous border, but we use this beautiful umbelliferous plant as a centerpiece in several of the boxwood-edged beds in the formal herb garden at Ballymaloe. Bees and hoverflies love the umbelliferous flower heads with clusters of whitish and greenish flowers.

It's a member of the cow parsley family and grows to a height of at least 60 inches. It grows wild in Finland, Sweden and Norway, but the area around Niort in Deux Sevres in western France is particularly famous for the quality of the products made from local angelica, which grows in abundance, having first been introduced to the area during the plague in 1604. I visited the area more than three decades ago and loved the fields of angelica. I bought a box of angelica with a scalloped doily edge, some angelica jam and a bottle of scary green liqueur called Angelique.

VARIETIES

Angelica sylvestris—this is the original form and the most widely grown. *Angelica sylvestris 'Purpurea'*—deep purple stems and umbels of purply-pink flowers, and is slightly shorter than the native variety *Angelica sylvestris*. It looks striking in a perennial border.

HOW TO GROW

Angelica likes moist, fertile soil. Ours thrives in full sun in warm, sheltered conditions in the herb garden, though I believe it generally prefers semi-shade. It flowers in the second year. It's easy to collect seed, but it deteriorates rapidly. Sow in early autumn for new plants and share with friends. The plant dies after flowering.

CONTAINER GROWING

A single plant can be grown in a large pot or half-barrel.

PESTS AND DISEASES

None that I know of, but it can be invasive. Cut off the flower heads before they go to seed.

HARVESTING

The stems may be cut in spring while they are fresh and green and before the plant flowers. Traditionally, angelica was supposed to flower on the feast of Michael the Archangel on 8 May, hence its name, but it's usually later in our garden.

GOOD FOR YOU...

All parts of the angelica plant—the roots, stalks, aromatic leaves, flowers and seeds –have both medicinal and culinary uses. Angelica helps to alleviate coughs, colds, fevers, colic and problems of the digestive system, and it purifies the blood. Diabetics should avoid angelica as it is thought to raise blood sugar in the urine.

WHAT TO DO WITH A GLUT

You are unlikely to have a glut, but you could always make lots of candied angelica and keep it to give as Christmas gifts, for decorating Christmas trifles, in nice little boxes.

IN THE KITCHEN

We use the young leaves in jams, marmalade, sorbets, fruit salads, custards, and ice cream, but the most common use is making candied angelica with the tender young shoots. It's a labor of love, but so worth it. The candied stems are used as an edible garnish for desserts and cakes. This bears no resemblance to the luminous green commercial version now available. The tender young leaves with their distinctive scent can be torn into salads alongside the tiny fresh flowers.

DID YOU KNOW?

It's supposed to be an aphrodisiac, an antidote to poisons and, should you need it, a protection against witches!

Angelica gives Bénédictine its characteristic flavor and it's also used in Chartreuse and vermouth.

Candied Angelica (right) is made from the hollow stalks of the plant.

In Finland, the leaves and stalks are enjoyed as vegetables, simply boiled until tender.

The addition of a little angelica to stewed rhubarb, gooseberries, currants, plums, and apples is thought to neutralize the acidity—it certainly works, and so reduces the amount of sugar needed. We also make angelica syrup and tisanes from the leaves. To make 1 cup **Angelica Tea**, infuse 1 teaspoon dried angelica root in 1 cup boiling water for 15 to 20 minutes, strain, and enjoy. It's a little bitter, but not unpalatable. For an **Angelica**

Tisane, pour boiling water over chopped fresh or crushed angelica leaves. Set aside to infuse for 3 to 4 minutes. Strain and drink.

The Lapps regard the stalks as a great delicacy and the Icelanders eat both the stems and roots raw with butter—try it, you'll find it's a delicious combination. The Norwegians use the roots in bread.

All parts of the angelica plant are edible, including the flowers and the seeds.

Candied Angelica

Homemade candied angelica will not be bright green like the commercial version you can buy in specialized stores, but is so delicious you may have to hide it. Use for cakes, decorating small cupcakes and trifles, or just for nibbling. We pick angelica stalks for candying in early summer, while they are still young. Lovage stalks may be candied in the same way.

young angelica stalks
granulated sugar
superfine sugar

Cut the angelica stalks into 3 to 6-inch lengths. Put into a stainless-steel saucepan, cover with fresh water, and bring to a boil. Drain and refresh the angelica under cold water. Then, if necessary, peel off the tough outer stems and fibers; a potato peeler works well for this.

Return the angelica pieces to the saucepan. Cover with boiling water and continue to cook for 4 to 5 minutes, by which time its color will have become a deeper green.

Drain the angelica again and pat dry with paper towels.

Sprinkle a layer of granulated sugar into a shallow dish and cover with the angelica. Repeat, using equal quantities of sugar to angelica. Finish with a layer of sugar and allow to macerate for 2 to 3 days.

Transfer the angelica and sugar to a deep saucepan. Heat gently and continue to simmer until the angelica is translucent. Remove the angelica pieces from the syrup. Spread out on a wire rack and let cool and dry, which takes about 30 minutes.

Toss the angelica in superfine sugar. Allow to dry completely before storing in an airtight container in a dry cupboard. It will keep for several years if necessary but, as ever, it is best to use it sooner rather than later.

Angelica & Almond Macaroon Cake

This recipe uses homemade Candied Angelica in an unusual fruitcake. I sometimes use the same macaroon topping on cupcakes or a madeira cake.

SERVES 8 TO 10

8 tablespoons (1 stick) butter

½ cup superfine sugar

1 organic egg yolk (use the white for the topping), plus 2 large organic eggs

1¼ cups all-purpose flour

¼ cup ground almonds

4 ounces Candied Angelica (page 437), finely chopped

⅔ cup golden raisins

⅓ cup raisins

⅓ cup currants

FOR THE MACAROON TOPPING

2 organic egg whites

⅔ cup superfine sugar

¾ cup ground almonds

a few drops of almond extract

¼ cup sliced almonds

Preheat the oven to 350°F and line the bottom and sides of a heavy 7-inch round cake pan with a double thickness of silicone paper.

Cream the butter, add the sugar, and beat until light and fluffy before adding the egg yolk and then the eggs, one at a time. Beat well between each addition. Stir in the flour and ground almonds, add the angelica, golden raisins, raisins, and currants and mix well. Turn into the prepared cake pan and smooth the top.

To make the macaroon topping, whisk the egg whites until just fluffy, then fold in the sugar, ground almonds, and almond extract. Spread evenly over the top of the cake. Sprinkle with the sliced almonds. Cover with a sheet of parchment paper and bake for 1¼ hours, then remove the paper and continue to bake for another 15 to 20 minutes to brown the top.

This cakes keeps really well in an airtight container but use within 7 to 10 days.

Rhubarb & Angelica Jam

This delicious jam should be made when both the rhubarb and angelica are young and not yet thick and tough.

MAKES 8 × 16-OUNCE JARS

4 pounds trimmed rhubarb

6 to 8 angelica stalks, finely chopped (approx. 6 tablespoons)

6½ cups granulated sugar

grated zest and juice of 2 lemons

1 teaspoon freshly grated ginger (optional)

Wipe the rhubarb and cut into 1-inch pieces. Put the rhubarb and angelica into a large bowl layered with the sugar, then add the lemon zest and juice and ginger, if using. Let stand overnight.

The next day, transfer to a preserving pan. Bring gently to a boil and continue to cook until it is a thick pulp—about 40 to 50 minutes. To test for a set, spoon a teaspoon of the hot jam onto a cold plate and set aside for a few minutes in a cool place. If setting point has been reached, the jam should wrinkle when pressed with a finger. (If the jam isn't set, return the pan to the heat and boil for a few minutes more, then test again.)

Pour the jam into hot, clean, sterilized jars, cover, and store in a dry, airy cupboard. It will keep for 3 to 5 months or longer, but, as ever, is most delicious when fresh.

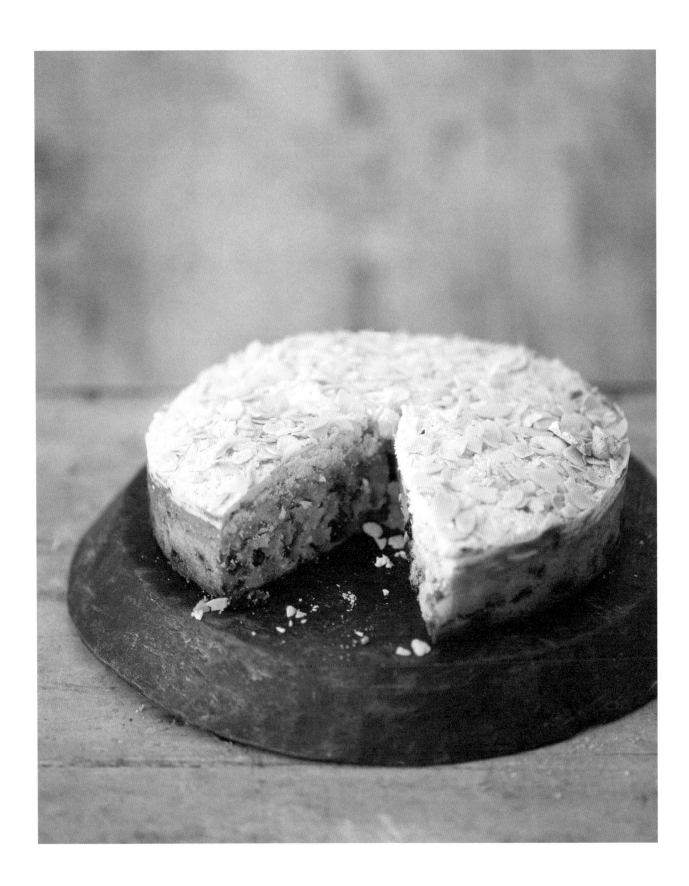

CHERVIL Anthriscus cerefolium ANNUAL (CAN BE GROWN AS A BIENNIAL)

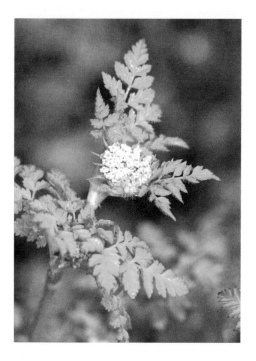

Chervil is one of the first herbs to emerge in spring—we use both the leaves and flowers.

Chervil is delicate, dainty and delicious, so deserves to be much better known. The slightly aniseed flavor is subtle and the feathery, almost lacy, leaves are light and elegant and make an appealing and delightful garnish. It's super easy to grow and not so easy to find, except in specialist food shops and greengrocers, so a brilliant choice to grow yourself. We use it in a variety of dishes.

VARIETIES

Anthriscus cerefolium—Hardy annual, which grows to 1 to 2 feet with tiny white flowers. Delicate, green, fern-like leaves that turn purply when the temperatures drop in late in autumn and winter.
Anthriscus cerefolium 'Crispum'—Curly form, but inferior flavor compared to the original.

HOW TO GROW

Sow early in spring into cells and then pot on into larger containers. Sow directly into the soil in late spring. Chervil can be grown in rows 10 to 12 inches apart or as a cut-and-come-again crop. It prefers semi-shade and light, moist soil. It can be sown under other crops to provide a little shade in midsummer.

CONTAINER GROWING

Chervil can be grown as a cut-and-come-again herb in a large container or bath.

PESTS AND DISEASES

We don't seem to have any problems, but apparently greenfly can be a problem. Wash gently with liquid horticultural soap.

HARVESTING

Snip off the leaves as you need them. The flavor is best before the chervil flowers, but of course one can use the delicate white flowers in salad and garnishes.

GOOD FOR YOU...

Another herb with lots of vitamin C, chervil also contains minerals including iron, carotene and magnesium. Chervil tea is reputed to aid digestion and to soothe liver complaints.

WHAT TO DO WITH A GLUT

We use chervil lavishly as a garnish and snip it into both herb and green salads. Introduce it to friends.

IN THE KITCHEN

Chervil is one of the classic French fines herbs so indispensable for **Omelet *Fines Herbes*** (page 447) and many soups and fish or chicken dishes. It looks like a feathery version of flat-leaf parsley, and I find myself using it more and more. Its mildly aniseed flavor is much more delicate than parsley and it therefore makes a more subtle and elegant garnish for many dishes. It is best served raw and fresh, added to a dish at the last moment. I love it added to crème fraîche to serve with bean and vegetable stew or to pop a blob onto a green soup. A little **Chervil Butter** is particularly delicious with pan-fried scallops or spooned over fresh fish. To make Chervil Butter, cream 3 tablespoons butter and stir 1 tablespoon finely chopped chervil into the butter. Add a little salt and freshly ground black pepper. To serve with radishes, split 15 to 20 fresh radishes in half lengthwise. Use a tiny nozzle to pipe a little riff of chervil butter onto the top of each radish. Add a flake or two of sea salt and, if you like, a little sprig of chervil leaf and flower.

DID YOU KNOW?

The oil that can be extracted from chervil has a similar smell to "myrrh," a resin from a small, thorny tree, which was one of the gifts brought by the Three Wise Men, so chervil oil was sometimes known as "myrrhis." In ancient times, chervil was believed to symbolise revitalisation and a new life.

Pickled Ox Tongue with Pickled Onion & Chervil Crème Fraîche

There's a great saying in Ireland when someone is about to venture home after a night of liquid socializing: "Ah, there'll be nothin' for you for dinner but hot tongue and cold shoulder." Order a pickled ox tongue from your butcher a week or so ahead unless you want to try pickling your own. A good way to use chervil, this is a delicate combination of flavors that complement the pickled ox tongue. The chervil crème fraîche is also good with fried or broiled fish, shellfish, meat, vegetables, and spicy bean stews.

. . . .

SERVES 8 TO 10

1 pickled ox tongue
Pickled Red Onions (page 00) and a salad
  of chervil sprigs, watercress, sorrel, and
  claytonia, to serve

FOR THE CHERVIL CRÈME FRAÎCHE
2 ounces chervil
1 cup crème fraîche
sea salt flakes and freshly ground black
  pepper
freshly squeezed lemon juice (optional)

Put the tongue into a narrow saucepan with high sides. Cover it with cold water, bring to a boil, cover the saucepan, and simmer for 4 to 4½ hours or until the tongue is tender and the skin will easily peel off the tip. Remove from the saucepan and set aside the liquid. As soon as the tongue is cool enough to handle, peel off the skin and remove all the little bones at the neck end. Sometimes I use a skewer to prod the meat to ensure no bones are left behind. Curl the tongue and press it into a small plastic bowl, then pour over a little of the cooking liquid. Nowadays the butcher often removes all the little bones. If this is the case the liquid may not set into a jelly without the help of gelatin—use 1 teaspoon to 1¼ cups liquid. Put a side plate or saucer on top and weigh down the tongue, then set aside to cool.

To make the chervil crème fraîche, chop the chervil, including a little stalk. Fold into the crème fraîche and season with salt and pepper. Taste and add a little lemon juice if necessary.

Serve the ox tongue thinly sliced with the Pickled Red Onions, chervil crème fraîche, and a little herb salad. The pickled ox tongue will keep for 5 to 6 days in the fridge.

These herbs can be easily confused, from left to right: flat-leaf parsley, chervil, and cilantro.

Cheese & Chervil Tart

A super way to use lots of chervil. If chervil is scarce, use a mixture of chervil, thyme, parsley, and a little French tarragon.

. . . .

SERVES 6 TO 8

FOR THE SHORTCRUST PASTRY DOUGH

1⅓ cups all-purpose, spelt, or whole
   wheat flour, sifted
5 tablespoons butter
pinch of salt
beaten egg or water, to bind

FOR THE FILLING

2 tablespoons butter
2 tablespoons all-purpose flour
⅔ cup heavy cream
sea salt and freshly ground black pepper
pinch of cayenne pepper
2 to 4 tablespoons chopped fresh chervil
¾ cup grated cheese, such as ½ cup gruyère
   and ¼ cup Parmesan or ¾ cup cheddar
2 organic egg yolks, beaten, plus 2 organic
   egg whites, stiffly whipped

Preheat the oven to 400°F.

Make the dough according to the instructions on page 36. Line a 7-inch pie pan with dough. Chill for 10 minutes. Bake blind for 20 to 25 minutes until the dough is almost fully cooked.

Meanwhile, melt the butter and stir in the flour. Whisk in the cream and bring to a boil. Season with salt and pepper and add the cayenne and the herbs. Cook gently for 4 to 5 minutes, then stir in the cheese and egg yolks. Set the mixture aside to cool, then fold in the egg whites. Pour the filling into the crust and bake for 12 to 15 minutes until risen and brown on top.

Serve warm with a little herb salad.

Oyster Shooters with Chervil

A deliciously light appetizer and another good way to use delicate chervil, this is an enchanting combination of flavors inspired by a recipe that Maggie Beer of Pheasant Farm in the Barossa Valley, Australia shared with us.

. . . .

MAKES 6 SHOOTERS

½ × ⅛-ounce gelatin leaf (or powder
   equivalent)
½ cup verjus or lemon juice
½ teaspoon superfine sugar
6 oysters
1 small shallot, finely chopped
1 tablespoon white wine vinegar
¼ teaspoon finely chopped thyme leaves
1 teaspoon chopped chervil, plus extra
   sprigs, to garnish
sea salt and freshly ground black pepper

Soak the gelatin leaf in cold water for a couple of minutes to soften. Heat the verjus or lemon juice and sugar in a small saucepan over high heat until the sugar dissolves, then set aside to cool a little. When the gelatin leaf is soft, discard the water and stir the gelatin into the lukewarm verjus until it dissolves.

Divide one third of the verjus mixture between 6 shot glasses and chill until the jelly sets. Keep the remaining two thirds at room temperature so that it doesn't set.

When the jelly is set in the glasses, open the oysters and arrange one on top of the jelly in each glass. Top with the remaining verjus mixture and chill until set.

Not long before serving, mix the shallot, vinegar, thyme, and chervil, then season to taste and set aside for 10 to 15 minutes for flavors to mingle.

Top each chilled shot glass with a little of the shallot mixture and a delicate sprig of chervil. Serve immediately.

HORSERADISH *Armoracia rusticana* PERENNIAL, ZONES 4–8

Horseradish is a member of the mustard family. The root has a hot, peppery flavor and varies in size and thickness depending on age. Fresh horseradish is not all that easy to find in the shops but it's ridiculously easy to grow. In fact, as many gardeners will know, the challenge is to actually stop it growing once it gets established. Only those who grow fresh horseradish know how deliciously pungent it can be. However, it does seem to fluctuate, the heat varying from soil to soil. Some plants can be fiendishly hot while others can be relatively mild, so adjust the quantity to taste.

VARIETIES

We grow both the common and variegated forms.

Amoracia rusticana—Large, bright green leaves similar to dock leaves, and small white flowers in summer. Taprooted.

Amoracia rusticana '**Variegata**'— Variegated form; large, dark green leaves splashed with cream. Very attractive looking, but spreads as vigorously as the plain variety.

HOW TO GROW

You certainly don't need green fingers to grow horseradish, but choose the spot carefully. It doesn't seem to be fussy about soil and will grow in full sun or semi-shade, but it will romp away once it gets going and can soon become a pest if it's not curtailed.

The easiest way is get started is to buy a plant or get a piece of root, which will sprout easily. Plant it upright in the soil, cover, firm and water well. Allow 18 to 20 inches between plants and let it establish for a year or so before you start to harvest the root.

CONTAINER GROWING

It will grow happily in a large container, which has the advantage of keeping it contained. A half-barrel works well, but make sure there are plenty of drainage holes in the base.

PESTS AND DISEASES

We haven't had any problems; in fact, it may help to keep pests away. I haven't tried any of these, but have heard that it can be used as a spray to treat brown rot on apple trees, or planted near potatoes to make them more disease resistant.

HARVESTING

The leaves resemble dock leaves, but are taller and coarser. In the early spring the young leaves are delicious snipped into salads. The leaves die down completely in winter. The roots can be dug at any time and the leaves will re-emerge in early spring. Try not to let it flower, which it does from early- to midsummer, because the roots will be woodier.

Harvest all year round as you need it—just dig up the taproot with a good, strong digging fork. The older the plants, the deeper they burrow into the ground and the woodier the roots become, so the more challenging to dig up. So it's definitely a good plan to try to dig out as much as you can every three years or so. Even a tiny bit of root will re-sprout so

Vigorous horseradish roots with young leaves emerging—use in salads when young and tender.

it's unlikely you'll ever need to replant horseradish again.

GOOD FOR YOU…

Horseradish really clears the sinuses! It is a good source of vitamin C, potassium, calcium and magnesium. It's also reputed to have antibacterial and diuretic properties and can aid digestion. The leaves can help in the treatment of chilblains, cuts and burns.

WHAT TO DO WITH A GLUT

Horseradish is perennial and the roots will happily stay in the ground getting fatter and tougher to dig until you are ready to harvest. If, however, you do have a glut, give it to friends or try selling it at a local farmers' market with instructions on how to grow or use in the kitchen. Once dug, it will keep for months provided it doesn't dry out. Like ginger, it can be well wrapped and frozen, but it becomes a bit soggy when it's defrosted so it's best to grate it straight from the freezer.

A piece of horseradish root will keep in a plastic bag or damp newspaper in your vegetable drawer in the fridge for three weeks or more, even months. Alternatively, wash, peel, grate and pack into a sterilised glass jars, add some salt and cover with good organic white wine vinegar. Use for horseradish sauce or cream, but omit vinegar and salt from the final recipe.

Wash and peel the root then grate, preferably on a rasp grater.

IN THE KITCHEN

Fresh horseradish is one of my secret weapons in the kitchen. I wouldn't be without a good clump in the garden and love to shred some of the young tender leaves into salads and mayo in early spring. The taste difference between homemade and shop-bought will astound you. Give the root a good scrub to clean off all the earth. Choose a swivel-top peeler to remove a thin outer layer, then use a rasp grater, rather than a tearing one, to grate the fibrous root. Grating or chopping horseradish releases volatile chemicals known as isothiocyanates, which clear the sinuses and may have you weeping and spluttering.

Horseradish leaves resemble giant dock leaves.

There are many more uses for horseradish other than as an accompaniment to roast beef, carpaccio and smoked and cured fish. The Italians love it with bollito misto. We also enjoy it with all kinds of sausages, pork, venison, beef and ox tongue and, of course, in beetroot and potato salad. You can also stir it into mashed potato. And then there's an apple and horseradish sauce that perks up roast pork in a zinging way. Try adding a couple of slices of horseradish to a bottle of vodka; left to infuse overnight or even for a few hours, it'll add extra oomph to a Bloody Mary.

To make **Horseradish Crème Fraîche** to go with beef, smoked sprats, mackerel, haddock and roast beetroot, put 2 tablespoons freshly grated horseradish into a bowl. Add a little freshly squeezed lemon juice, 1 teaspoon of honey and 8 ounces crème fraîche. Mix gently to combine. Season to taste with salt and freshly ground black pepper. Serves 6 to 8.

DID YOU KNOW?

Horseradish is a member of the *Cruciferae* family, which includes mustard, radishes and turnips. When the skin is broken and the root is grated, it releases sinigrin, an intensely volatile pungent compound akin to mustard oil which can make your eyes (and nose) water. It doesn't bother me much, but I've known people to wear goggles when they have to grate a large quantity.

Roasted Beet with Apple, Pomegranate Seeds, Mint & Horseradish Crème Fraîche

This combination of ingredients makes an irresistible appetizer but can also be served family-style for lunch or dinner.

. . . .

SERVES 8

2¼ pounds young beets
3 to 4 apples, peeled and diced into
   ¼-inch pieces
3 tablespoons extra virgin olive oil
½ to 1 tablespoon red wine vinegar
sea salt and freshly ground black pepper
1 pomegranate
2 to 3 handfuls of arugula
handful of mint leaves
2 tablespoons Iranian pistachios, halved
Horseradish Crème Fraîche (page 437) and
   slices of grilled sourdough , to serve

Preheat the oven to 450°F.

Wrap the beets in foil and roast for 30 minutes to 1 hour until soft and cooked through or until the skins will rub off.

Cut the beets into chunks and place in a bowl. Add the apple. Toss in oil and vinegar. Season with salt and pepper.

Halve the pomegranate and pop out the seeds.

Cover the bottom of each serving plate with arugula. Spread the beets and apple mixture over the leaves. Scatter the mint over the top and sprinkle with pomegranate seeds and pistachios.

Serve with Horseradish Crème Fraîche and some slices of grilled sourdough.

Pickled Ox Tongue with Beet Relish, Cucumber Pickle, Avocado & Watercress

It is such a pity that so many people decide that they don't like pickled ox tongue; it's so good and this is a particularly delicious combination. It can be served as an appetizer, a small plate, or a light lunch dish. The warm plate softens the chilled ox tongue and hugely enhances the overall eating experience.

. . . .

SERVES 8 TO 10

1 pickled ox tongue
2 firm but ripe avocados
Cucumber Pickle (page 137)
Beet & Ginger Relish (page 78)
Horseradish Crème Fraîche (page 437)
a few sprigs of watercress, to serve

A day or two ahead, put the tongue into a deep saucepan. Cover it completely with cold water. Bring to a boil, cover the saucepan, and simmer for 3 to 4 hours or until the skin will easily peel off the tip of the tongue. Remove the tongue from the saucepan and set aside the liquid. As soon as the tongue is cool enough to handle, peel off the skin and discard. Remove all the little bones at the neck end. Sometimes I use a skewer to prod the meat to ensure no bones are left behind. Curl the tongue and press it into a small plastic bowl. Pour over a little of the cooking liquid, put a side plate or saucer on top, and weigh down the tongue. Tongue will keep for up to a week in the fridge.

To serve, warm the plates. Thinly slice the tongue horizontally into rounds. Lay a slice on each of the plates. Peel and pit the avocados and cut into wedges. Top the tongue with a couple of wedges of avocado, a blob of Cucumber Pickle, Beet & Ginger Relish, a little Horseradish Crème Fraîche, and a few sprigs of watercress.

TARRAGON

Artemisia dracunculus PERENNIAL, ZONES 5–8

Although you won't reach for tarragon as often as chives, parsley or mint, for me, French tarragon (*estragon* in French) is one of the greatest culinary herbs. In fact it is indispensable in my kitchen—without it there would be no unctuous Béarnaise Béarnaise, the classic sauce created by Chef Collinet, also the creator of puffed potatoes (*pommes de terre soufflées*), to serve with a juicy steak or a rib of well-aged beef. It's got a beguiling perfumed flavor and can be used either fresh or cooked. It's one of the "famous five" *fines herbes* and is particularly beloved of French chefs, but you don't need to be a starchy chef to use it. It's got a mild anise seed, slightly liquorice flavor, which is great for chicken, fish and egg dishes. Any 12-week cookery student who can takes home a plant when they leave because "no home should be without tarragon".

VARIETIES

Artemisia dracunculus **var.** *sativa* **(French tarragon)**—half-hardy perennial. Far superior flavor to Russian tarragon so it's well worth growing, particularly as much of the French tarragon on sale in supermarkets is in fact Russian tarragon. Unfortunately, it cannot be grown from seed. A French tarragon plant will grow to about 2 to 3 feet and a width of 12 inches in two years. It has narrow leaves up to 2 inches long.

Artemisia dracunculoides **(Russian tarragon)**—hardy perennial. Russian tarragon grows taller than French tarragon to a height of 50 inches. It can be grown from seed. The leaves are slightly coarser and stronger in flavor, but less fragrant, and are long and narrow. Hardier than French tarragon, it originated in Siberia.

French tarragon.

Russian tarragon.

HOW TO GROW

FRENCH TARRAGON

French tarragon likes rich, fertile, well-drained soil, preferably with a neutral pH. It's quite drought tolerant. French tarragon does not produce seeds; it produces rhizomatous roots and is easily propagated by root cutting. We cut a plant, with a penknife or a gardener's knife, from a 5-inch square pot, into 4 to 6 × 1-inch pieces, then repot, usually with 100 per cent success rate. It dies back in late autumn and early winter but will re-emerge once again in spring.

RUSSIAN TARRAGON

In spring, sow the seed in seed trays or plugs. When the plants are large enough to handle, transplant 2 feet apart in the garden. Russian tarragon is hardier and more vigorous than French tarragon and dies down in winter. Don't water tarragon at night, it hates to have wet feet. If you have lots, the young stems can be cooked like asparagus and then tossed in melted butter to serve.

CONTAINER GROWING

Tarragon, any type can be grown outside in large containers, 10 to 12 inches in diameter. It's good to have a few extra plants to bring indoors in the winter. When the plant is dormant, keep it dry, but it will awaken a little earlier in a frost-free environment.

PESTS AND DISEASES

Rust can be a problem. This is a serious viral disease you certainly don't want to introduce into your garden. If you are buying a plant from a local garden center, examine it carefully. If your plant shows signs of rust, it will appear stunted and the leaves and stems, to a lesser degree, will be covered with a browny-orange rust colored powder. Dig it up and dispose of it with haste, not in the compost heap.

GOOD FOR YOU...

The phytonutrients and polyphenolic compounds within tarragon help to lower blood sugar levels. Tarragon is used as an appetite stimulant and in the treatment of anorexia. It is known to stimulate appetite. It contains vitamins C, A, and B, and minerals such as calcium, manganese, iron, potassium and zinc.

The essential oil eugonol in tarragon, which is antiseptic and inflammatory, has uses in dentistry to relieve the pain of surgery, extractions, root-canal treatment, fillings and to kill germs.

WHAT TO DO WITH A GLUT

When you can get fresh tarragon in summer, it is well worth picking and preserving for winter use. It is most abundant just before flowering in early August, so this is the best time to collect surplus growth. To make Tarragon Vinegar, strip the leaves from the tarragon plants. Measure them and crush them in your hands. Put them in Kilner jars or in jam jars with non-corrosive lids and fill the jars up with white wine vinegar. Allow 3 cups of vinegar to 2 cups of crushed leaves. After 2 weeks the vinegar will be ready for use. The tarragon can be extracted from the bottom of the jars, chopped up finely and used in Béarnaise sauces throughout the winter.Tarragon can also be frozen in ice cubes, but it's best just to make lots of tarragon vinegar, an essential ingredient for the basic reduction in Béarnaise sauce (page 39).

IN THE KITCHEN

Tarragon is heaven in many egg dishes; a little of the tender tips snipped into a scrambled egg or omelet raises it to a new level. Try it with turkey, guinea hen, or quail, as well as with chicken, shellfish, or tomatoes. A few leaves added to a green salad perfume it deliciously.

Casserole Roast Chicken with Tarragon

Use fragrant French tarragon here for the sublime perfumed flavor that we associate with this iconic dish. For those who are dairy intolerant, this dish can be made without cream, made just with chicken juices, stock, and fresh herbs.

SERVES 4 TO 6

1 × 5½ pound organic chicken (free-range if possible), wishbone removed and reserved for stock
sea salt and freshly ground black pepper
2 tablespoons chopped fresh French tarragon and 1 sprig of French tarragon, plus extra sprigs to garnish
2 tablespoons butter
⅔ cup cream
⅔ cup homemade chicken stock
roux (page 267, optional)

Preheat the oven to 350°F.

Season the cavity of the chicken with salt and pepper and stuff a sprig of tarragon inside. Smear ¾ tablespoon of the butter over the chicken breast. Mix half the chopped tarragon with the remaining butter. Place the chicken breast-side down in a casserole or Dutch oven and allow it to brown over gentle heat. Turn the chicken breast-side up and smear the tarragon butter over the breast and legs. Season with salt and pepper. Cover the pot and cook in the oven for 1¼ to 1½ hours. Transfer to a carving dish and rest for 10 to 15 minutes before carving.

Spoon the surplus fat from the juices and add the remaining chopped tarragon and the cream. If you need more sauce, add a little stock, then boil the sauce until it thickens slightly. Alternatively, bring the liquid to a boil and whisk in just enough roux to thicken the sauce (I prefer the latter). Season to taste.

Carve the chicken into 4 to 6 helpings with white and brown meat for each serving. Arrange on a serving dish, coat lightly with the sauce, and serve.

Oyster Mushrooms with Tarragon on Sourdough Toast

I am addicted to these mushrooms on toast. Fragrant extra virgin olive oil can, of course, be used here instead of foaming butter. Annual marjoram and thyme leaves are also super delicious in place of the tarragon.

SERVES 4

12 to 16 oyster mushrooms
3 tablespoons butter
4 slices of sourdough bread
1 tablespoon chopped tarragon sprigs
sea salt and freshly ground black pepper

Trim the stalks of the mushrooms into thin rounds, but leave the mushrooms intact. Melt the butter in a wide frying pan over fairly high heat. When it foams, arrange the mushrooms in a single layer, gills upward, and add the sliced stalks also. Sprinkle generously with salt and a little pepper, reduce the heat and cook for a few minutes, add the chopped tarragon, then turn over for another few minutes.

Meanwhile, heat a ridged grill pan over very high heat and toast the bread until it is well-charred. Arrange the mushrooms on top of the toast, lay the sprigs of tarragon over, and serve immediately. The sweet juices of the oyster mushrooms will soak into the toast.

Omelet *Fines Herbes*

A classic French omelet is the ultimate fast food, but many a travesty is served in its name. The secret is to have the pan hot enough and to use clarified butter if at all possible. Ordinary butter will burn if your pan is as hot as it ought to be. The omelet should be made in half the time it takes to read this introduction: 30 to 45 seconds. Your first omelet may not be a joy to behold, but persevere—practice makes perfect!

SERVES 1

2 large organic eggs
1 tablespoon water or milk
1 to 1½ tablespoons clarified butter or olive oil
1 teaspoon each chopped chives, chervil, tarragon, thyme, and flat-leaf parsley, plus extra to serve
sea salt and freshly ground black pepper

Warm a plate in the oven. Heat a 9-inch diameter nonstick omelet pan over high heat.

Meanwhile, whisk the eggs with the water or milk in a bowl until thoroughly mixed, but not too fluffy. Season with salt and pepper. Put the warm plate beside the pan.

Add the clarified butter or oil to the pan. As soon as it sizzles, pour in the egg mixture. It will start to cook immediately so quickly pull the edges of the omelet toward the center, tilting the pan so that the uncooked egg runs to the sides. Continue until most of the egg is set and will not run any more, then scatter the herbs over the surface. The center should still be moist.

To fold the omelet, flip the edge just below the handle of the pan into the center, then hold the handle of the pan so it is almost perpendicular over the plate, flip the omelet over again, then half roll, half slide the omelet onto the plate so that it lands folded into three.

Sprinkle a few more herbs over the top and serve immediately.

BORAGE *Borago officinalis* HARDY ANNUAL

Borage, also known as bugloss and burrage, has the prettiest blue, star-shaped flowers and slightly prickly leaves, but I can't say it's essential in the kitchen. In fact I cook with it rarely, but we have lots of borage scattered here and there throughout the farm and gardens because bees absolutely love and it also attracts blackfly so it's a brilliant companion plant to beans and strawberries. It seeds with gay abandon and can also be delightful in a flower border or cottage garden. Farmers can scatter the seeds here and there around the farm and in the hedgerows to attract beneficial insects to help with pollination.

In 2012, Isabella von Dellemann, a 12-week student from Italy, wanted to plant something at the school that she would be remembered by, so she planted a 100-foot row of borage in the vegetable field. We remember her fondly every summer; the borage flowers from mid- to late-summer and is a magnet for every bee in the neighbourhood—what a legacy to leave us.

VARIETIES

Borago officinalis (common borage)— Grows to 2 feet with bristly leaves and hollow stalks. Deep blue, star-shaped flowers throughout the summer. There's also a white version, *Borago officinalis* 'Alba' with white, star-shaped flowers.

HOW TO GROW

For an early crop, sow in plugs or pots in early spring. Harden off and transplant to its final position after all frost has passed. It will thrive on poor soil, sandy or chalky, and also in a pot. Alternatively wait until mid-spring and sow 2 inches deep and 2 feet apart directly into the soil in its final position. Borage germinates easily and quickly, but the seed is usually only viable for a year.

I love it to spread, but if you'd rather not have borage popping up all over your garden, deadhead the flowers and meticulously remove seed heads. Borage will flower cheerfully until late autumn when the first real frost will kill it.

CONTAINER GROWING

There are better herbs to grow in containers, but it would be pretty growing through other plants in a large barrel or trough, perhaps interspersed with nasturtiums.

Borage has slightly prickly leaves that have a distinctly cucumber flavor.

PESTS AND DISEASES

Blackfly can be a problem, but if you use it as a companion plant, close to broad or runner beans, it can be a bonus to host the pest. Our borage tends to get mildew late in the season, but we just live with it.

HARVESTING

The flowers and fresh leaves can be picked at any time.

GOOD FOR YOU...

Borage has many health benefits. Borage oil is the richest source of gamma lineolic acid, GLA, more than either blackcurrant or evening primrose oil, both of which are rich sources. GLA is an important polyunsaturated omega-6 fat that helps with anti-ageing and keeps skin and joints healthy. It also soothes arthritis. Borage also contains good levels of vitamins A, C, niacin, choline, thiamine, riboflavin and minerals.

IN THE KITCHEN

The young (slightly hairy) borage leaves have a distinct cucumber flavour. We shred them into salads and add to melted greens in a little olive oil or foaming butter. They are a traditional ingredient in Italian ribbolita. But it's the pretty blue, star-shaped flowers that feature most. We use the flowers in both sweet and savoury dishes and also crystallise them to decorate wee buns and cakes. They are particularly darling on white glacé icing and popped into ice cubes with a mint leaf to cool summer lemonades. Borage flowers are also delicious in a glass of Pimm's or floating on top of cold cucumber soup.

A Warm Salad of Chicken Livers with Ginger & Borage Flowers

This little salad takes minutes to make. The garlic/ginger mix lifts the flavour of the chicken livers immeasurably, and the borage flowers transform the salad into something extra special; you'll find yourself making it over and over again. This salad is also delicious with lambs' kidneys.

SERVES 4

approx. 4 handfuls of salad leaves, such as Lollo Rosso, claytonia, oakleaf, iceberg, butterhead or arugula
4 very fresh chicken livers
1 tablespoon butter
2 garlic cloves, finely chopped
1 teaspoon peeled and grated fresh ginger
borage or chive flowers or calendula petals, to garnish
sea salt and freshly ground black pepper

FOR THE DRESSING
2 tablespoons extra virgin olive oil
1 tablespoon red wine vinegar
¼ teaspoon Dijon mustard

Wash and dry the salad leaves and, if necessary, tear into bite-sized pieces.

Combine all the ingredients for the dressing, mix well and set aside.

Wash the livers and carefully remove any traces of green gall. Cut each liver into 4 pieces, dry and season with salt and pepper. Melt the butter in a frying pan over a medium heat, add the garlic and ginger and cook for 30 seconds, then add the livers and cook for 3 to 4 minutes until nicely brown on the outsides but still faintly pink in the centre (or cook to your taste).

Meanwhile, toss the salad leaves in the dressing, just enough to lightly coat the leaves.

To serve, put a little handful of salad into the centre of a large, white serving plate. Arrange the chicken livers on top and sprinkle with borage or chive flowers or calendula petals.

Ribollita

Ribollita is a Tuscan bread soup, a delicious example of *cucina povera*, peasant cooking, filling and hearty. Although it feels more like a winter soup, it can be eaten throughout the year, using whatever vegetables are in season and day-old bread. In winter, one might use cavolo nero; in spring and summer, nettles, cabbage, borage, spinach, and whatever wild herbs are available. Traditionally, this soup started the day before as a minestrone and then was reboiled—hence the name ribbolita—the next day with some additions.

SERVES 8

1 cup dried cannellini beans

1½ cups borlotti beans, fresh or dried and soaked overnight

2 fresh bouquet garni (1 bay leaf, 1 sprig of thyme, parsley stalks)

4 carrots, 2 cut in half, 2 peeled and cut into ¼-inch dice

1 onion, halved

2 tablespoons extra virgin olive oil, plus extra to serve

1 red onion, chopped

3 celery ribs, strings removed, cut into ¼-inch dice

3 garlic cloves, chopped

1 teaspoon ground fennel seeds

¼ teaspoon crushed red pepper

1 × 14-ounce can good-quality chopped tomatoes

sea salt and freshly ground black pepper

2½ cups homemade vegetable or chicken stock or the cooking water from the beans

3 ounces cavolo nero, leaves and stalks finely sliced

2 ounces borage or a mix of borage and spinach leaves

2 to 3 thick slices of good-quality stale bread, torn into chunks

Put the cannellini and borlotti beans into two saucepans with enough cold water to cover. Add the bouquet garni, halved carrots, and halved onion. Cook until the beans are soft. Fresh beans will take about 25 minutes, but dried beans can take up to an hour. Drain, reserving the cooking water for later (unless you are using stock). Discard the bouquet garnis, halved carrot, and onion.

Heat the oil in a saucepan, add the red onion, diced carrots, celery, and garlic, and stir in the ground fennel seeds and crushed red pepper. Cover and cook gently over low heat for 10 to 15 minutes or until just soft. Add the tomatoes and continue to simmer for another 5 minutes. Season with salt and freshly ground pepper.

Add the cooked and drained beans with 2½ cups cooking water or stock and return to a boil. Stir in the cavolo nero, borage, and spinach (if using). It looks like a lot, but don't worry, it will cook down.

Moisten the bread with a little stock or cooking water and add to the saucepan. The soup should be thick, but not dry, so add a little more liquid if you need to loosen it. Continue cooking for about 15 minutes until the soup is thick and silky. This is a thick soup similar in texture to *pappa al pomodoro*. Season to taste.

To serve, spoon into deep bowls and drizzle each with a little oil.

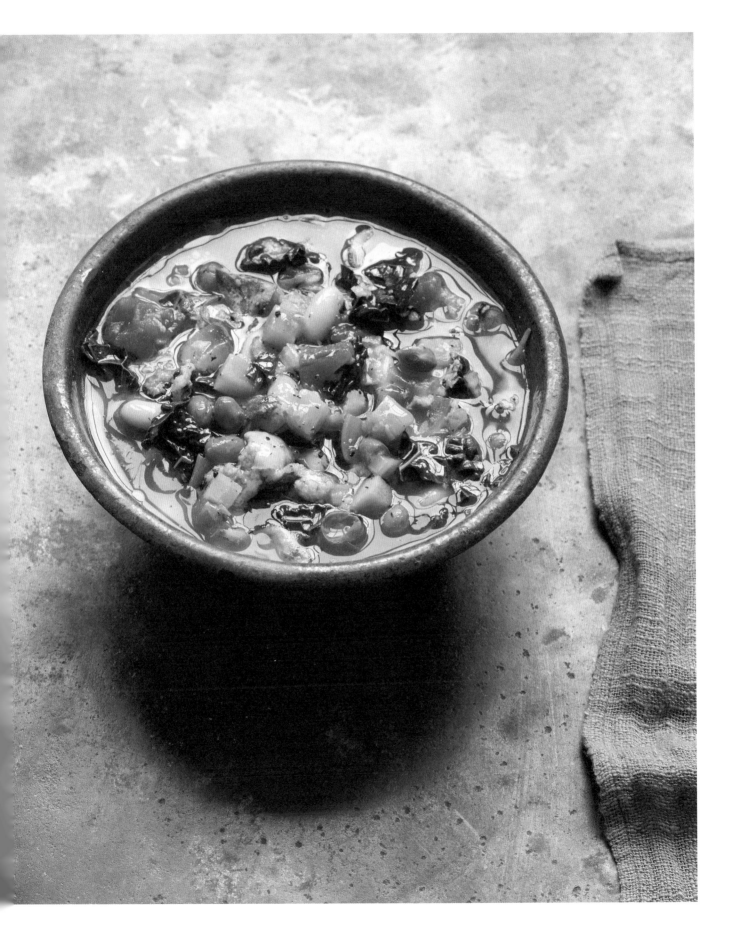

CARAWAY

Carum carvi HERBACEOUS BIENNIAL, ZONES 3–4

Caraway is certainly not an essential in your garden, but pretty and delicious and fun to grow. It's not just about the seeds either—all parts of the plant are edible: the roots, the young fern-like leaves, the pretty white flowers tinged with pink, and, of course, the seeds.

Just two or three plants would be enough to supply an average family with caraway seeds for a year. Home-grown are so much more aromatic than the caraway seeds you can buy. The crescent-shaped seeds, or achenes in botanical language, look similar to fennel and cumin, but taste entirely different. Caraway has many different names, including Persian cumin. It's part of the carrot and parsnip family and grows about 1½ to 2 feet tall with an umbelliferous flower head.

It's native to western Asia, North Africa, and Europe, so it will grow happily in vegetable or flower borders.

VARIETIES

I haven't come across different varieties. The variety we grow resembles a carrot plant with feathery leaves and white flowers in umbels.

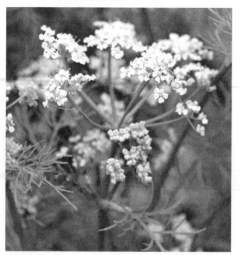

HOW TO GROW

Caraway thrives in full sun in well-drained soil. Sow the seeds ⅓ inch deep in autumn or spring. Thin to 8 to 12 inches apart. They may be slow to germinate, so don't let weeds smother them. Don't let the soil dry out while the young plants emerge and, if possible, avoid wetting the leaves too much while watering. Cut back in autumn and the plants will grow again the following spring.

CONTAINER GROWING

Caraway has a long taproot so the container would need to be quite deep— it's better grown in a herb bed or border.

PESTS AND DISEASES

Caraway seems resistant to most pests and diseases, even carrot root fly.

HARVESTING

Cut the seed heads before they get too brown. Hang them upside down in a dry place in a paper bag to collect any loose seeds. When they are fully dried out in a week or two, give them a good shake to extract the remaining seeds. Make sure

Caraway has pretty, umbelliferous flower heads. Enjoy them as well as the fragrant seeds.

they are fully dry before storing in an airtight tin or jar.

GOOD FOR YOU...

Caraway is used to aid digestion and prevent bloating, and is also included in some preparations to treat toothache. Caraway seed oil is used to treat fungal infections. The seeds are a rich source of fiber. Caraway also contains iron, calcium, potassium, zinc, selenium, magnesium and copper. The essential oil is sometimes used in perfume and soap-making and have been important in folk medicine for a long time. Caraway seeds are used to relieve menstrual pain and increase milk flow in nursing mothers.

WHAT TO DO WITH A GLUT

It is unlikely, but the seeds may, of course, be dried and stored.

IN THE KITCHEN

We use caraway seeds in cakes and bread, also in potato cakes and mashed potatoes. For **Caraway Seed Mashed Potatoes** for 4 to 6 people, add 1 tablespoon slightly crushed caraway seeds to 3 tablespoons melted butter, warm slightly, then add to 1 pound mashed potatoes.

Caraway seeds are also used in liqueurs and as a flavoring for cheeses and sauerkraut. The long taproots are similar to parsnips and carrots and can be cooked like them, but it is unlikely that the average gardener will be growing caraway in that sort of quantity.

Caraway is a familiar flavoring in rye bread. Caraway pudding, a rice pudding made with ground rice and water and flavored with caraway seeds, cinnamon, and a little sugar, is often served during Ramadan in the Middle East. The seeds can be made into a tea; crush lightly and infuse in boiling water.

Caraway Seed Cake

Caraway seed cake was a great favorite in Irish homes. I hated seed cake as a child, not least because my brothers joked that there were mouse droppings in it! Now it's one of my great favorites. My father had a passion for it, so it was always on offer when we went to visit our relatives on Sunday afternoons. The simple madeira cake is a perfect way to showcase the caraway flavor. Caraway seeds vary in intensity; homegrown seeds tend to be decidedly more aromatic than store-bought caraway, so use the minimum quantity if you are using homegrown.

SERVES 8 TO 10

12 tablespoons (1½ sticks) butter
¾ cup superfine sugar
3 large organic eggs
1¾ cups all-purpose flour
1 tablespoon ground almonds (optional)
pinch of salt
1 to 2 tablespoons caraway seeds, plus
    extra for sprinkling
½ teaspoon baking powder

Preheat the oven to 350°F. Line a 7-inch round, 3-inch deep cake pan with parchment paper.

Cream the butter, add the sugar, and beat until very soft and light. Whisk the eggs and gradually beat into the creamed mixture. Stir in most of the flour, then add the ground almonds (if using) and a good pinch of salt. Add the caraway seeds and the baking powder with the last of the flour. Turn the mixture into the prepared cake pan, sprinkle a few more caraway seeds on top, and bake for 50 minutes to 1 hour.

Let cool on a wire rack. This cake keeps well in an airtight container for a few days.

Caraway Angel Cake

This is another of Lydia Chatterton's recipes from *Home Notes* magazine, included in the scrapbook lent to me by Valerie Kingston of Glenilen Farm in Ireland when I was researching the revised edition of *Irish Traditional Cooking*. She suggests this as a splendid recipe to make use of egg whites when you are making a custard with egg yolks—the same would apply to ice cream. We love this cake; the candied peel gives a little extra edge and the egg whites lighten the texture.

SERVES 8 TO 10

3 tablespoons butter, plus extra
    for greasing
½ cup superfine sugar
⅔ cup milk
2 organic egg whites, stiffly whipped
1 teaspoon baking powder
pinch of salt
1¼ cups all-purpose flour
2 ounces candied peel, chopped
1 large teaspoon caraway seeds

Preheat the oven to 350°F. Grease and line a 7-inch round cake pan.

Beat the butter and sugar to a soft cream, stir in the milk gradually, and, when it is quite smooth, add the egg whites. Mix the baking powder and salt with the flour and beat into the butter mixture, then add the candied peel and caraway seeds. Pour into the prepared pan and bake for 50 minutes to 1 hour.

Cool on a wire rack. Serve with afternoon tea or as a dessert with summer berries or apple compote. Best fresh, but it will keep for a day or two in an airtight container.

DID YOU KNOW?
At least a quarter of the world's caraway production comes from Finland; the climate with long hours of sunshine there particularly suits their growth.

Emigrant's Soda Bread

At times of the year in Ireland when the men were working particularly hard in the fields, the farmer's wife would reward them with a richer bread than usual for tea. She might throw in a fistful of currants or raisins, some sugar, and an egg, if there was one to spare. The resulting bread had different names in different parts of the country—spotted dog, currie cake, railway cake, and so on. Currant bread was not just for haymaking and threshing, but was also a treat for Sundays and special occasions. Caraway seeds were added to the bread in Ireland long ago, but the tradition went by the wayside. Not so in America, where the Irish Americans added caraway seeds, to make Emigrant's Soda Bread.

MAKES 1 LOAF

3⅔ cups all-purpose flour, plus extra for
    dusting
1 to 2 tablespoons granulated sugar
1 level teaspoon salt
1 level teaspoon bread soda (baking soda),
    sifted
1 to 2 teaspoons caraway seeds
½ to ¾ cup golden raisins, raisins, or
    currants
1¼ cups sour milk or buttermilk
1 large organic egg (optional—you may
    not need all the milk if you use the egg)

Preheat the oven to 450°F.

Sift the dry ingredients into a bowl, add the caraway seeds and fruit, and mix well. Make a well in the center and pour most of the milk in at once with the egg (if using). Using one hand, mix in the flour from the sides of the bowl, adding more milk if necessary. The dough should be softish, not too wet and sticky. When it all comes together, turn it onto a floured surface and knead it lightly for a few seconds, just enough to tidy it up. Pat the dough into a round about 1½ inches deep and cut a deep cross on it. Bake for 15 minutes, then reduce the oven temperature to 400°F and continue to cook for about 30 minutes. If you are in doubt, tap the bottom of the loaf: if it is cooked, it will sound hollow.

Serve freshly baked, cut into thick slices and generously slathered with butter. Simply delicious!

Pumpkin Salad with Garlic, Harissa & Caraway

Antony Worrall Thompson, whose food I love, made this delicious salad as part of an antipasti during a guest chef appearance here at the school.

SERVES 4

1 tablespoon balsamic vinegar
1 tablespoon red wine vinegar
5 tablespoons extra virgin olive oil
2 garlic cloves, mashed with a little salt
4 teaspoons harissa paste
1¼ teaspoons ground caraway seeds
1 pound pumpkin, roasted, peeled,
    and mashed
salt and freshly ground black pepper
2 hard-boiled eggs, peeled and quartered
2 tablespoons chopped cilantro leaves

Mix together the vinegars, oil, garlic, harissa, and ground caraway seeds in a bowl. Add the pumpkin and combine. Season to taste with salt and pepper. Garnish with the hard-boiled eggs and the cilantro.

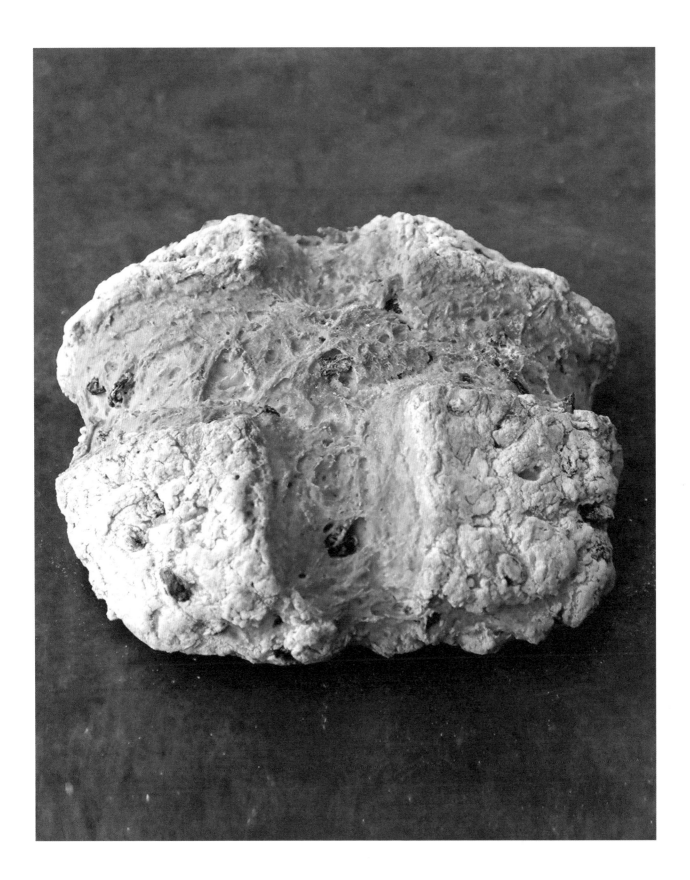

KAFFIR LIME (or makrut lime) *Citrus hystrix*

I love my lime leaf plant. It took me years to find one; before that I was constantly searching for a source of fresh lime leaves, but often had to settle for dried leaves which are only a pale substitute for fresh. It's such a joy to be able to snip a few leaves off the plant whenever I need to. *The Oxford Companion to Food* recommends the term makrut lime rather than kaffir lime (because the word kaffir is offensive to many people, having originally been used in an insulting way to describe colored people). It is native to Asia, including India, Nepal, Bangladesh, Thailand, Indonesia, Malaysia and the Philippines. The fragrant leaves of the wild lime tree are a very important flavoring in South-East Asian cuisines. There is nothing that comes close to the perfume and flavor so, now that plants are more readily available, it's really worth buying one and learning how to care for it.

VARIETIES

Citrus hystrix is a thorny bush that grows from 6 to 35 feet tall, with distinctively shaped, double-hinged leaves. The lower part is an oval and the top resembles the shape of a heart. The leaves and white flowers have an intensely citrus aromatic flavor. The small green fruits are knobbly and rough.

HOW TO GROW

Buy a plant from a reputable garden center and check the plant thoroughly to make sure it's not infected with any aphids or mealy bug. They like neutral or slightly acidic soil. Water with rain water if possible, but let the top layer of soil dry out between waterings. During the growing season—from spring to autumn—they benefit from a high organic nitrogen boost, chicken manure and a seaweed tonic. Try to mimic the humid conditions of South-East Asia as much as you possibly can.

CONTAINER GROWING

Small lime trees can be grown in pots outside or in large containers in a conservatory. I have several sizes, from 3 to 20 feet. They are happy outdoors in summer in a warm, sheltered area in full sun, but bring them indoors in mid-autumn and certainly before any threat of frost.

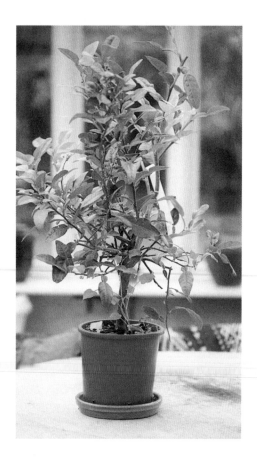

One of my lime leaf plants waiting to be repotted into a larger container.

PESTS AND DISEASES

Watch out for mealy bugs and scale insects which create a sticky black substance on the leaves. Use biological control (see pages 626–627) and wash the glossy green leaves with horticultural soap.

HARVESTING

Snip the glossy, double-hinged leaves leaves off as you need them. The leaves are highly aromatic and they keep well in damp kitchen paper or a resealable plastic bag in the fridge for a week or more.

GOOD FOR YOU...

Kaffir lime has many health benefits: the juice of the fruit is good to maintain healthy gums, detoxifies the blood, aids digestion, reduces stress, helps to enhance beautiful skin and healthy hair, and is used as an insect repellent.

WHAT TO DO WITH A GLUT?

Kaffir lime leaves freeze well—they are not as zesty and beautiful as fresh lime leaves, but far superior to dried. If you really have a surplus, add some to your bath water for a delightful perfume. We love the fragrant leaves infused in syrup for lemonade or to add a couple of leaves to a pot of jasmine rice.

DID YOU KNOW?

Kaffir lime has bleaching properties and can remove the toughest stains. The essential oil is extracted and used in many shampoos and cosmetic products. The oil is a hair and scalp cleaner.

IN THE KITCHEN

Lime leaves are an essential ingredient in many Southeast Asian dishes. They can be used in soup and stews; they are not eaten, but left behind in the bowl or on the plate. When lime leaves are used in salads or fishcakes, remove the spine, roll the leaves tightly, and shred as finely as possible.

Lime leaves are double-hinged so easy to recognize—watch out for thorns!

Tom Yum (Thai Sour Soup)

Another delicious way to showcase your fresh lime leaves—tom yum with homegrown lime leaves is serious one-upmanship!

. . . .

SERVES 5

3½ cups homemade chicken or fish stock
3 lemongrass stalks bruised and cut into 3-inch pieces
5 slices of fresh galangal
5 kaffir lime leaves, torn slightly
1 × 14-ounce can straw mushrooms, drained
2 ripe tomatoes, quartered
1¼ pounds uncooked shrimp, shelled and deveined
3 scallions, cut into 1-inch pieces
freshly squeezed juice of 1½ limes or lemons (approx. ½ cup)
¼ cup fish sauce (*nam pla*), or to taste
10 small bird's eye chiles, gently bruised
5 sprigs of cilantro to garnish
salt and freshly ground black pepper

Bring the chicken or fish stock (or the same quantity of water) to a boil, then add the lemongrass, galangal, and kaffir lime leaves. After a few seconds, add the mushrooms and tomatoes.

When the soup is boiling, add the shrimp and continue boiling over medium heat for 2 to 3 minutes until the shrimp are cooked. Remove from the heat. Pour the contents into a big bowl, then add the remaining ingredients. Season to taste with salt and pepper.

Garnish with cilantro and serve immediately.

Note: Tom Yum is served with the lemongrass, galangal, kaffir lime leaves, and chiles but they are normally not eaten—just left behind in the bowl.

Shredded Chicken & Shaved Coconut Salad

The fresh kaffir lime leaves are an essential element of this zingy Sri Lankan salad. They impart a haunting, lemon flavor.

SERVES 4

FOR THE SALAD

6 shallots, peeled, plus 3 shallots, finely sliced
extra virgin olive oil or peanut oil
4 chicken thighs or breasts
salt and freshly ground black pepper
1¾ to 2½ cups homemade chicken stock
6 scallions, finely sliced
2 red chiles, thinly sliced
1 cucumber, peeled and julienned
3 tablespoons mint leaves, shredded
5 kaffir lime leaves, spines removed and leaves very finely shredded
3 tablespoons finely shaved coconut and 2 tablespoons cilantro leaves, to serve

FOR THE DRESSING

½ cup coconut cream
approx. 2 tablespoons fish sauce (nam pla)
2 tablespoons palm sugar, or to taste
3 tablespoons lime juice, or to taste
1 red chile, thinly sliced
2 kaffir lime leaves, thinly shredded

Halve the 6 peeled shallots and slice thinly across the root. Spread out on paper towels to dry.

Heat 1 inch oil in a frying pan. Cook the shallots in batches for 4 to 5 minutes until crisp and golden, turning regularly. Spread on paper towels to crisp.

Season the chicken well. Fit into a small saucepan and cover with the stock. Bring to a boil and simmer for 20 to 30 minutes, or until the meat is cooked through and almost falling off the bones. Lift out and set aside to cool. Save the flavorful stock for use in another recipe.

Next, make the dressing: Mix all the ingredients together and season to taste with more fish sauce, lime juice, or palm sugar, as needed, to create a perfect sweet-sour, salty, and sharp balance.

Just before serving, make the salad: Shred the chicken, then mix with the remaining ingredients and toss with just enough dressing to lightly coat.

Arrange a little pyramid of the salad on each plate, then sprinkle the fried shallots and some coconut shavings over each one. Finish with a drizzle of the dressing and serve immediately with the cilantro leaves scattered over the top.

Mussels with Thai Flavors

We love this recipe. Use some of your precious fresh lime leaves to enhance the flavor.

SERVES 4 TO 6

4½ pounds mussels, cockles, or clams
2 tablespoons sunflower oil
6 garlic cloves, crushed
1 to 2 Thai red chiles, finely chopped
1 lemongrass stalk, chopped
1 tablespoon fish sauce (nam pla)
3 kaffir lime leaves
3 to 4 tablespoons chopped cilantro leaves

Check the mussels, cockles, or clams carefully, discarding any broken or open shells. Wash well, then drain.

Heat the oil over medium heat, add the garlic, chiles, and lemongrass, and cook for a minute or two. Add the fish sauce and kaffir lime leaves and then the shellfish. Cover with a folded kitchen towel or the lid of the pan. The shellfish will open in just a few minutes. Discard any that don't open.

Add the cilantro to the shellfish juices. Divide the shellfish among four hot plates, pour the hot juices over the shellfish, and serve immediately.

CILANTRO *Coriandrum sativum* ANNUAL

A crop of fresh cilantro leaves—we grow indoors year round and outdoors in summer.

You've got to grow your own cilantro, or coriander as it's known in the UK. I know it's an acquired taste at first but if your initial encounter did not convince you, keep on trying and suddenly you'll find that you crave the flavor you initially found soapy.

It is the most widely used herb in the world and an essential flavor in the food of the East, Far East and South America.

Every part of the plant is edible— roots, stalks, fresh leaves, both the pretty white flowers and the green seeds and, finally, the dried coriander seeds, which are used as a spice.

VARIETIES
Coriandrum sativum—Tender annual with white flowers in summer, which grows to about 2 feet.
Coriander sativum **Cruiser**—tidy, upright plant habit with good bolt resistance
Coriander sativum **Marino**—good production of seeds and leaves. Flowers are edible too.

HOW TO GROW
Cilantro is really easy to grow, but it runs to seed quickly, so plant it in succession from early spring to late autumn in a tunnel or greenhouse. This is not foolproof and whether you get seamless succession will depend on the weather. Cilantro needs a warm, sunny position and well-drained, light soil. Sow the seed directly in modular trays or in pots in early spring and transplant into the ground 6 to 8 inches apart in early summer. Cilantro does not like to have its roots disturbed.

CONTAINER GROWING
Cilantro will grow in a pot or container, but it's not particularly successful, so I wouldn't bother unless you have no other option.

PESTS AND DISEASES
None in our experience. Some gardeners have experienced a little greenfly if plants are too close together.

HARVESTING
Snip off the green leaves and stalks as you need them. The plant will eventually stretch and the shape of the leaf changes and becomes more fern-like. The flavor also changes and becomes more bitter as it flowers.

When the seeds change color and begin to dry, cut the stalks, tie together, and pop upside down into a paper bag and hang from the rafters or ceiling in a dry, airy place. The cilantro seeds will cure and can be used for seed or in cooking. They have a slightly burnt-orange taste. Store in airtight jars in a cool, dark place.

GOOD FOR YOU...
Cilantro is bursting with goodness, containing significant amounts of vitamins A and K, folate and potassium. It has many healing properties and research indicates that it helps to lower cholesterol, blood pressure and blood sugar levels, helps rid the body of heavy metals, protect against urinary tract infection, food poisoning, colon cancer and cardio-vascular disease.

WHAT TO DO WITH A GLUT
If you have a glut of leaves, use copious amounts in salads or make cilantro pesto or cilantro chutney. Leave to flower and go to seed and use as below. The flowers will turn into seed, which you can save for spice or next year's seed.

IN THE KITCHEN
It's difficult to think of any herb that provides as many options for the cook and pharmacist as cilantro. Young plants are somewhat mild in flavor, the roots provide oomph in a fresh spicy Thai green curry paste, stir-fries and soups. Unless you are close to an Asian food shop it will be difficult to find cilantro

DID YOU KNOW?
Cilantro has been used to relieve and prevent digestive problems for thousands of years. A little cilantro eaten with a spicy curry makes it more digestible.

roots. If you can't find cilantro roots, use the stems instead. We often chop up the stems with the leaves and scatter them over a myriad of Asian, Middle Eastern, Mediterranean and South American dishes.

The delicate white flowers have a haunting flavor and are so pretty scattered over starter plates and salads. Those that remain on the plants soon develop into fresh green seeds which have an intriguing flavor.

For **Pickled Green Coriander Seeds**, put ¼ cup white wine vinegar, ¼ cup water, 2 teaspoons pure salt (dairy salt) and 1 teaspoon granulated sugar into a saucepan. Bring almost to boiling point, to dissolve the salt and sugar, then remove from the heat and set aside to cool. Put 5 to 6 ounces green coriander seeds into one or two sterilized jars. Cover with the pickling liquid and the lid of the saucepan and leave for at least a week before using. They keep almost indefinitely but, as ever, use sooner rather than later. Add to mayonnaise or salsa, crush and add to marinades for fish or meat or scatter into grain or pearl barley salad..

Finally, there are the dried coriander seeds with their burnt-orange flavor— an essential ingredient in many curry powders and garam masala. Dry-roast and grind, add to vegetable stews, roast vegetables, homemade sausages and vinaigrettes. Carrot and cilantro soup sounds a bit clichéd these days, but that doesn't mean it's not delicious.

To make **Chilli and Cilantro Butter**, cream 8 tablespoons (1 stick) butter, add 1 finely chopped red or green chile (depending on the heat required) and 1 tablespoon chopped fresh cilantro (or marjoram if you prefer). Season with freshly ground black pepper and a few drops of lemon or lime juice. Delicious with Pan-grilled Mackerel (see page 00).

Cilantro flowers are super tasty in a salad, we also use them in flower arrangements.

Cucumber, Cilantro & Yogurt Raita

This cooling relish is good served with spicy food. We serve it with a myriad of curries and as a dip.

. . . .

SERVES 6

¼ medium-sized cucumber
½ tablespoon onion, finely chopped
pinch of salt
½ to 1 ripe tomato, diced
1 tablespoon chopped cilantro leaves or
   ½ tablespoon chopped flat-leaf parsley
   and ½ tablespoon chopped mint
⅔ cup plain yogurt
½ teaspoon cumin seeds

Peel the cucumber if you prefer, cut in half, and remove the seeds, then cut into ¼-inch dice. Put this into a bowl with the onion, sprinkle with salt, and allow to degorge for 5 to 10 minutes. Drain, then add the tomato, the cilantro or parsley, and mint and yogurt. Heat the cumin seeds in a dry frying pan over high heat for 30 seconds to 1 minute until fragrant, crush lightly with a mortar and pestle, and add to the raita. Season to taste with salt. Chill before serving. It can be made ahead and kept covered in the fridge for 2 to 3 days.

Roasted Salmon with Chermoula

Chermoula is a wonderfully versatile fresh herb and spicy sauce from Morocco and Tunisia. There are many versions; some include saffron, but we love this one which Asta and Camilla Plum cooked for us recently. It's fantastically versatile; we also slather it over butterflied chicken, a shoulder of lamb, or even chicken breasts. It uses both the stalks and leaves of cilantro. The spices are toasted separately, then ground together with a mortar and pestle or spice grinder.

. . . .

SERVES 8 TO 10

1 medium fish, preferably salmon, weighing
   about 4½ pounds
green salad, to serve

FOR THE CHERMOULA (MAKES 3 CUPS)
10 ounces cilantro sprigs, chopped, plus
   extra to garnish
¾ cup extra virgin olive oil
2 red chiles, coarsely chopped
2 tablespoons coriander seeds, toasted
2 tablespoons cumin seeds, toasted
1 tablespoon caraway seeds, toasted
1 tablespoon sweet paprika
zest of 3 organic lemons, plus juice of
   2 organic lemons
1 bulb of garlic, coarsely chopped
1 teaspoon sea salt

Cut deep slashes on each side of the fish and arrange in a roasting pan.

Process the ingredients for the chermoula to a fine paste in a food-processor. Smother the fish on both sides with about half of the mixture and let marinate for at least an hour.

Preheat the oven to 325°F and cook the fish for 35 to 40 minutes. Remove from the oven and spoon more chermoula over the surface of the salmon. Serve the fish warm or at room temperature with a green salad and the remainder of the chermoula. Garnish with a few cilantro leaves.,

Cilantro & Mint Relish

Another delicious recipe to serve with Indian dishes, such as pakoras, aloo tikki (page 224), and bhajis.

. . . .

6 tablespoons plain yogurt
1 tablespoon freshly squeezed lemon juice
2 heaping tablespoons chopped fresh mint
2 heaping tablespoons chopped fresh
   cilantro
1 green chile, finely chopped
salt, to taste

Mix all the ingredients together in a bowl and season to taste. Chill, cover, and use within a day or two.

Congee with Chicken, Shrimp, Mushrooms & Cilantro

Congee is a rice porridge—a kind of gruel, a staple breakfast food often eaten with bread sticks (known as *youtiao*) to dunk, in China and Hong Kong and many other Asian countries. I also love it as a soup. You can vary the additions—try some steamed or grilled fish or shellfish, or add some extra tasty tidbits, such as ground beef or pork, offal, a hard-boiled egg, and other vegetables, at the table.

. . . .

SERVES 4 TO 6

1½ cups jasmine rice, well washed and drained

3½ ounces raw chicken breast, finely shredded

3½ ounces raw or cooked shrimp

1 teaspoon fresh ginger, peeled and grated

1 red or green chile, thinly sliced (optional)

3½ ounces oyster or button mushrooms, thinly sliced

vegetable oil, for frying

sea salt and freshly ground black pepper

1 to 2 tablespoons toasted sesame oil

2 tablespoons thinly sliced scallions (they should be sliced thinly at an angle)

2 tablespoons cilantro leaves

Put the rice into a saucepan, cover with 8 cups of water, bring to a boil, cover, and simmer for 30 to 40 minutes until the rice is cooked and slightly soupy. Add the chicken, shrimp, ginger, and chile and cook for 4 to 5 minutes.

Meanwhile, sauté the mushrooms in a hot pan in a very little vegetable oil. Season with salt and pepper. Add to the soup, then taste for seasoning.

Ladle the soup into bowls, drizzle with a little sesame oil, and sprinkle with scallions and cilantro leaves. Serve this comforting and nourishing "soup" as soon as possible.

Fragrant Thai Meatballs with Cilantro & Peanut Sauce

Like many others, I am a great fan of Thai flavors. Everyone loves these meatballs when we make them; as ever, the fresh cilantro enlivens the dish.

SERVES 4 TO 6

FOR THE PEANUT SAUCE

1 tablespoon vegetable oil

1 tablespoon red curry paste

2 tablespoons crunchy peanut butter

1 tablespoon palm sugar

1 tablespoon lemon juice

1 cup coconut milk

FOR THE MEATBALLS

1 pound lean ground pork or beef

1 tablespoon chopped garlic

1 lemongrass stalk, finely chopped

4 scallions, finely chopped

1 tablespoon chopped fresh cilantro, plus
   extra sprigs to serve

2 tablespoons red curry paste

1 tablespoon lemon juice

1 tablespoon fish sauce (*nam pla*)

1 large organic egg

rice flour, for dusting

peanut or sunflower oil, for frying

sea salt and freshly ground black pepper

First make the peanut sauce: Heat the vegetable oil in a small saucepan, add the curry paste, and cook for 1 minute. Stir in the peanut butter, palm sugar, lemon juice, and coconut milk and bring to a boil. Reduce the heat and simmer for 5 minutes, or until the sauce thickens.

To make the meatballs, combine all the ingredients except for the flour and oil in a bowl and add some seasoning. Mix and blend everything together well. Fry off a little piece on a hot pan to check the seasoning. Taste and tweak if necessary. Roll and shape the meat mixture into small balls, each about the size of a walnut. Dust the meatballs with flour.

Heat about 2 inches of the peanut or sunflower oil in a wok until hot and deep-fry the meatballs in batches for 4 to 5 minutes until nicely browned and cooked through. Drain on paper towels.

Serve garnished with lots of cilantro and with the peanut sauce.

LEMONGRASS *Cymbopogon citratus* ZONES **10 - 11**

How quickly many formerly exotic ingredients have become mainstream. It doesn't seem all that long ago since I was trying to encourage stems of lemongrass to root in a glass of water. I remember my sister Elizabeth's delight when she got it to grow in the greenhouse in the early '80s. We were so proud of our couple of plants and showed them off. A couple of decades later one can buy plants in virtually every garden center and many supermarkets. It's no longer just adventurous chefs who add lemongrass to stocks, soups, stews, salads, ice creams and homemade lemonade, teas and tisanes.

VARIETIES

Lemongrass is a sub-tropical grass that grows all over Asia. There are about 50 species in the Poaceae family.
Cymbopogon citratus (**West Indian lemongrass**)—The one usually available in nurseries for culinary use.

Cymbopogon nardus (**Citronella grass**)— This species is grown mainly for use in medicine and as an insect deterrent; for example, in citronella candles which are brilliant for barbecues.

HOW TO GROW

Fine, healthy lemongrass plants are widely available, but if you would rather have the satisfaction of growing your own, buy nice, fresh-looking stalks in spring or early summer. Trim the base of each a little and put in a deep glass of water on a sunny windowsill. Roots will appear quite quickly from the base. When they are about 1 inch long, put them into 6-inch pots and repot them when they are about to be pot-bound. They will be happy in a greenhouse or in a hot, sunny, sheltered location in summer. Keep watered, but don't over-water. Bring indoors in winter, trim the leaves down to approximately 4 inches and keep watering to a minimum.

If planting into the ground, lemongrass likes rich, fertile soil; space 10 inches apart.

CONTAINER GROWING

Lemongrass will thrive happily in a large pot, given optimum conditions and good drainage.

PESTS AND DISEASES

Pests don't seem to bother lemongrass; in fact, the plant is known to deter insects.

HARVESTING

Allow the plants to establish; you can harvest the lemongrass when the base of the bulb is about $1/3$ inch thick or larger.

We have pots of lemongrass on windowsills all over the cookery school.

The foliage will be about 1 foot high by that stage. Cut the lemongrass stalks just below ground level; sometimes one can break a stalk off a clump.

The swollen base and about an inch above are the most tender. Trim the leaves; be careful, they can be sharp. Remove the tough outer stalks (add to the stock pot), and use the inner layer. The leaves can be added to the compost or strewn over the garden where they help to deter aphids.

GOOD FOR YOU...

In Maharashtra in India, lemongrass is used as an addition to tea and in a traditional herbal brew believed to relieve coughs and colds. It is also used in Ayurvedic medicine, again for nasal problems such as catarrh and congestion.

It is a good source of vitamins A and C, has a small percentage of B vitamins and also contains folate, folic acid, magnesium, zinc, copper, iron, phosphorous, calcium and manganese.

WHAT TO DO WITH A GLUT

This is unlikely, but lemongrass freezes quite well—freeze whole stalks or sliced lemongrass in resealable plastic bags. Use sooner rather than later. Lemongrass can also be dried by hanging upside down in a warm, dark place. It will last several months, but is obviously not like using it fresh as it has a weaker flavor.

IN THE KITCHEN

Lemongrass, which grows wild all over Asia, is an essential ingredient in many Asian dishes. Lemongrass seems exotic to us, but lemons are more a luxury in that part of the world. Add to soups, stews, and salads or use to make a syrup for homemade lemonade, infusions, and herbal teas.

Vietnamese Pork & Lemongrass Patties

Everyone loves these little pork patties; lemongrass lifts them to a different level. There's a nice kick of chile in the dipping sauce, but you can also add chile to the patties if you want a little more excitement in your life. A version of this dipping sauce is ever-present on restaurant tables in many Asian countries, including Thailand, Vietnam, Cambodia, and Laos. It's also great to use with grilled or fried meat or fish and, of course, spring rolls.

. . . .

SERVES 4 TO 6/MAKES APPROX. 16

FOR THE PATTIES

1 pound ground pork

2½ tablespoons shallots, chopped

2 lemongrass stalks, trimmed and very finely chopped

½ teaspoon salt

½ red chile, seeded and chopped (optional)

lots of freshly ground black pepper

FOR THE ASIAN DIPPING SAUCE

3 tablespoons fish sauce (*nam pla*)

3 tablespoons freshly squeezed lime or lemon juice

2 tablespoons granulated sugar, or to taste

1 garlic clove, crushed

3 to 4 fresh hot red or green chiles

Put all the ingredients for the patties into a food processor, season with pepper, and process for just a few seconds.

Heat a frying pan and cook a tiny piece of the patty mixture to check the seasoning, adjusting if necessary.

Make the meat mixture into patties up to 3½ inches in diameter and pan-grill for 5 minutes on each side. Alternatively, you can make the meat into balls about 2 inches in diameter and thread them onto well-soaked bamboo skewers and barbecue them for 10 to 15 minutes, turning on all sides.

To make the dipping sauce, combine the fish sauce, lime or lemon juice, sugar, and 3 tablespoons of warm water in a jar, then add the garlic. Mix well and pour into 4 to 6 individual bowls. Cut the chiles crosswise into very thin rounds and divide them among the bowls.

Serve the patties with the dipping sauce.

Lemongrass Lemonade

If you want to have access to more exotic ingredients in a rural area, the only solution is to grow them yourself. We've been growing lemongrass for several years and have so much now that we can afford to use it in all sorts of tasty ways. This is a refreshing and delicious drink.

. . . .

SERVES APPROX. 6

FOR THE LEMONGRASS SYRUP (MAKES APPROX. 3½ CUPS)

2½ cups cold water

2 cups granulated sugar

4 stems lemongrass, finely sliced

FOR THE LEMONADE

3 lemons

First make the syrup: Put 4 cups of water and sugar into a saucepan with the lemongrass. Bring slowly to a boil and simmer for 2 minutes. Set aside to cool completely.

For the lemonade, start by juicing the lemons. Then mix the lemon juice, water, and 1 cup cold lemongrass syrup in a bowl.

Keep the remainder (of the syrup) in the fridge for another day. Mix well, taste, and add more water if necessary. Serve chilled.

Cambodian Steamed Fish with Chili Oil

The fresh lime leaves and lemongrass add a magical flavor. Just one of the delicious ways I enjoyed fish in Cambodia.

SERVES 4

2 lemongrass stalks

1¾ cups coconut milk (organic if available)

2 tablespoons peeled and coarsely chopped fresh galangal or ginger

6 kaffir lime leaves

1 pound firm white fish fillets, such as monkfish, cod, sole, or turbot, skinned

salt and freshly ground black pepper

3 tablespoons finely sliced shallots

3 tablespoons fish sauce (*nam pla*)

2 tablespoons lime juice

1 tablespoon granulated sugar

2 teaspoons chili oil

a handful of cilantro leaves, to garnish

lime wedges, to serve

Trim and peel the lemongrass down to the tender whitish part. Crush with the blade of a knife and cut into 3-inch pieces. Put the lemongrass, coconut milk, galangal or ginger, and kaffir lime leaves or lime zest in a large pan. Bring to a boil, cover, and simmer for 30 minutes. Strain and discard the lemongrass, galangal or ginger, and kaffir lime leaves.

Pat the fish dry with paper towels.

Put a steamer over a wok or saucepan. Fill the wok or saucepan with 2 to 3 inches of water. Bring the water to a boil over high heat. Season the fish with salt and pepper and arrange it on a deep, heatproof plate, then spoon the coconut mixture on top. Add the shallots, fish or soy sauce, lime juice, and sugar. Put the plate of fish into the steamer. Cover tightly, and gently steam the fish until it is just cooked. Flat fish will take about 5 minutes to cook; thicker fish or fillets will take 8 to 12 minutes.

Remove the fish from steamer, divide among four hot plates, drizzle with a little chili oil, and garnish with a few cilantro leaves. Serve at once with lime wedges.

Asian Noodle Salad with Cilantro & Lime

There are many variations on this deliciously fresh-tasting noodle salad; shredded fresh lime leaves could also be added.

SERVES 8 TO 10

9 ounces thin rice noodles

2 carrots, coarsely grated

1 cucumber, cut into fine strips

8 scallions, diagonally sliced

½ lemongrass stalk, peeled and finely chopped

3 red chiles, seeded and finely sliced

⅓ cup chopped cilantro leaves

¼ cup torn mint leaves

¾ cup toasted peanuts, chopped

FOR THE DRESSING

½ cup freshly squeezed lime juice

½ cup fish sauce (*nam pla*)

4 teaspoons granulated sugar

Cook the noodles in a large saucepan of boiling water for 4 to 5 minutes until al dente. Drain, then refresh in cold water until completely cool. Drain again. Chop the noodles into smaller lengths.

Meanwhile, make the dressing: Mix the lime juice, fish sauce, and sugar together in a bowl until the sugar dissolves. Taste and tweak if necessary to balance the sweet, sour, salty, and sharp flavors.

Gently toss the noodles, carrots, cucumber, scallions, lemongrass, chiles, cilantro, and mint with the dressing until well mixed. Sprinkle with the toasted peanuts.

Serve chilled or at room temperature.

FLORENCE FENNEL

Foeniculum vulgare

PERENNIAL, ZONES 4–9

You must have at least one tall, feathery fennel plant. It will re-emerge every year in early spring to give you joy and many options in the kitchen. All parts of herb fennel are edible—stalks, leaves, flowers and seeds. It's a hardy perennial that has become naturalized in many parts of the world as diverse as California and West Cork where it grows wild along the roadside close to the coast, and occasionally on riverbanks. Fennel can also be grown as a hedge to hide a compost heap or to provide more privacy. In Sicily it is called *finocchio di montagna*, or mountain fennel. It grows wild in many areas and is used extensively in frittata and pasta dishes.

VARIETIES

There are many forms of fennel. We grow both herb and bulb fennel (see page 164).

Foeniculum vulgare var. *dulce* (**green fennel**)—the seeds from the green foliage varieties are used to produce fennel seeds for in spices and in medicine.

Foeniculum vulgare Preludio—uniform,

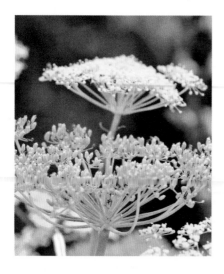

producing high yields of large, rounded bulbs.

Foeniculum vulgare (**common fennel**)— can grow to about 8 feet and so can provide a feathery centerpiece for a herb bed or a dramatic addition to a herbaceous border. This form is grown both as a herb and for its seeds. It does not produce a bulb.

Orazio—crisp and flavorful bulbs have a strong anise taste.

HOW TO GROW

How to grow fennel depends whether it's fennel herb or bulb (see page 164). For herb fennel, plant the seeds directly into rich moist soil or, better still, buy a couple of organic plants from a garden center. Plant 1 foot apart. Being native to the Mediterranean, it likes full sun, but keep it away from dill because they can cross-pollinate and the end result is not an improvement on either. Butterflies and moths love the stem. Fennel is an important plant for the larvae of some *lepidoptera* including the mouse moth and anise swallowtail who use it as a food plant. In midsummer cut back after flowering to encourage fresh growth— you will have another crop of flowers into early winter. Sometimes we cut back every second plant to have the best of both worlds.

CONTAINER GROWING

Herb fennel will also grow happily in a large, deep pot or half-barrel, 2 feet wide and at least 4 to 5 inches deep, but may need to be staked.

Fennel grows wild around Ireland—all parts of the plant are edible.

PESTS AND DISEASES

Fennel is generally trouble free.

HARVESTING

Use some of the feathery leaves of the herb fennel from the time they emerge.

The flowers are absolutely delicious. Pick them off and use them liberally in salads and for garnishing. Allow some to go to seed and harvest your own fennel seeds to add a delicious aniseed flavors to soups, stews and salads.

GOOD FOR YOU...

Fennel has many medicinal uses and it's rich in vitamin C, potassium and phytoestrogens. It's a known cure for colic and wind, an appetite suppressant, lowers blood pressure, boosts libido, and enlarges breasts and increases milk flow in breastfeeding mothers.

Fennel seeds are an important aid to digestion and are an essential ingredient of Indian pan which people love to chew after a meal.

WHAT TO DO WITH A GLUT

Save the seeds; they will keep for 6 to 12 months or longer if stored in a dark place in airtight jars, and can be eaten dried. Use the fronds lavishly in salads and flower arrangements. Harvest the pollen from the flowers and store carefully in small airtight jars.

IN THE KITCHEN

The young feathery green fronds look similar to dill, but taste distinctly different with an aniseed licorice flavor. The young flowers have a similar flavor and are delicious in salads and as a garnish for fish and pork, or snipped into mayonnaise. When the flower umbels open fully, snip them off carefully and lay them flower-side down on parchment or brown paper, to collect the pollen, which has an intense, sweet flavor. Chefs pay a fortune for this ingredient, but you can harvest it easily at home and store it in a glass jar. Sprinkle like "angel dust" over fish, chicken, roast pork, salads, or pasta. It sounds a bit dramatic to say you can use fennel pollen on almost everything, but keep it close by and you'll find its beguiling aniseed flavor adds a little magic to many dishes.

The flowers will turn into fennel seeds, which again can be harvested and eaten fresh or dried. Just hang the bunch of fennel upside down inside a brown paper bag with holes for air. The dry fennel seeds will collect in the bag and can be stored in a little jar. They are delicious with pork or fish; we also add them to homemade pork sausages and Italian salamis.

In Italy, fennel stalks are dried and used on the grill or as *spedino* (kebab sticks) to spear fresh fish for grilling.

When the flowers finish along come the powerful anise-flavoured fennel seeds.

Sicilian Pasta Salad with Sardines, Pine Nuts & Raisins

Italian pine nuts are now so excruciatingly expensive that we substitute cashews in many recipes—but try to use pine nuts here if you can find the long, slim, sweet Italian ones. Fresh sardines are, of course, best, if you can get ahold of them. Fennel grows wild all over the hills in Sicily so is an obvious addition to many dishes, including this classic.

SERVES 4 AS AN APPETIZER

2 tablespoons Italian pine nuts, toasted
extra virgin olive oil
½ to 1 red chile, finely chopped
2 tablespoons plump raisins
2 cups freshly cooked pasta (penne, orecchiette or shell), drained and tossed in olive oil
2 tablespoons chopped fresh flat-leaf parsley
2 tablespoons finely chopped fennel bulb, plus extra to serve
2 ripe tomatoes, diced and seasoned (optional)
freshly squeezed lemon juice
salt and freshly ground black pepper
4¼-ounce can of best-quality sardines in extra virgin olive oil
lemon segments, to serve

Toast the Italian pine nuts in a dry nonstick frying pan for a few minutes. They burn easily so keep an eye on them.

Heat a little oil in a frying pan, add the chile, raisins, and pine nuts. Add the pasta, parsley, and fennel and tomatoes (if using), then add more oil and some lemon juice. Season with salt and pepper, toss, and turn into a bowl. Add the sardines and toss again very gently.

Serve warm or at room temperature with lemon segments and some finely chopped fennel.

DID YOU KNOW?
During medieval times, fennel was used to ward off evil spirits. On Midsummer's Eve, herb fennel was hung over doors to ward off witches and evil spirits.

Pork Cooked in Milk with Fennel

Jane Baxter of Riverford Farm gave us this delicious recipe, but using lamb. We've substituted pork, and I use a mixture of belly or pork shoulder for extra juiciness. It may look slightly curdled, but it will taste delicious. The fennel adds a delicious extra anise element to this dish.

. . . .

SERVES 6

3 tablespoons fennel seeds, ground

3 tablespoons curly or flat-leaf parsley, chopped

3 garlic cloves, crushed

3 tablespoons olive oil

2¼ pounds pork shoulder or a mixture of shoulder and pork belly, trimmed and cut into 1½-inch chunks

1 teaspoon salt

2½ cups milk

¾ cup cream

2 tablespoons coarsely chopped fennel tops, wild fennel or dill

freshly ground black pepper

Mix together the fennel seeds, parsley, and garlic in a small bowl and set aside.

Heat the oil in a large saucepan until hot, then add half of the pork and cook until browned. Remove the pork from the pan, reduce the heat, and add the fennel seed mixture. Cook gently without coloring for 4 to 5 minutes.

Add the remaining pork and brown in the fennel paste. Return the rest of the pork to the saucepan with the cooking juices and add the salt and some pepper.

Add a little of the milk, using it to scrape any residue from around the pan. Add the remainder of the milk and the cream and bring to a very gentle simmer. Cover with a paper lid or cartouche and the lid of the pan, and leave barely simmering for 1 to 1½ hours on top of the stove or transfer to an oven preheated to 325°F until the meat is tender.

Remove the meat from the pan with a slotted spoon, cover, and set aside.

Reduce the pan juices over high heat until slightly thickened.

Return the pork to the sauce. Reheat for a few minutes. Season to taste. Sprinkle with lots of fennel tops, wild fennel, or dill and serve. A few fennel flowers scattered over the top are both delicious and appealing.

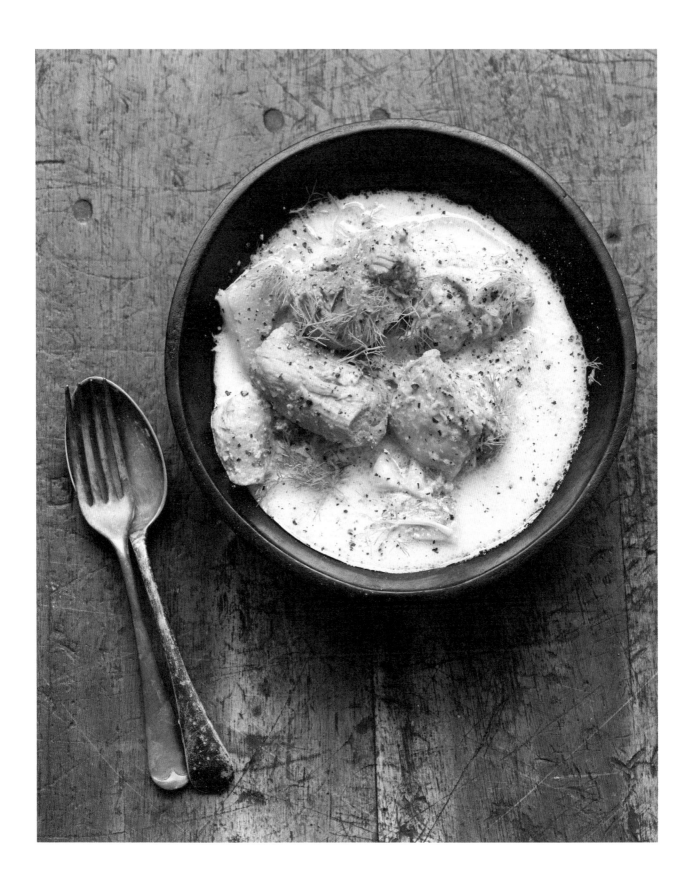

BAY *Laurus nobilis* PERENNIAL, ZONES 8–10

A mop head bay tree in the kitchen garden of the Ballymaloe Cookery School.

Bay is a deliciously aromatic evergreen tree, native to the Mediterranean region, which can grow to a height of 40 feet or more, so it can be a splendid specimen tree where space allows. From the cook's viewpoint, a little bay "tree" close to the kitchen door gives special joy. I just pop out and pick a glossy green leaf whenever I need it to flavor a dish. It can be trained into a pyramid or a mop head for aesthetic reasons—then you get double value for your bay, as it is both decorative and functional.

VARIETIES

There are many, but for the cook just two are particularly relevant. Both benefit from protection in winter in colder areas and can suffer from wind scorch, particularly in seaside areas.

However, they will recover in spring.
Laurus nobilis—Also known as sweet bay, with dark green, shiny leaves, small pale yellow flowers in spring and green berries that turn black in autumn.
Laurus nobilis **'Aurea'** —Golden leaves, similar to the above, with yellow flowers and black berries, very aromatic.
Lauraceae malabathrum—The Indian bay comes from the same family, The leaves (usually sold dried) are wider and longer than the regular bay, with three veins running down the center. They have a pronounced cinnamon aroma and flavor and can be used in soups, sauces and curries.

HOW TO GROW

You can grow bay from seed, but germination can be erratic and cuttings are difficult to strike, so I strongly recommend buying one or two strong, healthy plants. Plant in rich, fertile, well-drained soil in full sun and allow plenty of space. Mulch in spring to retain moisture.

In the soutehrnmost parts of the U.S., bay makes a splendid evergreen hedge. In other areas it can be kept in a greenhouse over the winter, and moved outdoors in summer. We have one planted near the greenhouse that gives us sprigs of green for small flower arrangements all year round.

CONTAINER GROWING

Bay is an ideal container plant. Mop head or pyramid-shaped bays look great alone or in pairs, framing a door or gateway.

Plant in half-barrels or large square planters. They can also be purely ornamental. They also look very effective planted as a centerpiece in a herb bed, as we do in the Ballymaloe Cooking School herb garden, to add height and structure in our formal herb beds. Bay in containers can be brought indoors to overwinter in extreme weather.

PESTS AND DISEASES

Bay is susceptible to scale insects which cause black sooty spots on the underside of the leaves and stem. Wash them off with a liquid horticultural soap.

HARVESTING

Bay can be harvested year round. Snip off a leaf or leaves as you need them. Prune in spring and late summer. It's vital to keep a standard or pyramid bay well pruned, otherwise it will lose its shape within a short time. Scatter the prunings on the compost heap.

GOOD FOR YOU...

Bay leaves are a good source of vitamins A, C, B6, calcium, iron, manganese and dietary fiber. They also contain copper, potassium, selenium, zinc and magnesium.

DID YOU KNOW?

Laurus nobilis is considered to be one of the oldest tree species. *Laurus* comes from the Latin meaning "praise" and *nobilis* means "famous" or "renowned." So athletes and poets were crowned with a wreath of laurels—Poet Laureate, baccalaureate....

The lauric acid in bay leaves is an insect repellent. Hang bunches in the kitchen to discourage flies.

WHAT TO DO WITH A GLUT

Bay is evergreen so just pick a few leaves as you need them. Make Bay Salt (page 472) from young growth in late spring or early summer. Dry bay leaves on a shelf over an Aga or radiator and store in jars for a couple of months to use in stews and casseroles, but I really prefer fresh bay to dried.

IN THE KITCHEN

Bay is an evergreen, so available to the cook year round. It has a strong, gutsy flavor so needs to be used judiciously. Often you just want a little hint of bay flavor, but in some dishes, such as Pollock with Cream and Bay Leaves, you really do want the flavor to predominate. Bay Salt is really worth making; it adds immeasurably to roasted chicken or pork.

Bay leaf is one of the constituents of a bouquet garni, which is essentially a little bouquet of herbs used in many classic French dishes such as boeuf bourgignon or cassoulet. There doesn't appear to be a generic recipe, but it always seems to include a sprig of thyme and a bay leaf. I also include parsley stalks, which have lots of flavor, and sometimes a sprig of tarragon or marjoram, and tie them all together with cotton string. If it's added to a large pot or casserole, it's a good idea to tie the bouquet garni to the handle so it's easy to fish out of the pot. The bouquet garni is always removed prior to consumption.

The glossy green leaves of Laurus nobilis.

Bay Leaf Custard Tart

The bay leaves flavor this custard tart deliciously—no need to serve extra cream or an accompaniment. Be generous with the bay leaves here—you want the flavor to be distinct. Full-fat heavy cream gives the best texture and flavor, but if you can't bear to use all cream, substitute ⅔ cup with whole milk.

SERVES 8

FOR THE SHORTCRUST PASTRY DOUGH
1⅓ cups all-purpose flour
5 tablespoons butter
pinch of salt
1 teaspoon superfine sugar
a little beaten egg or egg yolk, mixed with water, to bind
eggwash

FOR THE FILLING
2½ cups heavy cream
10 large bay leaves, lightly crushed
3 large whole organic eggs and 1 egg yolk
¼ cup superfine sugar

Make the shortcrust pastry dough and let rest in the fridge for 30 minutes.

Preheat the oven to 350°F.

Line a 9-inch tart pan with low sides and a removable bottom with the dough and chill for 10 minutes. Line with parchment paper, fill with baking beans, and bake blind for 25 to 30 minutes. Remove the paper and beans. Paint the tart base with a little eggwash and return to the oven for 3 to 4 minutes. Remove and let cool.

Reduce the oven temperature to 325°F.

Meanwhile, gently heat the cream with the bay leaves until it reaches the "shivery" stage, then let infuse for 15 to 20 minutes. Remove the bay leaves and discard.

Whisk the eggs well with sugar, then add the infused cream. Strain this mixture into the tart base and bake for 40 to 45 minutes until the custard is set. Remove from the oven, let cool, and serve at room temperature.

Roasted Stuffed Chicken with Bay Salt & Bay Leaves

Camilla Plum has a passion for herb salt and bay leaves. She showed us how to make this bay salt on one of her visits, stressing the importance of using the young growth. Bay salt keeps for 5 to 6 months or more.

. . . .

SERVES 4 TO 6

FOR THE BAY SALT

2 handfuls of young bay leaves,
  stalks removed

3 garlic cloves, crushed

½ cup Sel de Guérande, sea salt, or
  coarse gray salt from Trapani

FOR THE CHICKEN

1 × 3¼ to 5-pound free-range chicken,
  preferably organic

3 to 5 tablespoons soft butter

a little roux (optional, page 267)

salt and freshly ground black pepper

sprigs of bay, to garnish

crispy roasted potatoes, to serve

FOR THE STOCK

giblets (keep the liver for a chicken
  liver pâté) and wish bone

1 carrot, sliced

1 onion, sliced

1 celery rib

a few parsley stalks

a sprig of thyme

To make the bay salt, put the bay leaves, garlic, and half the salt in a food processor and pulse until juicy and green, then turn onto a plate. Add the remaining salt and dry on a flat platter for 4 to 5 days. Store in a glass jar or jars.

Remove the wish bone from the neck end of the chicken. This isn't at all essential, but it does make carving much easier later on. Tuck the wing tips underneath the chicken to make a neat shape and place the chicken in a roasting pan.

Season the cavity of the chicken with bay salt. Slather the breast and legs with the butter. Sprinkle generously with bay salt. Let sit for at least 30 minutes to 2 hours if possible.

To make the stock, put the giblets, wish bone, carrot, onion, celery, and herbs into a saucepan. Cover with cold water, bring to a boil, skim, and simmer gently while the chicken is roasting.

Preheat the oven to 350°F.

Weigh the chicken and allow about 30 minutes cooking time per 2¼ pounds plus 15 minutes extra. Baste the chicken a couple of times during the cooking with the buttery juices. The chicken is done when the juices are running clear. To test, prick the thickest part at the base of the thigh and examine the juices: they should be clear. Transfer the chicken to a carving dish, keep it warm, and let it rest while you make the gravy.

To make the gravy, spoon off the surplus fat from the roasting pan. Deglaze the pan juices with the fat-free chicken stock (you will need 2 to 2½ cups, depending on the size of the chicken). Using a whisk, stir and scrape well to dissolve the caramelized meat juices from the roasting pan. Boil it up well, season, and thicken with a little roux if you like. Season to taste. Serve in a hot gravy boat.

If possible, serve the chicken on a nice carving dish surrounded by crunchy roasted potatoes and lots of bay sprigs. Arm yourself with a sharp knife and bring it to the table. Carve as best you can and ignore rude remarks if you are still practicing, but do try to organize it so that each person gets some brown and some white meat. Serve with lots of gravy.

LOVAGE

Levisticum officinale PERENNIAL, ZONES 4–8

Lovage originated in the Mediterranean and western Asia and is another gem. Virtually trouble free, it is an almost forgotten celery-flavored herb that I wouldn't be without. It surely deserves to be much better known. I'm delighted to see it popping up on menus here and there and I regularly see plants for sale in garden centers, so snap one up and pop it into a spot in your garden in an area where it can re-emerge every year.

It's a tall, hardy perennial herb, a member of the Umbelliferae (carrot) family. The greenish yellow flower heads are up to 7 inches in diameter and are made up of hundreds of tiny florets, similar, though sturdier, than Queen Anne's Lace, carrot, parsley, angelica, dill or fennel. The leaves have an intriguing celery flavor and aroma. Someone once told me that lovage is one of the principal flavorings in Aromat, though I haven't been able to confirm that. The French call it *céleri batard*.

VARIETIES

Levisticum officinale—The only species within the genus *Levisticum*.

HOW TO GROW

Lovage likes rich, fertile soil and full sun. It will grow to about 6 feet. You could grow it from seed, but one plant is probably enough for most families. Plant it in the center or at the back of a vegetable bed or flower border, allow about 40 inches square to give it room to spread. If it does get too big, it can be split with a spade and divided during the winter months.

Like angelica, it survives well in a cold climate and winter frosts and pops out of the ground in early spring. The flowers attract lots of bees and butterflies.

Every part is edible and, if the soil is piled up against the base, the stems will be blanched and can be eaten like celery.

CONTAINER GROWING

Lovage can be grown in a large container, but remember it grows to a height of 60 inches so allow room for that when positioning it in your pot, and don't plant it in a light pot which could become top-heavy and keel over.

PESTS AND DISEASES

Lovage doesn't seem to be bothered by pests; in fact, it can attract beneficial insects such as hoverflies, which are predators for other insects, into the garden. It will also attract bees which will help with pollination.

HARVESTING

The stems may be used from early summer and, if they are cut down during the summer, there will be new young growth. Don't cut all the plants at the same time, so there will be sequence of young shoots. The leaves may be picked throughout the summer to give a celery flavor to soups etc.

GOOD FOR YOU...

Lovage plays a valuable part in supporting kidney and joint health. It fights against bacteria like E. coli and salmonella. It helps soothe the digestive tract and reduce bloating. It contains B complex vitamins and vitamin C, and

We snip fresh lovage into our green salads from spring to late summer—delicious.

can be used to make a herbal tea. It also contains quercetin which provides natural allergy support.

WHAT TO DO WITH A GLUT

It is unlikely that you will have a glut but if you want to keep some, the hollow stems can be candied like angelica (page 429), with delicious results.

IN THE KITCHEN

After its winter snooze, the young tender leaves are super delicious in a green salad, in soups, and shredded over meat and

bean stews. I'm addicted to lovage syrup drizzled on melon or ripe pears. Apart from salad, I also love the tender young leaves in stuffing, stir-fries, and omelets. The dried seeds can be used like celery seeds or fennel seeds in bread and

savory biscuits. Add the stalks to the stock pot, as well as, or instead of, celery. The flavor is more intense than celery, so use judiciously.

Gratin of Potato & Lovage

Serve this delicious gratin with a haunch of venison or a leg of mutton—divine.

SERVES 6

2 pounds similar-size potatoes
salt and freshly ground black pepper
1 cup whole milk
1 cup heavy cream
2 to 3 tablespoons chopped fresh lovage
1 small garlic clove, crushed
2 tablespoons freshly grated Parmesan
fresh lovage leaves

Peel the potatoes and slice them into rounds ¼-inch thick. Do not wash them. Dab them dry with a cloth. Spread them out on the worktop and season with salt and pepper, mixing it in with your hands.

Pour the milk into a saucepan, add the potatoes, and bring to a boil. Cover, reduce the heat, and simmer gently for 10 minutes.

Preheat the oven to 400°F.

Add the cream, chopped lovage, and garlic to the potatoes. Simmer for another 20 minutes, stirring occasionally, so the potatoes do not stick to the saucepan. As soon as the potatoes are cooked, take them out with a slotted spoon and put them into a large 6-inch square gratin dish or 6 × 5-inch small ovenproof dishes. Pour the creamy liquid over them. Sprinkle with the Parmesan. Heat in a bain-marie in the oven for 10 to 20 minutes until they are golden and bubbly on top.

Garnish with a few fresh lovage leaves.

Carrot & Lovage Soup

This soup may be served either hot or cold. Don't hesitate to put in a good pinch of sugar as it brings out the flavor. You can substitute mint or tarragon for the lovage. If you don't have your own home-grown carrots, seek out unwashed carrots if possible.

SERVES APPROX. 6

3 tablespoons butter
1¼ pounds carrots, chopped
  (about 4 cups)
4 ounces onions, chopped (about ⅔ cup)
5½ ounces potatoes, chopped
  (about 1 cup)
salt and freshly ground black pepper
pinch of sugar
sprig of lovage, plus 3 teaspoons chopped
  fresh lovage
4½ cups boiling homemade chicken or
  vegetable stock
¼ cup whole milk (optional)
a little lightly whipped cream or crème
  fraîche and sprigs of spearmint or
  chiffonade of lovage, to garnish

Melt the butter in a saucepan and when it foams add the chopped vegetables, then season with salt and pepper and add a good pinch of sugar. Add a sprig of lovage, then cover with parchment paper (to retain the steam) and a tight-fitting lid. Cook gently over low heat for about 10 minutes. Remove the lid, add the boiling stock, and cook until the vegetables are soft.

Pour into a liquidizer, then add the chopped lovage and purée until smooth. Season to taste. Add a little milk if necessary.

Garnish with a swirl of lightly whipped cream or crème frâiche and a sprig of spearmint or tarragon or chiffonade of fresh lovage.

LEMON BALM *Melissa officinalis* HARDY PERENNIAL, ZONES 3–7

Lemon balm might not have to be in your top ten "must-haves," but I just love it and so do the bees. our bees love the tiny white flowers. Given half a chance, lemon balm, or Melissa as it's also known, hops around the garden and is given to tucking itself here and there between the plants. It can become invasive, but the roots are shallow so it's easy to pull up, unlike horseradish. Lemon balm tisane has been a favorite after-dinner infusion at Ballymaloe House for several decades as it's known to aid digestion.

VARIETIES

These are the two varieties we enjoy because both have a distinct lemony fragrance and flavor.

Melissa officinalis—Soft, bright green leaves, almost heart-shaped, with a distinct lemony fragrance when crushed. Grows about 30 inches tall and has small white/pale yellow flowers.

Melissa officinalis 'Aurea'—Variegated, golden lemon balm with pretty yellow splashed leaves, about 2 feet tall.

HOW TO GROW

Lemon balm can be grown from seed in almost any type of soil, or one can divide established plants. However, unless you want to set up a stall at your local farmers' market or supply all

Lemon balm with its haunting lemon flavor and heart-shaped leaves is super easy to grow.

Variegated golden lemon balm—even prettier but with a similar flavor.

your friends, I suggest you just buy a healthy, preferably organic, plant from a reputable garden center.

Because it is native to the Mediterranean it enjoys a sunny position, but the leaves of the variegated form get scorched in the summer. It dies down in winter and it may need to be mulched for protection in cold areas.

CONTAINER GROWING

Lemon balm grows brilliantly in large pots or even in windowboxes. Water as needed in summer, but only sparingly during winter months.

PESTS AND DISEASES

We haven't encountered any pests, but it can be attacked by rust in which case it's necessary to dispose of the plant as soon as possible. Plant some lemon balm amid your flowers in a border, where it will self-seed and will fill any little gaps.

HARVESTING

Snip the leaves as needed. We have lots so we find sprigs of lemon balm really useful for small cut-flower arrangements also.

DID YOU KNOW?

Lemon balm was dedicated to the Roman goddess Diana by the Greeks, and used medicinally by them for over two thousand years.

Melissa, the generic name for lemon balm, comes from the Greek word for bee. The Greeks believed that if a bunch of lemon balm was put into an empty beehive it would encourage a swarm of bees to colonize it. I'm experimenting as I write...

GOOD FOR YOU...

LLemon balm has long been known as an aid to digestion and it helps to ease colic and flatulence. The essential oil made from lemon balm is highly regarded in aromatherapy and relieves nervous headaches, helps with insomnia and lifts the spirits of many who are feeling depressed.

I was delighted to learn recently that the ancient Greeks used lemon balm to improve their memories. Since the Middle Ages it has been considered to be a remedy for headaches, toothaches and depression and it helps to boost the immune system. So snip lots into your green salad and enjoy a cup of Lemon Balm Tea (page 480). It is also particularly recommended for those who suffer from cold sores. Prince Llewellyn of Glamorgan, who lived to the ripe old age of 108, attributed his longevity to a cup of lemon balm tea every day.

WHAT TO DO WITH A GLUT

Add it to salads, use as a garnish and enjoy it in lots of tisanes. We also use it in little flower posies.

IN THE KITCHEN

We've got lots of lemon balm, so we enjoy using some of the leaves in a green salad. They can also be used to garnish both sweet and savory dishes and are also adorable crystallized or frosted to decorate cakes and small treats.

Add a little to herb butter to roasted fish and enjoy some refreshing lemon balm tea by simply pouring boiling water over the slightly crushed fresh leaves in a cup or teapot. Add it to ice cubes to chill homemade lemonade. We also add it to the water pitchers in the cooking school at lunchtime.

Lemon Verbena & Lemon Balm Sorbet

Rory O'Connell serves this deliciously fresh sorbet as an appetizer in Ballymaloe in Ireland. It just flits across the tongue and scarcely needs to be swallowed. A perfect start to a late summer meal. Sweet geranium leaves (*Pelargonium graveolens*) also make a delicious sorbet—memorable served atop a fresh strawberry jelly.

. . . .

SERVES 8

1 cup granulated sugar
2½ cups cold water
2 large handfuls each of lemon verbena and lemon balm leaves, plus extra to garnish
freshly squeezed juice of 3 lemons
1 organic egg white (optional)
viola flowers (optional)

Put the first three ingredients into a nonreactive saucepan and bring slowly to a boil, then simmer for 2 to 3 minutes. Remove from the heat and set aside to get quite cold. Add the lemon juice.

Strain and freeze for 20 to 25 minutes in an ice-cream maker or sorbetière. If you don't have a sorbetière, simply freeze the sorbet in a bowl in the freezer. When it is semi-frozen, whisk until smooth and return to the freezer again. Whisk again when almost frozen and fold in the stiffly beaten egg white (if using). Keep in the freezer until needed.

Alternatively, if you have a food processor, simply freeze the sorbet completely in a pan, then break up and pulse for a few seconds in the processor, drop the lightly beaten egg white (if using) down the tube, pulse, and freeze again.

Serve in chilled glasses or chilled white china bowls. Garnish with lemon balm and verbena leaves and maybe a few viola flowers if available.

We also serve a splash of Champagne and sometimes a few pomegranate seeds with the sorbet.

LEMON BALM **479**

Home-smoked Salmon with Lemon Balm Butter

Fresh haddock or pollock are super delicious when hot-smoked. This is a tasty way to use lemon balm; the delicate fresh flavour complements the warm, lightly smoked fish.

. . . .

SERVES 6

FOR THE LEMON BALM BUTTER
4 tablespoons butter
4 teaspoons finely chopped lemon balm
a few drops of freshly squeezed lemon
   juice

FOR THE FISH
6 × 4-ounce fillets of salmon, haddock, or
   pollock, scaled but not skinned
pure salt

First make the lemon balm butter: Cream the butter, then stir in the lemon balm and the lemon juce, a few drops at a time. Roll into butter pats or form into a roll and wrap in parchment paper or foil, screwing each end so that it looks like a firecracker. Chill to harden.

Rub the skin and flesh of the fish with salt and set aside for 10 to 15 minutes while you prepare the smoker.

You don't need any special equipment—even a cookie sheet will do. Sprinkle 2 tablespoons of sawdust (we use apple wood) on the base of a rectangular cookie sheet or smoking box.

Dry the fillets with paper towels, place on a wire rack, and let dry in a cool, airy place for about 30 minutes. Put a wire rack onto the prepared pan/smoking box and lay the fish, flesh-side up, on top. Put the box over high heat for a minute or so until the sawdust starts to smolder. Cover the box. Smoke for 8 to 10 minutes, depending on the size of the fish, then turn off the heat and leave the fish to sit in the box for another 5 minutes.

Transfer the fish to one or several serving plates. Serve while still warm with a couple of slices of the lemon balm butter on top, and perhaps a Tomato and Basil Salad (see page 188), wilted greens, and some new potatoes.

Lemon Balm Tea

We love fresh-tasting herb teas and infusions. I'm very wary about ordering "herbal tea" in a restaurant, but one Paris restaurant I dined in recently served herb infusions in the most delightful way. The waiter came to the table with several china bowls of fresh herbs on a silver salver. With tiny silver tongs he put the guest's chosen herb into a little china teapot, poured in boiling water, and served it with a flourish. Exquisite.

. . . .

lemon balm, rosemary, sweet geranium,
   spearmint, lemon verbena, sage, fennel,
   peppermint leaves
cold water

Bring the water to a boil. Swirl some around a china teapot, then take a generous pinch of fresh herb leaves and crush them gently in your hand. The quantity will depend on the strength of the herb and how intense an infusion you enjoy. Put the herb leaves into the warmed pot. Pour the boiling water over the leaves, cover the teapot, and allow to infuse for 3 to 4 minutes. Serve immediately in china cups.

Alternatively, put a few leaves into a cup or mug and infuse as above.

MINT

Mentha sp. PERENNIAL, ZONES 5–9

I use tons of mint in both sweet and savoury dishes from the time it begins to peep up through the soil from its winter snooze. I cover a patch with a cloche to coax it out of the ground in order to have enough to make a little bowl of Myrtle's Mint Sauce to serve with our spring lamb on Easter Sunday.

Friends complain that it spreads, but plant it in an area where it doesn't matter and it can indeed romp away. Then use it with gay abandon in drinks, salads, tabbouleh, sauces, syrups, confectionery or fruit salads.

VARIETIES

There are literally hundreds of varieties of mint. Which varieties should you choose? Well, it depends on the available space. If I was only allowed one it would have to be the terrifically versatile spearmint *Mentha spicata*, valued not only for its culinary use, but also for medicinal and cosmetic uses. I find the form that has shiny leaves is infinitely more aromatic than the matte variety. If I could have just two, peppermint would be my next choice; it makes a delicious infusion and my brother Rory swears it's the best variety to use for Chocolate Mint Leaves, but I love spearmint also.

We grow apple mint, chocolate mint, After Eight mint, lemon mint, orange mint, basil mint, Moroccan mint, mojito mint, Bowles's mint, eau de cologne mint...far more than is necessary so the students can become familiar with different varieties and flavors.

Mentha spicata (**spearmint**)—Gets its name from the pointy "spear" tips on the leaves. It grows 12 to 40 inches tall and spreads by fleshy underground rhizomes.

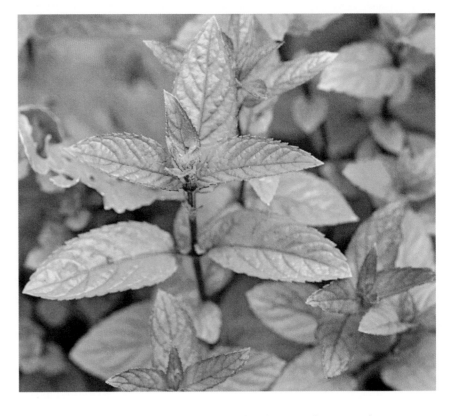

If you have space for just one, choose spearmint.

The leaves have a serrated edge and can be 2 to 3½ inches long and about ¾ inch across.

Mentha × piperita (**peppermint**)—Grows to 2 feet high and forms runners. Used for mint sauce, mint tea and for adding flavor to new potatoes and peas.

Mentha suaveolens (**apple mint**)—Also grows to about 2 feet, very invasive. It has woolly stems which sometimes gives it the name of woolly mint. The leaves are more rounded than spearmint. Lovely added to a pitcher of iced water or dried to make tea.

HOW TO GROW

Mint, like many herbs, is native to the Mediterranean. It's not that fussy about

DID YOU KNOW?

Mint is an ancient herb, much valued for its culinary, medicinal and aromatic properties. In some cultures mint is the symbol of hospitality—in ancient Greece it was rubbed on tables before the arrival of guests and in the Middle East a cup of mint tea is often offered to welcome visitors. The Native Americans valued it as a wild herb, even before the arrival of the colonists who brought it with them from the Old World. It is widely used in mouthwashes and toothpastes as a breath freshener.

soil, it loves sun, but will in fact tolerate some shade. It can be a real thug in the garden, so choose a spot carefully, where you don't mind if it spreads. Alternatively, plant it in a container, or curtail the roots with slates to a depth of 1 foot. It's best not to plant different varieties side by side, they cross-pollinate and lose their individuality, which results in a mishmash in a surprisingly short time.

Mint is really easy to grow and it's probably best to buy plants, preferably organic if you can find them. It can grow quite tall and has pretty purple flowers in summer and into autumn.

Transplant into larger pots or directly into the ground and allow the plant to establish before you start to pick.

Divide the plants every two years to stop the roots from getting all tangled.

CONTAINER GROWING

Where space is an issue mint is best planted in a container to curtail its spread. It will grow happily in a zinc bucket, timber box, a tub or half-barrel, on a balcony or close to your kitchen door ready for snipping. Mint can even be grown for a season or two in a hanging basket.

PESTS AND DISEASES

Mint rust can sometimes be a problem. Dig up and discard the plants immediately as the rust spreads. Burning off with a gas torch, if it's an option, effectively sterilises the ground.

Peppermint or spearmint, planted near roses, seems to deter aphids. The variegated apple mint, Mentha suaveolens 'Variegata', also looks lovely beneath the roses.

HARVESTING

Mint will start to peep up from the ground in mid-spring. Cut, it will keep on coming. It begins to die off in early winter and gradually becomes more

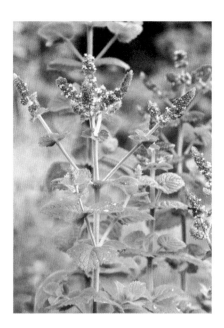

Bowles's mint has a furry underleaf.

distressed in appearance, particularly after a few nights' frost.

GOOD FOR YOU...

Mint has been cultivated for its medicinal properties since ancient times. It helps with digestion and can soothe stomachs. Peppermint oil can be soothing for those who suffer from motion sickness. It also has antibacterial properties and studies have found it can help relieve symptoms of irritable bowel syndrome. Mint is a source of manganese, copper and vitamin C.

WHAT TO DO WITH A GLUT

Mint can be chopped and fast frozen in ice cubes and used in mint sauce, soup or lemonades. Mint also dries quite well but, as ever, is only a shadow of the fresh herb. Make apple and mint jelly as one can never have too much. Use a handful in lemonade and green salads.

IN THE KITCHEN

There really is the world of difference,

Mentha suaveolens 'Variegata'—variegated apple mint also known as pineapple mint.

both in flavor and texture, between freshly picked homegrown mint and the commercial version. Use fistfuls in homemade lemonade, and add to anything from fruit salad to Vietnamese pork salad. Snip a little into jams and jellies. Round off the day with a fresh mint tea or some **Chocolate Mint Leaves**. Simply dip in melted dark chocolate and chill.

To make **Moroccan Mint Tea** for 4 people, heat a teapot with boiling water. Add 2 teaspoons Chinese green tea and 4 tablespoons chopped mint, preferably spearmint, to the pot. Fill with 3¾ cups boiling water. Let infuse and stand for 5 minutes. Pour the tea from a height into Moroccan glasses edged with gold. Add sugar to taste (in Morocco tea is supposed to be sweet).

For **Iced Mint Tea**, add the sugar to the pot with the tea and mint. After steeping, pour the tea through a strainer over cracked ice, so it cools quickly. Serve in cold glasses with ice cubes, decorated in the same way.

Thai Beef Salad

I love this warm, spicy beef salad. A super way to enjoy lots of fresh mint, basil and cilantro leaves.

. . . .

SERVES 6 TO 8

3 tablespoons Thai soy sauce

2 garlic cloves, crushed

2 tablespoons freshly squeezed lime juice

1 pound sirloin steak, cut into 2 steaks if more convenient

8 ounces salad leaves

1¼ ounces mint leaves

1 ounce basil leaves

1 ounce fresh cilantro leaves

1 small cucumber, cut in half lengthwise, then cut into ¼-inch slices at an angle

FOR THE DRESSING

1 to 2 red Thai chiles, chopped

3 tablespoons Thai soy sauce

2 tablespoons freshly squeezed lime juice

2 teaspoons palm sugar or brown sugar

2 kaffir lime leaves, spines removed and finely shredded

Mix the soy sauce, garlic, and lime juice together in a bowl, add the steak, and let marinate for 10 minutes.

Just before serving, preheat a grill-pan over high heat. Sear the steaks on both sides, then cook on the fat-side for 4 to 5 minutes until the fat is crisp, then continue to cook to your liking—no more than medium rare. Set aside to rest on an upturned plate while you make the dressing.

To make the dressing, combine the chiles, soy sauce, lime juice, sugar, and shredded kaffir lime leaves. Taste and balance the sweet, sour, salty, and sharp flavors if necessary.

Toss the salad leaves, mint, basil, cilantro, and cucumber together in a bowl. Sprinkle some dressing over the salad and toss. Arrange on a serving plate.

Slice the beef thinly and place on top of the salad. Serve at once.

Note: Thai mint and Thai basil are best here if you can find them, but spearmint and basil work well here too.

Mint Julep

The flavor of mint combines well with alcohol—think mojito. A good mint julep will transport you straight back to *Gone with the Wind*.

. . . .

SERVES 1

12 mint leaves

1 teaspoon superfine sugar

⅓ cup bourbon

2 tablespoons crushed ice

Put 8 mint leaves into a glass with the superfine sugar, then muddle with a drop of the bourbon until the leaves are nicely bruised. Fill the glass with crushed ice and add another 2 tablespoons bourbon. Stir until the glass has frosted and top off with the remaining bourbon. Decorate with the remaining mint leaves.

Crab, Shrimp & Pomelo Salad with Asian Dressing

Pomelo have a flavor reminiscent of grapes and grapefruit. We enjoyed them all over Myanmar and in salads in Thailand and Vietnam, often combined with shredded chicken or shellfish. Use red or pink grapefruit if you can't find a pomelo.

. . . .

SERVES 4

FOR THE DRESSING

3 tablespoons lime juice

3 tablespoons superfine sugar

2 tablespoons fish sauce (*nam pla*)

FOR THE POMELO SALAD

1 pomelo, peeled and shredded

10½ ounces cooked white crabmeat

a handful of dill, coarsely chopped

a handful of mint leaves, coarsely chopped

a handful of cilantro leaves, coarsely chopped, stems finely chopped, plus sprigs to garnish

2 to 3 large or 3 Asian shallots, sliced

1 large red chile, finely sliced

1 bird's eye chile, finely diced

2 tablespoons chopped salted peanuts

To make the dressing, combine all the ingredients in a bowl and stir together until the sugar dissolves. Taste and balance the sweet, sour, salty, and sharp flavors if necessary.

To assemble the salad, combine all the ingredients except the peanuts together in a wide bowl. Pour over just enough dressing to coat, toss gently, sprinkle with peanuts, and scatter some sprigs of cilantro over the top. (You can use Vietnamese cilantro—*persicaria odorata*—if available.)

Fresh Orange Gelée with Mint

Everyone loves gelée—you can imagine how good the spearmint is with the orange. You can also use 6 to 8 blood oranges.

. . . .

SERVES 6 TO 8

sunflower or vegetable oil, for oiling

6 organic oranges

1 cup syrup

freshly squeezed juice of 1 lemon

1 teaspoon Grand Marnier

2 rounded teaspoons gelatin

2 tablespoons cold water

sprigs of mint or lemon balm, to garnish

FOR THE SAUCE

freshly squeezed orange juice

superfine sugar, to taste (optional)

2 tablespoons chopped mint

Brush 6 to 8 × 3-ounce oval or round molds with oil.

Using a stainless steel grater, very carefully grate the zest from two of the oranges. Segment all 6 oranges and set aside.

Mix the syrup, orange zest, lemon juice, and Grand Marnier together well. Then strain the liquid off the oranges and measure 1¼ cups. Add the measured orange juice to the syrup mixture and set aside the remainder for the sauce.

Stir the gelatin with the cold water in a small bowl for a few minutes. Put the bowl into a saucepan of simmering water until all the gelatin crystals are dissolved. Mix with the orange liquid, stirring carefully. Add the orange segments and pour into the molds. Transfer to the fridge for 3 to 4 hours to set.

To make the sauce, measure 1 cup orange juice, taste, and sweeten with superfine sugar if necessary, then add the mint.

To serve, unmold the gelée onto individual plates. Pour a little sauce around each and garnish with mint leaves or variegated lemon balm.

Roasted Racks of Spring Lamb with Cucumber Neapolitana & Fresh Mint Chutney

At the school we do everything from scratch, but if that's not your scene many butchers will prepare a rack of lamb for you. Here we serve it with cucumber Neapolitana, a favorite vegetable stew, and zesty Fresh Mint Chutney.

SERVES 4 TO 6

2 prepared racks of spring lamb (6 cutlets each)
sprigs of mint, to garnish

FOR THE CUCUMBER NEAPOLITANA

3 teaspoons butter
1 onion (approx. 4 ounces), sliced
1 cucumber
4 very ripe tomatoes
salt and freshly ground black pepper
pinch of granulated sugar
¼ cup cream
1 tablespoon chopped mint
roux (optional, page 267)

FOR THE FRESH MINT CHUTNEY

1 green mango or 1 large apple, peeled and cored
a large handful of mint leaves, such as spearmint or Bowles's mint
⅓ cup chopped onion
2 tablespoons to ¼ cup superfine sugar (depending on tartness of apple)
cayenne pepper

Score the fat on the lamb and chill until needed.

Meanwhile, make the cucumber neopolitana: Melt the butter in a heavy-bottomed pot. When it foams, add the onion. Cover and cook for about 5 minutes until soft, but not colored.

Meanwhile, peel the cucumber and cut into ½-inch cubes; add to the onions, toss well, and continue to cook while you scald the tomatoes with water for 10 seconds. Peel the tomatoes and slice into the saucepan. Season with salt and pepper and add a pinch of sugar. Cover the saucepan and cook for a few minutes until the cucumber is tender and the tomatoes have softened, then add the cream and bring back to a boil. Add the mint. If the liquid is very thin, thicken it by carefully whisking in a little Roux. Cucumber neapolitana keeps for several days and may be reheated.

Preheat the oven to 425°F.

Sprinkle the racks of lamb with salt and pepper. Place them in a roasting pan, fat-side upward, and roast for 25 to 30 minutes, depending on the age of lamb and degree of doneness required. When cooked, transfer the lamb to a warm serving dish. Turn off the oven and let the lamb rest for 5 to 10 minutes before carving to allow the juices to redistribute evenly through the meat.

To make the fresh mint chutney, blend all the ingredients in a food processor, then season with salt and a little cayenne pepper.

Carve the lamb and serve 2 to 3 cutlets per person, depending on size. Serve with cucumber neapolitana and fresh mint.

CURRY LEAF *Murraya koenigii* PERENNIAL, ZONES 10–12

I love Indian and Sri Lankan food; fresh curry leaves are almost an essential ingredient in the latter and in South Indian food. You can buy dried curry leaves, but, when you are accustomed to fresh leaves, dried ones are a huge disappointment. Asian shops occasionally get a delivery of fresh curry leaves which freeze quite well but, as ever, there's nothing quite like the magic of fresh leaves—so, if you are a keen cook and live in a mild area, it's really worth growing your own. It has white flowers, but it's the leaves I'm really interested in. The blackberry-like fruit are also edible but the seeds are poisonous.

VARIETIES

There are three varieties:
Regular—Dark, shiny green leaves. Grows quickly and gets quite tall.
Dwarf—Lighter colour, longer leaves and not as tall.

Gamthi—Slow growing with fragrant thick leaves.

HOW TO GROW

Curry leaf is certainly not native to these parts, but if you can get your hands on a plant it can be grown indoors in a greenhouse. This tropical or sub-tropical plant grows into a large bush or small tree up to 13 feet high in its natural habitat, but I'm happy with a small bush. It is not frost tolerant.

Plant, not too deep, in slightly acidic soil, or a soil-based compost, with some horticultural grit added. Use a smallish pot, as it suits the plant to be slightly pot-bound. Feed it once a week with a liquid feed like a diluted seaweed feed to encourage leaf growth.

It is best to keep the plant on the dry

Keen cooks will want to track down a curry leaf plant—it's bliss to have a supply of fresh leaves.

side, almost letting it dry out between watering but keep an eye on it.

It needs temperatures of over 40°F to thrive and will suffer from sunburn if the temperature goes over 100°F. Don't leave young curry plants in direct sun as the leaves will scorch.

It can also be grown from seed, but is not easy to grow successfully—the seed needs to be very fresh and the temperature at least 68°F. Cuttings taken from fresh curry leaves can also be successful.

CONTAINER GROWING

It will grow well in a container and prefers to be slightly pot-bound.

PESTS AND DISEASES

The leaves may go slightly yellow or drop off while dormant during the winter season, so cut back on watering to prevent root rot. The plant may suffer from iron deficiency, so about six weeks give it a feed containing sulphate of iron.

HARVESTING

While the plant is getting established, pinch out the growing point to encourage a multi-branched plant

> **DID YOU KNOW?**
> Don't confuse curry leaf with the spiky leaves of the silver grey *Helichrysum italicum*, sometimes called the curry plant because of its strong curry smell. *Helichrysum* may be used in cooking, but is mostly used for medicinal purposes and the flowers can be used in pot pourri. Neither *Helichrysum* or curry leaf is an ingredient in curry powder.

encourage a multi-branched plant that will produce more leaves for harvesting. The more you use the plant, the bushier it will become. Snip off the leaves as needed.

GOOD FOR YOU...

Curry leaves have been used in Ayurvedic medicine for centuries, to control diabetes and it is rich in antioxidants, beta-carotene and vitamin C. Curry leaves also have anti-microbial, anti-inflammatory qualities. Studies on animals have shown hopeful results in preventing colon cancer and improving memory-boosting cholinergic activity in the brain.

WHAT TO DO WITH A GLUT

Freeze the leaves in plastic bags; they are not as good as fresh, but certainly better than dried.

IN THE KITCHEN

Use in soups, stews, sauces, and vegetable, meat, and fish dishes and to temper Indian dahls and curries. They will keep in sealed plastic bag for a couple of weeks. With a ready supply of fresh curry leaves, suddenly many hitherto impossible Sri Lankan curries and Indian dishes become possible. There is no substitute that I know of for fresh curry leaf.

Sun House Pineapple Curry

The Sun House in the fortified town of Galle in Sri Lanka is worth putting on your bucket list—this is one of the many delicious curries I enjoyed there. Curry leaves are an essential basic flavor in many Sri Lankan dishes.

. . . .

SERVES 6

¼ cup sunflower oil

3 garlic cloves, chopped

24 curry leaves

6-inch piece of pandanus leaf

¾ cup onions, sliced

2-inch piece of cinnamon stick, roasted

2 tablespoons medium Indian curry powder

1 teaspoon ground turmeric

1¾ cups coconut milk

1 unripe pineapple, cored and cut into chunks—3½ pounds whole weight, 1½ pounds prepared (about 4 cups)

1 green chile, sliced lengthwise

salt

1 teaspoon palm sugar

lots of cilantro leaves

boiled jasmine rice and a selection of other Sri Lankan curries, to serve

Heat the oil in a large wok, then add the garlic, curry leaves, and pandanus leaf to the wok and sauté for 1 minute. Then add the onion, cinnamon, curry powder, and turmeric. Cook for 1 minute until the mixture is fragrant.

Add the coconut milk, bring back to a boil, and allow to simmer for 2 minutes. Add the pineapple, chile, a generous pinch of salt, and the palm sugar. Bring back to a boil and simmer for 5 minutes. Transfer to a serving dish and scatter with lots of fresh cilantro.

Serve with jasmine rice and a selection of other Sri Lankan curries—garlic, beets, dhal, chicken, shrimp, or crab.

The same weight of canned pineapple can be used, but omit the sugar.

Taste and correct the seasoning as needed.

Sri Lankan Beet Curry

We love Sri Lankan vegetable curries and their clever use of spices and delicious flavors. Serve as an accompaniment as part of a curry feast or as a dish alone with a salad as below.

. . . .

SERVES 4

2 to 3 tablespoons sunflower oil
3 cloves of garlic, chopped
½ cup onions, chopped
5 curry leaves
3-inch piece of cinnamon stick
1¼ pounds beets, peeled and cut into
    1½-inch cubes
1½ teaspoons untoasted curry powder
10 fenugreek seeds
5 green chiles
salt and freshly ground black pepper
1 cup coconut milk, whisked

Heat oil in a deep frying pan over medium heat, add the garlic, onion, curry leaves, and cinnamon to the pan, stir, and cook for 2 minutes. Add the beets to the pan, stir, and add the curry powder, fenugreek seeds, chile, and some salt. Bring to a boil, add the coconut milk, and continue to cook for about 20 minutes until the beets are tender. Season to taste.

Martha's Orange Lentil Dahl

This super quick dahl is enhanced by the tempering of curry leaves and spices drizzled over the top.

. . . .

SERVES 6

¾ cup orange lentils
1¾ cups coconut milk
1 teaspoon ground turmeric
scant 1 teaspoon salt
1 tablespoon freshly squeezed lemon juice
1 teaspoon garam masala
6 slices of onion, sautéed until golden, and
    fresh cilantro or mint leaves, to garnish

FOR THE TEMPERING
3 tablespoons vegetable oil
6 to 8 fresh curry leaves
1 teaspoon cumin seeds
½ teaspoon cayenne pepper
1 teaspoon ground coriander

Cook the lentils with the coconut milk and 1¼ cups water in a heavy-bottomed pot, add the turmeric, bring to a boil, and simmer for 8 to 10 minutes by which time the lentils will be soft, almost mushy. When cooked, turn off the heat and add the salt, freshly squeezed lemon juice, and garam masala.

To make the tempering, heat the oil in a small frying pan, add the curry leaves followed by the cumin seeds, fry for 2 minutes, and remove from the heat. Add the cayenne and coriander, stir, and pour over the cooked lentils. Mix well and garnish with crispy onions and cilantro or mint leaves. Serve with basmati rice and tamarind and date chutney.

SWEET CICELY
Myrrhis odorata PERENNIAL, ZONES 5–9

Dainty sweet cicely—one of the first herbs to appear in spring.

Sweet cicely is also known as myrrh. I've had this old cottage-garden perennial ever since we designed and planted the formal herb garden in 1986. It's a little treasure that re-emerges in spring with fern-like leaves and fluffy white flowers. The leaves have a slightly sweet, aniseed and slightly liquorice flavor and help to cut the acidity in fruit tarts. It is known as a "sugar saver." This is a trouble-free plant that certainly deserves to be better known. The delicate lacy leaves are particularly pretty as a garnish for sweet dishes and are especially pretty when frosted with egg white and castor sugar.

HOW TO GROW

Sweet cicely is not fussy about soil, but it does best in semi-shade. The shiny black seeds don't remain viable for long, so you'll get best results from seeds that are grown 6 to 9 months after harvest. It needs cold, followed by warmth, to germinate. Sow one seed to a plug in autumn and leave outside for winter. Then plant 2 feet apart in spring when frosts have passed. Alternatively, divide a sweet cicely plant in autumn when the stalks have died down. It is one of the last plants to do so. If it's happy in your soil, it will probably spread itself around. Prune back after flowering to encourage new growth.

CONTAINER GROWING

Not ideal—sweet cicely has a long taproot so, if you are determined to grow it in a container, choose a deep one, put it in a shady spot and water it regularly.

PESTS AND DISEASES

We've never had a problem; it seems virtually pest and disease free.

HARVESTING

Snip off the pale green, fern-like leaves as needed. Use the flowers as a garnish. Both the green and black seeds are edible.

GOOD FOR YOU...

Several herbals mention that the roots, when boiled, were "very good for old people that are dull and without courage; it rejoiceth and comforteth the heart and increaseth their lust and strength." It's particularly important for diabetics as it sweetens without raising blood sugar levels. An ointment made from the roots of sweet cicely can be used on external wounds and ulcers. It is said that sweet cicely can also be used to treat hypertension and anxiety, ease coughing, calm the stomach and detoxify the urinary tract. A decoction can be made from the leaves and used externally to treat bruises, like a poultice.

WHAT TO DO WITH A GLUT

If you have a glut of sweet cicely, use the delicate leaves to garnish all your sweet confections. We also crystallise the fronds and the frosted results look exquisite on celebration cakes and desserts.

IN THE KITCHEN

All parts of sweet cicely are edible, although we find the leaves the most appealing. It's one of the few herbs that can be used for garnishing sweet and some savory dishes—both the flowers and the herbs can be used. Because the leaves have a sweet aniseedy flavor, one can add them to any poached fruit in quite large quantities to reduce the sugar needed. Jekka McVicar suggests combining with lemon balm to add a haunting flavor.

We also love to crystallize the leaves to decorate cakes and desserts. Leaves can be snipped into salads, scrambled

DID YOU KNOW?

In parts of Wales, sweet cicely is sometimes planted around the headstones in graveyards to commemorate and remember a loved one. It is one of the herbs used by the Carthusian monks in the making of the famous liqueur Chartreuse.

eggs, and omelets with a mixture of herbs. I've also tried rubbing the leaves on furniture as a polish, particularly for oak, but there are easier ways to polish your furniture. The fluffy white flowers are pretty scattered over summer fruit and salads.

The stalks of sweet cicely can be used in ice cream to give an aniseedy flavor, similar to Pernod.

Both the green and black seeds of sweet cicely are edible.

Sweet Cicely Custard

This basic custard is usually flavored with a vanilla bean, but can be made with any number of other ingredients, such as lemon or orange rind or mint. We love to infuse it with sweet cicely.

SERVES 6/MAKES APPROX. 2½ CUPS

1 ounce sweet cicely leaves and flower heads, crushed slightly
2½ cups cold milk
6 organic egg yolks
¼ cup superfine sugar

Put the sweet cicely into a saucepan with the milk. Bring almost to a boil. Set aside to infuse for 10 minutes.

Whisk the egg yolks with the sugar until thick and light. Whisk in half the warm milk and then whisk the mixture back into the remaining milk. Cook over very low heat, stirring constantly with a straight-ended wooden spoon, until the custard thickens slightly. Your finger should leave a clear trail when drawn across the back of the spoon.

Remove from the heat at once and strain into a cold bowl. Cool, cover, and chill in a bowl of iced water. The custard can be kept for up to 2 days in the fridge. Serve with poached rhubarb or rhubarb tart.

Carrageen Moss Pudding with Rhubarb & Sweet Cicely or Angelica Compote

My favorite way to eat sweet carrageen moss pudding is just with softly whipped cream and some brown sugar sprinkled over the top, but it's also very special with a fruit compote. Carrageen moss can also be flavored with fresh blackcurrant or fig leaves. The fruit I use varies with the season, but I'm giving this particular recipe for Rhubarb and Sweet Cicely or Angelica Compote because we use a wonderful variety of rhubarb that's been passed down through the Allen family from generation to generation; even when they moved, they brought their rhubarb and globe artichokes with them. If there's a particularly good variety of fruit or vegetable in your family, treasure it and make sure you pass it on.

. . . .

SERVES 6

¼ ounce cleaned, well-dried Irish (carrageen) moss (1 semi-closed fistful)

3¾ cups whole milk

1 vanilla bean or ½ teaspoon pure vanilla extract

1 large organic egg

1 tablespoon superfine sugar

softly whipped cream, to serve (optional)

FOR THE RHUBARB AND SWEET CICELY OR ANGELICA COMPOTE

1 pound red rhubarb

2 cups Stock Syrup (page 290)

4 to 6 sweet cicely leaves or 4 tablespoons of angelica, plus extra to garnish

Soak the Irish moss in a little bowl of tepid water for 10 minutes. It will swell and increase in size. Strain off the water and put the moss into a saucepan with the milk and the vanilla bean (if using). Bring to a boil and simmer very gently, covered, for 20 minutes. At that point and not before, separate the egg, put the yolk into a bowl, add the sugar and vanilla extract (if using), and whisk together for a few seconds, then pour the milk and carrageen moss through a strainer onto the egg yolk mixture, whisking all the time. By now the carrageen remaining in the strainer will be swollen and exuding jelly. You need to push as much of this as possible through the strainer, then whisk it into the egg and milk mixture. Test for a set in a chilled saucer as one would with gelatin. Whisk the egg white stiffly and fold, or fluff, it in gently; it will rise to make a fluffy top. Cover with plastic wrap and chill until ready to serve.

Follow the Rhubarb Compote recipe (page 374). Add the sweet cicely leaves or angelica leaves to the cold syrup and poach the fruit in the usual way.

Serve the carrageen pudding chilled with the compote and lots of softly whipped cream (if using), and garnish with extra sweet cicely or angelica leaves.

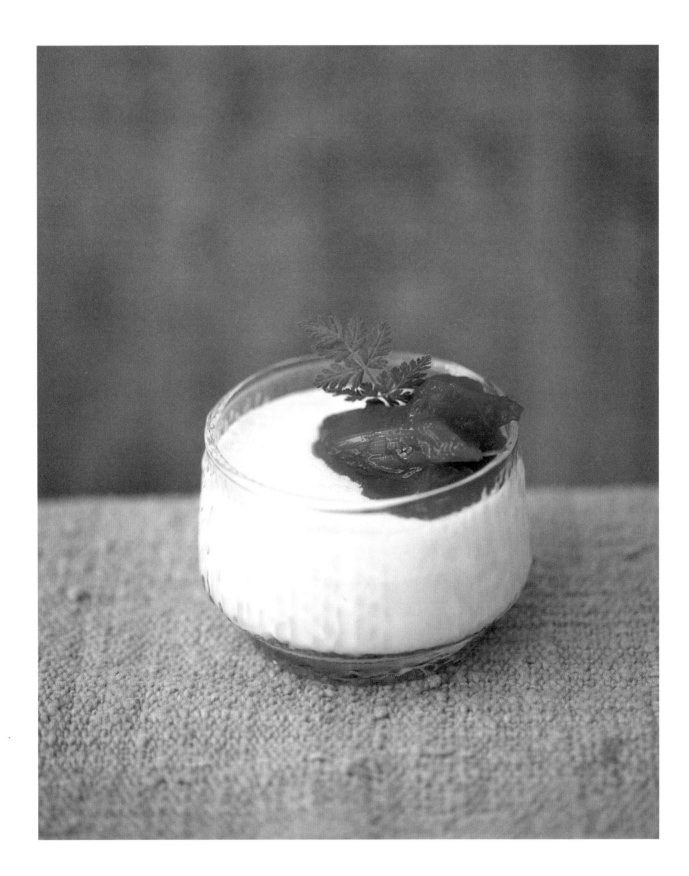

BASIL *Ocimum basilicum* ANNUAL

How we've all developed a love affair with basil. My first introduction to this quintessentially Italian herb was in the early 1980s when I did a cookery course with Marcella and Victor Hazan in Bologna. I had never tasted basil before, or indeed even heard of pesto, but by the end of the week-long course I felt I could never do without basil again. I bought some seeds in the market, brought them home and we've been growing several varieties of basil ever since. Even if you don't have a garden, it's worth growing a basil plant (in a large pot) on your sunniest window sill to add to tomato salads in summer.

We usually associate basil with Italy and Mediterranean countries, but it is also an essential herb in Thai, Vietnamese and Laotian cuisines.

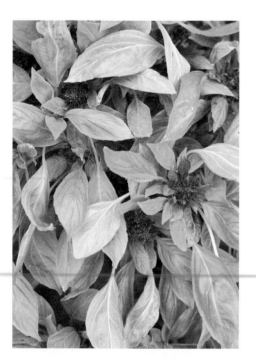

Thai basil has a distinct flavor which gives authenticity to Asian dishes.

VARIETIES

Ocimum basilicum 'Genovese'—All-purpose, best for pesto.

Ocimum basilicum 'Green Ruffles' and *O.b.* var. *purpurascens* 'Purple Ruffles'—Large, frilly, quilted leaves, spicy flavor but milder, good in containers.

Ocimum basilicum (sweet basil)—Large, soft leaves with an intense basil flavor.

Ocimum basilicum 'Dark Opal'—Dark purply-red leaves with a slight clovey flavor.

Ocimum citrodorum (lemon basil)—Distinct lemony flavor.

Ocimum minimum 'Greek'—Compact globular bush, excellent in pots. Tiny leaves on a dome shaped plant that grows about 8 inches tall. Strong, sweet basil flavour, white flowers.

Ocimum basilicum 'Cinnamon'—Spicy cinnamon smell and taste.

Ocimum 'African Blue'—Lavender blue flowers and purple-stained leaves. A large-leaved cultivar of Thai basil.

Ocimum basilicum var. *thrysifolia* 'Siam Queen'—(Thai basil)—Important for the authentic flavor of Thai food. The leaves are oval, the flowers pale purple and the flavor slightly reminiscent of anise.

Holy basil—Variety of *Ocimum tenuiflorum*, not to be confused with Thai basil, a variety of *Ocimum basilicum*, known as *bai horapa* in Thailand. There are now 60-plus distinct varieties, each with its own flavor, aroma, color and shape.

HOW TO GROW

Basil is a tender plant, native to the Mediterranean. It needs rich, well-drained soil. Basil is very sensitive to the cold, so wait until the weather is warmer to plant outside. Sow directly into the ground in early summer when all danger of frost has passed. Plant the seed ¼ inch deep at rate of 2 to 3 per inch, in rows 12 to 18 inches apart, depending on the variety. Lightly cover with soil.

We start the plants in the growing room in early spring, sowing seed in pots or plug trays and lightly cover with soil.

After six weeks, lightly prick out the seedlings and transplant into 3½-inch pots or directly into the ground. Once the basil plants have grown to 5 to 6 inches, transplant into large pots. Choose the sunniest location.

We do several sowings before early summer. Pinch out any flower heads as they appear to encourage new growth. Basil will continue to grow and flourish indoors until early autumn, but it is not tolerant of temperatures below 41°F. The first frost will kill every plant.

Interplant basil with tomatoes; it is said by many gardeners to improve the flavor and repel aphids.

CONTAINER GROWING

Basil will grow happily on a sunny window sill, but it's vital to have a large pot, at least 12 inches, otherwise it won't have enough nourishment and will be attacked by whitefly or greenfly.

PESTS AND DISEASES

Young plants can be susceptible to slugs. Basil grown in pots may be susceptible to whitefly or greenfly, particularly if the pot is not large enough. They need lots of good soil and plenty of water. Gently wash flies off with soapy water.

The young seedlings may also suffer from damping off, so don't plant too thickly or in wet compost, and avoid conditions that may be too humid.

HARVESTING

Pick the leaves regularly to encourage growth throughout the summer. Pinch out the growing point after six weeks to discourage flowering and encourage bushy growth.

GOOD FOR YOU...

Basil is an anti-inflammatory and a good source of vitamins A, C and K. It provides significant amounts of calcium, iron, magnesium and potassium. Basil is considered to be an aid to digestion and to help to ease stomach cramps and also relieve nausea.

Basil leaves are an insect repellent; we use lemon basil leaves on our breakfast buffet to deter flies during the warm summer months.

WHAT TO DO WITH A GLUT

Make lots of pesto and basil oil.

IN THE KITCHEN

Each type of basil has its own strong and distinct flavor, but the common *Ocimum basilicum* seems to have the best flavor for pesto. On my very first trip to Italy I learned that one tears, rather than chops, basil as it blackens almost instantaneously when chopped.

You can make **Pesto** in a food processor, however, I prefer to make it laboriously with a mortar and pestle; somehow it seems to taste so much more delicious. To make approx. 2 cups pesto in a food processor, pulse-blend 4 cups basil leaves with ¾ to 1 cup

Ocimum basilicum 'Dark Opal'.

extra virgin olive oil, 3 tablespoons Italian pine nuts and 2 large crushed garlic cloves. Transfer to a bowl and fold in ½ cup freshly grated Parmesan (Parmigiano Reggiano is best). Season to taste. Serve with pasta, goat cheese, tomatoes, and mozzarella. Red pesto is made with 'Dark Opal' or 'Purple Ruffles' basil leaves. Pesto keeps for weeks, covered with a layer of olive oil in a jar in the fridge. It also freezes well, but for best results don't add the grated Parmesan until it has defrosted. Freeze in small jars for convenience. If you can't find the long, slim Italian pine nuts, use cashews instead, rather than the Asian pine nuts. If you have difficulty in getting enough basil, use parsley, a mixture of parsley and mint, or parsley and cilantro—different but still delicious. For **Mint and Parsley Pesto**, substitute 2 cups mint and 2 cups parsley for the basil in the above recipe.

Basil may be used to flavor oil and oil may be used to preserve basil. If you have a large quantity of basil, you can preserve it in a jar with enough olive oil

Ocimum citrodorum *(lemon basil) in flower.*

to completely cover it for up to three months. Ensure the basil leaves are clean and dry. Alternatively, pour a little extra virgin olive oil from the bottle and stuff at least 8 to 10 basil leaves into the bottle, or more if you like. The basil must be covered by at least ½-inch of oil. Seal and store in a cold place. We sometimes fill bottles three quarters full and then chill them. When the oil solidifies somewhat, we top it off with another layer of oil. If the basil is not submerged in the oil, it will become moldy in a relatively short period of time. Use basil oil in salad dressings, vegetable stews, pasta sauces, or wherever else you wish.

Basil Butter is also easy to make, but adds magic to many dishes. Blend 16 tablespoons (2 sticks) butter, 2 cups basil leaves, and sea salt and freshly ground black pepper together in a food processor until combined. Fold in a roll and wrap in parchment and chill. Serve on grilled meat, lamb chops, or fried tomatoes.

The oils in basil are highly volatile so it's best to add basil toward the

Basil Ice Cream

This is a wonderfully rich ice cream. Unexpectedly delicious, we love it with precious ripe figs from the greenhouse. We usually use sweet basil for this recipe but each basil will produce a slightly different flavor.

. . . .

SERVES 6/MAKES 2½ CUPS

½ vanilla bean

2 cups basil leaves, torn

¾ cup whole milk

4 organic egg yolks

⅓ cup granulated sugar

¾ cup rich heavy cream, cold

ripe figs, quartered, to serve (optional)

Split the vanilla bean lengthwise and scrape the seeds into a heavy-bottomed pot. Add the basil, vanilla bean, and milk. Heat to just below boiling point and remove from the heat. Cover and set aside to steep for 10 minutes. Remove the vanilla bean and scrape again to release every bit of flavor. Add the scrapings to the milk and discard the bean.

Whisk the egg yolks and sugar together. In a bowl add the warm milk gradually, stirring constantly, until all the milk is added. Return to the saucepan and cook over low heat for 8 to 10 minutes, stirring constantly, until the custard coats the back of a spoon.

Pour the cream into a large bowl. Strain the basil custard into the cream. Mix well, then chill thoroughly.

Freeze according to the directions for your ice cream maker. Alternatively, pour into a plastic or stainless-steel bowl, cover tightly, and freeze for 1½ hours. Remove the bowl from the freezer and scrape the ice cream in from the edges of the bowl, continuing until smooth. Repeat two or three times until frozen solid.

Scoop into bowls or serve on chilled plates and top with ripe figs, if available.

Bocconcini, Olive, Sun-Blushed Tomato & Pesto Skewers

Bocconcini are baby mozzarella—great fun for salads, finger food, and some pasta dishes. However, they need a little bit of help from the flavor perspective. Pesto is great here.

. . . .

MAKES 20 SKEWERS

20 bocconcini

extra virgin olive oil

1 to 2 tablespoons Pesto (page 497)

20 to 40 basil leaves

20 Kalamata olives

20 sun-blushed tomatoes

sea salt

Drain the bocconcini and pop them into a bowl, then drizzle with oil and the Pesto. Toss to coat. Cover tightly and set aside to marinate for at least 5 minutes. The pesto will discolor if the bocconcini are tossed too far ahead of time.

Thread a bocconcini onto a bamboo cocktail or short satay stick, followed by a basil leaf, an olive, and, finally, a sun-blushed tomato. Repeat until you have threaded all the ingredients onto 20 sticks. Sprinkle with a little sea salt and serve as soon as possible.

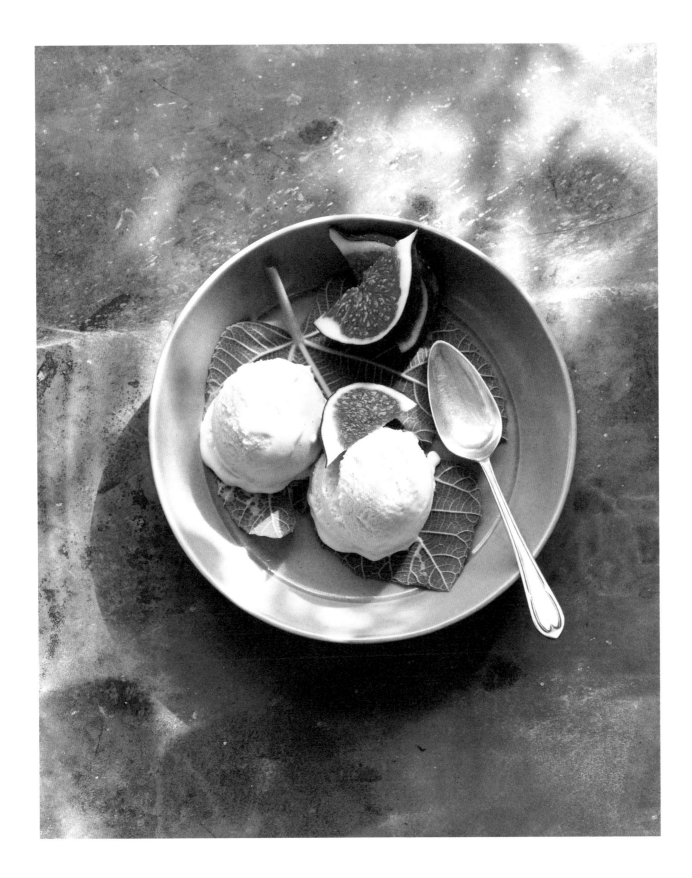

Pears Poached in a Basil Syrup

Many pears need a little help from aromatic herbs or spice. Basil gives a haunting, slightly spicy flavor to this delicious syrup, which makes it ideal for poaching the pears.

. . . .

SERVES 4

1 cup granulated sugar

2 cups water

6 to 8 sweet, lemon, or Thai basil leaves

3 tablespoons freshly squeezed lemon juice

4 firm pears, such as Bosc or Bartlett

Put the sugar, water, basil, and lemon juice into a shallow, wide pan; we use a stainless-steel sauté pan. Stir to dissolve the sugar and bring to a simmer.

Meanwhile, peel the pears, halve, and core them. As you cut them, put them into the simmering syrup, cut-side up.

Cover with parchment paper and the lid of the pan and cook gently for 20 to 30 minutes, spooning the syrup over them every now and then. Carefully remove the pears and arrange them in a serving dish in a single layer, cut-side down. Pour the syrup over the pears or reduce first (see below). Serve chilled.

This compote keeps for several weeks covered in the fridge.

For a more concentrated flavor, the syrup may be reduced a little after the pears have been transferred to a serving dish. Be careful not to cook it for too long or the syrup will caramelize.

VARIATIONS

Poached Pears with Saffron Syrup—Add 6 lightly crushed whole cardamom pods and ¼ teaspoon of good-quality saffron threads to the sugar, water, and lemon juice in the pan and proceed as above. If there is some syrup left over, use it to make pear and saffron gelée—use 3 teaspoons of gelatin to 2½ cups juice.

Poached Pears with Lemon—Simply add the thinly pared rind and juice of 1 lemon to the sugar, water, and lemon juice in the pan and proceed as above.

Poached Pears with Sweet Geranium Leaves—Add 3 to 4 large sweet geranium leaves to the water and sugar in the pan and proceed as above.

Poached Pears with Lemon Verbena Leaves—Add 4 to 6 lemon verbena leaves to the water and sugar in the pan, and proceed as above.

Poached Pears with Ginger—Add 1 inch thinly sliced fresh ginger to the sugar and water in the pan and proceed as above.

MARJORAM & OREGANO *Origanum* ANNUAL
AND PERENNIAL, ZONES 4–8

Another large and confusing family that includes one of my most favorite herbs—annual marjoram, also known as knotty marjoram or knot marjoram. Marjoram is native to the Mediterranean and is not anything like as well known as many of the other fresh herbs, but it's definitely one of my top ten must-have herbs.

VARIETIES
We grow three varieties of marjoram:
Origanum onites (**pot marjoram**)—Hardy perennial that grows to a height of about 18 inches. Small green leaves, pink/purple flowers in summer. A wild flavor, good in flower arrangements. Butterflies love it.
Origanum vulgare '**Aureum**' (**golden marjoram**)—Hardy perennial that can grow to 18 inches, but my cultivar is low growing and forms cushions of small golden leaves with pink/purple flowers in summer. It's best to plant in semi-shade otherwise the edge of the leaves get scorched by sun in summer.
Origanum majorana (**annual marjoram or knotted marjoram**)—We refer to this cultivar as annual marjoram to distinguish it from the others. In fact, it is half-hardy. It grows to about 12 inches and flowers in early summer, and has soft mid-green, highly aromatic leaves. It has by far the best flavor for cooking.

HOW TO GROW
Many of the *Origanum* genus can only be propagated by cuttings or division, but my favorite annual marjoram or knotty marjoram can be grown from seed. We sow in modules in the growing room in January, using seed compost. When the plants reach the leaf stage, about 3 inches tall in mid-spring, transplant into the greenhouse or tunnel, 12 inches apart.

We grow year round in the greenhouse, but don't over-water them.

Outdoors, sow in late spring in light loamy soil, 12 inches apart. Remove flowers to encourage more leaf growth.

CONTAINER GROWING
It can be grown in pots or troughs.

PESTS AND DISEASES
They can be affected by aphids; if this is limited to a few stems, the affected stems can be cut out and destroyed. Aphids can be hosed off with a heavy jet of water or, in worse cases, a biological soap solution may be used. Don't let the plants dry out during very hot dry weather; they will be stressed and maybe attacked by spider mite.

Mint rust can spread from affected mint if growing in the same area

HARVESTING
Snip as you need. The flowers of pot marjoram can be dried for flower arrangements.

Golden marjoram in full flower—it doesn't like full sun.

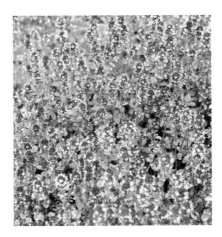

GOOD FOR YOU...
Marjoram contains high levels of vitamin A, vitamin K and many minerals, including iron, calcium, potassium, manganese, copper, zinc and magnesium. It is an important antiseptic owing to its high thymol content.

WHAT TO DO WITH A GLUT
The leaves dry reasonably well on the shelf above my ancient Aga. They can also be frozen. Marjoram Vinegar is very tasty. Just infuse the sprigs of marjoram in white wine vinegar.

IN THE KITCHEN
The aromatic leaves of annual marjoram are delicious with many meats, including lamb, chicken, turkey, and guinea hens. It has a particular affinity with zucchini, squash, white turnips, kohlrabi, corn, and roasted bell peppers and eggplant. Fresh marjoram leaves liven up salads and marjoram butter or oil adds zing to everything from charred onions and leeks to pasta and pilaf.

Knotted marjoram—origanum majorana –has tiny white flowers.

Salmoriglio

This herby Sicilian sauce is my go-to recipe to serve with pan-grilled meats and fish. This is a really good combination of herbs, but I sometimes use just annual marjoram because the flavor is so compelling.

MAKES APPROX. ⅓ CUP

1 tablespoon annual marjoram
2 teaspoons lemon thyme
2 teaspoons flat-leaf parsley
1 teaspoon sea salt
1 tablespoon freshly squeezed lemon juice
¼ cup extra virgin olive oil

Destalk the herbs and pound the leaves with the salt with a mortar and pestle until completely crushed. Add the lemon juice. Stir the oil into the mixture slowly. Season to taste.

Drizzle over pan-grilled meat or fish.

Lamb Chops with Chimichurri Sauce

Chimichurri is the quintessential Argentinian gaucho sauce, although it may be of Basque origin, because many from that region of Spain settled in Argentina in the nineteenth century. There are many local variations, but the essential ingredients are olive oil, parsley, and marjoram or oregano. It's great with beef or lamb, but also good with goat cheese.

SERVES 8

FOR THE CHIMICHURRI SAUCE

⅔ cup water
1 teaspoon salt
1 garlic bulb, cloves separated, peeled, and finely chopped
½ cup flat-leaf parsley leaves, finely chopped
2½ tablespoons marjoram leaves, finely chopped
1 to 2 teaspoons crushed red pepper
¼ cup red wine vinegar
½ cup extra virgin olive oil

FOR THE LAMB

8 to 16 lamb loin chops
extra virgin olive oil
2 tablespoons annual marjoram, chopped
sea salt and freshly ground black pepper
arugula, to serve

First, make the chimichurri sauce: Bring the water to a boil in a small saucepan. Add the salt and stir to dissolve. Remove from heat and set aside to cool (this is the *salmuera* brine). Put the garlic, parsley, and marjoram into a bowl and add the crushed pepper. Whisk in the vinegar and oil, then whisk in the salmuera brine to taste. Pour into a jar with a tight-fitting lid, cover, and store in the fridge. You can use chimichurri sauce as soon as it's made, but ideally it should be made at least one day ahead to allow the flavors to develop. It will keep in the fridge for 2 to 3 weeks.

Trim the chops of excess fat, then score the back fat. Take a flat dish or dishes large enough to take the chops in a single layer, brush with oil, and sprinkle with some of the marjoram. Season the chops on both sides with pepper, then place on top of the marjoram. Sprinkle some more marjoram on top and drizzle with oil. Let marinate for 1 hour or more.

Brush off any excess oil, then season well with sea salt. Pan-grill or grill on a rack 6 inches from the hot coals for 10 to 15 minutes, depending on the thickness and degree of doneness required. Serve the chops with lots of fresh arugula and the chimichurri sauce.

Turkey Baked with Marjoram

A splendidly flavorful dish, here the turkey is brined and roasted. There are several varieties of marjoram; the one we use for this recipe is the annual marjoram—*Origanum marjorana*—because it has the very best flavor. Tarragon, thyme, or watercress can all be used to change it up in a delicious way.

. . . .

SERVES 12 TO 14

1 × 10 to 12-pound free-range turkey, preferably organic
4½ cups salt
6 quarts water
sea salt and freshly ground black pepper
2 to 3 sprigs marjoram, plus extra to garnish
4 tablespoons finely chopped marjoram
8 tablespoons (1 stick) softened butter
3¾ cups roux (page 267, optional)

The day before, brine the turkey. Add the salt to the water and stir to dissolve. Put the turkey into a clean stainless-steel saucepan, plastic bucket, or pan. Cover with the brine and a lid and chill for 24 hours. This is, of course, optional, but it hugely enhances the flavor of the turkey and makes for moist, tender, and flavorful meat.

Preheat the oven to 350°F.

Drain the turkey and dry well. If possible, remove the wish bone from the neck end of the turkey for ease of carving. Also remove the fat from the vent end, season the cavity with salt and pepper, and stuff with 2 to 3 sprigs of marjoram. Smear the breast of the turkey with half the softened butter. Put the turkey, breast-side down, into a large Dutch oven and cook over gentle heat for 6 to 8 minutes or until the skin turns golden. Turn the other way up and smear the breast with 2 tablespoons of the chopped marjoram mixed with the remaining butter (sounds a lot, but the turkey is a large bird).

Season with lots of pepper and a little salt. Cover with parchment paper and a tight-fitting lid. Cook in the oven for 2 to 2½ hours.

Test to see if the turkey is cooked: the juices should be clear and there should be no trace of pink between the thigh and the breast. Transfer the turkey to a carving dish and let rest in a cool oven while the sauce is being made.

Remove all the fat from the top surface of the cooking juices. Add the cream, bring to a boil, taste, and reduce if necessary to strengthen the flavor. I really like to add a little roux to thicken the sauce to a light coating consistency. Add the remainder of the chopped marjoram and the juices from the carving dish to the sauce. Season to taste.

Carve the turkey and spoon the sauce over. Garnish with sprigs of fresh marjoram.

DID YOU KNOW?
The Ancient Greeks made wreaths and garlands from marjoram and used it as a symbol of peace, harmony, and happiness.

SCENTED GERANIUMS *Pelargonium* spp. PERENNIAL

Our students associate lemon scented geranium with Ballymaloe Cookery School.

On virtually every window sill in the cookery school there's a scented geranium of some kind, mostly *Pelargonium graveolens*, which we call sweet geranium or rose geranium, although it really ought to be called citrus geranium, because it has a distinct lemony aroma. We simply couldn't be without this geranium. It flavors syrup, tisanes, panna cotta, carrageen moss, fruit salads and is used for garnishing sweet dishes. Few plants give us so much pleasure or "bang for our buck."

VARIETIES

Pelargonium graveolens—Hardy, evergreen perennial; height about 2 feet, 40 inches wide; mauve flowers in summer; deeply cut, coarse-textured leaves.
Pelargonium 'Attar of Roses'—Hardy, evergreen perennial; grows up to 2 feet high and 12 inches wide; small pink flowers, the leaves smell of roses.
Pelargonium 'Chocolate Peppermint'—As above, with small, pale white/pink flowers, velvety green leaves and a chocolate peppermint aroma; fast growing.

HOW TO GROW

Scented geraniums are super easy to grow. You can grow by seed, but I recommend either buying a healthy plant or growing from a cutting.

Slice off a 4 to 6-inch long cutting with a sharp knife, strip off the bottom leaves and insert into a tray of potting compost at an angle, water and keep out of direct sunlight. It will root after 2 to 3 weeks.

In our mild climate, *Pelargonium graveolens* grows happily outside. It usually overwinters but occasionally a severe frost will kill even a well-established plant. However, it is not hardy in the U.S. except for extreme southern regions (zones 10–11).

CONTAINER GROWING

Scented geraniums make super house and pot plants. Just ensure they are in a large enough pot, in a mixture of potting compost and soil. Keep watered in summer, bring indoors before the first frost. As with all pelargoniums, keep watering to a minimum during autumn and winter.

PESTS AND DISEASES

Pelargoniums can be affected by whitefly, mostly as a result of being stressed by too small a pot or insufficient water or nourishment in summer. Grey mould can be caused by plants being over-watered. Remove affected leaves, allow the plant to dry and increase ventilation.

HARVESTING

We pick the leaves constantly during the year. Some of our plants scarcely get a chance to recover so we whip them off the window sills.

GOOD FOR YOU...

Geranium oil is used in aromatherapy. The *graveolens* species is reputed to produce one of the highest quality oils. It's said to calm and relax the body, and has anti-depressant, antiseptic and wound-healing properties. Back as far as Egyptian times it was used for enhancing healthy and beautiful skin, and today has uses in treating skin problems like eczema and dermatitis.

WHAT TO DO WITH A GLUT

We don't really have a glut, but if you do, make lots of sweet geranium syrup to use as a basis for homemade lemonade or cordials, or for poaching fresh fruit, particularly pears, apricots, peaches and apples. You can also take cuttings and give presents of this little gem to friends.

IN THE KITCHEN

No house should be without a *Pelargonium graveolens*. Apart from being a beautiful pot plant, the lemon-scented leaves can be used in many exciting ways and add a magical, haunting flavor to so many dishes. A few leaves added to a currant and berry salad or to apple sauce provide a certain *je ne sais quoi*. A few leaves in the cake pan underneath the mixture will perfume a cake deliciously. It also scents panna cotta or yogurt in a delicate and alluring way. Ice creams, sorbets, and granitas flavored with *Pelargonium graveolens* are irresistible.

Blackberry or Raspberry & Sweet Geranium Sugar Squares

This is a delicious way to use sweet geraniums. Blackberries and sweet geranium have a real affinity. This recipe is a variation on our basic bars, which we find super versatile.

. . . .

MAKES 24

12 tablespoons (1½ sticks) soft butter, plus extra for greasing
1 cup superfine sugar
2 large organic eggs
1⅓ cups self-rising flour
3 tablespoons chopped fresh sweet geranium leaves
1½ cups blackberries or raspberries

Preheat the oven to 350°F. Grease a 10 × 7-inch Swiss-roll pan.

Put the butter, ¾ cup of the superfine sugar, eggs, self-rising flour, and 2 tablespoons of the geranium leaves into a food processor. Pulse for a few seconds to amalgamate. Spread evenly in the prepared pan. Sprinkle the blackberries or raspberries as evenly as possible over the top. Bake for 25 to 30 minutes or until golden brown and well risen. Set aside to cool slightly.

Pulse the remainder of the superfine sugar in a food processor with the remainder of the geranium leaves. Sprinkle over the cake and serve cut into squares.

Lemon Posset with Rose or Sweet Geranium

This lemon posset recipe has done the rounds (was it Jane Grigson originally?), always lip-smackingly good, but it was Skye Gyngell who introduced us to this version scented with sweet geranium (*Pelargonium graveolens*) leaves. She, in turn, attributed it to Jeremy Lee, so on it goes.... Anyway it's sublime, so thank you all.

. . . .

SERVES 4

1¾ cups heavy cream
½ cup superfine sugar
5 rose or sweet geranium leaves, plus tiny rose or sweet geranium leaves, to garnish
¼ cup freshly squeezed lemon juice

Put the cream, sugar, and geranium leaves into a saucepan and bring to a simmer. Reduce the heat to low and cook, stirring often, for 5 minutes. Remove the pan from the heat, add the lemon juice, then strain into your serving dishes of choice. Cover and chill until set. Garnish each with a tiny geranium leaf to serve—frosted geranium leaves are even prettier.

DID YOU KNOW?
Scented geraniums are a large family that originated in South Africa. They were brought to England in the mid-seventeenth century, where the Victorians embraced them to scent their rooms, but it wasn't until the nineteenth century that the French perfume industry recognized their potential. Sometimes known as "the poor man's rose," sweet geranium oil is used occasionally instead of the more expensive rose oil.

PARSLEY *Petroselinum crispum* TENDER BIENNIAL, ANNUAL

Despite the wide choice of fresh herbs available nowadays, parsley is still the most widely used herb in these islands and was in fact the only herb that grew in our vegetable garden when I was little. It was chopped finely and used in copious quantities in Parsley Sauce to serve with Bacon and Cabbage and Champ—still one of my favorite comfort foods. Plant lots and lots so you can use it with gay abandon.

Although I grow more than 60 herbs in the formal potager in Kinoith, I can't imagine being without both curly and flat-leaf parsley. The latter, also called French parsley, is relatively new on the scene, maybe having been around for the past two decades. It's considered to be slightly posher than curly parsley—more cheffy—but I love both and don't discern a huge difference in flavor, although curly parsley appears to be slightly milder. The flavor and texture can vary depending on the soil it's grown in and whether it is grown indoors or outdoors, which seems to result in a stronger flavor.

VARIETIES

Petroselinum crispum (curly parsley)—Biennial, excellent flavor. Grows 12 to 16 inches with curly, bright green leaves and cream flowers in its second year.

Petroselinum crispum var. *neapolitanum* (flat-leaf or Italian parsley)—Biennial flat-leaved parsley, excellent flavor, great for bouquet garni.

Petroselinum crispum var. *tuberosum* (Hamburg parsley)—Perennial, but mostly grown as an annual. Also known as root parsley because the root grows to 5 to 6 inches long. It has a strong flavor and the leaves are quite coarse.

HOW TO GROW

You really need a year-round supply. Parsley is slow to germinate. Sow in pots rather than seed trays—like all of the Umbelliferae family, it dislikes being transplanted. We start it in early spring in the growing room, but a heated propagator will speed up germination, 2 to 3 weeks compared to 4 to 6 weeks without bottom heat.

When all risk of frost has passed (mid- to late-spring), plant in rich fertile soil, about 6 inches apart. It needs a little shade for summer, and a more sheltered, sunny spot for winter production. It may be necessary to water during a spell of hot weather.

Parsley will run to seed during the second year; dig it out and plant a new crop in different soil. Save the seeds; they have many uses—a tea made from crushed seeds is said to kill head lice.

CONTAINER GROWING

Parsley grows perfectly in large pots or containers. I have two old troughs close to the kitchen door—it's such a joy be able to dash out with a pair of scissors to snip what I need to incorporate into a dish seconds later. It's fantastically useful to have lots.

PESTS AND DISEASES

Given half a chance, slugs and snails will decimate young parsley plants, so take the usual precautions (see page 626).

HARVESTING

Snip the parsley, including the stalks, which has lots of flavor—use the stalks in a bouquet garni or add to the stockpot. Dig Hamburg parsley roots as required, harvest the remainder of the crop and store in sand until needed.

GOOD FOR YOU...

All types of parsley are rich in vitamins K, C, E and A, B6, B12, folate and iron. Parsley tea is a known diuretic and a treatment for urinary infections.

Flat-leaf parsley (left) and curly parsley (above).

WHAT TO DO WITH A GLUT?

It can be a feast or a famine with parsley. Make **Parsley Pesto** (see right). Pack chopped parsley into ice cube trays and freeze. Add lots to the green salad bowl or make a parsley salad and dress it with extra virgin olive oil, freshly squeezed lemon juice and lots of freshly grated parmesan. Parsley Soup is also fresh tasting and delicious. Top with a blob of horseradish cream.

IN THE KITCHEN

I scatter parsley into and over stews and casseroles, alone, or in tandem with garlic and lemon zest in the form of gremolata. Fistfuls go into **Tabbouleh** (below) and variations on the theme such as salsa verde, **Salmoriglio** (page 502), and **Gremolata** (see page 513).

Deep-fried sprigs can be delicious in a fritto misto; make sure they are dry before they go into the fryer otherwise they will splatter like crazy. Add to potato gnocchi and pasta sauces. As part of a fresh herb butter for fish, add toward the end for maximum freshness. Chop it freshly and add it to frittatas, pilaf, pilau, falafel, chopped salads, and the classic **Omelet Fines Herbes** (page 443), and not forgetting Parsley Sauce, still a family favorite all over these islands, and last, but certainly not least, the classic Maitre d'hotel butter.

When basil is scarce in the winter, make **Parsley Pesto**. To make 2 × 10-ounce jars, put ½ cup parsley, leaves only (no stalks), 1 to 2 crushed garlic cloves, ½ cup freshly grated Parmesan, and 3 tablespoons pine nuts into the bowl of a food processor. Pulse for a second or two, then add ¼ cup extra virgin olive oil and a little salt. Season to taste. Pour into a sterilized jar. Cover with oil and refrigerate. For **Parsley and Rocket Pesto**, use half parsley and half arugula in the same recipe.

Tabbouleh

Tabbouleh is made in every season, so we vary the additions accordingly. We love to add tomatoes in summer when they are really ripe. Little cauliflower or sprouting broccoli florets, blanched and refreshed, or roasted, also work well in the fall. Spices can also be added, as can almonds, pine nuts, or pomegranate molasses—but parsley is always the consistent and main ingredient in our tabbouleh.

SERVES 6

¾ cup coarse bulgur wheat
sea salt and freshly ground black pepper
1 tablespoon extra virgin olive oil
½ cup boiling water
⅔ cup pomegranate seeds
3½ ounces cucumber, cut in ¼-inch dice (about 1 cup)
3 scallions, white and green parts, sliced
½ cup flat-leaf parsley, chopped
½ cup mint, coarsely chopped
1 green chile, seeded and chopped
2 inner stalks of celery, finely sliced at an angle
lots of cilantro leaves and pita bread, to serve

FOR THE DRESSING

¼ cup extra virgin olive oil
zest and freshly squeezed juice of 1 lemon
1 generous tablespoon honey

Put the bulgur into a bowl. Add a good pinch of salt and the oil and toss until the grains are coated. Pour over the boiling water, cover with plastic wrap, and leave for 5 to 10 minutes. Fluff up the bulgur and set aside to cool. It will have doubled in volume and absorbed the water.

Next, make the dressing: Whisk the oil, lemon juice, and honey together.

Add the remaining ingredients to the bulgur. Spoon over the dressing, toss gently, and season to taste. Sprinkle some cilantro on top and serve on plates with pita bread.

DID YOU KNOW?
As with rosemary it is often said that parsley only grows well in the garden where the "women wear the trousers"!

Lamb Chops with Uchucuta Sauce

Uchucuta sauce is a Peruvian salsa packed with fresh herbs. Serve with steak or lamb chops, or just as a dip for potatoes or fresh vegetables. Fresh cheeses are made throughout the Andes mountain region. Cheese is added to the uchucuta, together with hot rocoto chile peppers and huacatay, an herb unique to that area. Here's a version with flat-leaf parsley, mint, and cilantro, based on a recipe from Martin Morales of Ceviche—my version is certainly not authentic, but it tastes delicious.

. . . .

SERVES 6

FOR THE UCHUCUTA SAUCE
1 cup feta
1 tablespoon extra virgin olive oil, plus
    extra for drizzling
1 tablespoon chili paste (I use harissa)
2 tablespoons crème fraîche
½ cup flat-leaf parsley leaves, finely
    chopped, plus extra sprigs to garnish
¼ cup cilantro leaves, finely chopped
¼ cup mint leaves, finely chopped
¼ cup tarragon leaves, finely chopped
¼ cup corn kernels
freshly squeezed juice of ½ lime
¼ cup cold water
sea salt and freshly ground black pepper

FOR THE LAMB
12 lamb chops
lemon wedges, to serve

To make the uchucuta sauce, crumble the feta into a blender and then add all the remaining ingredients. Blend until smooth. Season to taste.

Heat a grill-pan over high heat. Drizzle the lamb chops with a little oil, then season well with sea salt and freshly ground pepper. Cook for 3 to 4 minutes on each side, depending on the thickness and how you like them cooked.

Rest the lamb for a couple of minutes then serve with the uchucuta sauce and garnish with a few sprigs of flat-leaf parsley and lemon wedges.

Traditional Irish Bacon, Cabbage & Parsley Sauce

Our national dish of bacon and cabbage is real comfort food. When I serve this delicious traditional food for a dinner party everyone really dives in and loves it to bits. It's an excuse to have lots and lots of parsley sauce. It's best to add the parsley close to the end of cooking to retain its lively freshness.

SERVES 12 TO 15

4 to 5-pound slab of bacon, either smoked or unsmoked with the rind on and a nice covering of fat
boiled potatoes (optional)

FOR THE BUTTERED CABBAGE
1 pound Savoy cabbage
2 to 3 tablespoons butter
white pepper

FOR THE PARSLEY SAUCE
bouquet garni
a few slices of carrot (optional)
a few slices of onion (optional)
2½ cups full-fat cold milk
¼ cup roux (page 267)
½ to ¾ cup chopped fresh curly parsley
salt and freshly ground black pepper

Put the bacon in a large saucepan, cover with cold water, and bring slowly to a boil. If the bacon is very salty there will be a white froth on top of the water, in which case it is preferable to discard the water and start again. It may be necessary to change the water several times depending on how salty the bacon is. Finally, cover with hot water and simmer until almost cooked, allowing 20 minutes for every 1 pound.

Meanwhile, remove the outer leaves from the cabbage. Cut the cabbage into quarters, discarding the center core. Cut each quarter into thin strips across the grain. About 30 minutes before the bacon is cooked, add the cabbage. Continue to cook until the cabbage is soft and tender and the bacon is fully cooked through. Transfer the bacon to a hot plate and strain the water off the cabbage. Remove the rind from the bacon. Return the cabbage to the saucepan with the butter; season with white pepper.

To make the parsley sauce, put the herbs, vegetables (if using), and milk into a saucepan and bring to simmering point. Season and simmer for 4 to 5 minutes. Strain out the herbs and vegetables, return the milk to a boil, and whisk in the roux until the sauce is a light coating consistency. Season with salt and pepper. Add the chopped parsley and simmer over very low heat for 3 to 4 minutes.

Serve the cabbage with the bacon and, traditionally, boiled potatoes and lots of parsley sauce.

Rosé Veal Osso Buco with Gremolata

This Italian recipe is also lovely made with pork or lamb, but the original was made with milk-fed veal. The leftover meat and juices are delicious over pasta. Gremolata is a fresh-tasting mix of chopped parsley, garlic, and lemon zest, which adds a freshness to the dish. You can also sprinkle it over roast or braised meats, pastas, or anything pan-grilled—delicious!

SERVES 8

4 tablespoons extra virgin olive oil

3 onions, sliced

5 garlic cloves, chopped

2 red bell peppers, seeded and sliced

2 yellow bell peppers, seeded and sliced

2 bay leaves

1 sprig of thyme

1 × 14-ounce can chopped tomatoes

salt and freshly ground black pepper

2 tablespoons sweet or smoked paprika

3¾ cups homemade chicken stock

16 thick slices of rosé veal or pork shanks
  (you'll want 4 shanks for 8 people, ask
  the butcher to saw them into thick slices
  for you or do it yourself)

seasoned flour

2 cups dry white wine

1¼ cups sour cream

approx. ¼ cup roux (page 267)

pasta, rice, or mashed potatoes, to serve

FOR THE GREMOLATA

¼ cup parsley, preferably flat-leaf,
  chopped

1 generous teaspoon grated or finely
  chopped lemon zest

2 garlic cloves, finely chopped

Preheat the oven to 325°F.

Heat 2 tablespoons of the oil in a casserole or Dutch oven, add the onions and garlic, toss, cover, and cook over medium heat for 5 to 6 minutes. Add the bell peppers and continue to cook until the onions and peppers are soft. Add the bay leaves, thyme, and tomatoes with their juice. Add salt, pepper, and the paprika. Stir, then add the stock and bring to a boil.

Meanwhile, heat the remaining oil in a frying pan. Toss the veal or pork in seasoned flour. Sear the meat a few pieces at a time, and add to the tomato base.

Deglaze the pan with the wine and bring to a boil.

Dissolve the caramelized meat juices in the wine. Add to the pot. Cover and cook gently for 2 to 2½ hours.

To make the gremolata, mix all the ingredients together in a small bowl.

When the meat is almost falling from the bones, remove the veal or pork from the pot and set aside. Skim the fat off the cooking sauce, add the sour cream, return to a boil, and thicken lightly with roux. Season to taste. Return the pork shanks and their juices to the sauce. Simmer over medium heat until the meat heats through. Season to taste. Transfer to a shallow serving dish.

Serve one small and one large piece of shank per person alongside pasta, rice, or mashed potatoes. Sprinkle generously with Gremolata.

ROSEMARY

Rosmarinus officinalis TENDER PERENNIAL, ZONES 8–10

Everyone should have a rosemary bush, but the problem is it only thrives in a house where the woman wears the trousers, so if you want to know if you need "self-assertion" classes, just plant a rosemary bush! Rosemary is a fragrant evergreen shrub, native to the Mediterranean, with a strong flavor and pretty blue, purple, white or pink flowers in early summer. The leaves look like flat pine needles. If you have space consider planting a hedge of rosemary.

VARIETIES

There are two main types, upright and creeping varieties, and over 30 cultivars to choose from. There's also a gold variegated variety, but I prefer the green—it seems to be more aromatic.
Rosmarinus officinalis—Common upright variety.
Rosmarinus officinalis **Prostratus Group**—More low-growing variety.

HOW TO GROW

Choose the variety most suitable to your situation. The common *Rosmarinus officinalis* is probably the most useful, a sturdy shrub 40 to 60 inches tall and 24 to 40 inches wide, it will thrive in most well-drained soils, in a sunny position.

Choose *Rosemarinus officinalis* **Prostratus Group** for trailing down a wall or creeping over a bed. It can also be pruned into formal shapes or topiary.

CONTAINER GROWING

Rosemary will be happy in a large pot; keep it close to your kitchen door.

PESTS AND DISEASES

Rosemary is both pest resistant and drought tolerant.

HARVESTING

As with many herbs, the flavor and texture of rosemary varies through the season. The young growth in spring is softer with less aromatic oils. Later in the summer it becomes more potent and in winter the leaves are firmer and more robust in flavor.

GOOD FOR YOU...

There are numerous studies, but several have found that rosemary is good for the brain, improves digestion, helps to prevent brain ageing and protects against macular degeneration.

It is also believed to boost the immune system and improve blood circulation and is a rich source of antioxidants which play an important role in neutralising harmful particles called free radicals. It also contains iron, calcium and vitamin B6.

WHAT TO DO WITH GLUT

Rosemary can be picked year round. If the bush is becoming unruly, clip it and use the fresh rosemary sprigs in your bath or dry and add to the fire for a wonderful resinous aroma.

IN THE KITCHEN

Lamb with rosemary and garlic is a classic, but we find rosemary works well with chicken, fish, roasted vegetables, on focaccia, and even in soda bread.

Add a sprig or two of rosemary to a container of honey.

We also love rosemary oil; used judiciously it makes a delicious drizzle for lots of dishes, including salads, legumes, rice, and chunky soups. We use the woody stems as mini skewers and use the flowers for garnishing or salads.

Throw some woody sprigs onto the barbecue to infuse meats with a delicious flavor as they grill.

For **Tuscan Butter**, add some chopped rosemary and a pinch of crushed red pepper flakes to lard and spread on grilled sourdough. At Christmas, little sprigs of rosemary turned upside down resemble Christmas trees on the top of a Christmas cake.

A gutsy evergreen rosemary shrub. Enjoy the flowers as well as the leaves.

Zucchini Soup with Rosemary Oil & Croûtons

This soup tastes immeasurably better when made with the zucchini from your garden in summer. I purée the soup here, but it's also delicious served with the grated zucchini intact.

. . . .

SERVES 6 TO 8

3 tablespoons butter

4 ounces onions, cut into ¼-inch dice (about 1 cup)

5½ ounces potatoes, peeled and cut into ¼-inch dice (about 1 cup)

salt and freshly ground black pepper

1¼ pounds coarsely grated zucchini

3¾ cups boiling light chicken stock

1 to 2 sprigs of rosemary, plus flowers (optional), to garnish

1 cup whole milk (optional)

1½ cups whipped cream

FOR THE ROSEMARY CROÛTONS

1 to 2 × ¼-inch thick slices of white bread

¼ cup olive oil

½ tablespoon chopped fresh rosemary

FOR THE ROSEMARY OIL

3 tablespoons extra virgin olive oil

1 teaspoon finely chopped rosemary

Melt the butter in a heavy-bottomed pot. When it foams, add the onions and potatoes and turn them until well coated. Sprinkle with salt and pepper. Cover and cook over low heat for 5 to 7 minutes. Add the zucchini, stock, and rosemary sprigs. Boil for about 5 minutes until soft; be careful not to overcook or the vegetables will lose their flavor. Remove the rosemary sprigs, liquidize the soup, or strain it or put through a mouli. Adjust the seasoning and thin out with some milk if necessary.

Meanwhile, make the croûtons: Cut the bread into ¼-inch dice. Put the olive oil into a pan, add the chopped rosemary, and heat gently for 2 to 3 minutes. Strain out the rosemary, return the oil to the pan, and cook the croûtons over high heat, tossing continuously, for 2 to 3 minutes until crisp and golden. Drain on paper towels.

To make the rosemary oil, put the extra virgin olive oil and the chopped rosemary into a small saucepan, warm gently, and let infuse for a few minutes. Strain.

To serve, ladle the soup into bowls, put a blob of cream on each bowl of soup, and drizzle with some rosemary oil. Scatter with the croûtons and rosemary flowers, if using.

Chocolate & Rosemary Mousse

Lovely Jane Grigson, the legendary British cookbook writer, gave me this recipe, and from memory I think she got it from Franco Taruschio at the Walnut Tree restaurant in South Wales. It sounds odd, but it is strangely addictive.

. . . .

SERVES 8

1 cup superfine sugar

1 cup dry white wine

freshly squeezed juice of ½ lemon

2½ cups heavy cream

1 long branch of rosemary, plus extra sprigs, to decorate

6 ounces dark chocolate (we use Valrhona or Lindt, 52 percent cocoa solids is fine), chopped

heavy cream, to serve

Mix the sugar, wine, and lemon juice together in a stainless-steel saucepan, then stir over low heat until the sugar dissolves. Add the cream and bring to a boil—the mixture will thicken somewhat. Add the rosemary and chocolate. Stir, return to a boil, then reduce the heat and simmer very gently for 20 minutes. It should be the consistency of thick cream. Set aside to cool, tasting occasionally to see if the rosemary flavor is intense enough.

Pour through a strainer into 8 ramekins or little shot glasses. Cool, cover with plastic wrap, and chill until needed.

We serve it with heavy cream and a sprig of flowering rosemary.

Braised Lamb Shanks with Garlic, Rosemary & Beans

We also love lamb necks in this delicious gutsy recipe; they need long, slow cooking and benefit from the assertive flavors of rosemary and thyme. This dish tastes even better when cooked a few days ahead.

. . . .

SERVES 6

6 lamb shanks, weighing approx. 2¼ pounds

14 small sprigs of rosemary, plus extra to garnish

12 slivers of garlic

6 anchovy fillets, halved

sea salt and freshly ground black pepper

2 tablespoons goose or duck fat or olive oil

2 carrots, coarsely chopped

2 celery ribs, coarsely chopped

1 leek, coarsely chopped

1 onion, coarsely chopped

1 garlic bulb, halved horizontally

¾ cup bold red wine

⅔ cup homemade lamb or chicken stock

1 sprig of thyme, plus extra to garnish

2 bay leaves

2 strips of dried orange peel

green beans, to serve (optional)

FOR THE BEAN SAUCE

2 tablespoons extra virgin olive oil

3½ ounces bacon, cut into dice and blanched

½ carrot, finely diced

½ celery rib, finely diced

½ onion, finely diced

6 garlic cloves

4 very ripe tomatoes, peeled and diced or ½ × 14-ounce can tomatoes, plus juice

2 sprigs of thyme

leaves from 2 sprigs of rosemary, chopped

1 cup small white or borlotti beans, soaked overnight, drained, covered with fresh water, and boiled rapidly for 20 minutes

⅔ to 1⅓ cups homemade lamb or chicken stock

Preheat the oven to 300°F.

Remove most of the fat from each shank, then scrape the meat away from the bone to loosen it. Make two deep incisions in each side and insert a rosemary sprig and a sliver of garlic wrapped in half an anchovy fillet into each incision. Season the meat with salt and pepper. Heat the goose or duck fat or olive oil in a heavy sauté pan or casserole and sauté the meat for 5 to 10 minutes until well browned on all sides. Remove the meat from the pan. Add the carrots, celery, leek, onion, and garlic bulb and cook over high heat for another 5 minutes until well browned. Add the wine to the pan and bring to a boil, then stir for a minute or two. Add the stock, the remaining rosemary sprigs and the thyme, bay leaves, and orange peel to the pan, then place the lamb shanks on top. Cover and cook in the oven for 4 hours.

Meanwhile, make the sauce: Heat the extra virgin olive oil in a saucepan and brown the bacon in it. Then reduce the heat and add the carrot, celery, onion, and garlic cloves and cook for about 8 minutes or until the vegetables are soft. Add the tomatoes, beans, and enough stock to half cover the beans. Cover and simmer for 30 to 45 minutes or until the beans are cooked but still keep their shape. When the lamb has finished cooking, remove the thyme, bay leaves, and orange peel. Season to taste.

Serve the lamb shanks on a hot, deep dish with the beans and vegetables poured over and around. Garnish with sprigs of rosemary and thyme. There will be lots of delicious cooking juices in the braising pot. Drain, save, and use in a soup or as a basis for stews or gravy.

DID YOU KNOW?

Bees love rosemary flowers. Rosemary has a reputation for improving memory and students would entwine some sprigs in their hair. From the Middle Ages, rosemary was part of wedding ceremonies. The bride would wear a rosemary headpiece and the groom and wedding guests would tuck a sprig of rosemary into their lapel. We always include a sprig of rosemary in a wedding boquet as a love charm and in a funeral wreath as a symbol of fond remembrance. It also just happens to be part of the lyrics of my favorite Simon & Garfunkel song, "Scarborough Fair."

SORREL *Rumex* PERENNIAL

Common sorrel looks like spinach but the ends of the leaves are always pointed.

Sorrel may not be one of your must-have plants initially, but once you've got your essentials underway, I urge you to consider this hardy herbaceous perennial. It will become a dependable, trouble-free plant to add a distinctive, zingy lemon flavor to salads, sauces and juices. It is widely used in French cuisine. It takes its name from *surelle*, derived from *sur*, meaning "sour" in French. Its delightfully acid flavor was also enjoyed by the Romans who used it to impart a sharpness to food. Its clean, lemony flavor flits across the tongue, a perfect antidote to hearty winter flavors.

VARIETIES

Here are the varieties I enjoy
Rumex acetosa (**common sorrel**), zones 3–7—Leaves 6 to 8 inches long.
Rumex scutatus (**buckler leaf sorrel**), zones 5–8—Milder with smaller leaves shaped like an old buckler shield.
Rumex sanguineus (**red-veined dock**), zones 5–8—Beautiful, decorative, red-veined sorrel, equally at home in a flower border or vegetable patch. The baby leaves are beautiful in the salad bowl.
Rumex acetosella (**sheep's tongue sorrel**), zones 1–9—A small, arrow-shaped leaf that apparently resembles a sheep's tongue, hence the name. We love it in salads and on starter plates.

HOW TO GROW

Sorrel does best in acid soils, but it will also tolerate alkaline conditions. It is embarrassingly easy to grow, and almost impossible to buy, and can withstand hard frosts. One of the first leaves to unfurl itself in spring, it seems to do best in partial shade and usually starts to bolt in early summer. It self-seeds in midsummer so cut off the flowers unless you don't mind it running riot. The plants can be cut down to within 1 to 1½ inch of the ground and will re-sprout. It can be grown in open ground or in a vegetable bed.

CONTAINER GROWING

It will also grow in a large pot.

PESTS AND DISEASES

Slugs can attack young leaves, but once they are established they don't seem to have any problem.

HARVESTING

Just pick as you need. It tends to run to seed in early summer, so trim off the flower heads as soon as they appear.

Fresh, lemony leaves of bucker leaf sorrel are perfect for salads.

GOOD FOR YOU...

Sorrel is rich in vitamins C and A, B6 and 1, iron, magnesium, potassium and many beneficial organic compounds.

Do note that sorrel is rich in oxalic acid which gives it its distinctive, sharp taste. Oxalic acid can be a toxin so don't overdose on it. Those with certain medical conditions, such as gout, rheumatoid arthritis or kidney disease, are best advised to avoid sorrel altogether.

WHAT TO DO WITH A GLUT

Cook in lots of boiling salted water, drain well, purée and freeze to use in soups and sauces. Or thaw and serve in little bowls with lots of sugar and a blob of whipped cream like the Sami do.

IN THE KITCHEN

Use fresh sorrel in salads, soup, sauces, juices, and gratins. Its fresh green color turns to a sludgy brown when heated, because of the oxalic acid, but that doesn't affect the flavor in the least. Cook in stainless-steel as the acid reacts with aluminum.

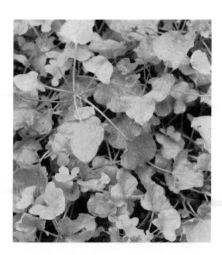

Salmon with Sorrel Sauce

Thanks to the Troisgros brothers. This classic, much-copied nouvelle cuisine recipe came to us via Declan Ryan of Arbutus Breads, who spent a happy stage in their kitchens in Roanne in the early '70s. The clean, sharp, lemony flavor of the sorrel delicately cuts the richness of the salmon.

SERVES 4

1½ pounds center cut of fresh wild
  salmon, off the bone
2½ cups fish stock
¼ cup dry white wine, such as a Sancerre
2 tablespoons vermouth, such as Noilly
  Prat
2 shallots, very finely chopped
1 cup sorrel
1½ cups heavy cream
3 tablespoons butter
freshly squeezed juice of ½ lemon
salt and freshly ground black pepper

Lay the piece of salmon lengthwise, skin-side down, on a cutting board. You'll need to get four escalopes out of this piece. For the first, hold the blade of the knife over the salmon as though you're about to cut it into two equal portions. Cut halfway down through the flesh and then swivel the knife 90 degrees so that it slices the salmon lengthwise toward the right. Transfer this escalope of salmon to a plate.

For the second escalope, continue to cut in the same place, down as far as, but not through, the skin. Just before the blade touches the skin, slide the knife 90 degrees right to slice the remaining salmon off the skin. Turn the intact piece of salmon around so it faces the same direction you were just working in and repeat this procedure until you have two more skinless escalopes. Cover and chill.

Put the stock, wine, vermouth, and shallots into a stainless-steel sauté pan. Bring it to a boil and reduce, uncovered, until you have a glistening syrup that is almost a glaze.

Meanwhile, string the sorrel to remove the stalks. Wash and tear the largest leaves into two or three pieces.

Add the cream and let it boil until the sauce is slightly thickened. Throw in the sorrel and, after 25 seconds, remove the pan from the heat and incorporate the butter in small pieces, shaking the pan back and forth to emulsify the sauce (don't use a whisk as this would break up the sorrel). Finish the sauce by adding a few drops of lemon juice, salt, and pepper.

Heat a nonstick frying pan. Season the salmon escalopes with salt and pepper on both sides and put them into the hot pan. After 25 seconds, turn them over and cook on the other side for just 15 seconds. The salmon must be slightly undercooked to remain moist and succulent.

This dish cannot be kept waiting and should be prepared at the last moment.

To serve, spoon the sauce over the bottom of 4 hot plates. Place the escalopes on top of the sauce with the best side uppermost. Sprinkle with a few sea salt flakes and serve immediately.

Broth of Sorrel, Tarragon & Cavolo Nero

I'm addicted to this light soup, one of the many delicious broths that my brother Rory loves to make. The sorrel melts and gets slimy, but with a tart, refreshing, and lemony flavor. The tarragon is sweet and highly scented. The cavolo nero is strong and deep in flavor and the three ingredients combine to give a rich balance of sweet, sour, and strong tastes. Remove the tough central rib from the cavolo nero and sorrel and tear into small, bite-sized pieces. Leave the tarragon leaves whole. Wild garlic leaves can be used instead of cavolo nero.

. . . .

SERVES 6

3 tablespoons butter
6 ounces potatoes, peeled and cut into
  neat ½-inch dice (about 1 cup)
2 garlic cloves, finely crushed
6 ounces onions, cut into neat ½-inch dice
  (about 1 cup)
salt and freshly ground black pepper
5 cups homemade chicken stock
1¼ cups torn sorrel leaves
2 tablespoons tarragon leaves
10½ ounces torn cavolo nero

Melt the butter in a large saucepan and allow to foam. Add the potatoes, garlic, and onions. Coat in the butter and season with salt and pepper. Cover with parchment paper and a tight-fitting lid. Cook over very low heat to allow the vegetables to cook gently until barely tender. This will take about 10 minutes. Don't overcook the vegetables, and allow the potato to collapse. Add the stock, stir gently, and bring to a simmer with the lid removed. Season to taste. This is the base and can be set aside until later.

To finish the soup, return the base to a boil. Add the herbs and cavolo nero and just allow to wilt. Taste and serve immediately.

Sorrel & Apple Juice

A clean fresh-tasting drink or an accompaniment to carrageen moss pudding.

. . . .

MAKES 2 TO 3 GLASSES

8 ounces sorrel, weighed after stalks have
  been removed
approx. 4 to 6 apples, depending on size

Destalk the sorrel and juice in a juice extractor; 8 ounces sorrel should yield 1½ cups sorrel juice.

Cut the apples into quarters or eighths. Make 1 cup apple juice.

Mix the two juices together.

Taste and enjoy as soon as possible, served chilled in small glasses.

SAGE *Salvia* PERENNIAL, ZONES 4–8

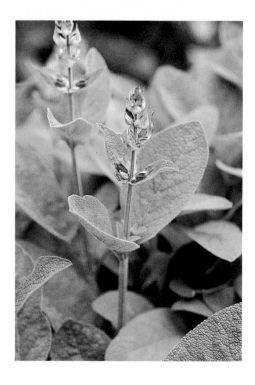

There are over 750 species of sage but salvia officinalis *is my favourite for culinary use.*

Sage is a feisty evergreen herb, with silvery grey, purple or variegated, textured leaves, depending on the variety. It has pretty purple-blue flowers for a few weeks in early summer. It's not everyone's favorite, which is totally understandable if your introduction to this herb has been a stuffing made with acrid dried sage. After that experience you may well wonder why you would ever bother to grow sage, but try frying a couple of eggs with crispy sage leaves and you'll reckon it's worth growing sage just for that experience alone. The Italians love sage and really know how to use it to maximise its attributes, but a roast goose or duck with a fresh sage and onion stuffing is also a feast.

VARIETIES

Salvia is a large and extended family. There are over 750 species and various forms grow all over the world. There are annual, biennial and perennial varieties to choose from.

We grow several in our perennial border and in pots around the school and five varieties in the formal herb garden.

Salvia officinalis (**common sage, or simply garden sage**)—Hardy, evergreen perennial with silver grey leaves and a strong, gutsy flavor. It grows 1 to 2 feet high and spreads each year unless judiciously pruned. Best for culinary use. The pretty blue flowers can also be used in salads and as a garnish. At Ballymaloe House we use sprigs of flowering sage to decorate the carving boards in early summer. There is also a white form of *salvia officinalis*, 'Albiflora', which is not so common.

Salvia officinalis '**Purpurascens**' (**purple sage**), **zones 6–9**—Dark purple leaves and deep blue flowers. Can also be grown from cuttings.

Salvia elegans (**pineapple sage**), **zones 8–10**—Beautiful scarlet flowers and a distinctly pineapple scent. Also beautiful grown as a pot plant. It attracts butterflies and hummingbirds. Common sage is much better to cook with.

Salvia officinalis '**Icterina**' (**golden sage**), **zones 4–8**—Hardy evergreen with small variegated leaves and pale purple-blue flowers. Can be grown from cuttings and has a good, if milder, flavor than the common sage.

Salvia sclarea (**clary sage**), **zones 5–9**—Hardy biennial which I particularly love because of its cheery purple, pink and white-splotched leaves.

Salvia sclarea var. *turkestanica* (**Italian Clary Sage**) **zones 4–10**—Tall pale pink flowers with large leaves. More decorative than functional in the kitchen, but particularly beautiful in the herbaceous border or just in a pot.

HOW TO GROW

Sage is native to the Mediterranean, so choose a sunny spot, neutral or mildly limy soil, not acid.

Common sage grows from seed. Sow in seed trays in a greenhouse or tunnel in early spring. The seeds are slow to germinate and benefit from being started in a heat propagator. Pot up and pot out after all risk of frost has passed. Plant 18 to 24 inches apart. However, if you just need one plant, buy a healthy, organic, common sage plant at a good garden center.

For other varieties, take cuttings in late spring and early summer from new growth. Using a peat compost, they root easily in 3 to 4 weeks. Alternatively, you can layer established sage branches in spring or autumn.

Prune in spring to encourage young growth otherwise the plant will get very gnarled and woody. It's worth replanting with new sage plants every 3 to 4 years.

CONTAINER GROWING

Sage will grow successfully in pots and containers, on its own or with other herbs. It's good to have a pot of sage near your kitchen door.

PESTS AND DISEASES

We haven't encountered any pest problems outdoors, but keep an eye on plants grown in pots for red spider. Wash the plants with a liquid horticultural soap as soon as you see the mites. Plant sage here and there through your cabbages to discourage white cabbage butterflies.

HARVESTING

We pick sage as we need it, year round. I really abhor the nasty acrid taste of dried sage and I'm sure it's responsible for putting many people off this delicious, feisty herb.

GOOD FOR YOU...

Sage is known to improve memory and brain power and possibly to slow the onset of cognitive diseases such as Alzheimer's. It also boosts the immune system. It is anti-inflammatory and has strong antioxidant compounds. Because of its significant level of vitamin K, it contributes to bone density. Sage can also help to prevent the onset of Type 2 diabetes and manage the condition. It contains vitamins B6, A and folate.

Sage is also known as "thinkers' tea" and is believed to help ease depression.

WHAT TO DO WITH A GLUT

One can pick sage year round, so I don't worry about a glut. Dry some leaves of pineapple sage for a pot pourri. Use sage to decorate buffets.

IN THE KITCHEN

Parsley, sage, rosemary, and thyme are there for the cook year round. Sage grows close to my kitchen door begging to be snipped. Fried eggs with sage are my go-to comfort food. Sage butter and sage oil enliven so many of my dishes, including pasta, risotto, and gnocchi.

The Italians really know how to use sage—think of saltimbocca, pappardelle with chicken livers and sage, and then there's the sage and anchovy sandwiches that I first ate in a little osteria in Volpaia in Tuscany. The gutsy flavor of the fragrant leaves complements offal dishes particularly, but it is surprisingly good with mushrooms, omelets, frittatas, and polenta.

I love to scatter the pretty blue flowers over a variety of dishes.

DID YOU KNOW?

The word sage is derived from the Latin *salvae*, "to heal or save." The Ancient Greeks used it to heal snakebites. The Romans, Celtic Druids, and Native Americans considered it sacred, and used it in their purification ceremonies. To be sage is to be wise.

Lambs' Liver with Crispy Sage Leaves

The robust flavor of sage works beautifully with lamb or veal liver, so keep a sage plant in a pot near your kitchen door. Sage leaves crisped in olive oil make an irresistible garnish.

SERVES 4

1 pound very fresh spring lambs' liver, cut into ½-inch slices
all-purpose flour, seasoned with salt and freshly ground black pepper
4 tablespoons extra virgin olive oil
12 sage leaves

Toss the liver in the seasoned flour and pat off the excess. Heat half the oil in a frying pan and add the liver. Sauté gently for 1 to 2 minutes on each side. Remove the liver while it is still slightly pink in the center.

Put the remaining oil in the pan, add the sage, and sizzle for a few seconds until crisp. Pour the oil, juices, and sage over the liver and serve immediately. Even if liver is perfectly cooked, it can toughen very quickly if kept hot.

Gillian's Ravioli with Sage Butter

Gillian Hegarty, a head chef at Ballymaloe House in Ireland, worked alongside Rose Grey and Ruth Rogers at the River Café for many years, where she learned how to make this exquisite pasta. We use the beautiful tender buffalo mozzarella from Macroom in West Cork and freshly plucked sage.

. . . .

SERVES 6 AS AN APPETIZER

FOR THE PASTA

1⅔ cups bread flour, plus extra for dusting

pinch of salt

1 whole large organic egg and 2 organic egg yolks

1 teaspoon olive oil

1 teaspoon cold water

semolina flour, for sprinkling

grated Parmesan, to serve

FOR THE FILLING

4 ounces buffalo ricotta

¼ cup mascarpone

¼ cup Parmesan, grated

freshly grated nutmeg

2 tablespoons chopped flat-leaf parsley

1 tablespoon chopped marjoram

1 teaspoon chopped mint

salt and freshly ground black pepper

FOR THE SAGE BUTTER

3 tablespoons butter

24 to 36 sage leaves (serve 4 to 6 sage leaves per portion depending on how strong the sage is), plus sage flowers to garnish (optional)

First make the pasta: Sift the bread flour into a bowl and add the salt. Make a well in the center, add the egg and egg yolks (no need to whisk them), oil, and water. Mix into a dough with your hand. The pasta should just come together, but shouldn't stick to your hand—if it does, add a little more flour. (If it is too dry, add a little extra egg white.) Knead for 10 minutes, or until it becomes elastic; it should be quite pliable. Wrap in plastic wrap and rest in the fridge for 20 minutes.

Roll the pasta by hand or in a pasta machine. To roll by hand, divide the dough in half. Dust each piece of dough with white flour before you roll each time. Roll out one piece at a time keeping the other piece covered with plastic wrap. Roll into a very thin sheet; you ought to be able to read the print on a matchbox through the pasta. A long, thin rolling pin is a great advantage, but you can manage perfectly well with an ordinary domestic rolling pin. To roll by pasta machine, roll the pasta to the lowest setting on the machine.

To make the filling, mix all the ingredients together. Season to taste.

Cut each sheet of pasta into smaller sheets, 8 inches long and about 4 inches wide. Place a teaspoon of filling along the top half of each sheet of pasta leaving 1-inch intervals. Fold the bottom half over the top half of each sheet and seal around the filling of each ravioli with your fingers. This is important to remove any air bubbles. Using a serrated pasta cutter, cut around each ravioli. Each ravioli should be about 3 inches square. Transfer to a pan sprinkled heavily with semolina flour.

To cook, just before serving, poach the ravioli in a large saucepan of boiling salted water (use 4.8 litres to 1 tablespoon of salt), for 1½ to 3 minutes, depending on how thin the pasta is, or until almost tender. The ravioli is cooked when it rises to the surface of the water.

To make the sage butter, put the butter and sage in a frying pan and melt slowly. Ensure it does not get too hot or it will become greasy.

When the ravioli is cooked, carefully transfer with a slotted spoon into the frying pan with a little extra pasta water. The pasta water emulsifies with the butter making a lighter sauce than if you were to use just butter.

Put 3 ravioli per person on a warm plate or in a wide soup bowl and spoon some sage butter over the ravioli. Serve 3 to 4 sage leaves per portion. Sprinkle a little Parmesan on top. Gillian didn't, but I love to sprinkle a few sage flowers over the pasta when they are in season.

Serve immediately.

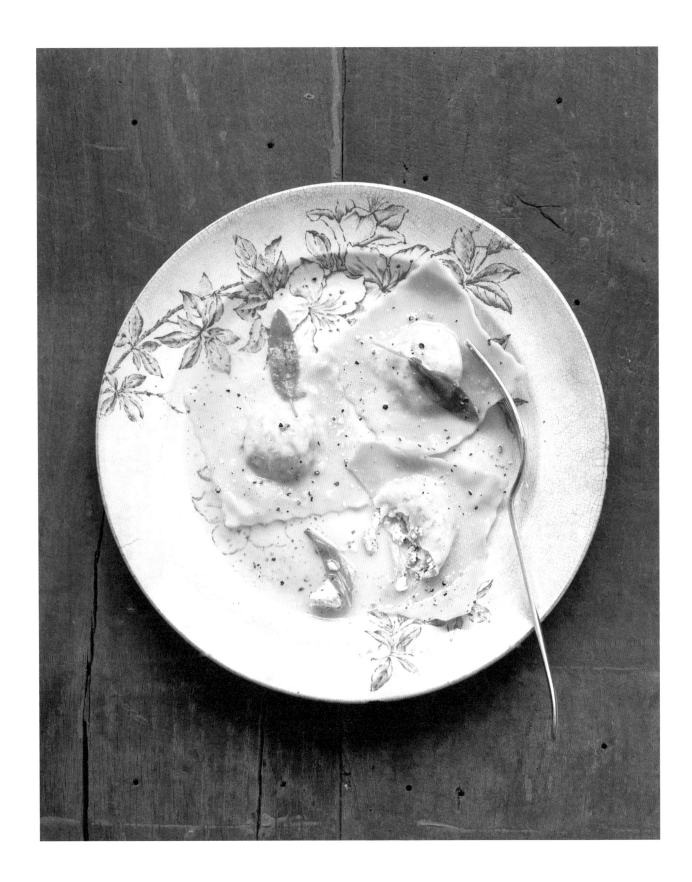

SAVORY *Satureja* PERENNIAL AND ANNUAL

Savory probably won't be one of your top ten must-have fresh herbs, but we grow both summer and winter savory—summer savory to enhance the flavor of beans and help with digestion, and winter savory to add to gutsy stews and casseroles. Of the two, summer savory is my favorite for cooking; the leaves are more tender and the flavor more appealing.

Winter savory is also one of the seven herbs that go to make up the Middle Eastern dried herb mixture *za'atar*, of which there are many versions. Summer and winter savory attract bees and other beneficial insects into the garden.

VARIETIES
There are several varieties of savory, but we grow two:

Satureja hortensis (**summer savory**) **annual**—Half-hardy annual, softish, oblong grey/green leaves and small white flowers with a dash of mauve in summer.
Satureja montana (**winter savory**) **zones 6–8**—Semi-evergreen, hardy perennial, grows to a height of 12 inches. Small white flowers with a slight splash of pink in summer, coarser, darker green oblong leaves.

HOW TO GROW
Both can be grown from seed, but I suggest just buying a couple of plants of each. They prefer poor, well-drained soil. Savory plants can be divided in spring, but may need to be protected in colder areas in winter with a mulch. We grow summer savory close to the beans to deter blackfly and other pests.

CONTAINER GROWING
Both types of savory can be grown in a container, but watch the watering.

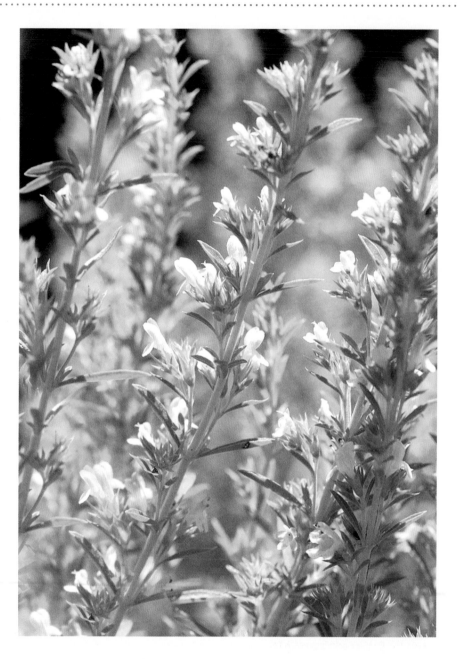

There's no need to feed, but they may need protection in winter.

Summer savory in full flower—it makes beans taste more "beany."

PESTS AND DISEASES
Savory doesn't seem to be bothered by pests and diseases.

HARVESTING
Keep snipping as you need and don't allow to flower if you want to encourage

new growth and maximum flavor. The leaves dry easily, store in airtight tins or jars in a cool, dry place.

GOOD FOR YOU...

Savory is both antibacterial and anti-fungal. It is rich in the B complex group of vitamins, plus vitamins A and C, niacin, thiamine and pyridoxine.

Savory relieves the pain of a bee sting. Rub it on the affected spot. A tea or tisane of summer savory stimulates the appetite.

IN THE KITCHEN

We love carrot and savory soup, and add a sprig of summer savory to fava beans and later to French beans to intensify their flavor. The young leaves can also be snipped into salads. Many bean and vegetable stews benefit from the unique flavor of savory. We also add it to meat marinades for summer barbecues.

Winter savory in flower—the flavor is more gutsy than the summer variety.

DID YOU KNOW?

The ancient Egyptians used savory in love potions and considered it an aphrodisiac. It has been used to flavor food for over two thousand years.

Labneh with Radishes, Mint, Summer Savory, Apple Syrup & Olive Oil

A delicious way to showcase your summer savory in this light, summery appetizer.

SERVES 5

1¼ cups labneh (page 291)
6 teaspoons apple syrup
⅓ cup extra virgin olive oil
10 radishes
10 mint leaves
10 tiny pieces of summer savory
10 to 16 cheese biscuits
sea salt and freshly ground black pepper

APPLE SYRUP (MAKES APPROX. ½ CUP)

3⅓ cups apple juice (from either eating or cooking apples)

To make the Apple Syrup, pour the apple juice into a wide stainless steel sauté pan. Bring to the boil and simmer until reduced to a thickish syrup, about 20 minutes.

Cool and pour into a sterilized glass bottle. Keeps for up to a year in a cold place or a fridge.

To serve, allow ¼ cup of Labneh per person and divide among chilled plates. Using a teaspoon, make a little indent in each portion of labneh and pour in the Apple Syrup followed by the oil. Place 2 radishes on each plate beside the labneh. Tear the mint leaves over the radishes and sprinkle on the summer savory. Place 2 to 3 cheese biscuits on the plates and finish off with a sprinkle of sea salt flakes and cracked black pepper.

Celeriac Soup with Winter Savory & Toasted Hazelnuts

Celeriac is in fact a celery root that looks a bit like a muddy turnip. Peel it thickly and use for soups or in salads, or just as a vegetable. This is a deliciously light soup, perfect for Christmas Day. Or you could serve it in espresso cups for a cocktail party. You can garnish the soup with Chorizo Crumbs (page 84), Crispy Sage Leaves (page 523), or Parsley, Arugula, or Kale Oil (page 81).

SERVES 6

3 tablespoons butter

5½ ounce potatoes, cut into ¼-inch dice (about 1 cup)

4 ounces onions, cut into ¼-inch dice (about 1 cup)

1 pound celeriac, cut into ¼-inch dice (about 3 cups)

sea salt and freshly ground black pepper

4½ cups hot Homemade Chicken or Vegetable Stock (page 00) or water

½ to 1 cup whole milk (optional)

1 to 2 tablespoons chopped winter savory

2 tablespoons hazelnuts

a few tablespoons heavy cream, to garnish

sprig of winter savory, to garnish

Melt the butter in a heavy-bottomed pot; when it foams, add the potatoes, onions, and celeriac and toss them in the butter until evenly coated. Season with salt and pepper. Cover with parchment paper (to keep in the steam) and the saucepan lid, and cook over low heat for about 10 minutes until the vegetables are soft, but not colored. Discard the parchment paper. Add the stock and cook for 8 to 10 minutes until the celeriac is soft.

Liquidize the soup in a blender or juicer; add a little more stock or milk to thin to the required consistency. Season to taste and add the winter savory.

Meanwhile, toast the hazelnuts on a baking sheet into a preheated 400°F oven for about 10 to 15 minutes or until the skins loosen. Remove the skins by rubbing the nuts on the corner of a kitchen towel. If they are not sufficiently toasted, return them to the oven until they become golden brown. Chop and set aside.

Serve the soup piping hot with a little bit of heavy cream on top. Sprinkle with the chopped hazelnuts and a sprig of winter savory.

Fava Beans with Summer Savory

Freshness is vitally important with fava beans; both flavor and texture change within hours of picking. A little summer savory added to the cooking water enormously enhances the flavor.

SERVES 6

2 to 3 sprigs of summer savory

4½ cups shelled fava beans

2 teaspoons butter

salt and freshly ground black pepper

Bring 2½ cups water to a rolling boil in a saucepan, then add 1 teaspoon of salt and the summer savory. Add the fava beans, return to a boil, and cook for 2 to 5 minutes, depending on size and freshness.

When cooked, taste and drain quickly, tossing in the butter and lots of pepper.

THYME *Thymus* spp. PERENNIAL

Left: *Make the most of pretty thyme flowers for garnishes and in salads.*
Right: *Lemon thyme in full flower.*

I hadn't really thought about how much I rely on thyme in my cooking until I started to write this entry. It's one of the supporting cast of flavors in so many of my dishes and part of the bouquet garni in stocks, stew, casseroles, pâtes and terrines. What would the famous Ballymaloe House chicken liver pâte or the onion and thyme leaf soup be without thyme leaves? In other instances it's not just a base flavor, it's a star, as in Roast Scallops with Butter and Thyme Leaves. Thyme comes from a huge botanical family; there are numerous species, very diverse in appearance, that thrive happily all over the world.

VARIETIES

We grow about 15 varieties, some just decorative and others functional as well. These are the varieties I use most for culinary purposes:

Thymus vulgaris (common thyme), zones 5–9—Evergreen, hardy perennial with small green, aromatic leaves and good,

gutsy flavor, this is thyme as far as most people are concerned. Pretty purple flowers.

Thymus citriodorus (lemon thyme), zones 5–8—Another favorite, evergreen hardy perennial, pink flowers in summer, 8 inches spread. Larger green leaves with a distinct lemon scent and flavor. 'Golden Queen' is a golden version of lemon thyme.

Thymus citriodorus 'Golden King', zones 5–8—Same as above, but with green and yellow variegated leaves. Also an excellent culinary thyme and so pretty for garnishing.

Thymus citriodorus 'Silver Queen', zones 5–8—Evergreen half-hardy, same height and spread as common thyme, silver-grey leaves, with a lemony scent and pink flowers in summer. We love this thyme and 'Silver Posie' also, which has pretty pink/pale flowers and variegated silver-grey leaves—good for cooking and garnishing.

Thymus herba-barona (caraway thyme), zones 4–8—Height ¾ inch, 8 inch

spread, leaves have a distinct caraway scent.

Thymus serpyllum (wild thyme, mother of thyme), zones 4–8—Low-growing cushions, grows on cliffs around the coast. Can be used for culinary purposes. Bees and other pollinating insects love the purple-violet flowers of thyme. Low-growing *Thymus caespititius* (zones 7–9) is particularly good for growing between paving stones, with pale pink flowers in summer.

HOW TO GROW

Thyme was originally native to the Mediterranean region. One can grow from seed or softwood cuttings but if you want a healthy variety of plants, source from a reliable garden center.

Creeping thyme can also be divided in early spring. Older woodier plants can also be propagated by layering. All thyme plants need poor (low-nutrient), free-draining soil. They simply won't thrive in rich soil and the flavor will also suffer. Being drought-loving plants, they can survive for a long time without water. They will need protection from excessive wind and rain and hard frost in winter. All thymes will rot and die if they become waterlogged, particularly in a cold winter.

To maintain thyme in best condition, trim after flowering to encourage new growth and stop the plant becoming too woody. You may want to replace old common thyme plants with new young plants every 1 to 2 years.

Thyme can grow squeezed into gaps between paving stones. A little thyme lawn or a thyme walk in different shades that flow into each other is a thing of real beauty. Can you imagine how lovely it is when in flower in a tapestry, creating a virtual tapestry of purple, pinks and mauves? Prince Charles's gardeners have created a beautiful thyme walk at Highgrove. But from the cook's perspective and if you are tight for space, have at least one common thyme, *Thymus vulgaris*.

CONTAINER GROWING

Thyme will thrive happily in pots, zinc buckets or galvanised basins. It thrives in poor, gravelly conditions and doesn't appreciate over-watering.

PESTS AND DISEASES

Aromatic plants do not normally suffer from pests and thyme is no exception, but if the soil is too rich, it struggles and can be attacked by aphids. Use a liquid horticultural soap. Some gardeners like to plant thyme close to cabbages to deter cabbage butterfly.

HARVESTING

Thyme is an evergreen so it can be picked year round. It's best snipped with a scissors. The plant can get damaged if roughly plucked in haste. As with all herbs, the flavor is best before the herb flowers but we use both; the flowers make a pretty garnish and also taste and look delicious, scattered over salads. Fresh thyme is best stored wrapped in damp kitchen paper.

GOOD FOR YOU...

Common thyme is both antibacterial, and anti-fungal so the essential oil is widely used in mouthwash, toothpastes, and massage oil. A thyme leaf tea is a good treatment for infected gums. Each variety has its own unique complement of nutrients—vitamin B complex, vitamins A, K, E, C and folic acid. Minerals include potassium, iron, calcium, manganese, magnesium and selenium.

WHAT TO DO WITH A GLUT

Thyme dries well just left out on a wire rack on a tray in a warm spot in your kitchen. It will dry in a few days. Store in an airtight container, like a sealed glass jar, in a cool dark place and use sooner rather than later. I just pop a few sprigs into a little pot on the shelf over the Aga and keep it topped up. I add the freshly dried leaves into a myriad of dishes.

IN THE KITCHEN

Thyme's gutsy flavor is accessible all year round. Apart from the obvious meat and vegetable stews, thyme enhances roasted vegetables, pasta, frittatas, quiches, and

Buttermilk Ice Cream with Olive Oil & Thyme Leaves

I got the recipe for this tasty ice cream from Randal Breski on a recent visit to New York. It's delicious paired with olive oil and lemon thyme or even common thyme.

SERVES 6

2½ cups heavy cream
1 cup granulated sugar
¼ teaspoon salt
3-inch strip of lemon peel
½ vanilla bean, split
8 large organic egg yolks
2½ cups buttermilk
6 to 8 teaspoons lemon or common
thyme leaves
fruity extra virgin olive oil

In a high-sided saucepan combine the cream and ¾ cup of the sugar with the salt, lemon peel, and vanilla bean and steep over low heat until the sugar dissolves.

In the bowl of a standing mixer, beat the egg yolks with the remaining sugar.

Very slowly add the hot cream mixture to the egg mixture, whisking constantly and being careful to not curdle the egg.

Once the two are combined, return the mixture to the saucepan and simmer over low heat until thick.

Strain the mixture and whisk in the buttermilk. Chill completely and then freeze in an ice cream maker according to the manufacturer's directions.

To serve, put some slightly soft ice cream into a wide bowl and spread it around the bowl. Sprinkle with the thyme and drizzle with oil.

Portobello Mushroom & Thyme Leaf Tart

Portobello mushrooms have tons more flavor than little white button mushrooms. A really flavorful tart, one of the few that tastes super warm or cold. Use cream; both the flavor and texture are quite different if you substitute milk. Tiny mushroom quiches may be served straight from the oven as appetizers before dinner or for a cocktail party.

SERVES 8 TO 10

FOR THE RICH SHORTCRUST PASTRY DOUGH
1⅓ cups all-purpose flour
8 tablespoons (1 stick) butter
water to bind or a mixture of water and
    beaten egg

FOR THE FILLING
1 pound Portobello or flat mushrooms
2 tablespoons butter
2 tablespoons olive oil
3 teaspoons thyme leaves
sea salt and freshly ground black pepper
2 cups light cream
6 organic eggs and 2 egg yolks
1 cup freshly grated Parmesan
good pinch of cayenne pepper
purple thyme flowers, to garnish (optional)
salad of organic leaves, to serve

Make the shortcrust pastry dough. Sift the flour into a bowl, cut the butter into cubes, and rub into the flour with your fingertips. Keep everything as cool as possible; if the fat is allowed to melt, the finished dough may be tough. When the mixture looks like coarse bread crumbs, stop. Whisk the egg or egg yolk and add 1 tablespoon of water. Using a fork or knife (whichever you feel most comfortable with), add just enough liquid to bring the dough together and mix. Then discard the fork or knife and collect the dough into a ball with your hands; this way you can judge more accurately if you need a few more drops of liquid. Although rather damp dough is easier to handle and roll out, the resulting crust can be tough and may well shrink out of shape as the water evaporates in the oven. A drier and more difficult-to-handle dough will give a crisper, shorter crust.

Cover the dough tightly with parchment paper and let rest in the fridge for at least 15 minutes. This will make the dough much less elastic and easier to roll.

Preheat the oven to 350°F.

Line a low-sided 10-inch flan ring or tart pan with pop-up base with the dough, cover with parchment paper, fill with baking beans, and bake blind for 25 minutes. The dough should be well cooked.

Meanwhile, chop the mushrooms finely, melt the butter in a frying pan, add the oil, and cook the mushrooms in batches over very high heat. Add the thyme and season with salt and pepper. Cook until all the juice has evaporated and then set aside to cool.

Whisk the cream in a bowl with the eggs and the extra egg yolks, then stir in the mushrooms and the Parmesan. Taste, then add the cayenne and more seasoning if necessary. Fry a spoonful to test the seasoning. Pour into the crust. Bake for about 30 to 40 minutes or until the filling is set and the top delicately brown.

Serve with a salad of organic leaves and garnish with thyme flowers (if available).

DID YOU KNOW?
Thyme has long been associated with courage—parsley for comfort, sage for strength, rosemary for love, and thyme for courage. Ladies gave it to their knights before they went into battle. The Ancient Egyptians used is as an embalming ingredient, the Ancient Greeks burned it as incense to give courage, and in the Middle Ages it was used as an aid to sleep.

GINGER *Zingiber officinale* PERENNIAL, ZONES 9–12

What would we do without ginger? We use it virtually every day in so many ways. It is a tropical plant, thought to have originated in southern Asia, so unless you have a greenhouse, tunnel or warm conservatory, you may need to settle for buying your rhizomes from a local greengrocer. However, do try to source organic ginger because commercial ginger is often treated with anti-sprouting chemicals to discourage it from sprouting. We are not self-sufficient for ginger, but we grow several ginger plants in pots in the greenhouse and conservatory. The plants reach a height of 40 to 50 inches, with beautiful yellow flowers. Ginger is closely related to galangal, turmeric and cardamom.

VARIETIES

There are more than 1,000 species but only one, *Zingiber officinale,* produces the rhizomes that are edible.

HOW TO GROW

Source some organic fresh ginger. Examine them well and choose rhizomes with emerging growth buds or "swollen" eyes. Fill a good-sized pot about 6 inches wide and deep—with rich, well-draining potting compost and vermiculite. Cut the ginger into pieces about 2 inches below the bud.

Plant in spring ¾ to 1 ¼ inches deep, with the bud facing upwards. Water and keep in a warm, sunny spot that gets a little shade in the afternoon. The soil should be kept a little moist but over-watering can rot the roots and will kill the plant. The sprouting times can vary tremendously, but it will certainly take a few weeks to emerge. Cover the pot with a loose plastic bag or place the pot on a propagator at 68°F to speed up the process.

CONTAINER GROWING

We grow some ginger in 18-inch pots in the greenhouse and in the conservatory of the cookery school, in semi-shade, so that the students can see what a ginger plant looks like. It's more a curiosity than a seriously productive plant. During the growing season we feed it every few weeks with a liquid fertilizer. Keep it lightly watered and it also likes

A healthy young ginger emerging—it will need to be transplanted into a larger pot soon.

to be misted with rain water. Keep it warm and fairly dry during the winter months, ideally at not less than 68°F and in full winter sun. This facilitates its normal dormancy process.

PESTS AND DISEASES

We haven't had a problem, but apparently red spider mite can be a problem in older plants. Keep well misted, use biological control or wash the leaves with horticultural soap, diluting to the manufacturer's instructions.

HARVESTING

It is best to allow the ginger to grow for a full season before harvesting. In autumn when the leaves begin to turn yellow, you can harvest some of your home-grown ginger. Shanagarry is not tropical so we don't get a large harvest, but it's fun to grow some of your own ginger and fascinating to see what the plant looks like. It makes a beautiful conservatory plant.

GOOD FOR YOU...

The health benefits of this ancient plant have been recognized for centuries. It is renowned as an anti-inflammatory, has antibiotic properties and is known to be an aid to digestion. It is an excellent source of vitamin C, magnesium and potassium, manganese and copper. It helps to prevent nausea and can relieve

DID YOU KNOW?

Ginger is known to be a very ancient plant and has been prized for its medicinal and culinary attributes in Asian cultures for thousands of years. It was traded with Europe in the first century AD as part of the lucrative spice trade and was greatly appreciated by the Romans. During the Middle Ages, ginger was expensive, one pound of ginger cost the same as the price of a sheep....

morning sickness, and several studies have shown it to be an effective pain reliever.

WHAT TO DO WITH A GLUT

Ginger freezes well for up to six months. Allow it to sprout and start some more plants.

IN THE KITCHEN

Ginger is indispensable for both sweet and savory dishes. So many Indian curries and dahls include a garlic and ginger paste, equal quantities of peeled and pounded or puréed garlic and ginger. Use immediately or spoon into a jar, cover with a layer of olive oil, and use within a day or two. This combination is widely used in Thai cooking as well. We add fresh ginger to cold and hot drinks and, of course, masala chai. It is a staple of Asian cooking, not just Indian food, but also Thai, Malaysian, Indonesian, Vietnamese, Burmese, Chinese, and Japanese.

It's also a popular spice in the Caribbean, where it grows wild in the lush tropical climate, and in the Middle East and in Western cuisine. Cooks and chefs from all over the world embrace fresh and dried ginger to enhance the flavor of their dishes—meat, fish and vegetables, cakes, pies, tarts, ice creams, ginger nuts, and gingerbread, which we are told was the invention of Queen Elizabeth I.

We love crystallized ginger, ginger lemonade, ginger beer, ginger wine, and what would sushi be without pickled ginger? We love to add a little freshly grated ginger to Melted Leeks (page 44), carrots, cabbage, stir-fries, and many other vegetables and salads and also water kefir and kombucha. As a cook, I couldn't imagine life without ginger....

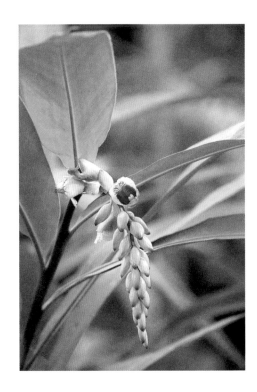

Blossom of the ginger plant.

Pickled Ginger

David Tanis made this fresh pickle to serve with scattered sushi here at the school.

· ·

MAKES 1 OUNCE

1 tablespoon granulated sugar

1 teaspoon salt

3 tablespoons rice vinegar

3-inch piece of fresh ginger, peeled and sliced as thin as possible (see note)

1 slice of red beet (optional, for colour)

Combine the sugar, salt and vinegar in a small jar and stir to dissolve the sugar and salt. Add the ginger and beet (if using). Make sure the ginger is completely submerged. Leave at room temperature for at least 1 hour or up to several hours, before serving. Keep any leftovers in the fridge.

Note: Use a mandolin or a sharp knife to cut the ginger into nearly paper-thin slices. Make slices along the grain, not across it.

Ginger & Saffron Lemonade

A deliciously refreshing ginger lemonade. It is simple to make and the pinch of saffron makes it more exotic.

. . . .

SERVES 10/MAKES 2 QUARTS

FOR THE GINGER SAFFRON SYRUP
1 cup granulated sugar
1 cup cold water
½ cup fresh ginger, peeled and thinly
    sliced
¼ teaspoon saffron

FOR THE LEMONADE
freshly squeezed juice of 4 lemons
5 cups still or sparkling water
ice cubes, to serve

First make the ginger saffron syrup: Put the sugar, water, ginger, and saffron into a saucepan. Bring slowly to a boil, then remove from the heat and set aside to cool. Strain—this should yield 2 cups syrup.

Add the lemon juice to the ginger saffron syrup and top off with the water. Serve with lots of ice.

Chettinad Shrimp Masala

A recipe from The Bangala in Chettinad. Here you have the classic ginger and garlic combination—which I enjoyed at a cooking class, in the courtyard of The Bangala—one of my favorite places to stay in Tamil Nadu.

. . . .

SERVES 4 TO 6

3 tablespoons vegetable oil
1 medium (approx. 3½ ounces) onion,
    finely chopped
½–1 teaspoon ground turmeric
½ teaspoon peeled and crushed ginger
1 teaspoon crushed garlic
2 teaspoons kashimiri mild chili powder
1 cup fresh tomato purée (made from
    peeled and chopped ripe tomatoes)
1 teaspoon sea salt, to taste
1¾ pounds cleaned, peeled and deveined
    shrimp
1 tablespoon cilantro leaves, chopped
paratha bread, to serve

Heat the oil in a large kadhai or wok over a high heat. When hot but not smoking, add the onion and sauté for a minute or two.

Add the turmeric, ginger, garlic and chili powder and cook for about 30 seconds. Pour in the fresh tomato purée, stir and cook. Add the salt and stir continuously until the oil separates around the edge and the mixture looks well cooked.

Add the shrimp carefully and mix until coated with the sauce. Cook gently for 4 to 5 minutes; be careful not to overcook the shrimp.

Transfer to a warm bowl and garnish with cilantro leaves. Serve hot with paratha bread.

WILD, FORAGED & NUTS

WILD GARLIC

Allium ursinum/tricocoum PERENNIAL, ZONES 4–9

We get super excited in early spring every year when we find the first little leaves of wild garlic popping up in the wood. For the next almost two months, wild garlic peppers much of what we eat in many different ways.

Wild garlic has been eaten since Mesolithic times, as is evident from an ancient settlement at Barkaer in Denmark. There are two plants that we refer to as wild garlic: *Allium ursinum* and *Allium triquetrum*. In the US, the native variety is *Allium tricoccum*, commonly known as ramps.

VARIETIES

Allium ursinum, Allium tricoccum, and *Allium triquetrum* are both perennial but they grow in quite different habitats.

Allium ursinum grows all over Ireland and is widespread in Europe and parts of the US. It grows in shady places, under the trees in deciduous woodlands,

perfuming the air with a distinct whiff of garlic. The leaves first emerge in early spring and the white, star-like flowers bloom several weeks later.

The tender spear-shaped leaves look remarkably like those of Lily-of-the-Valley—which is toxic, so be careful. If in doubt, rub the leaf between your fingers, it will release a distinctly garlic aroma. All parts are edible—the bulky stalk, leaves and flowers. It is also called devil's garlic, stinking jenny, ramsons, bear garlic, wood garlic, broad-leaved garlic, buckrams and bear leek.

In the US, where the entire plant is harvested and widely available early in the year in farmers' markets, there is concern that it will become extinct. However, in these islands it is more usual to harvest just the leaves and flowers. Cattle also relish the leaves, which flavor their milk with a distinct, not particularly appealing, garlic flavor, which was a seasonal speciality in nineteenth-century Switzerland. As children we hated it when the cows got into the wild garlic, though, because the milk would be, in our view, tainted for several days. Wild boar love it, too.

Allium triquetrum, which we also confusingly refer to as wild garlic, looks more like white bluebells and grows in quite a different habitat. It flourishes along roadside verges and river banks, particularly in coastal areas. *Triquetrum* refers to the three-cornered flower stalk, which is why it is also known as three-cornered leek, as well as onion weed. It too has pretty white flowers, similar in shape to bluebells, hence the common name white bells.

Allium ursinum, *unlike* Allium tricoccum *(ramps), has showy blooms that occur while the plant still has its leaves.*

All parts of the plant are edible—bulb, stalk, leaves and flowers—but we seem to use the flowers more than the leaves.

HOW TO GROW

Wild garlic is really worth growing if you don't have a patch in a wood close by. It's fun to forage for but it's also great to be able to just pop out to the garden to pick a few leaves to perk up a sandwich.

If you want to grow it at home, dig up a plant from a large clump in the wild, in an area where there's an abundance. Plant it in semi-shade, preferably under a deciduous tree. If it likes the spot, it will romp away, so plant it where you won't mind it spreading.

Allium ursinum has a beautiful pompom flower on a long triangular stem, with white star-like flowers that appear in late spring. These blooms last for 3 to 4 weeks before turning into knobbly green seed heads, which we also love to eat fresh or pickle. Once again, the bulbs transplant easily, so find a suitable spot on your property. This also spreads, which may or may not be a bonus.

GOOD FOR YOU...

Wild garlic has antibacterial, antibiotic and antiseptic properties. All garlic has the attribute of reducing blood pressure and as a result lessening the risk of

DID YOU KNOW?

Brown bears were known to have a taste for the bulbs and dig the ground for them, which gave wild garlic the Latin name of *Allium ursinum*, from *ursinus*, meaning "bear."

heart disease and stroke, but it is wild garlic that is reputed to have the biggest influence on blood pressure.

Wild garlic has high levels of folic acid, an essential B vitamin, and it also aids the digestion. It is a prebiotic so it is good for those who may recently have been on antibiotics because it helps restore the gut bacteria that antibiotics often decimate. Its mild antibacterial properties help ward off those end-of-winter colds.

WHAT TO DO WITH A GLUT

We use wild garlic every single day during its short season, in salads, wild garlic pesto, wild garlic mayo and wild garlic butter.

IN THE KITCHEN

Once the leaves of wild garlic, *Allium ursinum*, appear, we use them on a daily basis in soups, salad, pasta, wilted greens, and risotto. Julija goes into overdrive making wild garlic pesto, which our

students and hotel guests love. Customers in our farm shop and farmers' market stall put their names on a waiting list for the new season's pesto, which we can only make for 4 to 5 weeks in the spring.

The flavor of the leaves is best for the first few weeks then becomes less appealing as it gets stronger towards the end of the season.

The star-like white flowers of *Allium ursinum* and the bell-like flowers of *Allium triquetrum* are delicious and adorable sprinkled into the green salads or used as a garnish.

We make wild garlic butter to serve with lamb and pan-grilled fish, and we also wrap little fresh cheeses in the leaves.

The flat leaves of *Allium triquetrum* resemble garlic chives and can be used in the same way, snipped into a salad, pasta and rice dishes and, of course, stews and casseroles.

Just before eating toss the leaves in enough dressing to make the leaves

Allium triquetrum—a three-cornered lily which grows along the roadside verges in spring.

glisten—enjoy immediately before the leaves begin to wilt.

Spaghetti with Wild Garlic Pesto

Classic pesto is the wonderfully fragrant basil sauce of Genoa and Liguria, but we make many variations on the theme, all of which are irresistible with pasta. Here we use wild garlic, which we pick in early spring when the leaves are still young and tender. This cooking method is what we refer to as cheat's pasta, but it works brilliantly and rarely overcooks.

. . . .

SERVES 4 TO 6

1 generous tablespoon salt
1 pound spaghetti
approx. 2 heaped tablespoons Wild Garlic Pesto (page 542)
freshly grated Parmesan
wild garlic flowers (optional)

Bring 5 quarts water to a full rolling boil in a deep saucepan. Add the salt and the spaghetti and stir well. Return to the boil for just 2 minutes. Cover the saucepan with a tight-fitting lid, turn off the heat and allow the pasta to sit in the water for 10 minutes, by which time it should be al dente.

Drain the spaghetti immediately. Mix 2 tablespoons of the pasta cooking water with the pesto, toss with the spaghetti, sprinkle with lots of freshly grated Parmesan and wild garlic flowers, if available, and serve immediately.

Summer Minestrone Soup with Wild Garlic Pesto

We make huge pots of this soup, and I usually keep some in the freezer. Kielbasa is a Polish pork sausage which is now widely available; it gives a gutsy, slightly smoky flavor to the soup which, although satisfying, is by no means essential.

. . . .

SERVES 8 TO 9

8 ounces bacon, cut into ¼-inch lardons
2 tablespoons olive oil
½ pound onions, chopped
3 to 4 carrots, cut into ¼-inch dice
5 ribs celery, chopped into ¼-inch dice
2 parsnips, chopped into ¼-inch dice
white part of 1 leek, cut into approx.
   ¼-inch slices
1 kielbasa sausage or chorizo, cut into
   ¼-inch thin slices or dice
1 14-ounce can tomatoes
½ pound navy beans, cooked
7 cups homemade chicken stock
2 tablespoons chopped fresh parsley,
   to garnish
extra virgin olive oil, to drizzle (optional)
crusty bread, to serve
salt, freshly ground black pepper, and
   sugar, to taste

FOR THE WILD GARLIC PESTO

3 cups wild garlic or ramp leaves,
   de-stalked
¼ cup pine nuts or cashew nuts,
   finely chopped
1 garlic clove, crushed
¾ to 1 cup olive oil
½ cup freshly grated Parmesan

To make the wild garlic pesto, whizz the wild garlic, pine or cashew nuts, garlic, and olive oil in a food processor or pound with a mortar and pestle. Remove to a bowl and fold in the Parmesan cheese. Season to taste. Store in a sterilized jar in the fridge.

Blanch the chunky bacon lardons, rinse, and dry well. Put the olive oil in a saucepan, add the bacon and sauté over a medium heat until it becomes crisp and golden, then add the chopped onions, carrots, and celery. Cover and sweat for 5 minutes, then add the parsnips and finely sliced leeks. Cover and sweat for 5 minutes more. Add the Kabanossi sausage or chorizo. Chop the canned tomatoes and add to the rest of the vegetables with the beans. Season with salt, freshly ground pepper, and sugar, then add the chicken stock. Cook for about 20 minutes until all the vegetables are tender. Season to taste. Sprinkle with chopped parsley and drizzle with the wild garlic pesto or extra virgin olive oil. Serve with lots of crusty bread.

BITTER CRESS

Cardamine hirsuta HARDY PERENNIAL, ZONES 3–8

Did you know that this hardy weed is also referred to as hairy cress, land cress, hairy bitter cress, and lamb's cress? I bet it grows somewhere close to you—perhaps in your gravel paths or between paving stones or flower beds. It also grows on bare stone walls. We love this perky little plant and value it all the more because it's at its best in late autumn, winter and early spring when there are fewer good things to forage in the wild. It is unaffected by frost and will even survive and remain green under a shower of snow. It self-seeds all over the place, but look on that as a bonus rather than a nuisance—just eat your weeds.

WHERE/HOW IT GROWS

Winter cress grows in little rosettes or clusters and has a slightly mustardy flavor. The leaves are similar in composition to watercress or land cress, although much smaller. The top leaf, or lobe, is the largest and the leaves get smaller as they go down along the stem. The leaf stalks can grow to 4 inches long.

HARVESTING

We harvest the entire plant by pulling it out of the ground—roots and all—or we just snip off individual sprigs. Try to pick it before it flowers; like many plants, the flavor gets bitter as it runs to seed. The white flowers are also edible. American winter cress has yellow flowers.

DID YOU KNOW?
The Cherokee Indians used a tea brewed from the aerial parts (the parts exposed to the air) to purify the blood.

GOOD FOR YOU...

Like all members of mustard family, winter cress is loaded with nutrients and is rich in vitamins C, A and B—it was, in fact, one of the plants eaten to prevent scurvy when vitamin C was not readily available. The leaves are also a good source of calcium, potassium and fibre. In traditional herbal medicine it was used as a diuretic or expectorant.

Bitter cress grows in a rosette with white flowers, as with all cresses the top leaf is the largest.

IN THE KITCHEN

We love its peppery flavor in salads and starters and use it lavishly as a delicate garnish on winter starter plates. The flavor of bitter cress is often compared to arugula, so it can be used in a similar way; a little salad of quail eggs, tiny beets and bitter cress is delicious. Add it to frittatas and sandwiches as you would cress, sprinkle it over a forager's pizza, and it's also great to decorate deviled eggs. One can cook with winter cress, just adapt watercress recipes while the leaves are young and tender.

Forager's Salad

We use a mixture of foraged leaves for this salad. You are unlikely to have all of these so just add what you can find to a bowl of lettuces and salad leaves. In early spring we add some young beech and ground elder leaves. For maximum flavor, pick leaves when young; here the winter cress is past its best.

· ·

a selection of wild leaves such as:
dandelion
ground elder
wild garlic
wild watercress
land cress
bittercress
chickweed
wild sorrel, sheep's tongue or buckler leaf
navelwort
purslane
salad burnet
sweet cicely
lemon balm
lots of wild flowers, such as primroses

FOR THE DRESSING
3 tablespoons cold-pressed organic
  canola oil
1 tablespoon apple balsamic vinegar
pinch of salt and freshly ground black
  pepper

Allow a handful of wild leaves per person. Wash them carefully in cold water and dry them in a salad spinner. Keep chilled until ready to use.

To make the dressing, whisk the oil, vinegar, and salt to mix. Season to taste.

Toss the dried leaves in just enough of the dressing to make them glisten. Taste a leaf to check that the seasoning is correct. Serve immediately.

HAZELNUTS, COBNUTS, FILBERTS
LARGE FILBERTS

Corylus avellana, *Corylus maxima,* ZONES 3–9

The wild hazelnut has a long history in Ireland and their remains have been found in ancient cooking sites dating back to Neolithic times. The highly nutritious nuts have been a food source since we were hunter-gatherers and they still grow naturally on hillsides and in hedgerows all over the country. The hazel was known as the tree of knowledge in ancient Irish folklore and we are told the salmon of knowledge gained its wisdom by eating nine hazelnuts....

Collecting hazelnuts in autumn has been a favorite part of my foraging since I was old enough to toddle up Cullahill Mountain in Co Laois, in the Irish midlands (although mountain is rather a grand name for the hill). It's been covered with wild hazels as long as anyone can remember, and they could well be over a century old. Hazelnuts can be very long-lived.

Cobnuts (*Corylus avellana*) and filberts (*Corylus maxima*) are cultivated forms of the hazelnut. They have been grown since the sixteenth century, but the Kentish cobnut was introduced in the 1830s.

If you have the space, consider growing a nut garden. We inherited five old trees—a combination of hazelnuts, cobnuts and filberts. Each is a different size and shape and it's difficult to ascertain the exact variety of each apart from the cobnuts, which are relatively easy to recognise because the individual oval-shaped nuts are enclosed by a fibrous husk (involucre).

HOW TO GROW

Historically hazels are grown in coppices, but if they are planted further apart they will be more productive.

Hazelnuts, cobnuts or filberts can also be planted in a mixed hedge, but are usually not quite as productive grown this way. Plant them 60 to 80 inches apart or 10 to 16 feet apart when they are standing alone.

All nuts do best in well-drained fertile soil; they need a sheltered situation and a sunny location to produce well. Plant bare-rooted trees 10 to 16 feet apart between early winter and spring.

Cobnuts are not self-fertile so you will need to plant a pollinator from another variety of wild native hazel. For best

results plant 3 to 4 different cultivars in the same area. They will take 2 to 3 years to produce a crop.

As they get older, cut off any suckers that grow from the base, otherwise the trees will put all their energy into producing twigs and leaves rather than nuts.

HARVESTING

The nuts are encased in pale green shells which turn brown and become loose in the outer husks and eventually fall out onto the ground. The nuts of the wild hazelnut grow in clusters, while cobnuts and filberts grow singly.

They can be harvested from the tree or from the ground. Wear soft-soled shoes so you can feel the nuts that are obscured by grass. Resist the temptation to crack them with your teeth, use a nutcracker instead....

GOOD FOR YOU...

Hazelnuts, cobnuts and filberts are powerhouses of nutrition. They contain antioxidant properties and are particularly high in dietary fibre, protein and vitamin C and rich in mono-unsaturated fatty acids. As with olive oil, they contain oleic acid and are packed with B-complex vitamins such as riboflavin, niacin and thiamine. They are also an excellent source of iron, calcium, magnesium and potassium. Even though they are relatively high in fat, they contain no cholesterol.

WHAT TO DO WITH A GLUT

Store them in their shells in a cool dry place—I keep them in baskets

Unripe hazelnuts—the shells will gradually harden and change color as they ripen.

in my pantry. They keep for months, but will shrivel up somewhat in the shells, although they are still delicious. Alternatively, shell and freeze.

IN THE KITCHEN

Apart from nibbling a few every now and then for their abundant nutrients, we use them in both sweet and savory dishes.

Toss shelled hazelnuts or filberts into muesli and granola for breakfast or sprinkle toasted hazelnuts over thick unctuous yogurt and labneh and drizzle with honey. Add to salads, cakes, pastries, and biscuits. Make them into hazelnut praline or add to chocolate truffles. Decorate a coffee cake. Whizz them into a hazelnut butter. Roast, peel, and whizz with melted chocolate to make a chocolate and hazelnut spread—infinitely more delicious than anything you can buy. Fold into meringues... I love to serve new season's hazelnuts still in their husks with a cheese board, so family and friends can have the extra enjoyment of cracking the nuts.

To skin hazelnuts, preheat the oven to 350°F. Spread out the hazelnuts on a baking tray and roast for 10 to 15 minutes or until the skins start to loosen. Remove from the oven, rub off the skins in a tea towel, discard the "chaff," cool, and use as desired. Store in a glass jar with a sealed lid; they will keep 4 to 6 months but are most delicious when fresh.

Filberts (left) are longer and more tapered than hazelnuts (right) and fully enclosed by the husk.

DID YOU KNOW?

Hazel rods were considered to be a protection against evil spirits, and forked hazel twigs were, and still are, used by water diviners. A forked hazel twig is cut from a hazel tree and it is truly astonishing to see how the twig quivers in the water diviner's hand when there is water below the surface of the earth. The twig genuinely appears to have a life of its own. Some people have the gift, others do not, there doesn't seem to be a logical explanation.

Oatmeal & Apple Muesli with Hazelnuts

The best breakfast ever—made in minutes, super nourishing, and with a low GI index. In autumn a few blackberries are delicious added to the muesli.

SERVES 1 TO 2

3 heaped tablespoons rolled oats
1 to 2 dessert apples, such as Golden
    Delicious or McIntosh
approx. 1 teaspoon pure honey
2 tablespoons sliced hazelnuts
light cream and soft brown sugar, to serve

Soak the oatmeal in 6 tablespoons of water for 5 to 10 minutes. Meanwhile, grate the unpeeled apple on the coarse part of a grater (pick out the seeds if necessary.) Mix with the oatmeal. Sweeten to taste with honey—a scant teaspoon is usually enough but it depends on how sweet the apples are.

Add the hazelnuts and serve with light cream and a little soft brown sugar.

Chocolate & Hazelnut Squares

Super, simple, and delicious—easy to make. The hazelnuts and chocolate icing are an irresistible combination.

MAKES 24 TO 48, DEPENDING ON SIZE

12 tablespoons (1½ sticks) soft butter, plus extra for greasing

½ cup superfine sugar

2 organic eggs

½ cup self-rising flour

3 tablespoons cocoa powder

1 tablespoon milk

1 cup hazelnuts or pistachios, toasted and chopped or whole hazelnuts

dried rose petals, to decorate (optional)

FOR THE CHOCOLATE ICING

1¼ cups icing sugar

7 tablespoons butter

5 tablespoons cocoa powder

1 tablespoon milk

Preheat the oven to 350°F. Grease and line a jelly roll or sheet pan with parchment.

Put the butter, superfine sugar, eggs, self-rising flour, cocoa, and milk into a food processor. Whizz for a few seconds to amalgamate, then spread evenly on the pan. Bake for 20 to 25 minutes or until golden brown and well risen. Allow to cool then remove from the tin.

Meanwhile, mix all the ingredients for the icing. As soon as the cake has cooled, spread a thin layer of icing over the top and cut into squares. Pipe a swirl of chocolate icing in the center of each square if you wish, then sprinkle with toasted chopped hazelnuts or chopped pistachios or dried rose petals, if using. Alternatively, pop a whole toasted hazelnut in the center of each square for extra crunch and deliciousness.

Roast Parsnip, Apple & Toasted Hazelnut Salad

This recipe brings parsnips to a new level. Roasted hazelnuts add a delicious crunch, but walnuts or pecans are also good.

SERVES 8

2 large or 4 medium-sized parsnips

4 tablespoons extra virgin olive oil

4 apples, cut into eighths, cores removed

6 to 8 handfuls of watercress, arugula, or salad leaves

½ cup lightly toasted hazelnuts

crusty bread, to serve

sea salt and freshly ground black pepper

FOR THE DRESSING

1 garlic clove, crushed with a little salt

1 teaspoon English mustard

2 teaspoons honey

1 tablespoon lemon juice

4 tablespoons extra virgin olive oil

Preheat the oven to 400°F.

Peel and quarter the parsnips, remove and discard the woody cores if necessary, then chop the parsnips into roughly 1½-inch pieces. Put the parsnips on a large roasting tray in a single layer. Season with salt and freshly ground black pepper, drizzle with olive oil and toss to coat them. Roast for 10 minutes, remove from the oven and add the apple pieces and return to the oven for about 15 minutes or until everything is tender and golden.

Meanwhile, make the dressing by whisking all the ingredients together.

When the parsnip and apple pieces are fully cooked, transfer them to a salad bowl and toss them in the dressing. Season to taste.

Arrange the watercress, arugula, or a bed of salad leaves on a plate, top with the warm dressed parsnip and apple. Scatter with toasted hazelnuts and serve with crusty bread.

HAWTHORN

Crataegus monogyna, ZONES 7–10

The fruit of the hawthorn are known as haws.

This species is part of the huge Rosacea family of shrubs and small trees, often with thorny branches and small, mealy, berry-like fruit. This plant is known by many names: May bush, May blossom, whitethorn, bread and butter, haw bush and also quickthorn, because it grows rapidly. Hawthorn makes a brilliant impenetrable hedge should you need one... and lives for 100 to 200 years.

There is much folklore associated with the hawthorn. Old people believed that an abundant crop of haws heralded a hard winter, because nature was providing for the birds and wildlife. Blackbirds and mistle thrushes are particularly fond of the berries. When I was a child, an oft-repeated saying warned: "Ne'er cast a clout till May is out," which meant that we couldn't exchange our heavy winter clothes for summer dresses until the end of May.

The Maypole around which people danced was frequently made of hawthorn. Ancient Greeks carried it in wedding processions, and the superstition that it was the source of Jesus' crown of thorns provoked unease. Another account claims that St Joseph of Arimathea carried a hawthorn staff, and it's still a custom to send a sprig of Glastonbury thorn to the sovereign to decorate the Christmas table. Hawthorn or May bushes, particularly those near holy wells, are still decorated in many rural areas; people tie little bits of rag or ribbon to the branches to make a wish or ask for a cure.

WHERE/HOW IT GROWS

This small deciduous tree, 16 to 46 feet tall, is a common feature of the Irish countryside, being native to temperate regions of the northern hemisphere in Europe, Asia and North America.

It grows happily in hedgerows and is particularly associated with raths and fairy ring forts (see below).

HARVESTING

The hermaphrodite flowers cover the bush in late spring, when you should also harvest the young leaves. The flowers turn into hawberries in late autumn.

GOOD FOR YOU...

Hawthorn has had numerous medicinal uses through the ages. It is used in both Chinese and Japanese traditional medicine as an aid to digestion and as a heart tonic, and several studies suggest that it strengthens the cardiovascular system.

IN THE KITCHEN

We add the tender young leaves to salads in early spring to "improve the heart." Later in the season we use the fluffy white blossoms in a green salad.

Tiny, oval, dark red haw berries have a mealy texture and flavor reminiscent of over-ripe apples. They are "hard work" because there's very little to nibble from around the large stone in the center. We use them in jams and hedgerow, haw, and apple jelly as well as in haw syrup.

Haws are widely used in Chinese cooking to make a variety of snacks, jams, jellies, juices, and liqueurs. In Korea, a liqueur called Sansachun is made from the fruits. In Mexico haws are also used to make a Christmas punch and candies.

> ### DID YOU KNOW?
> *Sceac* is the Gaelic and colloquial name for hawthorn, which is intrinsically linked with superstitions in Ireland, both in folk memory and up to present times—as children we always believed fairies could be seen amongst hawthorn bushes. It is considered to be unlucky to cut down a hawthorn bush and many instances of ill fortune have been attributed to uprooting a tree or bulldozing a path where hawthorn regularly grows.
>
> *Beware, beware the hawthorn*
> *Lest it strike you down*
> *For if you take an axe to it*
> *You'll rue that you were born.*
> ("Hawthorn", Giles Watson, 2005)

Homemade Haw Brandy

Easy-peasy to make, this really impresses the pals! A very simple infusion. You can also experiment with other kinds of fruit using this basic technique. Vodka or gin work, too. I'm just tasting my last year's batch and it's smashing.

. . . .

MAKES APPROX. 3 CUPS

1 pound haws
½ cup granulated sugar
1¼ cups brandy

Wash the haws, or freeze them, then fill a 1-quart canning jar almost to the top with the haws. Add the sugar. Fill to the top with the brandy. Seal well and store in a cool, dark place for 3 to 4 months or longer if you have the patience. Shake it every now and then. Drink in small glasses.

Haw Gin

Enjoy it neat or put a measure of Haw gin in a glass with ice and a slice of lemon and top up with tonic. We also make haw vinegars using the infusion method with considerable success.

. . . .

MAKES APPROX. 3 CUPS

¾ pound haws
¾ to 1 cup granulated sugar
2½ cups gin

Wash and dry the haws and prick them in several places (we use a sterilized darning needle). Put the fruit into a sterilized 1-quart canning jar and cover with the sugar and gin. Seal tightly.

Shake the jar every couple of days to start with and then every now and then for 3 to 4 months, by which time it will be ready to strain and bottle. It will improve with age, so try to resist drinking it for another few months.

WALNUT

Juglans from the *Juglandaceae family,* DECIDUOUS ZONES 4–9

If you have the space, plant a walnut—it's a beautiful tree. I'm so glad that despite my misgivings at the thought of not having walnuts for ten or more years, a friend persuaded me to plant a walnut about twenty years ago. *Juglans regia*, the species I planted, loves the sheltered, moist, well-drained spot in the Pleasure Garden, and to my amazement produced a few nuts after about seven or eight years. Since then the harvest has been a bit random, but it produced abundant crops every couple of years—a feast or a famine! The students are intrigued to see them, as many have never seen walnuts growing before.

Of course, you can buy walnuts in their shells, but having said that they are only deliciously fresh and sweet for a couple of months in the year, from mid- to late autumn. The shelled walnuts you can buy in packages are often semi-rancid, but I find the organic ones are good, if triple the price. If you have your own raw walnuts, they will be organic and not irradiated or pasteurized as many of the walnuts on sale now are.

SPECIES AND VARIETIES

Choose the variety carefully because it takes about a decade or more for the tree to fruit, so you don't want to be disappointed when at last you have your long-awaited walnuts.

Juglans regia—The common (also called English) walnut, often thought to have a flavor superior to that of Juglans nigra.
Juglans nigra—Black walnut, this is a North American native. It is cold-hardy but needs hot summers to ripen the nuts properly.
Cascade—An English walnut with thin shells and plump, flavorful kernals.
Timber—A black walnut that grows very fast, producing thick-shelled small nuts.

HOW TO GROW

A walnut tree is easy to grow, but you do need space because most grow up to 20 feet tall in a decade, and can reach 130 feet high. They are very long-lived and can survive for a century or more. Choose a late-flowering variety best suited to the climate zone where you live (we are zone 8 to 10), choose a sheltered spot not prone to late frost with well-drained, moist, fertile soil. Walnut trees can be started in pots and transplanted while small into their chosen site.

Prune between midsummer and early autumn—don't leave it too late into winter as the cuts are prone to bleeding. Walnuts don't like hard pruning but it's

A cluster of unripe walnuts—the shell is hidden inside.

a good idea to remove dead or crossed branches. If you want to restrict the height of the tree, cut back the leader shoot, as this will encourage growth of side shoots.

HARVESTING

Pick some young walnuts for pickling in early summer—the skin will be soft and green. Pick the low-growing fruit first, as this will improve the rest of the crop.

In early autumn, you will notice some of the green husks starting to blacken and burst to reveal the walnuts' hard shells. Lay a blanket or tarpaulin under the tree and shake the branches. Remove the green husks as soon as possible to stop any fungal disease.

To store: lay the de-husked and washed walnuts in a single layer; I use flat baskets and leave them to dry for 3 to 4 days close to the Aga in my kitchen, then store them in a warm, dry place. They keep for a month.

PESTS AND DISEASES

Walnuts can be susceptible to some leaf blight and leaf hoppers but it's rarely a problem with individual trees.

GOOD FOR YOU...

Walnuts contain lots of vitamins C and E, folate and melatonin. A study by the American Chemical Society has shown that walnuts have a combination of more healthy antioxidants and higher-quality antioxidants than any other nut.

DID YOU KNOW?

Walnut blossom blooms late, which helps sustain the pollinating insects and bees for a longer time.

The fact that walnuts are not usually roasted before eating also increases their benefits, as roasting can reduce the quality of the antioxidants. Research has shown that eating walnuts 2 to 3 times a week can reduce the risk of developing type 2 diabetes. They are also known to improve brain function—have you noticed the shape resembles the brain?

IN THE KITCHEN

If you grow your own walnuts you will have the pleasure of making pickled walnuts from the young green nuts in early summer, an acquired but soon addictive taste. You will also be able to enjoy wet walnuts straight from the tree in mid-autumn, when the flavor is richer and more intense and the texture creamier. Peel off the thick green skin as soon as it begins to burst, insert the tip of a knife into the skin, twist and winkle out the nuts from each shell. You may want to peel the slightly bitter skin from the creamy walnut.

Caramelized marzipan walnuts make a gorgeous crunchy sweetmeat to nibble with a cup of coffee at the end of a meal. To make 20, sandwich 40 walnut halves together with about ¼ pound marzipan. Make a caramel with 1 cup granulated sugar and ½ cup water and coat the walnuts in the caramel. Leave to harden on an greased sheet pan, in a dry place. Serve in petits fours cases. Eat within a couple of hours otherwise they become tacky.

Walnuts bursting their outer casings to reveal the shell inside.

Penne with Beets, Goat Cheese & Walnuts

A rustic pasta dish that uses both the stalks and leaves of the beets as well as the roots. If you don't have fresh beet greens and stalks use ¾ pound Swiss chard or spinach stalks instead. The walnuts and melting goat cheese add a luxurious dimension to the finished dish.

SERVES 6

½ pound penne

¼ cup olive oil

2 garlic cloves, thinly sliced

¼ to ½ teaspoon crushed red pepper flakes

4 cooked beets, diced into ¼-inch dice, leaves and stalks cut into ½-inch pieces

1 tablespoon chopped fresh tarragon

½ cup cream or crème fraîche

pinch of sugar (optional)

4 ounces goat cheese

¼ cup walnuts, coarsely chopped and 1 tablespoon snipped flat-leaf parsley, to serve

sea salt and freshly ground black pepper

Bring 4 quarts water to a boil in a large saucepan, add 2 tablespoons salt and the penne, stir, and return to a boil for 4 minutes. Remove from the heat, cover the saucepan tightly and let sit for 8 to 10 minutes, until al dente.

Heat the oil in a skillet. Add the garlic and red pepper flakes, stir for a few seconds then toss in the beet stalks. Cook for 2 to 3 minutes, add the diced beets and leaves, stir, and cook for a couple of minutes until the leaves are wilted.

Drain the pasta well. Add to the skillet with the tarragon and cream or crème fraîche. Season with lots of salt and pepper. Taste, I sometimes add a pinch of sugar depending on the sweetness of the beets.

Transfer into a hot bowl. Add a few blobs of goat cheese. Sprinkle with chopped walnuts and lots of flat-leaf parsley to serve.

Caramel & Walnut Tart

A rich, irresistible tart. As ever, the quality and freshness of the walnuts really matter here. If you don't have enough of your own, seek out whole walnuts or shelled biodynamic walnuts, which seem to be the best quality among bought nuts.

. . . .

SERVES 8

FOR THE PASTRY

1 cup all-purpose flour, chilled, plus extra
   for dusting
5 tablespoons cold butter
2 tablespoons superfine sugar
1 organic egg, beaten

FOR THE FILLING

6 tablespoons superfine sugar
2 tablespoons butter
⅔ cup double cream
2 cups shelled walnuts

First make the pastry. Put the chilled flour into a bowl. Cut the butter into cubes, toss in the flour and rub in with your fingers until it resembles coarse breadcrumbs, then add the superfine sugar. Mix the beaten egg into the pastry, using just enough of it to bring it together as a dough. Wrap the ball of dough in parchment and chill in the fridge for 1 hour.

Preheat the oven to 350°F.

Roll out the pastry on a work surface dusted with flour, then use it to line a 9-inch tart pan with a removable base. Prick the pastry base gently with a fork, line it with parchment or silicone, fill with pie weights or dried beans and bake for 20 minutes. Reduce the temperature to 325°F. Remove the weights and parchment and return the pastry shell to the oven, then bake for 15 minutes more or until fully cooked.

Meanwhile, make the filling. Put the sugar in a heavy-bottomed saucepan, stir until it has dissolved and continue to cook until it reaches a rich caramel. Remove from the heat and cool for 5 minutes. Add the butter and cream, then return to the heat and stir until smooth—it becomes well blended and thick.

Spread the walnuts in an even layer in the cooked pastry shell. Pour the caramel over the nuts and leave to set for at least 1 hour in a cool place before serving.

Nocino—Walnut Liqueur

Nocino is made from green walnuts. Traditionally in Italy the walnuts are harvested on St John's Night—June 24—while the husks are still green. Superstition has it that the walnuts should be picked in odd numbers by a woman expert at the job. The walnuts should then be left on the grass overnight to absorb the dew of this very auspicious night. Experiment with spices—maybe a little ginger or star anise. I love to drink it chilled, as an aperitif, but it's also delicious drizzled over ice cream or panna cotta.

. . . .

MAKES 1 QUART

30 green walnuts
2 cups granulated sugar
½ vanilla bean
1 Sri Lankan cinnamon stick
5 cloves
zest of 1 organic orange, thinly shaved
1 quart vodka

Wash, dry, and quarter the walnuts. Put them into a large ceramic or glass jar. Add the sugar, vanilla bean, cinnamon, cloves, and thinly shaved orange zest.

Pour the vodka over the walnuts—it must cover them—then stir to start dissolving the sugar. Shake, cover, and leave to infuse for 6 to 8 weeks.

Strain through a fine sieve and pour the liquid into sterilized bottles and seal with stoppers or screw tops.

Store in a cool, dry place.

CRAB APPLES *Malus sylvestris* DECIDUOUS, ZONES 3–9

Red Sentinel—a splendid crab apple tree for any garden.

Crab apples are wild apple trees; the fruit varies in size but are usually small and tart. I long to go to Kazakhstan, generally considered to be the birthplace of the wild apple and where orchards with these trees still grow on the slopes of the Tien Shan mountain range which borders China and Kazakhstan. Malus sieversii is considered to be the most likely ancestor of our cultivated apple; hundreds of varieties are now endangered by over-grazing of livestock and housing development.

Apart from enjoying them as a decorative feature in the fruit garden, we use clusters of the berries for Christmas garlands and wreaths. We also use the prunings of both crab apples and apple wood to smoke foods; its slow-burning wood doesn't produce much flame but imparts a delicious flavor to the smoked foods.

VARIETIES

Lots of "cultivated" crab apples are available, including:

Golden Hornet—White flowers flushed with pink, lots of deep yellow fruit that rot faster than Red Sentinel.

Whitney—large harvest of red, goldball sized apples

Chestnut—produces small, pale yellow fruit with red blush. A good pollinator ofr other apples.

Dolgo—this beautiful tree sports bright red elongated and delcious fruit.

WHERE/HOW IT GROWS

Crab apple trees grow in hedgerows and ditches all around the British Isles and in many parts of Europe and America. We've got several wild crab apple trees in the hedges around the farm (they grow well on chalky soil and burst into white blossom in the spring), but we also planted two new hybrid varieties, "Red Sentinel" and "Golden Hornet," which are decorative as well as useful. The latter produces an abundance of small, yellow fruit about the size of a little walnut, which last for 2 to 3 weeks. The fruit of "Red Sentinel," however, will remain on the tree all through the late autumn and winter until the new leaves appear in early spring. They flower early and are a valuable attraction for pollinating insects and butterflies

If you're not sure if there's a crab apple tree in your area, watch out for the white blossom in the hedgerows early in the year so you can make a note of where to harvest the fruit in autumn.

HARVESTING

Crab apples or wild apples are in season in autumn and may be picked off the tree, but many grow quite high so they can be difficult to reach. However, the windfalls that lie on the ground are also worth collecting. Once the bruised bits are cut out and thrown into the compost bin, the remaining skin, seeds, and stalks are fine for making jellies.

GOOD FOR YOU...

Crab apples are rich in vitamin A, which is very beneficial as it contributes to good eye health and fights signs of ageing. They also contain vitamin C and iron. I haven't tried it but I've heard that unripe crab apples are good to help heal wounds—just put the cut apple on the wound and it helps it to close and heal. Ripe crab apples are also said to aid digestion and help prevent piles and diarrhoea.

WHAT TO DO WITH A GLUT

Use them to make Crab Apple Jelly or pickle them to serve with cheese or ham.

IN THE KITCHEN

We collect baskets of crab apples from a variety of trees with our autumn cookery students and foragers. The fruit from each tree tastes different, so we mix them randomly in jams and jellies. The flavor is greatly enhanced by roasting the fruits before puréeing.

Crab apples can be higher in pectin than many domestic apple varieties, so they are a huge asset when making autumn jams and jellies.

The individual berries make a delicious pickle to serve with glazed ham and other cold meats.

Some cider makers add a small percentage of crab apples to their brew to enhance the flavor.

Pickled Crab Apples

We use the ornamental crab apple "Red Sentinel" to make this delicious and pretty pickle. We love to serve it with a glazed ham or some cold pork or bacon.

. . . .

MAKES 10 PINT JARS

15 cloves

15 allspice berries

2 star anise pods

1-inch stick of cinnamon

5 cups apple cider or white wine vinegar

1 pound granulated sugar

3 to 4 pounds small crab apples

Tie the spices in a little cheesecloth bag. Put them into a stainless-steel saucepan with the vinegar and sugar and bring to a boil, stirring until the sugar dissolves.

Wash the crab apples and trim their stalks to 2 inches. Put them into a perforated wire basket (like a frying basket) and carefully lower them into the boiling vinegar. Leave for 5 minutes and remove before the skins start to crack. Put the apples into sterilized bottling or jam jars.

Meanwhile, boil down the vinegar and sugar until very syrupy, then cover the apples with it and close the lids immediately. Leave for months before using. In time the apples will leach their red color into the liquid, which makes a pretty pickle. Serve with pork or ham.

DID YOU KNOW?

Wild apple trees have several names, including silver bough, scribe tree, and wood apple.

WOOD SORREL *Oxalis* PERENNIAL, ZONES 6–9

Wood sorrel is part of a huge family of approximately 900 known species but it is super easy to recognize. The leaves look like those of a shamrock—hence the Irish name *Shamróg*—and it is widely believed that it may well have been this plant, with its distinctive clover-like leaf, that St Patrick used to explain the Trinity to the ancient Irish. Our grandchildren love to gather and taste them and use the white, yellow, pink, purple or red flowers and leaves to decorate mud pies.

VARIETIES

We have several types around us here. *Oxalis acetosella*, wood sorrel, grows in shady moist ground in woodlands or between damp mossy rocks. At Ballymaloe it grows all over the greenhouses, between the bays and plants. Once again, it's an opportunity to eat the weeds. The gardeners hike it out of the ground and encourage the students to do the same when they are harvesting leaves for the green salad. Although from a different family, it is

called sorrel because of its sour taste. *Oxalis corniculata* grows in the gravel outside the Pink Cottage. It too has the characteristic heart-shaped leaves and clean, fresh, lemony taste but winey-brown leaves and little yellow flowers. *Oxalis montana* grows a few miles away in Glenbower Wood and has bright green leaves and delicately streaked little purple and white flowers. It is also fresh-tasting and adorable.

HARVESTING

These varieties are in season all year round but flower from early summer to mid-autumn.

GOOD FOR YOU...

In common with many sour vegetables, oxalis has diuretic and anti-scorbutic (prevents scurvy) properties. It is high in vitamin C and historically it was used to treat scurvy, mouth ulcers, sore throats and nausea. A little is beneficial to health but those with kidney disorders or digestive problems are advised not to eat too much. The oxalic acid can affect those who suffer from gout. So, as ever, consume in moderation.

IN THE KITCHEN

We use the refreshing little leaves in salads and as a garnish; we love their sharp lemony taste in shellfish salads, particularly with the little pink shrimp from Ballycotton. For **Shrimp with Homemade Mayonnaise and Wood Sorrel** to serve 4, bring 2½ quarts water to a boil in a large saucepan, add 2 tablespoons salt, then toss in 36 to

Although associated with a woodland habit, wood sorrel grows abundantly in the greenhouse in between our crops.

Oxalis corniculata—*copper sorrel with yellow flowers.*

40 live or very fresh shrimp—they will change color from gray to pink almost instantly. Bring the water back to a boil and cook for just 2 to 3 minutes. The shrimp are cooked when there is no trace of black at the back of the head. Drain immediately and spread out on a large baking sheet to cool. When cold, serve with shells on, or peel them first. To peel, first remove the head, pinch the end of the tail and tug it; it will pull off half the shell. Remove the remainder of the shell with your fingers. Put 9 to 10 cooked whole shrimp on each plate. Spoon a tablespoon or two of Homemade Mayonnaise (page 196) into a little bowl or oyster shell on the side of the plate. Pop a wedge of lemon on the plate. Garnish with some fresh wild watercress or wood sorrel. Serve with fresh, crusty brown soda bread and Irish butter.

They also make a pretty decoration on cakes, especially on a St Patrick's Day cake or a naff tricolor jelly—green, white, and gold! All parts are edible but we just use the leaves and tiny flowers.

Labneh with Kumquat Compote & Wood Sorrel

Wood sorrel has tiny yellow flowers that look pretty but also have a delicious sharp, lemony flavor. This dish makes a perfect starter or dessert for St. Patrick's Day if you use green oxalis—green, white, and gold.

SERVES 4 TO 6

2 cups natural yogurt
Kumquat Compote (page 291)
wood sorrel or fresh mint leaves

Drip 2 cups natural yogurt in cheesecloth overnight (see page 291)—it will yield about 1 cup labneh. Add back a little whey if it is too thick. (Save the whey for drinks, homemade lemonade, pickles, or marinating meat or fish.)

To serve, put a good dollop of labneh on a cold plate. Drizzle some kumquat compote over the top and sides. Sprinkle a few wood sorrel leaves over the top for a St. Patrick's Day dessert with a fun twist.

DID YOU KNOW?
Wood sorrels are found all over the world and have been used in many traditional medicines. It is a well-known thirst-quencher and was considered to be an aphrodisiac by the Algonquin Indians.

PURSLANE *Portulaca oleracea,* ZONES 5–10

Another wild green which is well worth seeking out. It's one of our favorite summer greens—a forager's dream. However, gardeners consider purslane a pest because it spreads itself all over the greenhouse and along the paths, but I love it—especially because it's delicious and exceptionally nutritious. It is native to India and Persia but I've seen it growing all over the world from vineyards on the slopes of Mount Etna to cracks in the pavements in California.

This fleshy little succulent with a crunchy, mucilaginous texture and a lemony peppery flavor is a gem, but beware it can become invasive—once introduced it starts to romp along, so harvest it regularly. If I can sell my weeds I will really be making money!

According to the *Oxford Companion to Food*, there is evidence that purslane has been eaten for over 2,000 years; it was cultivated in Ancient Egypt and enjoyed by the Romans and Greeks, too.

VARIETIES

There are two kinds: summer and winter purslane.

Winter Purslane, Claytonia *(Claytonia perfoliata)* or Miner's lettuce—the latter colloquial name because it was used as a fresh salad leaf by miners in the 1849 Gold Rush in California, where its high vitamin C content prevented scurvy. It's a hardy annual and appears early in the year, a single leaf with a long tender stem, but by early summer it flowers and changes shape completely into a circular leaf with the tiny white flowers peeping up through the center.

Summer purslane *(Portulaca oleracea)*—A succulent plant and the most frequently reported weed species in the world. But there's a solution—if you can't beat weeds, enjoy eating them instead. It's got a slight lemony watercress or spinach flavor, crunchy and viscous.

HOW TO GROW

All purslane needs is a patch of clear, dry ground and sun. It loves our greenhouses and drives the gardeners mad because it pops up everywhere, but we do our best to keep eating it. It also springs up along paths; lots of people already have it and put huge effort into eradicating it without realising that it's edible. A sprawling succulent, it has yellow flowers and black seeds and prolifically reseeds itself. It transplants very easily.

CONTAINER GROWING

We also grow it in large wide pots on the balcony and on our windowsills, and also in smaller containers as a micro-green.

HARVESTING

Purslane is in season from midsummer until the first frosts come. Just snip tender young shoots with scissors.

Save seeds—collect pods near the end of summer and put them in a brown paper bag to dry.

GOOD FOR YOU...

If ever there was a contender for a 'superfood', purslane is it. A powerhouse of nutrients, with the highest dietary fibre level of any green plant, it is also high in omega-3 fatty acids but is a far cheaper source than salmon.

It contains lots of vitamins, including C, E (seven times more than spinach), A and B, plus magnesium, calcium, potassium, iron, riboflavin and phosphorus. It is also known to lower cholesterol.

Purslane, considered by many to be a noxious weed, but we enjoy at every opportunity.

According to the University of Texas, San Antonio, purslane contains 10 to 20 times more melatonin, an antioxidant, than any other vegetable or fruit.

In his book *In Defence of Food*, Michael Pollan referred to purslane as one of the two most nutritious plants on the planet, the other being lamb's quarters, pigs weed or fat hen.

IN THE KITCHEN

Purslane is now beginning to appear at farmers' markets and chefs are waking up to its possibilities. It's a juicy succulent with a slightly lemony flavor. Add it to your green salad or use it as a base for a starter; we love it mixed with watercress.

Purslane is mucilaginous, so it's great to thicken soups and stews. It also has a high pectin level which is known to lower cholesterol. One can also use it in Gazpacho and add it to Fattoush.

Lamb Koftas with Purslane Salad & Yogurt Dressing

This is another of Rory O'Connell's delicious recipes—roll the koftas into little balls the size of a large grape for this salad. They can, of course, be made larger, into burger or sausage shapes. Serve these strewn over a salad of purslane leaves with a yogurt dressing for a special treat.

MAKES 50 SMALL KOFTAS/SERVES 4

6 to 7 cups purslane, gently washed
  and dried
2 to 3 tablespoons Chile Oil (see below)
¼ cup hazelnuts, roasted, peeled and
  coarsely chopped
2 large pinches of roasted and ground
  cumin

FOR THE KOFTAS
1 pound ground lamb
1 medium onion, grated
1 garlic clove, grated on a microplane
2 tablespoons chopped hyssop or
  2 pinches of za'atar
1 red chile pepper, medium hot, finely
  chopped
1 teaspoon date syrup
olive oil, for frying
zest of 1 to 2 lemons
sea salt and freshly ground black pepper

FOR THE GARLIC AND YOGURT DRESSING
½ cup yogurt
¼ cup buttermilk
1 small garlic clove, crushed

FOR THE CHILE OIL
2 large red chile peppers
pinch of salt
⅔ cup olive oil

Mix all of the ingredients for the koftas together, except the oil and lemon zest. Cook a tiny piece in a skillet to check the flavor and adjust the seasoning accordingly. Form the mixture into little balls, approx. 1 to 2 tablespoons each, and store in the fridge on a parchment-lined tray.

To make the chile oil, chop the peppers (including the seeds) and add with a pinch of salt to the olive oil in a very small saucepan. Bring to a bare simmer and cook at the gentlest bubble for 5 minutes. Remove from the heat and, with the back of a spoon or a pestle, crush some of the peppers to break them up a little bit. Leave to cool completely and strain through a fine sieve again, using the back of a spoon or pestle to press some tiny bits of flesh through. I try to get about 1 teaspoon of the fine flesh through the sieve into the oil. Taste again and add a pinch of salt if necessary. Store in a sealed glass container such as a jam jar.

Mix the yogurt with the buttermilk and garlic and season gently with a pinch of salt and pepper.

Remove any long stalks from the purslane, chop finely, and add back to the leaves.

Toss the leaves gently in the yogurt dressing. Taste and add a pinch of salt if necessary. Spread out on a large flat serving dish. Drizzle with chile oil and scatter with the roasted hazelnuts. Finish the dish with the ground cumin dusted over the top.

To cook the koftas, heat a little olive oil in a heavy skillet or grill pan and cook them, turning regularly, until they feel slightly firm to the touch.

Scatter over the salad and sprinkle with very finely grated lemon zest. Serve immediately.

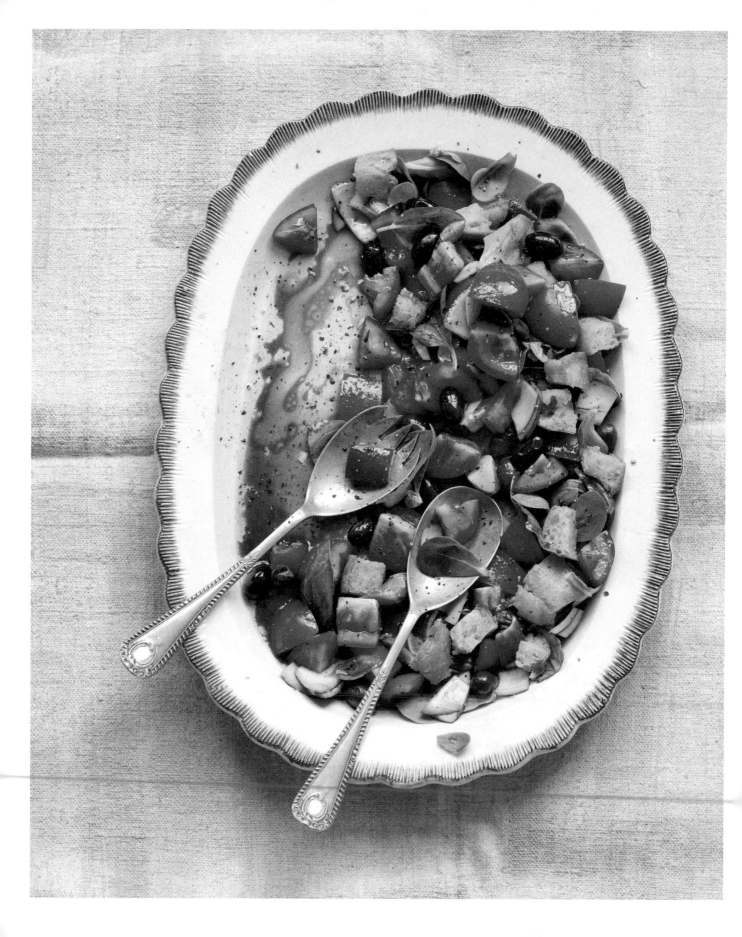

Panzanella (Tuscan Bread Salad)

A delicious way to use up slightly stale sourdough bread and enjoy lots of herbs and greens. We love to add little sprigs of purslane to add extra juiciness to both panzanella and fattoush.

SERVES 8

2 to 3 garlic cloves, thinly sliced
3 to 4 tablespoons extra virgin olive oil
¼ pound crusty sourdough bread, cut or
  torn into ½-inch cubes
1 red onion, roughly chopped
¼ cup pitted black olives
lots of basil leaves, torn into pieces,
  include some purple, opal, and lemon
  basil if available
a couple of handfuls of purslane
8 ripe medium-sized tomatoes, cut into
  quarters
2 tablespoons balsamic vinegar
1 tablespoon white wine vinegar
½ cup extra virgin olive oil
sea salt and freshly ground black pepper

Preheat the oven to 350°F.

Put the garlic and extra virgin olive oil in a large bowl. Add the bread cubes and toss to coat evenly. Spread on a baking sheet and bake for 4 to 5 minutes, just long enough to barely toast, they shouldn't be hard. Return the croutons to the bowl with the onion, olives, basil, purslane, and tomatoes. Whisk together the vinegars, olive oil, salt and pepper. Drizzle over the salad and toss gently. Season to taste. Serve soon.

DID YOU KNOW?
Purslane is known as one of Mahatma Gandhi's favorite foods; in an article in his magazine *Harijan*, he wrote about "the nourishing properties of the innumerable leaves that are to be found hidden among the grasses that grow wild in India." Purslane was also eaten by writer Henry David Thoreau when he lived at Walden Pond in Massachusetts. Harold McGee calls it pigweed in his book *On Food and Cooking*.

Purslane, Avocado & Cucumber Salad

The contrast of textures and flavors in this simple salad is really delicious. The crisp cucumber complements the creamy avocado and the juiciness of the succulent purslane. I sometimes add a few green grapes for an extra touch of sweetness.

SERVES 6 TO 8

1 cucumber
2 avocados
3 to 4 handfuls of purslane
flaky sea salt and freshly cracked pepper

FOR THE DRESSING
3 tablespoons extra virgin olive oil
1 tablespoon white wine vinegar

Top, tail, and halve the cucumber. Unless it's very fresh, scoop out the seeds—a melon baller or grapefruit spoon is good for this. Cut into ½-inch diagonal slices and transfer to a wide bowl.

Halve the avocados, remove the pits, peel, and cut into haphazard dice, about 2 to 3 inches. Add to the cucumber. Season with flaky sea salt and add some freshly cracked pepper. Add the sprigs of purslane.

Combine the dressing ingredients and drizzle over the salad. Toss gently. Season to taste. Arrange on individual plates and serve as soon as possible.

ALMOND
Prunus dulcis DECIDUOUS, ZONES 5–9

Almonds are native to the Middle East and South Asia, but don't let that put you off growing them. I'm sure it sounds frightfully exotic to have an almond tree in your garden, but ours are growing away happily here in Shanagarry, on the south coast of Ireland. I'm sure it's not as productive as the almond trees I saw laden with nuts in Regaleali, in Sicily, but nonetheless we are charmed to have some fruit and to be able to enjoy the young green almonds as well as the fresh mature nuts. They take about five years to fruit and are apparently quite long-lived, although my original almond tree keeled over after nine years. Botanically it is a stone fruit related to plums, apricots, peaches and cherries and the pink and white blossom is fragrant and beautiful.

Almond blossom.

VARIETIES

There are two types, sweet and bitter—avoid the latter, they have cyanide in them....

Most almond trees available for sale are grafted onto the rootstock of a plum variety called "St Julien."

All-in-One—Heat tolerant trees produces large crops of crisp nuts in September

Hall's Hardy—one of the most cold-tolerant almond trees, rodues large crops of delicious nuts in fall.

Garden Prince—the small, landscape worthy trees prduces generous crops in the third year and beyond.

HOW TO GROW

You'll need space as almond trees grow from 14 to 16 feet tall. They grow best in light, fertile, well-drained soil in full sun and, needless to say, they like a frost-free spot. Almonds thrive in Mediterranean climates with wet winters and hot summers.

Plant 13 feet apart in early spring; choose 2 to 3 if you can spare the space, as they are not self-fertile. Keep away from peaches, otherwise they may cross-pollinate and the nuts will be bitter.

CONTAINER GROWING

Choose a large pot and a dwarf variety such as Garden Prince, which grows to about 60 inches high and is self-pollinating. Water regularly during summer and mulch with compost or humus. Some varieties are just ornamental, so do check when you buy.

PESTS AND DISEASES

Peach leaf curl can attack almonds, so plant well away from a peach, also because they may cross-pollinate.

HARVESTING

We pick some of the fluffy green almonds off the tree in early summer and eat the milky nuts. The others are allowed to ripen on the tree until late summer into early autumn. When they are ripe the outer shell will dry and start to split; you can allow them to fall on the ground or pick them off the tree before the birds get them. If you have several trees you could put a tarpaulin on the ground and shake the nuts onto it as they do in almond orchards.

A healthy tree can produce between 33 to 55 pounds of nuts a year.

GOOD FOR YOU...

Almonds are high in monounsaturated fats, they have a low GI index and contain biotin, vitamin E, manganese, copper, vitamin B2, phosphorus and magnesium. Almonds are known to lower LDL cholesterol and reduce the risk of heart disease.

WHAT TO DO WITH A GLUT

It is unlikely that you will have more almonds than you can cope with, but they freeze very well. If you are lucky enough to have a surplus of almonds, as soon as possible after harvest, remove the outer husks, dry the nuts in their shells in an airy place, laid out on a wire rack in a single layer. Store shelled whole almonds in a tightly sealed container in a cool, dry place away from direct light. Almond pieces go rancid more quickly than whole almonds. Almonds in the shell have the longest shelf life.

If properly dried almonds can keep for up to 8 months, but be careful what you store them near as they will readily absorb other flavors.

IN THE KITCHEN

If you grow your own almonds you can try a rare delicacy: green almonds. Take a knife and cut through the protective outer green husk and taste the moist white flesh of the green almond inside. Eat them whole or sliced, dipped in sea salt. In the Mediterranean countries where they grow, they are eaten green husk and all when they are young and tender. The Greeks love them sprinkled with lemon juice and sea salt. The French like to marinate green almonds in verjus.

For those who are dairy intolerant, nut milks are a welcome addition to the diet—you can easily make your own **Almond Milk** and use it as a basis for smoothies and other nourishing drinks. For 1 quart milk, soak 1 cup skinned almonds overnight in cool water or for 1 to 2 hours in very hot, almost boiling water. Put the soaked then drained almonds, 1 quart spring or bottled water, and a pinch of sea salt, if using, into a blender. Blend until creamy and smooth and as much milky liquid as possible has been extracted from the almonds. Strain through cheesecloth, squeezing until all the liquid is extracted. The almond pulp may be used in baking if you wish, instead of milk. Put the strained almond milk into a glass bottle, cover tightly and store in the fridge. It's best used fresh but will keep for a few days. It tends to separate in the bottle so shake well before use. The milk can be flavored by adding strawberries, banana, or chocolate to taste and blending until smooth. Taste and add a little honey or lemon juice if needed.

Another deli or health-food-shop staple—but you can't imagine how easy it is to make—is **Almond Butter**.

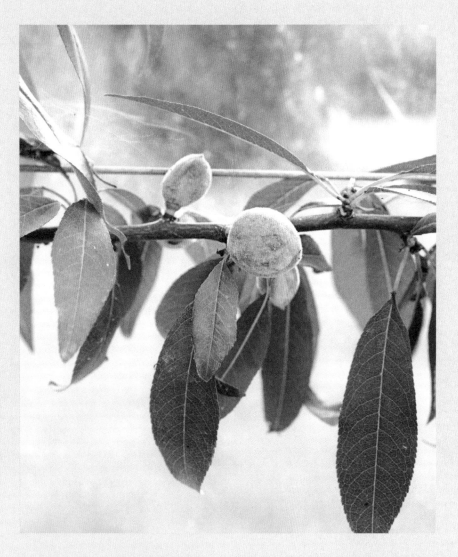

Young green almonds growing in the greenhouse.

Slather on toasted sourdough or use on sandwiches with cucumber and arugula. To make 1 pound, preheat the oven to 350°F. Spread 1 pound whole almonds on a baking sheet and roast for 10 to 12 minutes. Remove from the oven and let cool. Put the almonds and 1 tablespoon almond, sunflower, or peanut oil into a powerful blender or food processor and blend until smooth. Stop every now and then to scrape down the sides. Store in a clean, airtight jar in a fridge. It will keep for at least a month.

DID YOU KNOW?

Almonds were originally brought to California in the mid 1700s by the Spanish Franciscan missionaries. There are huge almond orchards in the San Joaquin and Sacramento valleys in California and millions of bees are transported across the state every year to help pollinate the trees.

Beet, Almond & Mint Salad

We're crazy about beets and continue to dream up new ways to enjoy them. This is a particularly delicious combination. Serve it as a starter or as part of a mezze.

. . . .

SERVES 4

3 tablespoons blanched, unskinned almonds or roasted Marcona almonds
1 pound cooked beets (page 75)
2 tablespoons shredded mint leaves
2 tablespoons fresh pomegranate seeds

FOR THE POMEGRANATE DRESSING
1 large pomegranate
1 tablespoon good red wine vinegar
2 tablespoons pomegranate molasses
4 tablespoons extra virgin olive oil
sea salt and freshly ground black pepper

If using blanched almonds, roast them in the oven at 300°F for 10 to 15 minutes, until golden brown. Remove and let cool, then roughly chop.

Peel and slice the beets into wedges.

To make the pomegranate dressing, cut the pomegranate in half and juice on a citrus juicer. Alternatively, remove the seeds and discard any bitter skin or white pith. Put the seeds in a nylon sieve and press them with the back of a spoon to extract all the juice, discarding any skin or hard seeds. Put the juice and the remaining dressing ingredients into a jam jar with a lid, season with salt and pepper, and shake well.

Pour the dressing over the beets, then scatter with the almonds, mint, and pomegranate seeds. Mix gently, taste, and serve.

Caramelized Almond Tart

A rich and beautiful tart; serve it alone or with a Kumquat Compote (page 291) and a dollop of crème fraîche.

. . . .

SERVES 6 TO 8

FOR THE PASTRY
½ cup (1 stick) cold butter, plus extra for greasing
½ cup all-purpose flour
2 tablespoons superfine sugar
1 organic egg yolk
drop of vanilla extract

FOR THE TOPPING
1¼ cup sliced almonds
6 tablespoons butter
2 tablespoons light brown sugar
2 tablespoons honey
1 tablespoon cream

softly whipped cream, to serve

Preheat the oven to 350°F. Grease a 9-inch springform pan.

Put the flour and superfine sugar into a bowl, rub in the butter and bind with the egg yolk and a drop of vanilla extract. This is a tricky pastry to handle, so if you like just press it into the greased pan. Prick the pastry and bake for 15 to 18 minutes, or until pale golden.

Cook the topping ingredients, except the cream, together over a low heat for 3 to 4 minutes until they are a pale straw color, then stir in the cream and cook for a few seconds longer. Spread the topping over the cooked base and bake until it is a deep golden-brown color—this can take anywhere from 8 to 15 minutes, depending on the length of time the original ingredients were cooked. Cool on a wire rack. Serve with softly whipped cream.

DAMSONS

Prunus domestica insititia HARDY DECIDUOUS FRUIT TREE, ZONES 5–9

A member of the rose family, tart, wild, bittersweet damsons are another autumn treat that bring memories of childhood flooding back. In a bountiful year we would pick bucketsful from the hedgerows around Nancy Roberts's field close to Cullahill Castle, just outside the little village of Cullahill in Co Laois, where I was born. Mummy made damson pies, tarts, crumbles and lots of jam, which was also a favorite of all my boarding school buddies which made me very popular at tea time—hugely important at school! For me, discovering a damson tree laden with fruit is the equivalent of winning the lotto.

Damsons are sometimes confused with bullaces, a wild plum originating from the same strain of *Prunus domestica.* Damsons are oval in shape and about the size of a walnut, while bullaces are rounder with smoother stones.

Immature damsons—ripe damsons have a black/purplish skin and yield to the touch.

VARIETIES

Shropshire prune—Very old variety with well-flavored blue-purple fruit. It's also known by other names, such as Damascene, Prune Damson or Westmoreland Damson. It was considered very suitable for canning.
Frogmore—Cultivar first grown in the Royal Garden at Frogmore in the nineteenth century. It ripens in early autumn.
King of the Damsons—Late-autumn variety also known as Bradley's King.
Merryweather—Twentieth-century cultivar with deep blue large fruit and sweet flesh when ripe.
Prune Damson can be cultivated. The latter tend to be considerably sweeter than their wild counterpart.
Blue Damson—large clusters of purple-blue fruit.

HOW TO GROW

I'm really keen on edible hedgerows, and as they are self-fertile a damson can be grown in hedgerows, as a lone tree or with other fruit trees such as apples, crab apples, Chaenomeles (Japanese quince), pears, medlar. They can also be trained into a bush pyramid or fan shape. They grow wild all around the countryside but many have been wantonly chopped down by "progressive" farmers removing hedges to increase the size of their fields.

CONTAINER GROWING

If you are tight for space, consider planting a miniature variety such as **Merryweather** on a dwarf St Julien A rootstock in a large pot or tub. Make sure there is ample drainage and apply a mulch of compost or well-rotted manure in spring.

PESTS AND DISEASES

Damsons are susceptible to the same pests and diseases as plums. They can be attacked by plum sawfly, which is difficult to treat organically but a pheromone trap may be used. An affected fruit, whether picked or on the ground, should be destroyed by burning to avoid spread of the fly.

Plant calendulas close by or spray with diluted washing-up liquid—1 teaspoon to 2 liters water.

They can also be attacked by aphids which may cause leaf curl.

Damsons may also be prone to silver leaf disease and powdery mildew. In the case of silver leaf it's best to remove and burn the tree. Don't plant the trees too closely together, allow plenty of air circulation which helps prevent powdery mildew, prune the center of the tree. Debris such as dead leaves should be picked up and disposed of as they can carry the spores of powdery mildew over the winter.

HARVESTING

Damsons will be ripe in early to mid-autumn, depending on the variety, and they need to be ripe, otherwise they can be mouth-puckeringly sour and tart. Soft plums with a dark dusky bloom can be eaten fresh from the tree or picked for cooking and preserving. Their fruiting pattern seems very unpredictable. The early blossoms are vulnerable to frost. If all the stars are aligned, one can have a bumper crop followed by years without a single fruit, so indulge when you can.

GOOD FOR YOU...

Rich in vitamin C and minerals such as potassium and phosphorus.

WHAT TO DO WITH A GLUT

Make lots of jam and damson pickle and damson cheese.

IN THE KITCHEN

Damsons have a high astringency that makes them perfect for cooking. Wild damsons are much more astringent and to my mind most delicious for cooking with than the much sweeter hybrids.

They are gorgeous simply stewed until they burst and served hot with icy-cold cream (see page 570). They make great cobblers and crumbles, pies, and tarts. Damson ice cream is good too, and a damson and apple sauce is perfection with a roast duck or goose. Damson jam is one of the best jams you'll ever make and damson vodka or gin will make Christmas presents guaranteed to endear you to your friends.

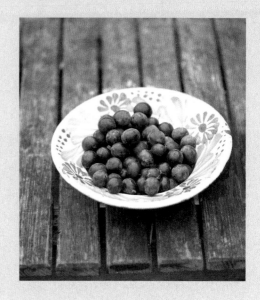

A bowl of perfectly ripe damsons.

Damson & Apple Tart

A brilliant way to make the most of a handful of damsons in a scarce year. The pastry is made by the creaming method, so people who are convinced that they suffer from "hot hands" don't have to worry about rubbing in the butter. It is quite simply the best pie pastry. Individual tarts may also be made.

SERVES 8 TO 12

FOR THE BREAK-ALL-THE-RULES PASTRY
16 tablespoons butter (2 sticks) butter
3 tablespoons superfine sugar
2 organic eggs
3 cups all-purpose flour, plus extra for
  dusting

FOR THE FILLING
1½ pounds cooking apples such as Gala
  or Rome
½ pound or more wild damsons
⅔ cup granulated sugar
eggwash, made with 1 beaten egg and a
  dash of milk
superfine sugar, for sprinkling
softly whipped cream and soft dark
  brown sugar (not Muscovado), to serve

Preheat the oven to 350°F.

First make the pastry. Cream the butter and sugar together by hand or with a stand or hand mixer (no need to overcream). Add the eggs and beat for several minutes. Reduce speed and mix in the flour. Turn out onto a square of plastic wrap. Flatten into a round, wrap tightly, and chill. This pastry needs to be chilled for at least 1 hour otherwise it is difficult to handle. Having said that, I have on occasions bunged all the ingredients into a food processor and whizz bang, whizz bang made the pastry in a matter of seconds, then rolled it out minutes later—albeit with a certain amount of difficulty. Even if it does break a little it responds very well to being patched and appears flawless and golden when it is fully baked.

To make the tart, roll out the pastry approximately less than a quarter-inch thick, and use about two-thirds of it to line a 7-inch × 11-inch brownie pan, a 9-inch round pan, or 9-inch square pan. Peel, quarter, and dice the apples into the tart, top with damsons (don't remove pits). Sprinkle with the granulated sugar. Cover with the rest of the pastry and seal edges. Decorate with pastry leaves, brush over the eggwash and bake in the oven for 45 minutes to 1 hour until the apples are tender.

When cooked, sprinkle lightly with superfine sugar, cut into squares, and serve with softly whipped cream and soft brown sugar.

Damson Compote with Icy Cold Cream

Poach the fruit whole—they'll taste better but, quite apart from that, you'll have the fun of playing "He loves me, he loves me not" as you count the pits on your plate! (You could just fix it by making sure you use an uneven number.) Greengages are also delicious cooked in this way. The fruit should be cooked in a stainless steel or enamel saucepan, never aluminum as the fruit will react with it.

SERVES 8

2 cups granulated sugar, a bit less if the fruit are very sweet
2 cups cold water
2 pounds fresh damsons
whipped cream, to serve

Put the sugar and water into a stainless steel saucepan and bring slowly to a boil. Add the damsons, cover the saucepan, and return to a boil. Simmer for 4 to 5 minutes, until the fruit begin to burst. Transfer into a bowl and serve warm with icy cold cream. Divine!

Poached damsons keep very well in the fridge and are delicious for breakfast (perhaps without the cream) or as a dessert.

VARIATION

Damson Fool—If you have the patience to remove the stones, the fruit can be puréed. When cold, mix with an equal quantity of whipped cream. Taste and serve with shortbread biscuits.

Damson Jam

My school friends and I used to collect damsons every year in Nancy Roberts's field near the old castle in Cullahill. First we ate so many we almost burst, the rest we brought home for Mummy to make into damson jam, my all-time favorite preserve. If you don't have enough damsons, add some Bramley apples. This also makes a delicious jam.

MAKES APPROX. 8 TO 9 POUNDS

butter, for greasing
6 pounds damsons
3 to 4 cups water
5 pounds granulated sugar

DID YOU KNOW?
Damsons (or bullaces) were used to dye the fabric for sailors' uniforms in the woolen industry in North Western England during World War I.

Grease a stainless steel stock pot to prevent the fruit sticking to the bottom.

Pick over the fruit carefully, wash and drain well, and discard any damaged damsons. Put the damsons and water into the stock pot and stew them gently for 10 to 15 minutes, until the skin breaks.

Preheat the oven to 350°F. Heat the sugar in the oven for 5 to 10 minutes, add it to the fruit and stir over a gentle heat until dissolved. Increase the heat and boil steadily, stirring frequently. Skim off the stones and scum as they rise to the top. After 15 minutes of boiling, test for a set by putting a spoonful of the jam on a chilled plate and letting it rest for a minute or two. If the jam wrinkles when pressed with a finger, it will set.

Pour into hot, sterilized jars and cover. Store in a cool, dry place and use within a couple of months, although it will keep until the beginning of the next season but gradually becomes less fresh-tasting.

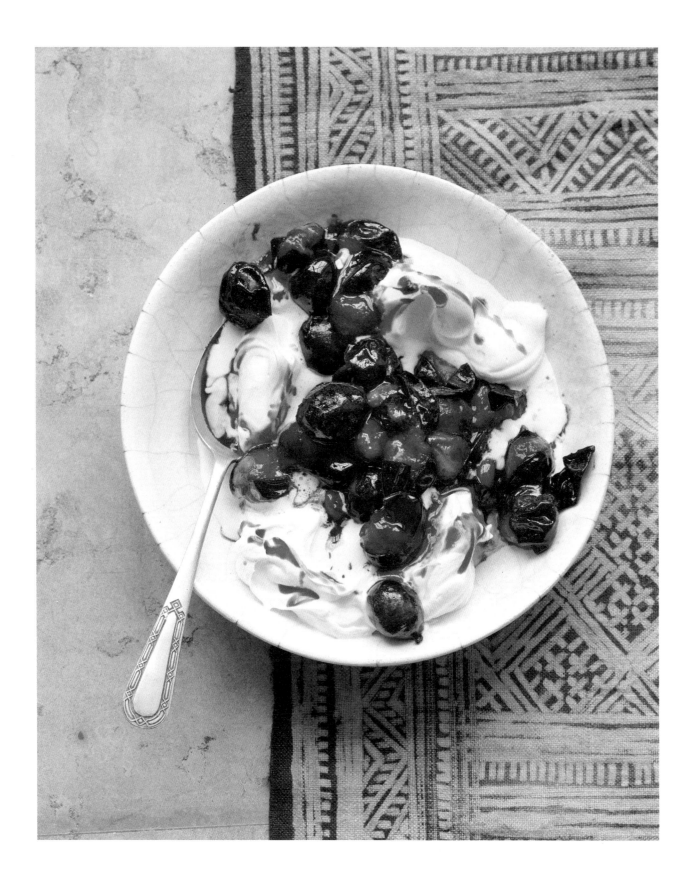

SLOES *Prunus spinosa* DECIDUOUS, ZONES 4–8

Sloes are the fruit of the blackthorn tree.

Sloes, the fruit of the blackthorn, are beloved of those of us in the UK who love to preserve and ferment. Try to make space for these plants (it is rare to find seeds in the US but you may sometimes find them from specialty sources), unless they already grow wild in a hedgerow in your neighborhood.

The blackthorn is a small-to-medium prickly bush, native to Europe as well as Asia and northwest Africa. It is also naturalized in New Zealand and northeastern America. It can grow to 13 feet tall if left unpruned.

Branches of sloes are gorgeous in flower arrangements and garlands. A prickly thorn hedge can be functional as well as decorative, as it creates a formidable deterrent to would-be intruders! The traditional Irish walking stick is made from the blackthorn.

VARIETIES

It's a wild plant, so there don't seem to be domestic cultivars available, although it is possible to take cuttings of wild trees to plant in the garden.

It is easy to get confused between the black- and whitethorn bushes; both have their place in an edible hedgerow, but in reality they are very different. The blackthorn produces the impossibly tart and tannic sloes, while whitethorn produces red mealy haws, beloved of the birds in late autumn (see pages 550–551). We use both in the kitchen and I encourage you to plant both in your hedgerow to add to the biodiversity of your area and to provide food for birds and insects, as well as for the enjoyment of all of us.

HOW TO GROW

Blackthorn will grow in virtually any soil. Because of its prickles, it's best planted in a perimeter hedge. The pretty, white, star-like flowers appear in spring on bare leaves. It is a good pollinator for apple trees.

HARVESTING

Whitethorn comes into leaf before blackthorn but the latter flowers on the prickly bare wood in early summer. Both have white blossom but the whitethorn is more profuse (see photos). Make a note of where the blackthorn bushes are when they blossom in spring so you'll know where to search for sloes in the autumn.

Sloes are generally ripe by mid-autumn when the small, tart, dark navy berries will be slightly soft. The bushes are prickly but it's easy to pick the sloes without getting prickled. In some years there's a bumper crop of the small, cloudy, dark-skinned berries. In other years the yield is so sparse it becomes frustrating to gather enough for even one batch of sloe gin.

GOOD FOR YOU...

Sloes are reputed to have properties of detoxification and blood purification—the flowers and fruit are rich in rutin and quercetin, which help prevent gout and rheumatism—though I don't know how much one would need to eat.

They are also said to improve digestion, relieve constipation, reduce bloating, and treat diarrhoea.

The fresh juice from pulped sloes may be used as a gargle for sore throats and a **Blackthorn Blossom Syrup** can be used for tonsillitis and laryngitis. Mix together 2¼ cups granulated sugar, 2 handfuls of sloe blossoms and 4½ quarts of boiling water and store in sterilised bottles. To use, dilute the syrup with water to gargle. It will taste horrible so it depends on how bad your tonsillitis or laryngitis is....

WHAT TO DO WITH A GLUT

Sloes freeze perfectly, in fact, many of my friends freeze them before they make sloe gin or vodka to simulate the first frost which helps to sweeten them.

IN THE KITCHEN

Sloe berries are mouth-puckeringly sour and bitter, but I will be forever indebted to whoever discovered that they are transformed by a spirit and add immeasurably to gin or vodka, jellies, vinegars, and sliders.

Apple, Sloe & Sweet Geranium Jelly

This apple jelly recipe is the most brilliant mother recipe to add all sorts of flavors to various dishes. If you have lots of sloes, increase the quantity here to half apples and sloes. Serve on scones, or with game, pork, duck, or guinea fowl.

MAKES 6 OR 7 ¾-POUND POTS

5 pounds crab apples or Bramley's Seedlings cooking apples, washed and quartered (no need to peel or core)

1 pound sloes

6 to 8 large sweet geranium leaves, plus extra as needed

2¾ quarts water

rind and juice of 2 unwaxed lemons

granulated sugar (1 pound to each 2½ cups of juice)

Put the apples in a large saucepan with the sloes, geranium leaves, water, and lemon rind and cook for 30 to 40 minutes, until it dissolves into a mush.

Turn the pulp into a jelly bag and leave to drip until all the juice has been extracted—usually overnight. Measure the juice into a preserving pan, allowing 1 pound sugar to each 20 ounces of juice.

Preheat the oven to 350°F. Heat the sugar in the oven for about 10 minutes. Squeeze the lemons, strain the juice, and add to the preserving pan with a few more geranium leaves if the flavor is still very mild. Bring to a boil and add the sugar. Stir over a gentle heat until the sugar is dissolved. Increase the heat and boil rapidly without stirring for 8 to 10 minutes. Remove the geranium leaves. Skim, test for a set by putting a teaspoonful on a chilled plate, and leave in a cool place for a few minutes. If the jam wrinkles when pushed with a finger, it has reached setting point. Pour the jelly into sterilized jars and top each jar with a sweet geranium leaf. Cover and seal immediately.

Store in a cool, dry cupboard; it will keep for up to a year, but for optimum flavor enjoy sooner rather than later.

DID YOU KNOW?
The blackthorn tree is called *Áirne* in Ireland and was often added to the illicit spirit *poitín* to make a potent drop to enjoy around Christmas. They often grew around ancient paths and forts and it is still considered to be unlucky to cut down a blackthorn tree. They make a useful cattleproof hedge or barrier.

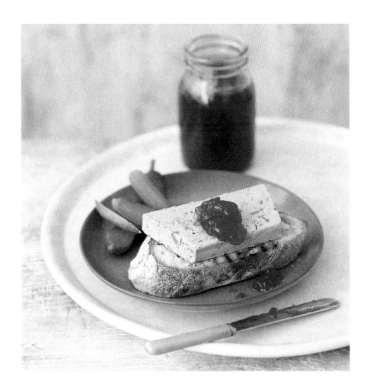

BLACKBERRY *Rubus fruticosus* HARDY PERENNIAL, ZONES 5–8

Those of us who live in the countryside have no difficulty finding blackberries. In autumn the hedgerows are full of tangles of prickly bramble bushes dripping with dark, juicy berries. For many it's their first introduction to gathering food in the wild. They taste so much more delicious when you collect them yourself, particularly if you gather a few friends and children together and bring a picnic. It always amazes me to see people buying plastic punnets of blackberries during the bramble season.

Cultivated blackberries are fine and plump, and it has to be said very delicious, but they are altogether a different thing to the wild fruit. Perhaps it's because they are so plentiful that they are so little prized. However, not everyone lives near a bramble patch so do consider growing a few cultivated blackberries in your garden. If you are thinking about making jam, bear in mind blackberries are low in pectin.

VARIETIES

Silvan—Large crops from mid- to late summer. Vigorous rambling plants that need staking.
Prime-Ark Traveler—produces good harvests of medium to large berries
Prime-Ark Freedom—Thornless canes, reistant to heat and humidty produce good crops of tasty berries.
Triple Crown—thornless canes produce juicy, sweet berries for up to five weeks.

HOW TO GROW

Blackberries need space and a really sturdy support system. They can be grown over arches, trellis or pergolas, or along fences and walls with strong wires. Choose a sunny spot—they can tolerate semi-shade but will be more productive and sweeter when they lap up full sun.

Although blackberries tolerate a variety of soil types, they thrive best in moisture-retentive, rich, fertile, free-draining soil. If your soil is heavy clay or sandy, add organic matter or some compost. Try to choose the best variety for your situation.

When well pruned and cared for, a blackberry bush can continue to be productive for 15 to 20 years and produce up to 10 pounds of fruit a year.

Erect 4 rows with high-tensile galvanised wire, use strong posts and space the rows 18 inches apart. Space the plants 8 to 13 feet apart depending on the vigor and growing habit of the cultivar.

Wild blackberries grow in urban areas and waste ground as well as the countryside.

Before planting in early spring, firm the ground and water well. Cut the blackberry plant back to 1 inch above soil level. This may seem quite drastic but it will ensure strong growth of the primary canes, which will fruit the following year. Tie up and train the canes as they grow. At the end of the season, cut out the fruiting canes and cut down to ground level depending on the cultivar. Mulch in early spring.

Wild blackberries are also super easy to find, not just in the countryside, they also grow freely on wasteground and corners of parkland, and sometimes around playgrounds.

PESTS AND DISEASES

Blackberries are usually trouble-free unless planted too close together. In wet summers, downy mildew can be a problem. Remove old branches and improve air circulation. If it is a recurring problem, start a new patch with disease-free plants in an area previously not affected by downy mildew.

HARVESTING

Blackberries ripen from mid-to-late summer onwards. Wild berries tend to be smaller and more intensely flavored than home-grown ones. Pick the individual fruit off the plant and check each one before putting them into your bowl. The center should not be stained with juice, which can be an indication that there are worms inside. Pick every 2 to 3 days to keep ahead of the birds. It is also good to pick some under-ripe berries when making jam; ripe blackberries are notoriously low in pectin but the under-ripe berries will help to increase the pectin levels—best to add some tart apples like Bramley's or crab apples to cut the sweetness and help the set.

GOOD FOR YOU...

Blackberries are another excellent source of nutrients, packed with vitamins and minerals. They are rich in vitamin C and vitamin K and also contain vitamins A, E, B3, B6, and folate. Minerals include calcium, iron, magnesium, phosphorous, potassium, and zinc. Blackberries are also a good source of dietary fibre.

WHAT TO DO WITH A GLUT

Blackberries freeze brilliantly—weigh them into bags in the quantities you will need for jam, jelly or cordial making.

IN THE KITCHEN

When I came to work in Ballymaloe House kitchen in the late 1960s, local children would come to the kitchen door in early autumn with tin cans brimming with freshly picked wild blackberries for Mrs. Allen. She'd weigh them, pay the children and put them on the menu in myriad ways—as blackberry jam and blackberry and apple compote for breakfast, a feather-light sponge with blackberries and cream for afternoon tea, blackberry and sweet geranium sorbet, flaky blackberry and apple tarts for dessert after dinner, crumbles and cobblers for lunch, and occasionally a soufflé omelette with blackberries and kirsch for some lucky guests. Blackberry wine is also worth considering, as is blackberry vodka. Blackberry and Sweet Geranium ice cubes are also cute...

DID YOU KNOW?

Irish folklore alleges that the *púca*, or the devil, spits on blackberries on St. Michael's Day, September 29, so one must on no account eat a blackberry after that date! Most folklore has a point, as by then the berries are often beginning to rot and many will be infested with worms and be somewhat bitter.

Blackberry, Apple & Sweet Geranium Jam

Blackberries are a bit low in pectin, so the apples here help the jam to set as well as adding extra flavor.

MAKES 9 OR 10 1-POUND JARS

2 pounds cooking apples, such as Bramley or Grenadier, washed, peeled, cored, and sliced

5 pounds blackberries

4 pounds granulated sugar (use ½ pound less if blackberries are sweet)

8 to 10 sweet geranium leaves

Stew the apples in a stainless steel saucepan with 1¼ cups water until soft; beat to a pulp. Cook the blackberries in a wide, low-sided, stainless steel saucepan until soft, adding about ½ cup water if the berries are dry. If you like, push them through a coarse sieve to remove seeds.

Preheat the oven to 350°F. Heat the sugar in a wide bowl in the oven for 10 minutes.

Put the blackberries into a clean, wide stainless steel saucepan or preserving pan with the apple pulp and the heated sugar. De-stalk and chop the sweet geranium leaves and add to the fruit. Stir over a gentle heat until the sugar is dissolved. Boil steadily for about 15 minutes. Skim the jam, test it for a set (425°F on a candy thermometer), or put a teaspoonful on a chilled plate and leave in a cool place for a few minutes. If the jam wrinkles when pushed with a finger, it has reached setting point. Put into warm, sterilized jars.

Store in a cool, dry place and, once opened, eat within a couple of weeks.

Wild Blackberry & Rose Petal Sponge

When the first blackberries ripen in the autumn we use them with softly whipped cream to fill this light fluffy sponge. The recipe may sound strange but the cake will be the lightest and most tender you've ever tasted.

. . . .

SERVES 6 TO 8

melted butter, for greasing
1¼ cups all-purpose flour, plus extra for dusting
3 organic eggs
1 cup granulated sugar
1 teaspoon baking powder
pale pink rose petals, fresh or crystallized

FOR THE FILLING
½ cup whipping cream
2 teaspoons confectioners sugar, plus extra for dusting
½ teaspoon rose water (optional)
½ to ¾ pound wild blackberries

Preheat the oven to 375°F. Brush two 8-inch round cake pans evenly with melted butter and dust with flour. I usually take the precaution of lining the base with a circle of parchment for guaranteed ease of removal later.

Separate the eggs. In the bowl of a stand mixer, whisk the yolks with the sugar for 2 minutes, then add ⅓ cup of water. Whisk for about 10 minutes until light and fluffy. Sift the flour and baking powder into the yolk mixture in batches. Whisk the egg whites until they hold a stiff peak. Gently fold them into the fluffy base. Pour into the prepared cake pans and bake for about 20 minutes until the center is firm and the edges begin to shrink in from the sides of the tin. Remove the cakes from the pans and cool on a wire rack.

Whip the cream, then add the confectioners sugar and a few drops of rose water (if using).

Sandwich the cold sponges together with the whipped cream and blackberries. Dust a little confectioners sugar over the top of the cake. Sprinkle with fresh or crystallized rose petals—it will look and taste enchanting.

Blackberry, Melon & Mint Salad

Simple but sooo delicious.... Just imagine the flavors together, fresh-tasting and juicy.

. . . .

SERVES 6

1 ripe cantaloupe, chilled
granulated sugar
freshly squeezed juice of 1 lemon
2 to 3 tablespoons torn or shredded mint
½ to ¾ pound freshly picked but not over-ripe blackberries

Cut the melon in half and remove the seeds, then cut into quarters, remove the peel and cut the flesh into ½-inch dice.

Put into a bowl, sprinkle with sugar and the freshly squeezed lemon juice. Toss gently and taste. The amount of sugar needed will depend on the sweetness of the melon.

Add the shredded mint and the blackberries and stir very gently to combine. Serve soon, chilled.

MARSH SAMPHIRE *Salicornia* ANNUAL,
ROCK SAMPHIRE *Crithmum maritimum*, PERENNIAL

Samphire can grow in abundance in coastal areas. Rock samphire grows among the rocks and shingle on the cliffs here in Ireland, although not in the U.S. Marsh samphire or glasswort, as its name suggests, grows in salt marshes close to the coast in Ireland and the U.S. Originally it was the food of the poor, free to those living by the sea, who picked it along the coastline. In Wales, lambs that feed on marsh samphire are much sought-after. It is becoming more available in markets as chefs rediscover these delicious wild plants.

Both varieties have been used since ancient times and there are many references in manuscript cookbooks, particularly for pickled samphire.

Samphires are just some of a number of Halophytes—"salt-tolerant" plants—that have adapted to grow in areas of high salinity; others are sea beet, sea purslane, sea mustard, Alexanders, and sea kale.

VARIETIES

Rock Samphire (*Crithmum maritimum*)—Sometimes called sea asparagus, this grows between the rocks, on cliffs, and on stone walls around the coast in Ireland. It comes from the Umbelliferae family and has dull green fleshy leaves. The leaves can be eaten fresh in salads, lightly cooked or pickled. When the yellow/green flowers appear the flavor becomes somewhat stronger and it has the aroma of a hardware shop, and the leaves become stringy and woody.

Marsh samphire (*Salicornia maritima*)—Also known as glasswort, because of its use in glass-making, this grows and thrives in marshy mud flats, estuaries, and areas close to the sea. Despite the name, it's not related to rock samphire and is in fact a member of the goosefoot family. It is a member of the beet family. It's a succulent that looks like a mini cactus but isn't at all prickly.

WHERE/HOW IT GROWS

Rock samphire grows in light, gravelly, well drained soil and likes full sun. Plant in spring or autumn.

Harvest the fleshy sprigs of rock samphire before it flowers.

Marsh samphire, on the other hand, grows in the salty marshes and coastal mud flats close to the sea.

HARVESTING

Harvest both types sustainably; pick or snip a few stems from each plant before it flowers. Rock samphire was once abundant, but because of over-harvesting it became virtually extinct.

Harvest marsh samphire from midsummer to early autumn—it is low-growing so this can be back-breaking work. It continues to grow until autumn but it's best in summer before it becomes too fibrous. Snip off each plant with scissors rather than pulling it up by the roots, so that the plant can grow again. Keep your ears tuned for the incoming tide.

GOOD FOR YOU...

Marsh samphire is rich in vitamins and minerals—vitamins C and A, magnesium, phosphorus, calcium, iodine, and iron—and full of phytochemicals that protect the liver, heart, and cellular DNA.

Rock samphire has diuretic and detoxifying properties and is good for liver function. It contains vitamin C and minerals such as iodine.

WHAT TO DO WITH A GLUT

If you are fortunate to have a glut, pickle or freeze the samphire. Just blanch and refresh, drain well, then open freeze on a tray and layer in plastic boxes before storing in the freezer.

IN THE KITCHEN

Young rock samphire takes only 2 to 4 minutes to cook in boiling (not salted) water, or you can steam it for the same length of time. Marsh samphire may take a little longer, particularly as it gets older. Tossed in extra virgin olive oil or a little butter, it is delicious in salad with warm smoked fish or shellfish, fava beans, or pickled eggs. Its salty flavor is particularly tempting with mutton or a slow-roasted shoulder of lamb.

We also love it with fish and chips.

Pickled samphire keeps for ages, certainly over a year if you really want to, but it is better to use it sooner rather than later.

Marsh samphire is so fun to eat; pick it up with your fingers and scrape it along your teeth to enjoy the succulent fleshy leaves, then discard the fibrous end.

Young marsh samphire looks like mini cacti.

Fava Beans with Rock Samphire, Cherry Tomatoes & Bocconcini

Freshness is vitally important with fava beans—both their flavor and texture change within hours of picking. A little summer savory added to the cooking water enormously enhances the flavor. If you can't find bocconcini (little balls of buffalo mozzarella), cut a larger ball of mozzarella into ½-inch cubes. I love the inclusion of succulent samphire here, but if perchance you don't have any or it's out of season, use purslane instead.

SERVES 8

½ pound rock or marsh samphire
2 to 3 sprigs of summer savory (optional)
1½ pounds young fava beans, shelled
extra virgin olive oil
16 cherry tomatoes
superfine sugar or honey (optional)
16 bocconcini
coriander flowers, if available
sea salt and freshly ground black pepper

Blanch the samphire in a pan of boiling water, then rinse in a bowl of cold water. Drain, and set aside.

Bring 1 quart water to a boil in a medium saucepan and add 1 teaspoon of salt and the summer savory (if using). Add the fava beans, return to a boil, and cook for 2 to 5 minutes, depending on size and freshness. Drain and rinse under the cold tap until cool enough to handle. Pop each bean out of its skin, then toss in extra virgin olive oil. Season with freshly ground pepper.

Slice the cherry tomatoes in half around the equator, season with salt and freshly ground pepper and maybe a pinch of sugar or a drizzle of honey, depending on the sweetness.

Add the tomatoes, bocconcini, and samphire to the beans and toss gently. Taste and tweak the seasoning if necessary. Sprinkle with fluffy white coriander flowers, if available.

Warm Smoked Pollock with Roast Peppers & Marsh or Rock Samphire

Marsh samphire is in season from mid- to late summer. Rock samphire may be substituted in spring and early summer before it flowers. Failing that, blanched and shocked French beans or asparagus work well. My brother Rory O'Connell first served this at a Long Table Dinner in the greenhouse, where it was a huge hit....

SERVES 8 AS A STARTER

1 to 1½ pounds pollock, skin on
2 red and yellow peppers
¼ to ½ pound marsh samphire
extra virgin olive oil
sea salt and freshly ground black pepper

DID YOU KNOW?
Rock samphire was served at the wedding of Prince Charles and Lady Diana. It came from the Norfolk estate owned by Queen Elizabeth. Marsh samphire was used as a source of soda ash in both soap-making and glass-making. Marsh samphire is also known as sea beans in the US.

You don't need any special equipment to hot-smoke fish—even a roasting pan will do.

Lay the fish filets flesh-side up on a tray, then sprinkle the unskinned pollock with salt as though you were seasoning generously. Leave for at least an hour but not more than 3 hours. Dry the fish with paper towels, place on a wire rack and leave to dry in a cool, airy place for about 30 minutes.

Preheat the oven to 475°F.

Put the peppers on a baking sheet and roast for 20 to 30 minutes, until the skin blisters and the flesh is soft.

Alternatively, put a wire rack over a mild gas flame and roast the pepper on all sides. When they are charred, remove. When roasted, put the peppers into a bowl and cover tightly with plastic wrap for a few minutes—this will make them much easier to peel. Peel, seed, and cut into strips.

To smoke the pollock, sprinkle 2 tablespoons of sawdust (we use apple wood) on the base of a rectangular roasting pan or smoking box. Put a wire rack into the pan and lay the fish, flesh-side up, on top. Put the box on a gas flame over a high heat for a minute or so until the sawdust starts to smolder. Cover the box with a lid or tightly with aluminum foil, then reduce the heat and smoke for 6 to 7 minutes. Turn off the heat and leave to sit, unopened, for 5 minutes.

Meanwhile, put the samphire into a saucepan of boiling water (not salted), return to a boil and simmer for 3 to 4 minutes or until tender. Drain the water (rinse under cold water if serving later). Toss the samphire in extra virgin olive but do not add salt because samphire has a natural salty tang.

To serve, divide the smoked pollock into nice flaky pieces, then arrange on a serving platter with strips of red and yellow pepper and sprigs of samphire on top. Drizzle with extra virgin olive oil and freshly ground pepper and a few flakes of sea salt.

ELDERBERRY *Sambucus nigra* PERENNIAL, ZONES 3–10

Elderberries are packed with goodness—have fun making gelatin, syrup, and wine.

Those of us who live in the countryside often have elder trees in abundance, but this plant grows everywhere and anywhere: in towns, villages, parks. Elder is native to Europe, Africa, part of Asia, and America, which delights our US students, who often encounter it for the first time when they are with us and love the cordials and granitas we make with it.

The leaves, stalks, and roots of the elder are toxic. However, the blossoms and berries can be enjoyed and have haunting flavors. The berries should be lightly cooked, as in their raw state they contain a chemical similar to cyanide.

WHERE/HOW IT GROWS
Elder grows in the woods and hedgerows, on the roadsides and on railway embankments, in urban and rural areas.

It's super easy to propagate; even a piece of twig stuck into the ground will often root.

VARIETIES
Nova—produces clusters of tender, sweet fruit for jams and jellies
York—bushes will tolerate dry or moist soil and can take some shade, produces tender fruit for cooking.

HARVESTING
The common elder bush produces white fluffy blossoms from late spring to early summer and we so look forward to the elderflowers, using them in myriad ways in the kitchen. Just snip off the flower heads on a sunny day when they are in full bloom. By autumn any flower heads left on the bushes will have turned into tiny black berries, which have a totally different flavor. Once again, we snip off the entire cluster of berries and strip them off the little head with fingers or the tines of a fork.

GOOD FOR YOU..
Elderberries have been used for centuries as a folk medicine and have many antibacterial and anti-viral properties; they also have a laxative effect and help to alleviate allergies and boost the immune system.

Recent research here in Ireland found that elderflower was effective in killing many common hospital bugs, including MRSA.

Berries from elder have even more health benefits than the flowers. They are rich in Vitamin C, and help to boost the immune system and cardiovascular

When elderflowers appear it's time to search for green gooseberries to make compote!

system and improve vision, plus they are good for rheumatism, colds, flu, viral infections, and tonsillitis. They are also used to lower cholesterol.

Elderberry syrup is great to guard against flu.

WHAT TO DO WITH A GLUT
Make lots of cordial and syrup from the flowers and berries. Each will taste totally different but will be delicious and nutritious in their own way.

IN THE KITCHEN
The black berries should always be cooked because some varieties are toxic when fresh. The common variety of elder (*Sambucus nigra*) is considered to be non-toxic but nonetheless the flavor is definitely improved when lightly cooked. The berries may also be dried and are surprisingly good added to scones or muffins.

Use elderflower blossom for cordials, champagne, syrups, fritters, and to flavor a whole host of other dishes, such as tarts, jellies, and sauces for game.

Elderflower Fritters with Elderflower Cream

These are very easy to make, very crisp and, once you've tasted one, you won't be able to stop! Serve with Green Gooseberry and Elderflower Compote (see page 390). In Germany these elderflower fritters are tossed in cinnamon sugar and called Hollerküchel.

SERVES 4

1 cup all-purpose flour
pinch of salt
1 organic egg
⅔ cup lukewarm water
8 to 12 elderflower heads
sunflower oil, for deep-frying
superfine sugar, for dusting
Green Gooseberry and Elderflower
Compote (page 390), to serve (optional)

FOR THE ELDERFLOWER CREAM
1 tablespoon elderflower cordial (see
    below)
¾ cup cream, softly whipped

Sift the flour and salt into a bowl. Make a well in the center and drop in the egg. Using a whisk, bring in the flour gradually from the edges, slowly adding in the water at the same time to make a smooth batter.

To make the elderflower cream, fold the cordial into the softly whipped cream, to taste.

Examine the elderflowers and shake them in case there are any insects, then rinse them in a bowl of water and shake dry. Inspect them again. Heat the oil in a deep-fat fryer to 350°F. Hold the flowers by the stalks and dip into the batter (add a little more water or milk if the batter is too thick) and shake off the excess. Fry for 2 to 3 minutes, until golden brown, in the hot oil. Drain on paper towels, toss in superfine sugar and serve immediately with elderflower cream and Green Gooseberry and Elderflower Compote, if using.

Elderflower Cordial

We make hundreds of gallons of elderflower cordial with the organic flowers that we snip from the hedgerows around the farm every year. It will keep for a year but is usually used up before the following year.

MAKES 1¾ QUARTS

20 elderflower heads
5 cups water
4 pounds granulated sugar
2 lemons
¼ cup citric acid

Examine the elderflowers and shake them in case there are any insects, then rinse them in a bowl of water and shake dry. Inspect them again. Bring the water to a boil in a stainless steel saucepan, add the sugar and stir to dissolve. Remove from the heat. Cool for 5 minutes.

Add the elderflower heads and stir. Grate in the zest of the lemons, then slice the fruit thinly and drop into the syrup. Stir in the citric acid, cover, and leave overnight to steep.

Next day, pour the liquid through a sieve and then a jelly bag. Save the lemon slices to add to homemade lemonade or gin and tonic. Pour the strained cordial into sterilized bottles. Cover, tighten, and store in a cool, dark place. Keep refrigerated and, once opened, consume within a couple of weeks.

To serve, dilute with water, wine or sparkling wine, about 1 part elderflower syrup to 8 parts water.

Elderflower Panna Cotta with Summer Berries

We also love this panna cotta with Green Gooseberry and Elderflower Compote (see page 390). The compote is also delicious served on its own with a little Elderflower Cream (see page 583) and maybe an elderflower fritter.

. . . .

SERVES 6 TO 8

non-scented oil, such as sunflower or peanut, for greasing

FOR THE PANNA COTTA

4 to 5 elderflower heads

2 quarts double cream

¼ cup superfine sugar

2 teaspoons gelatin

FOR THE SUMMER BERRIES

¾ pound fresh or frozen raspberries

½ to 1 cup confectioners sugar, or to taste, plus extra for dusting

1 pound mixed summer berries, such as small strawberries, raspberries, fraises du bois, blueberries, blackcurrants

fresh mint leaves and tiny sprigs of elderflower, to decorate

Lightly brush six to eight ½-cup molds with the oil.

Examine the elderflowers and shake them in case there are any insects, then rinse them in a bowl of water and shake dry. Inspect them again. Put the cream into a heavy-bottomed saucepan with the elderflower heads and superfine sugar. Set over a low heat and bring to the "shivery" stage. Remove from the heat and leave to infuse for 5 minutes.

Meanwhile, bloom the gelatin in a bowl with 3 tablespoons of water.

Strain the elderflower out of the cream. Set the bowl of gelatin in a saucepan over simmering water and stir until the gelatin is dissolved. Add a little of the cream to the gelatin, then pour in the rest of the cream and stir both mixtures together. Pour into the molds and leave until cold, then refrigerate until set, preferably overnight.

Pureé the raspberries in a blender or food processor with the confectioners sugar. Push through a sieve, and stir in the summer berries.

To serve, run a knife around the edge of the molds and turn out the panna cottas onto individual plates. Spoon a few berries onto the side of each then dust with confectioners sugar and tuck in a few fresh mint leaves and sprigs of elderflower.

Elderflower "Champagne"

This magical recipe transforms perfectly ordinary ingredients into a delicious sparkling drink. The children make it religiously every year and then share the bubbly with their friends. Despite the sparkle this drink is non-alcoholic. The bottles need to be strong and well sealed, otherwise the elderflower "champagne" will pop its cork.

. . . .

MAKES APPROX. 5 QUARTS

2 elderflower heads

1 lemon

1¼ pounds granulated sugar

2 tablespoons white wine vinegar

4½ quarts cold water

Examine the flowers and shake them in case there are any insects, then rinse them in a bowl of water and shake dry. Inspect them again.

Remove the peel from the lemon with a swivel-top peeler and squeeze the juice from the lemons. Put the peel into a bowl and add the elderflowers, lemon juice, sugar, vinegar, and cold water. Cover and leave for 24 hours, then strain into strong screw-top bottles. Lay them on their sides in a cool place and after 2 weeks the "champagne" should be sparkling and ready to drink.

ALEXANDERS
Smyrnium olusatrum Family *Apiaceae* ZONES 5–9

Alexanders are hardly recognized even though they grow freely all over the coastal countryside in Ireland. Introduced to the British Isles by the Romans who valued the plant as a "pot herb," they are now widespread in Europe, western Asia, and North Africa. Be careful when collecting, as the plant resembles poisonous wild dog (or spring) parsley and poison hemlock. Check a field guide if you are unsure. Or to you can grow your own from seed.

WHERE/HOW IT GROWS
Alexanders are a tall (up to 5 feet), lime green, umbelliferous plant with hollow stalks and large, yellow/green, multi-flowered heads.

HARVESTING
They are best harvested just before the buds burst into flower otherwise they can become bitter.

GOOD FOR YOU...
The plant was reputed to be good for digestion but nowadays it is rarely used in herbal medicine. Nicholas Culpeper, the well-known English herbalist, botanist, physician, and astrologer, included Alexanders in his book *The Complete Herbal*, published in 1652, which described the medicinal properties of all herbs and how to use them. He suggested using the powdered seed for 'flatulence, snakebite, and warming a cold stomach'.

IN THE KITCHEN
We use all parts—stalks, flowers, leaves—and later in the year you can roast the roots like parsnips. The dried seeds can be used as a spice like pepper.

The young leaves are good in salads but older ones need to be blanched first before being eaten as a vegetable or tossed into pasta with lots of grated

Look out for Alexanders growing by the roadside in coastal areas in late winter.

Parmesan or Pecorino cheese.

The stems can be picked and boiled, or very successfully candied like angelica and used to decorate cakes or served as a sweetmeat.

Roast Alexander Roots

Alexanders appear along the roadsides close to the coast just after Christmas. This is real hunter-gatherer stuff but they are properly delicious, so dig some up and have a little feast. Remember, all parts of the Alexander plant are edible. It has a flavor reminiscent of angelica and flat parsley, and the stem of Alexanders can be candied like angelica (see page 429). The flowers can be made into fritters like elderflower (see page 583).

SERVES 2

½ pound Alexander roots
2 tablespoons extra virgin olive oil
1 tablespoon fresh thyme leaves
sea salt and freshly ground black pepper

Preheat the oven to 350°F.

Scrub, peel, and slice the roots into ½-inch-thick slices. Dry.

Toss in the extra virgin olive oil and season with salt and freshly ground pepper. Sprinkle with thyme leaves and toss again. Roast for 20 to 25 minutes, depending on size.

Serve warm with lamb chops or roast chicken.

Alexander Tempura

One of the many ways we enjoy the tender young leaves of Alexanders.

SERVES 6

½ pound Alexander leaves or flowers, chopped or left whole
Aioli (page 195) or Asian Dipping Sauce (page 463), to serve
sea salt

FOR THE BATTER

1¼ cups white rice flour
2 tablespoons cornstarch
1 teaspoon baking powder
½ teaspoon cayenne pepper
1 cup cold sparkling water

Heat the oil in a deep frying pan to 375°F.

First make the batter. Mix the dry ingredients together in a bowl. Stir in the sparkling water with a wooden spoon, but don't overmix. Add the chopped Alexander leaves or dip the whole leaves or flowers into the batter.

Spoon scant tablespoons of the mixture into the frying panand cook for 3 to 4 minutes until lightly golden. Turn halfway through the cooking time. Drain on paper towels and sprinkle with a little salt.

Serve with Aioli or Asian Dipping Sauce.

CHICKWEED *Stellaria media* ANNUAL

Eat your weeds—the tender leaves of this invasive plant are delicious in salads and soups.

An invasive "weed" that thrives in most well-aerated soil, this low-growing plant provides an excellent ground cover (if you want it) and decreases insect damage to other plants.

It has several other common names, including mouse ear, chickenwort, and winterweed. Chickens love it and it has been grown as a cover crop for both human and poultry consumption.

WHERE/HOW IT GROWS

It grows in a wide variety of habitats in semi-cultivated ground and it's easy to pull. It's got pretty, white, star-shaped flowers, hence the name *Stellaria*, and grows up to 14 inches tall.

HARVESTING

Harvest in spring with a pair of scissors. It can be eaten all year round but it becomes straggly when it goes to seed.

GOOD FOR YOU...

Chickweed is high in vitamins, major minerals, and trace elements, particularly iron. It also contains beta carotene, calcium, potassium, oleic acid, and zinc.

IN THE KITCHEN

We use chickweed abundantly in our green salads and as a garnish. The delicate little pointy leaves are tender and delicious. It can also be used as a vegetable, wilted quickly in a little olive oil or butter.

Forager's Soup

Throughout the seasons one can gather wild greens on a walk in the countryside. Arm yourself with a good well-illustrated guide and be sure to identify carefully and, if in doubt, don't risk it until you are quite confident.

SERVES 6

4 tablespoons butter
1 medium potato, diced
1 small to medium onion, diced
4 cups hot light chicken stock
4 cups boiling full-fat milk
½ pound chopped greens, such as chickweed, Alexanders, nettles, wild sorrel, dandelions, wild garlic, watercress
extra virgin olive oil
2 ounces diced chorizo or lardons of bacon (optional)
wild garlic flowers, if available , to garnish
sea salt and freshly ground black pepper

Melt the butter in a heavy-bottomed saucepan. When it foams, add the potatoes and onions and stir them until well coated. Season. Cover and sweat over a gentle heat for 10 minutes. When the vegetables are almost soft but not colored, add the hot stock and boiling milk. Return to a boil and cook until the potatoes and onions are fully cooked. Add the greens and boil, uncovered, for 2 to 3 minutes, until they are just cooked. Do not overcook or the soup will lose its fresh green color. Purée the soup in a blender or with a stick blender. Season to taste.

Heat a little oil in a frying pan. Add the diced chorizo or lardons, cook over a low heat until the fat starts to run and the bacon is crisp. Drain on paper towels, saving the cooking oil. Sprinkle the crisp lardons and drizzle the oil over the top of each bowl and scatter a few wild garlic flowers over the top, if available.

DANDELIONS *Taraxacum officinale* ZONES 3–10

An ancient wild plant, but one that is easily recognisable to most people, although few would decide to nibble the leaves. The word dandelion is thought to have come from the French phrase "*dent de lion*," or "lion's tooth," which refers to the coarsely serrated leaves.

Dandelion belongs to one of the largest plant families, the *Asteraceae* family, which includes 22,000 species.

Dandelions have been gathered as a food source since the age of hunter-gatherers and have been valued as a medicine since ancient times.

WHERE/HOW IT GROWS
Although they now grow throughout the world, they are thought to have evolved 30 million years ago in Eurasia. Dandelions are hardy perennials and commonly regarded as a stubborn weed, but they add minerals and nitrogen to the soil and their long tap roots bring up nutrients for shallow-rooting plants. They are hardy and will grow almost anywhere. They are not fussy about soil conditions, but do best in rich, moist soil, in sun or partial shade. They are also a source of food for many insects and butterflies.

Dandelions, which many consider to be a pest, are grown commercially as a bitter salad green in France, the leaves are blanched to pale yellow which diminishes the bitterness somewhat. You can quite easily blanch dandelions in one's own garden or backyard, just cover the plant with a plastic bucket or lid, or a light saucepan lid to exclude the light. The dandelion leaves will blanch in a week or two, and become elongated and tender. Those growing in a shady area are likely to be more tender.

Dandelions are also a popular green in Italy, China, and India. The flowers open with the sun in the morning and close in the evening or when the weather changes.

HARVESTING
Pick the young leaves in early spring, you will find them very bitter when your first taste them but it's a quickly acquired taste and it's a green that can be very beneficial to one's health.

DID YOU KNOW?
Dandelion is called *pissenlit* in French, a reference to its powerful diuretic properties.

GOOD FOR YOU...
Dandelion leaves have twice as much iron as spinach. They are rich in vitamins A and B6, plus calcium, potassium, and manganese. It is also a powerful source of vitamin K; 110g contains up to five times the recommended daily intake.

The flowers are high in antioxidants. When I was a child the white milky sap was painted on warts and was said to dissolve them in eight days.

The roots, stalks, and flowers of dandelion constitute a complete protein.

IN THE KITCHEN
Blanched dandelion leaves are a delicious addition to salads, particularly in autumn and winter. We also love the wild leaves just as they are; if you enjoy the bitterness of chicory, you will also enjoy dandelion. Pop a few into a green salad or add to a forager's soup or wilted greens. We also add the flowers to water kefir.

Dandelion wine can also be very good made with the flowers, which we also use to make dandelion fritters.

All parts of dandelions are edible—the bitter leaves, flowers, and roots.

Dandelion Salad with Anchovy Dressing & Pangrattato

Use a mixture of blanched and unblanched dandelion leaves if available.

. . . .

SERVES 8

8 handfuls of dandelion leaves, cut or torn
    into generous bite-sized bits
1 to 2 handfuls of freshly grated Parmesan
Pangrattato (see below) or 40 croutons,
    approximately 1-inch square, cooked in
    extra virgin olive oil
16 anchovies
sea salt and freshly ground black pepper

FOR THE CAESAR DRESSING
1 (1.8-ounce) can anchovies
2 organic egg yolks
1 garlic clove, crushed
2 tablespoons freshly squeezed lemon
    juice
a generous pinch of English mustard
    powder
½ teaspoon salt
½ to 1 tablespoon Worcestershire sauce
½ to 1 tablespoon Tabasco sauce
¾ cup sunflower oil
¼ cup extra virgin olive oil
¼ cup cold water

FOR THE PANGRATTATO
4 tablespoons extra virgin olive oil
2 garlic cloves
1½ cups white bread crumbs
1 lemon

The Caesar dressing can be made in a food processor but it can also be made very quickly by hand. Drain the anchovies and crush lightly with a fork. Put into a bowl with the egg yolks, add the garlic, lemon juice, mustard powder, salt, Worcestershire and Tabasco sauces. Whisk all the ingredients together. As you whisk, add the oils, slowly at first, then a little faster as the emulsion forms. Finally, whisk in the water to make a spreadable consistency. Season to taste— this dressing should be highly flavored.

To make the pangrattato, heat the extra virgin olive in a frying pan, then add the garlic cloves and sauté until golden brown. Remove the garlic cloves and set aside. Add half the bread crumbs and stir over a medium heat until they turn golden. Spread out on a baking sheet, repeat with the remainder of the bread crumbs. Grate the garlic cloves over the bread crumbs. Finely grate the lemon zest over the crumbs also. Toss, season with salt, and taste.

Choose a bowl large enough to hold the salad comfortably, then sprinkle the leaves with enough dressing to coat them lightly. Add a handful of Parmesan. Toss gently and add the croutons (if using). Toss again. Divide among eight plates. Top each salad with a couple of anchovies and the pangrattato. Serve immediately.

Dandelion Flower Fritters

Picking dandelion flowers is an exciting way to introduce children to foraging. Get them to nibble a leaf and watch them scrunch up their faces. Children love these little fritters, and even from an early age they can help you make the batter.

. . . .

SERVES 4 TO 5

24 to 30 fully open dandelion flowers

sunflower oil, for deep-frying

Vanilla Sugar (made with a few vanilla beans buried in a tall jar of superfine sugar)

FOR THE BATTER

1 cup all-purpose flour

pinch of salt

1 organic egg

⅔ cup lukewarm water

First make the batter. Sift the flour and salt into a bowl. Make a well in the center and drop in the egg. Using a whisk, bring in the flour gradually from the edges, slowly adding in the water at the same time.

Shake the flowers just in case there are any insects hidden inside!

Heat the oil in a deep frying pan to 350°F or use a shallow pan with at least 1 inch oil.

Just before you are ready to eat, dip a few flowers in the batter (add a little more water or milk if the batter is too thick) and shake off any excess. Fry in the hot oil until puffed and crisp—about 2 minutes. Drain on paper towels. Toss the fritters in vanilla sugar and serve as soon as possible.

Dandelion Wine

A perfect wine to make if you have a glut of dandelion heads; make it in summer and it should be just right for drinking by mid-winter.

. . . .

MAKES ABOUT 6 QUARTS

1 pound dandelion flowers

juice and peel of 4 oranges (organic if possible), cut into thin slivers

2¾ pounds granulated sugar

1 teaspoon dried yeast

For best results pick the flowers in full sunshine at midday when they are fully open. Make the wine immediately.

Weigh the yellow dandelion heads and place in a large heatproof bowl. Discard as much green leaf as possible. Meanwhile, bring 6 cups of water to the boil.

Pour the boiling water over the flower heads. Leave to steep for 2 days. Don't exceed the time or what can be a delicious table wine may be spoiled. Tip into a large saucepan and bring to the boil, then add the thin slivers of the orange peel (no white pith) and continue to boil for 10 minutes.

Strain through cheesecloth onto the sugar in a large clean mixing bowl, stir to dissolve the sugar fully. When cool, add the juice from the oranges and the yeast. Transfer to a fermentation jar and fit an air-lock. Siphon off into clean bottles when the wine has cleared—which takes about 2 months. Store in a cool, dry place, and enjoy within a couple of months.

NAVELWORT

Umbilicus rupestris—Crassulaceae or Stonecrop family ZONES 6–9

We so look forward to seeing the first of the navelwort peeping out of the perimeter walls in midwinter. I first came across navelwort in Spain when I was walking in the oak forests in Andalucia. My friends who lives locally calls it the walker's friend, because it is beloved as a nibble to quench your thirst as you plod along the ancient cobbled paths.

I also came across a different form of navelwort in Burma. It's got a slightly larger and more tender leaf and grows wild in soil rather than in walls. The leaves were also scalloped but the texture was finer and not succulent. The Latin name is *Centella asiatica.* They were used in salad and dipped in a light tempura batter to make crispy fritters

WHERE/HOW IT GROWS

This delicious little succulent plant grows all over the British Isles, parts of south and western Europe and the Canary Islands. It is one of the first to emerge in winter. It grows between rocks and in damp crevices in old stone walls and in shady places. The round fleshy green leaves are slightly crimped at the edges, they are shallow-rooted and grow on a short fleshy stem.

The leaves can have a pinky-purplish tinge if the weather is cold at the beginning or end of the season, and the color lasts well into late summer.

DID YOU KNOW?

Here in Ireland we call this plant pennywort, although it is unrelated to the plant called pennywort in the US. The navelwort name comes from the indentation in the center of the leaf which resembles a navel.

HARVESTING

It is best before it flowers in early summer, when tall spikes appear with greenish-pink flowers which can be up to 10 inches long.

GOOD FOR YOU...

It's known to be anti-inflammatory, antibacterial, and an anti-viral agent. It aids digestion and is rich in B vitamins, calcium, phosphorus, zinc, magnesium, and other minerals. Studies have shown that eating a few leaves may sharpen the memory, combat Alzheimer's disease and help to lower blood pressure.

WHAT TO DO WITH A GLUT

Eat lots and lots in salads.

IN THE KITCHEN

We love navelwort; together with winter cress they are some of the earliest wild greens and are available to winter foragers. Navelwort has a delicate flavor, so we use the juicy leaves in salads, sandwiches, and to garnish plates. We also love them dipped in a light tempura batter and cooked as fritters or as part of a winter *fritto misto.*

The succulent leaves of navelwort grow on walls and at the bottom of trees in woodland.

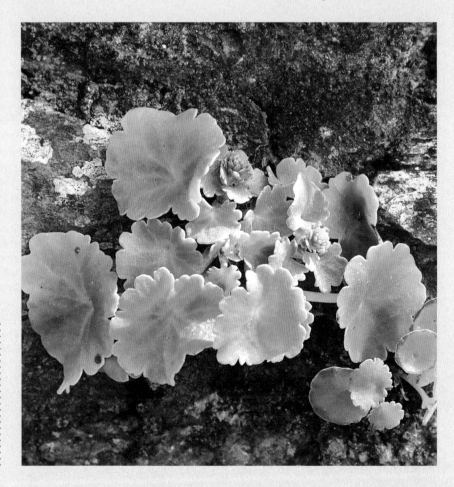

Burmese Navelwort Salad

Myanmar (previously Burma) is justly famous for its salads. Virtually every vegetable is made into a salad, and most include peanuts. Sometimes they scissor in some fish cakes—it sounds odd but it's delicious.

. . . .

SERVES 4

2 large garlic cloves
peanut oil, for frying
2 to 3 shallots, sliced, soaked in ice-cold
    water, and drained
¾ cup navelwort leaves
1 tablespoon freshly squeezed lime juice
2 teaspoons fermented bean paste
fish sauce or salt, to taste
1 large or 2 small tomatoes, halved and
    thinly sliced
2 to 3 tablespoons sesame seeds
1 tablespoon crushed peanuts

Slice the garlic into paper-thin slices and let dry on paper towels.

Heat some peanut oil in a frying pan and cook the garlic and shallots over medium heat until crisp and golden. Drain on paper towels.

Put the navelwort onto a plate. Sprinkle the oil used for cooking the garlic and shallots over the top, then the freshly squeezed lime juice, fermented bean paste, fish sauce or salt, thinly sliced tomato, and sesame seeds.

Toss and mix with your clean fingers as the Burmese do. Add most of the fried shallots and garlic and half of the peanuts. Toss again and season to taste.

Divide among 4 plates, sprinkle with the remainder of the fried shallots, garlic, and peanuts. Serve immediately, each salad is made to order.

Navelwort Fritters with Aioli

Navelwort grows in profusion on the stone walls around the School, and in woodlands and hedgerows around the countryside. We use it in salads but try it in these fritters, which I also came across on a trip to Myanmar. There they served them with a little Asian dipping sauce. The whole navelwort leaves are also irresistible.

. . . .

SERVES 6

olive or sunflower oil, for frying
1 cup navelwort leaves, chopped or left
    whole
Aioli (page 195) or Asian Dipping Sauce
    (page 463), to serve
sea salt

FOR THE BATTER
1¼ cups white rice flour
2 tablespoons cornstarch
1 teaspoon baking powder
½ teaspoon cayenne pepper
1 cup cold sparkling water

Heat the oil in a deep frying pan to 375°F.

First make the batter. Mix the dry ingredients together in a bowl. Stir in the sparkling water with a wooden spoon, but don't overmix. Add the chopped navelwort leaves or dip the whole leaves into the batter.

Spoon scant tablespoons of the mixture into the frying pan and cook for 3–4 minutes until lightly golden. Turn halfway through the cooking time. Drain on paper towels and sprinkle with a little salt.

Serve with Aioli or Asian Dipping Sauce.

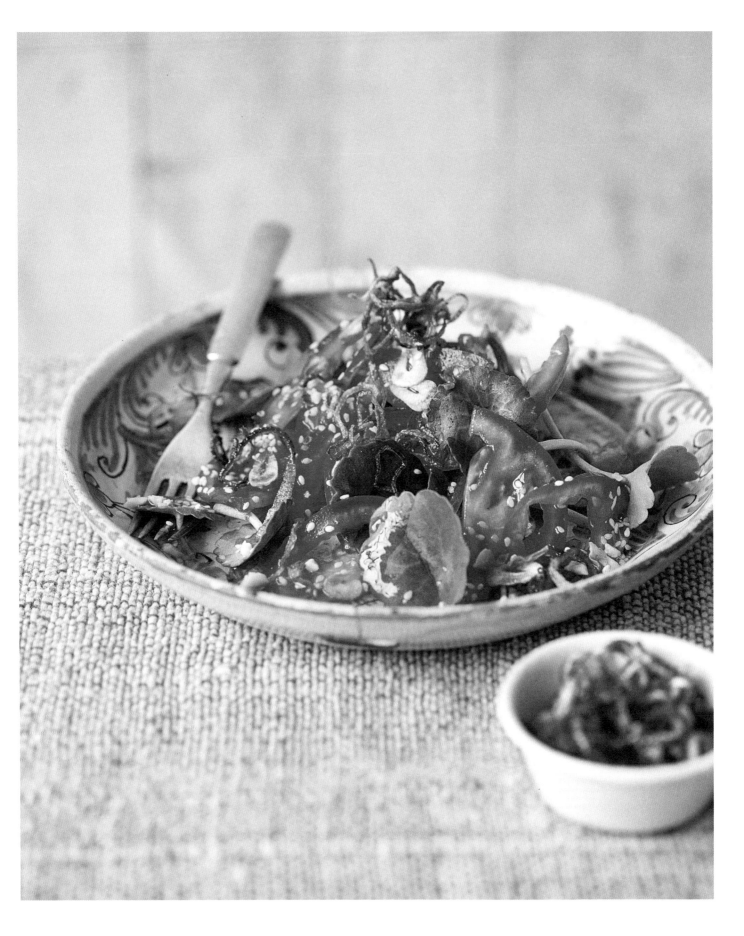

NETTLES   *Urtica dioica* PERENNIAL, ZONES 3–10

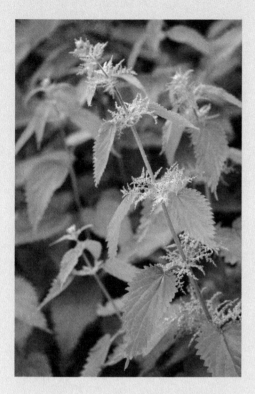

The common stinging nettle is a powerhouse of nutrients.

Can you imagine that I almost forgot to include nettles in this book? This chapter was just about completed when my editor sent an email to inquire why I hadn't included stinging nettles? Oops! The most obvious inclusion was almost forgotten.

It is a plant that irks the gardener, but it is also a delicious powerhouse of nutrients, so you should relish your weeds. In fact, nettles have been part of the Irish flora and diet for over 6,000 years—ever since the first farmers cleared the forests. There are many references to these plants in ancient manuscripts; monks added them to their pottages and knew the value of young nettles as a blood cleanser after the long winter months. This folk knowledge and these customs live on up to the present day when older people in particular will tell you of the tradition of eating "four feeds of nettles in the month of May to purify the blood and keep away the rheumatics." In fact, those who suffered would whip themselves with nettles to improve the condition.

Alexanders, ramps, and nettles are some of the earliest wild foods in the season; and now that foraging has become super cool, many chefs have also re-discovered wild food and have been incorporating these ingredients into their menus in myriad creative ways. We have seen the demand for organic nettles grow at our stall at the farmers' market in nearby Midleton.

HOW/WHERE IT GROWS

Nettles grow in profusion throughout temperate regions around the world and particularly flourish in nitrate-rich soil.

HARVESTING

Gather organic nettles in spring and early summer when the leaves are young and tender and the flavor is mild. Snip off the tender tips with scissors or secateurs from late winter onwards. It's best to harvest nettles before they flower.

The common nettle, *Urtica dioica*, is a stinging nettle, so wear long sleeves and long trousers when you are picking it—you'll also need gloves to protect your hands. If you do get stung, rub the affected area with a dock leaf (*Rumex obtusifolius*), because the sap will relieve the pain. Mother Nature has arranged that the antidote usually grows close by.

GOOD FOR YOU...

With their high iron (more than either kale or broccoli) and vitamin C content, nettles were, and still are, highly valued in folk medicine, and like many other wild foods they helped in some small measure to alleviate hunger during the Irish famine.

Herbalists confirm that as well as iron, nettles contain formic acid, histamine, ammonia, silicic acid, and potassium. Some of these compounds are known to alleviate rheumatism, sciatica, and other pains. They lower blood pressure and blood sugar levels, increase the haemoglobin in the blood, improve circulation, and purify the system—so our ancestors weren't far wrong.

DID YOU KNOW?

Fabric woven from nettle fiber has been found in burial sites that date back to the Bronze Age. There was an annual feast on Cape Clear, Oileán Chléire, an island off the West Cork coast, on May 1 called *Féile na Neantóg*. On that day all the children would have great sport chasing each other with bundles of stinging nettles. If they wet the nettles beforehand it put "extra heat" in them. They stung every inch of each other's bodies, and this was done with great glee and without a shred of remorse.

Islanders also fed nettles to their pigs and hens. Donnchadh O'Drisceóil described in his book *Aisti o Chléire* how he would search around the edge of the house and farm sheds for young nettles. The picked nettles were scalded and mixed with yellowmeal to entice the pigs to eat them and were prized as fodder.

Nettles are also a well-known and highly-regarded diuretic which helps to eliminate toxins from kidneys. They also aid digestion and are anecdotally used to eliminate worms.

WHAT TO DO WITH A GLUT

Make nettle beer, it's really good and can be drunk after just a couple of weeks. Gardeners will want to make **Nettle Plant Tea**, which is a splendid nitrogen-rich plant food. Just fill a bucket or a barrel with nettles—you could use the strimmer and then there will be a burst of fresh young growth—cover with rainwater and leave to steep for 2 to 3 weeks. (It will stink...!) Strain and bottle. To use, dilute the mixture at one part nettle concentrate to ten parts water and pour from a watering can with a rose nozzle.

IN THE KITCHEN

Every year we discover more ways to enjoy nettles. Needless to say, we don't eat them raw—they lose their sting as soon as they are cooked or even wilted on the pan with other greens.

Stinging nettle soup is delicious as it is, simply made with an onion and potato base or in conjunction with other greens, such as watercress, sorrel, or chickweed. Blanch the nettles well in boiling salted water and rinse, then purée or add to spinach and ricotta as a filling for cappelletti or tortellini. They also work well on pizza, and even though they are added raw, they lose their sting in the oven.

Nettle Pesto (see **Wild Garlic Pesto, page 542**) is surprisingly delicious. Serve it with pasta or drizzle it over potato soup. Add some leaves to spinach when making spanakopita or just creamed spinach, maybe one-third nettles to two-thirds spinach.

Fresh or Dried Nettle Tea can be an acquired taste, but it is super-nutritious and devotees swear by its health benefits. It's easy to make an infusion with fresh leaves, just put a few young leaves in a cup or a fistful in a tea pot, cover them with freshly boiled water and leave to macerate for a few minutes. Put through a tea strainer and enjoy.

Many people like to have a supply of dry leaves on hand for making tea. Pick lots of fresh leaves, then dry them overnight in a dehydrator. Alternatively, tie three or four stems together with cotton string. Hang to dry in the sun in a greenhouse, tunnel, conservatory, or sunny porch for 3 to 4 days. When crispy dry, crush over a bowl with gloved hands. Store in airtight jars in a cool, dry, dark place and make tea as above. You can also add a couple of teaspoons of dried nettles to the dry ingredients when making white soda bread.

Stinging Nettle Soup

We love this version, which includes leeks as well as onion and potato to give an extra silkiness to the texture and flavor to the soup. We use tender young nettle tops in spring.

. . . .

SERVES 6

3 tablespoons butter

1 large potato, peeled and chopped

1 small onion, chopped

1 small leek, chopped

1 quart chicken stock

1½ cups young nettles, washed and chopped

⅔ cup creamy milk

sea salt and freshly ground black pepper

nettle pesto (see above), to serve (optional)

Melt the butter in a heavy saucepan, and when it foams, add the potatoes, onions, and leeks, tossing them in the butter until well coated. Sprinkle with salt and freshly ground pepper. Cover with a circle of parchment (to keep in the steam) and the saucepan lid, and sweat over a gentle heat for 10 minutes, or until the vegetables are soft but not colored.

Discard the parchment, add the stock, and boil until the vegetables are just cooked, then add the nettle leaves. Simmer uncovered for just a few minutes. Do not overcook or the vegetables will lose their flavor. Add the creamy milk and purée. Season to taste. Serve hot with a drizzle of nettle pesto, if available.

Nettle & Ricotta Pizza

Alice Waters has incorporated local wild foods into her menu at Chez Panisse in Berkeley, California, for a very long time. On a recent trip I enjoyed this delicious pizza straight from the wood-burning oven.

. . . .

MAKES 1 PIZZA

2 ounces pizza dough (page 48)

cornmeal, for dusting

extra virgin olive oil, for brushing and drizzling

1 garlic clove, finely chopped

1 ounce fresh buffalo mozzarella, roughly grated

2 to 3 cups fresh young nettles

2 tablespoons ricotta or fresh goat cheese or curd

sea salt and freshly ground black pepper

Preheat the oven to 475°F with a heavy baking sheet inside.

Stretch or roll the dough into a thin round. Sprinkle a little cornmeal onto a paddle and lay the dough on top. Brush with extra virgin olive oil, sprinkle with chopped garlic and the mozzarella. Top with a mound of young nettles, then mist generously with water, season with salt and freshly ground pepper, and top with a few blobs of ricotta or goat cheese. Cook for 7 or 8 minutes, depending on the intensity of the heat.

Remove from the oven, drizzle with extra virgin olive oil and serve immediately with a few flakes of Maldon sea salt sprinkled over the top.

Roger's Nettle Beer

We're huge fans of Roger Phillips and found this recipe in his *Wild Food* book. It made delicious beer—sweet and fizzy, perfect for summertime. Unfortunately we bottled it before it had finished fermenting, and one night the glass bottles exploded. Oh well, practice makes perfect!

. . . .

MAKES ABOUT 12 QUARTS

100 nettle stalks, with leaves

2¾ pounds granulated sugar

5 tablespoons cream of tartar

1¼ tablespoons live yeast

Boil the nettles in a very large saucepan filled with 11½ quarts of water for 10 minutes. Drain and discard the leaves, then add the sugar and the cream of tartar to the liquid. Heat and stir until dissolved. Remove from the heat and leave until tepid, then add the yeast and stir well. Cover with cheesecloth and leave for a week.

Remove the scum from the surface and decant without disturbing the sediment. Bottle, cork, and secure the top. Leave at room temperature for about 2 weeks or until starting to bubble then drink within a few weeks.

EDIBLE FLOWERS

CALENDULA *Calendula officinalis* ANNUAL

Left: *French marigolds.*
Above: Calendula officinalis *also known as common or pot marigold.*

When I googled marigolds, the orange plastic dishwashing gloves popped up! Marigolds, like the word Kleenex, have entered into the language as a commonly used word. So what comes to mind when you see the word marigold?

For me, it's the cheery little pot marigold with bright orange flowers. But there's lots of confusion. Pot marigold or calendula, native to Europe, comes from the Asteraceae family, whereas the French marigold, an American native, is a member of the genus *Tagetes*. They are very different plants; calendula, my little cottage-garden friend, is edible, but most French marigolds aren't, which, despite their beauty and enormous variety, excludes them from this book.

There are 15 to 20 species of annual and perennial plants in the daisy family known as marigolds. The common name marigold refers to the Virgin Mary.

VARIETIES
Calendula arvensis (**Field marigold**)—Not easily available, looks good in borders.

Calendula officinalis (**Pot marigold**) comes in a wide range of oranges and yellows with great names like *Oopsy Daisy*, *Neon*, *Dandy*, and *Golden Prince*. There is also a dwarf selection which come under the *C. o. nana* strain, including *Candyman Orange* and *Lemon Daisy*.
Calendula **Touch of Red**—Special strain in which all the blooms have a touch of red on the petals. It includes *Touch of Red Orange*, *Touch of Red Buff*, *Touch of Red Mixed*, *Touch of Red Art Shades*.
Tagetes tenuifolia (**signet marigold**)—Smallest and daintiest marigold, used for rock gardens or to edge a bed. The flowers are edible.

HOW TO GROW
Calendula are easy to grow, in fact, once you have them in the garden they will seed quite happily. They like to grow in a sunny spot, and although they are not fussy about soil, ideally don't plant them in any that is prone to become waterlogged. They will happily grow alongside other flowers or vegetables.

Sow the seeds in spring after the last frost and gently water the seedbed immediately after planting.

Keep cutting the blooms to encourage more flowers and to prevent them forming too many seedheads—later in the season you may wish to save some of the seeds to sow the following year.

CONTAINER GROWING
All calendula can be grown in containers to good effect.

PESTS AND DISEASES
Calendulas are brilliant companion plants because they are naturally insect repellent, but the roots also repel nematodes and other pests for up to three years.

GOOD FOR YOU...
Calendula ointment is an effective treatment for a variety of skin problems; it may reduce inflammation and help wound healing. It is also used in the treatment of eczema, sunburn, and warts. Calendulas are also used in the treatment of conjunctivitis and other eye inflammation. Nutritionally, calendulas are a good source of carotenoids, especially in the form of lutein, which have strong antioxidant properties. They also provide vitamin C, phosphorous, potassium, and some flavonoids.

IN THE KITCHEN
Calendula petals are edible and can be used fresh or dried. We scatter them over salads all summer, sometimes in combination with blue cornflower petals. They can also be added to cookies and cakes and are used to color butter and cheese. Calendula tea is nutritious and delicious.

A Warm Salad of Chicken Livers & Calendula Petals

Cheery little orange calendula petals add color and a touch of magic to any salad. I sometimes grate some ginger over the chicken liver in the pan.

. . . .

SERVES 4

selection of lettuce and salad leaves, such as butterhead, iceberg, oakleaf, Lollo Rosso, curly endive, and mysticana

1 dessert apple, peeled and diced

approx. 1 tablespoon butter, plus extra for frying

pinch of sugar (optional)

4 to 6 fresh chicken livers (organic if possible)

1 tablespoon chopped chives, plus chive flowers and calendula petals, to garnish

salt and freshly ground black pepper

FOR THE DRESSING

3 tablespoons extra virgin olive oil

1 tablespoon red wine vinegar

a little Dijon mustard

Wash and dry the salad leaves and tear them into bite-sized pieces.

Whisk together the ingredients for the dressing.

Fry the apple in a little butter until just soft and almost golden, then taste—they may need a pinch of sugar. Keep warm.

Wash and dry the livers and divide each into 2 pieces. Just before you are ready to serve, melt the butter in a sauté pan, season the livers with salt and pepper and cook over low heat—they are very good when slightly pink in the center, but only if you like them that way.

While the livers are cooking, toss the salad leaves in just enough of the dressing to make the leaves glisten.

Divide the salad leaves among four large plates, sprinkle evenly with the fried apple and hot livers, then scatter over the chives, chive flowers, and calendula petals and serve immediately.

Note: One can do lots of variations on this starter, such as using duck livers or cooking the fillet pieces from the duck breasts quickly in a pan then slicing them onto the salad.

DUCK CONFIT SALAD

Ingredients as above but substitute 2 preserved duck legs for the livers.

Remove the duck legs from the fat (it may be necessary to melt some of it). Preheat the oven to 350°F. Roast the duck for 15 to 20 minutes and then cook for 4 to 5 minutes on a hot grill pan to crisp the skin. Strip the crispy duck from the bones and divide among the four plates of salad. Sprinkle with chives, chive flowers, and calendula petals and serve immediately.

DID YOU KNOW?

African calendula petals were added to chicken feed to make the yolks a darker yellow. In many Asian countries calendulas have special significance and in India they are considered sacred and honored and are used in religious ceremonies and as offerings at funerals and weddings. They are also used to make garlands to decorate religious statues and buildings and to welcome guests.

Calendula Shortbreads

These little biscuits are flecked with calendula petals, but I'm not sure from the flavor whether you would know they are there without being told. Nonetheless, they are delicious and look pretty with calendula sugar dusted over the top.

. . . .

MAKES 16 BISCUITS

1¼ cups plus 3 tablespoons all-purpose or
   spelt flour
3½ tablespoons superfine sugar
6 tablespoons (14g) calendula petals
½ cup (1 stick) cold butter

FOR THE CALENDULA SUGAR
calendula petals
¼ cup superfine sugar

Preheat the oven to 350°F.

Put the flour, sugar, and calendula petals into a bowl, then rub in the butter as for shortcrust pastry. Gather the mixture together and knead gently on a lightly floured surface. Roll out the pastry to ¼ inch thick, then cut into rounds with a 2½-inch cutter or into heart shapes. Bake for 15 to 18 minutes until pale brown, depending on the thickness of the cookies. Remove and cool on a wire rack.

While they cool, make the calendula sugar. Combine the calendula petals in a blender with the sugar and blend for a minute or two until just broken up.

Serve the biscuits with fruit fools, compotes, and ice creams and sprinkle calendula sugar over the top.

Note: Watch these cookies really carefully while they are baking; they burn easily. They should be a pale golden—any darker and they will be bitter. However, if they are too pale they will be undercooked and doughy.

CORNFLOWERS *Centaurea cyanus* ANNUAL

Cornflowers are super-easy and inexpensive to grow, and although we usually think of them as the color of Reckitt's Blue, they also come in pink, lavender, maroon, and white. Not only drop-dead gorgeous, they are also what we call a cut-and-come-again flower.

VARIETIES

Blue Boy—Classic blue cornflower, a double blue flower with multiple stems in the upper half, long season, 35 to 40 inches high.

Choice Mixed—Range of different shades including mauve, salmon pink, blue, violet, and pure white, 40 inches high.

Polka Dot—Another mixed variety with a dwarf habit, 12 inches high

HOW TO GROW

You can sow the seeds or spring—or in autumn in mild winter climates. If possible, autumn is best so the seeds can settle in before the frost, then they will develop strong roots when the soil warms up and burst into action in spring. Sow about ¼ inch deep, in rows 12 inches apart, just rake the seed in and barely cover them. Water in the seed. Alternatively, sow the seeds in pots in spring or directly into the flower beds or in a wild flower meadow. They like poor soil but need a sunny open spot to thrive. Cornflowers grow 6 to 14 inches high We also use them to edge paths in the kitchen garden where they also attract beneficial insects to help with pollination. Bees and butterflies love them.

CONTAINER GROWING

Cornflowers look great in containers. Sow in garden soil or multi purpose compost. Mix with common calendulas.

Beautiful centaurea cyanus *"Blue Boy"*.

PESTS AND DISEASES

We haven't had any bother at all.

HARVESTING

Cornflowers need to be cut constantly for maximum value. The more you cut the more blooms the plant will yield.

GOOD FOR YOU...

Cornflowers are said to ease tired or puffy eyes. Make an infusion with 2 tablespoons of petals and ½ cup water and simmer for 10 to 12 minutes. Strain, cool, and dab on with cotton wool. They contain gallic acid, vitamin C, phosphorous, and potassium

IN THE KITCHEN

We scatter the pretty blue flowers over deviled eggs, iced cakes, and wee cupcakes and salads. They are also great additions to drinks; freeze them in ice

Centaurea cyanus *"Choice Mixed"* come in an appealing range of colors.

cube trays with a little water and a fresh mint leaf, or sprinkle petals into homemade lemonades and cordials.

Coconut Cupcakes Sprinkled with Cornflowers

These were one of the big hits of our Airstream Dream Food Truck during the summer of 2016. Everyone loves these moist coconut cupcakes and they look so pretty with cornflower petals sprinkled over the top. If you don't have flower petals they will still be delicious of course.

MAKES AT LEAST 36 LARGE CUPCAKES

1½ cups (3 sticks) butter, at room temperature

2⅓ cups superfine sugar

5 organic eggs, at room temperature

1½ teaspoons vanilla extract

¼ teaspoon almond extract

3 cups all-purpose flour

1 teaspoon baking powder

½ teaspoon baking soda

½ teaspoon salt

¾ cup plus 1 tablespoon buttermilk

9 ounces desiccated coconut (we use frozen desiccated coconut, defrosted)

blue cornflower petals, to decorate

FOR THE CREAM CHEESE FROSTING

1½ cups (3 sticks) unsalted butter, at room temperature

1 pound cream cheese, at room temperature

1 teaspoon vanilla extract

⅛ teaspoon almond extract

5½ cups confectioners' sugar, sifted

Preheat the oven to 325°F. Line three 12-hole muffin cups with paper liners.

Cream the butter and sugar together in a bowl until light and fluffy. Beat in the eggs one at a time, scraping down the bowl after each addition. Add the vanilla and almond extracts and mix well.

Sift the flour, baking powder, baking soda, and salt together. Add the dry ingredients and the buttermilk in several stages: dry, wet, dry, wet, dry....Mix gently but thoroughly until just combined. Fold in 7 ounces of the coconut.

Fill each muffin cup two-thirds full with the mixture. Bake for 30 to 35 minutes until the tops are golden brown and the mixture is cooked through. Transfer to a wire rack to cool.

Meanwhile, make the frosting. Cream the butter until light and fluffy, then mix in the cream cheese, vanilla, and almond extracts. Fold in the confectioners' sugar and mix until smooth.

Pipe the frosting on top of each cooled cupcake and sprinkle each with some of the remaining coconut and the cornflower petals.

CHAMOMILE

Chamaemelum nobile ANNUAL AND PERENNIAL

Chamomile is the common name for several daisy-like plants in the Asteraceae family. It's so easy to grow, and you can harvest and dry the flower heads to make your own soporific chamomile tea, just like Peter Rabbit had in Beatrix Potter's children's books. Chamomile is naturally caffeine-free and has been used since ancient times for its calming properties. It's also called the "physician's plant" by gardeners who believe it helps to revive ailing plants when planted close to them.

VARIETIES

There are three main types:
Chaemaemelum nobile (**Roman chamomile**) perennial, zones 4–7—This is the original true chamomile and the best for chamomile tea.
Matricaria recutita (**German chamomile**), annual—Grows in a more upright fashion.
Anthemis tinctoria (**dyer's chamomile**), perennial, zones 3–7—Has yellow flowers and so-called because they can be used as a dye.

HOW TO GROW

Roman, German, and dyer's chamomile can be grown from seed. Sprinkle the seeds or even an old packet of chamomile tea over a patch of well-drained soil in spring. Water well and the seeds will germinate within a couple of weeks and keep you supplied with beautiful daisy-like flowers right through until the autumn. Bees love chamomile and the flowers look lovely in the garden or in the wild.

CONTAINER GROWING

Chamomile plants grow brilliantly in containers.

PESTS AND DISEASES

Chamomile isn't affected by many pests; in fact, it can be useful in companion planting as its strong scent can help keep pests away.

HARVESTING

Early summer is best for leaves, midsummer for the flowers. Chamomile tea can, of course, be made from fresh flowers, but it's also ridiculously easy to harvest and dry your own. Just snip off the plants' tips and hang up in a warm, airy spot to dry, then snip off the heads and store in a paper bag or a tin box.

DID YOU KNOW?

Chamomile is reputed to keep blonde hair bright, so try an infusion as a rinse (better than chemicals anyway!).

GOOD FOR YOU...

The list of chamomile's health benefits seems endless. According to an Ohio State University study, chamomile contains apigenin, which can halt the spread of cancer (apigenin is also abundant in parsley and celery). Yet another study at the University of Texas found that drinking chamomile tea helps to keep diabetes under control by decreasing blood glucose and insulin levels and improving antioxidant status. It's also known to soothe an upset stomach, ease menstrual cramps, make your hair shine, help with insomnia, and boost the immune system.

WHAT TO DO WITH A GLUT

Dry to use in making chamomile tea.

IN THE KITCHEN

Chamomile can be used fresh or dried. There are many more ways to use

Chamomile flowers ready for harvesting—just pick, dry and use to make "sleepy" tea.

chamomile than just making tea—you can use it in ice creams, panna cotta, and custards. Infuse 1¼ cups cream with 3 tablespoons fresh or 1½ tablespoons dried chamomile, warm gently, but don't allow to boil. Strain out the chamomile once it has infused. When it's cold, whip softly, serve with fruit salads, ice cream or panna cotta.

To make **Chamomile Tea**, put 1 to 2 teaspoons chamomile heads, depending on size, into a china teapot. Pour boiling water over the flowers and let infuse for 3 to 4 minutes. Strain into a cup or glass, add a little honey if you wish, sip, and savor.

Roasted Sweet Potatoes with Chamomile, Honey & Pumpkin Seed

Tender sweet potatoes, well caramelized at the edges, are a delicious accompaniment to grilled fish or roast belly of pork. This dish, which Eric Werner and Maya Henry of Hartwood in Mexico made for us when they came to Litfest 2016, is a take on a Mayan treat of charred camotes (sweet potatoes) topped with honey. They say: "A sprinkle of ground pumpkin seeds adds a contrasting crunch, while the dried chamomile brings floral and herbal notes. If you don't have fresh chamomile that you can dry yourself, or can't find dried chamomile at your local health-food shop or farmers' market, substitute chamomile tea, which is simply the dried flowers." Eric and Maya feel strongly, as I do, that it should be organic.

SERVES 4

4 sweet potatoes, scrubbed

1 teaspoon dried chamomile or the contents of 8 to 10 organic chamomile teabags

3-inch cinnamon stick

⅓ cup honey

¼ cup clarified butter, cut into pieces

¼ cup pumpkin seeds, roasted in a dry pan until lightly browned and then coarsely ground

flaky sea salt

Put the sweet potatoes into a saucepan just large enough to fit them and cover with water. Add half the chamomile, the cinnamon stick, and 2 tablespoons of the honey. Cover and bring to a boil, then simmer for 20 to 25 minutes until completely tender, but with the skins still intact. Remove the sweet potatoes from the cooking liquid. Reduce, the liquid with the lid off, by more than half, or until almost syrupy.

Meanwhile, preheat the oven to 475°F.

Heat a heavy roasting pan or gratin dish (we use a cast-iron grill pan) in the oven. Make a lengthwise slit along the top of each sweet potato. Add them to the hot pan, taking care not to burn yourself, then dot the top with the butter. Drizzle with a little honey and roast for about 5 minutes. Baste with the melted butter used to top the sweet potatoes and the remaining honey and 3 to 4 tablespoons of the cooking liquid. Roast for an additional 8 to 10 minutes until the sweet potatoes are nice and crispy around the edges. Remove from the oven and baste one last time.

Transfer the sweet potatoes to plates. Crumble the remaining chamomile over the sweet potatoes and dust them with the ground pumpkin seeds and a few flakes of sea salt.

Serve alone or as an accompaniment to roast belly of pork or grilled monkfish.

LAVENDER
Lavandula EVERGREEN SHRUB, ZONES 5–8

Lavender is deliciously fragrant and easy to grow. If you think of where it grows in abundance, like Provence, you'll know that it thrives on poor soil and is a drought-tolerant plant that loves lots of sun. Apart from purple, it also comes in shades of white, blue, pink, and mauve.

VARIETIES

Hidcote—Very popular cultivar, dense, dark violet flowers in early summer.
Loddon Blue—Violet-purple spikes, flowers midsummer.
Royal Purple—Grey/green foliage, long deep-purple flowers in early summer.
Hidcote Pink—Compact growth, dense spikes of pink flowers with slender silvery-grey leaves, flowers all summer.
Celestial Star—long thin spikes of white flowers

VARIETIES FOR A HEDGE

Miss Muffet—Violet-purple flowers.
Nana Alba—White flowers.
Little Lottie—Pink flowers.

HOW TO GROW

For a lavender hedge, plant 12 inches apart in spring when the soil is warming up.

CONTAINER GROWING

Lavender can be grown successfully in large pots. It's a beautifully fragrant plant to have on a balcony.

Use pots 12 to 16 inches wide and use poor, slightly gravelly soil or a loam-based compost. Most lavender works well in pots but growing this way is even more suitable for tender varieties such as Lavandula canariensis, L. lanata and L. pinnata. In very cold areas it's best to bring these frost-tender plants into a cold greenhouse for protection.

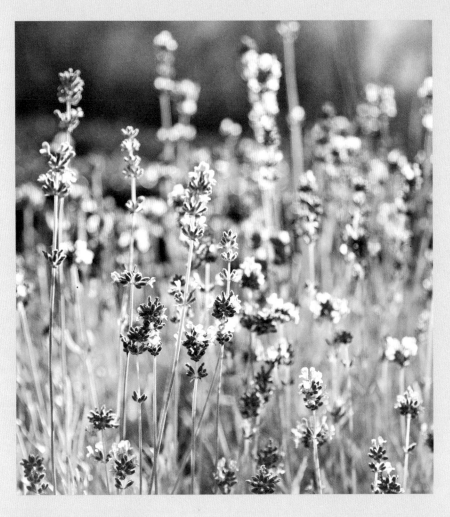

PESTS AND DISEASES

In wet heavy soil, lavender can suffer from root rot—remember it's native to the Mediterranean.

HARVESTING

For maximum flavor, snip off the flower before its bud breaks.

Lavender needs to be pruned in late summer after flowering to maintain the plant's shape and well-being. Snip off all the flower heads and about 10 inches of that year's growth.

Lavandula angustifolia *"Hidcote"*.

GOOD FOR YOU...

The name of this plant comes from the Latin verb lavare, meaning "to wash," so it is fitting that lavender is increasingly being grown for its essential oil, which is used both in beauty products and as a medicinal treatment. The essential oil has both antiseptic and anti-inflammatory properties and is used in the treatment of anxiety, insomnia, and depression. Studies also show that it may be used to treat stomach upsets and fungal infections. Lavender is said to contain vitamin A, calcium, and iron.

IN THE KITCHEN

We love lavender; we crystallize the fresh flower spikes and use them to decorate cakes. Harvest the flowers at the peak of perfection and dry on wire racks or trays in a warm airy place.

Use the fresh or dried buds to flavor ice creams, panna cotta, and custards.

Lavender syrup is easy to make and a delicious way to trap the fragrance of summer lavender in a bottle. Use to flavor Prosecco, then float some rose and lavender petals on top.

We have also had fun making lavender salt to sprinkle over a shoulder of lamb before cooking.

For lavender scones, add 2 tablespoons dried lavender to Mummy's Sweet Scone recipe (see page 402).

Homemade chocolates can also be flavored with lavender, then you can sprinkle a little more over the top.

For Lavender Lemonade, just add 2 tablespoons lavender flowers to 1¾ cups sugar dissolved in 2½ cups water.

A bunch of lavender drying—perfumes the air wonderfully.

Lavender Shortbread

The addition of rice flour to this shortbread recipe gives it an appealing texture and the lavender buds flavor it deliciously.

· ·

MAKES 24 TO 32 DEPENDING ON SIZE

2¾ cups all-purpose flour
good pinch of baking powder
½ cup superfine sugar
5½ tablespoons rice flour
good pinch of salt
2 to 3 tablespoons dried lavender
   (unopened lavender flowers)
1⅓ cups cold butter
vanilla or superfine sugar, for sprinkling

Preheat the oven to 300°F.

Sift the flour and baking powder into a bowl, then add the remaining dry ingredients and the lavender. Cut the butter into cubes and rub in until the whole mixture comes together (alternatively, combine everything together in a food processor and pulse to incorporate). Spread evenly into a 10 × 15-inch jelly roll pan and smooth it flat.

Bake for 1 to 1½ hours. (Alternatively, bake for 20 to 30 minutes at 350°F.) The shortbread should be pale golden but fully cooked through.

Cut into squares or bars while still hot. Sprinkle with vanilla or superfine sugar and let cool in the pan.

Honey & Lavender Ice Cream

Honey and lavender is a particularly delicious marriage of flavors. We make this richly scented ice cream when the lavender flowers are about to bloom in early summer. Lavender is at its most aromatic just before the flowers burst open. Serve on chilled plates and savor every mouthful.

SERVES 8 TO 10

1 cup milk

1¾ cups heavy cream

40 sprigs of fresh lavender or fewer if dried (use the blossom end only)

6 organic egg yolks

¾ cup honey (we use our own apple-blossom honey, although Provençal lavender honey would also be wonderful)

sprigs of fresh or frosted lavender (see below), to decorate

Put the milk and cream into a heavy-bottomed saucepan with the lavender, bring slowly to a boil, and let infuse for 15 to 20 minutes. This will both flavor and perfume the cream deliciously.

Whisk the egg yolks in a bowl, add a little of the lavender-flavored milk, then pour this into the saucepan and combine with the infused milk-cream mixture. Cook over low heat until the mixture barely thickens and lightly coats the back of a spoon (be careful not to let it curdle). Melt the honey gently, just to liquefy, then whisk it into the custard. Strain the custard to remove the lavender heads, pressing out every last drop.

Chill thoroughly, then process in an ice cream maker according to the manufacturer's directions.

Serve garnished with sprigs of fresh or frosted lavender (see below).

FROSTED LAVENDER

Frosted lavender sprigs are adorable and delicious to use as decoration. Pick lavender in dry weather while the flowers are still closed. Whisk a little egg white lightly and brush the entire lavender sprig with it. Sprinkling it all over with sifted superfine sugar. Lay the sprigs on parchment paper and let dry in a warm spot. Store in an airtight container.

Lavender Syrup

This syrup is delicious over ice cream or Labneh (page 291), or as a base for a sparkly aperitif. It is also good in cakes or over sliced peaches or nectarines in summer.

MAKES 3⅓ CUPS

2½ cups cold water

2 to 2¼ cups sugar

2 heaped tablespoons lavender flowers, gathered just before they open

a couple of very thin strips of lemon peel from 1 lemon

Put the water, sugar, and lavender into a saucepan and add the lemon peel. Warm slowly over medium heat, and when the sugar has dissolved, bring to a boil and boil for 5 to 6 minutes. Remove from the heat and let infuse for about 30 minutes.

Strain through a fine mesh sieve. Pour into sterilized bottles, cover, and store in a cool dry place or in the fridge if you have space. The syrup will keep for 3 months.

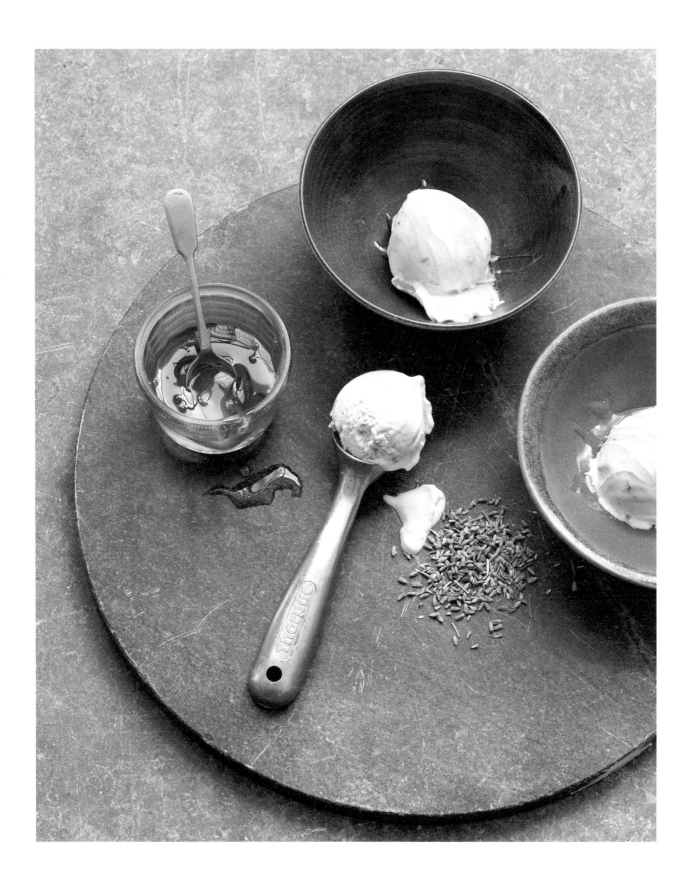

PRIMROSE

Primula vulgaris PERENNIAL, ZONES 4–8

Primroses, which bloom from early spring into summer, may be endangered in some areas, but are abundant in many parts of Ireland. The name comes from prima rosa, meaning the "first rose" in old French and medieval Latin, probably because this plant is one of the earliest spring flowers.

Primroses are one of my favorite flowers—both the leaves and flowers are edible.

VARIETIES

Breeding of named colored varieties became popular in the last century. There are many strains, known as polyanthus, which have been bred for early spring color and are also edible.

Crescendo Blue—early-blooming blue flowers on 6-inch tall plants.

Crescendo Yellow—bright, double, yellow flowers on 6-inch plants.

HOW TO GROW

Having first checked that primroses are not endangered in your area, dig up a little plant in the wild and plant it in a verge around your property. It may well naturalize and spread, as it does here. You can also buy seeds of wild primrose.

Primroses do best in moist but well-drained soil and they enjoy light shade.

HARVESTING

Just pick a little posy at a time as needed.

GOOD FOR YOU...

The leaves can be used for tea and the young flowers made into primrose wine, which was very popular in the past.

Primroses have a history of medicinal use, but this comes with a health warning as they contain a substance called salicylates, which would be detrimental to those with an allergy to aspirin or blood coagulation problems.

IN THE KITCHEN

The flowers are particularly pretty when crystallized and can be used to decorate iced cakes, but we also mix the leaves into the salad bowl and scatter them over panna cotta and buttermilk puddings. They are also adorable popped into ice cubes, perhaps with a mint or lemon balm leaf, too.

Buttermilk Pots with Primroses & Forget-Me-Nots

These buttermilk creams are also delicious with roast peaches, apricots, nectarines, or rhubarb in season.

SERVES 6

2 sheets of gelatin (use 3 sheets if you plan to unmold each one)
1½ cups buttermilk
⅓ cup superfine sugar
½ vanilla pod
1 cup heavy cream
Primroses, forget-me-nots, and mint leaves, to decorate

Soak the sheets of gelatin in cold water.

In a heavy-bottomed saucepan, bring 6 tablespoons of the buttermilk to a boil with the sugar and vanilla pod.

Drain the softened gelatin sheets and discard the water. Remove the saucepan from the heat, add the gelatin to the hot buttermilk, and stir until dissolved. Let cool, then whisk in the remaining buttermilk and the cream.

Scrape the seeds from the vanilla pod and add them to the mixture. Mix well. Pour into 6 small ramekins or molds, then cover and refrigerate until set.

To serve, sprinkle each little pot with primroses, forget-me-nots, and a few mint leaves. Alternatively, unmold into a deep soup plate and garnish as above.

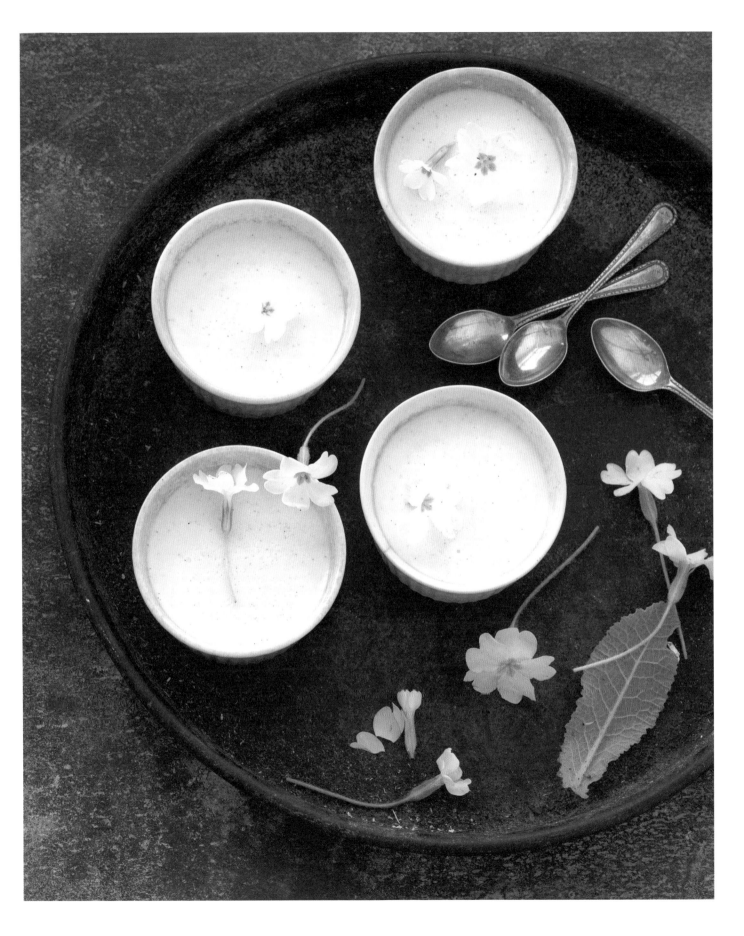

ROSES *Rosa* PERENNIAL, ZONES 2–9

All roses are edible, but the ones I like to use best are the deliciously perfumed old roses and china roses. As with all edible flowers, avoid blossoms that have been sprayed. The flavor and fragrance depends on the variety, color, and soil conditions. The fragrance seems to be more pronounced in the darker varieties. Pure rosewater is the distilled essence of roses so it is not easy to make at home.

VARIETIES

Rosa gallica var. officinalis—known as the Apothecary Rose, zones 4–9.
Rosa "Cardinal de Richelieu"
Rosa × centifolia—Cabbage rose, known for its healing powers and fragrance.
Rosa Chapeau de Napoléon.
Rosa × centifolia Muscosa.
Damask rose—specially good; Quatre Saisons.

Bourbon—Madame Isaac Péreire.
Rugosa—Martin Frobisher; Linda Campbell, zones 2–7
Hybrid Perpetual—Henry Nevard; Paul Neyron; Gloire de Ducher; Fairmount Red, the climber Reine de Violette

HOW TO GROW

Volumes have been written about growing roses, but cooks need to choose fragrant varieties. Roses are easy to grow and are tolerant of many conditions, but they thrive best in rich, fertile soil. They benefit from good soil preparation, so well-rotted manure or compost dug into the soil before planting will ensure strong growth. Buy healthy, preferably organic, plants—look out for disease-resistant varieties.

Dig a hole, roughly twice the size of the plant's root ball and deep enough to accommodate the plant. Tease out the roots so they spread out well. Keep mulched with a 3-inch layer of well-rotted stable manure, but clear it at least 4 inches away from the stem. Deadhead (remove spent flowers) throughout the season and keep watered if necessary, as roses are not drought tolerant.

CONTAINER GROWING

Roses can look beautiful grown in large terracotta pots, galvanized bins or timber barrels but should be watered and fed regularly. They can be planted all year round.

PESTS AND DISEASES

For all roses it is vital to have good airflow around the plant. Remember to

Sweet Ballymaloe Rose named by Eurotoque chefs to honor Myrtle Allen.

plant each one at least 12 to 14 inches from the next rose.

Black spot is easy to recognize, there will be black spots on the leaves. Plant chives and garlic chives close by. Tomatoes are also said to ward off black spot, but they do not make such a good combo.

Powdery mildew is a white, fuzzy looking mold on the leaves. Allow plenty of room around bushes to encourage air circulation. Remedies include spraying with a milk and water solution, garlic solution, baking soda, or compost tea.

To prevent aphids, Spray your roses with soapy water. Plant thyme, calendulas, and feverfew close by. Yarrow attracts ladybugs that feed on aphids.

Choose plants not just to enhance the beauty of the roses but to inhibit pests and attract beneficial insects. such as nigella ("Miss Jekyll Blue"), salvias, calendula, chives, basil, feverfew, centaurea, cornflowers, and nasturtiums.

HARVESTING

As with all edible flowers, it's best to harvest them in the morning after the dew has lifted. Snip the full bloom or just steal a few petals depending on your need. Watch out for earwigs!

Snip off the bitter white part of the base of each petal before using.

Rosehips are the seedpod of the flowers.

GOOD FOR YOU...

Apart from providing aesthetic appeal, rose petals and hips contribute to our overall wellbeing.

Rose petals have been used in Chinese medicine since as far back as 3,000 BC and are known to contain valuable nutrients. Adding some raw petals to your salad can help to fight heart disease and cancer, and boiling them in water makes an effective remedy for sore throats, and a strained infusion can help irregular periods and diarrhea.

Rose oil is used in aromatherapy and is a valuable ingredient in some facial preparations, although unadulterated good-quality oil is expensive.

Rosewater is used for skin treatment, particularly acne.

Rosehips are a very rich source of vitamin C and also flavonoids, tannins, and vitamins A, B1, B2, B3, and K, and are used to make rosehip syrup and apple and rosehip jellies.

IN THE KITCHEN
We use roses to flavor syrups and use rose petals in jams, and we sprinkle the flowers into both sweet and savory salads. Float them over homemade lemonades and fruit punches, or freeze them in ice cube trays, add them to jellies and ice creams, or use them to perfume butters and dips. Paint the petals with a little egg white and frost them with sugar to decorate cakes and desserts. In the autumn we use rosehips to make a vitamin-C-laden syrup.

Rose water is widely used in Middle Eastern cooking.

Rosa *"Madame Isaac Péreire"—fragrant old rose with an intense scent.*

Rose Petal Syrup

Pour a little of this rose petal syrup into a Champagne glass and top up with Cava or Prosecco to make a gorgeous perfumed aperitif. Stir, then float a rose petal on top.

MAKES 3⅓ CUPS

8 ounces fragrant rose petals from an old variety of unsprayed roses
2 cups cold water
3½ cups sugar, warmed
2 tablespoons freshly squeezed lemon juice

Put the petals into a stainless-steel saucepan with the water. Bring to a boil over medium heat and simmer gently for 20 to 30 minutes. Strain the petals through a sieve, pressing to get out as much of the liquid as possible. Add the warmed sugar and lemon juice, bring back to a boil, and simmer, uncovered, until thick and syrupy. Pour into sterilized bottles and seal. It will keep for months but enjoy sooner rather than later.

Chocolate Brownie with Pistachio & Rose Petals

This cake is based on a delicious spelt brownie recipe created by super baker Claire Ptak of Violet Cakes, in London. We've gilded the lily by adding a drizzle of ganache and sprinkling some coarsely chopped pistachio nuts and a few rose petals on top.

. . . .

MAKES 10 BROWNIES

¾ cup (1½ sticks) unsalted butter, cut into small pieces, plus extra for greasing

12 ounces dark chocolate (approx. 60 to 70% minimum cocoa solids), broken into pieces (we use Valrhona)

½ cup cocoa powder

1¾ cups white spelt flour

½ teaspoon baking powder

1 teaspoon salt (¾ teaspoon if using sea salt)

scant 2 cups superfine sugar

4 organic eggs (about 7 ounces)

2 teaspoons vanilla extract

⅓ cup pistachios, chopped, to decorate

1 tablespoon dried rose petals, to decorate

FOR THE CHOCOLATE GANACHE

½ cup cream

4 ounces dark chocolate, chopped into pieces

Preheat the oven to 350°F. Butter an 8 × 12-inch baking dish and line it with parchment paper.

In a heatproof bowl, melt the butter and chocolate over water that has been brought to the boil and then taken off the heat. Allow the mixture to rest, stirring occasionally as it melts.

In a separate bowl, sift together the cocoa, flour, and baking powder. Sprinkle over the salt.

In the bowl of a stand mixer fitted with the whisk attachment, whisk together the sugar, eggs, and vanilla until light and fluffy. Slowly add the melted chocolate mixture, followed by the dry ingredients, and pour into the prepared baking dish. Bake for 25 minutes—the brownies should be set but with a slight wobble.

Meanwhile, make the ganache. Put the cream into a heavy-bottomed stainless-steel saucepan and bring it almost to a boil. Remove from the heat and add the chocolate. With a wooden spoon, stir the chocolate into the cream until it is completely melted. Transfer the chocolate cream to a separate bowl and allow it to cool to room temperature.

Slather a little chocolate ganache on top of the brownies. Sprinkle with the pistachios and rose petals. Cut the brownies into squares and enjoy.

Camilla's Strawberry & Rose Petal Jam

When my friend Camilla Plum comes to stay she wanders through the farm and gardens and greenhouse, picking and collecting fresh ingredients, and cooks nonstop. Last summer, she filled her apron with rose petals from the old scented roses—she tossed them into a saucepan with some fresh strawberries and made this exquisite jam. We also made rose petal syrup and crystallized the petals to decorate desserts and cake. Use organic ingredients where possible.

. . . .

MAKES 2 OR 3 PINT JARS

2¼ cups granulated sugar
2¼ pounds strawberries, stemmed
4 cups unsprayed organic rose petals
juice of 1 lemon

Preheat the oven to 225°F. Scatter the sugar over a baking sheet and warm in the oven.

Put the strawberries in a wide stainless-steel saucepan and cook over high heat until the juices run and the fruit breaks down. Add the rose petals and hot sugar. Stir to dissolve the sugar, bring back to a boil, and continue to cook for 5 to 8 minutes until it reaches a set. Test for a set by putting about a teaspoon of jam on a cold plate, leaving it for a few minutes in a cool place. It should wrinkle when pressed with a finger. When at setting point, add the lemon juic and remove from the heat immediately. Pour into sterilized jars and store in a cool place for 3 to 4 months but enjoy sooner rather than later.

Apple, Rosehip & Rose Geranium Jelly

Rosehips, the seedpods of roses, come in all sizes. Depending on the variety, they can be tiny, or in the case of *Rosa rugosa*, the rosehips are fat and full of itchy seeds. As ever, choose rosehips from unsprayed roses. Bursting with vitamin C, this pale pink jelly is perfumed with the flavor of rose geranium leaves, but I sometimes add a few drops of rose water as well.

. . . .

MAKES 6 × ½-CUP JARS

4¾ pounds Granny Smith apples or a
  mixture of crab apples and Granny
  Smiths
¾ pound rosehips
6 to 8 rose geranium leaves (*Pelargonium
  graveolens*)
11¾ cups cold water
granulated sugar
6 to 8 sweet geranium leaves
juice of 1 lemons

Chop the unpeeled apples and the rosehips and place in a saucepan with the rose geranium leaves and the water. Bring to a boil and simmer until the fruit is completely soft, 1½ to 2 hours. Pour into a jelly bag or double layer of cheesecloth set over a large bowl and allow to drip overnight.

The next day, preheat the oven to 225°F. Measure the juice: for every 2½ cups juice measure 1¾ cups sugar. Scatter the sugar over a baking sheet and warm in the oven.

Put the sweet geranium leaves and the juice into a saucepan, and bring the liquid to the boil. Add the lemon juice and warm sugar. Cook until set (see above), about 20 minutes. Strain into sterilized jars, cover, and store in a cool, dry place. It will keep for 10 to 12 months but it's best eaten sooner.

NASTURTIUMS *Tropaeoleum majus* ANNUAL

There are both annual and perennial forms of nasturtiums; generally grown as annuals, in our relatively mild winters nasturtiums are perennial. Bright reds, yellows, oranges, and the more exotic wine and almost black, with bright green or cream-splashed variegated leaves. It's difficult to think of any other flower that delivers so much delight and value for a few pennies' worth of seed. This cheery little plant self-seeds, so once you introduce it to your garden, it will re-emerge every year and romp away.

All parts of the nasturtium are edible. They provide brilliant groundcover and are a useful companion plant to inhibit a variety of bugs and beetles, as their pepperiness inhibits blackfly.

VARIETIES

There are many forms—dwarf, semi-trailing and climbers—and they come in a range of vibrant colors.

Empress of India—Deep crimson flowers with dark leaves, semi-trailing.

Princess of India—Dwarf version of *Empress of India*.

Black Velvet—Velvety, reddish-black flowers.

Whirlybird—Very popular variety which comes in single colors like cherry red, or as mixed shades.

Try the peppery nasturtium seeds fresh as well as pickled.

Apricot Twist and Jewel of Africa—Tall climbing varieties, they will trail along the ground if unsupported.

Buttercream and Milkmaid—Two of the many creamy-yellow varieties.

Peach Melba—Bright, creamy-yellow with red blotches in the center, semi-double flowers.

HOW TO GROW

Nasturtiums are not in the least fussy about soil, in fact if anything they prefer poor soil, but do best in full sun. Sow seeds in pots or directly into the soil. They thrive on neglect and flower from late spring well into autumn to brighten your house and perk up food. The first frost will kill the leaves.

CONTAINER GROWING

Nasturtiums can be grown in pots, or in window boxes on a balcony, and will climb up any trellis, wall or support, or trail over a balcony or hang down a wall.

PESTS AND DISEASES

Slugs seem to ignore them but watch out for caterpillars towards the end of the season, as they will eat the leaves and make the plants unsightly looking. Plant a few nasturtiums close to your tomato plants to attract aphids.

HARVESTING

Pick the young leaves and add to salads. Pick the flowers as you need them during the summer. When they go to seed, from early autumn, collect the seeds—they can be enjoyed raw in salads, or pickled.

All parts of the cheery nasturtium are edible and high in anitoxidants.

GOOD FOR YOU...

Nasturtiums are high in antioxidants and vitamin C and act as a natural antibiotic. They are also used in Ayurvedic medicine for metabolic disorders, anemia, and kidney and bladder disorders.

WHAT TO DO WITH A GLUT

Make nasturtium pesto, nasturtium vinegar, and pickle or dry the seeds.

IN THE KITCHEN

Nasturtium leaves and flowers add a peppery flavor and bright splash of color to foraged salads. The seeds can be pickled or dried. To make two 7-ounce jars of nasturtium seed capers, put 10½ ounces nasturtium seeds into the sterilized jars, then add 1 large sprig of dill to each jar and cover with ½ cup white wine vinegar each. Let mature for a week. These keep for months. Sprinkle onto salads or serve with smoked fish, skate, or venison.

Risotto with Zucchini & Nasturtium Blossoms

The nasturtium flowers add both color and a peppery note here—the perfect foil for the creamy risotto.

SERVES 4 TO 6

¼ pound small zucchini

½ cup (1 stick) plus 1 tablespoon butter

1 onion, sliced

6 to 8 cups homemade chicken stock

2 cups Arborio, Carnaroli or Vialone Nano rice

½ cup plus 2 tablespoons dry white wine

6 to 8 zucchini blossoms

2 tablespoons chopped fresh annual marjoram

½ cup freshly grated Parmesan, plus extra to serve

8 to 10 nasturtium blossoms, torn

sea salt and freshly ground black pepper

Cut the zucchini in half lengthwise and then into ¼-inch-thick slices at an angle. Alternatively, just cut into ¼-inch dice.

Melt 4 tablespoons (½ stick) of the butter in a saucepan and cook the zucchini for 4 to 5 minutes until al dente.

Melt 2 tablespoons of the butter in a heavy-bottomed saucepan, add the onion, and sweat over low heat for a few minutes.

In another saucepan, bring the stock to the boil and then adjust the heat so it stays at a gentle simmer.

Add the rice to the onion, stir for a minute or two to coat the grains, then add the wine and continue to cook until the wine is almost fully absorbed. Season well with salt and pepper. Begin to add ladlefuls of the simmering stock, stirring all the time and making sure that the last addition has been almost absorbed before adding the next.

After about 12 minutes, when the rice is beginning to soften, add the cooked zucchini and cook for a few minutes more. When you are happy that it is just right, soft and wavy, stir in the zucchini blossoms, marjoram, and the remaining butter, then the Parmesan. Taste; it should be exquisite. Correct the seasoning if necessary.

Sprinkle the nasturtium blossoms over the top and serve immediately in warm bowls with an extra sprinkling of Parmesan.

Note: Other good things to add to risotto in the summer are broad beans, sugar peas, French beans, peas, and beet.

DID YOU KNOW?
Nasturtiums originated in South America and were brought to Spain by the conquistadors. Claude Monet loved nasturtiums and included them in paintings of his beautiful garden in Giverny in France.

VIOLETS

Viola odorata and V. sororia PERENNIAL, ZONES 3–8

Viola tricolor also known as heartsease and wild pansy.

I so love violets—the old-fashioned, sweet-smelling kind that are so rare nowadays. When I came to Kinoith they were romping around the neglected flower beds in Lydia's garden. I dug some up and divided and relocated them. Later I found that fragrant violets had been grown commercially on the farm in the 1920s as part of an East Cork violet project. They were bunched in the violet loft at the end of the coach yard, wrapped in a leaf and sent on the Innisfallen ferry boat from Cork to Fishguard, from where they made their way to the Covent Garden Market to be sold to adorn ladies' lapels.

I found references to picking and bunching violets in Wilson Strangman's diary (the previous owner of Kinoith) of the 1900s: "bunching violets again today". He obviously found it tedious!

VARIETIES

The original violet, *Viola odorata*, has deep purple flowers, but some specialist growers have developed a range of colors, including mauve and pink white, with names such as **"Becky Groves"** (pale pink), **"Beechy's Double White"**, **"Admiral Avellan"** (reddish purple), **"Dusky Maiden"** (pink). **"Konigin Charlotte"** is a very sweetly scented, mauve heritage variety. We use the cheery *Viola tricolor* fresh in salads and fresh or crystallized on top of wee buns and cakes (see right).

HOW TO GROW

Violets do well in light shade; they can create an enchanting, fragrant ground cover in woodland areas. They grow best in well-drained soil that is rich in organic matter, they need shade both in winter and summer. Plant in spring or autumn, but spring is preferable. Violets can seed themselves so if you don't want them to spread everywhere cut off the seedheads when the flowers have died.

CONTAINER GROWING

Violets can also be grown in containers.

PESTS AND DISEASES

The leaves may suffer an attack from spider mites.

HARVESTING

They will bloom in early spring and may be cut and bunched into little posies and wrapped with their own leaves. If picking them for culinary use, do this when the petals are dry.

GOOD FOR YOU...

Both the flowers and leaves are edible and are reputed to be rich in vitamins. Violets are sometimes used in herbal medicine; traditionally the leaves were used to treat abscesses, boils, and inflammations because of their cooling properties.

As far back as 1885, research has indicated the high vitamin content of violet leaves, and a study by Erichsen-Brown (1979) indicates that the basal leaves, if collected in spring, contain twice as much vitamin C as the same weight of oranges, and more than twice the amount of vitamin A, ounce for ounce, when compared with spinach! The same study says that Native Americans used violets in the treatment of cancer.

WHAT TO DO WITH A GLUT?

You don't have to pick them all, just enjoy the spectacle. Give presents of little posies to your friends. The flowers can also be crystallized. You could even start an artisan business like Le Petit Duc, in Remy-en-Provence.

IN THE KITCHEN

You can store crystallized violets in a tin for later use in cake decoration. Cupcakes with little crystallized violets on top are quite simply enchanting. Violet syrup makes a delicious base for a fizzy aperitif: just pour a little violet syrup into a Champagne flute and top with bubbly to taste. It'll be a scary shade of purple, so float a few fresh violets on top of each glass, if available.

Cupcakes with Crystallized Violets

Some of us have cupcake fatigue but these little fairy cakes are so cute and delicious we can't take them off the menu. If you have just one oven you may need to make the cupcakes in three separate batches. Depending on how the cakes are decorated, this can be any occasion—a wedding cake, christening, anniversary, children's party, sports day celebration.

MAKES 36 CUPCAKES

2 cups (4 sticks) butter, at room
    temperature
2¼ cups superfine sugar
3½ cups plus 2 tablespoons self-raising
    flour
6 large organic eggs
1½ teaspoons vanilla extract
6 tablespoons milk
crystallized primroses, violets, or lavender,
    to decorate

FOR THE LEMON ICING
1¾ cups confectioners' sugar
finely grated zest of 1 lemon
1½ cups freshly squeezed lemon juice

Preheat the oven to 375°F. Line three 12-hole muffin cups with paper liners.

Put all the ingredients except the milk into a food-processor and process until smooth. Scrape down the sides, then add the milk and process again. Divide the mixture evenly among the muffin cups and bake for 15 to 20 minutes until risen and golden. Remove from the tin and cool on a wire rack.

To make the lemon icing, sift the confectioners' sugar into a bowl. Add the lemon zest and enough lemon juice to make a softish icing.

Cover the tops of the cooled cakes with the lemon icing and decorate with the crystallized flowers.

DID YOU KNOW?
The scent of violets was very popular in late Victorian times and was widely used in perfume and cosmetics.

Violet flower syrup is a beautiful violet color when made; the addition of water lightens it to a lavender shade. Adding lemon juice changes it to magenta, or adding an alkaline substance will turn it green. Because of these properties it was at one time used as "litmus" paper before proper litmus papers existed.

APPENDIX

A BASIC TOOLKIT

Every gardener needs a basic toolkit, a few essential, indispensable items. Buy the very best you can afford so they will last a lifetime, or at least for many years, which they will if you buy top quality. Buy the basic essentials to start with, some items like trowels will be inexpensive, others like copper tools are costly but worth every penny.

Trowel – Copper if possible, they keep their edge and slide through the soil more easily.

Hoe – There are many types: Dutch hoes, onions hoes, draw hoes in various sizes. We have a variety, but the clear favorite are the copper swivel-top hoes that have a sharp blade that cuts easily through the soil when it's either pushed or pulled.

Digging fork – Choose one that feels comfortable to handle.

Shovel – A copper or stainless steel spade will last and are easier to use because the soil will adhere to the surface. Indispensable for digging holes for large plants or edging beds. Keep them sharp by using an edging stone.

Rake – Rakes have multiple uses: breaking up lumps to create a fine tilth, raking a bed after sowing, collecting up leaves and debris, and raking gravel. There are special long-pronged rakes for gathering leaves.

Dibber – Choose one with a pointed end and a longish wooden spade handle, it will be easier to grip. Invaluable for making holes for planting plugs and modules, garlic cloves and onion sets.

Wheelbarrow – Can be heavy plastic or zinc, a brilliantly useful tool for transporting weeds and plants, compost and manure, etc.

Plastic buckets – For collecting weeds and debris and carrying water.

Watering can – Pick one that you can comfortably carry when full – choose two kinds, one smaller and one larger.

Pruning shears – Choose the best you can buy, use for pruning and trimming.

Garden pocket knife – Brilliant to keep in your pocket to cut vegetables, train plants, and dead head flowers.

Seed trays – 6 x 9-inch trays are fine for microgreens and salad leaves, even radishes, but modular trays of different sizes are brilliant for individual plants.

We use 20 x 13 x 2-inch deep trays for lettuces, other salad greens and herbs and the same size but 3-inch deep for brassicas as they have a deeper root. You can push each plant out with a pencil, so there is minimum root disturbance when potting up.

Garden gloves – Buy a comfortable pair that are soft enough to garden in easily, they won't last indefinitely, so be prepared to replace when needed.

OTHER EQUIPMENT

A greenhouse – Every gardener's dream; glass admits more light than corrugated plastic. A polytunnel is cheaper, as it are lean-to structures. You can even buy a portable greenhouse complete with staging. Light plastic greenhouses can work in a sheltered yard but are not exactly durable.

South-facing cold frames – Bring on seedlings and protect crops from frost damage. Handy DIY gardeners can use old windows to construct a cold frame. The base can be constructed from bricks, blocks, or even planks.

Cloches – Good for growing salads in winter or protecting strawberries in summer and can be covered with polythene, landscape cloth, or mesh.

You can save money by using PVC water piping to create a frame. We weigh down mesh with fishermen's rope.

Hot box – These flexible plastic trash cans are also brilliant; one can even grow peas and cavolo nero in them, or even make compost. They need drainage holes.

Garden shed – Another brilliant asset, great for storing garden tools, drying onions, garlic, seeds, and depending on the shed, storing root crops, such as potatoes, carrots, and beets.

PESTS AND DISEASES

As ever, prevention is much better than cure. In an ideal world we would all plant our crops in optimum positions and conditions, water judiciously, keep on top of weeds and check the plant daily for signs of trouble ahead.

Winter cleaning and sterilizing programs in the greenhouse, tunnel and potting shed are vitally important. We steam-clean the greenhouse in winter when it is empty, the cover cloth also gets washed (we don't use any chemicals). The washing dislodges any over-wintering eggs and bugs. In the growing room the trays and pots are washed before re-use. It's important to keep utensils clean; don't leave half-empty pots or dead plants around the place. Check underneath your pots for sleeping slugs and dispose of them.

There are a myriad of pests and diseases to contend with; here I have selected just a few of the most common challenges. Do consult an authoritative gardening manual for more in-depth information (see Bibliography, page 639).

SLUGS AND SNAILS

I've asked my gardeners to share what we do about slugs because we don't seem to have many or sometimes any – it's all a bit embarrassing! I know it sounds completely unbelievable, but it's actually true. They are convinced that it is to do with the increasing fertility of the soil from multiple applications of compost and humus.

However, slugs are the bane of most gardeners' lives. They slither in at night and can do an extraordinary amount of damage in a short time. Here are three suggestions to prevent them attacking your precious plants:

1. Increase the fertility of your soil (see pages 16–18). Apart from that, presuming you don't wish to use any pesticides, there are various organic solutions all of which work well enough in small plots (see below).

2. Beer traps – Slugs and snails seem to love beer, so bury a can or even a deep paper cup in the soil, leaving about ½ inch of rim exposed, so as not to trap ground beetles that are the natural predators of slugs. The latter, you hope, will slip into the beer and drown.

3. Gardeners have also had certain success with crushed egg shells, charcoal, coffee grinds, coarse sand, and jagged gravel. Sprinkle them around the plants to make access difficult for slugs and snails. They don't like cat or dog hairs.

4. Slugs and snails like dark, moist, shady areas, so either keep the area weed-free or create little oases for them under upturned flower pots, cardboard boxes, wooden planks or grapefruit or orange rinds, even cabbage leaves. You can attract them further by adding a little tasty bait like cornmeal or dry pet food. Some gardeners go snail hunting at night with a torch and disposable gloves or tongs. They have various unmentionable ways of disposing of them, but you could feed them to birds, chickens, or ducks who are natural predators. It's best to add them to the compost heap. We have had ducks in the gardens and greenhouses from time to time, with considerable success. They love slugs but don't seem to damage the plants.

Frogs and toads are also partial to slugs so consider having a little decorative pond for them to live in.

Nematodes are microscopic parasitic worms that live in the soil. They enter the slugs while still underground and infect them with bacteria, the slug stops eating your plants in a few days and dies within a week. You can purchase them as we have done from time to time, but they die out as soon as they have eliminated their food supply, so if you have another infestation you will need to buy more. We spread them over the soil and water in.

Some plants also deter slugs – bitter greens and mustard leaves don't appeal to them, neither do they fancy garlic, chives, ginger, mint, or chicory (see companion planting, page 18).

You can make wormwood tea by steeping wormwood leaves in warm water overnight, or for 24 hours, then strain and mix again with soapy water. Spray on the ground or directly onto the slugs or snails. Vinegar water is also a deterrent. Salt is definitely effective and will kill slugs, but it is not to be recommended too much because it will contaminate the soil.

For a raised bed, attach a copper strip to the side and slugs and snails won't go over it. It can also be used directly on the soil to surround and protect a plant, but be careful of sharp edges.

There are several effective chemical solutions which if you choose to use should be done with care, adhering to the instructions. Slug pellets kill birds as well as slugs.

WHITE FLY

These unmistakable tiny white flies

attack greenhouse plants, suck the sap, and excrete a sticky sugar substance called honey dew. They attack tomatoes, cucumbers, and zucchini and congregate on the underside of the leaves. Look out for a black sooty mold, which indicates their presence.

They thrive in warm conditions so are not usually a problem outdoors in cooler climates. Try to avoid introducing them. They are exceedingly difficult to get rid of once they get into your greenhouse or tunnel. Weed control, good ventilation, and good hygiene are essential. We control them with the tiny parasitic wasp called *Encarsia formosa*, which attack the young white fly nymphs. It's essential to introduce them early enough; if the infestation is too great they can be overwhelmed.

White fly can survive the winter on host plants. We also hang sticky yellow sheets (sticky traps) among the plants to trap adult white fly. These are widely available from garden centers. Ladybugs, spiders, and dragonflies also help to control white fly naturally.

RED SPIDER MITE

This tiny, almost microscopic, red spider is another sap-sucking mite that attacks cucumbers, tomatoes, peaches, nectarines, eggplants, and peppers. In fact, few plants are immune. Look out for pale mottling on the upper leaves.

The mites are yellow-green at first and later in autumn turn red. Like white fly, they thrive in warm glasshouse or tunnel conditions. We use biological control, its natural predator, a predatory mite called *Phytoseiulus persimilis*. Remove infested plants in late summer and clean and disinfect whole area of weeds and debris, even plant ties.

APHIDS

There are many different types of aphid, including greenfly and blackfly, that can attack a range of different plants. They suck the sap from the plant, which reduces the plant vigor and leaves it susceptible to other diseases and viruses. Plants will have poor growth and can have a sticky substance on their leaves, which in turn can become a sooty mold. They will be most active outdoors from spring into summer but can persist all

year round on indoor plants.

They can be treated indoors by biological control with aphid predators such as parasitic wasps. Outside you can use soapy water or Pyrethrum.

GREENFLY

Greenfly are a type of aphid found in the garden during the summer. They will nibble at plants and suck the sap from leaves, they can also leave a sticky residue on the plants. This too reduces the vigor of the plants. Greenfly are frequently seen on roses during the summer. They can also attack vegetables such as cabbages and lettuces. If they are not badly infested, washing in cold, salty water can dislodge them.

To get rid of greenfly, clean the plant with warm soapy water from a spray bottle that will help control them, but it won't prevent them from coming in the first place. Keep an eye on greenfly-prone plants and as soon as you see some, squeeze them between your finger and thumb.

Ladybugs are the natural predator of greenfly. Encourage ladybugs, hoverflies, and other beneficial insects to your garden by planting marigolds, cosmos, dill, fennel, yarrow, or Queen Anne's lace. My grandchildren collect ladybugs for me, especially to feast on greenfly in case we have an infestation.

CATERPILLARS

The most common caterpillar that the home gardener encounters is that which hatches from the larvae of the white cabbage butterfly. Once you see white cabbage butterflies flitting around the garden it's time to be on guard – check the underside of the leaves of your cabbages and other brassicas – you will see clusters of tiny orange-colored eggs. The quickest remedy, if you are not too squeamish, is to squeeze them between your finger and thumb – you will need to do this regularly. Once they hatch, the little caterpillars will travel everywhere and have a voracious appetite. We grow a large area and a wide variety of brassicas, so we cover our plants with netting to keep the butterflies (and birds) off the plants. We find this works well, but inevitably a few butterflies manage to get in.

They are also partial to our

nasturtiums. The best thing is to pick off the caterpillars or, better still, have a competition for children to collect the fluffy caterpillars off the plants.

BIRDS

Cover brassicas or fruit with netting to protect them from birds. We have a pigeon problem here in Shanagarry, so we construct plastic hoops over every line of outdoor brassicas. We cover strawberries in a similar way to protect them from blackbirds and thrushes and weigh down the edges of the netting with leaded fishing rope.

Our blueberries are grown in a simple fruit cage with metal supports and chicken wire, otherwise we wouldn't have even one berry. In the Currant and Berry garden we have a blow-up figure that inflates every 5, 6, or 10 minutes and waves its floppy hands. It's quite effective at the beginning of the season but the birds get used to it and eventually it scares the garden visitors more than the birds… Thin strips of foil attached to the support wires which flap in the breeze also help, so a combination of ruses might be effective.

BLIGHT (*PHYTOPHTHORA INFESTANS*)

One of a number of blights that can affect many crops including potatoes and tomatoes. If you do get blight, you will notice dark brown blotches on the tips and edges of the leaves, white spores will develop in these areas and the stems will blacken. Cut off the affected stems. There is no known cure but several blight-resistant varieties of potato have been developed during the last couple of decades including **Sarpo Mira** and **Sarpoaona**. We have had considerable success with the Sarpo varieties and **Setanta** and **Cara** but even those have eventually succumbed in extreme blight conditions.

At the first sign of blight, we cut the stalks back to 2 inches above the ground and burn the leaves and stalks. The potatoes will continue to swell for a couple of weeks and develop a thicker skin; use the crop ASAP. Mulch the plant and water well. Prune out and destroy any affected material. The typical Irish summer –warm, humid weather – provides ideal conditions for blight.

Blight spreads rapidly and is virtually impossible to control organically. You can use the effective but still controversial Bordeaux mix of blue stone (copper sulphate), washing soda, and water (5: 6: 5 mix).

POWDERY MILDEW

A common fungal disease caused by a group of related fungi that thrive in hot, dry, overcrowded conditions. It covers the plants in a dusty white coating. Cucumbers, zucchini, and many other edible and ornamental crops can be affected. We remove affected leaves otherwise they will shrivel up and disintegrate. The crop can still be used.

DOWNY MILDEW

Downy mildew is common in the spring when there's frequent rain and cooler temperatures but is not usually a problem in drier, warmer weather. It's closely related to algae, so it needs water to spread and survive. It can appear as a downy growth on the lower leaves of a plant or as spots or mottling on the leaves. Water your plants around the roots, rather than watering from above, to minimize the amount of water lodging on the leaves. As ever, good hygiene helps—the disease overwinters on dead garden material, so an autumn tidy-up is a good idea. If downy mildew gets into a greenhouse, reduce the humidity and increase the air circulation.

CLUBROOT

Clubroot is a fungal disease to which all brassicas – cabbages, broccoli and their relations – are susceptible. It builds up in the soil, so it's vitally important to rotate crops. It can persist in the soil for up to 20 years; if the soil is acidic it helps to add lime.

Signs of clubroot include the growth above ground looking stunted and in hot weather it may wilt and the leaves may display a purplish tinge. Underground the root will be swollen and the finer roots will die. The plants will look unhealthy and the yield will be affected. It can occur when the weather is warm and humid, usually from midsummer into autumn. It's best to remove and destroy (don't put on compost heap).

NUTRITIONAL GLOSSARY & SOURCES

VITAMINS

Vitamin A—Supports healthy vision, neurological function, and healthy skin. It is a powerful antioxidant, and holds anti-inflammatory properties. It also helps your immune system combat illness and infection.

B vitamins—Give you energy and support brain function.

Thiamine (B1)—Helps break down and release energy from food and maintain a healthy nervous system.

Riboflavin (B2)—Aids the body in releasing energy from food and keeps the skin, eyes and nervous system healthy.

Niacin (B3)—Keeps both the skin and the nervous system healthy, and helps release energy from food; can help to lower cholesterol.

Pantothenic Acid (B5)—Needed to synthesize cholesterol. It helps to release energy from food, maintain a healthy digestive tract, create stress-related and sex hormones as well as red blood cells, and also aids the processing of other vitamins.

Pyridoxine (B6)—Assists the body in using and storing energy from carbohydrates and protein in food. It also helps to form hemoglobin (the substance in red blood cells that carries oxygen around the body).

Biotin (B7)—Helps the body break down fat and is necessary for cell growth

Folate/Folic Acid (B9)—Vital for growth—aids the body in creating healthy red blood cells and also reduces the risk of neural tube defects.

Vitamin C—One of the most powerful antioxidants, it protects against cell damage, supports the immune system, and aids the absorption of iron. It also helps with wound healing.

Vitamin D—Helps to regulate the amount of calcium and phosphate in the body to keep bones, teeth, and muscles healthy.

Vitamin E—Good for the heart and useful in countering antioxidant damage. Helps maintain healthy skin and eyes and strengthens the immune system.

Vitamin K—Needed for blood clotting and aids complete synthesis of proteins. May also help to keep bones healthy.

MINERALS

Potassium—Helps the heart work properly and moderates blood pressure. It also regulates the balance of fluids in the body, builds proteins and muscle, and breaks down and uses carbohydrates.

Iron—Important for making red blood cells and helping to prevent anemia.

Sodium—Maintains the correct balance of water and minerals in your body, controls blood pressure and volume and helps your muscles and nerves function properly.

Zinc—Supports the creation of new cells and enzymes, as well as the processing of carbohydrate, fat, and protein in food.

Copper—Helps produce red and white blood cells and activate the release of iron to form hemoglobin. It's important for infant growth, brain development, the immune system, and maintaining strong bones.

Calcium—Vital for building strong bones and teeth, and regulating muscle contractions, including heartbeat. It also makes sure blood clots normally. Calcium deficiency can lead to rickets.

Magnesium—Assists in turning food into energy and makes sure that the parathyroid glands (which produce hormones vital for bone health) work normally.

Phosphorous—Helps build strong teeth and bones, and release energy from food.

Manganese—Helps make and activate enzymes in the body.

Selenium—Prevents damage to cells and tissues and supports the immune system.

Iodine—Aids the body in producing thyroid hormones, which maintain healthy cells and metabolic rate.

Silica—Helps promote healthy blood vessel walls and keeps bones, tendons, blood vessels, cartilage, and artery walls healthy.

PROTEINS

Amino Acids—Build proteins, support your metabolism, and protect your heart.

Lysine—Increases the intestinal absorption of calcium and reduces its excretion.

Betaine—Has potential benefits for fighting heart disease, improves body composition and helps promote muscle gain and fat loss.

Fiber—Improves digestive health and aids in the prevention of heart disease, diabetes, weight gain and some cancers.

Inulin—Controls blood sugar and promotes digestive health by slowing digestion, increasing fullness, and removing cholesterol as it passes through the digestive tract.

Pectin—Helps support healthy cholesterol levels by lowering cholesterol, promotes stable glucose levels, and may protect against colon cancer.

PHYTONUTRIENTS

Sulforaphane—May prevent the development of cancer by stopping certain enzymes from activating carcinogenic agents in the body and increasing the body's production of other enzymes that clean carcinogens out of the system before they attack cells.

Chlorophyll—Helps with wound healing, deodorizing and detoxifying the body. It also has antioxidant properties and may prevent anemia.

Flavonoids—Have antioxidant and anti-inflammatory properties. Support both the cardiovascular and nervous systems and the detoxification of potentially tissue-damaging molecules.

Anthocyanins—Health-promoting flavonoids considered to protect against heart disease, cancer, inflammatory conditions, urinary tract infections...

Luteolin—Induces the production of nitric oxide.

Hesperidin—Helps alleviate haemorrhoids and chronic venous insufficiency.

Procyanidin—Has antioxidant properties.

Quercetin—Used for treating heart conditions, high cholesterol, heart disease, and circulation problems. It has antioxidant and anti-inflammatory properties and helps to fight allergies and pain.

Catechin—Antioxidant properties.

Bioflavanoids—Antioxidants which have anti-cancer properties. They contribute to good heart health and combat the build up of fatty material inside your arteries.

Flavones—Inhibit the activity of aromatase, so they have antiestrogenic effects.

Vicenin—Any particular class of flavonoid that carries some protection against radiation damage and is anti-inflammatory.

Allicin—Has potential to fight viral, bacterial and fungal infections. It also helps to lower cholesterol, aiding the prevention of heart-related conditions, and may support the overall health of the circulatory system, reducing the risk of heart attack and strokes.

Apigenin—Promotes neuronal differentiation, and is useful for the treatment of neurological diseases, disorders and injuries.

Rutin—Reduces inflammation and protects the cardiovascular system. Also has powerful antioxidant properties and helps your body to produce collagen and use vitamin C. It aids blood circulation, prevents blood clots, lowers cholesterol, and reduces arthritis pain.

CAROTENOIDS

Beta-carotene—Turns into vitamin A in the body and is a powerful antioxidant. It helps with vision, immunity, and general health.

Lutein—Promotes healthy vision and skin.

Lycopene—The most powerful antioxidant of the carotenoids. It may protect cells from damage and may help to prevent heart disease, certain cancers, infertility, and diabetes. Also used for cataracts and asthma.

OTHER NUTRIENTS/COMPOUNDS

Choline—Vital for the proper functioning of cells and for growth and development, the structure of cells, metabolism and liver function, nervous system activity and development, cancer prevention, and early growth and development. It is anti-inflammatory and deficiency can lead to liver disease and possibly neurological disorders.

Omega 3 (fatty acids)—Important for normal metabolism, and is beneficial for high cholesterol, cancer, diabetes, inflammation, arthritis, depression, and skin issues. It has also been shown to support weight loss.

Oleic acid (omega 9)— Reduces blood pressure and increases fat burning to aid weight loss. Can also help in the management of type 1 and type 2 diabetes by regulating blood glucose levels.

Gamma linolenic acid (GLA)—Can be useful for conditions that affect the skin. It is an omega-6 fatty acid which may reduce inflammation and is needed for normal cell growth.

Capsaicin—Acts as an antioxidant, assists digestion, and can help prevent bacterial infections. It is also used to strengthen lung tissues.

Isothiocyanates—Act as antioxidants and may have anti-inflammatory, anti-cancer, and antibacterial properties.

Eugenol—Acts as a good local antiseptic and analgesic, and is an antioxidant.

Monoterpenes—Have antibacterial and diuretic properties and aid pulmonary afflictions. They also have been found to prevent the carcinogenesis process

Limonene—May aid weight loss, treat and prevent cancer, and treat bronchitis.

Carvone—Works as a relaxant often used for the digestive system, and the treatment of coughs, asthma, and bronchitis.

Chlorogenic acid (Phenol)—An antioxidant, which can help to lower blood pressure and potentially have an anti-diabetic effect.

SEED AND PLANT SOURCES

Almost Eden Plants: almostedenplants.com

Aspinals Tree Nursery: aspinallstree.com

Baker Creek Heirloom Seeds: rareseeds.com

Brown Envelope Seeds: brownenvelopeseeds.com

Burpee: burpee.com

Burt Ridge Nursery And Orchards: burntridgenursery.com/Dave Wilson Nursery

Edible Landscaping: ediblelandscaping.com

Fedco Seeds: fedcoseeds.com

Fruit Hill Farm: fruithillfarm.com

Gurney's Seed and Nursery: gurneys.com

Harris Seeds: harrisseeds.com

High Country Gardens.com: highcountrygardens.com

High Mowing Seed Company: highmowingseeds.com

Johnny's Selected Seeds: johnnyseeds.com

Lake Valley Seeds: lakevalleyseed.com

Mountain Rose Herbs: mountainroseherbs.com

Nature Hills Nursery: naturehills.com

Nichols Garden Nursery: nicholsgardennursery.co

Pinetree Garden Seeds: www.superseeds.com

Plant Delights Nursery: plantdelights.com

Raintree Nursery: aintreenursery.com

Seed Savers Exchange: seedsavers.org

Seeds From Italy: growitalian.com

Stark Bros.: starkbros.com

Stokes: stokeseeds.com

Sustainable Seed Company: http://sustainableseedco.com/

Territorial Seed Company: territorialseed.com

Totally Tomatoes: totallytomato.co

Trees Of Antiquity: treesofantiquity.com

The Nursery at Tyty: tytyga.com

INDEX

BIBLIOGRAPHY

A History of Gardening in Ireland by Keith Lamb and Patrick Bowe (National Botanic Gardens, 1995)

A Taste of the Unexpected by Mark Diacono (Quadrille, 2010)

Charles Dowding's Vegetable Course by Charles Dowding (Frances Lincoln, 2012)

Charles Dowding's Vegetable Garden Diary by Charles Dowding (No Dig Garden, 2016)

Chez Panisse Vegetables by Alice Waters (HarperCollins, 1996)

The New Vegetables, Herbs & Fruit by Matthew Biggs, Jekka McVicar, and Bob Flowerdew (Firefly, 2016)

Creative Vegetable Gardening by Joy Larkcom (Mitchell Beazley, 2008)

Down to Earth by Madeleine Cardozo (Haxnicks, 2010)

From the Cook's Garden by Ellen Ecker Ogden (William Morrow, 2003)

Garden Feast by Melissa King (ABC Books, 2007)

Grow All You Can Eat in Three Square Feet (Dorling Kindersley, 2015)

Grow Your Own, Eat Your Own by Bob Flowerdew (Kyle Books, 2010)

Heirloom Vegetables by Sue Stickland (Prentice Hall & IBD, 1998)

How to Grow Winter Vegetables by Charles Dowding (Green Books, 2011)

In Defense of Food by Michael Pollan (Penguin Press, 2008)

Jekka's Complete Herb Book by Jekka McVicar (Revised Edition, in association with the Royal Horticultural Society, Kyle Books, 2007)

Kew on a Plate with Raymond Blanc by Raymond Blanc (Headline Books, 2015)

On Food and Cooking by Harold McGee (Scribner, 2004)

Oxford Companion to Food by Alan Davidson (Oxford University Press, 2006)

Petal, Leaf, Seed by Lia Leendertz (Kyle Books, 2016)

Salad Leaves for All Seasons by Charles Dowding (Green Books, 2008)

Stephanie Alexander's Kitchen Garden Companion by Stephanie Alexander (Quadrille, 2010)

The Allotment Cookbook Through the Year by Caroline Bretherten (Dorling Kindersley, 2011)

The Complete Gardener by Monty Don (Dorling Kindersley, 2003)

The Complete Herbal by Nicholas Culpeper (Wordsworth Reference, 2007)

The Cook's Garden by Lynda Brown (Ebury Press, 1990)

The Fruit Garden Displayed by Harry Baker (Cassell/Royal Horticultural Society, 1986)

The Fruit Tree Handbook by Ben Pike (Green Books, 2011)

The Good Revolution, Growing Healthy Food, People and Communities by Will Allen (Gotham Books, 2012)

The Great Vegetable Plot by Sarah Raven (BBC Books, 2011)

The Half Hour Allotment by Lia Leendertz, Royal Horticultural Society (Frances Lincoln, 2006)

The Modern Pantry by Anna Hansen (Ebury Press, 2012)

The Natural Cook by Tom Hunt (Quadrille, 2014)

The Royal Horticultural Society Allotment Handbook (Mitchell Beazley, 2010)

The Seasons on Henry's Farm by Terra Brockman (Agate Publishing, 2009)

The Wild Table by Connie Green and Sarah Scott (Viking Studio, 2010)

Trevor's Kitchen Garden by Trevor Sargent (Orpen Press, 2012)

Vegetables for the Irish Garden by Klaus Laitenberger (Milkwood Publishing, 2010)

Wild Food: A Complete Guide for Foragers by Roger Philips (Macmillan, 2014)

Window-box Allotment by Penelope Bennett (Ebury Press, 2001)

THANK YOU, THANK YOU...

This book has been more than two and a half years in the making and has grown and grown to the point where my "beyond patient" publisher Kyle Cathie has once again said, "that's it!"

Grow, Cook, Nourish is a book I've wanted to write for years. I so want to share the magic of growing and cooking and to encourage people to grow even a little of their own nourishing, wholesome, and super delicious food. But there are so many thank yous:

Our gardeners, Haulie Walsh, Eileen O'Donovan, and Susan Turner, thank you for being so patient with my endless questions and so generous with your knowledge and experience. Thank you also to Elizabeth Meagher for your advice on growing microgreens and to Bill Frazer for special insight into heritage apple varieties.

Each and every recipe was tested and retested at the Ballymaloe Cookery School by Emer O'Driscoll but also on occasions by Sorcha Moynihan, Pat Browne, Tracie Daly, Gary Masterson, and Annie Kehoe. Special thanks also to Rory O'Connell,

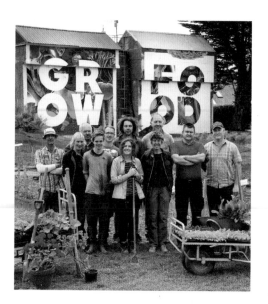

Rachel Allen, and Sharon Hogan for their unstinting support and encouragement.

Grow, Cook, Nourish includes many recipes from my travels, so special thanks to everyone who shared recipes and generously gave me permission to reproduce them in this book.

I've dedicated this book to my husband Tim and his extraordinary team of organic gardeners and farmers, who grow and harvest the most beautiful organic produce for us all to enjoy. Thank you each and every one, I feel beyond blessed to live in the midst of a 100-acre organic farm.

Clare Winfield, Tim Allen, and Daniel Callen collaborated on the garden photos and Clare photographed the food—thank you all.

The evocative drawings are the work of Ana Zaja Petrak. Special thanks to you and to Miranda Harvey for the design, Sunil Vijayakar for food styling, and Hannah Wilkinson and Polly Webb-Wilson for props.

Vicky Orchard had the unenviable task of editing this tome and trying to fit the reams of text into 640 pages. Thank you for your resilience and patience.

Last, but certainly not least, a huge thank you to Rosalie Dunne, whom I enticed out of retirement to help me with this book. Fortunately neither of us realised what a mammoth task we were embarking on or it might never have been started. Sixteen books later I'm still writing in long hand so all the copy has to typed, corrected, edited... Thank you Rosalie for your endurance and valuable research, which has contributed immeasurably to the finished manuscript.

Finally, once again, very special thanks to all my family for their constant encouragement and support and especially to Tim for creating a sustainable farm and garden to nourish us all.

PHOTO CREDITS

All photographs by Clare Winfield except for the following pages: **Daniel Callen**: 6; **Tim Allen**: 13 (top left and bottom right), 16, 17, 22, 26, 30, 31, 32, 38, 46, 47, 60, 65, 75, 80, 86, 87, 100, 104, 109, 119 (left and middle), 136, 137, 141, 151, 153, 157, 164, 169, 178 (left), 186, 187 (left), 199, 203, 220, 225, 230, 235, 242, 245, 248, 249, 250, 256, 268, 269, 282, 283 (top), 304 (bottom right), 316, 317, 318 (right), 324, 325 (left), 330, 331, 352, 364, 373, 379, 393 (right), 401, 414, 433, 436, 444 (bottom), 451, 453, 457, 462, 466, 467, 470, 505, 553, 568, 582, 586, 590, 593, 605 (top), 614, 617; **Alamy Stock Photo**: 56 (Tim Gainey), 57 (Nigel Cattlin), 64 (Elena Hramova), 68 (Rex May), 92 (Tim Gainey), 93 (Inga Spence), 96 (B Aldridge), 107 (Photos Horticultural/Avalon), 108 (GWI), 114 (Rex May), 124 (Inga Spence), 128 (left—Rex May; right—Lander Loeckx), 129 (Miriam Heppell), 133 (top right—Richard Becker), 154 (imageBROKER), 173 (Miyuki Satake), 179 (middle and right), 187 (right—Peter Jordan), 276 (Anne Gilbert), 286 (Sergey Sikharulidze), 280 (Eugen Wais), 296 (Tatyana Aleksieva-Sabeva), 297 (Charoen Pattarapitak), 300 (blickwinkel/Held), 308 (Tim Graham), 327 (Vladyslav Siaber), 334 (Wda Cache), 346 (CHROMORANGE), 347 (left—Rex May; right—Graham Prentice), 353 (top—FLPA; bottom—Nic Murray), 358 (Flowerphotos), 369 (top—Zoonar GmbH; bottom—Roger Holfert), 392 (Annie Eagle), 393 (left—Martin Hughes-Jones), 397 (middle—D. Hurst), 404 (Avalon/Photoshot License), 418 (Keith Burdett), 422 (Kevin Lang), 424 (Flowerphotos), 429 (Ketih M Law), 432 (blickwinkel/Hecker), 444 (top—Clare Gainey), 448 (Arco Images GmbH), 474 (Daniel Rönneberg), 478 (right—Flowerphotos), 483 (left—Garden World Images Ltd; right—Clare Gainey), 488 (Dinodia Photos), 492 (Organics image library), 493 (Rex May), 501 (right—blickwinkel/Teigler), 508 (left—Garden World Images Ltd/), 522 (imageBROKER), 523 (GFK-Flora), 526 (Zoonar GmbH), 527 (Premium Stock Photography GmbH), 530 (right—mauritius images GmbH), 535 (Johannes Hansen), 540 (Steffen Hauser/botanikfoto), 541 (Bob Gibbons), 544 (Marcus Harrison), 564 (Philip Jones), 572 (Eye Ubiquitous), 574 (FLPA), 596 (MBP-Plants); **GAP Photos**: 133 (bottom left—Jonathan Buckley), 397 (left—Maddie Thornhill; right—Clive Nichols); **Elizabeth Allen**: 262; **Shutterstock**: 314 (Vladimir Gjorgiev); **Peter Cassidy**: 578, 579; **Laura Edwards**: 610.